Comparative Reflections in Private Law

Professor Simon Whittaker

Comparative Reflections in Private Law

Essays in Honour of Simon Whittaker

Edited by

MARCO CAPPELLETTI
Tutorial Fellow in Law, Worcester College, Oxford University, UK

CIARA KENNEFICK
Associate Professor of Law, Oxford University, UK

DOROTA LECZYKIEWICZ
Associate Professor of Law, Oxford University, UK

OXFORD
UNIVERSITY PRESS

OXFORD
UNIVERSITY PRESS

Great Clarendon Street, Oxford, OX2 6DP,
United Kingdom

Oxford University Press is a department of the University of Oxford.
It furthers the University's objective of excellence in research, scholarship,
and education by publishing worldwide. Oxford is a registered trade mark of
Oxford University Press in the UK and in certain other countries.

Published in the United States of America by Oxford University Press
198 Madison Avenue, New York, NY 10016, United States of America.

British Library Cataloguing in Publication Data
Data available

Library of Congress Control Number: 2025947719

ISBN 9780198959137

DOI: 10.1093/9780198959168.001.0001

Printed and bound by
CPI Group (UK) Ltd., Croydon, CR0 4YY

MIX
Paper | Supporting responsible forestry
FSC® C013604
FSC www.fsc.org

The manufacturer's authorised representative in the EU for product safety is
Oxford University Press España S.A. of Parque Empresarial San Fernando de Henares,
Avenida de Castilla, 2 – 28830 Madrid (www.oup.es/en or product.safety@oup.com).
OUP España S.A. also acts as importer into Spain of products made by the manufacturer.

Preface

The idea for this book first took shape in 2023, as a way of marking the retirement of Professor Simon Whittaker and paying tribute to his outstanding contributions to comparative law. The first drafts of the twelve chapters that make up this collection were presented and discussed in depth at a colloquium held at St John's College, Oxford, on 25–27 September 2023. As editors of the book, we are very grateful to St John's College and the Faculty of Law at the University of Oxford for generously funding this event.

Following the colloquium, the contributors revised their papers in light of the rich discussions that took place there, as well as of subsequent comments from the editors. We are also very grateful to Jordan English for having contributed written comments on one of the chapters, and to all those who made suggestions or comments to the individual contributors. While it is not possible to name everyone here, acknowledgements have been included in the chapters themselves.

Editing legal texts, each one about more than one jurisdiction, is a particular challenge given the diversity of terminology and sources. In this respect we owe special thanks to Giorgia Bucaria and Benedict Stanley for their help in preparing the manuscript for publication. That help was invaluable. Funding for this editorial assistance was kindly provided by Christ Church, Oxford; the John O'Connor Research Fund of St Peter's College, Oxford; and the Faculty of Law, to all of which we are also very grateful.

We are also grateful to Armando Román Zozaya of the Law Faculty for valuable assistance in facilitating the use of the funding we had secured. Finally, our sincere thanks go to Matthew Williams at Oxford University Press, whose support for this project has been unwavering from its inception.

Marco Cappelletti
Ciara Kennefick
Dorota Leczykiewicz
30 June 2025

Contents

List of Contributors

Hugh Beale KC (Hon), FBA is Professor Emeritus at the University of Warwick and Visiting Professor and Senior Research Fellow at Harris Manchester College, Oxford

John Bell KC (Hon), FBA is Professor of Law Emeritus at the University of Cambridge

Jean-Sébastien Borghetti is Professor of Private Law at the Université Paris-Panthéon-Assas

Marco Cappelletti is Tutorial Fellow in Law at Worcester College, University of Oxford

John Cartwright is Emeritus Professor of the Law of Contract at the University of Oxford

Matthew Dyson is Professor of Civil and Criminal Law at the University of Oxford and Fellow of Corpus Christi College, Oxford, and Global Professor of Law at the University of Notre Dame (London Law Programme)

Michele Graziadei is Professor of Comparative Law at the University of Torino and Professor of Law at the Collegio Carlo Alberto

Ciara Kennefick is Associate Professor of Law at the University of Oxford and Official Student (Tutorial Fellow) in Law at Christ Church, Oxford

Yves-Marie Laithier is Professor of Law at the University of Paris-Panthéon-Assas

Dorota Leczykiewicz is Associate Professor of Law at the University of Oxford and Official Fellow in Law at St Peter's College, Oxford

Barbara Pozzo is Professor of Comparative Law at the Università dell'Insubria

Solène Rowan is Professor of Law at King's College London and Law Commissioner for Commercial and Common Law, Law Commission of England & Wales

Pietro Sirena is Dean and Full Professor of Civil Law, Comparative Private Law, and Banking Law at Bocconi Law School

Introduction: Simon Whittaker and Comparative Law

Simon Whittaker is a world-leading scholar of comparative law. The present book aims to celebrate his outstanding contribution to the field by presenting twelve chapters in comparative private law by scholars who were, each in their own way, profoundly influenced by Simon and his scholarship. The three editors of this book—Marco Cappelletti, Ciara Kennefick, and Dorota Leczykiewicz—completed their doctoral theses under the supervision of Professor Whittaker. In this editorial role, they have endeavoured to emulate the rigour, originality, and elegance which characterizes Professor Whittaker's extensive oeuvre in comparative law.

The motivation for this book was the desire on the part of the editors to mark, in a suitable way, Simon's retirement in 2023 from his Tutorial Fellowship in St John's College, Oxford, and his post at the University, a joint appointment which he had held since 1987. In the University, Simon was successively (CUF) Lecturer in Law from 1987, Reader in European Comparative Law from 2001, and Professor of European Comparative Law from 2008.

Therefore, from 1987 to 2023, Simon was a central figure in comparative law at Oxford. With colleagues in Oxford and Paris, he organized conferences and edited books which examined from a comparative perspective the most significant changes to the French Civil Code since the Napoleonic era. With colleagues in other institutions, he wrote books on French law and good faith in European legal systems. Simon is also the sole author of a magisterial monograph on product liability which presents a deeply learned and comparative analysis of the laws of England, France, and the European Union on this subject. Oxford University Press published that monograph, along with the two editions of *Principles of French Law* which he composed with two colleagues. It is, therefore, particularly appropriate that the present collection of essays in honour of Simon also be published by this leading press. His immense academic activity at Oxford from 1987 to 2023 made a significant contribution to the construction of a close, warm, and productive comparative law community extending outwards from Oxford across continental Europe. Professor Whittaker's colleagues and former students are still reaping the benefits of their membership of this unique community.

Mastery of one's own legal system is a necessary condition for excellence in comparative law, as Simon's scholarship demonstrates particularly powerfully. His

Comparative Reflections in Private Law. Edited by: Marco Cappelletti, Ciara Kennefick, and Dorota Leczykiewicz, Oxford University Press.
DOI: 10.1093/9780198959168.001.0001

significant contributions to English private law include several chapters in *Chitty on Contract*, the leading treatise on the English law of contract; indeed, his studies of English law are themselves often enriched by his comparative insights.

Simon's first contribution to comparative law was the doctoral thesis which he defended in Oxford in 1987 under the supervision of Professor Bernard Rudden, at that time the holder of the Chair in Comparative Law. The title of the thesis is 'The Relationship between Contract and Tort: A Comparative Study of French and English Law'. Fittingly, each of the three sections in the present book addresses these themes, which continued to shape Simon's academic journey thereafter: contract law, tort law, and what lies between and beyond them. English law and French law are, naturally, prominent, but a wide range of other legal systems are examined in addition to EU law.

Each of the chapters in this book celebrates Simon's rich scholarship in different ways. French law features in all chapters and plays a central role in several chapters, in recognition of Simon's extensive and impressive contribution to the study of French private law, or civil law, as continental lawyers would insist. His work has brought to English and international audiences a deeper and more nuanced appreciation of the French legal tradition, particularly its understanding of the boundary between contract and tort as well as that between regulatory and private law. All chapters pay tribute to Simon by employing a wide variety of comparative approaches—historical, doctrinal, and conceptual—to significant topics in contract, tort, and unjust enrichment. Each chapter is an attempt to emulate Simon's comparative scholarship not only in its substantive coverage and contextual sensitivity, but also in the depth with which it presents private law rules as expressions of historical processes and normative preferences.

The book is divided into three Parts: I. Contract Law; II. Tort Law; and III. Between and Beyond Contract and Tort.

The Part on Contract Law starts with a chapter by John Bell: 'Pragmatism in French Law: The Case of Mistake' pays tribute to Simon's scholarship by rejecting simplistic contrasts between English and French law and painting a more nuanced picture of the features and patterns characterizing the French legal tradition. The chapter returns to a well-known characterization of French law as 'principled', in contrast with English law, which has traditionally been regarded as having a more pragmatic bent. Bell challenges this contrast by tracing the pragmatic elements in French contract law. As a case study, the essay examines the interpretation of the French concept of *erreur* (mistake) under article 1110 of the French Civil Code from 1804 before the provision was revised in 2016. This is a particularly acute example of judicial law-making in French private law. The chapter offers an in-depth analysis of individual cases, on such issues relating to the doctrine of mistake as the interpretation of 'substance', substantial qualities, and mistake as to value, in order to establish if they display a consistently principled approach or are more open to pragmatic considerations. The conclusion is that French case law displays a high level of pragmatism, not always directly visible but nonetheless discernible. Bell contrasts the approach of French judges with that of French legal scholars, who display a much more rigid attitude towards departures from a principled stance. However, scholarly accounts do consider judicial development of the law, incorporating pragmatic concerns. The chapter engages with a long-standing theme within legal scholarship, namely the question of the weight which should be given to conceptual consistency and fact-specific fairness, and the tension that arises where rigid adherence to a 'consistent line of principle', as Bell has called it, would generate a morally or socially unfair result.

The second essay in the book, 'A Dangerous Method: Genealogy in the Interpretation of Contracts' by Michele Graziadei, looks at contractual interpretation from a historical perspective, framing its inquiry as a search for the genealogy of the practices we observe in different contract laws today. The chapter first identifies these interpretative practices and then examines different jurisdictions to establish which approaches were adopted in different periods. The chapter offers a nuanced picture of both English law and civil law jurisdictions. Both, in their own way, are fragmented: the former through competing doctrines, the latter under the umbrella of principles which are, seemingly, of general application. The chapter pays particular attention to the question of ambiguity, that is, when and how different legal systems define its existence and the appropriate response thereto. It also reflects on the different approaches to the parties' intentions—whether intention is considered relevant, and how a legal system goes about establishing its content. A further dimension which the chapter addresses is the reasons for the adoption or rejection of particular approaches, such as rules on evidence, the boundary between private law and administrative law, and the overall conception of contract. In all these observations, the author finds inspiration or support in Simon's work, such as the latter's article on 'Contracts, Contract Law and Contractual Principle' in John Cartwright and Simon Whittaker (eds), *The Code Napoléon Rewritten: French Contract Law after the 2016 Reforms* (Hart Publishing 2017), or 'Public and Private Law-making: Subordinate Legislation, Contracts and the Status of "Student Rules"' (2001) Oxford Journal of Legal Studies 103. However, the chapter also shows that, regardless of these differences, common law and civil law jurisdictions historically used the same sources for inspiration.

The third chapter in the book, 'Remedies for Defects in the Formation of a Contract: Learning by Comparing' by John Cartwright, is a more direct comparison between the two legal systems which, more than any others, have occupied Simon's academic career: English and French law. The chapter compares the remedies for defects in the formation of a contract in English law and French law, but more fundamentally, it reflects on the terminology that a comparative lawyer should use when describing various legal phenomena in a neutral way. It engages with Simon's contribution to *Chitty on Contracts*, a leading reference work on contract law in England and Wales, in which Simon has authored a number of chapters in the 'General Principles' and 'Specific Contracts' volumes. Cartwright engages in particular with the first chapter in *Chitty*, 'Contract Law and "Contracts"', where Simon defines and discusses such phenomena as void, voidable, and unenforceable contracts. The essay also draws on the author's conversations with Simon during seminars taught together at Oxford, and their various joint projects, including the translation of the reformed French Civil Code provisions adopted in 2016 ('The Law of Contract, the General Regime of Obligations and Proof of Obligations', *Ordonnance* no 2016-131 of 10 February 2016, with Bénédicte Fauvarque-Cosson). As the title of Cartwright's chapter suggests, his objective is to establish if the French experience with the remedy of relative nullity could be useful in addressing the difficulties which English law faces with the categories of void contracts and those which are voidable. The chapter suggests that the purpose of the distinction between void and voidable contracts could become clearer if English law not only looked to its 'internal policies' but also drew on approaches found in other jurisdictions.

The next chapter in the book, 'Performance, Reasonableness, and Proportionality: English and French Remedies Law' by Solène Rowan, moves to issues relating to performance, and it is another contribution which, following Simon's own work, offers a direct comparison of English and French law. The chapter starts by recalling Simon's insightful observation about the contrast between French law—which emphasizes the right to perform, including that of the debtor—and English law, which focuses more on balancing the interests of both parties ('Contributory Fault and Mitigation, Rights and Reasonableness: Comparisons between English and French Law' in Luboš Tichý (ed), *Causation in Law* (Konrad Adenauer Stiftung 2007) 149). Rowan also draws on Simon's assessment of the limited role of reasonableness in the French law of contractual remedies, particularly when compared with its role in English law. So framed, the chapter observes that English law's gradual recognition of an 'interest in obtaining performance' has not been matched, unlike in French law, by a similar recognition of an interest in 'rendering performance', a concept which has rarely received attention in English law and remains underdeveloped. On the French side, the chapter traces the increasing significance of reasonableness and the closely related concept of proportionality, which was officially introduced into the French Civil Code by the 2016 reforms. Rowan concludes that these reforms brought French law closer to English law, but a strong contrast remains because of English law's mitigation principle, which continues to have no place in French law.

Yves-Marie Laithier, in his chapter 'The Impact of Illegality in French Contract Law: A Reflexive Endeavour', also offers a direct French to English law comparison, this time focusing on illegality of contracts. Laithier highlights a contrast between the generality of the French approach, which overtly uses broad codified principles and leaves the detail to be worked out in judicial decisions, and the English approach, judge-made at its inception, which has opted for a more concrete framework that accepts a range of possible consequences of illegality. Inspired by Simon's chapter 'Theory and Practice of the "General Clause" in English Law: General Norms and the Structuring of Judicial Discretion' in Stefan Grundmann and Denis Mazeaud (eds), *General Clauses and Standards in European Contract Law* (Kluwer Law International 2006) 57, the chapter considers the role of case law in defining general clauses, such the codified rule in French law which renders illegal contracts non-existent, with all the familiar problems it generates in terms of retroactive application and overruling. The chapter signals what lessons French law can draw from the English approach, which is characterized by greater variability, making a distinction between situations where illegality exists at the time the contract is entered into and those in which illegality arises subsequently. In a conflict between the policy of protecting society from illegal transactions and sanctioning contracts which are against public policy, and that favouring the preservation of contractual relationships into which the parties have voluntarily entered, the law needs to strike a balance. Laithier's chapter is an invitation for French law to adopt a more nuanced approach, following the example of English law—a proposal that seems to be gaining recognition in France.

The Part on Contract Law concludes with a chapter by Hugh Beale—'Doctrines of Change of Circumstances, Covid-19 and Special Measures'—which explores the doctrine of change of circumstances from a comparative perspective. In its approach, the chapter is inspired by Simon's monograph on product liability (*Liability for Products: English Law, French Law and European Harmonisation* (OUP 2005)). The specific factual situation with which the essay engages is the set of restrictions introduced during the COVID-19 pandemic, and the extent to which—and the manner in which—the doctrine of change of circumstances was used in different jurisdictions to respond to the resulting curtailment of economic activity. The chapter begins by reflecting on the development of the doctrine of change of circumstances by German scholars between the two World Wars, its reception in many civil law systems—either through legislation or case law—and its absence from the traditional common law systems, where the nearest equivalent is the doctrine of frustration of the 'contractual venture'. Beale then traces the use of the doctrine of change of circumstances in different countries affected by COVID-19 restrictions. His discussion reveals that its deployment has not been uniform. Beale observes that behind the appearance of unity lies a wide range of approaches. He posits that these differences are due to different views about which risks should ordinarily be borne by each party. In the same context, and in light of the absence of any tradition of judicial adjustment of contracts in the common law, Beale shows that commercial parties in England and Wales tended to respond by renegotiating their contracts 'in the hope of keeping their commercial relationship going'. His chapter also offers a reflection on the different levels of transparency in English and civil law judicial decisions. Perhaps expressing a frustration common among

English lawyers, Beale observes: 'I was struck yet again by the difficulty of getting into the mindset of judges and lawyers from other jurisdictions, for example as to what risks parties are expected to bear', singling out Simon as a scholar who has been able to achieve precisely that kind of understanding in his writing.

One of the editors of the present book, Dorota Leczykiewicz, has the honour of opening the Tort Law Part of the book with an essay entitled 'Violation of a Right and Tort Law'. The chapter is a tribute to Simon, the author's former DPhil supervisor. First, the chapter expressly adopts Simon's approach to comparative law as a study of the ways in which lawyers from different jurisdictions approach legal questions (*Liability for Products*). Secondly, it keeps categories distinct by separating non-contractual liability from other forms of liability, even if the areas covered by non-contractual rules across the jurisdictions which are compared do not fully overlap. Thirdly, the chapter adopts an inclusive definition of a lawmaker as covering both the legislator and judges. Within these parameters, the chapter conducts a comparative inquiry into the role which violation of a right plays in German, English, and French tort law. The chapter compares these three tort laws through the prism of the three possible functions that violation of a right may perform: structural, doctrinal, and rhetorical. The chapter notes the centrality of rights in German tort law and argues that in that system, unlike in the other two legal systems, all three functions are present. In contrast, English law is characterized by the dominance of the doctrinal and rhetorical function. An argument in favour of the structural function can be found only in academic writings. In relation to French law, the chapter identifies a localized rather than a general role for the violation of a right, performing only a doctrinal function. Throughout, the chapter compares the ways in which the three legal systems define rights relevant to their tort laws, locate their sources, and conceptualize their violation. It concludes by reflecting on the factors that contribute to the emergence of rights-based reasoning, ranging from a legal system's readiness to express normative ideas overtly, to its willingness to introduce concepts that would be universal across the entirety of its tort law—or at least the default core—and to the desire to limit at least overt judicial recourse to policy arguments.

The next chapter in the Tort Law Part, 'Foreseeability in the Law of Torts: A Comparative Analysis' by Marco Cappelletti—also one of the editors of the present book and Simon's former DPhil supervisee—is a comparison between English and French tort law. The chapter draws on Simon's book *Liability for Products*, not only in its approach to comparative law—which emphasizes differences as an opportunity to enrich the debates in each of the compared laws both in terms of policy and technique—but also in substance. Cappelletti refers to Simon's account of both the English law of negligence and the French law of extracontractual liability, as well as to Simon's more general observations on the role of fact in the formulation of English tort law rules, and its relative absence in French law. The chapter reveals that in English law, foreseeability is a pervasive and structuring principle—central to a range of tort law doctrines, such as the standard of 'reasonable care' in the tort of negligence, remoteness of damage, and defences. This evaluation of English law is contrasted with French law, where Cappelletti observes a more limited engagement with foreseeability. He attributes it to the broad and pliable conception of *faute* (fault) in French law and to the central role of strict liability rules, for which conduct-based evaluations are often irrelevant. Cappelletti also notes the academic debate in France concerning the role of foreseeability in causation and defences, a role which is overtly recognized in English case law. Cappelletti posits a number of factors to explain these differences, including a stronger ethos of social solidarity in the French system, where the compensation and spreading of losses are fundamental aims of tort law. This stands in contrast to the English perspective, which tends to begin with the question of why the defendant should be liable and which views foreseeability mainly as a means of restricting the range of situations in which liability arises and of limiting its scope.

The next chapter, 'Justifying the Denial of Compensation for Pure Economic Loss' by Jean-Sébastien Borghetti, returns to a long-standing theme in comparative law, namely, the unequal recoverability of pure economic loss in different jurisdictions—a topic which Simon has addressed in many of his publications, most notably in *Liability for Products*. Pure economic loss, especially its treatment by French law, has also been a recurring theme in books co-edited by Simon: *Principles of French Law* (OUP 1998 and 2008, with John Bell and Sophie Boyron), *The Development of Product Liability* (CUP 2010), *The Code Napoléon Rewritten: French Contract Law after the 2016 Reforms* (Hart Publishing 2017, with John Cartwright and Bénédict Fauvarque-Cosson), and *French Civil Liability in Comparative Perspective* (Hart Publishing 2019, with Jean-Sébastien Borghetti). Borghetti, one of Simon's co-authors and co-editors, returns to the topic by discussing French civil liability law, which seemingly places no official limit on the compensation of pure economic loss. The author notes that debates in French scholarship indicate that there is an appetite for the formal introduction of restrictions on the recoverability of pure economic loss. This task could be facilitated by the fact that French law's conceptual framework already includes elements suggesting that not every interest deserves the same level of protection. Borghetti pays special attention to the distinction in French law between *dommage*, understood as the primary harm caused by the damaging act and consisting in the violation of a legally protected interest, and *préjudice*, which refers to the negative consequences flowing from that harm. This distinction creates intellectual space for a discussion of the interferences which should be regarded as *dommage*—a question that requires reflection on the nature of the underlying interest in question and on the reasons why the law ought to protect it. Yet Borghetti recognizes that these terms serve only as headings under which substantive issues must be worked out. He concludes by observing that, despite English law's progress in identifying which economic interests deserve protection in the law of negligence, it is unlikely that a single theory or approach could provide all the answers—or, in his words, 'spare courts and lawyers the effort of engaging in such a discussion'.

The last chapter in the Tort Law Part—'A "Pilfered Ginger": Tort Claims for Harm Caused by Products Involving Illegality' by Matthew Dyson—focuses our attention on the curious absence of the defence of illegality in tort law claims arising from harm caused by a product. The inspiration for the chapter is, once again, Simon's *Liability for Products*. Following Simon's example, Dyson looks for relevant ideas, regardless of where they 'sit in a legal system', while remaining attentive to the doctrinal structures used by the jurisdictions under examination. In that regard, Dyson's chapter offers unparalleled richness: it examines the English law of illegality and product liability, and then compares it with a broad range of jurisdictions, with a special focus on the United States. The chapter argues that the special rules imposing strict liability for defective or harmful products explain why illegality claims do not arise in these jurisdictions, suggesting that illegality better suits a fault-based regime. In addition, Dyson observes that illegality has 'vaguer boundaries in tort'. He suggests that it is likely that other mechanisms, legal or non-legal, are addressing the concerns that would otherwise fall under the banner of 'illegality'. In the spirit of reflective comparative law that characterizes Simon's scholarship, the chapter also offers some thoughts on why civil law systems have not developed an equally robust defence of illegality, concluding that the explanation lies in the way in which they apply positive conditions of liability, such as unlawfulness, fault, causation, or damage.

Pietro Sirena's chapter, 'The Subsidiarity of Unjustified Enrichment', opens the final Part of the book, 'Between and Beyond Contract and Tort', which is dedicated to themes that transcend domestic contract and tort law systems. The chapter offers a critical review of the doctrine of subsidiarity in the law of unjustified enrichment. While it focuses on a single legal proposition—that unjust enrichment should not be available when the matter is covered by a contractual, property law or tortious remedy—it examines this proposition in a wide range of jurisdictions, including Italian, French, German, English, and Portuguese law. The chapter engages with Simon's scholarship on French law. Simon provided an excellent account of the French law of unjust enrichment, understood as part of the law of obligations, in the book *Principles of French Law*, co-authored and co-edited with John Bell and Sophie Boyron. Sirena goes through different contexts in which subsidiarity of a restitutionary claim has been invoked, including three-party cases and situations covered by property law. In all these areas, the subsidiarity rule is intended to curb the expansion of unjust enrichment. Sirena's comparative analysis reveals that in all the jurisdictions which he examines, there is a trend in judicial decisions and scholarly discourse towards restricting or even abandoning the subsidiarity rule, due to its negative effect on efforts to define the boundaries of unjustified enrichment independently from other areas of the law. Sirena concludes by arguing that the subsidiarity rule should be abandoned because the task of limiting the scope of unjust enrichment can be achieved through a clear articulation of the essential elements of that claim. In Sirena's view, subsidiarity is an historical artefact that no longer serves any useful function.

A book honouring Simon Whittaker would not be complete without a chapter on the European harmonization of contract law, a theme to which Simon has devoted many of his publications, consistently highlighting the difficulty of achieving fully harmonized contractual rules and a uniformly applied body of consumer law. This sentiment is shared by the final chapter in the book, 'Harmonizing Contract Law without a Common Terminology: Comparative Law Perspectives' by Barbara Pozzo. The chapter examines the various strands of the EU's contract law harmonization project, along with its national counterparts in the form of national implementations of EU directives and the national scholarly response to these measures, many of which introduce not only substantively unfamiliar but also conceptually disruptive elements into domestic law. The chapter relies markedly on two strands of Simon's scholarship. First, it benefits from the lucid and learned accounts of English contract and consumer law that Simon has made available to international audiences (for example, in 'Distinctive Features of the New Consumer Contract Law' (2017) 133 Law Quarterly Review 47). Secondly, the chapter engages with Simon's writings on European proposals on the codification of contract law, which aimed—among other things—to provide EU contract law legislation with a settled and uniform terminology with the hope that such a shared vocabulary would enhance coherence and support national legislators in implementing EU measures. Simon was famously critical of these attempts, as reflected in key publications as 'The Proposed "Common European Sales Law": Legal Framework and the Agreement of the Parties' (2012) 75 Modern Law Review 578, 'The Optional Instrument of European Contract Law and Freedom of Contract' (2011) European Review of Contract Law 371, 'On the Development of European Standard Contract Terms' (2006) 2 Journal of European Contract Law 51, and 'A Framework of Principle for European Contract Law' (2009) 125 Law Quarterly Review 616. Pozzo generally agrees that the creation of a common terminology for EU contract law remains a difficult challenge, and that existing mechanisms such as the various interpretative methods mandated by the Court of Justice of the EU to address the issue of multilingualism can assist national lawyers only to a limited extent. EU law's multilingualism is both a source of richness and an obstacle on the path to achieving truly harmonized contract law. A particularly interesting theme in the chapter is the role of specially devised legal English, abstracted from its common law cultural heritage and emerging as a neutral intermediary among the different civilian jurisdictions that, alongside the EU legislative measures, form part of the overarching European legal order. The way English has been used in the preparation of the different measures, with the ambition to express a private law that can be accepted as representative of all EU Member States' jurisdictions, suggests that there is a need for a shared frame of reference expressed in neutral language that can inform national definitions and the use of central contract law concepts. Pozzo concludes by reflecting on the role of legal education in enabling dialogue among different national legal traditions—a goal to which Simon has devoted a large part of his academic career. He has not only written about English law for foreign audiences, and about French law for the common law world, but taught comparative and European private law to generations of undergraduate and graduate students at Oxford. All students who have benefited from Simon's teaching are well equipped to build bridges of understanding across diverse legal systems.

There is, however, another way in which Simon's formative influence will continue: it is through the generous, rigorous, and supportive way in which he supervised the three editors of the present book, his former DPhil students at the University of Oxford. We are deeply grateful to Simon for the dedication he showed to each of us as a doctoral supervisor, for the learning he imparted, and for the ethos of comparative law scholarship he instilled in us. We are committed to carrying forward that ethos, sharing it with a new generation of students, doctoral supervisees, and academic colleagues.

PART I
CONTRACT LAW

1

Pragmatism in French Law

The Case of Mistake

John Bell

Just before Simon Whittaker joined the Oxford Law Faculty as a lecturer, a project came to an end which involved leading contract lawyers from France and England. The project lasted more than two years and involved several two-day meetings to discuss prepared and pre-circulated papers. Its output was published as *Contract Law Today* in 1989.[1] The conclusions of the project examined not only contract law in the two countries, but more general features of English and French legal reasoning. The study claimed to provide 'many examples of the traditional contrast between the conceptualism of French law and the pragmatism of English law'.[2] The French approach is variously described in those conclusions as 'dogmatic', one of 'conceptualism', and reliant on 'greater use of abstract principles'.[3] All the same, the authors suggested that the contrast should not be exaggerated and that it was 'a matter of tendencies not clear-cut contrasts'.[4] Pragmatism could be found in the topics discussed in French contract law:

> A realistic appraisal must also take into account the tendency within any legal system for judges to balance the use of traditional concepts with their intuitive feeling of justice. The foreign observer will note that the French judge is adept at this process. If the victim of a loss should receive compensation, the judge will somehow find a way to award it.[5]

Although in formal reasons for their decisions French judges stick to citing the Code, that does not mean that pragmatic and consequentialist reasons play no part in decisions:

[1] Donald Harris and Denis Tallon, *Contract Law Today: Anglo-French Comparisons* (Clarendon Press 1989). A French version was published as Donald Harris and Denis Tallon, *Le Contrat aujourd'hui: comparaisons franco-anglaises* (LGDJ 1987). The present author was a member of this project.

[2] ibid 386–87.

[3] ibid 387–89.

[4] ibid 391.

[5] ibid 389.

John Bell, *Pragmatism in French Law* In: *Comparative Reflections in Private Law*. Edited by: Marco Cappelletti, Ciara Kennefick, and Dorota Leczykiewicz, Oxford University Press. © Marco Cappelletti, Ciara Kennefick, and Dorota Leczykiewicz 2026. DOI: 10.1093/9780198959168.003.0002

> Our discussions led to the conclusion that French judges and lawyers are as much concerned with the consequences of applying rules as are the English, and that this factor has a significant effect on the solution of legal problems.[6]

This concern about conceptualism and pragmatism in legal reasoning was reflected in the contemporaneous *Hamlyn Lectures* which were delivered by one of the main participants in the project, Atiyah.[7] Although mainly about English law, the published version of the lectures begins with the observation that the contrast between continental theoretical approaches and English pragmatism may be overstated, and Atiyah hoped that his reflections on English law 'with the occasional side glance abroad' might enrich comparative law.[8] 'If this is not a comparative method in its own right', he wrote, 'I hope at least to provide some of the material for a comparative study from those who can then approach the same questions from the other side.'[9]

In a sense, this chapter is a belated response to Atiyah's challenge. Neither *Contract Law Today* nor the *Hamlyn Lectures* provided a developed discussion of pragmatism in French contract law, although the matter was discussed extensively in the project group. The chapter tries to go some way to rectifying that by examining one topic identified by Harris and Tallon as reflecting a contrast between the French use of theory and English pragmatism: the law on mistake, and misrepresentation.[10] It is a topic on which two of the French participants in the project, Ghestin and Tallon, had written extensively. Although this is not recorded specifically in the published work, the views of Ghestin and Tallon, as well as those of Atiyah and Nicholas, diverged on where the balance lies between principle and pragmatism in the French approach. As will be seen, Nicholas did analyse French law on this topic in his subsequent work.[11]

The purpose of this chapter is to examine how far the conclusions of *Contract Law Today* are right about French law. To do this, I will take one topic—mistake—and examine some leading case law up until the reform of the Code in 2016. Given that the wording of the provisions on mistake changed substantially in 2016 and there is an insufficiently large body of case law to examine on the new provisions, I will not make any effort to examine the post-2016 case law. The advantage of the topic is that it relates directly to writing by Ghestin, Nicholas, and Tallon, all participants in the project. The judicial development of the doctrine of mistake (*erreur*) in French contract law was described by Ghestin as 'one of the most characteristic examples of the creation of law by case law'.[12] But he also argued strongly against

[6] ibid 390.
[7] PS Atiyah, *Pragmatism and Theory in English Law* (Stevens 1987).
[8] ibid 2–3.
[9] ibid 3.
[10] Harris and Tallon (n 1) 387.
[11] Barry Nicholas, *The French Law of Contract* (2nd edn, OUP 1992) 20–23.
[12] Jacques Ghestin, *La notion de l'erreur dans le droit positif actuel* (LGDJ 1963) 3.

the idea that judicial decisions should be based on the issue of which party most merited protection.

The method of this research has been to make use of the analytical framework developed by Atiyah and used in the *Contract Law Today* project with some insights from Fortsakis on the French side. I will argue that the framework helps us to understand what happened in the French codified private law of contract. Although there is usually a contrast between deduction from principles in code-based systems and induction from concrete cases in non-code-based systems such as English law and French administrative law, the differences in reasoning are not as clear-cut. I suggest that judicial reasoning in French contract law is frequently pragmatic. Judges choose between the conceptual tools available to them in order to achieve fair results. French scholarly writing, on the other hand, is more concerned with conceptual clarity and the integrity of the system of the Code. But, even here, the direction of the law is given by the judges, and the scholars tend to follow this lead in their formulation of concepts.

I. The Problem: Principle or Pragmatism

Atiyah argued in his inaugural lecture in 1978 that English judges adopted a 'pragmatic' approach to contract law, rather than a 'principled' approach.[13] He distinguished the two approaches in the following way:

> A decision on principle is a decision determined by the hortatory effect which the court wishes its decision to have in the future; a pragmatic decision is a decision designed to achieve justice in the particular circumstances of the case, irrespective of the possible impact of the decision in the future.[14]

In Atiyah's view, the law has two functions. First, there is the *dispute settlement* function through which particular disputes are resolved. Secondly, there is a *hortatory* function which is part of a complex of mechanisms providing incentives and disincentives to certain forms of conduct, expressed in the form of principles. Judicial decision-making has to seek a balance between these functions. Atiyah realized that the two functions he described are ideal types and that actual situations are more complex. For a start, legal rules can rarely be stated definitively without qualification or amendment in the light of other principles of the law.[15] So there needs to be adaptation of the written text of the law or a precedent. On the other hand, pure pragmatism is not acceptable. Law is a purposeful enterprise

[13] PS Atiyah, *From Principles to Pragmatism* (Clarendon Press 1978).
[14] ibid 5.
[15] Atiyah (n 7) 50.

and exists for reasons. Judges are required to base decisions on reasons which are exposed to criticism and refutation.[16] To let decisions be based on pragmatic assessment of the facts alone would risk arbitrary discretion and would be a form of unacceptable elitism.[17] The key question is how the balance is struck.

Nicholas suggested that the distinction was really between applying principles or concepts 'logically' and applying them 'pragmatically' in the light of the fairness of consequences.[18] He suggested further that French judges tended to be pragmatic (despite the format of judgments), while the scholarly writers (*la doctrine*) tended to focus on concepts and principles.[19] The two approaches reflect different ways of giving direction to the law. An English judge who was also a scholarly writer, Lord Justice Robert Goff, as he then was, argued that 'it is important that the dominant element in the development of the law should be professional reaction to fact situations rather than theoretical development of legal principles'.[20] As I have argued elsewhere, such an approach is not peculiar to English law but is shared by French law.[21] Similarly to Goff, judge Chenot argued that judges and not the 'makers of systems' (*faiseurs de systèmes*), as he described the scholarly writers,[22] should be the leaders in shaping French administrative law. Both English law and French administrative law are not codified systems. Judges thus have been responsible for developing concepts and theories, as well as for applying them. The view of Goff suggests that it is the function of judges and not just scholars to create the theoretical framework of the law, its hortatory part. But does this apply equally in a codified system, such as French (private) contract law?

A former president of the *Cour de cassation* did not think that the development of concepts or theory had a place in private law judgments. For him, judgments had to focus on '"the plea, all the plea, and nothing but the plea" that is the RULE which judges have handed on like a sacred flame ... The Cour de cassation—our Cour de cassation—should not embrace in its midst the "makers of systems"'.[23] By contrast, the annual report for that court in 1975 remarked: 'we are pleased to emphasize that ... while remaining within its role, our Court contributes to the gradual creation of the new state of law which will shape the society of tomorrow'.[24]

[16] ibid 144.

[17] ibid.

[18] Nicholas (n 11) 21.

[19] ibid 21–22.

[20] Robert Goff, 'In Search of Principle' (1983) 69 Proceedings of the British Academy 169, 185–86.

[21] See John Bell, 'English Law and French Law—Not So Different?' (1995) Current Legal Problems 64.

[22] A critique by B Chenot in his argument as *commissaire du gouvernement* in the *Gicquel* case: Conseil d'Etat 10 February 1950, Lebon 100 ('this case-law which never articulates the theoretical reasons for its choice leaves the makers of systems in confusion ...') (all translations are mine unless otherwise stated). Leading scholar Jean Rivero responded with Jean Rivero, 'Apologie pour les "faiseurs de systèmes"' in Recueil Dalloz de doctrine, de jurisprudence et de législation, 1951, Chr 99.

[23] Pierre Drai, 'La Cour de cassation face à la doctrine' in *Droits, no 20: Doctrine et Recherche en Droit* (PUF 1994) 107, 109.

[24] Cour de cassation, *Rapport annuel 1975* (La documentation française 1976) 101.

The very function of the *Cour de cassation* is to provide coherence to the case law emerging from the different regional *cours d'appel*. So the tension is not only between the roles of judges and scholars but also within the mission of the higher private law courts in France.

Atiyah's tension between 'principle' or 'theory' and 'pragmatism' is found also in contemporaneous writing on French administrative law by Fortsakis. Fortsakis argued that the law needed both conceptualism and empiricism.[25] For him, conceptualism provides the legal basis for decisions and empiricism the flexibility in the application of rules. The question, as in England, was how far the lead in developing theory was to be taken by the legal scholars, rather than by the judges. Fortsakis saw the roles of developing concepts and being pragmatic as shared between judges and scholars. But his primary interest was to show the influence of scholars on case law, a matter that is difficult in France because judgments do not cite sources other than legislation or the Constitution and even the *rapporteur public* (previously called the *commissaire du gouvernement* in administrative law) rarely cites the scholarly sources for their ideas.[26]

Although typically concerned with legal principles, scholars also explained legal rules in terms of the practical effects and consequences of law. A major role of the French scholar since the beginning of the nineteenth century has been as *arrêtiste*, the writer of commentaries on cases. This shows just how central the judicial engagement with fact situations is to scholarly debate. Scholars are able to situate a legal problem in its economic and social context. This is an extension of 'practical knowledge'[27] about the cases that come to court. As the leading private law scholar Carbonnier wrote, 'The *arrêtiste* is a jurist and as such is involved in the struggle for the law, or even for the just solution, and has the vocation to orient case law'.[28] Legal scholars are even more strongly connected to the practical side of law by their role as consultants to practitioners in individual cases.[29] Their very status as professors has long provided this consultant role and it forms a significant part of the activity of many scholars. The engagement of scholars in treatises and theses builds on this judicial engagement with the practicalities of legal life as exhibited in cases with which these scholars are deeply familiar through their work as *arrêtistes* and as consultants. All the same, the thesis and treatise writer have a distinct mission.

[25] Théodore Fortsakis, *Conceptualisme et empiricisme en droit administratif français* (LGDJ 1987) 1, 449.

[26] ibid 32–35.

[27] See Alain Bernard and Yves Poirmeur, 'Doctrine civiliste et production normative' in Yves Poirmeur (ed), *La Doctrine Juridique* (PUF 1993) 127, 145–50.

[28] Jean Carbonnier, 'Notes sur des notes d'arrêts. Chronique pour le cinquantième anniversaire de l'entrée du Doyen René Savatier au Dalloz', Recueil Dalloz-Sirey 1970, Chr 137, 138. French cases are often published with notes by scholars (the *arrêtiste*) which provide an explanation of the decision which is not apparent from the laconic style of the judgments, particularly those written before the reform of judgment writing in 2019.

[29] Bernard and Poirmeur (n 27) 152–53; Philippe Jestaz and Christophe Jamin, *La Doctrine* (Dalloz 2004) 238–39.

That mission is to bring out of the ideal aspects of the law 'a logical and coherent law, morally justified, socially just and effectively applied'.[30] Some judicial decisions might be rejected and some rough edges knocked off case law interpretations of the Code in order to make the law more systematic. Thus, the makers of systems are very much informed by the facts, even if they are not constrained by them. It is this ideal of coherence and logical structure which Atiyah captured in his notion of the hortatory function of law. That focus on principle and on the hortatory function of law is in tension with what the French judge considers the mission of the court—to deal with the arguments as presented and to resolve the dispute in front of them.[31]

The doctrine of *erreur* ('mistake') in France up to 2016 illustrates how the scholarly and judicial functions interact. But it also illustrates the way in which the conceptual structure of the Code was adjusted to meet practical issues. Section II shows that the conceptual structure of the 1804 Code was unclear both in relation to mistake and in relation to cognate concepts. Section III shows how scholarly writing tried to rationalize these different concepts into a coherent system, but judges focused on resolving disputes pragmatically. This then led scholars to re-assess their schemes in order to accommodate the practicalities of life illustrated by litigation. Section IV then reflects on the picture which emerges.

II. The Doctrine of Mistake in the Civil Code of 1804–2016

Until the reforms of 2016, the doctrine of mistake was contained in article 1110 of the Civil Code of 1804. That text read:

> Error is a cause of nullity of an agreement only when it touches the very substance of the thing which is its subject-matter. It is not a cause of nullity when it touches only the person with whom there was an intention to contract, unless considerations concerning such person were the principal reason for the agreement.

This text contained ambiguity in terms of its overall policy. On the one hand, it stressed the importance of the certainty of transactions by trying to narrow the scope of mistake to those situations '*only* when it touches the very substance of the thing' or '*only* the person with whom there was an intention to contract'.[32] On the other hand, article 1108 Cc listed as first among the four *essential* conditions for a binding contract 'The consent of the party who binds himself'. This suggests an attention not just to the objective terms of the contract, but to the subjective

[30] Bernard and Poirmeur (n 27) 150. See also Philippe Jestaz, 'Déclin de la doctrine?' in *Droits* (n 23) 85, 89: the role of doctrine is 'to structure the legal universe by giving it a logical coherence'; Jestaz and Jamin (n 29) 228–32.

[31] See Drai (n 23).

[32] Emphasis added.

consent of the contracting party and its genuineness. The ambiguity in the policy was reflected in the preparatory works of the Code. Bigot de Préameneu argued in the committee formulating the text: 'Mistake in the reasons for a contract is only a cause of nullity in those cases where the truth of these reasons can be considered as a precondition on which it is clear that the parties wanted their contract to depend.'[33] By contrast, Mouricault argued before the Tribune that 'mistake should relate to the very substance of the thing or to the reason determining the agreement.'[34] The former narrows mistake to where a feature is an agreed term of a contract, whereas the latter is broader and focuses on any significant reason which is the basis for the consent of the parties. The text was approved without resolving this ambiguity.[35] The pre-existing law had been equally inconclusive, and the ambiguity was not resolved by the new Code. So, the Code started off by being ambiguous about what it wanted to sanction and for what reason. It contained less principle and conceptual clarity than might first appear.

The 1804 Code then had a number of other provisions and concepts which were partly connected with mistake. The first was *dol* or fraud, where a mistake induced by the defendant's deliberate manoeuvres is sanctioned as such. Article 1116 Cc provided: 'Fraud is a cause for nullity of an agreement when the manoeuvres used by one of the parties are such that it is evident that, without such manoeuvres, the other party would not have contracted.' So, there was no need for the mistake to be limited to a term of the contract or a substantial quality of the thing to be acquired. Bad behaviour inducing consent sufficed.

Mistakes may arise not only from what the seller has said but also from typical expectations in the market of what a product is like. If the product sold was defective, then that itself provided a reason for terminating a contract. So article 1641 Cc provided:

> The seller is held to guarantee against hidden defects in the thing sold which render it improper for the use for which it was intended, or which so diminish this use that the buyer would not have bought it, or would only have given a lower price, if he had known of them.

If the buyer had the opportunity to inspect, then he would be deemed to have accepted the risk that there was a defect (article 1643 Cc).

This guarantee against hidden defects did not need to be stated expressly by the parties. It was taken for granted. Other expectations were often stated expressly as terms of the contract. If the seller failed to deliver what the other party expected

[33] PA Fenet, *Recueil complet des travaux préparatoires du Code civil*, vol 13 (Zeller, Osnabrück edition 1968) 223.
[34] ibid 417.
[35] Ghestin (n 12) 31.

from the terms of the contract, then that party could ask for the contract to be terminated under article 1184 Cc:

> A resolutory condition is always implied in bilateral contracts in cases in which one of the two parties does not perform his undertaking. In such cases, the contract is not terminated as a matter of law. The party for whom the undertaking has not been performed has the choice either to force the other to perform the undertaking when it is possible or to claim termination of the contract with damages.

The contract would not come to an end automatically as under article 1110 Cc, but a court would have to approve its termination and could choose to give the defendant more time to perform. By contrast, an undervalue was rarely to be treated as a factor which vitiated consent: '*Lésion* vitiates agreements only in certain contracts or with regard to certain persons.'[36] As will be seen, mistake as to value was seen as a factor which did not lead to nullity of a contract.

So, the law on mistake was not only unclear in its meaning, but had to be related to a number of other concepts within the Civil Code. This left significant scope for interpretation by scholars and by judges both in setting out the conceptual structure of the Code and in resolving pragmatically individual cases.

III. How the Text Developed

The application of the text of article 1110 Cc was not linear or coherent. The cases illustrate the way in which there was a lack of consistency in the classification by the courts of facts into conceptual categories. The categories set out in the Civil Code seemed less determinative of the solutions adopted by the courts in individual cases than the judges' sense of what was the fair outcome to be reached. In addition, scholarship contained debates which, over the years, changed in emphasis on how to interpret article 1110 Cc. The scholarly debates and judicial decisions can be grouped around certain dominant concepts. But it will be seen that, whatever the aspiration of doctrinal writers, the case law applying those concepts was much messier.

A. 'Substance'

The text of article 1110 Cc, set out above at the beginning of section II, required that a relevant mistake 'touch[…] the very substance of the thing which is its

[36] Art 1118 Cc.

subject matter'. One of the most significant evolutions in the doctrinal interpretation of this provision was the debate about the meaning of the 'substance' of the thing. A narrow approach would be that substance meant the subject matter (*objet*) of the contract, viewed objectively. For example, in 1832 the sale of the office of *huissier* (a court officer with some similar functions to bailiff) at a gross undervalue was held not to constitute mistake as there was no mistake as to the subject matter (the office) that was being sold or about the subject matter (the price) which was promised in return.[37] The mistake did not relate to the *substance* itself. In a view much relied on by French scholars, the early nineteenth-century German scholar von Savigny[38] adopted the more expansive interpretation that substance meant not just the physical object, but also what was the general opinion of the public of what belonged to the description of the thing, the feature making the subject matter of the contract distinctive in the market. By contrast, a more subjective view focused on the qualities of the thing which had led *this* buyer to enter into the contract, a view entertained before the Revolution by Pothier. In his view, 'Mistake annuls a contract not only when it relates to the thing itself, but also when it relates to the quality of the thing which the parties principally had in mind, and which constitutes the substance of the thing'.[39]

That approach was much more focused on consensus between these particular parties and was more subjective. These different positions continued to be debated in scholarly writing well into the twentieth century. In 1902, the fifth edition of Aubry and Rau's treatise sets them out and shows the strength of support in scholarly writing and in case law at the time in a very lengthy footnote.[40] Indeed, Ghestin showed that the emphasis on an objective view of substance had not totally gone away even in the late twentieth century, though it was definitely the view of a minority.[41] Drawing on Pothier, there were two categories excluded from the concept of substance, namely 'accidental qualities' and personal motives (*mobiles*) for a transaction.[42] Writing in the early twentieth century, Josserand argued that 'substance' was not simply the objective and abstract subject matter of the contract but had to be viewed from the subjective and particular perspective of the party making the contract. 'We mean', Josserand said, the qualities 'susceptible of infinite

[37] Req 17 May 1832, *Metayer*, S 1832.1.849.

[38] Friedrich Carl von Savigny, *Traité de droit romain*, vol 3 (Firmin Didot 1845) did not think that Roman law revealed that there was a general rule in favour of the nullity of contracts for mistake (at 350). There were certain situations in which a contract would not be enforced. The main general points related to either fraud or where a particular state of affairs was an agreed condition for an obligation to arise (at 339–40). He noted that error with respect to value was not enough to justify the nullity of a contract (at 348).

[39] Robert-Joseph Pothier, *Traité des obligations* (Debure 1763) pt 1, ch 1, s 18.

[40] C Aubry and C Rau, *Cours de droit civil d'après la méthode de Zachariae*, vol 4 (5th edn, revised by G Rau and C Falcimaigne, Marchal & Billard 1902) 490–91, note 1 *quinquies*.

[41] Jacques Ghestin, *Traité de droit civil, la Formation du Contrat*, vol 1 (4th edn, Jacques Ghestin, Grégoire Loiseau and Yves-Marie Serinet eds, LGDJ 2013) 900–901.

[42] Pothier (n 39) s 18, p 29 and s 20, p 32.

variety, which are given to the thing by the contracting party who views it through this or that specific angle according to his desires'.[43] It was Josserand's view that *erreur* covers any mistake where the thing lacks the properties in view of which it was bought.[44]

Although the conceptual debate continued in scholarly writing for more than a century, the courts were not particularly interested in articulating their choice of approach in terms of a standard formulation. While the 'personal motives' (*mobiles*) which had persuaded the party to make a contract were clearly not relevant to a finding of mistake, the (subjective) purpose which the party had in mind was often held to have defined the subject matter of the contract and so defined its substance. Examples after the Second World War included the farmer who bought a draught mare for his farm; the dealer claimed, but did not warrant, the mare to be about 12 years old. The mare died eight days after the sale of old age. She must have been much older. The dealer was a professional and had acquired the animal for 48,000 Fr, but had resold it to the claimant for 108,000 Fr. In this case court found both a mistake as to a substantial quality and fraud with regard to the age of the animal.[45] Similarly, the sale of a farm was nullified for mistake when its condition was not suitable for a working farm, although this requirement was not specifically mentioned in the contract.[46] There was a great deal of rubbish on the land, which had not been mentioned; most of the vines and orchards needed to be torn up; and only a third of the cattle were suitable. The price to be paid was only suited to a working farm.

Although appealing to this interpretation of the concept of substance within the Code, courts actually gave it divergent applications to facts that appeared relatively similar. Cases on the authenticity of paintings provide numerous examples.[47] For example, in a case of 1856, the seller had written a letter to the buyer saying that he had paintings by painters of great repute including named painters. The paintings were bought without attribution in the contract. All the same, the contract was annulled. The *cour d'appel* of Paris argued that both good faith and the law required it to treat attribution as an essential condition for works which derive their principal value from the name and reputation of their painters.[48] The note by the *arrêtiste* to the case pointed out the diversity of the reasoning in the (then) recent cases.[49] A few years earlier a court had proclaimed that 'it is obvious that the name of an artist appearing at the foot of the painting does not constitute a substantial

[43] DP 1932.1.129 note Josserand.
[44] Here he cites CA Paris 19 July 1890, DP 1892.2.257.
[45] Cass (1) civ 27 April 1953, *Besnier c Edmond*, D 1953.440.
[46] Cass Soc 4 May 1956, *Vidal c Sanchez-Boxa*, D 1957.313.
[47] Jules-Joseph-Edmond Millet, *De l'erreur et de la bonne foi en droit romain et droit français* (Thesis, Faculté de droit de Paris 1871) 155–56 provided an early discussion. Ghestin (n 41) 900–901 provides two pages of very detailed footnotes, offering 36 example cases, most of which are from after 1980.
[48] CA Paris 29 March 1856, *Leroy d'Etoilles c Remilleux*, S 1856.2.304.
[49] On the *arrêtiste*, see n 28.

quality of that painting', but the note writer criticized this, while considering that the decision was right on its facts.[50] Indeed, there are other examples of attribution apparently authenticated by a signature being treated as a substantial quality of the works of art and so justifying a nullity when it is false.[51] These cases illustrate the fluidity of the concept of 'substance' and the essentially pragmatic character of its judicial application in individual cases. The cases illustrate also the way 'substance' became less an objective feature of the subject matter of the contract, but more the feature which had subjective importance for the parties.

The eventual move in scholarly writing had the effect of liberalizing the text of article 1110 Cc and enabling a wider range of situations to be included. In particular, the concept moved from a focus on the material features of the subject matter of the contract to the factors which had influenced the parties to make the contract. The concept did not control the direction in which the law was applied in the courts and decisions such as those just discussed were often more flexible in achieving justice in the particular case. As Beale rightly concludes, '[g]iven the extended notion of substance which has been accepted, it is not always easy to distinguish a mistake of substance from mere mistake in motive'.[52]

B. Mistake as to a substantial quality and mistake as to value

From the earliest times, the Code was interpreted to mean that a mistake as to value did not invalidate a contract.[53] Nullity for sale at an undervalue (*lésion*) was limited, by articles 1118 and 1674–1685, to the sale of land. That position continued to be retained formally by authors and courts throughout the period under discussion. But the courts became flexible in differentiating what was treated as a pure mistake as to value from situations in which a substantial mismatch in value between the real worth of the subject matter of the contract and the contractual price provided evidence of a mistake as to substantial qualities.

Scholarly writing moved towards the end of the nineteenth century to use the term 'substantial qualities' instead of 'substance'.[54] This reflected the inability to make a sharp distinction between the objective and subjective aspects of the subject matter of the contract. As a case note pointed out:

[50] Trib de Seine 28 January 1848, *Durand-Ruel*, S 1848.2.99.

[51] See for example CA Bordeaux 13 November 1905, *Pommiès c Ellissen*, DP 1908.2.287; also CA Paris 5 March 1890, *Berlino c Poulet*, S 1890.2.133.

[52] Hugh Beale, *Mistake and Non-disclosure of Facts* (OUP 2012) 44. Beale was another member of the *Contract Law Today* group.

[53] Cass civ 4 June 1810, *Grand c Grand-Maison*, S 1809-11.1.192. See also Cass civ 31 October 1811, *Fusi c Perret*, S 1809-1811.1.416.

[54] See nn 40–43.

> Whatever opinion you adopt to define 'substance', one has to recognise that a non-substantial quality may on occasion become the determining reason for the agreement and to admit that a mistake on this point is a cause of nullity, even if it is not an error about the substance properly so-called.[55]

Even if textbook authors such as Aubry and Rau tried to hold onto the idea that 'substance' was different from 'substantial qualities' until the beginning of the twentieth century, courts predominantly interpreted article 1110 Cc as being concerned with 'substantial qualities' from 1875.[56] Ghestin noted that this happened because courts focused on assessing 'substance' not in the abstract, but concretely in relation to the factors which had determined the consent of this contracting party.[57] Thus, although the concepts which define mistake were clear in scholarly writing, their essential sensitivity to the facts of the case enabled courts to be pragmatic in their application.

As Tallon pointed out,[58] the judicial assessment of facts was of central importance to the outcome of cases. The flexibility of concepts was enhanced by the flexibility of the judicial interpretation of facts. The sovereignty of the lower court judge in assessing the facts was recognized by the *Cour de cassation* from the beginning of the Civil Code: 'it is for the conscience of the judges to assess the merits of the facts on which the alleged fraud is founded.'[59] Often we find similar facts decided by different courts with different results. For instance, the sale of the same encyclopaedia by doorstep salesmen could be treated differently. In 1875, a contract provided for the 1871 edition of the *Encyclopédie du 19ème siècle*, and it was annulled for mistake when the volume turned out to be an older edition than the sample with a new cover.[60] On the other hand, in a case of 1884 the volumes delivered were less good in terms of the quality of paper and engravings than the sample, but it was treated as substantially the same and so no mistake as to a substantial quality could be found.[61]

It was suggested in one case that the price for the subject matter of the contract may, in itself, be an indicator of a mistake. In that case, the claimant signed a contract for a summer let of a villa at 6,000 F for July 1964. The villa was in a poor state of repair. The *cour d'appel* found an error with respect to a substantial quality 'of which the price formed one of the indicative elements'.[62] Other decisions rarely

[55] DP 1895.2.417.
[56] Ghestin (n 41) 974–80.
[57] ibid 979–80.
[58] See n 110.
[59] Cass civ 28 brumaire An XIV, *Billoin c Villavicensio et Leroy*, SV XIII-1808.1.180. Also, Cass civ 2 fructidor An XIII, *Larrigues c Laffond*, SV XIII-1808.1.155.
[60] Cass civ 24 February 1875, *De Lamothe c Lagardière*, DP 1875.1.464.
[61] CA Riom 12 May 1884, S 1885.2.13.
[62] Cass civ (3) 29 November 1968, *Berthon c Vanden-Borre*, GP 1969.1.63.

articulate the point so clearly, but the decision is not unusual in its approach,[63] an approach upheld by the *Cour de cassation* in that case.

One of the most commonly litigated areas has been the authenticity of paintings or of other artistic productions. The topic has long been the subject of scholarly study.[64] The most common approach by the courts was to examine the status of the parties. If one party was a professional or otherwise expert, then the failure to notice that an object was not genuine was treated either as fault on their part or simply as a risk which they took. This was already seen in the case of the two jewellers contracting with each other in 1811.[65] Of course, under article 1110 Cc, the court was not concerned with finding fault, merely with interpreting whether the circumstances gave rise to a genuine mistake.[66] All the same, the status of a person as an expert was likely to weigh against a finding of a genuine mistake. Where a non-expert deliberately sought to purchase from an antique dealer, it was clear that he was wanting to buy antiques, and the actual purchase of modern replicas was thus a mistake on which the purchaser could rely.[67] Relying on common opinion in the trade might be evidence of mistake, such as where the claimant's agent relied on long established expert reports that proved to be wrong about the authenticity of a painting.[68] Chairs appearing to have originated under Louis XV did not prevent nullity when it was discovered during renovation that they had been altered at a later period.[69] These examples show the importance of the nuances of facts in determining whether a mistake vitiating a contract would be found or not.

At first sight, a mistake about the attribution of a painting by the seller might well appear to be a mistake as to value not substantial qualities, because all are agreed on the identity of the object which is for sale. Of course, any mistake as to a substantial quality will affect the value of the performance to be tendered. But not every mistake as to the valuation of a performance is a mistake about essential qualities. In terms of principle, only mistakes as to substantial qualities counted. The courts muddied the waters by drawing a distinction between a mistaken valuation and a mistake in understanding the facts on which the valuation is based. This is illustrated by the *Poussin* saga.[70] In 1968, the husband and wife Saint-Arroman sold

[63] See already CA Paris 29 March 1856 (n 48), and CA Paris 9 January 1849 DP 1849.2.67.

[64] See especially Marthe Fournier, *De la protection des parties dans la vente des antiquités et des objets d'art* (thesis, Université de Dijon 1936).

[65] See *Fusi c Perret* (n 53).

[66] See Cass civ 25 July 1900, *Berheim c Tardif*, DP 1904.1.611, quashing a rejection of a claim for mistake on the ground that the expert had been imprudent in not checking the painting.

[67] CA Bordeaux 13 November 1905, *Pommiès c Ellissen*, DP 1908.2.287 (sale of engravings by a professional antique dealer with a hint of fraud: the goods were the 'product of gross deception and of a trade lacking scruples', but no finding of fraud was made against the dealer). See also CA Orléans 21 January 1931, *Chocquel c Camirel*, DH 1931.172.

[68] CA Paris 22 February 1950, *Delton c Franchelli & Blaison*, D 1950.1.269.

[69] Cass civ (1) 23 February 1970, *Aubin de la Messuzière c Chalon*, JCP 1970.II.16347.

[70] Cass civ (1) 22 February 1978, D 1978.601 note Malinvaud; Cass civ (1) 13 December 1983, D 1984.340 note Aubert; and CA Versailles 7 January 1987, GP 1987.1.34. For details, see Ghestin (n 41) 892–93.

a painting at auction for 2,200 F. There had been a tradition in the family that the painting was by Poussin, but the auctioneer's expert reported that it was merely by the School of Caracci, and the painting was so described in the catalogue. The French state exercised its right of pre-emption and so became the substitute buyer. Their experts conducted research, and, within a fortnight, the painting was exhibited in the Louvre as by Poussin. The sellers brought an action to have the sale annulled for mistake. After 15 years, during which period there were two decisions of the *Cour de cassation* and four in other courts, they succeeded. The painting was returned and so was the price of 2,200 F. The wife (the husband having died) was then able to sell the painting to a Swiss gallery for 7.4 million F. The final and successful ground for annulment was that the determining consideration for the sellers was the erroneous view, caused by the auctioneer's expert, that the painting could not be by Poussin. That finding of the *cour d'appel* of Amiens was adopted, but the *Cour de cassation* rejected the lower court's additional ruling that the seller could only obtain a nullity when the mistake had been caused by fraud on the part of the buyer. The case was remitted to the *cour d'appel* of Versailles, which gave judgment for the seller. The attribution of the painting changed a substantial quality of the item that was being bought and sold and did not just affect its valuation. The mistake was not purely subjective but was evidenced by the description given to the item in the sale catalogue. In effect, there is a kind of circularity. The quality of a thing determined its price. But the price was an indicator of the quality the thing was supposed to have according to the contract.[71]

The conceptual structure may have been open-textured and have allowed flexibility but the real determinant of the decision was the assessment of facts. The *Poussin* saga can be contrasted with the *Fragonard* case. The saga of Fragonard's painting *The Bolt* reveals the flexibility with which facts were interpreted to come to a just decision within the concepts associated with mistake. The estate of a deceased art collector, Vincent, sold the painting at auction in 1933. Six expert opinions had been obtained and it was sold for 67,000 (old) francs (equivalent to 6,700 (new) francs) as attributed to Fragonard. It was bought by a rich art collector who died in 1966. The heir of the collector, Sportuno-Coty, put the painting up for auction in 1969, after two further expert reports excluded its being by Fragonard. It was bought by Heim, a gallery director, for 55,000 F (new francs). Heim proceeded to have the painting restored.[72] Heim then resold it in 1974 to the Louvre for 5,150,000 F. Sporturno-Coty then began proceedings to have the sale to Heim annulled for mistake. His claim was rejected by the first instance court but allowed

[71] See Alain Piedelièvre, 'Le dernier état de la jurisprudence "Poussin"' GP 1987.1.196. The fact that the mistake was made by the seller was not peculiar to the *Poussin* case, because agreements relating to succession in the early nineteenth century also were annulled at the behest of the seller: see n 3. See generally Ghestin (n 41) 931–35 on mistake as to one's own performance.

[72] The same agent had been involved in the purchase of the Poussin painting in the case previously mentioned at much the same time.

by the *cour d'appel* of Paris.[73] Because the painting now belonged to the State, Heim was ordered to pay Sporturno-Coty 5,095,000 F by way of restitution by equivalent. This decision was upheld by the *Cour de cassation* in 1979.[74] The key finding was that the common intention of the parties was that the painting could not be by Fragonard and so there was no risk of authenticity involved. The Vincent family, representing the original vendors, then brought an action against Spoturno-Coty seeking to annul the sale of 1933. The action failed because the *cour d'appel* of Paris considered that the description 'attributed to Fragonard' in the auction catalogue implied some doubt about the authenticity of the painting and that the seller was thus taking a risk that what he put up for sale might be a Fragonard.[75]

So, in relation to sales of the same painting, we get different findings of fact as to whether there was doubt as to the authenticity of the painting and acceptance of the risk that it might be genuine or whether both parties were convinced that it could not be genuine. Indeed, the same divergence of views occurred with the three *cours d'appel* which heard the *Poussin* case.[76] Ghestin considered that the key issue was whether the risk that the painting was not genuine was part of the contract or not.[77] He illustrated this with a case of a portrait of Monet which was sold as the work of one painter, but after the sale was attributed by experts to a lesser-known painter. The seller and buyer then came to a settlement under which the seller remitted 150,000 F and the buyer kept the painting. Even later, experts discovered that it was a self-portrait by Monet and so worth vastly more than the settlement price. The courts refused the seller's request to annul the settlement on

[73] See 'Faits et jugements. La vente d'un Fragonard annulée', *Le Monde* 25 April 1978: https://www.lemonde.fr/archives/article/1978/04/25/faits-et-jugements-la-vente-d-un-fragonard-annulee_3128168_1819218.html (accessed 2 April 2025)

[74] Cass civ (1) 16 October 1979, *Heim c Sporturno-Coty*, GP 1980.1 somm 60. For a discussion see Pierre Legrand, 'The Case for Judicial Revision of Contracts in French Law (and Beyond)' (1989) McGill Law Journal 908, 921. Bizarrely, Avocat-général Gulphe in his *conclusions* in the Poussin case, Cass civ (1) 13 December 1983, *Epoux Saint-Arroman c Réunion des Musées nationaux*, JCP 1984. II.20186 mentions the Tribunal civil decision in this Fragonard case (21 January 1976) (see 'Les "qualités substantielles" d'un tableau de Fragonard', *Le Monde* 1–2 February 1976, https://www.lemonde.fr/archives/article/1976/02/02/les-qualites-substantielles-d-un-tableau-de-fragonard_2958933_1819218.html, accessed 2 April 2025), but not its reversal by the *cour d'appel* in 1978 or the decision of the *Cour de cassation* in 1979. He sought to distinguish the two cases when, by the time he was writing, they were coming out with the same result!

[75] Cass civ (1) 24 March 1987, *Vincent c Spoturno-Coty*, JCP 1989.II.21300 and critical observations by Vieville-Miravette. For an explanation of the history of the authenticity of this painting, see '"Le Verrou" de Fragonard contesté. Fausse histoire de faux', Le Monde, Paris, 5 November 1988, https://www.lemonde.fr/archives/article/1988/11/05/le-verrou-de-fragonard-conteste-fausse-histoire-de-faux_4124570_1819218.html (accessed 17 July 2023) and '"Le Verrou" fin de la polémique?', Le Monde (Paris, 16 February 1989, https://www.lemonde.fr/archives/article/1988/11/05/le-verrou-de-fragonard-conteste-fausse-histoire-de-faux_4124570_1819218.html (accessed 17 July 2023).

[76] cf CA Paris 2 February 1976 (referred to in the *Cour de cassation* decision of 1978, and holding that it was not proved that there was a mistake); CA Amiens 1 February 1982, Gazette du Palais 1982.1.134 (no mistake because the attribution of the painting to Poussin was doubtful); CA Versailles 7 January 1987, GP 1987.1.34 (the seller was under the mistaken opinion that the painting could absolutely not be a Poussin).

[77] Ghestin (n 41) 880–84, 1037.

the ground that risk as to authenticity had been a key part of the contract, even if not in the way that the real facts had turned out to be.[78]

The cases of Fragonard, Poussin, and Monet illustrate the way in which judges (or settlements) achieved fairness by accompanying any order to return the subject matter of the contract with an allowance for the effort put in by the purchaser in establishing the authenticity of the painting, such as by restoration work. This was shown in the first Fragonard case, in the famous Poussin case, and in a later Poussin case concerning *The Flight into Egypt*. In the last case, the work of the expert was remunerated by an *actio de in rem verso*.[79]

In summary, the development of the concept of 'substance' in scholarly writing from objective to subjective and thence to 'substantial qualities' continued to exclude mistake as to value. But the malleability of these different concepts enabled the courts to categorize facts in such a way as to achieve what they considered to be a fair outcome, even if this came close to what scholars would have considered to be 'mistake as to value'. Indeed, textbooks would illustrate the law by citing the judicial categorization of facts in particular cases and the case notes to the judicial decision would not criticize the results. In consequence, some of the conceptual clarity was lost. As was noted above,[80] under the Civil Code sale at an undervalue only vitiated the contract in the very limited circumstances of *lésion* (article 1118). To allow 'mistake as to value' under article 1110 would be to undermine this careful restriction of the scope of *lésion*.

C. Consent

A dominant idea in nineteenth-century contract law was the protection of consent. As noted in section II,[81] article 1108 of the Civil Code made the consent of the parties as an essential requirement for formation of the contract. Article 1110 Cc appeared then as an elaboration of this idea. The idea that contract was based on the consent of the parties had its secular origins in the works of Domat and Pothier.[82] Pothier wrote: 'Mistake is the most significant factor vitiating consent, because contracts are formed by consent of the parties; and there cannot be consent where the parties are mistaken about the subject matter of their contract.'[83] This perspective was reinforced and qualified by debates in Germany in the 1880s and 1890s

[78] Cass civ (1) 28 March 2008, JCP 2008.II.10101 note Serinet; Ghestin (n 41) 881–82 and 1037.

[79] See CA Paris 27 February 1998, D 1998.IR.93; Cass civ (1) 17 September 2003, JCP 2004.1.123 observations by Serinet.

[80] See text to n 36.

[81] See p 7.

[82] Jean Domat, *Les Loix civiles dans leur ordre naturel* (Coignard 1689) book 1, pt 1, title 8, p 20 and Pothier (n 39) s 4. More generally see G Rouhette, 'The Obligatory Force of Contract in French Law' in Harris and Tallon (n 1) 38, esp 44–50.

[83] Pothier (n 39) s 17.

on the adoption of a civil code. The German Civil Code (BGB)'s provisions on mistake were focused on protecting genuine consent.[84] Parties who could demonstrate lack of consent could escape the contract under §119 BGB but might have to pay damages for fault in disappointing legitimate interests in the security of the contract under §122 BGB. French scholars, notably Saleilles, found attractive this combination of protecting consent but sanctioning fault in contracting, but this combination was not within the formal wording of the French Code of 1804.[85] As Rouhette pointed out, consent did not so much become the law for the parties, but rather its force was restricted by law.[86]

The tension between these two ideas of protecting consent and protecting legal certainty was reflected in the way judicial decisions were justified. The force of consent was limited by pragmatic considerations of fairness. Unreasonable subjective beliefs could not be allowed to undermine the validity of the contract. Thus, where a painting was bought at auction as 'signed G. Courbet, attributed to Courbet', the contract could not be annulled when the painting did not turn out to be original. The claimant was an art lover from a sophisticated background and ought to have known that the description did not warrant the authenticity of the attribution or the signature.[87] Even more clearly, the purchase of land for which the seller had valid title could not be annulled for mistake because the property had originally been expropriated from the church. The fact that this origin would have affected the consent of the purchaser, a staunch Catholic, did not amount to mistake vitiating the contract.[88]

Furthermore, a focus on consent is restricted by the evidence admitted to prove a mistake. It is clear that French courts did not search out the genuineness of subjective consent. The evidence on which they relied was objective. Thus, in Pothier's own example, the seller presented the specific objects to the buyer as silver candlesticks, though they both did not know that they were merely silver gilt and in fact made of brass.[89] He contrasted this with a wrong opinion as to whether a book sold was good or bad, which is a matter of subjective taste.[90] The objective elements lay in what the seller said and how this defines the subject matter of the contract. These were the basis on which mistake had to be proved. In this area, the concept of consent was really over-inclusive and so was narrowed carefully by judges in assessing individual cases.

[84] Basil S Markesinis, Hannes Unberath, and Angus C Johnston, *The German Law of Contract—A Comparative Treatise* (2nd edn, Hart Publishing 2006) 43–46.
[85] Ghestin (n 12) 134–35 suggests that Ripert and Josserand also embraced these ideas.
[86] Rouhette (n 82) 44–45.
[87] Cass civ (1) 16 December 1964, *de Causans c Villet*, D 1965.136. Similarly, Cass civ (1) 2 March 1964, Revue trimestrielle de droit civil 1965, 112 (purchase of land by an architect who should have been able to assess for himself whether land was suitable for the building he envisaged).
[88] CA Bordeaux 15 June 1926, *Drouyn*, S 1926.2.119.
[89] Pothier (n 39) s 18.
[90] ibid.

D. Cause

There is a tension between the objective description of the subject matter of the contract, the description under which it is marketable, and the subjective intentions of the parties, which define their consent. At the turn of the twentieth century, scholarly writing tried to resolve this by focusing on the *cause* of the contract, the legal reason why a party made the contract and why it is enforced. In Capitant's view, cases of mistake overlapped with the absence of *cause*.[91] For this he cited a scholarly article of 1904 and the theses of his star pupils.[92] For Capitant, mistake as to the substance or as to the substantial qualities of the subject matter of the contract was a mistake of fact, and it could only be justified as a ground of nullity by reference to *cause*, that is, the legal goal which the party had set for themselves. Legal certainty could only be protected if mistake were limited to factors relating to the fundamental reason why the contract was being made—its *cause*.

Illustrations of this idea in the case law often related to mistakes as to the moral obligations of the parties. For example, a young man agreed to pay an annuity to a woman to look after a child which she claimed resulted from their casual sexual relations. The contract was set aside for lack of *cause* under article 1131 Cc on the ground that it was unlikely that he was the father of the child and so there was no natural obligation that provided a (moral) reason for the commitment to pay the annuity.[93] But a mistake as to *cause* depended on the mistake affecting the nature of the agreement. In this case, the mistake did affect the nature of the transaction. The young man thought he was satisfying a moral obligation to his child, but in fact there was no such obligation. Similarly, the cinema owner who agreed to pay a performer for belongings destroyed in a fire on the ground that, as bailee, he was legally obliged to do so was able to obtain nullity for mistake when he realized that he had no such legal obligation to compensate the performer for his loss.[94] In another case, a farmer who paid twice for insuring his crop was able to obtain nullity of the second transaction.[95] The farmer was clearly getting nothing extra for his policy, and that is the classic area for *cause*.

For Capitant, nullity for error of law was also only possible where it related to one of the elements of the objective manifestation of the will, that is, the goal which the contracting party has set. In some cases, appeal to mistake was seen as

[91] Henri Capitant, *De la cause des obligations* (Dalloz 1923) 212. The idea of a focus on *cause* is found in early editions of Aubry and Rau: see Millet (n 47) 142–43.

[92] Joseph Delachenal, 'Influence exercée par l'Article 1110 du Code civil sur la détermination de la cause en matière de donation', Revue critique de législation et de jurisprudence 1904, 596; and the theses of Raymond Célice, *L'erreur dans les contrats. Etude de jurisprudence française* (Paris 1922) and Jacques Maury, *Essai sur la notion d'équivalence en droit civil français* (Toulouse 1920).

[93] Req 7 July 1931, DH 1931.445; CA Paris 3 February 1944, DA 1944.71.

[94] Req 1 July 1924, *Dumaine c Duribreux*, DH 1924.509.

[95] Req 6 June 1932, *Cie La Nationale*, S 1933.1.31: here the farmer took out a policy in ignorance of the fact that his mother (to whom he was now heir) had taken out an identical policy before her death.

an example of mistake as to the *cause*. Thus, an agreement under which one heir was to satisfy a legacy to his co-heir was annulled for mistake because the legacy was legally invalid for lack of due form.[96] Indeed, many of the early mistake cases concerned errors in interpreting the law of succession. Complexity arose from the regional laws governing marital property and succession before the Revolution of 1789. For instance, a father assumed wrongly that the marital joint property regime that he and his wife entered in 1783 under the custom of Brittany continued after his wife's death in 1791. He dissolved the co-property in 1836 and transferred half to his daughter, co-heir to his wife. This error was described by the lower court as 'the sole *cause* of the consent' and this justified the nullity of the contract of division of the property.[97]

This conceptual idea encountered two objections. First, within the conceptual scheme of the Code, this would collapse mistake under article 1110 Cc into article 1131 Cc on *cause*, making the former almost redundant. To avoid this, Aubry and Rau had carefully differentiated mistake as to the characteristics of the *cause*, which led to nullity under article 1110 Cc, and mistake as to the existence of a *cause*, which rendered a contract a nullity from the start under article 1131 Cc, on which the cases just cited turned.[98] For them, only the former was an instance of mistake within article 1110 Cc. Secondly, it simply did not fit the range of cases where the courts wished to nullify a contract. As Josserand pointed out in 1932,[99] it might sometimes be expedient to collapse a mistake as to the content of the subject matter of the contract into the theory of *cause*, and sometimes this was done in the case law. For example, in 1895 the *cour d'appel* of Orléans relied on both articles 1110 and 1131 Cc to annul the purchase of land by an elderly parish priest.[100] It was understood by both buyer and seller that he wished to build a parish school on the land. But it was not legally possible to comply with planning norms for such an enterprise. The court found that there was a false *cause* for the transaction, which, at the time, was an easier route to a remedy than mistake as to the substance of the contract.

Conceptually, this was hard to justify. Josserand noted that such an approach would, however, have the effect of characterizing *cause* not as the objective nature of the transaction (fulfilling an *obligation naturelle*, ie, an obligation stemming from a moral or social requirement, or making a sale of land as opposed to a lease)

[96] Cass civ 28 May 1888, *Faget*, S 1889.1.248. Also, Req 13 December 1927, *Dlles Speady*, S 1928.1.125 where a contract was signed on the inaccurate assurance by their notary that a lease on the property was invalid.

[97] Cass civ 12 March 1845, *Leroux*, S 1845.1.524. Cf Cass civ 4 June 1810, *Grand c Grand-Maison*, S 1809-11.1.192.

[98] See Aubry and Rau (n 40) 495, fn 6.

[99] DP 1932.1.129 note Josserand.

[100] CA Orléans 18 January 1895, *Serain c Lapérotte*, DP 1895.2.417. But cf *Fusi c Perret* (n 53), where the credulity of one jeweller in buying jewels at an excessive price from another jeweller was not held to constitute fraud or mistake.

but as the driving and determining subjective reason for the transaction: 'the cause which drives and determines consent' (*la cause dite impulsive et déterminante*). In the *Villa Jacqueline* case on which Josserand was commenting, the mistake was about the surface area of a parcel of land. The description given in precontractual information (but not included in the terms of the notarized contract) would have enabled the purchaser to resell the land as building plots. But the smaller, actual size made this purpose unrealizable. In the *Villa Jacqueline* case, there was clearly a misrepresentation by the seller in a newspaper advertisement about the size of the plot of land for sale. This case was resolved by reference to 'substantial qualities' and not by reference to *cause*. In the 1895 case, the eighty-year-old priest had a deep trust in the seller, though no fraudulent manoeuvres could be shown. In any formal terms, both transactions were sales of clearly defined and agreed plots of land. But what might have been taken to be secondary considerations—the size of the plot—became treated as the determining reason in the mind of the purchaser for the contract, justifying the use of mistake to annul it. But only in the 1895 case was *cause* invoked as a ground for nullity. The judges seemed to be using the categories of *erreur*, *dol*, and lack of *cause* without any clear reference to principle. They seemed to have a clear sense of where the just solution of a case lay and were using the legal categories to provide a formal justification for the solution they wished to reach.

The cases illustrated Josserand's more general argument that subjective motives tended to have a significant place in the case law.[101] *Cause*, the goal which the party set out in the contract, and which manifested their will, became transformed into the subjective description of the subject matter they were purchasing.

So, *cause* might be a relevant category for mistake, but it was not an exclusive category. Despite the efforts of eminent scholars to offer *cause* as a principled framework for *erreur*, courts rarely appealed to the concept, but more generally adopted a more pragmatic approach to its application alongside other ideas.

E. Fraud and mistake

Fraud (*dol*) has always been an easier route to nullity than mistake. Judges may therefore have been pragmatic in classifying an error by a victim as 'fraud' under article 1116 Cc rather than as 'mistake' under article 1110 Cc. Article 1116 Cc required manoeuvres and fraudulent behaviour, which are questions of fact, focusing attention to the moral character of the behaviour of the parties. Where the parties were on an equal footing as professionals and there were no manoeuvres, the courts refused to find fraud.[102] But in other cases, evidence of extreme reliance

[101] See Louis Josserand, *Les mobiles dans les actes juridiques du droit privé* (Dalloz 1928).
[102] *Fusi c Perret* (n 53).

on the transferee was considered to amount to *dol*. For example, an eighty-year-old priest, who had been in England since the Revolution, transferred his family property in France to the defendant. He complained about the way the transaction was brought about in a codicil to his will, so his heirs were able to use this to demonstrate fraud.[103] Equally, *dol* was found where a drinking companion obtained from his cousin a lease on unusually advantageous terms including an advance payment of two years' rent. The cousin's guardian (*tuteur*) was able to have the transaction annulled for fraud as a disguised loan on the ground that the transaction was made without legal advice and there were significant drinking debts owed for which the cousin needed money.[104]

Each of these cases were mistakes by the seller about the value of what they were selling. Such mistakes were inadmissible as mistake under article 1110 Cc but gained a remedy by the court's decision to categorize the facts as fraud. Each of these decisions of the *Cour de cassation* also made the point that the lower court judges were sovereign in their assessment of the findings of fact both with respect to whether there were fraudulent manoeuvres and whether the victim would not have contracted without them. The concept is not articulated further in these decisions, but the *Cour de cassation* was content to leave the direction of the law to the assessments of facts by the lower courts. The advantages for the litigants were pragmatic not conceptual. Although *dol* required particularly bad behaviour to be shown, it did not require a mistake as to a substantial quality of the thing and it provided an easier route to damages linked to the nullity of the transaction.[105]

F. Term of the contract and hidden defects

One of the ways in which the subjective element of mistake could be kept within bounds was by insisting that the relevant characteristic had been agreed as central to the contract, as a term. There would thus be evidence of the importance of this feature at the time the contract was made and what the understandings of the parties were. But this approach seems to link nullity for mistake with failure to deliver what was promised. Both might be based on erroneous assumptions, but they are distinct ideas. A failure to deliver what was explicitly promised constituted non-delivery for which article 1184 Cc provided a discretionary power in the judge to terminate the contract for breach and award damages, or to grant the debtor more time to perform. In the case of unexplicit terms of the contract, articles 1641–1648

[103] Req 2 March 1840, *Guilbert c Delanoë*, S 1840.1.408. The rapporteur Lasagni in the case (the lead judge for the case) cites other cases where excessive influence was not treated as enough to constitute fraud: Cass civ 4 June 1810, *Grand c Grand-Maison*, S 1809-11.1.192; and Req 5 December 1838, *Bourdonnay et Moisson c Bourdonnay-Duclésio*, S 1838.1.951.

[104] Cass civ 5 August 1840, *Lechaffotec c Lechaffotec*, S 1840.1.907.

[105] Nicholas (n 11) 101 and 110–12.

Cc made provision for hidden defects. The contract might be terminated or there might be a reduction in the price. Both of these provisions gave discretionary power to the judge. By contrast, it was established very early on that the judge had no discretion on how to sanction nullity for mistake. If nullity were claimed, then nullity must be awarded.[106]

There were clearly different reasons for claiming non-delivery or a hidden defect. Non-delivery provided a contractual basis for damages for consequential loss, including loss of profits, under article 1184(3) Cc. A hidden defect gave rise to a possible claim to reduce the price. Article 1648 Cc on hidden defects gave rise to a claim for 'costs incurred in the sale'. Originally this was merely the expenses of making the transaction, but, later, courts tried to expand this to cover consequential loss. However, they then preferred to presume a professional seller to be in bad faith in selling goods which were defective, and this gave rise to a wider range of claims for damages under article 1645 Cc.[107] By contrast, any damages associated with nullity for mistake would be delictual under article 1382 Cc. It is often the different remedies sought by the parties that lead to differences in the technique adopted by the court.

Authors were clear that mistake and hidden defects were different issues. For example, the leading writer on sale, Troplong, argued that a mistake as to the authenticity of a painting could not be a hidden defect for the purposes of article 1641 Cc. The defect was not hidden because knowledgeable buyers knew how to recognize genuine old masters and would be expected to notice the defect.[108] The remark drew on an early case which refused to find a hidden defect when a painting did not turn out to be by a famous artist.[109] But such a comment left open the issue of mistake.

Ghestin noted that the courts took different attitudes in different periods to the question of whether the claimant was able to base a claim on both *erreur* and hidden defects at the same time or was required to choose between them. He noted that most authors treated them as clearly distinct causes of action.[110] Until 1950 the courts were flexible, as they were again between 1980 and the 1990s, but at other times they have been more rigid.[111] This suggests that the interpretation of the law was driven less by conceptual concerns and more by policy factors.

Tallon argued against the distinction supported by Hamel in the latter's edition of Planiol et Ripert,[112] that mistake took account of the subjective dimension

[106] Cass civ 4 vendémiaire An VII, *Guignard et Bellot c Granger et Maurey*, S 1791-XII.1.103: the lower court was required to grant nullity within the prescription period for factors vitiating consent under article 46 of the *ordonnance sur la reformation de la justice, fait à Lyon 13 juin 1510*.

[107] See Jacques Ghestin and Bernard Desche, *Traité des contrats. La vente* (LGDJ 1990) 899–902.

[108] R-T Troplong, *De la Vente*, vol 2 (Hingray 1835) no 555.

[109] CA Paris 17 April 1813, SV 1814.2.85.

[110] Ghestin (n 12) 344–45.

[111] Ghestin (n 41) 1057–67.

[112] Joseph Hamel, 'La Vente' in Marcel Planiol and Georges Ripert, *Traité pratique de droit civil français*, vol X (2nd edn, LGDJ 1956) pt 1.

of a contract whereas the guarantee against hidden defects took account of the economic dimension, and so they were conceptually distinct. For Tallon, such a conceptual distinction failed to take account of the way the judges' sovereign assessment of facts enabled similar facts to be placed under different conceptual categories in order to reach pragmatically fair solutions.[113] He gave agricultural seed as examples. The delivery of *autumn* wheat instead of *spring* wheat was held to be mistake under article 1110 Cc.[114] The delivery of *fodder* beetroot (mangel wurzels) instead of *kitchen* beetroot was held to be non-performance under article 1184 Cc.[115] The delivery of Russian hemp seed instead of hemp seed from Tours was held to be a hidden defect under article 1641 Cc.[116] In most cases, a claim for non-performance of the contract would be most suitable, since the seeds would have been planted and so restitution after nullity would be impossible. In the first mentioned case, the first instance court found no hidden defect, but mistake in relation to an essential feature of the purposes for which the product was destined. The *cour d'appel* awarded damages for failure to provide information, even though there was no mistake or hidden defect. The *Cour de cassation* upheld the award of damages, but for non-delivery. Everyone agreed compensation should be paid, but the legal basis varied. A later example concerned the sale by auction of Louis XV armchairs, described as *marquises*. After restoration work had been undertaken by the buyer, it was discovered that they had either been enlarged *bergères* or came from a different period. The first instance court granted termination for breach of contract under article 1184 Cc. The *cour d'appel* awarded nullity for mistake but refused damages for breach of the guarantee against hidden defects in sale. The *Cour de cassation* quashed the latter finding and, when the case was remitted to a different *cour d'appel*, the lower court awarded damages for breach of the guarantee against hidden defects under article 1641 Cc.[117]

These cases illustrate the way in which there was a lack of consistency in the classification by the courts of facts into conceptual categories. Whatever the clarity of concepts explained in the scholarly textbooks and articles, the courts seemed to make use of whichever category provided the fairest solution. Such an approach reinforces the analysis expressed by Ghestin that much judicial attention is focused on the fairness of the outcome of the case, an approach which he regretted.[118]

[113] D Tallon, 'Erreur sur la substance et garantie des vices dans la vente mobilière' in *Dix ans de conférences d'agrégation. Etudes de droit commercial offertes à Joseph Hamel* (Dalloz 1961) 435–57.

[114] Cass civ 24 June 1867, *Demoulin c Cadiet*, DP 1867.1.248. The case note points out that the solution fitted Troplong's book on sale (see n 108) and that Troplong was the first President of the *Cour de cassation* deciding this case!

[115] CA Paris 11 March 1947, D 1949.148.

[116] Req 28 April 1873, DP 1873.1.470. See also Cass civ 22 March 1853, *Dubuc c Leborgne*, S 1853.1.480.

[117] See Cass civ (1) 23 February 1970, *Aubin de la Messuzière c Chalon*, JCP 1970.II.16347 and CA Reims 25 June 1974, JCP 1975.II.18120.

[118] Ghestin (n 12) 355.

IV. Pragmatism at Work

This chapter has highlighted two features of the French law on mistake. First, it has provided illustrations of how courts in the period up to 2016 proceeded pragmatically in resolving cases and were consistent in their appeal to conceptual categories. Secondly, although scholarly writers had tried to systematize the law in terms of principle using certain key concepts they had to acknowledge the way courts decided cases and adjust their presentation accordingly. Although it is traditional to see scholarly writing as a dominant influence in French law, as Fortsakis tried in relation to administrative law,[119] in many ways the direction to the law is given by the courts.

A. Principle and pragmatism

The tension between the faithful adherence to concepts and principles on the one hand and pragmatic attention to fairness in the individual case has been seen in the discussion in section III. Judicial decisions did not seem to choose consistently one set of concepts or principles over others.

In particular, section III showed numerous instances where courts seemed to have chosen a conceptual category pragmatically in order to achieve a fair result and did not follow 'logically' the requirements for applying that concept that scholarly writers had outlined. In particular, this was shown by the discussion of 'substantial qualities' and *cause*,[120] and by Tallon's discussion of the relationship between mistake, breach of contract and remedies for hidden defects.[121] In addition, concepts such as 'consent' and 'fraud' were open-textured notions which allowed courts to analyse the facts with a view to achieving a fair result. Judicial reasoning did not elaborate any criteria for the application of these concepts.[122] The use of the concept of the 'substance' of the contract was treated in a similar way.[123]

Aspects of fairness were added to the specific requirements of the provisions on mistake in the Civil Code by way of judicial interpretation. The mistake of one party must, at least, have been known by the other, even if the dominant view was that the issue need not be an agreed term of the contract. As was seen earlier, unexpressed unilateral mistakes do not count.[124] Furthermore, mistakes that were not excusable did not count. This was not directly a finding of fault, but there is a strong sense from Pothier onwards that people should look after their own affairs

[119] See n 25.
[120] See nn 98–100 and accompanying text.
[121] See nn 112–116 and accompanying text.
[122] See sections III.C and III.E.
[123] See eg nn 45–46 and accompanying text.
[124] See eg n 88.

and not complain when they make a miscalculation.[125] The courts were equally adept at compensating a purchaser when a contract was nullified for mistake, at least where the purchaser had contributed to the value of a painting by his efforts. Therefore, there was the possibility of compensating the party who was not at the origin of the mistake, albeit not as explicitly as in German law. The contours of a framework did exist for fair re-adjustment of a situation where an unexpected gain or loss had arisen.[126] The cases also showed the ability of the courts to categorize facts flexibly in order to fit them within particular conceptual categories. This was seen especially in the many cases concerning works of art.[127]

The failure of judges to adhere consistently to principle was criticized by Ghestin in his 1963 thesis. He suggested that it was tempting to conclude that 'by an intuitive perception of the concrete situation, the judge should choose between the two parties the one who deserved to be protected'.[128] But leaving everything to judicial impressionism, he thought, would undermine the ability of individuals to know their legal situation in advance. For him, the hortatory function of law remained dominant.

However, the role of the hortatory function of law depends on how far those affected depend on the legal rule. Does it seem from the case law that people were failing to perform contracts because they claimed that they had made a mistake? Or is it that they were seeking a remedy for the poor outcomes of performed contracts? In the *Contract Law Today* discussions, Rudden argued against Atiyah's view that contract law had a predominantly remedial function by emphasizing that the executory contract is the typical contract.[129] But, in the cases typical of the French law of mistake, relatively few reported cases were executory contracts. For example, of the fifty cases studied in depth for this chapter, only two were completely executory contracts.[130] A further two were annuities which had begun to be paid, but were stopped after a small number of payments and the claimant was suing for continuing payment.[131] The vast majority of cases where mistake was raised were situations where a contract had been performed and then one party had discovered an important fact which made the transaction unfair. All the cases on the authenticity of paintings and other works of art were of this kind, as were all the cases concerning rights of succession. In the case of executed contracts, there is no question of refusing nullity for mistake in order to encourage people to perform their contracts. Rather, the question before the court was whether it was unfair to

125 For example, Pothier (n 39) s 31.
126 For example, the cases of the armchairs (see nn 69 and 117), *Poussin* and *Fragonard* (nn 70–75).
127 See nn 47–49, 63–68, 69–72, and 59–60.
128 Ghestin (n 12) 355.
129 Bernard Rudden, 'The Domain of Contract: English Report' in Harris and Tallon (n 1) 81, 84–89.
130 Cass 24 June 1873, *Société Young's Paraffin*, D 1874.1.17 (an English company refused to deliver paraffin free of customs duty where, unknown to the parties, the rate of duty had been raised from 5% to 37% by the French Parliament) and Req 1 July 1924 (n 1).
131 Req 7 July 1931; and CA Paris 3 February 1944 (n 93).

leave an unexpected gain or loss where it had fallen or to adjust the situation of the parties to achieve a fair result. To that extent Ghestin's concern about the need to protect contractual certainty was overstated. Pragmatism in the provision of remedies may have been appropriate in executed contracts.

To be fair to Ghestin, he did argue that contract law is a balance between three social values: freedom of contract, social utility (especially the public interest and certainty in contract), and fairness.[132] Much of his discussion was on the balance between the latter two. For Ghestin, contractual justice is severely limited by the priority of the social utility of contract.[133] But in the case of mistake, the argument from social utility may be less strong than he thought.

B. Scholarly writing and the courts

As noted above, Nicholas argued that conceptualization was primarily a function undertaken in scholarly writing.[134] The broad policy and conceptual categories for the application of the doctrine of mistake in French law were laid down early. The pre-Revolutionary doctrine and the authors of the Civil Code favoured the protection of the sanctity of agreements. Parties were free to contract, but their agreement bound them (article 1134(1) Cc). As a matter of principle, the authors of the Civil Code did not focus on subjective mistake, however genuine.[135] This line of reasoning was maintained by scholars until the turn of the twentieth century. For example, in the fifth edition of Aubry and Rau in 1902,[136] the editors argued that the subject matter of the contract involved not only the material content, but also the objective properties which, according to 'common knowledge' (*notions communes*), the item should have. But they acknowledged that there was a second view expressed in scholarly opinion which focused on the qualities either which individualized the subject matter or which reflected the purposes which the buyer principally had in mind when making the contract. Such subjective approaches were, in the view of those textbook authors, incompatible with the wording of article 1110 Cc and the intentions expressed in the preparatory works by the authors of the Code. But they had to acknowledge that the case law favoured the second view. Courts looked at what the parties had treated as the necessary elements of their agreement. The book then cited twenty-nine cases in which the editors (both members of the *Cour de cassation*) had noted this phenomenon. This illustrates the way in which conceptual tidiness in scholarly writing was less influential in shaping the direction of the law than the efforts of courts to achieve just results.

132 Ghestin (n 41) 447–49.
133 Ghestin (n 41) 449.
134 See n 19 and accompanying text.
135 See nn 33–34 and accompanying text.
136 Aubry and Rau (n 40).

The way in which the development of the law was more focused on achieving the fair practical solution to a case, rather than consistency in the use of concepts, is illustrated by the fact that the majority of the cases discussed in that edition of Aubry and Rau came from the lower courts, the judges of fact.

In section III, subsection D, we saw how scholarly attempts to give coherence to the use of mistake by reference to the doctrine of *cause* did not succeed. There were, indeed, some instances where the courts based their reasoning on *cause*, but such usage was patchy and never became dominant. Other scholars, such as Josserand, also disagreed with an appeal to *cause* to ground decisions on mistake. It is interesting to note that these scholars criticized the appeal to *cause* on the ground that it did not fit judicial practice.[137]

In section III, subsection E, we looked at the inter-relationship between mistake and remedies for hidden defects. Scholarly writers tried to insist on the separation of the two concepts. But the work of Tallon showed that courts did not consistently respect the distinction. Even Ghestin, who had championed the cause of conceptual clarity in his thesis of 1963, was prepared in later years to acknowledge the lack of conceptual clarity in judicial practice. Indeed, he was prepared to concede privately in the *Contract Law Today* discussions that the lack of conceptual clarity might have been in part the result of the role of professors as consultants to lawyers for the parties. Their advice to *avocats* on the choice of grounds for a claim or an appeal was often tactical—choosing the best concept that would give success to the client of the *avocat* they were advising.

V. Conclusion

The balance between principle and pragmatism is struck in different ways in different legal systems, between different legal issues within the same legal system, and between different groups of actors, such as academics and judges. The study of *erreur* shows that it is the ambition of scholarly writing to offer coherence and direction to the law. Conceptual categories have their origins in the Civil Code and in scholarly writing, often going back before the Code. But, however carefully drafted, these conceptual categories do not represent the driving force of the law. Their open texture and the conflicts between them open scope for variation in interpretation by courts. Faced with specific fact situations, the courts' unease with the results that would follow from a rigid adherence to conceptual principles leads them to adopt a more flexible approach. In the period studied here, the courts seemed to seek ways of redefining the meaning of the concepts, even if they remained faithful to the (loose) wording of article 1110 Cc. In addition, the

[137] See nn 98–99.

application of concepts requires specific findings of fact. The courts were able to make different determinations of fact to ensure an appropriate outcome. Indeed, as Tallon pointed out,[138] they seemed to be able to interpret very similar facts to achieve different outcomes.

Leading writers such as Ghestin emphasize the hortatory role of the law in ensuring legal certainty. But if the majority of cases coming forward relate to executed contracts, then the encouragement factor is less important than the dispute resolution role. In that role, fairness all round is achieved by giving a framework for settlement which may include recognition of the contribution which the buyer has made to the subject matter, such as through restoration which has contributed to establishing the authenticity of a painting. For the most part, cases of *erreur* are dealing with unexpected gains. Expected gains or losses were often handled under the concept of risk accepted as part of the contract or under the concept of *dol* if there had been exploitation of the ignorance of one party. In dealing with unexpected gains, the hortatory function of the law was less prominent. The idea of justice was more prominent and Ghestin identified this as choosing which party merits the most protection.

Going back to Lord Goff, in this area, it could well be said that the driving force of the law has been judicial reaction to concrete situations. Indeed, the amount of attention which scholarly writers give to the cases and their attempts to identify the dominant trend in the case law suggests that fitting an account of the law to the cases is almost as much a feature of French scholarly writing as it is of English law. Since scholars make a considerable part of their living as consultants or commentators in the very cases to which they try to fit conceptual frameworks in their textbooks, it could be said that they contribute to their own difficulties in making coherent sense of the law.

This overview of one specific area of law suggests that we need a more nuanced picture of the differences between English law and French law. It is an agenda that Simon Whittaker has set for us, but which needs to be pursued with careful attention to judicial decisions and case commentaries rather than just to what is said in textbooks.

[138] See n 113.

2

A Dangerous Method

Genealogy in the Interpretation of Contracts

*Michele Graziadei**

I. Introduction

Language, hailed as the greatest tool for human communication, has a complex and nuanced nature, which explains why it is also a source of confusion and miscommunication. Words are slippery, the implicit dimensions of interpersonal communications are often underestimated, and the meaning of a text can be elusive. Unsurprisingly, determining what the parties agreed while concluding a contract is an important question, frequently discussed and litigated in many jurisdictions. Nonetheless, certain issues related to the interpretation of contracts have little to do with language usage, or proficiency in a particular language. Instead, they arise from different conceptions of contracts, their underlying functions and ideals,[1] and from practical considerations, such as those concerning the costs of litigation and its efficiency as a means of dispute resolution.[2]

Even within a single jurisdiction there are different views about issues such as the weight to give to the parties' intentions, legal certainty, commercial practicability, fairness, expediency, considerations as to costs, and procedure in adjudicating disputes as to the interpretation of contracts. Controversies concerning the definition of these factors are far from rare. Where to draw the line in contentious cases often depends on the interaction of all these factors. With respect to the interpretation of contracts, the tendency to rationalize the law, to present it as a coherent whole, may hide its many purposes and consequent disagreements. The variety of notes that are simultaneously played in each legal system to fulfil disparate requirements

* All the translations in the text and in the footnotes are mine, except otherwise stated. My thanks to Marco Cappelletti, Ciara Kennefick, Dorota Leczykiewicz, Joshua Getzler, and Johanna McCunn for their helpful comments. The usual disclaimer applies.

[1] Simon Whittaker, 'Contracts, Contract Law and Contractual Principle' in John Cartwright and Simon Whittaker (eds), *The Code Napoléon Rewritten: French Contract Law after the 2016 Reforms* (Hart Publishing 2017) 29.

[2] Nicholas A Tiverios, 'Accuracy, Utility and Gateways: Justifications(?) for Controlling the Use of Surrounding Circumstances in Contractual Interpretation' (2021) 43 Sidney Law Review 547, 562ff; Remus Valsan, 'The Law and Economics of Contract Interpretation' in Jaap Baaij, David Cabrelli, and Laura Macgregor (eds), *Interpretation of Commercial Contracts in European Private Law* (Intersentia 2020) 31.

Michele Graziadei, *A Dangerous Method* In: *Comparative Reflections in Private Law*. Edited by: Marco Cappelletti, Ciara Kennefick, and Dorota Leczykiewicz, Oxford University Press. © Marco Cappelletti, Ciara Kennefick, and Dorota Leczykiewicz 2026. DOI: 10.1093/9780198959168.003.0003

of justice should not be lost or suppressed.[3] While it is tempting to contrast the different legal philosophies that inform contract law in different legal systems, caution is advised. The notion that each legal culture offers a different philosophical response to the interpretation of contracts may seem appealing at first sight, but this may only be an *ex post facto* rationalization of a complex set of factors at work to provide an intelligible framework for a particular rule.[4]

The comparative law literature on the interpretation of contracts recognizes a certain degree of convergence in the way contracts are interpreted in different legal systems, but it also notes some salient differences.[5] Of course, this is not just a matter of curiosity. For conflict of laws purposes, a contract governed by a foreign law must also be interpreted in accordance with that law.[6] The distinct approaches to contractual interpretation that prevail in different jurisdictions have an impact on the outcome of disputes. The rise of specialized courts in some continental European countries, such as France, Germany, and the Netherlands, which operate in English to attract English-speaking litigants, adds a new dimension to the issue.[7] It is not uncommon for a contract governed by a foreign law to be interpreted by the court in a way that still reflects an unconscious national bias in the interpretation process.[8]

[3] Nick Sage, 'Reconciling Contract Law's Objective and Subjective Standards' (2023) 86 Modern Law Review 1422.

[4] Catherine Valcke, 'Contractual Interpretation at Common Law and Civil Law: An Exercise in Comparative Legal Rhetoric' in Jason W Neyers, Richard Bronaugh, and Stephen GA Pitel (eds), *Exploring Contract Law* (Hart Publishing 2009) 77; Catherine Valcke, 'Convergence and Divergence of the English, French, and German Conceptions of Contract' (2008) 16 European Review of Private Law 29, and see Lord Hoffmann's remarks in *Chartbrook Ltd v Persimmon Homes Ltd* [2009] UKHL 38, [2009] 1 AC 1101, [39].

[5] See eg Silvia Ferreri, *L'intepretazione del contratto internazionale da parte del giudice italiano* (CEDAM 2000); Eric Clive, 'Interpretation' in Hector L MacQueen and Reinhard Zimmermann (eds), *European Contract Law: Scots and South African Perspectives* (Edinburgh UP 2006) 176; Stefan Vogenauer, 'Interpretation of Contracts: Concluding Comparative Observations' in Andrew Burrows and Edwin Peel (eds), *Contract Terms* (OUP 2007) 123; Valcke, 'Contractual Interpretation' (n 4); Giuditta Cordero-Moss, 'Interpretation of Contracts in International Commercial Arbitration: Diversity on More than One Level' (2014) 22 European Review of Private Law 35; Aurelio Gentili, *Senso e consenso: Storia, teoria e tecnica dell'interpretazione dei contratti*, vol 1 and 2 (Giappichelli 2015); Gerard McMeel, *The Construction of Contracts: Interpretation, Implication, and Rectification* (3rd edn, OUP 2017); Stefan Vogenauer, 'Interpretation' in Nils Jansen and Reinhard Zimmermann (eds), *Commentaries on European Contract Law* (OUP 2018) 740; Catherine Pédamon, 'Judicial Interpretation of Commercial Contracts in English and French Law: A Comparative Perspective' (2021) 23 European Business Law Review 1093; Solène Rowan, 'Observations on the Reform of the French Law on Contractual Interpretation' in Sophie Turenne (ed), *Reasons and Context in Comparative Law: Essays in Honour of John Bell* (CUP 2023) 123.

[6] Regulation (EC) No 593/2008 of the European Parliament and of the Council of 17 June 2008 on the law applicable to contractual obligations (Rome I), OJ L 177, 4.7.2008, p 6, art 1(a).

[7] On these courts: Albert Henke, Marco Torsello, and Elena Zucconi Galli Fonseca (eds), *International Commercial Courts: A Paradigm for the Future of Adjudication?* (ESI 2024); Man Yip and Giesela Rühl (eds), *New International Commercial Courts: A Comparative Perspective* (Intersentia 2024).

[8] See n 160.

The purpose of this chapter is to highlight what was common to several legal systems with respect to the interpretation of contracts before a heightened sense of separateness and diversity among them began to materialize in the latter part of the nineteenth century. My discussion will mostly focus on English and French law, with occasional incursions into other legal systems that offer interesting insights on specific points.[9]

As to the method followed, this is a study in genealogy, aimed at tracing doctrines and rules rooted in the past, to appreciate better the (relative) value of present conceptions and solutions. Far from being a unique sample of this kind of research, this contribution falls in line with other, similar research. It is well known that certain maxims used as canons of interpretation (often still expressed in Latin) are shared across legal systems, and that this is not by chance. *Verba cartarum fortius accipitur contra proferentem* ('the words of documents are to be taken strongly against the one who proffers them');[10] *verba sunt intelligenda ut res magis valeat quam pereat* ('an interpretation which upholds the validity of a transaction is to be preferred to one which would render it ineffective');[11] *falsa demonstratio non nocet cum de corpore constat* ('a false description does not vitiate when there is no doubt which person is meant'),[12] and so on are part of the tools of the trade in many jurisdictions. It is also known that similar principles on the interpretation of contracts often derive from the Roman law and its afterlife in the epoch of the *ius commune*, when canon law also contributed to the elaboration of this important legacy. This kind of learning was once inscribed, both on the Continent and in England, within a wider intellectual framework that valued maxims as a way of thinking about and explaining the law.[13] In that world, it was firmly believed that to depart from the words of a text as they were written was to resort to a dangerous method

[9] Valcke, 'Contractual Interpretation' (n 4), and Vogenauer, 'Interpretation' (n 5) have already examined German law in depth, which dispenses me from trying to add to the points they made.

[10] The Latin maxim was introduced into English law by Lord Coke and Lord Bacon. See *Oxonica Energy Ltd v Neuftec Ltd* [2008] EWHC 2127 (Pat) (Peter Prescott QC sitting as a judge of the Chancery Division); Joanna McCunn, 'The *Contra Proferentem* Rule: Contract Law's Great Survivor' (2019) 39 Oxford Journal of Legal Studies 483.

[11] This is the translation of the maxim given by a majority of the Supreme Court in *Enka Insaat ve Sanayi v OOO Insurance Company Chubb* [2020] UKSC 38, [2020] 1 WLR 4117, [95].

[12] Rix LJ translated the principle as 'a plain misdescription did no harm' in *Gesner Investments Ltd v Bombardier Inc* [2011] EWCA Civ 1118, [19].

[13] Adolfo Giuliani, 'Knowing Through Maxims', <http://dx.doi.org/10.2139/ssrn.4814874> accessed 2 May 2024. On the nature and the role played by legal maxims in English law, see Ian Williams, 'The Role of Rules: Legal Maxims in Early-modern Common Law Principle and Practice' in Maksymilian del Mar and Michael Lobban (eds), *Law in Theory and History: New Essays on a Neglected Dialogue* (Hart Publishing 2016) 188. On the diverging approach to legal maxims in the common and in the civil law tradition after the renaissance, see Andreas Blank, 'Leibniz, Locke, and the Early Modern Controversy over Legal Maxims' (2015) 41 History of European Ideas 1080. The relationship between English law and the *ius commune* in the sixteenth and seventeenth century is examined under a new light by David J Ibbetson, 'The Renaissance of English Legal History' [2021] Cambridge Law Journal 91; John Baker, *The Oxford History of the Laws of England*, vol 2 (OUP 2003) 3–52. For a broader, penetrating enquiring into the intellectual framework mentioned in the text, see James Gordley, *The Philosophical Origins of Modern Contract Doctrine* (OUP 1991).

of interpretation,[14] and the title of this chapter reflects the enduring tension with respect to challenges to literal adherence to textual language over time. Lawyers have always expressed fear that the unbridled search for meaning in written text could be disruptive of their art or profession and undermine the practical function of the law. And yet, despite intimations that such method should be avoided, the interpretation of contracts was never a simple matter of strict adherence to a written text. Having said this, some shared principles of interpretation have solid historical roots both in the civil law and in the common law tradition.[15] In the following pages I intend to cast more light on this background. Failure to appreciate the genealogy of the law on contractual interpretation may lead to misapprehensions regarding what the courts say and do. Prior historical research in this area of the law supports a similar conclusion.[16]

Here I shall discuss only the problems involved in determining what the parties intended when they agreed on a particular written text, without taking a broader approach to the construction of contracts.[17] A broader approach would involve the discussion of several other issues, mostly related to a normative approach to determining the content of a contract, such as the analysis of, for example, the role of good faith or commercial reasonableness in the interpretation of contracts. Secondly, my aim is not to be exhaustive, but rather, as I said, to give an example of what this type of research reveals. If productive, this research sheds light on how variations along some common lines emerge over time. What is found beneath the surface of the law may help us to understand better what we share and why, or how divergences arise. It may even provide a form of denouement. Is this not what comparative law is supposed to do?

Let me add that with this text I intend to honour a scholar to whom I owe more than I can express here, both in intellectual terms and for a friendship that I treasure, and that goes back to the very first steps of our academic lives.

II. Text and Context

What is the relationship between the text of the contract and its context? This crucial question has been the subject of intense debate in England in recent decades.

[14] See text to nn 38, 46, 82.

[15] See eg McCunn (n 10). On the related subject of the interpretation of statutes, see the landmark comparative study by Stefan Vogenauer, *Die Auslegung von Gesetzen in England und auf dem Kontinent* (Mohr Siebeck 2001).

[16] Joanna McCunn, 'Revolutions in Contractual Interpretation' in Andrew Robertson, Graham Virgo, and Sarah Worthington (eds), *A Historical Perspective in Revolution and Evolution in Private Law* (Hart Publishing 2018) 141; Joanna McCunn, *The Interpretation of Deeds and Wills at Common Law, c. 1536–c. 1616* (PhD thesis, University of Cambridge 2019) casts further light on the subject from the perspective of a common lawyer.

[17] cf Ewan McKendrick, 'Express Terms' in Hugh Beale (ed), *Chitty on Contracts* (35th edn, Sweet & Maxwell 2023) para 16-047.

Both the Supreme Court and the Court of Appeal have repeatedly had the opportunity to state and restate the principles governing the interpretation of contracts.[18] Lord Hoffmann vigorously defended the idea that a contractual text is to be read in context, and that 'background will always play some part in determining what the speaker or notional author used the words to mean'.[19] Not everybody agrees. Lord Sumption criticized Lord Hoffmann because in dealing with contractual interpretation the court should not have too ample opportunity to override the 'autonomous meaning' of the words used by parties to frame their contract.[20] Although both Lord Hoffmann and Lord Sumption support an objective theory of contract interpretation, ascertaining the meaning of contractual texts under each of their approaches tends to be done differently. Careful consideration of these different positions highlights some possible points of contact but also reveals disagreement.[21] If words have an autonomous meaning and the text agreed upon appears to be self-sufficient, in principle interpreters should not look beyond it. At most, the background context is to be examined to clarify the meaning of the words employed in the contractual document. One could, however, reply that any text is a set of symbols, and symbols by their very nature must be interpreted. Therefore, the words employed within a text do not rigidly delineate a clear-cut boundary for the interpreter when it comes to ascribing meaning to them, as Lord Hoffmann maintained.

From a comparative and historical perspective, these debates are far from unprecedented. The questions raised before English courts on the interpretation of contracts are inherently multi-jurisdictional; it is therefore instructive to consider them in a broader setting. In order to do so, a few preliminary clarifications are helpful. First, different legal systems adopt a more or less expansive view of the proper scope of the interpretation of contracts.[22] At a higher level of generality, contract is not a uniform concept across legal systems, and the scope of contractual

[18] *Investors Compensation Scheme Ltd v West Bromwich Building Society* [1997] UKHL 28, [1998] 1 WLR 896; *Chartbrook Ltd v Persimmon Homes Ltd* [2008] EWCA Civ 183, [2008] 2 All ER (Comm) 387; *In Re Sigma Finance Corporation* [2009] UKSC 2, [2010] 1 All ER 571; *Rainy Sky SA v Kookmin Bank* [2011] UKSC 50, [2011] 1 WLR 2900; *Arnold v Britton* [2015] UKSC 36, [2015] AC 1619; *Wood v Capita Insurance Services Ltd* [2017] UKSC 24, [2017] AC 1173; *Sara & Hossein Asset Holdings Ltd v Blacks Outdoor Retail Ltd* [2023] UKSC 2, [2023] 1 WLR 575; *Dassault Aviation SA v Mitsui Sumitomo Insurance Co Ltd* [2024] EWCA Civ 5, [2024] 2 WLR 833, [115].

[19] Leonard Hoffmann, 'Language and Lawyers' (2018) 134 Law Quarterly Review 553, 560.

[20] Lord Sumption, 'A Question of Taste: the UK Supreme Court and the Interpretation of Contracts' in Daniel Clarry (ed), *The UK Supreme Court Yearbook: Volume 8 (2016–2017)* (Appellate Press 2018) 75.

[21] Ewan McKendrick, 'Interpretation' in William Day and Sarah Worthington (eds), *Challenging Private Law: Lord Sumption on the Supreme Court* (Hart Publishing 2020) 3, 4ff.

[22] Vogenauer, 'Interpretation of Contracts' (n 5). See eg *Marks & Spencer Plc v BNP Paribas Securities Services Trust Co (Jersey) Ltd* [2015] UKSC 72, [2016] AC 742 [26] (Lord Neuberger) (supporting the distinction between 'interpretation' and 'implication of terms in fact' because 'construing the words used and implying additional words are different processes governed by different rules'). This decision rejects Lord Hoffmann's approach to the same issue in *Attorney General of Belize v Belize Telecom Ltd (Belize)* [2009] UKPC 10, [2009] 1 WLR 1988.

liability is thus variable. To overcome this difficulty in the application of EU legislation, such as the Rome I Regulation on the law applicable to contractual obligations,[23] the Court of Justice of the EU has developed an autonomous concept of contract.[24] Furthermore, while certain contractual matters in some legal systems fall within the scope of civil or commercial law, in other jurisdictions they may appear in an entirely different guise, governed by public or administrative law.[25] Even within a single legal system, the concept of contract is not uniform from the point of view of the rules on contractual interpretation. Different rules of interpretation may apply to different types of contracts (eg commercial and consumer contracts, employment contracts, standard form contracts, etc). Different rules on evidence and procedure play a role in this context as well.[26] English law is a case in point as the interpretation of oral or partly oral contracts is governed by rules that differ in certain respects from those applicable to written contracts. While extrinsic evidence concerning the subsequent conduct of the parties is not admissible for interpreting written contracts,[27] such evidence is admissible in the case of oral or partly oral contracts.[28] This difference has historical roots, but has received recent judicial support on the basis of various practical considerations.[29] In both France and Italy, evidence given in writing or orally is not admissible for adding to or contradicting a written contract.[30] The very idea that the interpretation of contracts should be governed by rules varies from jurisdiction to jurisdiction and is not universally accepted. An English court now applies 'principles' of interpretation to contracts, while the old idea that contracts should be interpreted by applying 'rules' of interpretation has fallen out of favour: precedents in this area of the law provide 'guidelines' to the court, rather than rules to be applied.[31] Elsewhere, articles of the civil codes on the interpretation of contracts may be considered more

[23] Regulation (EC) No 593/2008 on the law applicable to contractual obligations (n 6).

[24] Case C-147/12 *Östergötlands Fastigheter AB v Frank Koot, Evergreen Investments BV*, ECLI:EU:C:2013:490, para 33.

[25] Simon Whittaker, 'Public and Private Law-making: Subordinate Legislation, Contracts and the Status of "Student Rules"' (2001) Oxford Journal of Legal Studies 103.

[26] Joshua Getzler, 'Interpretation, Evidence, and the Discovery of Contractual Intention' in Simone Degeling, James Edelman, and James Goudkamp (eds), *Contract in Commercial Law* (Thomson Reuters 2016) 121.

[27] See text to nn 167–170.

[28] *Bottrill v Harling* [2015] EWCA Civ 564; *BVM Management Ltd v Roger Yeomans (t/a Great Hall at Mains)* [2011] EWCA Civ 1254. Nonetheless, the construction of an oral contract is in other respects subject to the same rules applicable to contractual documents: *Khan v Kahn* [2008] Bus LR D73 (Arden LJ).

[29] *Thorner v Major* [2009] UKHL 18, [2009] 1 WLR 776, [83] (Lord Neuberger, albeit a claim in proprietary estoppel rather than contract). See also Lord Neuberger, *The Impact of Pre-and Post-contractual Conduct on Contractual Interpretation* (Banking Services and Finance Law Association Conference, Queenstown, 11 August 2014) (<https://www.supremecourt.uk/docs/speech-140811.pdf> accessed 5 November 2024) paras 8–14.

[30] Art 1359 Cc (France); art 2722 of the Italian Civil Code. Several exceptions mitigate this prohibition, which in France does not apply to commercial contracts, but I need not consider them here.

[31] McKendrick (n 17) para 16-048, where he also states that *contra proferentem* is still considered more in the nature of a rule than of a principle.

as a source of practical advice to the court on how to perform that task than strictly binding rules of law.[32]

Once all this has been duly noted, it is still possible to identify cases which, in all the legal systems discussed in this chapter, would be classified as instances of contract interpretation, where the primary focus is on what the parties said and did, and what they meant by those actions and words.[33] It is to this material that I now turn.

III. Acte Clair

So how do you interpret contractual language? The tendency to assume that the text agreed upon by the parties to the contract has a stand-alone meaning, independent of the context in which the contract was concluded, has a distinguished historical pedigree in the civil law. Recent legal reforms in France and in Belgium show that it also has a contemporary dimension. The French reform of the law of obligations of 2016 introduced into the French Civil Code (Cc) a provision forbidding the interpretation of clear and unambiguous contractual terms: 'Clear and unambiguous terms are not subject to interpretation as doing so risks their distortion.'[34] The new Belgian Civil Code has a modified version of the same provision, drafted in less peremptory terms. Contracts evidenced in writing must not be interpreted in a way which is manifestly irreconcilable with the scope of their written text, having regard to the factors intrinsic to the text and the circumstances in which it was drafted and performed.[35] By expressly referring to the circumstances surrounding the text and the conclusion of the contract, the Belgian Code appears to be more open than the French Code to the consideration of extra-textual factors in attributing meaning to the contractual text. On the other hand, the different wording of these two provisions does not necessarily reflect a fundamentally different approach to the issue. It may simply be the result of different drafting styles. In any case, these recent enactments can hardly be regarded as innovations. Rather, they represent a restatement of the law as it developed under the original text of the French Civil Code because the *Cour de cassation* established a similar rule in the

[32] On the evolution of French law on this point, see Cyril Grimaldi, 'La valeur normative des directives d'interprétation', Revue des contrats 2015, No 1, 154.

[33] On the distinction between interpretation and construction of contracts, see Nicholas A Tiverios, 'A Uniform Hermeneutic Thesis: Objectivity and the High Court of Australia's Approach to Interpretation Across the Private Law' (2021) 40 University of Queensland Law Journal 141.

[34] 'On ne peut interpréter les clauses claires et précises à peine de dénaturation' (art 1192 Cc). Translation by John Cartwright, Bénédicte Fauvarque-Cosson, and Simon Whittaker, in 'Appendix' to Cartwright and Whittaker (n 1) 434.

[35] '[O]n ne peut donner du contrat une interprétation manifestement inconciliable avec la portée de cet écrit, compte tenu des éléments intrinsèques à celui-ci et des circonstances dans lesquelles il a été établi et exécuté.' (art 5.64(2) Belgian Civil Code). The code is bilingual, and the French and the Dutch language versions are equally authentic.

second half of the nineteenth century.[36] It has recently been stated that this rule protects what the parties intended and that it would, for example, counteract the tendency emerging in the lower courts to manipulate contractual interpretation to meet requirements of fairness.[37]

Behind these rules of interpretation, which emphasize adherence to the words used by the parties to a contract, lies an old argument for adherence to the text. It was developed by the young Marcus Tullius Cicero a little over two thousand years ago in *De inventione*, a handbook for orators that he wrote around 86–84 BC. In *De Inventione*, Cicero addressed a variety of topics, including how to handle controversies arising from the asserted divergence between an author's intention and the written word. Cicero shows how an advocate should argue the point in favour of adherence to the text. He suggests that the wording of a text is the controlling factor in determining intent and that:

> If the writer is alleged to have meant one thing and written another, the advocate who follows the letter will say: it is not for us to dispute the intention of someone who has left us evidence of that intention precisely to prevent us from doing so . . . much inconvenience would result if it should be established as a principle that we may depart from the written word.[38]

The new rules in the French and Belgian Civil Codes, which reinforce the notion that clear words are a limit for the interpreter, are thus supported by a long line of authorities. Maxims such as *in claris non fit interpretatio* ('in clear cases no interpretation is allowed'), *interpretatio cessat in claris* ('interpretation ceases when things are clear'), *quando verba sunt clara, non admittitur mentis interpretatio* ('when the words are clear, no interpretation of intent is allowed'), all reflect an objective approach to the reading of legal texts. During the epoch of the *ius commune* similar maxims were often indistinctly referred to in the interpretation

[36] Cass civ 15 April 1872, DP 1872 I 176; S 1872 1 232. Art 1378 of the Dutch Civil Code of 1838 followed the *ius commune* tradition by providing that 'If words of a contract are clear one cannot deviate from them by interpretation'. The original version of the French Civil Code did not incorporate a similar rule, despite proposals in favour of it. See further on this point, Massimo Brutti, *Interpretare i contratti. La tradizione, le regole* (Giappichelli 2017) 134ff. Giovanni Chiodi, 'Interpretazione dei contratti e poteri del giudice: riletture del codice civile in Francia e in Italia tra Otto e Novecento' in Mauro Pennasilico (ed), *L'interpretazione tra legge e contratto. Dialogando con Aurelio Gentili. Atti del convegno, Bari, 29–30 settembre 2016* (ESI 2019) 51.

[37] François Terré and others, *Droit civil: Les obligations* (12th edn, Dalloz 2019) para 618.

[38] Marcus Tullius Cicero, *De inventione* (HM Hubbel tr, Harvard UP 1949) book II, chapter 44, section 128. On the Roman law and the intellectual tradition behind this text, which is indebted to the art of rhetoric, see: Brutti (n 36) 36ff, 54ff; Reinhard Zimmermann, *The Law of Obligations: Roman Foundations of the Civilian Traditions* (Juta & Co 1990) 622ff. The historiography on the interpretation of wills and contracts in Roman law is discussed in Giovanni Chiodi, *L'interpretazione del testamento nel pensiero dei glossatori* (Giuffrè 1997) 16ff; Cicero's *De inventione* was used as a textbook at Bologna in the twelfth century: Ronald G Witt, *The Two Latin Cultures and the Foundation of Renaissance Humanism in Medieval Italy* (CUP 2012) 423–24.

of provisions of law, or private documents, such as wills and contracts.[39] The elaboration of canons of interpretation favoured a similar transversal approach. Until 1916, the Austrian Civil Code of 1811 still reflected this overall tendency by extending to the interpretation of contracts the provision of the code on statutory interpretation.[40] In England as well, Lord Blackburn held that statutes should be interpreted just like contracts or wills, by having regard to intention as expressed by the words used.[41]

Going back in time, Justinian's Digest contains fragments that favour an approach to the interpretation of private acts that prescribes adherence to the text; for example: '[w]hen there is no ambiguity in the words, the question of intent should not be considered.'[42] This opinion from Paulus was given on a testamentary matter, but a long series of academic and practical commentaries of the epoch of the *ius commune* support its application to other private acts such as contracts (and, once more, to normative enactments too).[43] In testamentary matters the idea of reliance on the meaning of the words of the testament, except when it was clear that the testator had a different intention, was also expressed by Marcellus, another prominent Roman jurist: '[o]ne ought only to depart from the sense of the words when it is clear that the testator meant something else.'[44]

Eventually, *Le droit des gens, ou Principes de la loi naturelle* by Vattel, a very popular and influential book on public international law based on natural law principles, first published in London in 1758, supported the same principle for the case in which the drafter of a treaty used 'clear and precise terms' (*termes clairs et précis*).[45] With little adaptation, in 2016 these words found their way into the text of the new provision of article 1192 Cc. It is worth reading in full the relevant excerpt from Vattel's great work:[46]

[39] Giovanni Rossi, 'Il giurista al banco di lavoro: L'interpretazione dei negozi giuridici privati nelle "Vaticanae lucubrationes de tacitis et ambiguis conventionibus" di Francesco Mantica' in Marco Cavina (ed), *Francesco Mantica (1534–1614). Vicende umane e vicende culturali di un giurista della controriforma* (Pàtron 2011) 73, 88. This does not mean that the medieval jurists were blind to the different problems raised by the interpretation of a will and the interpretation of a contract: Chiodi (n 38) 225.

[40] ABGB, §914. This provision was amended in 1916 to bring it in line with §133 of the BGB. Both now provide that the focus of interpretation should be on determining the true intention behind a declaration, rather than strictly adhering to its literal wording.

[41] *River Wear Comm'rs v Adamson* (1877) 2 App Cas 743. Cf Jonathan Green, 'The Misunderstood History of Interpretation in England' (2024) 56 Arizona State Law Journal 911.

[42] 'Cum in verbis nulla ambiguitas est, non debet admitti voluntatis quaestio' (D. 32.25.1).

[43] Rossi (n 39) 86–88.

[44] 'Non aliter a significatione verborum recedi oportet quam cum manifestum est aliud sensisse testatorem' (D. 32.1.69). Translation by Alan Watson (ed), *The Digest of Justinian*, vol 3 (rev English ed, University of Pennsylvania Press 1998).

[45] As mentioned above in text to nn 39–41, in this epoch certain maxims of interpretation were held to be of general application.

[46] Emer de Vattel, *Le droit des gens ou principes de la loi naturelle, appliqués à la conduite & aux affaires des Nations & des Souveraines*, vol 1 (Londres 1758) 461.

> The first general maxim of interpretation is, that *It is not allowable to interpret what has no need of interpretation*[.] When a deed is worded in clear and precise terms,—when its meaning is evident and leads to no absurd conclusion—there can be no reason for refusing to admit the meaning which such deed naturally presents. To go elsewhere in search of conjectures, in order to restrict or extend it, is but an attempt to elude it. If this dangerous method be once admitted, there will be no deed which it will not render useless.[47]

Vattel does not cite any Roman law source on this point, but the pertinent references must have been obvious to his readers. Paulus's fragment mentioned above is directly on the point. The second key reference is Venuleius' opinion on the origins of the saying *in certis non est locus coniecturae* ('in things certain there is no room for conjecture').[48] Vattel is alert to the risks inherent in the 'dangerous method'[49] of challenging the manifest meaning carried by the clear and precise terms of an instrument where there are no obvious reasons to set it aside. Follow that dangerous method—this is Vattel's conclusion—and any document shall not be worth the paper it is written on. In advancing this point, Vattel was essentially rehearsing Cicero's old argument in *De inventione:*

> much inconvenience would result if it should be established as a principle that we may depart from the written word. For those who draw up a written document will not feel that what they have written will be fixed and unalterable, and judges will have no sure guide to follow if [they] depart from the written word.[50]

Jurists of the natural law school who wrote before Vattel had already advanced similar opinions. Pufendorf had done so in his *De jure naturae et gentium libri octo,*[51] and Wolff's monumental *Jus naturae methodo scientifica pertractatum* followed the same line of thought.[52]

Before proceeding further, let us pause to consider a linguistic point. The abovementioned fragment by the Roman jurist Paulus dealt with a case in which the

[47] Emer de Vattel, *The Law of Nations: or, Principles of the Law of Nature, applied to the Conduct and Affairs of Nations and Sovereigns* (1st edn, Sweet, Stevens, and Maxwell 1834, Joseph Chitty ed, CUP 2015) 213–14.

[48] D. 45.1.137.2. As shown by Chiodi (n 38) 113, fn 18, 166ff, 574ff, and Ian Maclean, *Interpretation and Meaning in the Renaissance: The Case of Law* (CUP 1992) 101ff, *coniectura* is a word with a precise technical meaning, indicating what is probable rather than what is certain, and is also used in relation to the interpretation of ambiguous texts contained in legal documents that raised questions of proof. This use goes back to Quintilianus, *Institutio Oratoria*, 3.6.43 (which was published ca 96 AD at the latest).

[49] See n 47.

[50] Cicero (n 38) book II, chapter 44, section 128.

[51] Samuel Puffendorf, *De jure naturae et gentium libri octo* (London/Amsterdam 1672), book 5, ch 12, s 13.

[52] Christian Wolff, *Jus naturae methodo scientifica pertractatum. Pars Septima* (Halle 1740) ch 4, para 822 (at p 491).

testator's words were not ambiguous. This is why he advised against raising a question concerning the will behind the words. Article 1192 Cc avoids the reference to ambiguity and speaks instead of *clauses claires et précises* ('terms that are clear and precise'), as Vattel did. The term *ambiguitas* had a rich background for the Roman jurists.[53] The jurists were acquainted with the philosophical and rhetorical traditions that distinguished various types of ambiguity. Ambiguity was therefore a key term in the discussion of similar problems in antiquity and interpreters struggled, for example, to distinguish *ambiguitas* ('ambiguity') from *obscuritas* ('obscurity').[54] Eventually, however, the discussions of the medieval jurists of similar problems turned as well on whether the dispute related to a document containing *verba clara* ('clear words') or not. *Verba clara* would not tolerate *interpretatio* ('interpretation') or *coniecturae* ('conjectures'), and they should therefore be taken by the judge for what they said, at face value.[55] Bartolus de Saxoferrato is explicit on this point: 'Likewise, if the words were perfectly clear and [the judge] wanted to interpret them differently, it would not be permitted.'[56] By the end of the renaissance period Jason of Mayno (Giason del Maino) made the same point, summing up the doctrine of his time with reference to the interpretation of a judgment:

> Where the words are clear, interpretation does not apply ... nor is there room for conjectures ... when the wording of a judgment is clear, it cannot be interpreted differently by the judge who delivered it, and thus no external interpretation of the word in the judgment can be made by the judge who issued it.[57]

The maxim *in claris non fit interpretatio* ('in clear cases no interpretation is allowed') handed down by the medieval interpreters to their successors emerged in this context.[58] From the linguistic point of view it is curious that the English translation of the reformed French Civil Code by Cartwright, Fauvarque-Cosson, and

[53] Anthony Ossa-Richardson, *A History of Ambiguity* (Princeton UP 2019) 77ff.

[54] Sebastiano Tafaro, *Il giurista e l'ambiguità': ambigere, ambiguitas, ambiguus* (Cacucci 1993); Chiodi (n 38) 107ff, 119ff (on the glossators), 131ff (on the influence of Aristotle's philosophy through the logicians); Saverio Masuelli, 'Regole per l'interpretazione nel diritto romano e nella tradizione romanistica. II. Regole per l'interpretazione in presenza di "oscurità"', Rivista di diritto romano 2015, 15, 1.

[55] Andrea Massironi, *Nell'officina dell'interprete: La qualificazione del contratto nel diritto comune (secoli XIV–XVI)* (Giuffrè 2021) 145ff; Chiodi (n 38) 232ff, 245. Both authors show that the principle was far from absolute.

[56] 'Item si verba essent omino clara et ipse [iudex] vellet aliter interpretari, non admitteretur'. Bartolus de Saxoferrato, *In secundam digesti novi partem* (Venetiis 1570) f 233va, comment to D. 49.1.4 pr, n. 7. See also comment to D. 45.1.99 pr, de verborum obligationibus l quicquid adstringendae, pr., and Maclean (n 48) 89ff ('The self-evident text').

[57] Giason del Maino, *In secundam digesti novi partem commentaria* (Venetiis 1590) Comment to D. 45.1.99 pr, de verborum obligationibus l. quicquid astringendae, n 4.

[58] Saverio Masuelli, '*In claris non fit interpretatio*: Alle origini del brocardo', Rivista di diritto romano 2012, no 2, 401, traces the origins of the maxim back to Cicero (n 38) book II, chapter 44, section 128: 'when the document is plain and the accused confesses everything, then the judge ought to comply with the law and not interpret it.'

Whittaker draws on the classical precedent provided by Latin. The English version of the expression *clauses claires et précises* used in article 1192 Cc is translated as 'clear and unambiguous terms'.[59] The translation thus draws upon the legacy of the Latin sources to the English language.[60]

Which terms can then be considered 'clear and unambiguous' (*claires et précises*)? If the historical materials are set aside for a moment and the question is posed with reference to French law, it appears that the *Cour de cassation* proceeds in this matter in a rather firm way,[61] although academic commentators maintain that the distinction is not as simple and clear-cut.[62]

The point that is not made in this discussion is that clarity and precision are not just a matter of linguistics. True, some contractual texts are unclear because of garbled language, but the text agreed by the parties to a contract may be clear from a linguistic point of view, and yet neither clear nor precise for legal purposes. This will be the case in particular where extrinsic circumstances—whether antecedent, contemporaneous, or subsequent to the conclusion of the contract—raise serious doubts as to whether a particular result which would be warranted by the text was actually intended by the parties to the contract. If there is sufficient reason to believe that the parties would have excluded such an outcome, there is a legitimate reason to doubt whether the text of the contract stands as written, although the possibility that one side agreed to something which, in hindsight, did not serve its interests should not in principle be ruled out.[63]

In the civil law tradition, the view that *verba clara* ('clear words') are not to be interpreted applies only where those words are taken to be a manifestation of the parties' will. Even a clear and unambiguous expression is not decisive whenever extra-textual indicia cast doubt on the existence of a corresponding intention. The text may then be set aside in the name of the need to adhere to the actual intention of the parties. The adage *in conventionibus contrahentium voluntatem potius quam verba spectari placuit* ('In agreements between contracting parties, intention rather than the actual words must be considered') can be invoked to support this conclusion.[64]

This leads me to conclude that the principle in *claris non fit interpretatio* is best understood as a dialectical argument. Its weight had to be assessed by the medieval interpreters on a case-by-case basis, in relation to the situation at hand and the specific facts of the case. It was not a hard and fast rule.[65] Essentially, medieval

[59] Cartwright and Whittaker (n 1) 492 for the text of art 1192 Cc.
[60] See n 42.
[61] See eg Cass civ (1) 30 January 2019 no 18-10796; Cass civ (1) 10 December 1991 no 90-14.519.
[62] See eg Terré and others (n 37) para 618.
[63] The point is highlighted (once more) in *PA(GI) Limited v Cigna Insurance Services (Europe) Limited* [2023] EWHC 1360 (Comm).
[64] D. 50.16.219 (translation by Watson (n 44)). Art 1188(1) Cc and art 1362(1) of the Italian Civil Code follow this old text closely.
[65] Massironi (n 55) 162.

jurists and their successors engaged in balancing acts when interpreting a particular text. Consequently, courts might set aside clear words to reach an outcome that the words did not necessarily support, provided there were sufficient arguments to do so. This maxim was a rule of thumb that allowed the search for an alternative whenever there were sufficient indications that such an alternative was based on weighty considerations. Quite paradoxically, one could argue that when the parties' intentions could not be firmly established, the wording of the text was all that an interpreter had. Thus, the operative meaning of the maxim recommending against the interpretation of clear words seems rather to be: *in dubio non est recedendum a verbis* ('in case of doubt, one must not depart from the words').[66]

The 'proper meaning of words' (*propria verborum significatione*) could therefore be abandoned if it was certain that it did not correspond to the parties' will.[67] On the other hand, it had to be respected if there was uncertainty on this point. The Spanish Civil Code follows this line of thought:

> If the terms of a contract are clear and leave no doubt about the intention of the parties, the literal meaning of its clauses shall be followed. If the words appear to be contrary to the evident intention of the parties, the latter shall prevail over the former.[68]

Under this provision, the text of the contract expressed in clear terms governs the case, unless there are doubts as to the intention of the parties. But to prevail over the letter of the terms, a contrary intention of the parties must be evident. Once more, the notion that a contrary intention must be 'evident'[69] to lead to a different interpretation of the contract has a distinguished antecedent. In this case it is Domat's *Les lois civiles dans leur ordre naturel*, first published in 1689: 'If the words of a Covenant appear to be contrary to the intention of the Contracters, which is otherways evident, we must follow this intention, rather than the words.'[70]

[66] ibid 165. The maxim can be traced to D. 32.69 pr concerning Marcellus' opinion on the interpretation of testaments: 'one should not deviate from the meaning of words in a will, unless the testator's different intention was evident' ('Non aliter a significatione verborum recedi oportet, quam cum manifestum est aliud sensisse testatorem').

[67] On the proper meaning of words with respect to wills, see Chiodi (n 38) 231ff, 245ff. He clarifies that doubts about the meaning of the text opened up the interpretative exercise (ibid 557ff).

[68] Spanish Civil Code, art 1281.

[69] ibid.

[70] Jean Domat, *The Civil Law in Its Natural Order: Together with the Publick Law* (William Strahan tr, London 1722) book I, tit I, s II, §11 (p 39), 4th Rule. The marginal note to the text is: 'The Intention to be preferred to the Expression.' Domat cites various fragments of the Digest in support of this opinion. In the same section of his work, s 8, he argues that it is by the common intention of the contracting parties 'that we are to explain whatever may be obscure or doubtful in the Covenant.' For a deeper examination of Domat's literalist approach to the interpretation of contracts and his use of the Roman sources, see Brutti (n 35) 106ff (compared to Domat's doctrine, Pothier's doctrine is more open to a subjective interpretation of the contractual text, and is therefore more innovative: ibid 122ff); Valentina Calderai, *Interpretazione dei contratti e argomentazione giuridica* (Giappichelli 2008) 21ff.

An allegation aimed at showing that the text of the contract does not reflect the common intention of the contracting parties can succeed only if that intention is evident.

So far, the intention of the parties has been treated as a self-evident verbal formula. How nice it would be if it were![71] Arguments made to attack the apparent meaning of the text of the contract may in fact use different understandings of the parties' intention. This may lead to alternative interpretations of the contract. The unreasonableness of the meaning apparently given by the text (which would be absurd in the circumstances, a commercial nonsense, etc) can thus be contrasted with the reasonableness of an alternative solution allegedly also based on the parties' intention.[72] This strategy can be supported by inferences based on factors external to the text of the contract. They can lead to the construction of a plausible but hypothetical will, as in *Anglo Continental Educational Group (GB) Ltd v Capital Homes (Southern)* Ltd.[73] In this case the Court of Appeal rejected both parties' interpretation of the contract, preferring 'an interpretation which produces a result that the parties are likely to have agreed over an improbable result'.[74] The 2016 reform of the French law of obligations takes a position on this issue. The new provision of article 1188(2) Cc helps to disentangle the different meanings that a reference to the parties' intention has in different contexts. This is a step in a new direction, towards greater conceptual clarity, as discussed below.[75]

IV. Our English Brethren

As mentioned in the previous section, on the Continent the medieval interpreters took over from the Roman law *ambiguitas* as one of the key terms in the discussion of problems concerning the interpretation of legal documents.[76] They also thought that, where the words employed by the drafter of the instrument were clear enough, there was no reason to look for an alternative meaning by way of interpretation. On the other hand, the meaning of obscure words was to be collected by exposing the intention of the parties (as reconstructed by the court with the aid of presumptions). This approach was followed in 1536 by Fitzherbert and Baldwin JJ to interpret a bond in *Bold v Molineux*.[77] In 1555 the same Court of

[71] For an excellent critical discussion of this point, see Valcke (n 4).
[72] *Mannai Investment Co Ltd v Eagle Star Assurance* [1997] AC 749, 771 (Lord Steyn).
[73] [2009] EWCA Civ 218, [2009] CP Rep 30.
[74] ibid [13] (Lady Arden).
[75] See text to n 158.
[76] On the medieval and early modern jurists' struggles to define ambiguity: Ossa-Richardson (n 53) 82–83.
[77] (1536) Dy 14b, 73 ER 31. Fizherbert and Baldwin JJ take as a starting point of their judgment what was the common opinion in the *ius commune*: 'if a condition, or words in deeds and statutes, have a meaning, they do not want interpretation; but if the words do not bear apparent meaning, but obscure,

Common Pleas in *Throckmerton v Tracy*[78] decided in the clearest terms that it is the intention of the parties that drives the interpretation of words if it appears that words in a deed are used in an inappropriate way.[79] Fulbecke's *A Direction or Preparative to the Study of the Lawe*, first published in 1600,[80] shows that this is an orthodox view in England as well, just like in the civil law. In his work, Fulbecke pronounced it 'foolish' to doubt the meaning of words where it was 'plain and manifest'.[81] He held that, 'when the words of a covenant or devise be clear and manifest, we follow the literal sense of them without further investigation, because in things that be certain, and apparent, there is no place for conjecture'.[82] In the same year, *Butt's Case* reached a similar conclusion: 'the law will not make an exposition against the express words and intent of the parties, when it may stand with the rule of law *quoties in verbis nulla est ambiguitas, ibi nulla expositio contra verba expressa fienda est*.'[83]

This is almost a paraphrase of Paulus' famous opinion in D. 32.25.1. Indeed, the word exposition is a calque from *expositio*, the term that was used in the *ius commune* to refer to 'the process of explanation of an insufficiently clear text... addressed to the dissolution of its literal ambiguities'.[84]

Edrich's Case,[85] decided three years later, was the occasion for the Court of Common Pleas to apply the same reasoning to the interpretation of a statute, pointing out the danger of setting aside the words of statute without good reasons. In this case, the judges said:

then the intention of the makers and parties shall be expounded': ibid, Dy 18a, 73 ER 37. For a full discussion of this case see McCunn, *Deeds and Wills* (n 16) 41, 44–45, 49.

[78] (1555) Plow 145, 75 ER 222.

[79] On this case, see Joanna McCunn, 'Contractual interpretation: from the Tudors to Lord Hoffmann' (University of Bristol Law School Blog, 15 January 2018); <https://legalresearch.blogs.bris.ac.uk/2018/01/contractual-interpretation-from-the-tudors-to-lord-hoffmann/> accessed 13 October 2024; McCunn, 'Revolutions' (n 16) 145–47. McCunn holds that the 'central place' these cases give to the parties' intentions 'is entirely typical of interpretation cases from the period' (ibid 147). In *Lampen v Clobery* (1683) 2 Ch Cas 155, 22 ER 892 counsel cites Mantica, a civilian author, on the interpretation of a will, to emphasize the necessity of adhering to the words used in it. The title of Francesco Mantica's treatise, which is not given in the report, is: *Tractatus de coniecturis vltimarum voluntatum: in libros duodecim distinctus* (Ludguni 1581).

[80] William Fulbecke, *A Direction or Preparative to the Study of the Lawe* (London 1600). The fundamental study on this text is by Johanna McCunn, '"An art obscured with difficult cases": Interpretation and Rhetoric in Fulbecke's Direction' in Sophie Turenne (ed), *Reasons and Context in Comparative Law: Essays in Honour of John Bell* (CUP 2023) 94.

[81] Fulbecke (n 80) 30.

[82] ibid 33v. (The spelling of the words has been modernized.)

[83] *Butt's Case* (1600) 7 Co Rep 23a, 24a, 77 ER 445, 447. The Latin maxim in the case translates as: 'when in the words there is no ambiguity, then no construction contrary to the expressed words is to be made.'

[84] Adolfo Giuliani, 'From Presumption to Interpretation' in Ferdinando Treggiari (ed), *Giuristi dell'Università di Perugia* (Aracne 2010) 447, 455.

[85] (1603) 5 Co Rep 118a, 77 ER 238.

> they ought not to make any construction against the express letter of the statute; for nothing can so express the meaning of the makers of the Act, as their own direct words, for *index animi sermo* [('speech is the mirror of the mind')]. And it would be dangerous to give scope to make a construction in any case against the express words, when the meaning of the makers doth not appear to the contrary, and when no inconvenience will thereupon follow; and therefore in such cases *a verbis legis non est recedendum* [('there must be no departure from the words of the law')].[86]

The Latin maxim *quoties in verbis nulla est ambiguitas, ibi nulla expositio contra verba expressa fienda est*,[87] which excludes the possibility of interpreting a text contrary to its unambiguous, express words, was included in Coke's commentary on *Littleton's Tenures*[88] and cited in (at least) eight cases, including cases dealing with contracts, up to 1834 in *Jesse v Roy*.[89] The maxim according to which there must be no departure from the words of the law (*a verbis legis non est recedendum*) in *Edrich's Case* was regularly cited over the centuries. It is in the collection of legal maxims published by Wingate in 1658,[90] and it then features in Broom's *Legal Maxims* published in 1845.[91] The saying *index animi sermo* ('discourse is the index of the mind') is noteworthy as well. It compendiously expresses the notion that words communicate intention and must therefore be taken to express it. Its remote origins lie in *De Moribus*, a collection of 145 moral maxims composed by an unknown author around the year 600 CE, where it features as *imago animis sermo est* ('discourse [is] an image of the mind').[92] The exact textual precedent is provided by Petrarch, the Italian initiator of humanism, whose books Coke owned.[93] During his lifetime, Petrarch published a first collection of his letters under the title *Epistolae familiaris* composed between 1325 and 1366. While discussing the relationship between philosophy and rhetoric in a letter to his fellow student

[86] (1603) 5 Co Rep 118b, 77 ER 239.

[87] For the translation of the maxim, see n 83.

[88] Co Litt 147a.

[89] *Lanyon v Carne* (1699) 2 Wms Saund 165, 85 ER 912; *Thomlinson v Dighton* (1711) 10 Modern 31, 88 ER 631; *Hervey v Aston* (1738) West T Hard 350, 25 ER 975; *Spencer v All Souls College* (1762) Wilm 163, 97 ER 64; *Tankerville (Lord) v Wingfield* (1773) 2 Bro & B 498n, 129 ER 1058; *Cholmondeley v Clinton* (1820) 2 Jac & W 1, 37 ER 527; *Smith d. Jersey (Earl of) v Doe* (1821) 7 Price 379; 146 ER 1005; *Jesse v Roy* (1834) 1 Cr M & R 316, 149 ER 1101 (citation by counsel, at 330, 1106, the Court agrees at 344, 1112: 'The language of this contract is clear and distinct, and the plaintiff cannot recover').

[90] Edmund Wingate, *Maximes of Reason, or, The Reason of the Common Law of England* (London 1658) 25 (maxim 16).

[91] Herbert Broom, *A Selection of Legal Maxims, Classified and Illustrated* (Maxwell & Son 1845) 268.

[92] *De Moribus* was wrongly ascribed to Seneca in some old editions; it is currently attributed to an unknown author. I have consulted the text at: <https://www.thelatinlibrary.com/sen/sen.proverbs.shtml>, accessed 24 September 2024. In this text the maxim can be found at nos 72–73.

[93] WO Hassall (ed), *A Catalogue of the Library of Sir Edward Coke* (Yale UP 1950), lists two works under the name of Petrarch. I could not consult the list of books owned by Sir Edward Coke, Chief Justice, internal Holkham Hall list (as updated on 13 June 2018) cited by Ian King, 'The Legal Writing of Sir Edward Coke, the Anglo-Saxons, and Lex Terrae' (2024) 39 The Seventeenth Century 329.

Tommaso da Messina, Petrarch summed up the relationship between words and thought with the aphorism *index animi sermo.*[94]

While all these sources emphasize fidelity to the text as the primary principle of interpretation, McCunn's meticulous analysis of sixteenth-century cases reveals that, much like their continental European counterparts, English lawyers of the time often prioritized the parties' clear intentions over the literal wording of the document.[95] Fulbecke's *Direction* is eloquent on this point. He reports the argument that 'words were invented, that they might shew the meaning of the parties, therefore we must not regard that which is probable, but that which the words do sound'.[96] But then he goes on to show how it happens that the 'words do give place to the meaning':[97]

> To this I answere, that there ought to be no departing from the words, and from the true propertie, unlesse there bee apparant proofe of an other meaning: l. non alit . . . ff. de leg. 3 but where an other meaning doth appeare, there the toung yeeldeth to the heart, and the words do give place to the meaning.[98]

The jurists of the *ius commune* would have not been surprised by the way English lawyers approached the problem of interpreting private instruments. They could have easily agreed with a statement of the law such as that of Coleridge J in *Shore v Wilson*:

> I believe the authorities to be numerous and clear (too numerous and clear to make it convenient or necessary to cite them), that where language is used in a deed which in its primary meaning is unambiguous, and in which that meaning is not excluded by the context, and is sensible with reference to the extrinsic circumstances in which the writer was placed at the time of writing, such primary meaning must be taken, conclusively, to be that in which the writer used it; such meaning, in that case, conclusively states the writer's intention, and no evidence is receivable to show that in fact the writer used it in any other sense, or had any other intention.[99]

[94] Francis Petrarch, *Epistolae familiaris* (letter 9 to Tommaso da Messina). I consulted the edition of the letter published in Heinrich F Plett, *Rhetoric and Renaissance Culture* (De Gruyter 2004) 80ff.

[95] McCunn, 'Revolutions' (n 16) 144ff. The path-breaking study by Maclean (n 48) is still of fundamental importance to an understanding of the intellectual context.

[96] Fulbecke (n 80) 34.

[97] ibid.

[98] ibid. Fulbecke's citation (l. non alit . . . ff. de leg. 3) is to D. 32.69 pr (see n 66).

[99] (1842) 9 Cl & Fin 354, 555, 8 ER 450, 517–18. James Edelman, 'The Interpretation of Written Contracts' in Charles Mitchell and Stephen Watterson (eds), *The World of Maritime and Commercial Contracts: Essays in Honour of Francis Rose* (Hart Publishing 2020) 230, analyses the same case focusing on the speech of Tindal CJ.

On both sides of the Channel the applicable principles were very much the same during the period considered. The primary principle was strict adherence to the text. However, in cases of ambiguity or substantial doubts about its intended meaning—such as when a text seems nonsensical given the surrounding circumstances—extrinsic evidence could be admitted to clarify the text. In the last edition of 1928, an old work such as *Norton on Deeds* contains a statement of the law that still shows more than a trace of the old thinking:

> When the words used in a deed are in their literal meaning unambiguous, and when such meaning is not excluded by the context, and is sensible with respect to the circumstances of the parties at the time of executing the deed, such literal meaning must be taken to be that in which the parties used the words.[100]

The qualifications to the general rule are many and substantial in a work that should be—as McMeel noted—'a bastion of literalism'.[101] The same author remarks: 'It may be that the differences between the traditional approach and the modern approach are largely differences of emphasis.'[102]

V. Of Pleading and Evidence

In England, questions relating to the interpretation of documents such as wills, deeds, and written contracts were considered early on in pleading and evidence. During the Renaissance, a profound change in mentality steered the law towards a more favourable view of the evidential value of written documents over oral testimony.[103] This evolution of the law introduced a new challenge: whether extrinsic oral evidence could be accepted to clarify the intent behind an ambiguous written text. *Lord Cheyney's Case*,[104] decided by the Court of Wards in 1591, provided a first useful indication of how to bypass the procedural obstacle posed by the exclusionary rule against oral evidence that had meanwhile emerged.

Sir Thomas Cheyney's will left property to his son Henry and to Henry's heirs, with a remainder to Thomas Cheyney of Woodley and his male heirs, subject to the condition 'that he or they, or any of them, shall not alien, discontinue etc'.[105] Did this condition apply only to the remainderman and his male heirs, or did it also extend to his son Henry? Wray and Anderson CJ, on conference with other

[100] Robert F Norton, *A Treatise on Deeds* (2nd edn, Sweet & Maxwell 1928) 63.
[101] McMeel (n 5) para 1-40.
[102] ibid.
[103] Heather MacNeil, 'From the Memory of the Act to the Act Itself. The Evolution of Written Records as Proof of Jural Acts in England, 11th to 17th Century' (2006) 2 Archival Science 213.
[104] (1591) 5 Co Rep 68a, 77 ER 158.
[105] ibid.

Justices, resolved that proof by witness of the intent and meaning of the devisor was not admissible against the written words in the will, thus affirming the exclusionary rule mentioned above:

> for the will concerning lands, etc ... ought to be in writing, and the construction of wills ought to be collected from the words of the will in writing, and not by any averment out of it; for it would be full of great inconvenience that none should know by the written words of a will what construction to make or advice to give, but it should be controlled by collateral averments out of the will.[106]

The Court thus applied the precedent established in *Vernon's Case* in 1572.[107] Having stated the rule, the Court then proceeded to carve out an exception for the case where the testator, due to ignorance of a particular fact, had omitted to address a specific possibility in his will:

> but if a man has two sons, both baptized by the name of John, and conceiving that the elder (who had been long absent) is dead, devises his land by his will in writing to his son John generally, and in truth the elder is living; in this case the younger son may, in pleading or in evidence, allege the devise to him, and if it be denied, he may produce witnesses to prove his father's intent, that he thought the other to be dead.[108]

In such a case, parol evidence would have been admissible to prove the intention behind the words of the document.

A few years later, Bacon's *Maximes of the Lawe* discussed the same problem more systematically, by distinguishing between two types of ambiguity: 'latent ambiguity' and 'patent ambiguity'.[109] Bacon wrote his tract after the decision in *Lord Cheyney's Case* but before the death of Elizabeth I, to whom the work was dedicated; the manuscript was therefore probably first composed in 1596 or 1597 and later revised, to be published posthumously in 1630. In this work, Maxim nr 25 encapsulated the guidance given to resolve ambiguity in similar cases: 'Latent ambiguity in words is resolved by verification, for what becomes ambiguous because of a fact is resolved by verifying that fact.'[110]

[106] ibid. Ossa-Richardson (n 53) 87, fn 60 notes the similarity, in substance and phrasing, to Cicero (n 38) book II, chapter 44, section 128.

[107] (1572) 4 Co Rep 1a, 76 ER 845.

[108] (1591) 5 Co Rep 68a, 77 ER 158.

[109] Ossa-Richardson (n 53) 84–86 provides an excellent discussion of the intellectual context to which this work belonged. Ibbetson (n 13) 95 notes that 'Francis Bacon freely borrowed Roman texts alongside English materials in his *Maxims of the Law*', and that 'Rule 11, for example, is identical to D.50.17.8' (ibid fn 17).

[110] 'Ambiguitas verborum latens verificatione suppletur; nam quod ex facto oritur ambiguum verificatione facti tollitur.' Francis Bacon's tract was first published in 1630 and then appeared in several editions. My citations are to Francis Bacon, 'The Maxims of the Law' in James Spedding and others (eds), *The Works of Francis Bacon*, vol 7 (London 1859) 307, 385. Until the publication of the complete

As Bacon explained, ambiguity is of two kinds: patent and latent. Patent ambiguity 'is that which appears to be ambiguous upon the deed or instrument';[111] in other words, it is a formal property of the text. Latent ambiguity occurs instead where the deed or instrument 'seemeth certain and without ambiguity', and yet 'there is some collateral matter out of the deed, that breedeth the ambiguity'.[112] *Lord Cheyney's Case* provided an example of these two forms of ambiguity. The testator's will was affected by patent ambiguity, while the hypothetical case discussed by the Court in the same litigation provided an example of latent ambiguity. Following that precedent, but without citing it,[113] Bacon maintained that extrinsic evidence could resolve a latent ambiguity, because such an ambiguity is related to a matter of fact, that can be verified by oral evidence, which is therefore admissible in such a case;[114] on the other hand, oral evidence would be inadmissible for the resolution of a patent ambiguity, because such evidence would render 'hollow' a document of higher probative value such as a deed.[115]

As Ossa-Richardson has shown, for a little over a century, litigants and the courts ignored Bacon's work. From the last quarter of the eighteenth century, however, it began to be cited in the law reports as a valuable statement of the law. The question of whether the ambiguity was inherent in the text or due to circumstances external to it became central to the examination of the admissibility of extrinsic evidence.[116] Only in the latter case—a case of latent ambiguity—could the admission of extrinsic evidence (hopefully) clarify the intention of the party to the document before the court. If, on the other hand, the text suffered from a patent ambiguity, either the court could interpret it in such a way as to arrive at a coherent and specific meaning without recourse to extrinsic evidence, or the instrument was void for want of a discernible meaning shared by the parties. This doctrine was applied to both wills and contracts.[117] By the nineteenth century, it had become a commonplace and was thus codified in the Indian Evidence Act 1872, ss 93–7. This legislation is still in force in several Asian and African jurisdictions.[118]

Oxford Francis Bacon, this remained the standard edition. As the text explains, the maxim reflects the substance of the judgment in *Lord Cheyney's Case* (n 104), while its language is that of philosophical discussions. A possible source for such language is Jacopo Zabarella's Commentary of Aristotle's *Posteriors Analytics*: Iacobi Zabarellae, *In duos Aristotelis libros posteriores analyticos commentarii* (Padua 1582) 56, where the author distinguishes various forms of errors (patent and latent) in propositions.

[111] Bacon (n 110) 385.
[112] ibid.
[113] The hostility between Coke and Bacon is well known: Peter Grajzl and Peter Murrell, 'Characterizing a Legal–Intellectual Culture: Bacon, Coke, and Seventeenth-century England' (2021) 15 Cliometrica 43, 46ff and may perhaps be a reason for the omission.
[114] Bacon (n 110) 385.
[115] ibid.
[116] Ossa-Richardson (n 53) 88–91.
[117] ibid. Stephen Martin Leake, *A Digest of Principles of the Law of Contracts* (3rd edn, Steven & Sons 1892) 181–83.
[118] Yihan Goh, 'Contractual Interpretation in Indian Evidence Act Jurisdictions: Compatibility with Modern Contextual Approach?' (2013) 13 Oxford University Commonwealth Law Journal 17.

One of the nineteenth-century cases that illustrates the distinction between patent and latent ambiguity is *Raffles v Wichelhaus*,[119] a decision that has been rescued from obscurity by subsequent academic commentary.[120] Here, the existence of two ships named *Peerless*, both of which were to carry cotton from Bombay to Liverpool—one departing in October and another departing in December—gave rise to a contractual dispute over the sale of cotton on board one of them. Counsel for the defendant described the fact that the contract did not clarify which ship the parties had in mind as a latent ambiguity. Counsel for the plaintiff objected that the defendant had 'no right to contradict by parol evidence a written contract good upon the face of it'.[121] On demurrer, the Exchequer Court delivered a judgment for the defendants whose counsel argued the following:

> the moment it appears that two ships called the 'Peerless' were about to sail from Bombay there is a latent ambiguity, and parol evidence may be given for the purpose of shewing that the defendant meant one 'Peerless', and the plaintiff another. That being so, there was no consen[s]us ad idem, and therefore no binding contract.—He was then stopped by the Court.[122]

The Court simply held: 'There must be judgment for the defendants'.[123]

Later cases show that courts upheld the distinction between patent and latent ambiguity as applicable law until at least the first two decades of the twentieth century.[124]

Much water has passed under the bridge since this distinction was first adopted by the courts, and several decisions have since declared it outdated and useless. In *L G Schuler AG v Wickman Machine Tool Sales Ltd*, Lord Simon of Glaisdale maintained that the old learning evoked by the couplet patent ambiguity–latent ambiguity was of no value:

> the distinctions between patent ambiguities, latent ambiguities and equivocations as regards admissibility of evidence are based on outmoded and highly technical and artificial rules and introduce absurd refinements.[125]

[119] (1864) 2 H & C 906; 159 ER 375.

[120] AW Brian Simpson, '*The Beauty of Obscurity*: Raffles v Wichelhaus and Busch (1864)' in AW Brian Simpson, *Leading Cases in the Common Law* (OUP 1995) 135; and Catharine MacMillan, *Mistakes in Contract Law* (Hart Publishing 2010) 186ff provide a full analysis of the background of the case and of what seems to have been the reasoning of the Court, as well as of its reception in the legal literature, which framed the case as one of contractual mistake.

[121] *Raffles* (n 119) at 2 H & C 907, 159 ER 375: '. . . the defendant has no right to contradict by parol evidence a written contract good upon the face of it.'

[122] ibid at 2 H & C 908, 159 ER 376.

[123] ibid.

[124] *GWR v Bristol Corporation* (1918) 87 Law Journal Ch 414, 429 (Lord Wrenbury).

[125] [1974] AC 235, 268.

In *Mannai Investment Co Ltd v Eagle Star Life Assurance Co Ltd*, Lord Hoffmann condemned the distinction because it sanctioned a rule that was:

> not merely capricious but also . . . incoherent. It is based upon an ancient fallacy which assumes that descriptions and proper names can somehow inherently refer to people or things. In fact, of course, words do not in themselves refer to anything; it is people who *use* words to refer to things.[126]

In *Sans Souci Ltd v VRL Services Ltd*, Lord Sumption said:

> It is generally unhelpful to look for an 'ambiguity', if by that is meant an expression capable of more than one meaning simply as a matter of language . . . The real issue is whether the meaning of the language is open to question. There are many reasons why it may be open to question, which are not limited to cases of ambiguity.[127]

A leading treatise on the interpretation of contracts illustrates the distinction between 'patent ambiguity' and 'latent ambiguity' only to declare it irrelevant.[128]

Why do the courts now disavow and condemn in such strong terms a distinction that was honoured over several centuries? What is the 'ancient fallacy' mentioned by Lord Hoffmann in his speech? The misconception lies in assuming that a single, self-standing meaning, tied to the use of certain words, exists or can be achieved. Summing up nineteenth-century debates on this matter, it is the fallacy of missing the fact that there can only be some person's meaning.[129] The fallacy, therefore, lies in the assumption that there is a final or correct meaning of a word or phrase that exists independently of human use and interpretation.

The criticism of the traditional distinctions advanced in these terms was to have an impact many years later with the reform of the law concerning the interpretation of wills. The Administration of Justice Act 1982, s 21 now provides that extrinsic evidence, including evidence of the testator's intention, is admissible as an aid to interpretation where a will is either meaningless or ambiguous, either from its wording or from surrounding circumstances established by evidence other than the testator's intention.[130]

However, while testators could never be called to the witness stand in disputes as to the meaning of words in a will, for the obvious reason that they are no longer

[126] [1997] AC 749, 778 (emphasis in the original).

[127] [2012] UKPC 6, [14] (on appeal from Jamaica).

[128] Kim Lewison, *The Interpretation of Contracts* (8th edn, Sweet & Maxwell 2024) para 8.12: 'The traditional distinction between these two types of ambiguity does not appear to have survived into the modern law.'

[129] Ossa-Richardson (n 53) 91–96.

[130] See eg *Partington v Rossiter* [2021] EWCA Civ 1564, [2022] Ch 43.

living, the situation is rather different with respect to *inter vivos* transactions such as contracts. With respect to contracts, the parties may be alive and willing to testify when a dispute as to the interpretation of the contractual document arises.

Perhaps this distinction between testamentary dispositions and *inter vivos* transactions helps explain why, since the late nineteenth century, English law has adopted an objective approach to the interpretation of contracts as a starting point, whereas French law seems to adopt a subjective perspective, requiring the court to first determine the parties' common intention. In this respect, the institutional setting in which judges operated cast a long shadow on how the law is presented in each jurisdiction, as explained in the following section.

VI. Procedure as a Key to Substantive Law

Beginning in the late sixteenth century, civil litigation in England underwent a transformation, with the emergence of new procedural norms.[131] Within the common law courts, the notion of a party's oath lost its standing in the context of jury trials, finding its proper place exclusively within the old and obsolete trial form of wager of law. Consequently, parties were disqualified as witnesses before the common law courts in jury trials 'at least by the time of Eli[z]abeth, as early as 1582' and this was then 'a thing well understood and accepted'.[132] In the following century this evolution was rationalized by asserting that a party could not be relied upon to speak the truth.[133] Their exclusion as witnesses was considered to be essential to protect legal proceedings from falsehood and to avoid the risk of perjury. As a result of this development, by the mid-seventeenth century interested non-parties were also disqualified from testifying on the same grounds.[134]

The importance of these rules in the context of contract litigation should not be overlooked. They enabled common law courts, up until the mid-nineteenth century, to interpret contractual language while avoiding what was perceived to be the quagmire of a party's participation in the litigation as a witness in the case. English law was not isolated in adopting these rules.[135] Drawing upon the legacy of the

[131] John H Langbein, 'Historical Foundations of the Law of Evidence: A View from the Ryder Sources' (1996) 96 Columbia Law Review 1168; Joel N Bodansky, 'The Abolition of the Party-Witness Disqualification: An Historical Survey' (1981) 70 Kentucky Law Journal 91.

[132] John Henry Wigmore, *A Treatise on the System of Evidence in Trials at Common Law*, vol 2 (3rd edn, Little Brown 1940) 680 at §575, fn 21, citing *Dymoke's Case* (1582) Savile pl 81, 123 ER 997. Baker (n 13) vol 6, 364, fn 122, refers the reader to the *Diversite de Courtz* (1530) sig C3v for the same rule. Wigmore notes some later rulings in which the parties themselves are offered as witnesses, eg *Smith's Case* (1611) 12 Co Rep 69, 77 ER 1347, and *Howard v Bell* (1617) Hob 91, 80 ER 241.

[133] James Oldham, 'Truth-telling in the Eighteenth-century English Courtroom' (1994) 12 Law and History Review 95, 107ff.

[134] Wigmore (n 132) 680 at §575.

[135] After a thorough review of the sources, Michael RT Macnair, *The Law of Proof in Early Modern Equity* (Dunker & Humblot 1999) 185ff, 230, rejects Wigmore's arguments against a roman-canon law

Roman law, the civil law in the same period prohibited witnesses from testifying in their own cases (*nullus idoneous testis in res sua intelligitur*).[136] The law of evidence in civilian jurisdictions such as France or Italy also disqualified both parties and interested non-parties as witnesses.[137] Actually, the prohibition on hearing parties or interested non-parties as witnesses still operates today, both under the French Civil Code (articles 1381 and 1386) and the Italian Code of Civil Procedure (article 246).[138] Therefore, up until the mid-nineteenth century, courts on both sides of the Channel consistently excluded testimony from the parties involved in the dispute when pronouncing on the interpretation of their contract.

While France and Italy have not changed the law on this subject, England reformed the law of evidence during the first half of the nineteenth century with several Acts passed between 1843 and 1851. This legislation abolished most of the exclusionary rules of evidence criticized by the Benthamite reformers and their followers.[139] The abolition of the rules on the disqualification of parties as witnesses came last, with the Evidence Act 1851, s 2. The new rules were not favoured by many lawyers, and they were not popular with several judges who were against the abolition of the old rules.[140] What probably played in favour of this last reform was the success of the new rules in the county courts and in arbitration proceedings.[141]

With this reform, the English rules on evidence began to diverge significantly from those in France and Italy. As seen previously, in both France and Italy, parties remain disqualified from giving evidence as witnesses, whereas under English law parties' testimony is now admissible. This means that, in principle, nothing prevents parties from testifying about their intentions when entering into a contract under English procedural law. However, contract law evolved in England so to avoid this.[142] A case involving the formation of a contract, *Smith v Hughes*,[143]

influence in this matter, concluding that 'there is some direct evidence of borrowing from the learned laws' in both Chancery practice and common law.

[136] D. 22.5.10.

[137] Massimiliano Bina, 'La scommessa del giudizio. Sapere della parte come fonte di prova', Judicium, Il Processo civile in Italia e in Europa 2022, 1.

[138] Valcke, 'Contractual Interpretation' (n 4) 89–91, duly notes the 'segregating tendency' prevailing in French law that makes these and other similar rules on evidence wholly autonomous from the rules on the interpretation of contracts contained in the Civil Code, which marks a contrast with the common law approach to this matter.

[139] On these reforms, see Patrick Polden, 'The Superior Courts of Common Law' in William Cornish and others (eds), *The Oxford History of the Laws of England*, vol 11 (OUP 2010) 570, 604–18; Christopher Allen, *The Law of Evidence in Victorian England* (CUP 1997).

[140] Allen (n 139) 117–19, mentions the opposition of the Lord Chancellor Truro and notes that Chief Justice Denman was worried because it appeared that many judges were determined to defeat the proposed legislation in its operation; Polden (n 139) 609.

[141] Allen (n 139) 183; Polden (n 139) 609–10.

[142] cf Sage (n 3) 1437–38; Joseph M Perillo, 'The Origins of the Objective Theory of Contract Formation and Interpretation' (2000) 69 Fordham Law Review 427, 460–61, considers the objective theory of contract formation and interpretation as a response to the relaxed rules of evidence permitting parties to testify.

[143] (1871) LR 6 QB 597. The case concerned an oral sale by sample and was tried with a jury. MacMillan (n 120) 207–13 provides a full discussion of it, showing how Blackburn's judgment was

provided a statement of substantive law leading to this conclusion. According to it, the interpretation of a contract does not hinge upon the actual intention of the parties but is rather determined by the contractual terms as they would be understood by a reasonable person in the position of the promisee. This is Blackburn J's judgment in that case:

> If, whatever a man's real intention may be, he so conducts himself that a reasonable man would believe that he was assenting to the terms proposed by the other party and that other party upon that belief enters into the contract with him, the man thus conducting himself would be equally bound as if he had intended to agree to the other party's terms.[144]

This statement of the law effectively ruled out allowing parties to testify about their intentions when the issue is how to interpret a contract. While the decline of jury trials in contractual matters during the second half of the nineteenth century provided judges with greater opportunities to elaborate on canons of interpretation,[145] this approach aligned English law again with French and Italian law in operative terms.[146]

Simon Whittaker noticed the importance of this side of the story for determining the approach of the court to the interpretation of contracts in France. As Rowan wrote in her instructive contribution on the subject:

> I am grateful to Professor Whittaker for commenting that there is a key irony in that whilst French courts seek to identify the actual intentions of the parties rather than what was written, the courts in practice do not take direct evidence of this intention. There are no witness statements by the parties as to what one or other (or both) intended. Civil decisions are made on the basis of a dossier of documents. In other words, the nature of the French civil process leads to a fundamentally objective set of evidence of intention.[147]

influenced by Judah Benjamin, *A Treatise on the Law of Sale of Personal Property* (London 1868); John Phillips, 'Smith v Hughes (1871)' in Charles Mitchell and Paul Mitchell (eds), *Landmark Cases in the Law of Contract* (Hart Publishing 2008) 205, explains why Blackburn was not following Archdeacon Paley, *Principles of Moral and Political Philosophy* (London 1785) on this point.

[144] (1871) LR 6 QB 597, 607. Blackburn J immediately qualified the statement when discussing mistake as to the terms, for which subjectivity is relevant.

[145] David Ibbetson, *A Historical Introduction to the Law of Obligations* (OUP 1999) 221.

[146] On the other hand, the test for rectification of a contract is subjective, not objective: *FSHC Group Holdings Ltd v GLAS Trust Corp Ltd* [2019] EWCA Civ 1361, [2020] Ch 365. On this case: Edelman (n 99). Warren Swain, 'Not Worth the Paper It's Written On: Contractual Rectification—A Historical Account' (2023) 17 Journal of Equity 161, notes that, prior to Henry Ballow, *Treatise of Equity* (London 1737), interpretation likely provided some of the solutions now obtained through rectification.

[147] Rowan (n 5) 128, fn 28.

As mentioned above, in England the same outcome results from the rules that give prominence to the standard of the reasonable person in contract formation and interpretation.[148]

One may gloss this conclusion by noting that in France and Italy pre-contractual documents produced by the parties can still be used to aid in the interpretation of a contract, while this is excluded in England.[149] However, in many cases, the objective standard does not lead to a different result than a subjective approach to interpretation. A subjective method typically also relies on the wording of the contract itself. It is only in particular cases that the two methods yield diverging results, when there are doubts concerning the meaning of those words. Cases such as *Chartbrook v Persimmon*,[150] which reject the use of evidence from pre-contractual negotiations and adhere to an objective approach to interpretation, show that such an approach may match the actual meaning of the agreement.[151]

There is therefore much to be said for the conclusion that a divergent path of development with respect to the rules of evidence in these jurisdictions is at the origins of the different ways in which the interpretation of contracts has been conceptualized since the last quarter of the nineteenth century in England, France, and Italy.

VII. Convergence?

While the interpretation of contracts in England has evolved since the nineteenth century, the legacy of the past has not completely vanished.[152] In England, it is still impermissible to make reference to preliminary negotiations to prove what one party thought of the contract or the meaning of its terms. In *Chartbrook v Persimmon Homes Ltd*[153] Lord Hoffmann confirmed this exclusionary rule, while

[148] See eg *Sirius International Insurance Company v FIR General Insurance Limited* [2004) UKHL 54, [2004] 1 WLR 3251, [18] (Lord Steyn).

[149] See text to n 148.

[150] [2009] UKHL 38, [2009] 1 AC 1101.

[151] On *Chartbrook*, see text to nn 153 to 156, 174 to 176.

[152] Lord Hoffmann's speech in *ICS Ltd v West Bromwich Building Society* [1998] 1 WLR 896, is considered not dissimilar from Blackburn's judgment 'with some embellishment' by Phillips (n 143) 213. This is just one of many judicial statements that insist on the objective nature of interpretation: see Lewison (n 128) para 2-14.

[153] *Chartbrook* (n 150). In *Union of Shop, Distributive and Allied Workers v Tesco Stores Ltd* [2022] EWCA Civ 978, [2022] IRLR 844, Bean LJ stated at [35]: 'In some circumstances pre-contractual statements which demonstrate the *mutual* intention of both parties may be admissible, but it must be clear that both parties had the same intention' (emphasis in the original). On the facts, the parties had no such intention, but if taken at face value, this statement would much diminish the effect of the exclusionary rule as established by the House of Lords and by the UK Supreme Court (but the judge may have had in rectification in mind). On appeal, a unanimous Supreme Court ruled that an implied term was essential to prevent Tesco from ending employment with the intent of taking away the employees' entitlement to 'retained pay' that had been promised as a 'permanent benefit' and thus reinstated the first instance judgment: *Tesco Stores Ltd v Union of Shop, Distributive and Allied Workers and others*

making clear that in other respects the law had changed, and that contract interpretation was now free from the strictures of the past:

> What is clear . . . is that there is not, so to speak, a limit to the amount of red ink or verbal rearrangement or correction which the court is allowed. All that is required is that it should be clear that something has gone wrong with the language and that it should be clear what a reasonable person would have understood the parties to have meant.[154]

To draw upon Lord Hoffmann's metaphor, more recent cases show that there is, after all, a limit to the amount of red ink a court would employ to interpret a contract, at least for some English judges.[155] Still, the objective approach to the interpretation of contracts now makes significant concessions to the consideration of subjective factors relating to knowledge that a reasonable person would have if put in the same position of the parties while making the contract, ie, knowledge about the 'factual matrix' of it.[156] But, as mentioned above, in France and Italy a party would not be heard as a witness to their own intentions when making the contract, nor would they be allowed to testify as to the meaning that was attributed by that same party to the contractual terms.

Meanwhile, the French reform of the law of obligations of 2016 added a second paragraph to article 1188 Cc. According to it, if the common intention of the parties cannot be ascertained, the contract must be interpreted in the sense that a reasonable person in the same situation would have given to it. This new provision acknowledges that in certain cases it is impossible to find out what was 'the common intention of the parties'.[157] In such a case, reference to the meaning that a reasonable person placed in the same situation would give to the contract is a clear indication of the objective test that the Court must apply. The test points to a hypothetical intention. Indeed, the new provision is strikingly close to the principle set out by Lord Hoffmann in *Investors Compensation Scheme Ltd v West Bromwich Building Society*:

> Interpretation is the ascertainment of the meaning which the document would convey to a reasonable person having all the background knowledge which would

[2024] UKSC 28, [2024] IRLR 998. The whole litigation is a nice example of how different techniques may be used to achieve a certain result.

154 *Chartbrook* (n 150) [25], 1114G.
155 See *Sara & Hossein Asset Holdings Ltd* (n 18) (Lord Briggs' dissent in particular) and the note by Liza Bond, 'Between Scylla and Charybdis in Contractual Interpretation' (2023) 82 Cambridge Law Journal 220.
156 Whether this approach is actually new is disputed: Thomas Bingham, 'A New Thing Under the Sun? The Interpretation of Contracts and the ICS Decision' (2008) 12 Edinburgh Law Review 374.
157 Art 1188(1) Cc.

reasonably have been available to the parties in the situation in which they were at the time of the contract.[158]

Actually, model soft law texts consulted during the work on the French reform provided textual precedents that are even closer to the wording of article 1188(2) Cc.[159] Of course, if the French and English reasonable persons were to draw identical inferences from the same facts, the law in the two jurisdictions would be in perfect agreement on this issue. Nevertheless, deep-rooted interpretive habits and mentalities can lead to divergent practical outcomes even where there is the appearance of convergence among the laws that are compared.[160] English judges disagree even when applying the same law.[161] The best we can hope for, therefore, is that instructive comparisons will advance cross-jurisdictional communication to facilitate mutual learning in this area of the law.

VIII. Divergence?

So far, I have discussed a few general principles governing the interpretation of contracts. I now intend to show that discussing the genealogy of the law can cast some light on specific problems too. The topic chosen for this purpose is whether or not the parties' subsequent conduct is admissible as an aid to the interpretation of their intentions.

A few civil codes make express reference to this aid in the interpretation of contracts. The Spanish Civil Code, for example, provides: 'To determine the intent of the contracting parties, primary attention should be given to their actions, both contemporaneous with and subsequent to the contract.'[162] Similarly, the Italian Civil Code provides: 'To determine the common intention of the parties, their overall conduct, including that subsequent to the conclusion of the contract, must be examined.'[163] But even where the codes stay silent, as in France, reference to the parties' subsequent conduct to interpret a contract is considered admissible as an aid to interpretation.[164]

[158] [1998] 1 WLR 896, 912.

[159] Rowan (n 5) 133.

[160] *Dallah Real Estate and Tourism Holding Co v Ministry of Religious Affairs, Government of Pakistan* [2010] UKSC 46, [2011] 1 AC 763, [15]. In that case, the UK Supreme Court, applying French law, purported to apply the French subjective approach to interpretation but then upheld a formal and literal reading of the agreement, thus reaching a decision conflicting with the previous decision rendered by the Paris *cour d'appel* in the same case. Pierre Mayer, 'Conflicting Decisions in International Commercial Arbitration' (2013) 4 Journal of International Dispute Settlement 407, 412, comments that this reflects 'the irreconcilable difference in the legal cultures of the judges'.

[161] *Sara & Hossein Asset Holdings Ltd* (n 18) (Lord Briggs' dissent) and the lower courts in *Chartbrook* (n 150).

[162] Spanish Civil Code, art 1282.

[163] Italian Civil Code, art 1362.

[164] See eg Terré and others (n 37) para 618.

On the other hand, English law takes a narrower view of what is relevant to or admissible in the interpretation of a contract. As mentioned above, in principle the background of the contract—described as 'absolutely anything which would have affected the way in which the language of the document would have been understood by a reasonable man'—[165]can be considered in the interpretation of a contract. Nonetheless, evidence of both the parties' previous negotiations and of their precontractual declarations are inadmissible in the interpretation of a concluded written contract (although evidence that the parties negotiated on the basis of an agreed meaning is admissible in support of a claim of estoppel or rectification[166]).

As to the parties' subsequent conduct, in *James Miller and Partners Ltd v Whitworth Street Estates (Manchester) Ltd*[167] the House of Lords upheld the rule that such conduct must be excluded as evidence in the interpretation of a written contract. As Lord Reid explained: 'Otherwise one might have the result that a contract meant one thing the day it was signed, but by reason of subsequent events meant something different a month or a year later.'[168] The fact that several jurisdictions reject the rule supported in this decision casts doubt on the logical validity of the argument advanced in these terms. This exclusion probably owes more to policy considerations than to any logical argument.[169] Indeed, this is one of those cases where different opinions on the same issue coexist within the same legal system. Lord Nicholls, writing extrajudicially, remarked that evidence provided by subsequent conduct of the parties is a tool for determining the meaning of the language they used at the relevant time: 'Evidence of the parties' subsequent conduct is sought to be used as a means of identifying the meaning which the language of the contract has borne from its inception.'[170] This is also how a scholar or a judge coming from a civil law jurisdiction would justify the admissibility of evidence regarding the subsequent conduct of the parties.

It is certainly not for me to enter into the debate as to whether or not the rule so far upheld by the courts escapes criticism. However, it may be instructive to note the tendency prevailing in England to compartmentalize or group together under certain categories several rules in order to rationalize aspects of the law relating to the interpretation of contracts. In an important recent article, Sage refers to this

[165] *Investors Compensation Scheme* (n 18) 912 (Lord Hoffmann).

[166] *Northrop Grumman Mission Systems Europe Ltd v BAE Systems (Al Diriyah C41) Ltd* [2014] EWHC 2955 (TCC), 156 Con LR 118; *Re Rhino Enterprises Properties Ltd & Anor* [2020] EWHC 2370 (Ch), [2022] BCC 78, aff'd sub nom *Scholefield v Smith* [2022] EWCA Civ 824, [2023] 1 All ER 480.

[167] [1970] AC 572.

[168] ibid 603.

[169] The Court of Appeal did not exclude the possibility that the law might develop in a different direction in the future in *Brian Maggs v Guy Marsh* [2006] EWCA Civ 1058, [2006] BLR 395. Lord Reid's statement was exposed as problematic by Tipping J in *Wholesale Distributors v Gibbon* [2007] NZSC 37, [59].

[170] Lord Nicholls, 'My Kingdom for a House: The Meaning of Words' (2005) 121 Law Quarterly Review 577, 589; cf Yihan Goh, 'Towards a Consistent Use of Subsequent Conduct in Singapore Contract Law' (2017) Journal of Business Law 387, 413.

technique as 'hiving off'.[171] If I am not misinterpreting him, by resorting to this technique, rules that could be grouped under the same heading are shifted to distinct departments of normative theory, so as to avoid their collision with prevailing doctrine. For example, a leading English textbook lists eight different exceptions to the rule excluding evidence of subsequent conduct in the interpretation of contracts.[172] By way of contrast, civilian jurisdictions such as France or Italy typically adopt a more abstract and general approach to the subject, aiming at a comprehensive framework leading to a more uniform set of applicable principles and rules of interpretation, although in these jurisdictions too one may detect a certain 'segregating tendency' at work that may surprise a foreign observer.[173]

Maintaining intellectual boundaries to isolate one set of rules from other adjacent sets demands intellectual dexterity, and perhaps, on occasion, a willing suspension of disbelief. *Chartbrook v Persimmon Homes Ltd*[174] provides a good example of how this technique works. In *Chartbrook*, Lord Hoffmann held that:

> statements in the course of pre-contractual negotiations will be drenched in subjectivity and may, if oral, be very much in dispute ... [Hence their inadmissibility as evidence is] justified in the more general interest of economy and predictability in obtaining advice and adjudicating disputes.[175]

Baroness Hale's speech in the same case shows how operation of the traditional rule affirmed in these terms may be subtly qualified by the oblique influence of a different rule, concerning the rectification of contracts:

> I have to confess that I would not have found it quite so easy to reach this conclusion [ie, the conclusion reached by the Court as to the interpretation of the contract] had we not been made aware of the agreement which the parties had reached on this aspect of their bargain during the negotiations which led up to the formal contract. On any objective view, that made the matter crystal clear.[176]

What is the message underlying this candid statement? By introducing a claim for rectification in such cases, the content of prior negotiations between the parties indirectly comes to the attention of the Court. Although the Court does not address the claim for rectification when dealing with contract interpretation, the evidence

171 Sage (n 3) 1438ff.
172 McKendrick (n 17) para 16-061.
173 Valcke, 'Contractual Interpretation' (n 4) 90.
174 *Chartbrook* (n 150).
175 ibid [38].
176 ibid [99]. Cf *Monsolar IQ Ltd v Woden Park Ltd* [2021] EWCA Civ 961, [2022] 2 P & CR 10 (correction of a drafting error by way of interpretation). Lorna Richardson, 'Correction by Construction: Dealing with Drafting Errors by Way of Interpretation' (2023) 27 Edinburgh Law Review 90.

presented to support it can still indirectly influence the Court, as Baroness Hale honestly acknowledged in her speech.

Compartmentalization operates to exclude the relevance of parties' subsequent conduct unless, for instance, the issue pertains to the formation rather than the interpretation of a contract. When the issue concerns whether there was a contract and what the contract terms were,[177] evidence of subsequent conduct is admissible. It is also admissible when such conduct raises an estoppel,[178] but then again estoppel belongs to a doctrinally distinct area of the law. Although doctrinally satisfying, just like Cinderella's coach, this method only leads so far. The increased costs and predictability argument:

> ignores the reality that many interpretation disputes will be accompanied by alternative claims for rectification of the written contract and possibly also misrepresentation or estoppel, under which evidence of all the negotiations and surrounding circumstances must be received. Accordingly, excluding such evidence for the purpose of interpretation disputes will not have the effect of reducing the length and cost of civil trials.[179]

With these remarks in mind, let us examine how English law started from a common ground with French and Italian law in considering the parties' post-contractual conduct as an aid in the interpretation of a contract, but then abandoned this position when it began to distinguish between different types of conduct and factual situations.

Although the French Civil Code does not explicitly address this issue, the first interpreters of the Code did not dispute that the parties' subsequent conduct could provide an aid in the interpretation of contracts. Toullier, for example, is explicit on the point:

> When an instrument contains an obscure or ambiguous clause, the most reliable way to ascertain its true meaning is to focus on who has possession and the interpretation that the parties themselves have made of the instrument, as reflected

[177] *Wilson v Maynard Shipbuilding Consultants AB* [1978] QB 665, 675, 677; *Todd v British Midland Airways Ltd* [1978] ICR 959, 964, 967; *Mears v Safecar Security Ltd* [1983] QB 54, 77; *Great North Eastern Ry Ltd v Avon Insurance Plc* [2001] EWCA Civ 780, [2001] 2 Lloyd's Rep 649 [29]; *Lawlor v Sandvik Mining and Construction Mobile Crushers and Screens Ltd* [2012] EWHC 1188 (QB), [2012] 2 Lloyd's Rep 25, [12], [47].

[178] *Amalgamated Investments v Texas Commerce Bank* [1982] QB 84, 119 (estoppel by convention); *Carmichael v National Power Plc* [1999] 1 WLR 2042, 2051.

[179] David McLauchlan, 'Contractual Interpretation: What Is It About?' (2009) 31 Sydney Law Review 5, 37. According to Tiverios (n 2) 566 (who in turn cites McLauchlan), 'it has become common practice in Australia for cautious trial judges to allow all pre-contractual wide context materials to be adduced as evidence. This is for the principal reason that if the trial judge errs in applying the ambiguity gateway, then the appeal court can interpret the contract in light of the full set of prescribed clues'.

> in how they implemented it. For as Dumoulin states, 'such is presumed to be the antecedent title, as appears from the use and possession'.[180]

The maxim often cited in this context, *præsumitur præcessisse titulus, qualis apparet usus et possessio* ('such is presumed to be the antecedent title, as appears from the use and possession'), probably first addressed the evidential challenges raised by land transfers. These transfers often gave rise to doubts, which could be resolved by proof of possession.[181] Under the Code, the same maxim was however smoothly applied to the interpretation of contracts. Demolombe, for example, eulogizes the same interpretative principle in emphatic words with respect to agreements in general.[182]

The doctrine followed by these authors was well received in Italy under the Civil Code of 1865, which, like the French Civil Code, was silent on the matter.[183] In both France and Italy, the justification for this principle of interpretation was based partly on arguments which, in the English context, would point towards the principle of estoppel, since reliance on subsequent conduct is mentioned as a key factor in determining the intentions of the parties.[184] Article 1282 of the Spanish Civil Code and article 1362 of the Italian Civil Code now in force thus simply confirmed once more that this rule was applicable to contracts in general.

The rule by which in litigation concerning a conveyance of land it is permissible to have regard to extraneous evidence, including evidence of a subsequent conduct, where the information contained in the conveyance is unclear or ambiguous has been affirmed in England in *Ali v Lane*[185] and in *Haycocks v Neville*,[186] as well as by more recent cases.[187] The scope of application of the rule is, however, currently limited to the interpretation of conveyances of land, contrary to the broader approach prevailing in France, in Italy, and in Spain. In *Ali v Lane* the judge relied

[180] Charles Bonaventure Marie Toullier, *Le droit civil français suivant l'ordre du code*, vol 3, tome 2 (Tarlier 1830) 447 at nr 320.

[181] This is the case discussed by Philippe Antoine Merlin, *Recueil Alphabétique Des Questions De Droit*, Vol 2 (Danel, Rondonneau, Porthmann 1802) 418.

[182] Charles Demolombe, *Cours de Code Napoléon, XXV: Traité des contrats ou des obligations conventionnelles*, vol 2, (Paris 1845), 42 at nr 36. This is cited by the Supreme Court of Canada in *The City of Quebec v The North Shore Railway Company* (1897) 27 SCR 102, 124 (a case involving an ambiguous land transfer).

[183] Giorgio Giorgi, *Teoria delle obbligazioni*, vol 4 (7th edn, F.lli Cammelli 1908) 199, at nr 184.

[184] Demolombe (n 182) 42, at nr 36; Cesare Grassetti, *L'interpretazione del negozio giuridico con particolare riguardo ai contratti* (CEDAM 1938) 205–206.

[185] [2007] EWCA Civ 1532 [2007], 1 P & CR 26.

[186] [2007] EWCA Civ 78, [2007] 12 EG 56.

[187] *Bradford v James* [2008] BLR 538; *Piper v Wakeford* [2008] EWCA Civ 1378, [2009] 1 P & CR DG16; *Norman v Sparling* [2014] EWCA Civ 1152, [2015] 1 P & CR 6.

on a counsel's reference to trace the rule back to the nineteenth-century case of *St Leonards v Ashburner*.[188] Nevertheless, there are indications suggesting that its application was once broader.[189] *Watcham v Attorney General of East Africa Protectorate*[190] in particular suggested the latter possibility. Nonetheless, in *L Schuler AG v Wickman Machine Tools Sales Limited*[191] the House of Lords held that precedents concerning proof of subsequent conduct as an aid to the interpretation of a conveyance did not apply to contracts. The Court of Appeal had reached a different conclusion. Denning LJ, whose view on the point was rejected by the House of Lords, later voiced his reservations about what appeared to him to be a newly minted exclusionary rule:

> For many years I thought that when the meaning of a contract was uncertain you could look at the subsequent conduct of the parties so as to ascertain it. That seemed to me sensible enough. The parties themselves should know what they mean by their words better than anyone else.[192]

Meanwhile, in *St Edmundsbury and Ipswich Diocesan Board of Finance and Another v Clark*,[193] Megarry J offered a justification for confining in its own niche the admission of evidence relating to subsequent conduct as an aid to the interpretation of a conveyance:

> One may accept to the full that it does not apply to commercial contracts or, for that matter, to any language of obligation, whatever the document. If the question is what one party is obliged to do under some document, the effect of measuring the obligation by what in fact that person has done under the document is to convert into a binding obligation what may have been done as of grace or to promote good relations or to avoid argument.[194]

This is good sense, and it may even be considered plausible from the point of view of how social interaction unfolds in context, but does it square with the theory that a court should not investigate the subjective intentions of a party when dealing with the interpretation of contracts?

188 (1869) 21 LT 595.

189 Lewison (n 128) para 3-184. In support, Lewison cites Lord Atkinson in *Houlder Brothers & Co v Public Works Commissioners* [1908] AC 276 (a case of a charterparty).

190 [1919] AC 533.

191 [1974] AC 235.

192 *Amalgamated Investment & Property Co Ltd v Texas Commerce International Bank Ltd* [1982] QB 84, 119. See also *Port Sudan Cotton Co v Govindaswamy Chettiar & Sons* [1977] 2 Lloyd's Rep 5, 11.

193 *St Edmundsbury and Ipswich Diocesan Board of Finance v Clark (No 2)* [1973] 1 WLR 1572.

194 ibid 1585.

IX. Conclusion

I am willing to concede that exploring the genealogy of the law may not be of any immediate practical use, but it does at least highlight the limits of any attempt to inject into it more coherence than it can sustain. How to conceptualize what is ambiguous depends on which theory of language prevails; how to ascertain intention requires a theory of the role that such a factor plays in contracts. But there is no single, definitive answer to these big questions. In this regard, both common law and civil law lawyers are immersed in the same environment. As such, they have long looked to the same sources for inspiration, particularly when it comes to the issues discussed in this chapter. Of course, law is not just a matter of ideas. It is also bound up with particular procedures and institutions, and is administered in particular places, within institutional frameworks created by and for particular communities. These are facts that make a difference in relation to the subject at hand, although, as I have tried to show, a degree of convergence has been maintained in spite of change. Whereas in legal systems which have codified the law of contractual interpretation there still is reliance on broad generalities which are put into practice in a relatively unstructured way, in England the same field appears to be much more fragmented, with a very large number of competing doctrines and techniques which may potentially bear on the problem of resolving a dispute about the meaning of particular words in a contract. The official portrait of the legal system that is conveyed by so many statements about objectivity as the polar star in the interpretation of contracts is just a part of a much larger picture that has been built up by adding precedent to precedent, and by framing and reframing legal doctrine and procedural rules. The finer distinctions that have been developed within that broader framework show the vestigial traces of the past. In its own way, genealogy silently rules.

3

Remedies for Defects in the Formation of a Contract

Learning by Comparing

John Cartwright

The purpose of this chapter is to consider the remedies for defects in the formation of a contract, and to consider what legal systems can learn from each other in making such a comparison. The focus is on what English law can learn from a comparison with civil law systems, and in particular France. This seemed to me to be the natural focus for my contribution to this book. Over the years, Simon Whittaker and I have taught comparative law together at Oxford, with a focus on the comparison of French and English contract law, and as a (rather broad) generalization we tended to divide the topics of our lectures and seminars so that I took the first half of the life of the contract and Simon took the second half—a division which would generally be recognized by French lawyers as between the formation of the contract, and its effects.[1] This does not mean, however, that we simply worked separately: and I must put on record how much I learnt from Simon during the course of our work together, not only in our teaching but also in research projects, including the translations we made of proposed and enacted reforms of the French Civil Code.[2]

I. Terminology and Context

A. Remedies for defects in formation: terminology

At the outset we need to be clear about the terminology that will be used in this chapter, and the risks associated with the choice of terminology.

[1] See eg François Terré and others, *Droit civil: Les obligations* (13th edn, Dalloz 2022) paras 17–895 (*Le contrat*), divided into sub-title 1 (*La formation du contract*: paras 129–595) and sub-title 2 (*Les effets du contrat*: paras 596–895). The French Civil Code (Cc) (after its reform in 2016/2018) divides the provisions on contract into four chapters: introductory provisions (arts 1101–1111-1), formation of contracts (arts 1112–1187), contractual interpretation (arts 1188–1192) and the effects of contracts (arts 1193–1231-7).

[2] See n 7.

John Cartwright, *Remedies for Defects in the Formation of a Contract* In: *Comparative Reflections in Private Law*.
Edited by: Marco Cappelletti, Ciara Kennefick, and Dorota Leczykiewicz, Oxford University Press.
 DOI: 10.1093/9780198959168.003.0004

We adopt the term 'remedies' as the overarching term as it is generally used within English law. Although there has been some debate in France,[3] the term generally used in the French tradition—and still used in the latest reforms of the Civil Code—is 'sanctions' (*les sanctions*).[4] The choice of language can be significant, 'sanction' reflecting a more morally loaded notion[5] than the morally neutral idea of a 'remedy' applied to solve, or cure, a problem. In the context of our discussion, however, the use of the English terminology in discussing legal systems outside England, as well as English law, should not cause a distraction or give rise to any significant loss of nuance.

More problematic, though, is the terminology to be used when discussing in the English language the remedies that are used by non-Anglophone legal systems. A well-known hazard for the comparative lawyer is the use of terminology taken from one legal system to identify things or concepts used in another legal system. The reader who does not know the foreign system may draw erroneous conclusions from apparently familiar terms, and it may be better to use neutral terms by way of translation, or at least to take care in describing and defining for the English reader the elements and characteristics of the foreign concept even if the foreign language term is retained—but certainly not to adopt a technical English term for the foreign system where it may mislead. In translating the French contract law reforms of 2016/2018[6] into English, Simon Whittaker and I discussed on many occasions how to deal with this, and in this chapter the general approach—and the terminology that we adopted in the published translations[7]—is generally used. And so, for example, terms such as 'void' and 'voidable' are used only in relation to English law and never as a translation of the French remedy of *nullité*, which can be

[3] See esp Denis Tallon, 'L'inexécution du contrat: pour une autre prestation', Revue trimestrielle de droit civil 1994, 223, proposing the use of the term *remède*. In the run-up to the reform of the Civil Code in 2016 (see n 6) this term was also used by the Avant-projet Terré: François Terré (ed), *Pour une réforme du droit des contrats* (Dalloz 2009) 24–25, 256–60 (draft arts 97, 102, discussed by Philippe Rémy) and by the Ministry of Justice in its Report to the President of the Republic explaining the text of the reform: Report to the President on *Ordonnance* no 2016-131 of 10 February 2016. It is not however used in the Code itself, which continues to refer to *les sanctions* (see text to n 4).

[4] The term is used in a broad sense to refer to any measure justified by the violation of an obligation and, more generally, to any means of ensuring that a right or an obligation is respected and enforced: see Gérard Cornu, *Vocabulaire juridique* (14th edn, Presses Universitaires de France 2022) 'Sanction, I.2 and I.3'. Within contract law, the term is used in relation to remedies for non-performance (breach) of the contract, as well as formation. For references within the French Civil Code see the heading of section 4 (arts 1178ff Cc) of Chapter II (formation of contracts), and the text of art 1217 Cc in section 5 (contractual non-performance) of Chapter IV (the effects of contracts).

[5] 'Sanction' can carry the idea that that the defendant against whom it is ordered is a wrongdoer, although this does not mean that it is seen in punitive terms. See also n 8.

[6] *Ordonnance* no 2016-131 of 10 February 2016 (2016 *Ordonnance*), amended by *Loi* no 2018-287 of 20 April 2018 (2018 *Loi*).

[7] For the translation of the 2016 *Ordonnance* by John Cartwright, Bénédicte Fauvarque-Cosson, and Simon Whittaker, see the Appendix to John Cartwright and Simon Whittaker (eds), *The Code Napoléon Rewritten: French Contract Law after the 2016 Reforms* (Hart Publishing 2017), and for the revised translation of the reforms as amended by the 2018 *Loi*, see John Cartwright, Bénédicte Fauvarque-Cosson, and Simon Whittaker, 'The new provisions of the Code civil created by Ordonnance no

translated by the (to the English legal ear) neutral 'nullity' but then also needs to be explained so that the English reader understands the characteristics and nuances of the term.

B. Remedies in the context of the rules for formation

The context for the discussion in this chapter is the formation of the contract, and in particular defects in the formation of a contract which has, or appears to have, been concluded. We are not considering problems which may arise during contractual negotiations which fail—the area which generally goes under the heading of precontractual liability,[8] providing remedies for the party who admits that the negotiations did not result in a concluded contract but seeks redress for losses such as expenses wasted during the failed negotiations, or even the loss of the benefit of the hoped-for contract which did not materialize.

The focus of the discussion is not the substantive rules for formation of the contract, but the remedies available to one party (or, sometimes, each party) in a case where those rules are not (or not fully) complied with, or where the conduct of one party during the process of formation of the contract can be raised by the other to challenge the validity or some other aspect of their contract. This is the practical question which arises from problems in formation of the contract: the parties need to know what remedy they may claim when the defect in formation is discovered—and systems generally recognize a range of remedies which may be sought, depending on the circumstances.[9] However, in any legal system it is

2016-131 of 10 February 2016 and including revisions made to the text by Loi no 2018-287 of 20 April 2018 translated into English' <https://www.justice.gouv.fr/sites/default/files/migrations/textes/art_pix/Translationrevised2018final.pdf> accessed 6 November 2025. Translations of the French Civil Code in this chapter are taken from this translation. For the translation by John Cartwright and Simon Whittaker of the earlier proposals for reform (Pierre Catala (ed), *Avant-projet de réforme du droit des obligations et de la prescription: Rapport remis au Garde des Sceaux* (Documentation française 2005) (the Avant-projet Catala)), see the Appendix to John Cartwright, Stefan Vogenauer, and Simon Whittaker (eds), *Reforming the French Law of Obligations: Comparative Reflections on the Avant-projet de réforme du droit des obligations et de la prescription ('the Avant-projet Catala')* (Hart Publishing 2009). For discussion of the difficulties of translation, see John Cartwright and Simon Whittaker, 'Introduction to the English Translation' in François Ancel and Bénédicte Fauvarque-Cosson (eds), *Le Nouveau Droit des Contrats: Guide Bilingue à l'Usage des Praticiens* (LGDJ 2019) 431ff, esp 442–45 (discussing *les sanctions*); Simon Whittaker and John Cartwright, 'Translating the *Avant-projet de réforme*' in Cartwright, Vogenauer, and Whittaker, ibid 425–44.

[8] See eg John Cartwright and Martijn Hesselink (eds), *Precontractual Liability in European Private Law* (CUP 2008).

[9] cf John Cartwright and Martin Schmidt-Kessel, 'Defects in Consent: Mistake, Fraud, Threats, Unfair Exploitation' in Gerhard Dannemann and Stefan Vogenauer (eds), *The Common European Sales Law in Context: Interactions with English and German Law* (OUP 2013) 373, 376 ('The practical importance of mistake, fraud, threats or unfair exploitation is the remedial consequences which are thereby available to one or both parties') and the general approach taken in that chapter, which discusses English law and German law, as well as the Draft Common Frame of Reference (Christian

impossible to consider the remedies for defects in the formation of the contract without also considering the substantive rules for formation. A remedy is designed to address a particular problem, and therefore understanding the nature of the remedies and their operation relies on first understanding the problem that needs to be addressed. To that extent, although the aim of this chapter is to draw comparisons across legal systems about the different remedies for defects in the formation of the contract, and from that to see what lessons one legal system can learn from another, we shall need to broaden the discussion from remedies to the rules for formation of the contract.

C. The remedies chosen for discussion

In this chapter, the term 'remedies' is used in a broad sense, covering both active remedies (effected by court order or by act of party) and passive remedies (consequences provided by the law without the need for intervention of either the court or a party), including remedies which operate at different levels. For example, in English law the effect of a misrepresentation on a contract may be to render it *voidable*; the way in which the avoidance of the contract is effected is through its *rescission*; and a consequence of rescission may be that one or both parties must make *restitution*. Among these, it might be most usual to refer to rescission as the remedy for misrepresentation; it is rescission that the misrepresentee seeks as the (active) remedy for the misrepresentation, with the contract being voidable as merely a (passive) legal consequence of the misrepresentation and restitution being either a precondition for obtaining the remedy of rescission (therefore part of the remedy of rescission rather than being an independent remedy in itself) or at most a second-order remedy which follows only if the primary remedy of rescission is effected. However, for the purposes of discussion in this chapter, we include within the broad categorization of remedies all three: not only rescission of the contract, but also the voidability of the contract, as well as restitution following rescission. It is necessary to draw the scope of the discussion widely, not only in order to make an effective comparison with the remedies for defects in formation of a contract in other legal systems, but also to discuss fully how the defects in formation work within English law, particularly in understanding the relationship between void contracts and voidable contracts.

von Bar, Eric Clive, and Hans Schulte-Nölke (eds), *Principles, Definitions and Model Rules of European Private Law: Draft Common Frame of Reference (DCFR)* (Sellier 2009)) and the European Commission's proposal for a Common European Sales Law (European Commission, Proposal for a Regulation of the European Parliament and of the Council on a Common European Sales Law', COM/2011/0635 final, 2011/0284).

The principal focus in English law will be the distinction between void contracts, voidable contracts, and unenforceable contracts, drawing by way of comparison on the French remedies of absolute and relative nullity of the contract. In section II, we consider the principal categorization of contracts as void, voidable, and unenforceable within English law, with some comparison with the approach to categorization taken in French law. In section III, we look in more detail at particular difficulties which arise in the categorization of void contracts within English law, to see what might be learnt from a comparative study.

II. Void, Voidable, and Unenforceable: Comparing the Categories

A. Categories defined by degrees of defect

The classification of contracts as void, voidable, or unenforceable is set out very helpfully in *Chitty on Contracts*, in a chapter written by Simon Whittaker:[10]

> A void contract is strictly a contradiction in terms, because if a contract is truly void it is not a contract at all; but the term is a useful one and well understood by lawyers. Properly speaking, a void contract should produce no legal effects whatsoever. Neither party should be able to sue the other on the contract...
>
> A voidable contract is one where one or more of its parties have the power, by a manifestation of election to do so, to avoid the legal relations created by the contract; or by affirmation of the contract to extinguish the power of avoidance... But until the right of avoidance is exercised, the contract is valid...
>
> Unenforceable contracts are valid in all respects except that one or both parties cannot be sued on the contract... In some cases the defect of unenforceability is curable... An unenforceable contract may be indirectly enforceable by means other than bringing an action.

These different degrees of defect in the contract—'degrees of imperfection'[11]—are well established in English law, and something similar will be recognized by lawyers from civil law jurisdictions, although there are some well-known traps in making the comparison. The void/voidable distinction can too easily be assimilated unthinkingly with the distinctions between (for example) *la nullité absolue* and *la nullité relative* in French or Belgian law; *la nulidad* and *la anulabilidad* in Spanish law; *Nichtigkeit* and *Anfechtbarkeit* in German law; *nietigheid* and *vernietigbaarheid* in Dutch law. The English terminology should not be used

[10] Simon Whittaker, 'Contract Law and "Contracts"' in Hugh Beale (ed), *Chitty on Contracts* (35th edn, Sweet & Maxwell 2023) paras 1-093, 1-095, 1-097 (footnotes omitted).

[11] ibid para 1-091.

to translate such technical terms within other systems and, indeed, the way in which these distinctions operate within each system varies as regards the restrictions placed on effecting the annulment of the contract, such as whether or not a court order is required, and whether the remedy can be sought by only the contracting parties or also by third parties with an interest related to the contract or by public authorities where the public interest is engaged; and what further legal consequences flow from finding that the contract is or (by act of party or by court order) becomes a nullity, either automatically or if the claimant so requests. Each legal system will also have developed its own theory of nullity to explain why its rules operate as they do, not as an isolated set of rules but integrated into the system's general rules of contract law—and, indeed, how contract relates to other areas of law such as property law. A complete survey of such theories, and the differences between the different systems' approaches, is far beyond the scope of this chapter, and we focus on the French approach by comparison with English law.

The idea of degrees of defect in the contract was expressed very well in the context of French law by Carbonnier:[12]

> The contract is invalid if, at the moment of its formation, one of its essential conditions is absent, or if one of those conditions is vitiated. The generic sanction is invalidity. Within this, we can rationally distinguish three degrees in a *decrescendo* of force: *inexistence, absolute nullity, relative nullity* . . . It should be noticed, however, that inexistence (nothing has been effected, *nihil actum est*, no need for a court order to establish what does not exist) is a notion that has been rejected by many writers: they include it within absolute nullity.

This is a logical framework for analysing defects in formation of the contract, which relates the legal consequence, as regards the validity of the contract, to the nature of the defect in the process of its formation. Some defects in formation are so serious as to prevent the contract being formed at all; the contract is inexistent. Other defects do not prevent its formation but the contract, which exists, contains a defect which may later be activated to nullify the contract, although if it is not activated the contract continues in force and effect as if it had been properly formed. And within the defects that affect the contract without preventing its formation, there are also differences, referred to by Carbonnier by the distinction between absolute and relative nullity, which depend on the different circumstances in which the formation of the contract is regarded as defective in law.

[12] Jean Carbonnier, *Droit civil, Les Obligations*, vol 2 (22nd edn, Presses Universitaires de France 2000) para 104 (translation by the author).

B. The French approach to degrees of defect in the contract

In the passage quoted above, Carbonnier noted that the framework which he presented was not universally accepted—and in particular that the notion of inexistence, distinct from absolute nullity, was rejected by many authors. For many years there has been significant debate among French authors about this[13] and more generally about how to formulate the theory of nullity, including the distinction between absolute and relative nullity.[14] The reform of the French Civil Code in 2016/2018[15] has provided answers to some of the questions raised by this debate. Some aspects of the reform are new, but many set out the position as it had generally been accepted by the case law and by many writers by the time of the reform,[16] and for our purposes it is sufficient to note the position following the reform.

The Civil Code does not explicitly contemplate inexistence as a remedy for defects in formation. The definition of a contract and the requirements for its formation are set out: a contract is 'a concordance of wills of two or more persons intended to create, modify, transfer or extinguish obligations'[17] and is 'formed by the meeting of an offer and an acceptance by which the parties demonstrate their will to be bound'.[18] From this we might infer that the absence of agreement—the absence of will or the absence of consent of one or both parties—would negative the formation of the contract, although this is not explicit and the text of the Code muddies the waters. It treats the requirement of consent (both the existence of consent and the lack of a defect in consent)[19] as a condition not of the existence of the contract but of its validity;[20] as also are the requirements that the parties have

[13] For references to the debate about whether inexistence exists as a sanction separate from nullity, see Terré and others (n 1) para 140; Jacques Ghestin, Grégoire Loiseau, and Yves-Marie Serinet, *La formation du contrat, L'objet et la cause—Les nullités*, vol 2 (4th edn, LGDJ 2013) 824–35; Philippe Malaurie, Laurent Aynès, and Philippe Stoffel-Munck, *Droit des obligations* (13th edn, LGDJ 2024) para 408, noting that this debate lost much of its interest when the law of prescription was reformed in 2008 to provide a unified regime for all personal actions and those relating to movable property (see art 2224 Cc); before that reform, there were separate prescription periods for relative nullity (5 years) and absolute nullity (30 years) and it was argued by some writers that there was no prescription at all for inexistence where no judicial decision was called for.

[14] For references to the debate about the theory of nullity, and the development from the 19th century 'classical' doctrine to the 'modern' theory during the 20th century, see Terré and others (n 1) paras 139–42; and for a detailed account, see Ghestin, Loiseau, and Serinet (n 13) 789–835.

[15] See n 6.

[16] In spite of the reform, debates continue: see eg Laurent Aynès and others, 'Les nullités absolues: quel avenir?', Revue des contrats 2019, no 3, 127. For detailed critical discussion of the reform, article by article, and giving further references, see Olivier Deshayes, Thomas Genicon, and Yves-Marie Laithier, *Réforme du droit des contrats, du régime générale et de la preuve des obligations* (2nd edn, LexisNexis 2018) 362–91; Gaël Chantepie and Mathias Latina, *Le nouveau droit des obligations* (2nd edn, Dalloz 2018) 410–37.

[17] Art 1101 Cc.

[18] Art 1113 Cc.

[19] cf the headings of art 1129 Cc ('Existence of consent', dealing with mental capacity, although the text of the article refers to validity of consent) and arts 1130ff ('Defects in consent').

[20] cf Chantepie and Latina (n 16) para 285 (criticizing the reform on the basis that the consent of the parties is not a condition of validity of the contract but a condition of its formation); cf however, Terré and others (n 1) para 130.

capacity to contract, and that the contract have a lawful and sufficiently certain content.[21] And the general remedy for failure to satisfy the conditions required for validity of a contract[22]—as well as the general remedy for failure to comply with any (exceptional) requirement of formality in formation of the contract[23]—is nullity.

In the reformed French Code, nullity now has its own detailed section as one of the sanctions for defects in formation of the contract.[24] Indeed, it is the only such sanction listed apart from *la caducité*, where a contract which has been validly formed lapses if one of its essential elements disappears, a curiously placed provision since it is not a response to a defect in formation.[25] Nullity is therefore clearly the dominant remedy, and for the first time the Code sets out its features.

A key feature of this modern theory of nullity[26] is the distinction between absolute and relative nullity: nullity is *absolute* where the rule that is violated has as its object the safeguard of the public interest, and it is *relative* where the rule that is violated has as its sole object the safeguard of a private interest.[27] In consequence, absolute nullity may be claimed by any person who can demonstrate an interest (including a public official acting in the public interest), and it cannot be excluded by the parties' affirmation of the contract,[28] whereas relative nullity may be claimed only by the party whom the legal rule that has been violated was designed to protect, and it may be remedied by affirmation by that party.[29] This distinction between absolute and relative nullity is reinforced in other sections of the reformed Code, and is fundamental to the French vision of the purpose of nullity as a remedy (*sanction*) within the formation of the contract.[30]

[21] Arts 1128 (requirements for validity of a contract), 1145 ff (capacity), 1162 ff (content).
[22] Art 1178 Cc.
[23] Art 1172 Cc.
[24] Arts 1178 to 1185 Cc.
[25] Arts 1186 to 1187. Lapse puts an end to the contract, emphasizing that it is a defect not at the moment of formation but later, when the circumstances change. The reformed Belgian Civil Code (see n 33) correctly treats lapse not within formation of the contract, but as a ground of extinction of the obligation: arts 5.244, 5.265–5.267.
[26] See n 14. Clarification of the rules concerning nullity was one of the aims of the reform set out in the legislation which authorized the procedure of reform by an *Ordonnance*: *Loi* no 2015-177 of 16 February 2015, art 8.
[27] Art 1179 Cc. The language of the text here is significant: the question is not whether the public or private interest is engaged on the facts of the case, but how the *rule* which has been violated was formulated, and it is relative nullity only if the rule has the private interest as *its sole object*: Deshayes, Genicon, and Laithier (n 16) 374–76.
[28] Art 1180 Cc.
[29] Art 1181 Cc.
[30] For explicit grounds of relative nullity, see arts 1131 (defects in consent) and 1147 (lack of capacity to contract). The Code also provides for nullity in various contexts without specifying whether it is absolute or relative, but this will be determined by the general test for the distinction (art 1179 Cc, n 27): see eg arts 1124 (contract concluded in breach of unilateral promise with a third party who knew of its existence); 1172 (contract not complying with legislative requirements of formality); 1202 (certain types of contract where part of the price is concealed); 1216-2 (assignment of contract not in writing); 1304-2 (obligation subject to a condition whose satisfaction depends on the will of the debtor alone); 1322 (assignment of rights not in writing); 1327 (assignment of debt not in writing).

The remedy of nullity (whether absolute or relative) also has other distinctive features in French law, which help us to see its nature and how it fits within the French vision of contract. Perhaps the most distinctive feature is that, although the law defines the circumstances when the contract is *nul* (a nullity), this identifies only the potential for the contract to be annulled. Annulment of the contract is never automatic but must be activated—and unless it is agreed by the parties, it must be declared by a judicial decision.[31] The role of the court is significant. There is a notable reluctance to place remedies in the hands of only one of the contracting parties, even where the law recognizes the right to the remedy for a party who can establish the necessary factual basis of the claim. The contract, once created, normally requires either a contractual or a judicial release. French law does admit self-help remedies in certain contexts and, indeed, the reforms of 2016/2018 expanded the circumstances in which a party to a contract can effect certain remedies without recourse to the courts, most notably in allowing a party to terminate a contract for the other party's non-performance by giving notice to the other as an alternative to seeking a court order.[32] But nullity remains a judicial remedy, emphasizing the reluctance of French law to diminish the court's power over the contract.[33]

The effect of nullity, once declared, is retroactive—as might be expected: given that the defect is in the formation of the contract, the natural consequence in any legal system is that the contract should be treated as if it had never existed.[34] Similarly, it is not surprising that a secondary remedy following the annulment should be restitution of the parties' performances already carried out under the contract.[35] The 2016/2018 reform has put in place a new Chapter dealing with Restitution (*les restitutions*) within the Title of the Code dealing with the General Regime of Obligations,[36] which applies in a range of cases including nullity of the contract. The Chapter contains various rules for the calculation of restitution, but for the purposes of our comparison with English law in this chapter, two points are relevant. First, this is a set of rules which apply as an automatic (secondary) remedy in a case where a contract is annulled. Second, the general rule is that restitution of a thing (other than a sum of money) takes place in kind or, where this is

[31] Art 1178 Cc.

[32] Arts 1226 and 1227 Cc. According to the text of the Code as it stood before the reform, termination (*résolution*) required a court order: art 1184(3) of the 1804 Code. However, termination by notice (*résolution unilaterale*) had already become established in practice: Solène Rowan, 'Termination for Non-performance' in Cartwright and Whittaker, *The Code Napoléon Rewritten* (n 7) 317, 320.

[33] Belgian law, by contrast, now accepts that a contract, as long as it is not contained in a formal notarized instrument (*acte authentique*), can be annulled by notice: see art 5.59(3) of the Belgian Civil Code, in force since 1 January 2023. In Belgium this was seen as a logical step for nullity if termination of the contract by notice was also to be accepted: see the commentary on the draft articles of the reform presented to the Belgian Chambre des Représentants during the Parliamentary process: Chambre des Représentants de Belgique, 'Proposition de Loi portant le Livre 5 "Les obligations" du Code civil' DOC 55 1806/010, 6 April 2022, 69.

[34] Art 1178(2) Cc.

[35] Art 1178(3) Cc.

[36] Arts 1352–1352-9 Cc.

impossible, by value assessed at the date of the restitution.[37] Although restitution in kind is the natural remedy, as a means of reversing (literally) the performance carried out under the contract in order to return to the pre-contract position, substitute restitution (in money) is seen as a natural alternative. This allows the contract to be annulled even where the reversal of literal performance is not possible, while providing the court with a mechanism to assess the value to be paid by way of restitution, thereby avoiding the loss or unjust enrichment that might follow from either a denial of nullity or a denial of restitution in kind.

A final feature of the remedy of nullity which we should note is that it may be partial, as well as of the whole contract: where a ground of nullity affects only one or more terms of the contract, it entails the nullity of the whole contract only if this term or these terms constituted a decisive factor in the undertaking of the parties, or of one of them.[38] This may reflect a more general approach in French law where the focus is on the obligation as much as on the contract as a whole. But it also leans in favour of keeping the contract alive where it is appropriate and possible to do so, while still addressing the problem to which the ground of nullity is addressed. It is linked[39] to a similar desire to maintain the contract where there is a challenge only to an individual clause or clauses of the contract not by way of a ground of nullity, but on some other basis provided by the law, such as the unfairness of a clause which may result in the clause being 'deemed not written' (*réputée non écrite*).[40]

C. The English approach to degrees of defect in the contract

We have already seen that English law traditionally sees degrees of defect in the formation of a contract: void contracts, voidable contracts, and unenforceable contracts.[41] We shall see further comparisons with French law in section III, but we can already notice that there are some similarities in the general approach of English law to the classification of defects, but also some significant differences.

Void contracts present certain problems in English law. As Simon Whittaker wrote in *Chitty on Contracts*,[42] they are a contradiction in terms: a void contract is not, strictly speaking, a contract at all. This appears at first sight rather similar to the difficulty that French law has had with the notion of inexistence of the contract,

[37] Art 1352 Cc. This provision enacts a position that had already been adopted by the case law: see eg Cass civ (1) 11 June 2002, JCP 2002.IV.2323.

[38] Art 1184(1) Cc.

[39] Art 1184(2) Cc.

[40] See eg art 1171 Cc, which provides that in a standard-form contract, any term which is non-negotiable and determined in advance by one of the parties and which creates a significant imbalance in the rights and obligations of the parties to the contract (not relating to the main subject matter or the adequacy of the price) is deemed not written.

[41] See section II.A.

[42] See text to n 10.

but it is much more complicated than that. Inexistence has been marginalized in the French doctrinal thinking in favour of nullity (in its different forms).[43] Void contracts, by contrast, are well recognized in English law, and for the most part their characteristics are well defined and understood by lawyers—although we shall see in section III that there are some real difficulties in the way in which the classification of contracts as void is used within the English law of contract.

We generally use the term void to refer to a transaction which has the outward appearance of being a contract between the parties, although there is a defect in its formation which is so serious as to prevent a contract coming into existence. In that sense, this is English law's inexistent contract. There are contexts in which we would not refer to a contract being void but simply say that there is no contract—which generally describes the fact that one of the conditions of formation of a contract in English law[44] has evidently not been fulfilled. But there can be a cross-over of terminology. For example, sometimes we say that there is no contract for lack of consideration, but sometimes we say that a contract is void for lack of consideration. These two phrases are describing the same thing: that even if there might be an appearance of a contract, in law the parties' actions have not created contractual obligations.[45] A contract in English law, as in any legal system, is a source of legal obligations on one or both parties in favour of the other(s). If the contract is void, no such obligations have been created.

There are some significant consequences of the (apparent) contract being void. As a general rule, there is no need for any judicial intervention, even to declare the contract to be void: the contract being void is a passive legal consequence which requires no active legal remedy.[46] A court may resolve a dispute between the parties by determining that the contract is, and always was, void. But the court order does not in itself make the contract void. A court may become involved to deal with the consequences of the contract being void: there may be a need to cancel documents or consequential transactions which were entered into by the parties

[43] See section II.B.

[44] Given the absence of a Code or any other legislative definition, the requirements for the formation of a contract in English law are established by the case law. It is generally accepted that formation of a contract requires a sufficiently complete and certain agreement between the parties, objectively ascertained and normally established through the acceptance by one party of an offer made by the other, and consideration provided by each party for the undertakings of the other: see eg Jack Beatson, Andrew Burrows, and John Cartwright, *Anson's Law of Contract* (31st edn, OUP 2020) chs 2 and 4. No particular formality is normally required, although there are exceptional requirements of form, set by statute, for particular types of contract such as a contract relating to land, which does not come into existence unless it is made in writing and signed by or on behalf of each party: Law of Property (Miscellaneous Provisions) Act 1989 s 2; Beatson, Burrows, and Cartwright (n 44) ch 3.

[45] cf *Dunlop Pneumatic Tyre Co Ltd v Selfridge & Co Ltd* [1957] AC 847 (HL), 853 where Viscount Haldane LC said that it is a 'fundamental principle' of English law that a person who has not given consideration cannot enforce a contract not under seal (ie not executed as a deed). This refers to the contract not being enforceable by the party in the absence of consideration, but the context of the case is not about the formation of a contract but who can enforce a contract (and in particular the other 'fundamental principle' to which Viscount Haldane refers, the common law doctrine of privity of contract).

[46] See section I.C for the broad notion of remedy used in this chapter.

and even third parties on the mistaken assumption that the contract was valid;[47] and the fact that the contract was void may give rise to a claim for restitution, for example where money has been paid, or services have been performed, under the terms of the void contract.[48]

If the contract is void, then (strictly speaking) it is equally so for both parties and for any third parties who might be affected by the putative contract, and the parties themselves have no power to affirm it. If they decide to cure the defect which rendered the contract void rather than valid, they may create a contract, but it is a new contract.[49] There are, however, situations in which the fact that the contract is void is not taken to its apparently logical conclusion, and the courts will limit the circumstances in which one or other party is allowed to rely on the contract being void.[50]

A very significant consequence of a contract being void is in the law of property. Legal systems fall into different groups in the way in which they treat the relationship between a contract to transfer property (real or personal) and the transfer of the property rights themselves.[51] In English law, where the contract is for the sale of goods, the general rule is that the contract does not (unlike French law)[52] in itself transfer the property in the goods, but property is transferred to the buyer when the parties to the contract intend it to do so. In practice, however, the property will often pass when the contract is made because, in the absence of contrary intention, in an unconditional contract for the sale of specific goods in a deliverable state the parties are deemed to intend property to pass when the contract is made.[53] A consequence of this, however, is that if the contract of sale is void, then there is no contract by which the property can pass.[54] This becomes critical where the void contract forms part of a chain. In English law the general rule is that one cannot pass better title to property than one has oneself,[55] and there is no general rule along the lines accepted in civil law legal systems, including French law,[56] that

[47] See eg *British Red Cross v Werry* [2017] EWHC 875 (Ch), [2017] WTLR 441 (an agreement, which had been embodied in a court order pursuant to which a deed of trust had been entered into for the distribution of property, was void for mistake: the court order and the deed of trust were set aside).

[48] See eg *Rover International Ltd v Cannon Film Sales Ltd* [1989] 1 WLR 912 (CA).

[49] *Lever Bros Ltd v Bell* [1931] 1 KB 557 (CA), 585 (Scrutton LJ).

[50] See n 101.

[51] See Birke Häcker, 'Contract and Conveyance, The Further Repercussions of Different Transfer Systems' in John Cartwright and Ángel M López y López (eds), *Property and Contract: Comparative Reflections on English Law and Spanish Law* (Hart Publishing 2021) 89, 92–101, discussing the approaches taken in France ('a pure causal consensual system'), Germany ('a fully-fledged principle of abstraction'), Austria ('an example of separation without abstraction'), and England ('a muddle?').

[52] See art 1196 Cc, discussed by Geneviève Helleringer, 'The Proprietary Effects of Contracts' in Cartwright and Whittaker, *The Code Napoléon Rewritten* (n 7) 207.

[53] Sale of Goods Act 1979, ss 17 and 18, Rule 1.

[54] There is an argument that property may pass by other means outside the operation of the (void) contract, such as by delivery, but this is not settled: see Häcker (n 51) 101.

[55] 'Nemo dat quod non habet'; in the context of contracts for the sale of goods, see Sale of Goods Act 1979, s 21(1).

[56] Art 2276 Cc. For a detailed comparative discussion, see Häcker (n 51) 124–35.

in the case of movable property the person who receives property in good faith without notice of the fact that the transferor has no title, or a defect in title, can acquire good and indefeasible title by receiving possession of the property. In English law, the seller under a void contract therefore retains title to the goods not only as against the immediate purchaser but also against sub-purchasers along a chain of contracts, even if they are in good faith.

Voidable contracts appear to be a much more straightforward category than void contracts. Even the language here is helpful—we are concerned with a contract that has been formed: it is not void *ab initio* but is capable of being made void in the sense that the contract is retrospectively avoided (annulled). However, there are some uncertainties about the nature and effects of a voidable contract, and about the operation of the remedy (*rescission* of the contract) by which the (voidable) contract is avoided. Some of these uncertainties flow from two characteristics of the English legal system.

First, there is the fact that there is no Code or other legislation setting out the general law of contract, and therefore no legislative definition of the characteristics of a voidable contract or its avoidance, which means that we depend on the case law to answer our questions—and sometimes the courts have either declined to address important issues which are not necessary for their decisions, or questions have simply not (yet) arisen in reported litigation, either at all, or only at the level of the lower courts without there being authoritative guidance from the Supreme Court. A second characteristic is the distinction within the case law between rules and remedies developed by the courts of common law and those developed by the courts of equity. This is not the place to discuss the history of this jurisdictional division,[57] but it must be recognized that the history lives on in the modern law in many areas, including the rules relating to voidable contracts.

These two characteristics sometimes together contribute to a single uncertainty in the law of voidable contracts. For example, both the courts of common law and the courts of equity developed the law to recognize circumstances in which a defect in formation would render the contract voidable, but they applied different tests not only to define the circumstances in which the contract was thus vitiated but also the way in which the remedy of avoidance should work. Pre-contractual misrepresentation by one party to the other was accepted as a ground on which the contract was (from the moment of its formation) voidable, but the common law required a misrepresentation to be fraudulent; the courts of equity allowed a non-fraudulent misrepresentation to vitiate the contract. Since the late nineteenth century all courts have applied both common law and equity in their decisions,[58]

[57] John Baker, *An Introduction to English Legal History* (5th edn, OUP 2019) chs 2, 6.

[58] Judicature Acts 1873 and 1875: the courts were unified into a single court structure, inheriting the law developed at both common law and in equity, but in case of conflict the equitable rules were to prevail. This provision is now found in the Senior Courts Act 1981, s 49.

and this would appear to suggest that the claimant who can establish any misrepresentation, even innocent, can take advantage of the less strict equitable rule and obtain rescission. That, indeed, is the general rule but in the modern law there are—or, at least, there may be—lingering differences in the rules for the remedy of rescission depending on whether the claim is one which is brought under the old common law authorities or the equitable authorities. For example,[59] in 1963 in *Car and Universal Finance Co Ltd v Caldwell*[60] the Court of Appeal decided that the seller of a car who was the victim of a fraudulent misrepresentation by the buyer had the right to rescind the contract without first obtaining a court order, not only (as the cases had already held) by giving notice to the buyer of his decision to rescind or, if the buyer could not be found, by simply retaking possession of the car, but also by taking reasonable steps to try to trace the buyer or the car if neither could be found.[61] This developed the law on rescission of a voidable contract with the authority of the Court of Appeal, and it has been followed in England in another similar case of fraud,[62] but the point has not yet arisen for decision in the Supreme Court. Indeed, there are in-built limits to the authority of the decision in *Car and Universal Finance Co Ltd v Caldwell*. The case involved a contract which was voidable for fraud, and it is not clear whether the decision would also apply to rescission for a non-fraudulent misrepresentation: one of the judges expressly declined to consider this question since it did not arise.[63] Much more important, however, is the broader question of whether the general common law rule that rescission can be obtained by notification to the other party and without a court order applies at all in the case of a non-fraudulent misrepresentation which relies (historically) on the case law from the equitable jurisdiction. There are indications in the modern law that judges assume that in this respect[64] there should be no distinction between fraudulent and non-fraudulent misrepresentations, and therefore that rescission should generally be available by notice rather than by a court order.[65] But this is not settled with sufficient authority to avoid a continuing debate

[59] For another problem recently raised by the Court of Appeal, see *IGE USA Investments Ltd v Revenue and Customs Commissioners* [2021] EWCA Civ 534, [2021] Ch 423 [6] (*IGE USA Investments*) criticizing the uncertainty over whether the statutory limitation period for claims in the tort of deceit should be applied by analogy to claims to equitable rescission for fraud.

[60] *Car and Universal Finance Co Ltd v Caldwell* [1965] 1 QB 525 (CA).

[61] The Court held that rescission was effected by the buyer contacting the police and the Automobile Association to try to trace the owner or the car. However, Davies LJ doubted whether there was very clear existing authority allowing retaking of the property rather than giving notice: *Car and Universal Finance Co Ltd v Caldwell* (n 60) 558.

[62] *Newtons of Wembley Ltd v Williams* [1965] 1 QB 560 (CA), in which the trial judge and one of the judges in the Court of Appeal also sat in the Court of Appeal in *Car and Universal Finance Co Ltd v Caldwell* (n 60).

[63] *Car and Universal Finance Co Ltd v Caldwell* (n 60) 555 (Upjohn LJ).

[64] There are a range of other rules for rescission of a contract for misrepresentation which the courts do apply more favourably to the victim of fraud than to one who is misled innocently: see John Cartwright, *Misrepresentation, Mistake and Non-disclosure* (7th edn, Sweet & Maxwell 2025) para 4-31.

[65] eg *TSB Bank Plc v Camfield* [1995] 1 WLR 430 (CA) 438 (Roch LJ: 'the right to set aside or rescind the transaction is that of the representee, not that of the court. The court's role in a disputed case will be to decide whether the representee has lawfully rescinded the transaction or is entitled to rescind it').

and, indeed, the Court of Appeal has recently said that the authorities are in such a state of disarray that only the Supreme Court can reconcile them.[66] This is a matter of significant practical importance which needs to be resolved: allowing rescission by notification provides the victim of the misrepresentation with a speedy and efficient remedy—and, indeed, fits with a general spirit of the common law of contract in allowing self-help remedies where there is no good reason to insist on judicial intervention, such as in the termination of a contract by notification to the party in breach.[67] We have seen that in French law the remedy of nullity cannot be effected by notice by one party alone but requires a court order, although this appears to reflect a different general approach in France to the relationship between the parties (and their contract) and the court.[68]

There are some other features of the remedy of rescission of a voidable contract which should be noted, by contrast with what we have already seen of the remedy of nullity of a contract in French law.

First, English law has not developed a general remedy of partial rescission: where a contract is voidable it is the whole contract, not merely individual terms of the contract, that are affected, and the whole contract will be avoided if rescission is effected. Even if the ground of rescission affects only part of the contract, the party with the right to rescind cannot avoid one part of a contract and affirm another part, unless the parts are so severable from each other as to form two independent contracts.[69] This reflects a general approach of English law in seeing the contract as a whole, rather than focusing on individual obligations,[70] as well as a reluctance to intervene in such a way as to re-write the balance of the parties' bargain.[71] There are certain situations where English law does allow a challenge to individual contract terms. In the case of a term of a contract which is illegal or contrary to public policy, the courts have developed a rule by which they may sever the contract and

[66] *IGE USA Investments* (n 59) [91] (Henderson LJ). Permission to appeal to the Supreme Court in *IGE USA Investments* was granted on 8 July 2021, but the appeal was settled without a hearing. For further references to the debate on this issue in the cases and in academic writing, see Cartwright (n 64) para 4-19.

[67] cf the rationale of allowing immediate termination for anticipatory breach by notification to the party in breach: *Hochster v De La Tour* (1853) 2 El & Bl 678, 689; 118 ER 922, 926 (Lord Campbell CJ: 'But it is surely much more rational, and more for the benefit of both parties, that, after the renunciation of the agreement by the defendant, the plaintiff should be at liberty to consider himself absolved from any future performance of it, retaining his right to sue for any damage he has suffered from the breach of it. Thus, instead of remaining idle and laying out money in preparations which must be useless, he is at liberty to seek service under another employer, which would go in mitigation of the damages to which he would otherwise be entitled for a breach of the contract').

[68] See text to nn 31–33, noting also the different approach now taken in Belgian law.

[69] *United Shoe Machinery Co of Canada v Brunet* [1909] AC 330, 340.

[70] For example, although it is based on a non-performance of a particular obligation, we speak of breach of contract, or frustration of the contract; and consideration is necessary for formation of the contract, rather than being allocated to individual obligations for which it is given in exchange.

[71] *Marme Inversiones 2007 SL v Natwest Markets Plc* [2019] EWHC 366 (Comm) [338] (Picken J: 'The underlying principle is that a party seeking rescission should not be allowed to pick and choose which parts of the transaction to perform since that would involve rewriting the parties' bargain').

allow it to continue with the offending term disregarded, but only if the term can (literally) be removed without rewriting any other words of the contract, and if the offending clause does not form the main consideration of the contract and can be removed without constituting a major change in the overall effect of the agreement.[72] And there are situations in which a particular type of term might be targeted by statute and made ineffective while leaving the rest of the contract intact.[73] But the courts have developed no such general doctrine relating to rescission of voidable contracts.

The second notable feature of the remedy of rescission is that (as we have seen in French law) it is linked to the (second-order) remedy of restitution by one or both parties of benefits they have received by performance of the contract which is rescinded. But, unlike in French law, impossibility of making restitution is a bar to the remedy of rescission, and English law has not yet, at least,[74] developed a general doctrine of restitution by value (money-equivalent) where restitution in specie of performance that has already been effected is no longer possible. The courts have found some ways to soften this rule, applying the test of impossibility rather flexibly, and using other remedies alongside rescission to achieve a satisfactory solution.[75] But there is no direct solution along the lines taken by French law.

A further limit on the availability of rescission is the rule that the remedy will be barred if it would prejudice the rights of innocent third parties. A particular instance of this is where the contract is for the sale of goods and the seller had a defective (voidable) title to the goods: the purchaser who has bought in good faith and without notice of the seller's defect of title still acquires a good title to the goods. This rule lay behind the litigation in *Car and Universal Finance Co Ltd v Caldwell*.[76] We have seen already that in the case of a contract for the sale of goods, the buyer's title can depend on the validity of the contract of sale; and if the contract is void, there is no contract to pass the property in the goods.[77] Where, however, the contract is not void but voidable, it is a contract unless and until it is rescinded; and if it is rescinded, the contract is retrospectively avoided. But this means that the transfer of title to the property is also avoided by the rescission of the contract. If the purchaser has already sold the goods to an innocent (good faith) sub-purchaser before the initial contract of sale is rescinded, the title to the

[72] Beatson, Burrows, and Cartwright (n 44) 423–26.

[73] eg in the case of certain exclusion or limitation clauses, or other unfair terms, under the Unfair Contract Terms Act 1977 or the Consumer Rights Act 2015.

[74] cf Birke Häcker, *Consequences of Impaired Consent Transfers* (Hart Publishing 2013) 109–13, arguing that the requirement to make restitution following rescission of the contract should now be seen as part of the law of unjust enrichment.

[75] See Cartwright (n 64) paras 4-56 to 4-61. This is another area within the remedy of rescission where there were differences between the approaches taken by the courts of common law and equity, and between the approaches to fraudulent and non-fraudulent misrepresentation, some of which still linger in the modern law.

[76] See n 60.

[77] See text to n 54.

goods has passed along the chain and cannot be recalled from the sub-purchaser. In *Car and Universal Finance Co Ltd* the property in the car hinged on whether there had been a rescission before such a sub-sale to an innocent third party, which made it crucial to determine whether the party with the right to rescind can do so without having to take the time to go to court to obtain an order. In their development of rules within contract law, the courts can sometimes be influenced by the impact the development will have in other areas, such as property law.[78]

Unenforceable contracts are a different matter. In terms of their potency, we could say that they fall somewhere between void and voidable: unlike void contracts, they satisfy the basic rules for the formation of contracts and do create obligations, but already from the moment of their formation they are defective as regards some of their immediate effects (enforceability by one or both parties) whereas the voidable contract is valid and fully effective but potentially defeasible if the ground of voidability is later activated in order to rescind the contract ab initio.

But the grounds for categorization of contracts as unenforceable are rather different from void and voidable contracts. Many grounds of unenforceability are statutory, and the statute will define the defect in the contract or in its method of formation and (either explicitly by the terms of the statute, or by its interpretation by case law) this may sometimes be curable so as to render the contract wholly binding and enforceable.[79] The grounds of unenforceability are sometimes designed to protect one or both parties, such as the cautionary function of formality in the formation of certain kinds of contract.[80] Others may be designed to further a broader public interest, such as where the contract or one or more of its terms are illegal (including the terms being contrary to public policy). This latter case is a question of the substance of the contract rather than the process of its formation and therefore raises some different issues, but there is clearly an overlap here with matters which would be dealt with in French law by the remedy of nullity—absolute nullity, since that remedy is a response to the violation of rule which has as its object the safeguard of the public interest.

For our purposes, it is interesting to note that, while the French response in such a case is to nullify the contract, English law is more nuanced.[81] The consequences of illegality may be defined by a statute, and in some instances the statute may provide that the contract is void.[82] But in the absence of statutory provision the general

[78] See generally Häcker (n 51).

[79] eg the requirements of writing set out in the Statute of Frauds 1677 as a condition of enforceability of certain kinds of contract could be satisfied not only by the contract itself being in writing, but also by a written memorandum or note of it, which could be executed later. Only s 4 of the Statute of Frauds now remains, in relation to contracts of guarantee, but in the modern law there are also other contracts for which statute has set a requirement of writing as a condition of enforceability. See generally John Cartwright, *Formation and Variation of Contracts* (4th edn, Sweet & Maxwell Ltd 2024) ch 6.

[80] See Cartwright (n 79) paras 4-03, 6-06.

[81] Beatson, Burrows, and Cartwright (n 44) 410–26.

[82] eg Marine Insurance Act 1906, s 4(1) ('Every contract of marine insurance by way of gaming or wagering is void').

approach in the modern law is not to think in terms of the contract itself being void but to consider whether allowing a party to bring a claim relating to the contract would be 'harmful to the integrity of the legal system', applying a range of factors set out by the Supreme Court: the underlying purpose of the prohibition which has been transgressed and whether that purpose will be enhanced by denial of the claim; any other relevant public policy on which the denial of the claim may have an impact; and whether denial of the claim would be a proportionate response to the illegality, bearing in mind that punishment is a matter for the criminal courts.[83] We have seen that one critical issue in relation to the categorization of contracts as void or voidable in English law is the impact on the passing of property where the contract is one pursuant to which property was intended to pass. This is less of an issue in the case of illegality: since the contract is not void, there is no inherent obstacle to property passing, even if other claims by the parties to enforce the contract might otherwise be denied.[84]

III. English Law: Learning by Comparing? Void Contracts and Relatively Void Contracts?

Section II included discussion of some general points of comparison between the nature and effect of the remedies for defects in formation of the contract in French law and English law. In the course of that discussion, we saw that English law had unresolved difficulties in relation to some remedies, and in particular void contracts. In this section we consider particular problems that arise in the operation of void contracts in English law, which raise some doubts about the general effect of a contract being void and the relationship between void contracts and voidable contracts. Although there is no question of simply borrowing from French law, where the remedy of nullity is embedded in the French vision of contract which has many significant differences from the English vision, it may yet be possible to draw some inspiration from the current thinking in French law, and in particular its modern theory of nullities,[85] to consider how English law might re-think some of its difficulties in this area.

There are two very different types of situation in which a contract can be void in English law: first, where there is no properly constituted contract at all because one or more of the conditions required for the formation of a contract have not been complied with; and second, where the elements required for the formation of the contract have apparently been satisfied but there is some other defect which is so

[83] *Patel v Mirza* [2016] UKSC 42, [2017] AC 467, [120].

[84] *Tinsley v Milligan* [1994] 1 AC 340 (HL), in which the result would still be the same today: *Patel v Mirza* (n 83) [112].

[85] See n 14.

serious as to prevent the parties' obligations ever coming into existence as a matter of law. In the modern law, these two situations come together in the context of *mistake* as a vitiating factor in a contract.[86] The difference between the two situations was expressed by Lord Atkin in *Bell v Lever Bros Ltd*:[87] a mistake may *negative* consent, or it may *nullify* consent. The example he gave of a mistake which negatives consent was a mistake as to the identity of the other contracting party: the belief by A that A is contracting with B, whereas in fact A is contracting with C, where it is clear that the intention of A was to contract only with B. And the example of a mistake which nullified consent was where both parties are in fact agreed about the subject matter of a contract of sale of goods, but the goods have already perished at the time of the contract. As Lord Atkin put it, 'a consent to transfer or take delivery of something not existent is deemed useless, the consent is nullified'.[88] The first of these two examples involves a failure to satisfy one of the conditions for the formation of a contract—in the case of a mistake of identity, when A mistakes B for C, there is no contract because there are no two parties who intended to contract with each other, and this lack of a common intention is as much an obstacle to the formation of a contract as the failure of parties to agree on the terms of the contract: there is a failure of offer and acceptance.[89] Although the test for the formation of a contract in English law is objective, not purely subjective, and therefore a contract can be found where one party reasonably (but erroneously) believes that the other party is agreeing with him,[90] a mistake can prevent the parties being in sufficient agreement—and therefore prevent there being a contract—where one party knows or ought to know that the other is mistaken about the terms,[91] or where the parties are simply at cross-purposes about the terms.[92]

In the second example, however, there is a contract: there is agreement, formed through offer and acceptance, and each party provides consideration in the

[86] In relation to lack of consideration, there is no doubt that the contract is void (or, otherwise put, just not formed—inexistent): cf n 45 and preceding text. As regards defects in formation other than mistake—misrepresentation, duress, undue influence, unconscionable bargains—it is clear that the contract is voidable, not void: see Beatson, Burrows, and Cartwright (n 44) chs 9 and 10. Lack of capacity is more complicated and whether the contract is void, voidable, or unenforceable depends on the ground of incapacity: ibid ch 7.

[87] *Bell v Lever Bros Ltd* [1932] AC 161, 217.

[88] ibid. There are in fact broader questions of risk allocation in such a case: a contract for non-existent goods can be valid (not void) if one party, typically, the seller, has guaranteed their existence and thereby undertaken the risk: *McRae v Commonwealth Disposals Commission* (1951) 84 CLR 377; *Associated Japanese Bank (International) Ltd v Crédit du Nord SA* [1989] 1 WLR 255, 268; *Great Peace Shipping Ltd v Tsavliris Salvage (International) Ltd (The Great Peace)* [2002] EWCA Civ 1407, [2003] QB 679, [84]. But where there is no express or implied allocation of risk, the contract may be void for lack of subject matter.

[89] *Cundy v Lindsay* (1878) 3 App Cas 459; *Shogun Finance Ltd v Hudson* [2003] UKHL 62; [2004] 1 AC 919, [55], [170], [191]. The *Shogun* case raises a number of difficulties and has been controversial, but the detail is not of concern here; see Cartwright (n 64) ch 14, esp paras 14-34 to 14-43.

[90] *Smith v Hughes* (1871) LR 6 QB 597, 607.

[91] *Hartog v Colin & Shields* [1939] 3 All ER 566, 568.

[92] *Falck v Williams* [1900] AC 176.

promise to provide the goods or to pay for them. The fact that the contract cannot be performed because of the non-existence of the goods where it is not within the risk undertaken by either party does not prevent the conditions for formation of the contract being satisfied. But it renders the contract void. The circumstances in which this will be satisfied are narrow—and deliberately so, since the courts have made clear their reluctance to allow a mistake to be void by reason of a mistake as to fact or law (rather than a mistake as to terms or identity), on the basis that it risks undermining the binding force of contracts.[93] It has, however, been said that the doctrine of mistake is not limited to cases where the subject matter of the contract does not exist, but extends to cases of mistake about the qualities of the subject matter, as long as it is 'the mistake of both parties, and is as to the existence of some quality which makes the thing without the quality essentially different from the thing as it was believed to be';[94] or where there is a common mistake (outside the risk or fault of either party) which renders performance of the contract impossible—but this extends to not just physical impossibility but also impossibility as regards the purpose of the contract.[95]

There is a very clear tension here: the courts express reluctance to allow mistake of fact or law relating to the subject matter to operate, but leave open the door to a limited scope of (shared) mistake being sufficiently serious to render the contract void—although it is a door that has hardly been opened in the reported cases. Much more doctrinal ink has been spilled in debating this topic[96] than judicial ink in deciding cases. There are practical reasons why the courts have not needed to deal with it—including the fact that many cases of mistake can be solved satisfactorily through other claims, either remedies for breach of contract where there is an express or implied term of the contract allocating the risk of the mistake to one of the parties, or rescission of the contract where the claimant's mistake was provoked by the defendant's misrepresentation, rendering the contract voidable. In English law, the misrepresentation need not be fraudulent, and the availability of rescission is at least part of the explanation why the significant number of cases which are litigated in France under the heading of mistake as to the essential qualities of the subject matter do not appear under that heading in the English law

[93] *Bell v Lever Bros Ltd* (n 87) 224 (Lord Atkin: 'it is of paramount importance that contracts should be observed, and that if parties honestly comply with the essentials of the formation of contracts—i.e., agree in the same terms on the same subject matter—they are bound, and must rely on the stipulations of the contract for protection from the effect of facts unknown to them').

[94] *Bell v Lever Bros Ltd* (n 87) 217–18 (Lord Atkin).

[95] The 'contractual adventure': *The Great Peace* (n 88) [76].

[96] To which the present author has contributed: John Cartwright, '*Solle v Butcher* and the Doctrine of Mistake in Contract' (1987) 103 Law Quarterly Review 594. See also, eg, Christopher J Slade, 'The Myth of Mistake in the English Law of Contract' (1954) 70 Law Quarterly Review 385; PS Atiyah and FAR Bennion, 'Mistake in the Construction of Contracts' (1961) 24 Modern Law Review 421; JC Smith, 'Contracts – Mistake, Frustration and Implied Terms' (1994) 110 Law Quarterly Review 400; Jonathan Morgan, 'Common Mistake in Contract: Rare Success and Common Misapprehensions' [2018] Cambridge Law Journal 559.

reports.[97] But there are also other explanations. The general significance of mistake as a vitiating factor in French law is in sharp contrast to its narrow scope in English law because of a different vision of the role of the parties' (subjective) consent in the formation of the contract: in French thinking, mistake naturally undermines a contract,[98] whereas the English approach is not only more objective in its determination of the existence of the contract but it also more strongly and openly favours a policy of holding parties to contracts where there is no good reason to allow them to escape—and a purely internal mistake, even one shared with the other party, is not seen as a good enough reason. If the other party is responsible for it—as by making a misrepresentation—that changes the picture. But mistakes do not generally deserve a remedy.[99]

Even if we accept this position of policy and limit the right of parties to rely on their own mistakes rather than on the other party's misconduct in inducing the contract, there is still a contradiction as long as we allow such a mistake to operate at all: the actionable mistake makes the contract void, whereas the other party's misrepresentation which induced the mistake, where the merits of intervention are clearly stronger on this English vision of responsibility in formation of the contract, only makes it voidable—and we have seen that the consequences of a contract being void are much more problematic than it being voidable.[100] This contradiction does not arise in France because all the defects in formation of the contract are met by a single response: nullity, which does not contain the sharp-edged distinction between void and voidable contracts. It may well be that one of the reasons for the English courts' reluctance to allow mistake of fact or law as a defect in a contract is the remedy and its consequences: property may not pass pursuant to the contract, both parties are equally affected by it being void, there is no right to affirm the contract, and so on. But this is to put the matter the wrong way round. English law could simply reject mistake of fact or law as the basis of a remedy for a defect in the contract, leaving only breach of contract and misrepresentation. But

[97] John Cartwright, 'Defects of Consent and Security of Contract: French and English Law Compared' in Peter Birks and Arianna Pretto (eds), *Themes in Comparative Law in Honour of Bernard Rudden* (OUP 2002) 153, discussing the provisions of the Code before the 2016/2018 reforms. In the reformed Code, see now art 1132 Cc ('Mistake of law or of fact, as long as it is not inexcusable, is a ground of nullity of the contract where it bears on the essential qualities of the act of performance owed or of the other contracting party').

[98] cf Robert Joseph Pothier, *Traité des Obligations* (Debure l'aîné 1761) para 17: 'mistake is the greatest defect that can affect a contract, for contracts are formed by the consent of the parties, and there cannot be consent when the parties have made a mistake about the subject matter of their agreement' (translation by the author). However, Pothier had a view of the scope of actionable mistakes very different from (and narrower than) the modern French law: Barry Nicholas, *The French Law of Contract* (2nd edn, Clarendon Press 1992) 85–86; and, indeed, Pothier drew a distinction between mistakes and other defects in formation which gives the appearance of being closer to the English position: mistake prevented a contract being formed (absence of consent), but fraud and duress did not prevent consent and therefore the contract was formed even though it was vitiated: Pothier (n 98) paras 21, 29.

[99] Cartwright (n 64) paras 12-13 to 12-16.

[100] Section II.C.

if there should be a good reason to allow a party to escape the contract on the basis of mistake, the remedy should respond appropriately. Given that the essence of a mistake is that it is the misunderstanding of one party that leads that party to regret the contract and therefore to seek to avoid it (even if we add the limitation that it should be a shared mistake in order to be actionable), the more natural remedy should be not that the contract is void, but that it is voidable. This would align with other defects in formation, to which this kind of mistake is more closely related than cases where the contract is void because the conditions for formation of the contract have not been satisfied; it would not have the automatic (and sometimes undesirable) consequences that void contracts are seen to have; and it would focus on providing a remedy for the party who seeks it, and who deserves to be protected: in the French thinking, it is a form of *relative* nullity.[101] Reverting to Lord Atkin's idea:[102] if mistakes operate at all, they operate to negative the consent or to nullify it. Negation of consent (or, rather, negation of the contract by reason of a failure of one of its conditions of formation) is the traditional void contract—a form of inexistence of the contract. It is not the way modern French law thinks, preferring nullity over inexistence for defects of formation generally. But in English law the contract being void (inexistent) where the consent is negated makes sense. Nullification of consent, however, has the potential to be rethought. Even the language carries echoes of a remedy which is different from the inexistent (void) contract. Perhaps we can think of it more as a 'relatively void' contract. But the simpler approach would be just to bring it into the fold of voidable contracts.

It must be admitted that this suggestion is a form of heresy: in the second half of the twentieth century, beginning in 1949 with his judgment in *Solle v Butcher*,[103] Lord Denning tried to shift the remedy for common mistake of fact from the contract being void to it being voidable, but this was roundly rejected by the Court of Appeal in 2002 in *The Great Peace*.[104] However, Lord Denning may have overcooked his argument. In *Solle v Butcher* and the (relatively few) cases which discussed and developed it, not only was the argument that a fundamental common mistake of fact rendered the contract voidable (rather than void), but also, through the application of the test for mistake set out by Lord Denning, the scope of actionable mistakes appeared to be widening (thus increasing the threat to the binding

[101] There are aspects of the doctrine of mistake which already align with this thinking—such as the rule that, even though the mistake of fact must be common (shared) if it is to be actionable, the remedy still depends on the merits of the individual party's claim to the contract being void: the claimant's fault in making the mistake, or in having caused the (common) mistake, may act as a bar to the remedy even if the other party might be able to claim that the contract is void: see *Associated Japanese Bank (International) Ltd v Crédit du Nord SA* (n 88) 268. There are also other examples of situations where courts traditionally hold a contract void for mistake which might better be seen as voidable because the underlying policy is to protect one of the parties: see eg the doctrine of *non est factum*, discussed in Cartwright (n 64) para 13-63.

[102] See text to n 87.

[103] *Solle v Butcher* [1950] 1 KB 671, 693, discussed in Cartwright (n 64) para 15-31.

[104] *The Great Peace* (n 88).

force of contract), and the remedy of rescission for mistake was within the discretion of the court which could make associated orders designed, in effect, to re-write the contract to eliminate the mistake—a role which the English courts generally decline in the context of contract law.[105] Given also the apparent sidestepping of the authority of the existing case law in order to effect this development of rescission for mistake, it is not surprising that the Court of Appeal, in a commercial case and emphasizing the importance of commercial certainty, rejected Lord Denning's approach and reasserted what they saw as the orthodoxy that the only remedy for common mistake of fact is that the contract is void—and that it is to be kept narrow, and not a matter of judicial discretion.[106]

There is clearly room for disagreement about the proper scope of the doctrine of mistake of fact and the appropriate remedy (void/voidable); and some courts in other common law jurisdictions have so far preferred to retain Lord Denning's approach and have declined to follow *The Great Peace*.[107] In English law, the Supreme Court has not yet been invited to consider these developments since the House of Lords last pronounced on the matter in 1932.[108] The suggestion in this chapter is that any reconsideration of the remedies for defects in the formation of contracts, such as the distinction between void contracts and voidable contracts, could learn not just from a review of the internal policies of the English law of contract, but also from thinking more broadly about the purpose of such distinctions in light of comparisons with the approaches taken in other jurisdictions, including those within the civil law tradition.

[105] See the cases from *Solle v Butcher* to *The Great Peace*, discussed in Cartwright (n 64) para 15-32. The equitable remedy of rectification is designed to re-write the contract, but this is in order to bring a written document into line with the parties' agreement, not to allow the courts to override the agreement: Cartwright (n 64) paras 13-38, 13-47.

[106] *The Great Peace* (n 88). Toulson J, the judge at first instance in the case ([2001] All ER (D) 152 (Nov) [120]) had been even more forthright in rejecting Lord Denning's approach to common mistake of fact: 'Bluntly, the difficulty about this form of the doctrine is that it puts palm tree justice in place of party autonomy.'

[107] Cartwright (n 64) para 15-34, fn 183.

[108] *Bell v Lever Bros Ltd* (n 87).

4

Performance, Reasonableness, and Proportionality

English and French Remedies Law

Solène Rowan

I. Introduction

In 'Contributory Fault and Mitigation, Rights and Reasonableness: Comparisons between English and French Law',[1] Simon Whittaker contrasted English and French law in the following way:

> There is ... a concern in French law for ... the rights of parties to a contract to performance of its obligations, whereas English law is more concerned to balance the interest of parties ... by reference to a standard of reasonableness.[2]
>
> While the grand declarations of principle ... invoke the creditor's right to performance, French law is also very much concerned to protect the debtor's right to perform ... By contrast, English law protects the rights of creditors to 'performance' by allowing them freely to obtain a substitute elsewhere, protecting the rights of debtors by subjecting this to the standard of reasonableness.[3]

Reading these observations—on the first occasion as a doctoral student at the University of Cambridge—was a pivotal moment in the development of my scholarship. It crystallized in my mind the distinction between two contractual 'rights': the 'right to obtain performance' of the promisee and the 'right to render performance' of the promisor. This distinction had, and still has, rarely been made in English academic literature or case law.

Simon Whittaker's work also brought to my attention the relatively minor role that reasonableness, a concept that is at the heart of English remedies law, had in French law. There were circumstances in which reasonableness would be an

[1] Simon Whittaker, 'Contributory Fault and Mitigation, Rights and Reasonableness: Comparisons between English and French Law' in Luboš Tichý (ed), *Causation in Law* (Konrad Adenauer Stiftung 2007) 149.
[2] ibid 150.
[3] ibid 170.

Solène Rowan, *Performance, Reasonableness, and Proportionality* In: *Comparative Reflections in Private Law*.
Edited by: Marco Cappelletti, Ciara Kennefick, and Dorota Leczykiewicz, Oxford University Press.
 DOI: 10.1093/9780198959168.003.0005

important moderating force in English law, yet would play no role in France. These two themes—the performance interest and the significance of reasonableness—would become important in my doctoral thesis and my later scholarship.

This chapter surveys some key developments relating to these themes that have taken place during Simon Whittaker's career. It examines how the protection of contractual performance and the role of reasonableness in the context of remedies have evolved in England and France over recent decades. The analysis begins with English law. It shows that while reasonableness remains central in the English law of remedies, over time greater protection has been afforded to contractual performance. In particular, there has been a notable trend—both in the authorities and the academic literature—towards recognizing that the promisee has an 'interest in obtaining performance' that is worthy of protection. However, the corresponding interest of the promisor in 'rendering performance' has rarely received attention and remains an underdeveloped concept.

The focus then moves to France, where the commitment to performance remains strong, but reasonableness now plays a more prominent role in remedies law. Reasonableness, and the closely related concept of proportionality, were introduced to the provisions on remedies by the 2016 reforms of the contract law section of the French Civil Code (Cc) as limiting mechanisms to achieve greater balance between the competing interests of the parties. The aim was to avoid extreme outcomes that subjugate the interests of the defaulting promisor to those of the injured party.

These evolutions have undoubtedly brought about a *rapprochement* between English and French law. However, as will be suggested by way of concluding remarks, the contrast encapsulated by Simon Whittaker in the passage set out above remains generally true. This is mainly now due to the mitigation principle, which is rooted in reasonableness, still playing a central role in English law, yet having no place in French law. The mitigation principle dictates the behaviour expected of the injured party following breach. Its introduction in France would enhance the role of reasonableness but is an unlikely prospect.

II. The Performance Interest in English law

The 'performance interest', meaning the interest in obtaining the performance of the promisee, has attracted increasing attention in English law in recent decades. It is an expression that is used with growing frequency in academic literature and authorities, reflecting a greater awareness that performance, rather than its mere monetary equivalent, has intrinsic value. This contrasts with the comparatively sparse coverage of the lesser-known and seldom discussed interest of the promisor in rendering performance.

A. The origins of the performance interest in English contract law

To refer to a *right* to contractual performance is not 'the natural mode of expression of the common lawyer'.[4] Instead, what one finds in the literature and case law is reference to the 'performance interest' or the 'interest in performance'. These expressions are relatively recent additions to the academic and judicial lexicon, having originated in Friedmann's seminal article 'The Performance Interest in Contract Damages',[5] where the following description is proffered:

> The essence of a contract is performance. Contracts are made in order to be performed. This is usually the one and only ground for their formation. Ordinarily, a person enters into a contract because he is interested in getting that which the other party has to offer and because he places a higher value on the other party's performance than on the cost and trouble he will incur to obtain it. This interest in getting the promised performance . . . is the only pure contractual interest.[6]

The performance interest therefore refers to the interest of the promisee in obtaining the performance which they are promised under the contract.[7] It is their interest in having the contract duly performed, which includes both the interest in receiving the benefit to which they are contractually entitled and in being compensated for loss caused by the breach.[8]

A premise of Friedmann's article is that although 'performance interest' and the more familiar 'expectation interest' may be synonymous, the former is a more accurate characterization of the entitlement of the injured party. The word 'expectation' has connotations of a prospect which is unsupported by a contract. It does not accurately portray the enforceability of the promise that gives rise to the interest.[9]

[4] ibid 161.

[5] Daniel Friedmann, 'The Performance Interest in Contract Damages' (1995) 111 Law Quarterly Review 628 criticizing LL Fuller and William R Perdue, 'The Reliance Interest in Damages' (1936–37) 46 Yale Law Journal 52 and 373.

[6] Friedmann (n 5) 629.

[7] For a similar definition in the case law, see *Alfred McAlpine Construction Ltd v Panatown Ltd* [2001] AC 518 (HL) 577 (Lord Browne-Wilkinson).

[8] Some commentators have attributed a narrower meaning to the performance interest, drawing a distinction with what they consider to be another contractual interest, the compensation interest: Charlie Webb, 'Performance and Compensation: An Analysis of Contract Damages and Contractual Obligation' (2006) Oxford Journal of Legal Studies 41; Brian Coote, 'Contract Damages, *Ruxley* and the Performance Interest' [1997] Cambridge Law Journal 537, where the 'performance interest' is differentiated from the 'wider expectation interest', which also covers consequential loss. See also David Winterton, *Money Awards in Contract Law* (Hart Publishing 2017).

[9] Friedmann (n 5) 634–35.

Nowadays, the expression 'performance interest' is increasingly used in academic literature[10] and the case law.[11] It has firmly become part of the contract law lexicon, frequently being used interchangeably with 'expectation interest'.[12] This is because the semantic distinction between 'expectation interest' and 'performance interest' is often irrelevant to the question of which remedy should be granted. In most circumstances, a breach of contract is remedied by compensatory damages, which is very much the remedy of choice in English law. It is perceived to be adequate and effective, particularly where the parties enter into a contract for profit and their 'contractual expectations' are, or their 'interest in obtaining performance' is, financial. Damages are the monetary equivalent of performance.

B. The growing recognition of the interest in obtaining performance

There are however some circumstances where the objectives of the parties are wider than financial gain, and damages are not an adequate remedial response to breach. It is here that the courts have been creative in granting relief and have tended to use the term 'performance interest' to signal that the contractual interest in question is in obtaining performance itself or a monetary remedy that is more robust than mere compensation.

(i) Interest in obtaining performance that goes beyond compensation

In recent times the courts have shown a growing readiness to acknowledge that the parties can have broader contractual aims than to make a financial gain. This might be subjective, non-financial, or not easily measurable in terms of market value. As Lord Bridge observed in *Ruxley Electronics and Construction Ltd v Forsyth*,[13] the law relating to damages for breach of contract normally proceeds 'on the assumption that each contracting party's interest in the bargain [is] purely commercial and that the loss resulting from a breach of contract is measurable in purely economic terms. But this assumption may not always be appropriate.'[14]

Where compensatory damages are insufficient to protect contractual expectations, the authorities have increasingly leaned towards a broader approach to the

[10] eg Andrew Burrows, *Remedies for Torts and Breach of Contract* (4th edn, OUP 2019) 189–90; Ewan McKendrick, *Contract Law: Text, Cases, and Materials* (10th edn, OUP 2022) 925; Janet O'Sullivan, 'Reflections on the Role of Restitutionary Damages to Protect Contractual Expectations' in David Johnston and Reinhard Zimmermann (eds), *Unjustified Enrichment: Key Issues in Comparative Perspective* (CUP 2002) 327, 334.

[11] eg *McAlpine Construction* (n 7) 546 (Lord Goff); *Earl's Terrace Properties Ltd v Nilsson Design Ltd* [2004] EWHC 136 (QB) [76]–[78] (HHJ Thornton QC).

[12] *AG of Trinidad and Tobago v Trinsalvage Enterprises Ltd* [2023] UKPC 26 (PC); *McAlpine Construction* (n 7).

[13] [1996] AC 344 (HL).

[14] ibid 353 (Lord Bridge).

concept of loss and the recognition that performance can have intrinsic value. This has been particularly apparent in the creation of exceptions to the general principle that non-pecuniary loss does not sound in damages,[15] the suggestion that defeated expectations may amount to loss,[16] and gain-based monetary awards.[17]

An early example of this readiness to acknowledge that loss is not always financial and that the parties may have an interest in obtaining performance itself is exemplified in *Ruxley Electronics and Construction Ltd v Forsyth*.[18] In this case, the promisor, a building contractor, constructed a swimming pool for the promisee. In breach of the provision that the pool should have a maximum depth of seven feet six inches, the promisor constructed the pool to a maximum depth of six feet. As the pool was safe for swimming and diving, and the resale value of the property was unaffected, the performance rendered was equivalent in value to the promised performance and no financial loss was suffered.

Acknowledging that the subjective value and the market value of performance are not always equal, the House of Lords held the amenity that the promisee had lost in consequence of the breach to be recoverable. Lord Mustill embraced the concept of 'consumer surplus',[19] which is the subjective value obtained from performance over and above the utility associated with the market price,[20] and stated:

> The law must cater for those occasions where the value of the promise to the promisee exceeds the financial enhancement of his position which full performance must secure. This excess, often referred to in the literature as the 'consumer surplus' . . . is usually incapable of precise valuation in terms of money, exactly because it represents a personal, subjective and non-monetary gain. Nevertheless where it exists the law should recognise it and compensate the promisee if the misperformance takes it away.[21]

The House of Lords' expansive analysis of the loss suffered filled a gap in the protection of the performance interest. It recognized that performance beyond economic benefit is worthy of protection.

The contract for the benefit of third parties is another context in which it has been recognized that performance has inherent value. In third party contracts, the promisee enters into the contract and pays for the consideration moving from the

[15] This head of loss does not generally sound in damages by virtue of the principle in *Addis v Gramophone Co Ltd* [1909] AC 488 (HL) that a wrongfully dismissed employee cannot be compensated for the manner of their dismissal, injury to their feelings, or loss of reputation. See the exceptions created in *Ruxley* (n 13); *Watts v Morrow* [1991] 1 WLR 1421; *Farley v Skinner* [2002] 2 AC 732 (HL).

[16] *McAlpine Construction* (n 7) (Lord Goff and Lord Millett).

[17] *AG v Blake* [2001] 1 AC 268 (HL).

[18] *Ruxley* (n 13).

[19] ibid 360 (Lord Mustill).

[20] Donald Harris, Anthony Ogus, and Jennifer Phillips, 'Contract Remedies and the Consumer Surplus' (1979) 95 Law Quarterly Review 581.

[21] *Ruxley* (n 13) 360–61 (Lord Mustill).

promisor, yet this consideration is for the benefit of a third party. In the event of default, the promisee may suffer no financial loss, and absent privity of contract, the third party may have no enforceable rights against the promisor. A recurrent question is whether the promisee may recover substantial damages for breach where the only financial loss caused by the breach is borne by the third party.

There has been support for the view that, in these hard cases, the protection of performance should go beyond compensation for financial loss. In *Linden Gardens Trust Ltd v Lenesta Sludge Disposals Ltd* (consolidated with *St Martins Property Corp Ltd v Sir Robert McAlpine Ltd*), Lord Griffiths stated that not receiving the promised performance could, without more, constitute loss, giving rise to an entitlement of substantial damages.[22] In *McAlpine Construction*,[23] Lord Goff and Lord Millett, who were in the minority, drew upon Lord Griffith's view that an enforceable promise should confer an entitlement to the promised performance. Lord Millett characterized the argument that the absence of financial loss should prevent the recovery of damages as being 'the product of the narrow accountants' balance sheet quantification of loss which measures the loss suffered by the promisee by the diminution in his overall financial position resulting from the breach'.[24] He went on to say:

> in certain kinds of contract at least, the right to performance has a value . . . There has for some time been a growing consensus among academic writers that English law adopts an unduly narrow approach to the concept of loss, and that it ought to recognise that the performance of a contractual obligation may have an economic value of its own which is capable of sounding in damages.[25]

This is a wide conception of loss that emphasizes the right to performance rather than the financial benefit of performance.[26] A breach of contract can constitute a loss of the performance interest.[27]

Another example of the legitimate interest in obtaining performance having played a significant role is in the context of restitutionary monetary awards. In the well-known case of *Attorney General v Blake*,[28] a majority of the House of Lords invoked the discretionary remedy of an account of profits to order the disgorgement

[22] [1994] 1 AC 85 (HL).
[23] *McAlpine Construction* (n 7).
[24] ibid 588 (Lord Millett).
[25] ibid 587 (Lord Millett).
[26] Coote (n 8) 550–51, for whom the real problem lies in the courts confusing, in some contexts, bargained-for contractual rights (benefits in law) and the enjoyment of the fruits of performance (benefits in fact); Catherine Mitchell, 'Remedial Inadequacy in Contract and the Role of Restitutionary Damages' (1999) 15 Journal of Contract Law 133, 149–50; more generally see Solène Rowan, *Remedies for Breach of Contract: A Comparative Analysis of the Protection of Performance* (OUP 2012) ch 4.
[27] The promisee 'although not himself suffering the pecuniary damage [suffers] his own damage being the loss of his performance interest': *McAlpine Construction* (n 7) 577 (Lord Browne-Wilkinson).
[28] [2001] 1 AC 268 (HL).

of gains made by a spy from the publication of information that he had agreed with the Crown to keep secret. Lord Nicholls, giving the leading judgment, said:

> An award of damages, assessed by reference to financial loss, is not always 'adequate' as a remedy for a breach of contract. The law recognises that a party to a contract may have an interest in performance which is not readily measurable in terms of money.[29]
>
> In the same way as a plaintiff's interest in performance of a contract may render it just and equitable for the court to make an order for specific performance or grant an injunction, so the plaintiff's interest in performance may make it just and equitable that the defendant should retain no benefit from his breach of contract.[30]

Lord Nicholls explicitly acknowledged that the existing remedial regime for breach of contract is not always fit for the purpose of safeguarding the performance interest. This was critical to his conviction that gain-based awards are justifiable.

That a party may have an interest that goes beyond financial reparation was reiterated by the Supreme Court when considering 'negotiating damages' awards in *Morris Garner v One Step (Support) Ltd*,[31] even though the court distanced itself from *Blake*[32] and refused to base their availability on whether the injured party has shown a legitimate interest in preventing the profit-making activity of the defaulting party.[33] Negotiating damages compensate the injured party for the hypothetical price that they would have been willing to accept to release the defaulting party from the obligation that was breached, and in many cases they have been assessed as a proportion of the defaulting party's profits from the breach. The Supreme Court limited the availability of negotiating damages to 'where the loss suffered by the claimant is appropriately measured by reference to the economic value of the right which has been breached'.[34]

(ii) Growing significance of the performance interest in the context of penalties

The increased recognition that contracting parties can have an interest that goes beyond compensation in the above hard cases was borne out of a desire to find satisfactory solutions as they occasionally arose. Recently, this recognition has extended more widely. The performance interest has gained mainstream importance in the context of agreed damages clauses and is now at the heart of the new law

[29] ibid 282 (Lord Nicholls).
[30] ibid 285 (Lord Nicholls).
[31] [2018] UKSC 20, [2019] AC 649. See [31]–[40] (Lord Reed); [110]–[111] (Lord Sumption).
[32] ibid [90], [97] (Lord Reed).
[33] ibid.
[34] ibid [91] (Lord Reed).

on penalties. In *Cavendish Square Holding BV v Talal El Makdessi*,[35] the Supreme Court held that an over-compensatory damages clause can be valid where it creates a secondary obligation that serves a legitimate interest of the injured party in the performance of the contract and imposes a detriment that is not extravagant, exorbitant, or unconscionable in comparison with the interest protected.[36] This is a departure from the previous rule under which any clause that went beyond compensation was automatically unenforceable.[37]

In rationalizing the new rule, the Supreme Court emphasized that while in many cases compensation adequately serves the legitimate interest of the injured party,[38] there may be circumstances in which they have an interest in the enforcement of the primary obligation which is not satisfied by the recovery of compensatory damages.[39] Where this is the case, a damages clause that has no relationship with loss and which aims to deter breach may be justified.[40] As Lord Neuberger and Lord Sumption said in the principal judgment given jointly:

> A damages clause may properly be justified by some other consideration than the desire to recover compensation for a breach. This must depend on whether the innocent party has a legitimate interest in performance extending beyond the prospect of pecuniary compensation flowing directly from the breach in question.[41]
>
> [The innocent party's] interest is in performance or in some appropriate alternative to performance. In the case of a straightforward damages clause, that interest will rarely extend beyond compensation for the breach . . . But compensation is not necessarily the only legitimate interest that the innocent party may have in the performance of the defaulter's primary obligations.[42]

Compensation therefore remains the central remedial response and is considered to be satisfactory in most situations. However, where it fails to protect the broader contractual objectives of the parties, stronger protection of performance is appropriate. The distinguishing characteristic of damages clauses is that it is the parties themselves rather than the courts that identify this need. Since *Makdessi*, the

[35] With its conjoined appeal *ParkingEye Ltd v Beavis* [2016] AC 172.
[36] Solène Rowan, 'The "Legitimate Interest in Performance" in the Law on Penalties' (2019) 78 Cambridge Law Journal 148.
[37] Note however that there was growing recognition that the pre-emptive invalidation of all damages clauses to neutralize occasional unfairness was a crude solution and the courts had been showing growing tolerance towards wide but not oppressive clauses: *Philips Hong Kong Ltd v The AG of Hong Kong* (1993) 61 BLR 41 (PC); *Murray v Leisureplay plc* [2005] EWCA Civ 963 (CA).
[38] *Makdessi* (n 35) [32] (Lord Neuberger and Lord Sumption); [255] (Lord Hodge).
[39] ibid [28]–[32], [99] (Lord Neuberger and Lord Sumption); [152] (Lord Mance); [255] (Lord Hodge).
[40] ibid.
[41] ibid [28].
[42] ibid [32].

courts will help them to meet the need and achieve better protection of performance by enforcing damages clauses more extensively and flexibly.

The new approach to penalties reflects a more liberal approach to the contractual wishes of the parties and their possible reasons for agreeing to a damages clause that goes beyond compensation. Its effect is to give the courts greater flexibility and increase the prospects of damages clauses being enforced. This in turn gives the parties more scope to reinforce the protection of their contractual interests. They can tailor the level of protection to reflect their particular circumstances.

In view of its central role in the new test on penalties, the concept of 'legitimate interest in performance' has gained considerable practical importance. The injured party's entitlement to rely on a damages clause now turns on the extent of their legitimate interest in performance, which in each case the court must measure with a view to determining whether the normal compensatory measure should be departed from.

C. The interest of the promisor in rendering performance

The expression 'performance interest' has been mainly associated with the interest of the promisee in obtaining performance. There has been comparatively little emphasis on, and indeed barely any mention of, the corresponding 'interest in rendering performance' of the promisor in academic literature[43] or the case law.[44] As Treitel has pointed out in the context of termination, 'Anglo-American courts are ... less concerned with the protection of the debtor than either German or French law. Their emphasis tends ... to be on speedy and convenient remedies for the creditor'.[45]

Despite this apparent indifference, it is relatively uncontroversial that the promisor whose obligation under the contract is to deliver the goods, services, or other consideration may themselves wish to insist on rendering that performance. They may wish to do so for any number of reasons. Usually only by performing will they be entitled to receive the reciprocal consideration promised under the contract. They might also want to protect their reputation or be able to honour commitments made to third parties in connection with the contract. It may be that they have incurred expenses in advance of performance that would otherwise be wasted. Members of their workforce who would have had a role in

[43] An exception is Qiao Liu, 'The *White & Carter* Principle: A Restatement' (2011) 74 Modern Law Review 171.

[44] But see the use of legitimate interest in the context of *White and Carter (Councils) Ltd v McGregor* [1962] AC 413 (HL) (Lord Reid's speech).

[45] GH Treitel, *Remedies for Breach of Contract: A Comparative Account* (Clarendon Press 1988) para 259.

performing the contract may end up being idle and unproductive to their own detriment.

That the promisor may have an interest in performing their side of the contract has been recognized in at least one context, that of repudiatory breach. The interest in rendering performance has had a role where, following one party's repudiation, the other party seeks to affirm the contract, perform their remaining obligations, and sue for the contract price. In *White and Carter (Councils) Ltd v McGregor*, it was held that where a repudiatory breach is not accepted, the contract remains alive for the benefit of both parties. The promisor can insist on performing their contractual obligations, albeit subject to two limitations: first, performance by the promisor should not require the co-operation of the other party; second, they must have a 'legitimate interest in performing' the contract rather than claiming damages.[46]

While *White and Carter* has been affirmed in later cases,[47] the courts have never satisfactorily unpacked the notion of legitimate interest in this context. Its meaning or origins were not explained in *White and Carter* and no clear definition or guidance has emerged in subsequent cases.[48] The only light that has been shed relates to when a legitimate interest will arise. There is no legitimate interest in keeping the contract alive where damages are an adequate remedy and insistence on performing is 'wholly unreasonable', a 'commercial absurdity', or 'perverse'.[49] This suggests that the concept of legitimate interest is narrow and the protection of that interest strong. In most circumstances, the promisor should be able to insist on performance and claim the agreed price. Performance is the rule and a finding that there is no interest in performing will be rare.[50] It is not sufficient to show that the promisor might mitigate their loss and claim damages for any shortfall or that they behaved unreasonably in the conventional sense of the term.[51] The degree of unreasonableness in their election to keep the contract alive must be severe for the courts to interfere.[52]

[46] *White and Carter* (n 44) 431 (Lord Reid).

[47] The main ones being *Isabella Shipowner SA v Shagang Shipping Co Ltd* ('The Aquafaith') [2012] 1 CLC 899 [44] (Cooke J); *Gator Shipping Corporation v Trans-Asiatic Oil Ltd* ('The Odenfeld') [1978] 2 Lloyd's Rep 357 (QB) and *Ocean Marine Navigation Ltd v Koch Carbon Inc* ('The Dynamic') [2003] EWHC 1936 (Comm).

[48] The absence of any clear definition of legitimate interest in this context and the difficulty in articulating its meaning have also led to criticism. Lord Reid's qualification has been described as a 'puzzle' and as 'vague', by JW Carter, 'White and Carter v McGregor—How Unreasonable?' (2012) 128 Law Quarterly Review 490, 491, and as 'unintelligible and elusive' and suffering from 'severe obscurity', by Liu (n 43) 171.

[49] *The Aquafaith* (n 47) [44] (Cooke J); see also *The Odenfeld* (n 47) and *The Dynamic* (n 47).

[50] *The Aquafaith* (n 47) [46] (Cooke J).

[51] ibid [42] (Cooke J). See also *Reichman v Beveridge* [2007] Bus LR 412 (CA).

[52] ibid.

D. Obtaining performance v rendering performance: a distinction poorly articulated

The comparative lack of focus on the interest of the promisor in rendering performance may explain why its relationship with the interest in obtaining performance has seldomly been articulated, or even properly understood, in England.[53] This is most evident from the nexus that the Supreme Court in *Makdessi* sought to draw between the performance interest in the context of damages clauses and that in *White and Carter*.

In laying down the new rule on penalties that damages clauses are valid where they serve a legitimate interest in performance, the Supreme Court pointed, albeit in relatively general terms, to the requirement of a legitimate interest in *White and Carter*. Yet, the reference to *White and Carter* in this context seems incongruous. The legitimate interest in performance in the areas of repudiatory breach and agreed damages clauses are different. The use of the same or similar terms should not simply be assumed to mean that the concepts can be equated.

Makdessi was concerned with a damages clause, which is a secondary obligation that provides for the consequences of breach[54] and is designed to protect the contractual expectations of the injured party in case of default. In that respect, it protects the injured party's interest in obtaining performance. Only exceptionally does the injured party have a legitimate interest in the counterparty's performance that goes beyond compensation following a breach (of any kind). In contrast, the legitimate interest of *White and Carter* is concerned with the interest of the promisor in rendering performance, that is, in performing their own primary obligations under the contract. The key question is whether they can insist on performing their side of the bargain. They are almost always considered to have a legitimate interest in performing their own obligations following the counterparty's repudiation.

The only parallels that can be drawn between the two contexts are at a relatively high level. One is that at the heart of both legitimate interests is the performance of the contract and the protection of the party who wants performance to occur. In *White and Carter*, this was the party who wished to perform their obligations so as to earn the contract price.[55] With damages clauses, it is the beneficiary of the promise to perform that is seeking to obtain the promised performance.

Another parallel is that in both contexts the court must determine whether compensation is an adequate remedial response to which the injured party should be confined. In the context of *White and Carter*, the question is whether they can

[53] It is however addressed in Liu (n 43); Simon Whittaker, 'Performance of Another's Obligation: French and English Law Contrasted' in Johnston and Zimmerman (n 10) 433; and Rowan (n 26) 5 and 99–105.

[54] *Makdessi* (n 35) [32] (Lord Neuberger and Lord Sumption); [241] (Lord Hodge).

[55] Liu (n 43).

perform in order to obtain the contract price so as not to be restricted to mere compensation.[56] With damages clauses, it is whether the parties can agree to a remedy that goes beyond compensation. The perceived parallels drawn by the Supreme Court between the performance interest in the context of damages clauses and that in *White and Carter* should therefore be scrutinized carefully and not simply accepted as correct on the basis of a premise that is superficially attractive but on close examination turns out to be substantively false or at best doubtful.

III. The Growing Significance of Reasonableness and Proportionality in the French Law of Contractual Remedies

While the extent of the protection afforded to the performance interest has evolved in England, so too has the role of reasonableness and the closely related concept of proportionality in France, both of which have recently acquired a central role in French remedies law. Replacement and specific enforcement are the most striking examples of the remedies that are now subject to these standards.[57] There have also been calls to extend their application to compensatory damages.

A. Reasonableness in the context of 'replacement'

Reasonableness has made a remarkable emergence in the context of the remedy of 'replacement' (*faculté de remplacement*) following the 2016 overhaul of contract law. Where the defaulting promisor is required to indemnify the injured party in respect of the cost of employing a third party to perform the obligation that has been breached,[58] replacement must now occur within a reasonable time and at a reasonable cost. New article 1222 Cc provides that:

> Having given notice to perform, a creditor may also himself, within a reasonable time and at a reasonable cost, have an obligation performed or, with the prior authorisation of the court, may have something which has been done in breach of an obligation destroyed. He may claim reimbursement of sums of money employed for this purpose from the debtor.[59]

[56] *MSC Mediterranean Shipping Co SA v Cottonex Anstalt* [2017] 1 All ER (Comm) 483 (CA) [40] (Moore-Bick LJ).

[57] See also the law relating to price reduction (art 1223 Cc), which confers on the injured party a right to accept performance that falls short of the contractually agreed standard but at a lower price. The reduction must be in proportion to the shortcomings in the performance: Solène Rowan, *The New French Law of Contract* (OUP 2022) 210–13 and 248–54.

[58] Rowan (n 57) 208–10; Whittaker (n 53) 450.

[59] Throughout this chapter, I have relied upon, and cited from, the translation of the new articles of the Code civil by John Cartwright, Bénédicte Fauvarque-Cosson, and Simon Whittaker, 'The new

There was no such requirement in the 1804 Civil Code. Under old article 1144 Cc, replacement was available to the injured party subject to judicial approval.[60] Applying for the permission of the court was the sole limitation on the availability of the remedy. It served to ensure that the ouster of the defaulting promisor from the contract was not arbitrary.[61] The court would verify that they could not perform or refused to perform in order to protect their 'interest in rendering performance'.[62]

Since the 2016 reform of contract law, there is no need for the injured party to seek judicial approval in order to obtain replacement performance. The safeguard against the perceived risk of the defaulting party being ousted from the contract arbitrarily is now provided through two main requirements in article 1222 Cc. First, as with other remedies, replacement is conditional upon the injured party serving a notice on the defaulting party giving them a reasonable time to render performance (*mise en demeure*). Only where the refusal or the failure to perform persists can the injured party enter into a substitute contract.[63] Second, the requirement that replacement must occur within a reasonable time and at a reasonable cost operates to protect the defaulting party against abuse. Although article 1222 Cc is silent on the criteria to be applied in assessing reasonableness, it has been interpreted as meaning that there should be an exercise in balancing the interests of the parties, in particular 'checking that the costs incurred by the defaulting party are not exorbitant, and that the injured party does not obtain, by means of indirect performance, a more valuable counter-performance than the one originally due'.[64]

The 2016 reforms have brought French law closer to English law. The need for court approval under the 1804 Code was extraordinary to common lawyers. An injured party in England generally has to be proactive in replacing the performance that was to be rendered by the defaulting promisor in reasonable mitigation of their loss.[65] The court verifies whether the injured party has acted reasonably,

provisions of the Code civil created by Ordonnance no 2016-131 of 10 February 2016 and including revisions made to the text by Loi no 2018-287 of 20 April 2018 translated into English' (<http://www.textes.justice.gouv.fr/art_pix/THE-LAW-OF-CONTRACT-2-5-16.pdf> (2016 version) and <http://www.textes.justice.gouv.fr/art_pix/Translationrevised2018final.pdf> (2018 version). I am very grateful to them for giving me permission to use their translation.

[60] Former arts 1143 and 1144 Cc. This was subject to two exceptions: first, where termination was required urgently (Cass civ 2 July 1945, RTD civ 1946.39 obs J Carbonnier) and second, in the context of commercial sales (Cass civ 7 December 1951, RTD civ 1952.242); Didier Plantamp, 'Le particularisme du remplacement dans la vente commerciale', D 2000 Chron 243.

[61] Cass soc 5 Jun 1953, D 1953.601; Cass civ (3) 20 March 1991, RTD civ 1991.735 obs J Mestre.

[62] Whittaker (n 53) 452.

[63] Yves-Marie Laithier, 'Exécution Forcée en Nature' in John Cartwright and Simon Whittaker (eds), *The Code Napoléon Rewritten: French Contract Law after the 2016 Reforms* (Hart Publishing 2017) 257, 264; Gaël Chantepie and Mathias Latina, *La réforme du droit des obligations, Commentaire théorique et pratique dans l'ordre du Code civil* (2nd edn, Dalloz 2018) para 639; Marianne Faure-Abbad, 'Article 1222: la faculté de remplacement', Revue des contrats 2015, no 3, 784.

[64] Laithier (n 63) 264; Chantepie and Latina (n 63) para 639.

[65] Whittaker (n 53) 449–50.

albeit their actions are only subjected to judicial control a posteriori.[66] This judicial control now occurs in France at this later stage too.

B. Proportionality in the context of specific enforcement

Comparable to the reasonableness standard of article 1222 Cc is the new requirement of proportionality in the context of specific enforcement. The remedy, which is of central importance in French law, is now unavailable where there is a 'manifest disproportion' between the cost of performance and the interest of the injured party in obtaining it.[67] Article 1221 Cc provides:

> A creditor of an obligation may, having given notice to perform, seek performance in kind unless performance is impossible or if there is a manifest disproportion between its cost to the debtor acting in good faith and its interest for the creditor.[68]

This new exception to the availability of specific enforcement is among the most notable changes made by the 2016 reforms of the Civil Code.[69] Previously, the court did not have any discretion as to whether to grant specific enforcement. An order could not be resisted on the ground of disproportionality. Nor was there an undue hardship bar, meaning that the remedy could be obtained even at the financial ruin of the contract-breaker.[70]

As with replacement, this new limitation on the availability of specific enforcement has brought French law closer to English law. In England, specific performance will generally be refused where it would cause oppression to the defaulting party[71] or give rise to cost that is wholly out of proportion to the benefit to the injured party.[72] The courts also have regard to any hardship that might be occasioned to third parties.[73]

No guidance was provided by the drafters of the French reforms either as to the factors that are relevant to assessing the interest of the injured party or to the meaning of manifest disproportion. Commentators have anticipated that relevant

[66] ibid 456. See also Simon Whittaker, 'Les sanctions de l'inexécution des contrats. Droit anglais' in Marcel Fontaine and Geneviève Viney (eds), *Les sanctions de l'inexécution des obligations contractuelles, Etudes de droit comparé* (Bruyant and LGDJ 2001) 977, 1012.

[67] Art 1221 Cc.

[68] ibid.

[69] Rowan (n 57) 198–208.

[70] Cass civ (3) 3 December 1969, Bull civ III no 2.

[71] *Francis v Cowcliffe* [1976] 33 P & CR 368 (Ch); *Patel v Ali* [1984] Ch 283; *Wedgwood v Adams* (1843) 49 ER 958, 960 (Lord Langdale MR).

[72] *Tito v Waddell (No 2)* [1977] Ch 106, 325–28 (Megarry V-C).

[73] *Co-op Insurance Society Ltd v Argyll Stores Holdings Ltd* [1998] AC 1 (HL).

factors are likely to include the seriousness of the breach, the extent of the injured party's loss, the level of difficulty in obtaining the promised performance elsewhere, whether the injured party would themselves be in breach of a separate contract with a third party (for example where there are back-to-back contracts) and the risk of under-compensation if compensatory damages were awarded.[74] As for manifest disproportion, there is consensus that it must be blatant, in the sense of 'certain, evident and flagrant',[75] which serves to limit the scope of the exception.[76]

The practical impact of the new 'manifest disproportion' exception remains to be seen. At the time of the reforms, it had been predicted that the exception would be interpreted narrowly by French courts, and specific enforcement would be refused in extreme cases only.[77] In the words of Deshayes, Genicon, and Laithier:

> the exception is not a principle that is in competition with the binding force of contract and the general availability of specific enforcement . . . It would be a mistake to infer that specific enforcement will be ruled out every time compensatory damages are adequate to fulfil the expectations of the injured party.[78]

The same is true where a replacement can be obtained in the marketplace or the cost of the remedy is high. It has also been said that 'this limitation is meant to operate at the margin',[79] and is 'exceptional' in character.[80]

However, these predictions may turn out to be incorrect. Indeed, the first two decisions on the effect of article 1221 Cc, which were related and handed down on the same day by the *Cour de cassation*,[81] seem to have embraced a broad interpretation of the exception. In the first case, a building company had acquired a plot of land on a housing estate for the purpose of redevelopment. It demolished a villa on the land and erected a block of six flats with a swimming pool. In the second case, a (different) building company redeveloped in a similar way another plot of land on the same estate, constructing a block of seven flats with garages. Both developments were in breach of contractual provisions regulating the estate, which required the footprint of any new buildings to be no more than a particular size. The claimants, who were living in a neighbouring property on the housing estate, sued both companies, seeking an order for the demolition of the two blocks of flats or damages in the alternative.

[74] Olivier Deshayes, Thomas Genicon, and Yves-Marie Laithier, *Réforme du droit des contrats, du régime général et de la preuve des obligations* (2nd edn, LexisNexis 2018) 555; Laithier (n 63) 285.
[75] Chantepie and Latina (n 63) para 638.
[76] Deshayes, Genicon, and Laithier (n 75) 555.
[77] Chantepie and Latina (n 63) para 639; Deshayes, Genicon, and Laithier (n 75) 485–88.
[78] Deshayes, Genicon, and Laithier (n 75) 549.
[79] ibid.
[80] Laithier (n 63) 263.
[81] Cass civ (3) 13 July 2022 no 21-16.407, and Cass civ (3) 13 July 2022 no 21.16-408.

The Aix-en-Provence *cour d'appel* refused to order the demolition of the buildings on two grounds.[82] First, demolition was impossible in practice as the flats were inhabited. Second, it found demolition to be 'totally disproportionate'.[83] This was because the breach did not lead to 'an objective loss' (*une situation objectivement préjudiciable*): the buildings did not block the view of the claimants; they were built in the spirit of the housing estate; and no other neighbour had complained about them. Instead, the claimants were simply unhappy with the new buildings, which they subjectively 'perceived negatively' (*un ressenti négatif*) to be less 'middle-class' or 'bourgeois' than the villas.[84] In these circumstances, there was a manifest disproportion between the cost of the demolition for the defaulting promisor and the benefit to the injured parties. Awards of compensatory damages of €20,000 and €50,000 respectively were made.

The *Cour de cassation* affirmed both decisions. It held that since the claimants had sought the demolition of the blocks of flats solely to avoid the inconvenience of a new neighbourhood, the *cour d'appel* was correct to find that there was 'a manifest disproportion between the cost of demolition for the defaulting promisor and its interest for the injured party'.[85]

These decisions are remarkable for three reasons. First, new article 1221 Cc, which came into effect on 1 October 2016 and applies only to contracts entered into after this date, was inapplicable on the facts since the contract had been entered into prior to this date, yet both the *cour d'appel* and *Cour de cassation* used its exact wording as the basis of their decisions, thereby applying the article in anticipation of its coming into effect.[86] Second, it was open to the *Cour de cassation* to reach the same outcome without relying on the 'manifest disproportion' exception. What they could have done was to rely on impossibility (as did the Aix-en-Provence *cour d'appel*), which is an uncontroversial exception to the availability of specific enforcement. Indeed, impossibility was cited by the *cour d'appel* as an additional reason for rejecting demolition, yet the *Cour de cassation* relied on the 'manifest disproportion' exception as a sole ground for its decision,[87] ignoring impossibility. The use of the very same terms and the identical reasoning in both of decisions was undoubtedly intended to send a strong message.

Lastly, the decisions represent a significant break from the past. Before the 2016 reforms, injunctions requiring the demolition of buildings constructed in breach of contract were the norm, regardless of any disproportion. In one case, for example, the *Cour de cassation* quashed the refusal of the Aix-en-Provence *cour*

[82] CA Aix-en-Provence ch. 1-5 11-03-2021.
[83] Cass civ (3) 13 July 2022 no 21-16.407 citing the CA of Aix-en-Provence at [8].
[84] ibid [7].
[85] Cass civ (3) 13 July 2022 no 21-16.407 at [8]–[9].
[86] Thomas Genicon, 'Exécution forcée en nature du contrat: une violation anticipée du nouvel article 1221 du code civil?', D 2022.1647.
[87] ibid.

d'appel to order the demolition of 418 houses built in breach of contract. It was irrelevant that the project had been partly financed with public funds, and was for social purposes.[88] In another, the *Cour de cassation* ordered the demolition of an extension to a shopping centre built in breach of contract, pointedly taking no account of the implications for around ten shopkeepers, whose shops would be destroyed as a result of the order, even though they were not parties to the litigation. It also ignored the financial detriment that would be occasioned to the lessees of other shops during the reinstatement works.[89]

The two recent decisions of the *Cour de cassation* suggest that the practical impact of article 1221 Cc on the right of injured party to obtain performance will be real. This has drawn criticism. Commenting on the two decisions, Genicon observed that article 1221 should not be used as 'a tool to re-evaluate (devalue?) contractual rights'.[90] There should continue to be a right to specific enforcement. In his view, article 1221 was introduced merely as a safeguard for defaulting parties against injured parties who act in bad faith. This behaviour, he argues, was not present on the facts of the two cases. He also contends that requiring that performance bring an objective benefit is a 'nonsense'.[91] The right to performance should not be eroded by courts making assessments of the utility of the benefit that is expected from the contract. Whether or not the expected benefit is legitimate in the eyes of others should have no bearing.[92]

C. Reasonableness and proportionality in the context of compensatory damages?

The 2016 reforms did not amend in any significant respect the provisions of the Civil Code on compensatory and agreed damages, apart from some terminological changes and reordering. Both forms of liability were held over by the drafters to be addressed together with extra-contractual liability by a later and broader reform of civil liability in France.[93] The result is that, in contrast with replacement and specific enforcement, neither reasonableness nor proportionality were introduced in respect of compensation. Interestingly, however, French courts have recently

[88] Cass civ (3) 18 March 1974, Bull civ III no 127.
[89] Cass civ (3) 3 April 1996, Bull civ III no 91.
[90] Genicon (n 87) 1649.
[91] ibid 1649–54.
[92] ibid.
[93] Ministère de la Justice, *Projet de réforme de la responsabilité civile*, 13 March 2017; Simon Whittaker and Jean-Sébastien Borghetti (trs), *Reform Bill on Civil Liability (March 2017)*, <http://www.textes.justice.gouv.fr/art_pix/reform_bill_on_civil_liability_march_2017.pdf> accessed 15 November 2024.

begun to extend these requirements to compensatory damages, pending the enactment of the reforms.

The aim of damages is to provide the injured party with the sum of money that is necessary to put them in the position in which they would have been had the contract been performed.[94] Compensation should be full (*principe de réparation intégrale du préjudice*) and commensurate with the loss suffered (*tout le préjudice mais rien que le préjudice*).[95]

It generally falls to the courts of first instance and lower appeal courts to determine the loss that has been suffered and quantify an appropriate award (*pouvoir souverain d'appréciation des juges du fond*).[96] There is a broad power to decide between the principal measures of damages, which are cost of cure and diminution in value.[97] Reasonableness has generally not played a role in the choice between these measures. Unlike in English law, cost of cure damages have not been refused on the ground of unreasonableness or disproportionality. It is generally irrelevant to the assessment of damages that the cost of repair is high[98] or significantly in excess of the original contract price.[99]

The unfettered availability of cost of cure damages is at variance with the newly conditional availability of the analogous remedy of replacement under article 1222 Cc, as described earlier. In common with cost of cure damages, replacement involves a monetary award to enable the injured party to obtain substitute performance, subject however to a requirement that this occurs 'within a reasonable time and at a reasonable cost' as article 1222 Cc specifies. Yet, while the injured party must act reasonably when claiming the cost of replacement, there is no such requirement where they claim cost of cure damages. For remedies that achieve substantially the same outcome to have such divergent threshold requirements is surprising, particularly since the injured party has an entirely free choice of remedy in France.[100] This inconsistency risks leading to the cost of cure damages being constantly favoured over replacement, all other things being equal.

A similar incongruity exists between the unfettered availability of cost of cure damages and the 'manifest disproportion' exception of article 1221 Cc relating to specific enforcement. This has been brought to light by the *Cour de cassation* in

[94] For an example of an express affirmation by a French court of this proposition, see Cass civ (3) 9 January 1991, Bull civ III no 12.

[95] New art 1231-2 Cc, which substantially reproduces old art 1149 Cc.

[96] Andrea Pinna, *La mesure du préjudice contractuel* (LGDJ Paris 2007). But see Louis Thibierge, 'La mesure des dommages-intérêts: question de fait ou question de droit? Libres réflexions au travers du prisme de la minimisation du préjudice', Revue des contrats 2019, no 1, 193.

[97] Pinna (n 97) paras 92–122.

[98] Cass civ (3) 11 January 1984, Rev Droit Immob 1984.191; Cass civ (3) 9 December 1975, JCP 1976.IV.43; Pinna (n 97) para 137.

[99] Cass civ (1) 12 October 1961, Bull civ I no 455.

[100] Under art 1217 Cc. See Laithier (n 63) 264; Bernard Haftel 'La responsabilité contractuelle', Revue des contrats 2017, no 4, 143, [14].

a recent case of 6 July 2023.[101] The promisor, a building contractor, constructed a house that did not comply with contractual specifications. The ceilings were 5 centimetres too low on the ground floor, having been built at a height of 2.48 metres instead of 2.53 metres, and 30 centimetres too low on the first floor, being 2.20–22 metres high instead of the contractually agreed 2.50 metres.

The *Cour de cassation* quashed the decision of the Rennes *cour d'appel* to award damages for the cost of demolishing and rebuilding the entire house. It held that the cost of demolition and reconstruction could not be ordered where it was disproportionate to the loss suffered.[102] In explaining its decision, the Court expressly acknowledged the contradiction introduced by the reforms, noting that a claim for specific enforcement is subject to a proportionality requirement, but where the claim is for compensation, the cost of demolishing and rebuilding is not subject to any such limit.[103] It stated:

> the difference of treatment regarding the rights and obligations of the parties who are in a similar situation and the role of the court does not appear to be justified[104] . . . a court dealing with a claim for the demolition and reconstruction of a defective building must consider whether there is a manifest disproportion between its cost to the debtor acting in good faith and its interest for the creditor considering the loss suffered as a result of the defect, regardless of whether the claim is for specific enforcement on the basis of old article 1184 or new article 1221 or a compensatory damages claim for the cost of demolition and reconstruction.[105]

The *Cour de cassation* concluded that the *cour d'appel* had been wrong in not considering disproportion when awarding damages.

This decision is remarkable for two reasons. First, it introduces disproportion as a limiting factor in the context of compensatory damages, despite there being no provision to this effect in the Civil Code. Second, it represents a significant break from its previous decisions. In one case, for example, the *Cour de cassation* upheld a decision of the Angers *cour d'appel* to award the cost of demolishing and reconstructing a house which, in breach of contract, had been built to a height that was just over a metre beneath the agreed specification. It was irrelevant that the house was fit for purpose.[106] In another case, the *Cour de cassation* quashed the refusal of the Montpellier *cour d'appel* to award damages to remedy the non-conformity of a roof to contractual specification, despite the roof being perfectly adequate.[107]

[101] Cass civ (3) 6 July 2023 no 22-10.884.
[102] Citing Cass civ (3) 17 November 2021 no 20-17.218.
[103] Cass civ (3) 6 July 2023 no 22-10.884 at [10].
[104] ibid [11].
[105] ibid [12].
[106] Cass civ (3) 5 December 1979, JCP 1981.II.19605. See also Cass civ (3) 6 May 1981, Juris-Data no 1981-001783.
[107] Cass civ (3) 22 October 2002, Rev Droit Immob 2003.95.

Whether the drafters of the reforms directed their minds to this incongruity is unclear. It has, however, been discussed at length by commentators, attracting considerable criticism. This is reflected in the following rhetorical question posed by Laithier:

> is it possible to assess the damages at the level of the cost of repair or replacement where the magnitude of this cost partly explains the refusal of enforced performance in kind? Would it be legally or economically coherent to accept this limitation in respect of performance in kind but to refuse it in calculating the amount of damages?[108]

One neat solution to the incongruity might be for the injured party to be under a general requirement to act reasonably to mitigate their loss following a breach. Mitigation requires the injured party to take reasonable steps to minimize their loss or to forbear from taking unreasonable steps that increase their loss.[109] There is presently no such duty in French law, mainly out of a concern not to burden the injured party with responsibility for reducing the liability of the defaulting party.[110] Instead the injured party is free to choose their preferred remedies, as enshrined in article 1217 Cc, and they are not required to seek substitute performance even if this would be reasonable. This is made clear in the context of replacement, where the text of article 1222 Cc provides that the injured party 'may' have the obligation performed by a third party. It confers a right but without imposing any duty to enter into a substitute transaction. The injured party can therefore 'prefer direct enforced performance in kind by his debtor (under article 1221) rather than seek a substitute solution himself'.[111]

[108] Laithier (n 63) 284; See also Jean-Sébastien Borghetti, 'Faut-il distinguer les dommages et intérêts compensatoires des dommages et intérêts en lieu et place de la prestation?', Revue des contrats 2016, no 4, 787.

[109] On the effect in English law of mitigation on the injured party's choice of remedies, see Solène Rowan, 'Damages' in Hugh Beale (ed), *Chitty on Contracts* (35th edn, Sweet & Maxwell 2023) 2219, para 30-124.

[110] See generally, Solène Le Pautremat, 'Mitigation of Damage: A French Perspective' (2006) 55 International and Comparative Law Quarterly 205; Yves-Marie Laithier, 'La *Cour de cassation* refuse d'imposer au créancier le devoir de minimiser le dommage', Revue des contrats 2010, no 1, 52; Olivier Deshayes, 'L'introduction de l'obligation de modérer son dommage en matière contractuelle—Rapport français', Revue des contrats 2010, no 3, 1139; Yves-Marie Laithier, 'Les sanctions de l'inexécution du contrat', Revue des contrats 2016, no Hors-série, 39; Haftel (n 101) 143; Borghetti (n 109) 787; Olivier Deshayes '"Existe-t-il un devoir de minimiser son dommage en matière contractuelle?"—Une question mal posée', Revue des contrats 2014, no 1, 27; Louis Thibierge, 'La mesure des dommages-intérêts: question de fait ou question de droit? Libres réflexions au travers du prisme de la minimisation du préjudice', Revue des contrats 2019, no 1, 193; Geneviève Viney, 'La victime n'est pas tenue de limiter son préjudice dans l'intérêt du responsable', Revue des contrats 2015, no 1, 24.

[111] Laithier (n 63) 264.

IV. Concluding Comparative Observations

The rules on remedies in both England and France have evolved in a number of notable respects in recent decades. In England, compensation remains at the heart of the remedial response and is generally regarded as protecting the performance interest satisfactorily in most situations. However, where it falls short, there is now acceptance that stronger protection of performance is necessary. This has led to calls for the courts to grapple with the fundamental question of what constitutes loss and for remedies for breach of contract to be reinforced. In France, requirements of reasonableness and proportionality have been introduced in respect of some remedies. The moderating force of these new standards seeks to balance more fairly the competing interests of the parties and avoid extreme outcomes.

On one view, these evolutions achieve a *rapprochement* between English and French law. The greater recognition that performance has intrinsic value and the increased protection of contractual interests has brought English law closer to the performance-orientated remedial approach in France. Similarly, the new limitations on the availability of replacement and specific enforcement have brought French law closer to English law, in which both compensation to enable the injured party to obtain substitute performance from a third party[112] and specific enforcement are subject to requirements of reasonableness and proportionality.[113]

Nevertheless, there continue to be significant differences between the two jurisdictions regarding both the protection of performance and the role of reasonableness and proportionality. Despite the moderating force of these new standards, the French law of remedies is still much more protective of performance than English law. This is apparent in various aspects of the French approach. One is the general requirement upon the injured party to give notice before seeking the remedy requiring that performance be effected within a reasonable period of time (*mise en demeure*). This affords the defaulting party additional time and another opportunity to perform. The effect is to give 'priority to performance'[114] over other remedies, constraining at least initially their freedom of action.

Other aspects illustrating the commitment of French law to performance include the cardinal role of specific enforcement, which is available for almost all contracts; a generous approach to damages in which non-pecuniary loss generally sounds in damages; and termination being a remedy of last resort. Where termination is unwarranted, the courts have large powers such as being able to resurrect the contract or award grace periods. The emphasis remains on upholding

[112] *Radford v De Froberville* [1977] 1 WLR 1262 (Ch) 1270 (Oliver J); *Ruxley* (n 13).

[113] *Francis* (n 72); *Patel* (72); *Wedgwood* (n 72) 960 (Lord Langdale MR); *Tito* (n 73) 325–28 (Megarry V-C); *Argyll* (n 74).

[114] Borghetti (n 109) paras 10–11.

performance where possible. Introducing reasonableness and proportionality as moderating forces has not fundamentally recast the philosophy underlying French law.

In the same vein, reasonableness still has a much more prominent role in England than in France. This is primarily due to the existence of and the significant role played by the doctrine of mitigation of loss, fundamental to which is a requirement that the injured party act reasonably following breach.[115] In practice, this can often mean that the injured party is required to enter into a substitute transaction with a third party.[116] Obtaining performance and reallocating resources elsewhere are frequently regarded as more efficient and less wasteful than insisting on performance by the defaulting party. Only where it is reasonable to invite or accept the late or defective performance of the defaulting party can their performance be required.[117] The centrality of mitigation fits coherently and consistently in the wider framework of contractual remedies in English law, dovetailing neatly with the limited availability of specific performance and the narrowness of the restrictions on the right to terminate.[118]

It is uncertain whether mitigation will be seen in France in the future. The introduction of a doctrine of mitigation is proposed in the pending Reform Bill on Civil Liability.[119] It contains two provisions—articles 1237 and 1263—that together would introduce a duty to mitigate into French law in both a contractual and an extra-contractual context:

> Art. 1237.—Expenses incurred by a claimant in order to prevent the imminent occurrence of harm or to avoid it getting worse, as well as in order to reduce its consequences, constitute a reparable loss as long as they were reasonably undertaken.
>
> Art. 1263.—Except in the case of personal injuries, damages are reduced where the victim did not take safe and reasonable measures, notably having regard to his ability to pay, appropriate to avoid an increase in his own loss.[120]

If enacted, these provisions would increase the role of reasonableness in the French law of remedies. However, it is unclear whether the Reform Bill will be implemented.[121] Unlike the exception in article 1221 Cc, the *Cour de cassation* has not

[115] *British Westinghouse Electric & Manufacturing Co Ltd v Underground Electric Railways Co Ltd (No 2)* [1912] AC 673 (HL) 689.

[116] Whittaker (n 1) 161.

[117] *Sotiros Shipping Inc v Sameiet Solholt (The 'Solholt')* [1983] 1 Lloyd's Rep 605.

[118] Solène Rowan, 'Resisting Termination: Some Comparative Observations' in Andrew Dyson, James Goudkamp, and Frederick Wilmot-Smith (eds), *Defences in Contract* (Hart Publishing 2017) 163.

[119] Art 1263 Cc of the Draft Reform Project of Civil Liability; see Borghetti (n 109) paras 19–26.

[120] *Projet de réforme de la responsabilité civile* (n 94); Whittaker and Borghetti (n 94).

[121] In July 2020, several senators who were impatient to see reforms enacted put forward proposals amending the 2017 reforms: Commission des Lois (Sénat), *23 propositions pour simplifier la vie des*

started introducing it in advance, and to the contrary appears to have shown some doubts about it. This can be seen, for example, in a decision in 2020[122]—some three years after the publication of the reform proposals—relating to a contract for the sale and maintenance of a catamaran that proved to be defective. Overturning the decision of the Paris *cour d'appel*, the *Cour de cassation* held that the buyer could recover damages in respect of losses that resulted from the vessel being under repair, and therefore unavailable, for a prolonged period, which would have been avoided if the buyer had arranged for the vessel to be repaired more promptly. The buyer was not under any obligation to take steps to repair the catamaran and was entitled to compensation for all of the losses flowing from the breach.

In conclusion, the contrast between English and French law articulated by Simon Whittaker in 2007 broadly remains,[123] albeit with a degree of erosion from developments in both jurisdictions over the course of his career. It remains to be seen whether this trend will continue or whether the contrast will stand the test of much more time.

Français en facilitant la réparation des dommages, 22 July 2020. This was followed by a bill (*Proposition de loi*): Sénat, *Proposition de loi portant réforme de la responsabilité civile, Texte* no 678, 29 July 2020.

[122] Cass com 23 Sept 2020 no 15-28.898; for more recent decisions, see Marie Dugué, 'Obligation de minimiser le dommage en matière contractuelle: où en est-on?', Revue des contrats 2023, no 1, 34.

[123] Whittaker (n 1).

5

The Impact of Illegality in French Contract Law

A Reflexive Endeavour

Yves-Marie Laithier

I. Introduction

As Husa rightly observed in his *Introduction to Comparative Law*, foreign law is like a 'mirror' in which we see our own law.[1] Indeed, one of the main benefits of analysing foreign systems is to gain a better understanding of one's own law. Naturally, having a better understanding of foreign law in itself is an objective of a comparative study, but it is usually a first step. Following what might be called a 'reflexive' approach, comparison also (mainly?) serves to 'illuminate our understanding of our own' law, to use the words of Lord Goff in a famous case.[2] Simon Whittaker is perfectly aware of this. Thanks to his remarkable knowledge of civil law in general and French law in particular, he has examined the existence of a 'Period of Grace' in English law[3] or the exact place of good faith in the performance of certain types of 'commercial contracts' in English law,[4] to give but a few examples.

Bearing this advantage in mind, it may be fruitful for a French lawyer considering his own law on the illegality of contracts to observe carefully the presentation and developments of this subject in English law. However, at first sight, the use of English law as a 'mirror' in this particular case may be surprising, for three reasons.

First, 'it is not easy to set out in clear terms what the law is on "illegality" in relation to contracts'.[5] The law is considered to be 'complex' and full of distinctions 'that have tended to confuse rather than illuminate'.[6] It is true that the *Patel v Mirza* decision,[7] handed down in 2016, made a major change. This very significant

[1] Jaakko Husa, *Introduction to Comparative Law* (2nd edn, Hart Publishing 2023) 95–96.
[2] *White v Jones* [1995] 2 AC 207, 263 (Lord Goff).
[3] Simon Whittaker, 'A "Period of Grace" for Contractual Performance' in Mads T Andenas and others (eds), *Liber Amicorum Guido Alpa: Private Law Beyond the National Systems* (BIICL 2007) 1083.
[4] Simon Whittaker, 'Unfair Terms in Commercial Contracts and the Two Laws of Competition: French Law and English Law Contrasted' (2019) 39 Oxford Journal of Legal Studies 404.
[5] Jack Beatson, Andrew Burrows, and John Cartwright, *Anson's Law of Contract* (31st edn, OUP 2020) 405.
[6] ibid.
[7] *Patel v Mirza* [2016] UKSC 42, [2017] AC 467.

Yves-Marie Laithier, *The Impact of Illegality in French Contract Law* In: *Comparative Reflections in Private Law*.
Edited by: Marco Cappelletti, Ciara Kennefick, and Dorota Leczykiewicz, Oxford University Press.
 DOI: 10.1093/9780198959168.003.0006

decision was praised by many commentators for the 'clarification'[8] it brought compared with previous law[9] and for the flexibility introduced by the Supreme Court of the United Kingdom.[10] But the decision also had its critics, starting with Lord Sumption who, with the benefit of a few years' distance, considered '*Patel v Mirza* to be the worst decision of the Supreme Court in the realm of private law for a generation'.[11] Without being so critical, it should be recognized that the approach based on a range of factors, by being more discretionary, is likely to generate uncertainty rather than alleviate it. Moreover, *Patel v Mirza*, as significant as it is, leaves a number of questions unresolved, particularly in contractual matters.[12]

Secondly, if we look not at illegality in general but at its effect on the contract, a certain lack of clarity persists in English law. The most visible sign of this confusion is the terminology. Several technical terms may be used to describe the effect of illegality on the contract: 'void contract', 'voidable contract', or 'unenforceable contract'. In principle, each of these terms has its own meaning. None is an exact synonym of the other.[13] Nevertheless, in matters of illegality, the use of these words is sometimes imprecise. 'Void' may well replace 'unenforceable', for example. As Lord Burrows points out, 'as far as English law is concerned these labels in the context of illegality have not been rigorously distinguished and tend to be used interchangeably'.[14] All this may seem trivial. But, as is often the case, terminological imprecision can reveal substantial hesitations. To give but one example, Häcker points out that the words 'void' and 'unenforceable' have 'radically divergent implications for the law of unjust enrichment'.[15] Aware of the difficulties of classifying defects in contracts, English lawyers are able to avoid the many pitfalls.[16] But the task requires great attention from outside observers.

Thirdly, the approach to illegality in French contract law is general, based on broad principles, whereas English law is characterized by a more concrete

[8] Hugh Beale (ed), *Chitty on Contracts* (35th edn, Sweet & Maxwell 2023) para 19-006.

[9] Lord Burrows describes the former law as follows: 'The truth is that the common law in this area had become a nightmarish mess that was not only complex and unclear but also produced a mode of reasoning that did not appear to reflect the underlying issues that, standing back from the detail, one would have expected to be relevant' (Andrew Burrows, 'The Illegality Defence in the Courts Today' in Edwin Peel and Rebecca Probert (eds), *Shaping the Law of Obligations: Essays in Honour of Professor Ewan McKendrick KC* (OUP 2023) 59, 60.

[10] See Andrew Burrows, 'A New Dawn for the Law of Illegality' in Sarah Green and Alan Bogg (eds), *Illegality after* Patel v Mirza (Hart Publishing 2018) 23, 24.

[11] Lord Sumption, 'Introduction' in William Day and Sarah Worthington (eds), *Challenging Private Law: Lord Sumption on the Supreme Court* (Hart Publishing 2020) 1, 2.

[12] Janet O'Sullivan, 'Illegality and Contractual Enforcement after *Patel v Mirza*' in Green and Bogg (n 10) 165, 186 ('*Patel* offers no concrete clarification of the correct approach to illegality and contract enforcement . . . Time will tell, no doubt, but for now Norris J was certainly right that the question remains "uncertain to an exceptional degree"').

[13] See eg Beale (n 8) paras 1-093–1-097.

[14] Burrows (n 10) 25.

[15] Birke Häcker, 'The Impact of Illegality and Immorality on Contract and Restitution from a Civilian Angle' in Green and Bogg (n 10) 331, 336.

[16] See John Cartwright, 'Remedies for Defects in the Formation of a Contract: Learning by Comparing', this book, ch 3.

approach focusing on the many possible consequences of illegality for the parties. French lawyers generally take the view that an unlawful contract is a contract that should be deleted, or, to use a term of art, 'annulled'. As Malaurie—a prominent French jurist—observed in his doctoral thesis, '*nullity* is the most logical measure ... it will be the normal sanction, annihilating an act that the Law does not want'.[17] This somewhat blunt statement is justified by the defence of the public interest, or *ordre public*. The effect of illegality in English law is presented less categorically, especially since *Patel v Mirza*. As Cartwright observes:

> in the absence of statutory provision the general approach in the modern law is not to think in terms of the contract itself being void but to consider whether allowing a party to bring a claim relating to the contract would be 'harmful to the integrity of the legal system'.[18]

This approach might leave a French lawyer somewhat sceptical. He or she might not pay further attention to it, considering that it expresses a truism—if the contract is *illegal*, the *integrity* of the legal system is necessarily *harmed*—and that the illegal contract must simply disappear from the legal system.

However, notwithstanding the above observations, it is fairly obvious that the French lawyer would find it helpful to look in the 'mirror' of English law. In so doing, he or she would become aware of two issues which are similar—because they both concern the impact of illegality on the contract—but distinct.

The first issue has to do with the temporal scope of illegality. Here there is a striking difference between the incomplete presentation found in French legal literature and the systematic and comprehensive presentation found in English legal writings. The structure of the French Civil Code (the Code civil (Cc)) explains, at least in part, this difference. Following the articles of the Code civil, whether before or after the Reform of 10 February 2016,[19] French authors treat the absence of illegality as a condition of the validity of the contract. This focus on validity is easy to understand. One of the most fundamental rules—and probably one of the most famous—of the Code civil is that only contracts 'lawfully formed have the force of legislation for those who have made them' (article 1103 Cc). This provision draws a line between contracts that are 'legally formed', ie validly formed, and those that

[17] Philippe Malaurie, *L'ordre public et le contrat* (Éditions Matot-Braine 1953) 203 (emphasis added).
[18] Cartwright (n 16) 81–82.
[19] On this reform, see John Cartwright and Simon Whittaker (eds), *The Code Napoléon Rewritten: French Contract Law after the 2016 Reforms* (Hart Publishing 2017). Translations in this chapter of the Code civil concerning the law of contract are taken from the translation by John Cartwright, Bénédicte Fauvarque-Cosson, and Simon Whittaker, 'The new provisions of the Code civil created by Ordonnance no 2016-131 of 10 February 2016 and including revisions made to the text by Loi no 2018-287 of 20 April 2018 translated into English' <https://www.justice.gouv.fr/sites/default/files/migrations/textes/art_pix/Translationrevised2018final.pdf> accessed 7 November 2025. Other translations in this chapter are the author's, unless otherwise indicated.

are not. For the contract to be valid, its content must be 'lawful' (article 1128(3) Cc). Some further clarification is provided by article 1162 Cc, which states that 'a contract cannot derogate from public policy either by its stipulations or by its purpose, whether or not this was known by all the parties'. On the basis of these provisions, French authors equate illegality with the question of the validity of the contract. A little further on, the Code civil provides that 'a contract which does not satisfy the conditions required for its validity is a nullity' (article 1178(1) Cc). Most French authors see 'nullity' as the 'standard sanction'[20] or 'the sanction most consistent with the prohibitions established by the law'.[21] These authors then establish a second connection, this time between the validity of the contract and its nullity. The combination of these two connections explains why illegality is most commonly seen as a condition that the parties failed to respect when concluding the contract. Illegality and nullity seem to form a couple. It is within this latter framework—the one linking illegality and nullity—that most academic work is carried out. Academic research focuses on two main themes: the first concerns what is meant by illegality (the literature, which is rich, is mainly devoted to the elusive and evolving concept of *ordre public*), and the second concerns the theory of nullities, in particular the distinction between 'absolute' and 'relative nullity'.

By comparison, the study of illegality in English contract law is not confined within such narrow limits. Admittedly, it has been pointed out that 'the vast bulk of the law is concerned with the effect of illegality on a contract and on consequential restitution (ie the recovery of benefits conferred under the contract)'.[22] But the study of illegality in English contract law is broader. Unlike in French legal literature, it is not limited to the situation in which illegality exists at the time the contract is made. On the contrary, it is common practice in English law to distinguish between *ab initio* illegality and supervening illegality, that is, where only the performance of the contract is legally prohibited. Far from being purely theoretical, this distinction is fundamental since the same legal rules do not apply in both situations.[23]

This distinction undoubtedly makes sense in French law both because illegality can *in fact* also occur after the contract has been concluded and because the applicable rules are not identical *in law*. For example, nullity—a sanction by definition specific to the lack of validity of a contract—is clearly inapplicable in cases of supervening illegality. The purpose of looking at English law is therefore not to introduce but rather to highlight (or emphasize) this distinction in French law. In other words, the comparison acts here as a revealing device.

[20] Bertrand Fages, *Droit des obligations* (15th edn, Lextenso 2025) para 195 ('*sanction de référence*').

[21] Jacques Ghestin, Grégoire Loiseau, and Yves-Marie Serinet, *La formation du contrat*, vol 2, *L'objet et la cause—Les nullités* (4th edn, LGDJ 2013) para 2013.

[22] Beatson, Burrows, and Cartwright (n 5) 405.

[23] See eg ibid 405 and 477–78; Edwin Peel, *Treitel on the Law of Contract* (16th edn, Sweet & Maxwell 2025) paras 11-019–11-020 and 19-045–19-053.

The second issue relates to policy considerations. Since the public interest is part of the notion of illegality, it seems essential, in order to protect the public interest effectively, that a contract which transgresses a prohibition should not produce effects. Under French law, this apparently simple and logical reasoning strengthens the role of nullity. It should be recalled that in France, a contract is primarily regarded as an act involving obligations.[24] If that act is illegal, it is necessary to ensure that those obligations no longer exist. This is exactly what nullity does: 'an annulled contract is deemed never to have existed' (article 1178(2) Cc). And while it is true that restitution may be made where one of the parties or both had begun to perform the annulled contract, such restitution has no other justification or purpose than to make it appear as if the contract had never been concluded.

In English law, the impact of illegality is not as radical as the defence of the public interest might suggest. On the contrary, it has been pointed out that after *Patel v Mirza*, the enforcement of an illegal contract is likely to be permitted 'in a wider range of circumstances'.[25] It is clearer than ever, since that decision, that antecedent illegality 'is not of itself necessarily regarded as a ground of invalidity'.[26] Claimants may enforce their claims notwithstanding their own illegal conduct. The same is true in cases of supervening illegality: the effects of such illegality 'may vary according to the type of illegality in question'[27] and more broadly according to the circumstances. For example, property may pass pursuant to the contract in the case of illegality.[28] Similarly, under certain conditions, the courts 'may "sever" the contract and allow it to continue with the offending term disregarded'.[29]

Once again, a look at English law leads to a reconsideration of the usual presentation of French law and helps to show that, in an increasing number of situations, nullity—that is, the retroactive annulment of the whole contract—is being set aside in favour of other remedies which are more balanced and allow the contract to produce certain effects. French law has certainly not formalized the discretionary or multi-factorial approach adopted by the Supreme Court of the United Kingdom, nor is there such a thing as a 'case-by-case approach of nullity'.[30] But in

[24] See eg Alain Bénabent, *Droit des obligations* (21st edn, Lextenso 2025) para 16; François Terré and others, *Les obligations* (13th edn, Dalloz 2022) para 78.

[25] Mindy Chen-Wishart, *Contract Law* (7th edn, OUP 2022) 490.

[26] Edwin Peel, *Frustration and Force Majeure* (4th edn, Sweet & Maxwell 2022) para 8-005.

[27] ibid.

[28] See Cartwright (n 16) 82.

[29] ibid 79–80.

[30] Laurent Aynès, Philippe Malaurie, and Philippe Stoffel-Munck, *Droit des obligations* (13th edn, Lextenso 2024) para 410. This case-by-case approach would mean leaving the judge, who has found that the conditions for nullity have been met, a discretion to grant or refuse nullity. For example, the judge could refuse nullity if the failure to comply with a formal requirement imposed by law has not, in the case before him, caused harm to the claimant. The reform of nullities in company law resulting from an *Ordonnance* no 2025-229 of 12 March 2025 (which came into force on 1 October 2025) illustrates this approach, since the new art 1844-12-1 Cc makes nullity subject to a threefold test (has the irregularity caused a harm? Did it influence the decision taken? Is the nullity not disproportionate?) This last test clearly leaves it to the judge to decide whether to uphold the nullity in each case. The example is also interesting in that it shows the sharp contrast with general (*droit commun*) contract law.

its own way, French law also displays pragmatism. The need to remove the contract from the legal order because it is illegal is by no means the only policy considered. In many situations, the contract still produces effects both in the case of antecedent illegality (II) and in the case of subsequent illegality (III).

II. Antecedent Illegality

The situation considered here is one in which the contract is illegal at the time it is formed. What we would like to emphasize in the discussion that follows is that there are a number of decisions in French law which show that, despite the illegality, nullity is avoided. No more than in English law is a contract 'tainted by illegality', to quote Lord Toulson,[31] doomed to disappear in French law. It can produce effects other than restitution following nullity.[32] In other words, although the contract 'derogates from public policy either by its stipulations or by its purpose' (article 1162 Cc), it is enforceable in whole or in part. To highlight this trend, which reflects the flexibility shown by the French courts, two situations can be distinguished: one in which the illegality has disappeared by the time the court is required to give its decision (A) and one in which the illegality still exists at that time (B).

A. The subsequent disappearance of illegality

Changes in the law are constant. For this reason, it is possible that a contract that was illegal when it was entered into may no longer be unlawful when the time comes for its performance or when a claim to enforce the agreement is brought. For example, a statute which required an authorization is repealed at the time when what was promised is due. What happens then to the contract? To answer this question, should only the date on which the contract was concluded be taken into account? Or should the present be given precedence over the past and it be held that since the basis of the illegality has disappeared, the contract is enforceable?

There does not seem to be any authority for the position in English law where the contract was unlawful at the time it was entered into but subsequently becomes

For a detailed analysis of this reform, see eg Caroline Coupet and France Drummond, 'L'ordonnance Nullités: une réforme radicale', Bulletin Joly Sociétés 2025, no 5, 29; Bruno Dondero, 'L'ordonnance réformant les nullités en droit des sociétés. Modifications du droit commun des nullités', Semaine juridique—Entreprise et affaires 2025, no 16, 1116.

[31] *Patel v Mirza* (n 7) [9].

[32] Art 1178(3) Cc: 'Acts of performance which have been carried out give rise to restitution under the conditions provided by articles 1352 to 1352-9.'

lawful. In a Consultation Paper entitled *Illegal Transactions: The Effect of Illegality on Contracts*, published in 1999, the English Law Commission considered this problem and provisionally proposed that 'a contract that involves conduct which, though previously unlawful, is lawful when performed . . . should be fully enforceable'[33] unless it is otherwise contrary to public policy. The same view is shared today by Peel, according to whom 'so long as the act in question is lawful *when it is done*, no useful purpose is served by holding the contract invalid'.[34]

The French Civil Code ignores the matter, probably because it was not considered important enough by its drafters. As Whittaker has pointed out, Portalis constantly advised against detailed regulation in the Code civil.[35] Echoing the teaching of Portalis, who praised the necessary complementarity between the Code civil—an instrument doomed to be incomplete—and case law in the process of law-making, the *Cour de cassation* has provided some answers to the issue raised. It has done so on two occasions, some twenty years apart.

In a case decided in 1998, the claimant was an astrologer who, having decided to stop her activities, introduced her successor to her clients in exchange for a sum of money. As she had not been paid, she went to court to claim payment of the agreed price. The Bordeaux *cour d'appel* dismissed her claim.[36] The *cour d'appel* held that the profession of astrologer was prohibited under the Criminal Code and therefore 'annulled' the contract between the two astrologers on the grounds of statutory illegality. As the contract was 'annulled', the claim for payment of the agreed price could not succeed. The claimant's *pourvoi en cassation*[37] was also dismissed by the *Cour de cassation*, although in the meantime the legislative ban had been repealed.[38] 'Nullity' for 'cause illicite' (an unlawful *cause*)[39] was justified in law according to that court. This apparently means that the validity of the contract is to be assessed—solely—in the light of the rules in force at the time it was concluded. Whether or not the illegality subsequently disappears is irrelevant—or so it seems.

The solution reached by the *Cour de cassation* in two cases handed down on 19 May 2021 is different. In these cases, non-physicians wanted to open a beauty salon offering 'pulsed light' hair removal methods. Franchise agreements were signed for this purpose in 2014. Having failed to secure the funding they had hoped for,

[33] Law Commission, *Illegal Transactions: The Effect of Illegality on Contracts and Trusts* (Law Com CP no 154, 1999) para 7.105.

[34] Peel (n 23) para 11-022.

[35] Simon Whittaker, 'Theory and Practice of the "General Clause" in English Law: General Norms and the Structuring of Judicial Discretion' in Stefan Grundmann and Denis Mazeaud (eds), *General Clauses and Standards in European Law* (Kluwer Law International 2006) 57, 76.

[36] CA Bordeaux 10 January 1996, Juris-Data no 1996-040092.

[37] A *pourvoi en cassation* is a type of appeal in the English sense of the term, but it is different from an *appel* in the sense that the *Cour de cassation* is a judge of the law and not of the fact. It quashes rulings of appeal courts for error of law.

[38] See Cass civ (1) 10 February 1998 no 96-15.275. All French cases handed down by the *Cour de cassation* mentioned in this chapter are available at www.legifrance.gouv.fr.

[39] See the former art 1131 Cc.

the non-physicians (now also franchisees) took legal action in 2015 and sought to be released from their commitments, arguing that hair removal using pulsed light was an activity prohibited to non-physicians and that the subject of the contract therefore fell within the scope of the illegal practice of medicine. Meanwhile, on 31 March 2020, the Criminal Division of the *Cour de cassation* reversed its position and ruled that this technique could be carried out without the requirement of being a physician.[40] The ground of illegality had thus disappeared between the moment the contracts were concluded and the moment they had to be performed. In view of the 1998 decision, it was likely that the nullity of the contract would have been declared. This time, however, the *Cour de cassation* ruled against nullity as the illegal nature of the activity forming the subject matter of the contracts had disappeared.[41]

Three observations can be made. First, the position of French law is not very clear. Everything depends on the way in which the decisions just mentioned are understood. Two analyses can be submitted. The first analysis is that the 2021 rulings introduce an implicit distinction based on the nature of the modified law. If the modified rule is legislative in nature—that is, a statute passed by Parliament—nullity remains an available sanction because legislation 'has no retroactive effect' (article 2 Cc), unless otherwise provided. This is illustrated by the case decided in 1998. If the modified rule is established by case law (the judge allows what he previously banned), nullity is ruled out because, in principle, the overruling has retroactive effect. This is reflected in the two cases decided in 2021.[42] The second analysis, however, is the following: the 2021 decisions are the only ones that reflect positive law and the 1998 case must be ignored (even if the *Cour de cassation* does not explicitly acknowledge it). In this scenario, it must be admitted that, as a general rule in French law, nullity is now excluded where the illegality that existed at the time the contract was entered into subsequently disappeared. The contract is enforceable.

Secondly, French scholars are divided as to which solution to adopt. Some are of the opinion that the validity of the contract must be assessed once and for all at the time of its conclusion.[43] The main argument in support of this view is that

[40] See Cass crim 31 March 2020 no 19-85.121.

[41] See Cass civ (1) 19 May 2021 no 19-25.749; Cass civ (1) 19 May 2021 no 20-17.779.

[42] The retroactivity of a judicial decision overruling a precedent is familiar to English readers. Its possible consequences for the validity of an agreement are well illustrated by *Kleinwort Benson Ltd v Lincoln City Council* [1999] 2 AC 349 (HL), even if the situation is somewhat the opposite of that submitted to the *Cour de cassation* in the 2021 decisions. In the French decisions, the overruling in 2020 enabled the *Cour de cassation* in 2021 to hold valid contracts entered into in 2014 which were clearly unlawful under positive law in 2014 but which were no longer unlawful since the retroactive change in 2020. In *Kleinwort Benson*, the parties had believed—as everyone else did—that the agreements were lawful at the time they were entered into between 1982 and 1985, whereas as a result of a 1991 decision of the House of Lords they were not and, according to the majority, never had been, so that the claimant could rely on a mistake of law enabling him to obtain restitution.

[43] See eg Jean-Luc Aubert, Jacques Flour, and Eric Savaux, *Les obligations. L'acte juridique* (18th edn, Dalloz 2024) para 597.

just because the illegality disappeared later does not mean that it did not exist and should lose its force. In other words, just because the illegality no longer appears justified today does not mean that it was not justified yesterday.[44] There is no need to rewrite the past. Others defend the opposite solution: it is absurd to prevent the contract from producing its effects when the legislator or the judge has dispensed with the illegality.[45] Why not allow the enforceability of the contract if its performance is no longer contrary to the law or public policy?

Thirdly, the two most recent decisions of the *Cour de cassation* illustrate the phenomenon mentioned at the end of the introduction, namely the setting aside of nullity in a situation where it is undeniable that the contract has not been lawfully formed, which, in consequence, allows the parties to enforce it. Similar consequences can be observed when the law has not changed, and the contract remains unlawful.

B. The ongoing illegality

This time, the comparison between English and French law is based on more reliable (in the sense of less hypothetical) factors. Indeed, as regards the situation in which the illegality remains in force, in both systems there are not only academic opinions but also legislative and judge-made rules of positive law.

In English law, the basic and undisputed rule is that 'a court will never "enforce" an illegal contract in the sense of ordering a party actually to do something that is unlawful or contrary to public policy' but—and these are important qualifications—it may still award damages for breach of contract or the agreed sum.[46] The illegality may arise by statute. For example, the Human Tissue Act 2004 prohibits commercial dealings in human material. Unless someone has been authorized so to deal by the Human Tissue Authority, a purchaser would not be able to get an order actually transferring such material from the seller.[47] The statute may provide the consequence of the illegality of the contract. If the effect of illegality has not been laid down by the statute, it will be determined according to common law.[48] There is no need to expand on this. What deserve more attention from a French observer's point of view are the following two points.

The first is the adoption of a flexible approach by the Supreme Court in *Patel v Mirza*. What is striking about this case from a French perspective is that instead of deciding that the effect of illegality is necessarily to render the contract invalid, the Supreme Court chose to adopt a policy-based approach. The Court held that

44 See Ghestin, Loiseau, and Serinet (n 21) para 2496.
45 See eg Terré and others (n 24) para 524.
46 Peel (n 23) para 11-070.
47 Human Tissue Act 2004, s 32.
48 See Burrows (n 9) 67–68.

in order to decide whether restitution of the benefits conferred by one party to the other under an illegal contract is available, a range of factors has to be considered: (i) the underlying purpose of the illegality in question; (ii) other public policies on which the denial of the claim may have an impact; (iii) the need to avoid a result that would be disproportionate to the illegality.[49] To decide whether denying the claim would be proportionate, several factors may be considered, such as the seriousness of the illegal conduct, its centrality to the claim, whether or not the conduct was intentional, and so on.[50] Although the direct issue dealt with in *Patel v Mirza* concerned restitution of money paid under a contract, this policy-based approach is applicable to the enforcement of a contract as well.[51] Some commentators welcome this broad scope. They argue that 'because the variables involved in respect of a contract claim are so great, the majority's approach is even more obviously to be welcomed in respect of enforcement of a contract than in respect of restitution of an unjust enrichment'.[52]

Secondly, it has been suggested that the new approach (adopted in *Patel v Mirza*) 'will limit the cases in which the defence [of illegality] can succeed'.[53] To add to this prediction, and without even waiting for it to come true, it should be observed that there are already a number of situations in English law in which an illegal contract produces consequences.

For example, a statute may prescribe that a particular term only is void so that the rest of the contract is enforceable. For example, section 142(1) of the Equality Act 2010 provides that 'a term of a contract is unenforceable against a person in so far as it constitutes, promotes or provides for treatment of that or another person that is of a description prohibited by this Act'.[54] And the following section states

[49] The test to be applied is summarized in *Patel v Mirza* (n 7) [120] as follows: 'The essential rationale of the illegality doctrine is that it would be contrary to the public interest to enforce a claim if to do so would be harmful to the integrity of the legal system (or, possibly, certain aspects of public morality, the boundaries of which have never been made entirely clear and which do not arise for consideration in this case). In assessing whether the public interest would be harmed in that way, it is necessary a) to consider the underlying purpose of the prohibition which has been transgressed and whether that purpose will be enhanced by denial of the claim, b) to consider any other relevant public policy on which the denial of the claim may have an impact and c) to consider whether denial of the claim would be a proportionate response to the illegality, bearing in mind that punishment is a matter for the criminal courts. Within that framework, various factors may be relevant, but it would be a mistake to suggest that the court is free to decide a case in an undisciplined way. The public interest is best served by a principled and transparent assessment of the considerations identified, rather by than the application of a formal approach capable of producing results which may appear arbitrary, unjust or disproportionate' (Lord Toulson).

[50] ibid.

[51] See eg *Litkraft Ltd v Cottrell* [2023] EWHC 465 (Comm) [162]: 'In light of these factors and applying the test in *Patel v Mirza*, the Defendants fail to persuade me that a fee sharing agreement between a claims management company and a firm of solicitors should be treated as being unenforceable at the suit of the claims management company where the illegality alleged is the solicitors' obligation to notify the client of the agreement has not been discharged'.

[52] Beatson, Burrows, and Cartwright (n 5) 420.

[53] John Cartwright, *Contract Law, An Introduction to the English Law of Contract for the Civil Lawyer* (4th edn, Hart Publishing 2023) 204.

[54] Equality Act 2010, s 142(1).

that 'the county court or the sheriff may, on an application by a person who has an interest in a contract or other agreement which includes a term that is unenforceable as a result of section 142, make an order for the term to be removed or modified'.[55]

Similarly, at common law there is a doctrine of severance which allows one or more terms of a contract to be severed on the grounds that they are illegal, leaving the rest of the contract intact. Several conditions must be met: severance must be in accordance with public policy; it must be possible to remove the objectionable part without affecting the meaning or altering the nature of the contract; and the offending term must not form the main consideration of the contract.[56] If these conditions are met—something that a severability provision[57] can perhaps[58] facilitate—the remaining part of the contract is enforceable.[59]

Another illustration concerns the transfer of property under an illegal contract. As Cartwright observes, 'since the contract is not void, there is no inherent obstacle to property passing'.[60] A buyer cannot claim the delivery of goods 'from a seller who has never delivered them at all'.[61] But if the goods sold are delivered under an illegal contract, the buyer 'can recover them or their value if they are later taken away from him by the seller'.[62]

With some analytical finesse, it may be argued that 'although this results in an illegal contract having some legal consequences, this in no way constitutes enforcement'.[63] A French jurist, used to considering the 'effects' of illegality in a more comprehensive way, may be forgiven if he or she considers that some of these 'legal consequences' are very similar to those produced by the enforcement of the contract.

In French law, there is neither in the Code civil nor in the case law of the *Cour de cassation* an approach similar to that adopted in *Patel v Mirza*, that is, one openly favouring discretion. On the face of it, therefore, the difference is clear. In French law, the effect of illegality on the contract is apparently simpler: a contract which is from the beginning illegal is invalid. And we have seen first that 'a contract which

[55] Equality Act 2010, s 143(1).

[56] See eg Beatson, Burrows, and Cartwright (n 5) 423–26.

[57] See Cartwright (n 53) 204: 'In order to avoid the risk of a whole contract being void or unenforceable on the basis of a particular provision, it is common for negotiated commercial contracts to contain an express provision to the effect that if any term of the contract is found to be illegal, invalid or unenforceable, in whole or in part, it shall be severed and deemed not to form part of the contract'.

[58] See Edwin Peel, 'The Common Law Tradition: Application of Boilerplate Clauses under English Law' in Giuditta Cordero-Moss (ed), *Boilerplate Clauses, International Commercial Contracts and the Applicable Law* (CUP 2011) 129, 136 ('there is little, if any, direct judicial consideration of such clauses').

[59] See, eg, on the power of the court to sever the offending clause from the rest of the contract (in a restraint of trade case), *Egon Zehnder Ltd v Tillman* [2019] UKSC 32, [2020] AC 154.

[60] Cartwright (n 16) 82.

[61] Peel (n 23) para 11-100.

[62] ibid.

[63] Beale (n 8) para 19-050.

does not satisfy the conditions required for its validity is a nullity' (article 1178(1) Cc) and, secondly, that 'an annulled contract is deemed never to have existed' (article 1178(2) Cc).

But, and this is where the difference between English law and French law needs to be put into perspective, the legal consequences of illegality are not as systematic or as radical as the provisions of the Code civil might suggest. It should be noted at the outset that in French law nullity is a judicial sanction. Article 1178(1) Cc states: 'nullity must be declared by a court'. This has at least two consequences. First, as long as there is no judicial decision, the illegal contract exists in the legal order. It produces its effects normally, bearing in mind on the one hand that it is not certain that a court will ever intervene, and, on the other hand that a claim for 'nullity' is subject to prescription (usually five years starting from the date on which the claimant knew or should have known the facts enabling him to exercise his right[64]). Secondly, the judicial nature of nullity gives the judge a key role: it is up to them to determine whether one of the conditions of validity of the contract has been infringed ('illegality' in our context) and, if so, to decide what consequences should be drawn.

It is precisely this last point that needs to be emphasized: although the contract is illegal from the beginning, the court may decide not to annul it. As the contract is not 'deleted' from the legal order, it produces effects. Several techniques are used to achieve this result. Here are some examples.

A first method—similar to severability in English law—is what might be called 'amputation'. This involves removing the term or terms that are illegal while maintaining the rest of the contract.[65] More exactly, there are two techniques that are close in fact but not identical in law. The first is 'deemed not written'. As the name suggests, this involves treating the provision as if it did not exist. The second is the nullity of the term. The distinction between these two techniques may seem to be sophistry and unnecessary since both mechanisms lead to the same result: the definitive removal of one or more terms. But there are significant legal differences. First, the term deemed unwritten is a sanction which is totally detached from the intention of the parties,[66] whereas the choice between the nullity of the whole contract or the nullity of a single term depends on whether the term 'constituted a decisive factor in the undertaking of the parties, or of one of them' (article 1184(1) Cc) and on an objective factor relating to the 'purposes of the rule not followed' (article 1184(2) Cc). The conditions for the nullity of a term are therefore more difficult to meet than those for 'deemed unwritten', a sanction that requires only that it be provided for by statute or case law. Secondly, unlike the nullity of a

[64] See art 2224 Cc.

[65] See eg Terré and others (n 24) paras 572–574.

[66] See Olivier Deshayes, Thomas Genicon, and Yves-Marie Laithier, *Réforme du droit des contrats, du régime général et de la preuve des obligations* (2nd edn, LexisNexis 2018) 387.

term, 'deemed unwritten' is a remedy that is not judicial; it takes effect without the need to go to court, which is why extinctive prescription does not apply.[67]

A second method is to carry out a substitution, that is, to replace the illegal element by a legal element. For example, if the parties have agreed that the value of a monetary obligation depends on an illegal index,[68] the judge may replace the illegal index with a legal index after checking that this does not betray the common intention of the parties.[69]

A third method involves shifting the debate from the formation of the contract to its performance. For example, in French contract law, that which are called 'perpetual commitments' are prohibited.[70] A breach of this prohibition could have been sanctioned by the nullity of the contract. This would have been logical since one of the conditions of the validity of the contract has been violated. But the *Cour de cassation* opted instead for unilateral termination of the contract.[71] The rule is now enshrined in the Code civil (article 1210). It could be argued that in both cases (nullity and termination), the contract comes to an end, and that the situation is therefore similar in practice. But what is similar is not identical. The fact is that the definition of a 'perpetual' commitment is not clear in French case law[72] (the concept of 'perpetual' in law is not the same thing as 'indefinite' duration—discussed below in section III). This uncertainty puts the parties in an uncomfortable situation. Unlike nullity, which is a judicial sanction, termination is a self-help remedy.[73] It is therefore the contracting party who bears the risk of deciding whether or not to terminate the contract. This is a difficult decision, precisely because the notion of a perpetual commitment is uncertain. The contracting party is likely to hesitate to terminate on this ground—a hesitation that has no place in the context of nullity, where it is for the court to decide, and which therefore has the effect (whenever there is significant doubt) in practice of maintaining the contract.

A fourth method is to make a 'reduction'.[74] This technique is adequate when the illegality arises from the fact that one of the elements of the contract exceeds a permitted threshold. The situation where a statute sets a maximum duration for the validity of a contract provides a good illustration of the mechanism. For example,

[67] See eg Cass civ (1) 30 March 2022 no 19-17.996.

[68] To limit the risk of inflationary effects, art L112-2 of the Monetary and Financial Code requires the indexation clause to refer to the price of goods or services directly related to the subject of the contract or the activity of one of the parties.

[69] See Cass civ (3) 22 July 1987 no 84-10.548.

[70] See art 1210 Cc. The Code civil does not provide a definition of perpetual commitments. Perpetuity depends on the context. If the co-contractor is a human being, a commitment for a very long term, for example sixty years, may be considered perpetual. In general, the question is more subtle and involves determining whether the renewal clauses actually allow one of the parties to withdraw from the contract. See eg Cass com 11 May 2022 no 19-22.015.

[71] See eg Cass com 21 Sept 2022 no 20-16.994.

[72] See n 70.

[73] See eg Flour, Aubert, and Savaux (n 43) para 699. See also arts 1210–1211 Cc.

[74] See eg Terré and others (n 24) para 575.

for certain contracts, article L 330-1 of the French Commercial Code limits the validity of the exclusivity clause to a maximum of ten years. If the term of the contract is longer than the maximum authorized period, the court may reduce it to ten years, thereby avoiding the nullity of the contract.[75] Similarly, when the maximum duration of the rental of an advertising space is set by legislation at six years,[76] the *Cour de cassation* decided that the courts must reduce the duration of the contract rather than declaring it annulled.[77] As Genicon has rightly pointed out, in this type of situation the sanction shifts from nullity for illegality to 'revision for illegality'.[78]

As a final example, it may be observed that the *Cour de cassation* sometimes simply rules out nullity without giving any technical justification. The contract is annulled for policy reasons that are not spelled out. For example, in a case where a lubricant supplier had routinely granted cash loans to parties who had entered into exclusive supply contracts with him, it was found that this regular practice infringed article L511-5 of the Monetary and Financial Code, which established a monopoly of credit institutions for this type of transaction.[79] Under French law, this violation exposes the lubricant supplier to criminal liability. But what about the loan contracts? This was the question submitted to the court. The guarantors argued that these contracts should be annulled because they were illegal, and that they were therefore released from their obligations to repay the loan if the borrowers defaulted. The *Cour de cassation* rejected their claims. It held that contracts entered into in breach of the banking monopoly should not be annulled.[80] The decision is formulated in clear terms but without any explanation. In practice, it means that lenders can receive the benefit of the contracts (the interest) and keep it in full, unless they are sentenced to pay criminal fines. The result is quite surprising if one bears in mind that the loan contracts are illegal. It may be thought—but this is only a supposition—that the *Cour de cassation* did not want guarantors to be able to escape so easily from their obligations and, above all, that the defence of the banking monopoly is more a matter for criminal law (where the public interest prevails) than for civil law (where the private interest predominates). Still, this is a further illustration of a contract which, although concluded in violation of the law, produces its effects.

The decline of nullity as a sanction for illegal contracts can probably be explained by a variety of reasons. Since nullity is a judicial sanction, one reason is to avoid, where possible, the need for a trial which, while perhaps not as costly on

[75] See eg Cass com 10 Feb 1998 no 95-21.906.
[76] Art L581-25(1) Code de l'environnement.
[77] See Cass civ (1) 13 Nov 2002 no 99-21.816.
[78] Thomas Genicon, 'De la nullité partielle à la clause réputée "partiellement" non écrite', Revue des contrats 2010, no 4, 1199, 1206. The phrase 'revision for illegality' echoes the famous discussion in the French legal literature on 'revision for unforeseeable supervening circumstances' (or *révision pour imprévision*).
[79] See Cass com 15 June 2022 no 20-22.160; and Ass plén 4 March 2005 no 03-11.725.
[80] ibid.

average in France as in England, is often lengthy because of the slowness of the judicial institutions and the ease with which appeals can be made in French law. Another possible explanation lies in the desire to avoid as far as possible the opportunistic use of nullity, a sanction which is often sought by a contracting party who intends to escape from his obligations after having realized that the contract is not as profitable or useful as he had expected when it was made or if it turns out to be contrary to his interests (as the guarantors understood in the last case referred to). The decline in nullity can also be explained by the need to safeguard the interests of third parties. This is the reason commonly given for the rarity of nullity in company law.[81]

We will conclude these remarks on antecedent illegality by pointing out that even if, in contrast to the Supreme Court of the United Kingdom in *Patel v Mirza*, the *Cour de cassation* does not explicitly accept a broad discretionary power in relation to the effects of illegality—a step which would be difficult to take because it would be a considerable departure from the provisions of the Code civil—it nevertheless manages to show flexibility in that it does not hesitate to give effect to the contract by various methods. The same *favor contractus* can be observed when the illegality arises after the contract has been entered into.

III. Subsequent Illegality

Subsequent illegality occurs when there is a change in the law and contractual performance becomes legally impossible. The performance undertaken is forbidden (for example, trading with the enemy) or the promisor is deprived of control over the subject matter of the contract (for example, where land subject to a restrictive covenant against building is compulsorily acquired by the state). Subsequent illegality is a long-standing phenomenon that continues today (embargoes against Iran or Russia are good examples) and is not peculiar to a single legal system. This is why the gap between the great attention paid to this topic in English law, on the one hand, and the lack of interest shown in it by French authors, on the other, is so striking. This is yet another reason justifying what we described at the beginning of this chapter as a 'reflexive' comparison—that is, a comparison with a foreign system to gain a better understanding of one's own law—and therefore consideration of the possible fate of supervening illegality in French law. In light of English law, two issues can be addressed. First, what would be the legal basis (*fondement*)[82]

[81] See eg Philippe Merle and Anne Fauchon, *Droit commercial. Sociétés commerciales* (28th edn, Dalloz 2024) para 86.

[82] The word *fondement*, which is very common in French legal discourse, is polysemous. This makes it very difficult, or indeed impossible, to translate into English. See Richard Hyland, 'The *Fondement*' in Alexandra Popovici, Lionel Smith, and Régine Tremblay (eds), *Les intraduisibles en droit civil* (Editions Thémis 2014) 75. In a broad sense, the word can refer either to a general principle that is said to govern a

in French law of the rules applicable to a contract which ceases to be lawful (A)? Second, what would be in French law the effects of subsequent illegality both on the contract itself and the parties (B)?

A. The legal basis of subsequent illegality

In English law, subsequent illegality is dealt with under the doctrine of frustration. This topic is the subject of numerous studies, some of them very extensive,[83] and illustrated by a significant number of cases. Only two brief reminders will be given here. For the doctrine of frustration to be applicable in this context, (i) the prohibition must exist and (ii) it must be supervening. First, the prohibition itself must exist and be valid. If for one reason or another, the legislation rendering the existing contract illegal is invalid, the contract is not frustrated.[84] Secondly, the illegality must be subsequent and not antecedent. In theory, the distinction is clear: illegality is subsequent if the prohibition is imposed after the contract was made. But the distinction can become blurred in certain situations, as, for example, where a licence is required at the time of contracting and was easily granted up to that time but is now refused following a change of government policy.[85] The contract may be frustrated (for supervening illegality) even though the change of policy is not the result of a new statute or regulation.[86] A similar difficulty may arise where a law prohibiting performance of the contract has been passed at the time of contracting but shall come into force at a later date. If a new order is necessary for bringing into force the legislation that prohibits performance and if such an order is made after the contract is entered into, the doctrine of frustration for supervening illegality may be applied by a court.[87]

In French law, there are two possible 'doctrines'—or, as a French lawyer would say, two 'legal bases'—for resolving the problem raised by a subsequent illegality: force majeure and lapse (*caducité*). Before showing how both are relevant, it is important to stress that nullity is unquestionably excluded in this hypothesis. The reason is simple: nullity is a sanction applicable only for defects in the formation of the contract. It should also be noted by way of preliminary observation that, under French law, a contract can always be revoked by the parties' mutual consent (see article 1193 Cc) and each party may put an end to the contract at any

legal concept or to a general justification. In a stricter sense, it refers to the legal basis on which a concept or set of rules of positive law rests.

[83] See eg Peel (n 26) ch 8.
[84] ibid para 8-003.
[85] ibid para 8-041.
[86] ibid.
[87] ibid para 8-044.

time where it is concluded for an indefinite duration (see article 1211 Cc). There is therefore nothing to prevent a willing party (or willing parties) from putting an end to the contract if it turns out that the contract has become illegal. Having said this, let us return to force majeure and lapse.

The first mechanism is force majeure. In contractual matters, force majeure means that the debtor is prevented from performing his obligation.[88] This prevention, which is at the heart of the concept of force majeure, must have been caused by an event the nature of which is not specified in the Code civil. Consequently, in the silence of the Code, there is nothing that precludes the event—and consequently the prevention—from being of a legal nature. For example, force majeure occurs if, after the lease contract has been signed, local authorities are unable to issue the licences that the lessor needs in order to fulfil his obligation to plant vines on the entire leased plot.[89] Similarly, force majeure is applicable where, as a result of measures taken by the French government in order to comply with new rules on the non-proliferation of nuclear weapons, the performance of several contracts for the supply of study plans and technical assistance for the creation of a plant for the reprocessing of irradiated fuel in Pakistan is prevented.[90]

The main effect of force majeure is the termination of the contract. The general rule is set out in article 1218(2) Cc. This general rule (*droit commun*) may be modified or clarified by more specific rules. For example, there is a particular rule for contracts of charter and carriage by sea—a type of contract frequently encountered in English case law on this matter—which explicitly addresses (which is rare in French law) the event of subsequent illegality. The decree states that 'the contract shall be terminated without damages on either side if, before the departure of the vessel, there occurs a prohibition of trade with the country for which it is intended or any other event of force majeure which makes it impossible to carry out the voyage'.[91]

The second mechanism is lapse. By definition, this concept applies to a contract which has been 'validly formed' (article 1186(1) Cc). This is a point in common with the concept of force majeure mentioned above. Another common feature with force majeure is the extinction of the juridical act: 'lapse puts an end to the contract', states article 1187 Cc. The advantage of lapse in comparison with force majeure lies in the fact that it is subject to different conditions which are prima facie easier to meet. For a contract to lapse, it is sufficient for 'one of its essential elements' (article 1186(1) Cc) to disappear. Article 1128 Cc provides that legality

[88] See art 1218(1) Cc: 'In contractual matters, there is force majeure where an event beyond the control of the debtor, which could not reasonably have been foreseen at the time of the conclusion of the contract and whose effects could not be avoided by appropriate measures, prevents performance of his obligation by the debtor.'

[89] See Cass civ (3) 15 November 2005 no 04-17.213.

[90] See CA Paris 13 July 1987, JurisData no 1987-024165.

[91] Décret no 66-1078 of 31 December 1966 on contracts of charter and maritime transport, art 12.

of content is one of the conditions 'necessary for the validity of a contract'. As a result, a contract that has been lawfully formed is valid but lapses if its 'content' (ie its stipulations or purpose) becomes unlawful. It is clear from these provisions of the Code civil that the legality of the contract is not just a condition of its validity, as French writers usually assert; legality is also a condition of the continued existence of the contract. It may be added that where several contracts can serve to implement a particular economic strategy, which is not unusual, article 1186(2) Cc provides for more detailed rules. In short, contracts may lapse if performance of one of the contracts is rendered impossible by the disappearance of another, or if performance of one of the contracts which has disappeared was a key condition of a party's consent, provided in each case that the other party against whom lapse is claimed was aware of the existence of the overall economic strategy at the time they gave their consent. It follows from this provision that—in the absence of a severability clause—subsequent illegality may result in the termination of the entire set of contracts.

Let us suppose, for instance, that several legally distinct but economically interdependent contracts are entered into: one relates to the sale of a number of aircraft by company A to company B, which then leases them to company C for a period of ten years, and a third contract provides, for the same period, for the direct sale by company A to company C of spare parts essential to the maintenance and proper operation of the planes. If during this period all commercial dealings with company C are prohibited as a result of a ban imposed on it, there is a risk that all the contracts will lapse, including the sale between companies A and B (company B being able to argue that the performance of the lease was a determining condition of its consent to the purchase of the aircraft and that the global nature of the operation was known to company A at the time it gave its consent to the sale). This brings us to a closer look at the effects of the subsequent illegality.

B. The effects of subsequent illegality

Overall, the law regarding the effects of antecedent illegality is consistent with that of subsequent illegality: in both situations, the courts' approach is flexible. This flexibility can be observed in both English and French law.

In English law, under the doctrine of frustration, a contract may be discharged by supervening illegality. Frustration brings the contract to an end with effect from the time of the frustrating event. Therefore, after the occurrence of the frustrating event, both parties are relieved from further performance.[92] As a general rule, 'the

[92] See Beatson, Burrows, and Cartwright (n 5) 494.

contract cannot be kept alive or revived at the option of either party; neither can the court keep the contract on foot'.[93]

However, a subsequent illegality will frustrate the contract only if it makes the performance of the obligations radically different from that originally undertaken. When deciding whether or not a contract has been frustrated, courts adopt—once again—a 'multi-factorial approach'.[94] According to Rix LJ, factors taken into account include:

> the terms of the contract itself, its matrix or context, the parties' knowledge, expectations, assumptions and contemplations, in particular as to risk, as at the time of contract, at any rate so far as these can be ascribed mutually and objectively, and then the nature of the supervening event, and the parties' reasonable and objectively ascertainable calculations as to the possibilities of future performance in the new circumstances.[95]

Just as antecedent illegality is not necessarily a ground of invalidity,[96] 'a contract will not be discharged *merely* because a supervening prohibition has made full and exact performance in some respect unlawful'.[97]

Three brief illustrations of this approach can be given. First, for there to be frustration, partial illegality must defeat the 'main object of the contract'.[98] This means that if the illegality does not affect its main purpose, the contract is not discharged.[99] Secondly, where the part of the contract which becomes unlawful is severable and the performance of the remaining part would still make commercial sense, then only the illegal part of the contract is discharged and the rest remains enforceable.[100] For example, it has been held that while the scope of an insurance contract was reduced as a result of the Financial Restrictions (Iran) Order 2009 made pursuant to the Counter-Terrorism Act 2008, the cover for bunker oil pollution remained lawful and was not dependent on the other parts of the contract which were no longer lawful; therefore, the contract was not discharged by frustration.[101] Thirdly, temporary illegality does not necessarily frustrate the contract. It depends on the length of the illegality. For example, the House of Lords held that a 99-year lease had not been frustrated since government restrictions preventing its performance covered only a small part of the term.[102]

93 Chen-Wishart (n 25) 324.
94 Peel (n 23) para 19-008.
95 *The Sea Angel* [2007] EWCA Civ 547 [111], as cited in Peel (n 23) para 19-008.
96 See n 26.
97 Peel (n 26) para 8-045 (emphasis added).
98 *Denny Mott & Dickson Ltd v James B Fraser & Co Ltd* [1944] AC 265, 271 (Viscount Simon).
99 On 'partial illegality', see Peel (n 26) para 8-046.
100 For a detailed discussion and references, see ibid paras 8-047–8-050.
101 *Islamic Republic of Iran Shipping Lines v Steamship Mutual Underwriting Association (Bermuda) Ltd* [2010] EWHC 2661 (Comm) [114]–[126].
102 *Cricklewood Property & Investment Trust Ltd v Leighton's Investment Trust Ltd* [1945] AC 221.

In French law, as in the case of antecedent illegality,[103] there is no *Cour de cassation* decision giving courts a discretionary power to determine the effects of subsequent illegality. Nor does any ruling provide for the adoption of a 'multi-factorial' approach. The truth is that there are very few cases on subsequent illegality in French law.

Notwithstanding this relative uncertainty due to the lack of precision in the provisions of the Code civil and the absence of significant authority, it should be emphasized that 'the end of the contract'—which is the effect provided for by the Code civil both in the event of permanent force majeure (the contract is terminated and 'termination puts an end to the contract' pursuant to article 1229 Cc) and in the event of lapse (article 1187 Cc)—is a harsh outcome that can be avoided in a number of situations. The French approach is therefore not as rigid as one might think prima facie. The common basis underlying these situations is that it seems fair and worthwhile to 'keep the contract alive' despite the fact that the illegality affects its performance. There are a number of possible ways of achieving this. Here are a few illustrations relating to force majeure and lapse.

We have seen that force majeure requires by definition an event which 'prevents performance of his obligation by the debtor' (article 1218(1) Cc).[104] It is generally accepted that the prevention must be absolute (this is one of the differences between force majeure and *imprévision*).[105] Consequently, a party will not be excused if the supervening illegality simply makes performance more difficult or more onerous (for example, a law prohibiting delivery of goods at a particular place does not prevent delivery elsewhere, unless the place now prohibited has been designated by the parties as the only possible one). Moreover, even if force majeure is established, the contract may not be terminated if the prevention is temporary. Depending on the nature of the prohibition and on the length and the effect of the delay, a temporary illegality may merely suspend the performance of the contract (article 1218(2) Cc). As the contract is suspended but not terminated, the parties are not released from their obligations. They must perform the contract once the illegality ceases.[106] However, it has to be admitted that the Code civil's distinction between 'temporary' prevention and 'permanent' prevention is somewhat simplistic: first, because it is not necessarily easy to know the exact duration of the prevention (eg, how long will the prohibitions or restrictions imposed on Russia and Russian companies last after the invasion of Ukraine?); secondly, because the duration of the prevention must always be compared with the content of the contract

[103] See text following n 65.

[104] See n 88.

[105] See eg Bénabent (n 24) para 359; Fages (n 20) para 323. See also Hugh Beale, 'Doctrines of Change of Circumstance, Covid-19 and Special Measures', this book, ch 6.

[106] In English law, an express clause providing that supervening illegality is to suspend the contract may be given effect in certain circumstances. See Peel (n 26) para 8-077.

to determine whether the suspension—and therefore future performance—is in the interests of the parties.

As regards lapse, the law is still uncertain. Two observations can be made. First, the Code civil provides that lapse puts an end to the contract but does not specify how lapse operates. Is the contract ended automatically? Does 'lapse' need to be invoked? Can it be invoked by either party? As in the case of nullity,[107] is a court decision required? In other words, is lapse a self-help remedy or a judicial remedy? These are important questions that have not yet been resolved. Until the *Cour de cassation* clarifies these issues, suffice it to say that the more obstacles there are, the greater the likelihood that the contract will continue. Secondly, it will be interesting to know whether lapse can produce an effect other than 'termination of the contract'—the only effect mentioned in article 1187 of the Code civil. Drawing a comparison with the alternative sanctions to the extinction of the contract in the case of antecedent illegality[108] but also with the English doctrine of frustration for supervening illegality,[109] the question may be raised whether, in the case of subsequent illegality in French law, the terms can be adjusted in order to comply with the new law. The contract would be maintained but its content would be modified to become lawful. If, for example, a contract is for the sale abroad of 2,000 tonnes of a product and a new law prohibits the export of more than 1,000 tonnes of that type of product, it would be possible, following this line of reasoning and in the absence of a non-severability clause, to bring the contract into conformity—thus limiting the sale to 1,000 tonnes and modifying the price accordingly—instead of terminating it. Whether this solution will one day be accepted by the *Cour de cassation* is uncertain. If it were, the *Cour de cassation* would have to clarify whether, in the event of partial illegality, the debtor has an option between simply terminating the contract or 'bringing it into conformity'.

To complete the study of the effects of subsequent illegality, two final points can be made. The first concerns the consequences for the defendant of maintaining the contract. If despite the subsequent illegality the contract is not terminated, it is, of course, still binding (article 1103 Cc). This awkward situation, in which conflicting considerations coexist—the need to comply with the new law and the binding nature of the contract—may give rise to some uncertainty. There are situations that are simpler than others, such as those where contractual provisions are deemed

107 See text preceding n 64.

108 See nn 65ff.

109 See Peel (n 26) para 8-047, regarding the prohibition of the export of soyabean meal save in restricted circumstances by the United States authorities after floods in the Mississippi valley: 'The position may be illustrated by reference to the soyabean cases, in many of which the American export restrictions ultimately applied to no more than 60% of the quantity sold. The actual decisions in those cases turned on the operation of the express prohibition and force majeure clauses in the contracts. But the present point is that such a prohibition would not in any event affect the seller's liability to deliver the 40% which could lawfully be delivered. In this respect, the effect of the prohibition would be the same as that of partial physical impossibility caused (for example) by partial failure of a specified crop.'

not to have been written or where there is a temporary force majeure. In the first case, the Code civil provides that 'the contract is upheld where legislation deems a contract term not written' (article 1183(2) Cc). In the second case, the Code civil provides that in principle only 'performance of the obligation is suspended' (article 1218(2) Cc).[110] But in other situations, such as where the subsequent illegality affects a minor obligation or where no request has been made to the court for the contract to lapse (assuming that this sanction is judicial), difficulties may arise. If an action is brought on the basis that the contract is enforceable, can the defendant raise illegality as a defence? A distinction can be made here between a claim for performance in kind and a claim for compensatory damages.

As far as performance in kind is concerned, the defendant should be able to argue fairly easily that this remedy is 'impossible' under article 1221 of the Code civil. The *Cour de cassation* has long accepted that the impossibility of specific performance can be of a legal—and not just a physical—nature. It can therefore be said that the subsequent illegality of the obligation in question makes it legally impossible to enforce it *in specie*.[111]

As far as compensatory damages are concerned, and in the absence of any specific provisions in the Code civil, the following reasoning can be put forward. In order to obtain compensatory damages, the loss must be legally 'reparable'. To be reparable, a number of conditions must be satisfied, including the lawfulness of the injured interest.[112] If the obligation that has not been performed is no longer lawful because of a subsequent change in the law, then the loss (ie the protected interest) caused by its non-performance is no longer lawful either. Consequently, there can be no damages for compensation[113] for what is sometimes referred to—in English law—as the 'performance interest'.[114]

[110] In English law, a temporary illegality which is not serious enough to frustrate the contract may give the party whose performance is made unlawful a temporary excuse. See Peel (n 26) para 8-066.

[111] See eg Fages (n 20) para 297, who illustrates the concept of legal impossibility by giving as an example the case where the 'promised service has in the meantime become prohibited'. See eg Cass civ (1) 18 Dec 2024 no 24-14.751, concerning restrictions on the distribution of drinking water suddenly imposed by the public authorities due to exceptional drought conditions.

[112] See eg Philippe le Tourneau (ed), *Droit de la responsabilité et des contrats, Régimes d'indemnisation* (14th edn, Dalloz 2025) para 2123.11. Art 1235 of the 'Reform Bill on Civil Liability' (*Sénat, Proposition de loi portant réforme de la responsabilité civile*, no 678, 29 July 2020) makes this condition more explicit: 'Any certain loss is reparable where it results from harm and consists of any injury to a lawful interest, whether patrimonial or extra-patrimonial' (translation by Simon Whittaker in consultation with Jean-Sébastien Borghetti, in Jean-Sébastien Borghetti and Simon Whittaker (eds), *French Civil Liability in Comparative Perspective* (Hart Publishing 2019) 477, 480. On the legality of the loss, see Dorota Leczykiewicz, 'Loss and Its Compensation in the Proposed New French Regime of Extra-contractual Liability' in Borghetti and Whittaker (n 112) 181, 192–93.

[113] In English law, where supervening illegality does not discharge the contract, specific performance of the part which has become illegal will not be ordered and it has been argued that neither should the defendant be held liable in damages. See Peel (n 26) para 8-068.

[114] See eg *Attorney General of Trinidad and Tobago v Trinsalvage Enterprises Ltd* [2023] UKPC 26 [28] (Lord Burrows): 'It is trite law that, in general, the aim of contractual remedies is to put the claimant into as good a position as if the contract had been performed . . . This has sometimes been referred to as the protection of the claimant's expectation or performance interest.'

The second point concerns contractual provisions relating to the effects of subsequent illegality. This is a topic largely ignored in French law and one on which English experience is enlightening.[115] For example, the new prohibition may provide for a system of exemption if a request is made.[116] A contractual provision might specify the standard of duty which one of the parties must meet when it is asking for an exemption. It might be supplemented by another provision covering non-performance—such as a liquidated damages clause, for example. Other kinds of provisions are also possible. Admittedly, a contractual term cannot impose a duty on a party to perform an obligation that has become illegal—to continue, for example, to supply a pesticide that is now banned. But a clause could provide for the payment of a sum of money in the event of subsequent illegality. It is a way to allocate the loss. For example, in cases in which performance of the contract is made illegal by supervening prohibitions of export or import, a provision may specify that the party who can no longer deliver the goods must pay the other party a sum of money.[117] Save where this sort of clause is expressly prohibited by the new law, there is no reason to deprive it of its effect. It does not contravene the prohibition (the import or export of the goods in the example). It merely modifies its consequences. This shows, in a very interesting way, that any illegality is not in itself incompatible with the exercise of freedom of contract.

IV. Conclusion

Illegality, whether antecedent or subsequent, creates a conflict between two policies. On the one hand, there is the scrupulous defence of public policy and, more broadly, the fact that legality should lead to the 'removal' from the legal order of any contract that is or becomes illegal; on the other hand, taking a more cautious approach, not all illegalities are equally important. Depending on their content and scope, some are more serious than others. It is therefore easier to understand why the contract, despite the illegality that taints it, might not be 'annulled', 'terminated', or 'discharged', but instead 'kept alive'. How is this conflict solved in English and French law? We do not claim, as some functionalists would,[118] that the two

[115] On this type of clause and stressing the distinction to be made between cases of 'trading with the enemy' and other forms of supervening illegality, see Peel (n 26) paras 8-008 and 8-076–8-077.

[116] ibid para 8-069.

[117] See, in English law, *Johnson Matthey Bankers Ltd v State Trading Corp of India Ltd* [1984] 1 Lloyd's Rep 427, 435, suggesting that an express provision which specifies that the party whose performance has become illegal must pay a sum of money (an invoicing back clause) is not contrary to public policy and can therefore be given effect.

[118] See Konrad Zweigert and Hein Kötz, *An Introduction to Comparative Law* (Tony Weir tr, 3rd edn, OUP 1998) 39.

legal systems, despite their historical, structural, and conceptual differences, reach the same solutions. Their differences cannot be denied or underestimated. It is nonetheless true that there is a tendency in French law to uphold a contract which has been affected by antecedent or subsequent illegality, and this tendency is also perceptible in English law.

6

Doctrines of Change of Circumstances, Covid-19, and Special Measures

Hugh Beale

Foreword

It is an honour and a great pleasure to contribute to this *Festschrift* for Simon Whittaker. I have had the privilege of working with Simon in a number of contexts. He is the single largest contributor to *Chitty on Contracts*, for which he has produced original and ground-breaking analysis, for example on the role of good faith in English law and on the application of the reasonableness test under the Unfair Contracts Terms Act 1977, to say nothing of his wholly new chapter on Consumer Contracts, which inter alia gives the most penetrating analysis I have seen of the relevant case law of the Court of Justice of the European Union. For a time, he and I were both members of the Expert Group established by the European Commission to draft a Feasibility Study for the proposed Common European Sales Law, and we enjoyed long discussions not only at the meetings but on our train journeys to and from Brussels. I have been involved in the fascinating workshops that Simon and John Cartwright organized to discuss recent reforms of the French Civil Code, and I have developed an enormous respect for Simon as a comparative lawyer. To my mind, his book on *Liability for Products*,[1] and in particular its close examination of the context within which the French law operates, is a model of comparative law. Simon is a great scholar.

I. Introduction

If we look across jurisdictions in Europe and jurisdictions that have inherited or have been heavily influenced by various European laws of contract, and apply the functional approach of stripping away differences in concepts and terminology and

[1] Simon Whittaker, *Liability for Products: English Law, French Law, and European Harmonisation* (OUP 2005).

Hugh Beale, *Doctrines of Change of Circumstances, Covid-19, and Special Measures* In: *Comparative Reflections in Private Law*. Edited by: Marco Cappelletti, Ciara Kennefick, and Dorota Leczykiewicz, Oxford University Press.
 DOI: 10.1093/9780198959168.003.0007

concentrating on the outcomes in particular cases,[2] we find that the laws of contract have a great deal in common. This is what has made it possible to draft restatements of the law of contract such as the Principles of European Contract Law[3] or the UNIDROIT Principles of International Commercial Contracts.[4] For example, though they use different mechanisms, all the systems that I have studied reach the result that if a change makes the contract factually impossible or legally impermissible to perform and if that change occurs after the contract was made, was unforeseen, was not the result of anything done by either party, and was outside the normal risks, a party who is unable to perform will neither be required to do so nor be liable to pay damages for breach of contract for failing to perform; and the counterparty may be released from its obligations also.[5] However, on a number of key issues, outcomes seem to differ markedly between the domestic laws of contract. On these issues the drafters of the Restatements had either to make a choice or to find a compromise that the members of the relevant group felt that they could live with. One of these areas is the effect of changed circumstances (or *imprévision*, as it is termed in French law[6])—that is, whether a party can obtain relief if the contract, though not impossible, becomes much more burdensome for the party to perform, or the performance the party is to receive becomes much less worthwhile, because of a change in circumstances that the parties had not foreseen and that neither of them had brought about nor could have done anything about.[7] Many civilian systems provide relief for the party affected, commonly by allowing the court, if the parties themselves fail to agree on a solution, to adapt the contract so as to enable its continuation, or to terminate it. The common law is quite different: standard doctrine is that in this kind of case, the common law (other than in the US[8]) gives no

[2] See Konrad Zweigert and Hein Kötz, *An Introduction to Comparative Law* (Tony Weir tr, 3rd edn, OUP 1998) 33–47. The method is critiqued by Ralf Michaels, 'The Functional Method of Comparative Law' in Mathias Reimann and Reinhard Zimmermann (eds), *The Oxford Handbook of Comparative Law* (2nd edn, OUP 2019) 339.

[3] Ole Lando and Hugh Beale (eds), *Principles of European Contract Law, Parts I and II* (Kluwer 2000); Ole Lando and others (eds), *Principles of European Contract Law, Part III* (Kluwer 2003) (PECL).

[4] Unidroit Principles of International Commercial Contracts 2016 (UPICC).

[5] For a brief summary, see the Notes to PECL, art 8:108. The reasoning used to reach these outcomes differs from one system to another: see Hugh Beale and others (eds), *Cases, Materials and Text on Contract Law* (3rd edn, Hart Publishing 2019) ch 28.

[6] To simplify things, I will use the phrase 'change of circumstances' to cover the various versions of the doctrine.

[7] The doctrine is normally separate from that of impossibility. Exceptionally, art 533 of the Civil Code of the People's Republic of China combines the two doctrines, so it seems that there can be adjustment of the contract terms in cases of force majeure where that is feasible.

[8] In the US, §2-615 of the Uniform Commercial Code uses the word 'impracticable' rather than 'impossible'; this is now also the language used in *Restatement 2d of Contracts*, §261. E Allan Farnsworth, *Contracts* (4th edn, Aspen 2004) 627–28 points out that the Commentary to §2-615 UCC says that this might cover a marked increase in the cost of performance and that some courts have allowed this—eg, *Florida Power & Light Co v Westinghouse Elec Corp* 826 F 2d 239 (4th Cir 1987)—but that many courts have refused to do so.

relief—though the common law will give effect to provisions such as adverse change[9] or hardship[10] clauses if they were included in the contract.

Originally, my aim was that this chapter should address two questions. The first was whether jurisdictions that recognize change of circumstances have used the doctrine to solve cases arising from the restrictions on economic activity imposed by governments in response to the Covid-19 epidemic, when those restrictions did not render the contract impossible[11] but made performance much more onerous for one party. The second question was, where the doctrine of change of circumstances was used, how the outcomes reached compare to the effects of the special measures that were adopted in many systems, both in those which recognize change of circumstances and those, including of course England and Wales, that do not.

However, I was soon to discover that there are so many variations in the way national laws allow relief for change of circumstances—differences in the mechanisms used, in the scope of application of the rules, in the remedies available and in the way in which the doctrine, or perhaps I should say doctrines, seem to be applied—that the first half of the chapter is devoted to the doctrine in general. Even so, space does not permit anything like a complete account,[12] so I give just an outline with illustrations of the principal complexities and variations. It will be seen that in some respects it is very difficult to make reliable comparisons, in particular of the ways the doctrine is applied in practice.

I also found such variety among the special measures that I cannot describe even a few schemes in any detail. Instead, I pick a number of general characteristics by which to compare the schemes to each other, and their outcomes to those that a variety of other systems would reach under their general law.

[9] They are commonly found in agreements for the sale and purchase of a business. Typically, if there has been a material adverse change, the purchaser is not obliged to go ahead. For a recent example see *BM Brazil 1 Fundo De Investimento Em Participacoes Multistrategia v Sibanye BM Brazil (Pty) Ltd* [2024] EWHC 2566 (Comm).

[10] Such clauses may refer any issues that arise to be determined by a third person, eg *Superior Overseas Development Corp v British Gas Corp* [1982] 1 Lloyd's Rep 262 (CA); or they may oblige the parties to renegotiate the contract, often in good faith. The effect of this is discussed in Beale and others (n 5) 1255.

[11] Cases in which the Covid-19 restrictions rendered contracts permanently or temporarily impossible are explored in Hugh Beale and Christian Twigg-Flesner, 'COVID-19 and English Contract Law' in Ewoud Hondius and others (eds), *Coronavirus and the Law in Europe* (Intersentia 2021) 461, 463–71, and in many other chapters of that volume.

[12] Much fuller treatment of change of circumstances will be found in Denis M Philippe, *Changement de circonstances et bouleversement de l'économie contractuelle* (Bruylant 1986); Ewoud Hondius and Christoph Grigoleit (eds), *Unexpected Circumstances in European Contract Law* (CUP 2011); RA Momberg Uribe, *The Effect of a Change of Circumstances on the Binding Force of Contracts: Comparative Perspectives* (Intersentia 2011); Hein Kötz, *European Contract Law* (2nd edn, OUP 2017) ch 15; Gareth H Jones and Peter Schlechtriem, 'Breach of Contract and the Relevance of Fault' in *International Encyclopaedia of Comparative Law*, vol 7, 'Contracts in General' (K Zweigert and Ulrich Drobnig eds, Arthur T von Mehren vol ed, Brill 1999) paras 216–234.

I have attempted to cover a range of systems in Europe and in Asia. I am not able to read most of the languages, so that I have to rely on secondary sources in English. I am fortunate to be able to draw on two particularly useful sources. The first is the volume *Coronavirus and the Law in Europe*,[13] which contains reports from various jurisdictions in Europe. The second is the collection of papers in the fifth volume in the Studies in the Contract Laws of Asia series, *Changing and Ending Contracts*.[14] I want to acknowledge immediately how much I have taken from these two sources. I have also been helped by subsequent correspondence with a number of the contributors to the volumes and with other colleagues.[15]

II. Change of Circumstances: An Introduction

By no means all civil codes contain articles giving relief for change of circumstances, particularly those following the Napoleonic tradition, though France itself adopted the doctrine of *imprévision* when the Code civil (Cc) was reformed in 2016.[16] However, in a significant number of civilian jurisdictions scholarly legal writing has argued in favour of change of circumstances and the cases show the courts apply it or something similar.

This was the case with the first adoption of the civilian doctrine, at least in its modern form, in Germany.[17] There was no reference to change of circumstances in the German Civil Code, the *Bürgerliches Gesetzbuch* (BGB), as it was adopted in 1900. Windscheid[18] had promoted the doctrine of *Voraussetzung* (presupposition), which was derived from the ancient notion of *rebus sic stantibus*, that (broadly speaking) each party's will was conditional on the circumstances in which they would have to perform remaining broadly the same. The drafters of the BGB

[13] Hondius and others (n 11).

[14] Mindy Chen-Wishart, Dora Neo, and Stefan Vogenauer (eds), *Studies in the Contract Laws of Asia V: Changing and Ending Contracts* (OUP, forthcoming) ('*Changing and Ending Contracts*').

[15] I take sole responsibility for any errors or misunderstandings.

[16] Traditionally the French courts refused to make adjustments in light of changed circumstances (see the *Canal de Craponne* case, Cass civ 6 March 1876, D 1876.I.93) unless the contract was one to provide a public service. Public law contracts come under the jurisdiction of the *Conseil d'Etat*, which might adjust the contract in order to ensure that the service remained available. On this, see *Gaz de Bordeaux*, Conseil d'Etat, 30 March 1916, S 1916.III.17, and the discussion in Barry Nicholas, *The French Law of Contract* (2nd edn, Clarendon Press 1992) 209–10. However, occasionally the civil courts had held that good faith required the renegotiation of a contract, eg Cass civ (1) 16 March 2004, D 2004.1754, or even that a change might deprive the contract of *cause*: Cass com 29 June 2010 no 09-67369, unpublished.

[17] The development of the doctrine in Germany (before 1995) is explained in Werner Lorenz, 'Contract Modification as a Result of Change of Circumstances' in Jack Beatson and Daniel Friedmann (eds), *Good Faith and Fault in Contract Law* (OUP 1995) 357, and in somewhat more detail in Basil S Markesinis, Hannes Unberath, and Angus C Johnston, *The German Law of Contract* (2nd edn, Hart Publishing 2006) 320–33. This section of my chapter draws gratefully on these sources.

[18] Markesinis, Unberath, and Johnston (n 17) 321 refer to Bernhard Windscheid, *Die Lehre des römischen Rechts von der Voraussetzung* (Buddeus 1850) and Bernhard Windscheid, *Lehrbuch des Pandektenrechts*, II (Theodor Kipp ed, 8th edn, Rütten & Loening 1900).

omitted this idea on the ground that it would be wrong to allow one party to shift a contractual risk to the other.[19] But the *Reichsgericht* (RG), relying on the requirement of good faith set out in § 242 BGB, adopted the theory of *Geschäftsgrundlage* (basis of the transaction) put forward by Oertmann.[20] This differed from the previous theory in that a party's assumption must have been manifested during negotiations and acquiesced in by the other—'in essence, Oertmann had shifted from the hopes and expectations of the parties (stressed by [Windscheid]) to the obvious effects which the changed circumstances had had on the transaction.'[21]

The German courts first used this doctrine in cases arising from the period of economic turbulence following the First World War and again after the Second World War and after Reunification, but it was not brought into the BGB[22] until 2002. In the meantime, the doctrine had been adopted in many other jurisdictions, either in legislation[23] or by legal scholarship and case law.[24]

III. Change of Circumstances: An Outline of Current Doctrines

§ 313 BGB[25] may be taken as a classic version of the doctrine:

[19] Markesinis, Unberath, and Johnston (n 17) 321, who note also the (somewhat contradictory) argument that the court could imply a reservation of the right to terminate where this seemed just and equitable.

[20] Paul Oertmann, *Die Geschäftsgrundlage: Ein neuer Rechtsbegriff* (A Deichert 1921).

[21] Markesinis, Unberath, and Johnston (n 17) 322, who point out a number of difficulties that Oertmann's theory does not solve.

[22] §313 BGB. For the text of the article see text to n 27.

[23] For instance, Lithuania: art 6.204 Lithuanian Civil Code; The Netherlands: art 6:258 *Burgerlijk Wetboek* (BW); Hungary: art 6.192 Hungarian Civil Code; Italy: art 1467 Italian Civil Code; Greece: art 388 Greek Civil Code; Poland: art 357 Polish Civil Code, on which, see Aneta Wiewiórowska-Domagalaska, '"Corona Contract Law" in Poland: When Pandemic Meets Politics' in Hondius and others (n 11) 219, 233; Portugal: art 437 Portuguese Civil Code. Art 112 of the Slovenian Code of Obligations provides for rescission of the contract but not its amendment.

[24] For instance, Spain: see Carmen Jerez, María Kubica, and Albert Ruda, 'Force Majeure and Hardship in the Corona Crisis: Some Contract Law Reflections on ELI Principle no 13' in Hondius and others (n 11) 603, 606–07 and Antoni Rubi-Puig, 'Coronavirus' Impact on Broadcasting Rights for the Spanish Professional Football League' in Hondius and others (n 11) 627, 642–43 (describing the Supreme Court's decisions as 'pendulant'), and Hondius and Grigoleit (n 12) 126–33; Austria and Switzerland (seemingly referred to as *rebus sic stantibus* but the substance seems the same): see Andreas Furrer, Angelika Layr, and Jeremias Wartmann, 'Impossibility, Force Majeure and COVID-19 under Swiss and Austrian Contract Laws' in Hondius and others (n 11) 719, 737–39. Unusually for a civil law jurisdiction, Czech law does not recognize change of circumstances, though it does allow for termination if the purpose expressed in the contract is frustrated: Hondius and Grigoleit (n 12) 92–95. The Scandinavian systems do not recognize change of circumstances but have a doctrine of assumptions that may perform a similar function, see text to n 75.

[25] Other recent enactments of the doctrine are to be found in France in art 1195 Cc (2016) and in Belgium in art 5.74 of the new Belgian Civil Code (2023). In both systems earlier case law had shown some movement towards adoption of the doctrine; for France, see n 19, and for Belgium see text to n 84 and Denis M Philippe, 'The Impact of the Coronavirus Crisis on the Analysis and Drafting of Contract Clauses: Force Majeure, Hardship and Deferral of Obligations' in Hondius and others (n 11) 527, 547–48.

Interference with the basis of the transaction

(1) If circumstances that became the basis of a contract have undergone serious change since the contract was concluded and if the parties would not have concluded the contract or would have concluded it with different contents had they foreseen this change, then adaptation of the contract may be demanded to the extent that, taking account of all the circumstances of the specific case, in particular the contractual or statutory distribution of risk, one of the parties cannot reasonably be required to uphold the contract without alteration.
(2) It is equivalent to a change of circumstances if material conceptions that have become the basis of the contract are found to be incorrect.[26]
(3) If adaptation of the contract is not possible or if one party cannot reasonably be required to accept it, then the disadvantaged party may rescind the contract. In the case of continuing obligations, the right to terminate takes the place of the right of rescission.[27]

I will leave aside the question of remedies for the moment, merely noting that § 313 envisages either adaptation of the contract, if necessary by a court order, or its ending. Instead, I will concentrate on the requirements that must be satisfied for relief to be available. In article 6:111 of the PECL they are summarized thus:

(2) ... [P]erformance of the contract becomes excessively onerous[28] because of a change of circumstances, and

[26] I will leave aside § 313(2), as it concerns what common lawyers would call common mistake rather than changed circumstances. It reflects the fact that the courts in Germany and some other countries whose contract law is heavily influenced by the German model have applied change of circumstances to cases where the circumstances that have turned out to be very different to what was contemplated by the contract already existed at the time the contract was made, eg BGH, 13 November 1975, NJW 1976, 565: Beale and others (n 5) 554–58; Markesinis, Unberath, and Johnston (n 17) 346–48 and case no 105. To a common lawyer that would be a case of common mistake, but there are difficulties in applying the BGB's articles on mistake in this situation. § 119(2) BGB allows a party to avoid a contract that it has entered under a mistake as to 'such characteristics of a person or a thing as are regarded as essential in business dealings'; but the avoiding party must compensate the other party for its reliance loss unless the other party knew or ought to have known of the mistake, § 122 BGB. That does not seem a fair result in the case of a shared mistake.

[27] This and other translations of the BGB are taken from the German Federal Ministry of Justice website, <https://www.gesetze-im-internet.de/englisch_bgb/> accessed 15 December 2024.

[28] This includes where the performance will be less valuable to the creditor, not just where the cost of performance by the debtor has increased, see PECL art 6:111(1). It has been argued by Tom Hick, 'The Coronacrisis and Its Impact on Creditors: Frustration of Purpose' (2002) 30 European Review of Private Law 389 that art 1195 Cc, which refers only to performance becoming more onerous, is confined to cases in which the debtor's obligation has become more onerous, but Jean-Sébastien Borghetti, 'Non-performance and the Change of Circumstances under French Law' in Hondius and others (n 11) 509, 519 says that art 1195 Cc must be read in the same way as PECL Art 6:111. This must be right: the provision of the PECL, the UPICC and the DCFR all apply to both cases, and the reform

(a) the change of circumstances occurred after the time of conclusion of the contract,
(b) the possibility of a change of circumstances was not one which could reasonably have been taken into account at the time of conclusion of the contract, and
(c) the risk of the change of circumstances is not one which, according to the contract, the party affected should be required to bear.

This seems broadly to represent the position in the jurisdictions whose case law or legal scholarship recognize change of circumstances, not only in Europe[29] but in many other systems around the world.[30] What is stressed in many systems, however, is that this formula cannot be applied in a mechanical fashion: the detailed circumstances of each case must be considered.[31]

IV. Variety and Complexity in the Doctrine of Change of Circumstances

In national laws there are various complications and variations.

A. An extended notion of impossibility

A number of jurisdictions have treated changes that make it very much harder for one party to perform the contract as a form of impossibility, often referred to as

is seen as following those models: see eg François Ancel, Bénédicte Fauvarque-Cosson, and Juliette Gest, *Aux sources de la réforme du droit des contract* (Dalloz 2017) 176–77, at least in broad terms; see Bénédicte Fauvarque-Cosson, 'Does Review on the Ground of Imprévision Breach the Principle of the Binding Force of Contracts?' in John Cartwright and Simon Whittaker (eds), *The Code Napoleon Rewritten* (Hart Publishing 2017) 187–88. For further accounts of art 1195 Cc in English, see Catherine Pédamon and Radosveta Vassileva, 'Contractual Performance in Covid-19 Times: Does Anglo-French Legal History Repeat Itself?' (2021) 29(1) European Review of Private Law 3, 26–29; Solène Rowan, *The New French Law of Contract* (OUP 2022) 181–91.

[29] See eg The Netherlands: Harriët Schelhaas, 'The Decision of the German Bundesgerichtshof of 12 January 2022 on Lease and Corona from a Dutch Perspective' (2023) 31 European Review of Private Law 615, 622–23.

[30] For instance, in China, Indonesia, Japan, the Philippines, South Korea, Taiwan, and Vietnam; see respectively the following chapters in the forthcoming *Changing and Ending Contracts* (n 14): Lei Wang, 'Change of Circumstances in China's Civil Legislation and Judicial Practice'; Gary F Bell, 'Change of Circumstances in the Indonesian Law of Obligations'; Eriko Taoka, 'Ending and Changing Performance under Japanese Law'; Ma Ngina Teresa V Chan-Gonzaga, 'Revision of Contracts in the Philippines: The Ramifications of a Change of Circumstances'; Youngjoon Kwon, 'Change of Circumstances: Korea'; Tsung-fu Chen, 'The Doctrine of Change of Circumstances in Taiwanese Law'; Giang Nam Do, 'Change of Circumstances under Vietnamese Contract Law'.

[31] For an example, see the German BGH's approach to leases affected by Covid-19 restrictions (text to n 136).

economic impossibility. This was the approach first used by the German courts, when dealing with commodity shortages after the First World War: if, though literally possible, performance would be totally different—for example, a seller could only supply the material contracted for if it re-purchased goods it had already sold to another buyer—the *Reichsgericht* treated the case as one of practical impossibility.[32] They refused relief, in contrast, in 'tin' cases, when tin remained available in the market, though at a much higher price.[33] In Germany the economic impossibility approach has been superseded by change of circumstances, partly because of the difficulty in defining what should amount to economic impossibility[34] and partly because impossibility leads to the party affected being released from the contract, which was not always considered appropriate; it might be better to adjust the contract.[35] However, relief on the ground of economic impossibility still seems to be contemplated in some jurisdictions.[36]

Economic impossibility represents one side of the coin. The other is the buyer who, because of the change of circumstances, no longer has any use for the goods or services it has agreed to buy. In this case it seems that the German courts were less inclined to give relief before the introduction of change of circumstances, arguing that that the risk should fall on the buyer.[37] Under the newer doctrine a number of cases seem to have allowed it. An example is the 'drill hammers' case,[38] in which a buyer in West Berlin agreed that the seller would make and supply a large number of drill hammers, both parties knowing that the buyer intended to resell the hammers to mines in East Germany. That became impossible[39] because of the blockade of Berlin. The old-fashioned design of the drill hammers meant that there was no market for them in the West. The *Bundesgerichtshof* (BGH) granted the buyer some relief: it had to pay for the drills that had been manufactured to date but was released from any obligation in respect of the remainder. However, the notion that

[32] See eg RG 23 February 1904, RGZ 57, 116, described by Markesinis, Unberath, and Johnston (n 17) 326.

[33] See eg RG 21 March 1916, RGZ 88, 172, described in Markesinis, Unberath, and Johnston (n 17) 327.

[34] See Markesinis, Unberath, and Johnston (n 17) 327–28.

[35] See eg BGH 23 November 1951, JZ 1952, 145, cited, along with similar decisions, by Markesinis, Unberath, and Johnston (n 17) 332.

[36] See eg Austria: Hondius and Grigoleit (n 12) 65; Hungary: Attila Menyhárd, 'The Impacts of COVID-19 in Hungarian Contract Law' in Hondius and others (n 11) 759, 767. Borghetti (n 28) 516 cites a number of French cases before 2016 that seemed ready to take this approach, but argues that it should not be accepted.

[37] Markesinis, Unberath, and Johnston (n 17) 342. But see Menyhárd (n 36) 767, citing Hungarian SC Legf Bir Pfv VIII, 20.056/2007, sz 2007 no 370.

[38] BGH 16 January 1953, MDR 1953, 282. Translations of the case can be found in Markesinis, Unberath, and Johnston (n 17) case no 101, and in Beale and others (n 5) 1226. It seems to be doubted by Lorenz (n 17) 373, on the ground that the buyer should normally take the risk of not being able to use the goods.

[39] Or it may already have been impossible by the time the contract was made: the court held that the timing did not matter: see n 26.

a party may not rely on its own 'economic distress and lack of liquidity'[40] keeps resurfacing as a limit on the applicability of § 313 BGB.[41]

It is ironic that frustration of purpose is the one situation in which courts in the common law countries have given relief when the contract can still be performed in a literal sense but has become pointless. This is sometimes seized on by civilian commentators as showing that the English doctrine of frustration applies to cases in which a party's performance 'has now been rendered valueless by subsequent unexpected events'.[42] They do not always seem to grasp either the fragility of the doctrine, resting as it does almost entirely on the Coronation cases,[43] nor the fact that in *Krell v Henry*[44] the renter's purpose was not just known to the other party, it was shared by him.[45] The owner of the flat would not have wanted strangers in his flat for the days of the coronation (it was not a standard rental, as the nights were excluded) if there were no coronation taking place.[46] I cannot see an English court holding that the contract in the drill hammers case, for instance, had been frustrated.

B. Limits on type of cases

I have found two types of case which in some systems seem to be excluded from the application of the doctrine.[47] The first I have noted already: a party may not rely on its own economic distress and lack of liquidity.[48] This seems to be derived from doctrines of impossibility and force majeure, under which it was often said that

[40] Martin Schmidt-Kessel and Christina Möllnitz, 'Particular Corona Contract Law in Germany: Why Does General Contract Law not Suffice?' in Hondius and others (n 11) 699, 705.

[41] See text to n 52.

[42] Kötz (n 12) 279; see also ibid 285–87. To be fair, in the later discussion Kötz says that the purpose of the agreement must be known to both parties and the party relying on the doctrine must not have assumed the 'risk' of the purpose being frustrated (ibid 287). But I doubt that knowledge of a purpose suffices: see text to nn 43–46.

[43] See Hugh Beale (gen ed), *Chitty on Contracts* (35th edn, Sweet & Maxwell 2023) para 27-034; also Guenter Treitel, *Frustration and Force Majeure* (3rd edn, Sweet & Maxwell 2014) ch 7.

[44] [1903] 2 KB 740.

[45] Vaughan Williams LJ said: 'the taking place of those processions . . . was regarded by both contracting parties as the foundation of the contract' (ibid 750), and the procession was the basis of the contract 'as much for the lessor as the hirer' (ibid 751).

[46] This seems to be the best way of distinguishing the case from *Herne Bay Steamboat Co v Hutton* [1903] 2 KB 683. In the *Herne Bay* case (which was decided by the same three Lord Justices), the plaintiffs' steamboat was engaged by the defendant to take passengers from Herne Bay 'for the purpose of viewing the Naval Review at Spithead and for a day's cruise round the fleet'. The review was cancelled but the Court of Appeal held that the contract had not been frustrated: 'the purpose of Mr. Hutton, whether of seeing the naval review or of going round the fleet with a party of paying guests, does not lay the foundation of the contract within the authorities' (ibid 689).

[47] There may also be legislative exclusions. For example, art 1195 Cc does not apply to (broadly speaking) financial services contracts: art L211- 40-1 of the French Monetary and Financial Code.

[48] See text to n 52.

payment of money is never impossible.[49] Some commentators argue that the same exclusion applies to change of circumstances,[50] and the Supreme Court of Slovenia has refused relief in such a case.[51] If this limit applies, it seems to make the doctrine unbalanced: why should a seller who is having great difficulty in obtaining goods qualify for possible relief, but not a buyer who no longer has a market in which to resell the goods and therefore cannot pay for them? It is possible that the argument that a debtor cannot rely on its own lack of funds is linked to another argument that is commonly made, namely that the change of circumstances must be one that affects more than just the particular contractual relationship; it must affect the market generally.[52]

A second limit is less clear. Does the doctrine apply only when the excessive cost to one party is matched by a gain to the other, and therefore not if the change has not brought about any enrichment of the other party? We saw that one of the reasons for the German courts' shift from economic impossibility to change of circumstances was that it was thought more appropriate to adjust the contract than to terminate it;[53] and I understand that Oertmann and Krückmann argued that the doctrine should aim to reverse disproportionality between performance and counter-performance.[54] Many of the cases that confronted the German courts when hyperinflation struck after the First World War involved disproportion of this kind;[55] Markesinis describes this as the first of three main groups of cases.[56] Some commentators appear to suggest that disproportionality is an essential

[49] See Kötz (n 12) 245.

[50] Borghetti (n 28) 516 seems to regard the rule as limiting art 1195 Cc as well as art 1218 Cc; similarly Guido Alpa, 'Remarks on the Effects of the Pandemic on Long-term Contracts' in Hondius and others (n 11) 553, 562 (speaking about Italy), 'paying the amount in legal currency is never excessive onerousness'; Henrique S Antunes, 'Portugal's COVID-19 Legislation and the Challenges Raised for the Change of Circumstances Regime' in Hondius and others (n 11) 677, 682 (about Portugal); Maciej Zachariasiewicz, 'The Lease of Commercial Premises in Time of COVID-19: The Decision of the German Bundesgerichtshof of 12 January 2022 from a Polish Perspective' (2023) 31 European Review of Private Law 627, 638.

[51] Miha Juhart, 'Deferral of Payments under a Credit Agreement as an Extraordinary Measure Due to the Epidemic: A Slovenian Approach' in Hondius and others (n 11) 779, 781, citing decision III Ips 17/1993 of 7 April 1993.

[52] For example, Zachariasiewicz (n 50) 634.

[53] See text to n 35.

[54] Markesinis, Unberath, and Johnston (n 17) 328.

[55] For example, the highly controversial decision (at the time) of the *Reichsgericht*, RG 28 November 1923, RGZ 107,78 (translated in Markesinis, Unberath, and Johnston (n 17) case no 99), in which the defendant mortgagee refused to return the deeds of the land after the plaintiff had paid just the nominal amounts owed in *Reichsmark* (RM), which had depreciated tenfold between the date of the mortgage and the date for repayment (and which by 1923 had fallen from 4.2 to the US dollar in 1914 to 98m RM to the dollar: see Markesinis, Unberath, and Johnston (n 17) 329), so the repayment to the mortgagee would be almost worthless, while the land was (in nominal terms) worth much more than it had been. The court held that the principle of good faith embodied in § 242 BGB required that the debt be revalorized, good faith even overriding legislation of 1909 stating that paper RM were legal tender.

[56] Markesinis, Unberath, and Johnston (n 17) 325, the others being frustration of purpose and common mistake (on which see n 26).

ingredient.[57] If the doctrine is limited in this way, it would seem to exclude some of the cases in which the seller is having difficulty in obtaining supplies, as there may be no enrichment to a buyer who intends to use the goods itself. There would be a corresponding benefit, however, if the shortage of goods has caused their market price to go up and the buyer will be able to resell them for much more than would have been the case without the change of circumstances. It may well be that the court is far more likely to grant relief when the change has resulted in a disproportion, but I doubt many systems impose any formal limit of the kind I have described.[58] Recent decisions of the German BGH and of the Dutch Supreme Court (the *Hoge Raad*) show that there is no restriction of this kind in those systems. As we will see later,[59] they have held that relief from paying the full rent can be given when Covid-19 restrictions prevented a tenant from making use of the rented premises as intended, a situation which does not seem to involve any benefit to the landlord.[60] Rather, the question was when it is appropriate that the parties 'share the pain'.[61]

C. Variations in remedies

(i) Termination only

We saw earlier that one reason why the German RG abandoned the doctrine of economic impossibility in favour of the doctrine of change of circumstances was that termination of the contract (automatic if the contract had become wholly impossible; at the creditor's choice if it was partly impossible) was seen as less appropriate than adjustment of it, by the court if necessary, so as to preserve the contractual relationship if possible.[62] The BGB, the French Civil Code, and the PECL all allow for adjustment by the court if necessary. However, there are some

[57] For example, Antunes (n 50) 682, though arguing that this should not be the case; Letizia Coppo, 'The Impact of Pandemics on the Landlord–Tenant Relationship: An Italian Reading of the German Federal Court's Solution' (2023) 31 European Review of Private Law 601, 609–10.

[58] Scholars in Taiwan seem to have argued that 'the balance between the performance and the counter-performance [must lose] its adequacy to the parties'; but Chen (n 30) adds: 'That is, the disadvantaged party has to endure an extreme burden, while the other party has merely suffered slightly, and the equilibrium of the contract is affected unreasonably.' This may be only a requirement that the change has not hurt both parties, rather than one that the other party be gaining from the change. Certainly, any gain to the other party must be taken into account when fixing the amount of any adjustment to the contract: Supreme Court 103 Tai-shang No 983 Civil Judgment (2014), quoted ibid.

[59] See text to nn 128–139.

[60] Coppo (n 57) 609.

[61] See Schelhaas (n 29) 625.

[62] See text to n 35.

legislative provisions that only allow for termination.[63] Article 1467 of the Italian Civil Code provides:

> In contracts with continuous or periodical performance, or performance deferred to a later time, if extraordinary and unforeseeable events make one party's performance excessively onerous, that party may request the termination of the contract with the effects laid down in article 1458. Termination cannot be requested if the supervening onerousness falls within the normal sphere of contractual risk. The other party may avoid termination by offering to modify the terms of the contract equitably.[64]

So, if the other party offers a modification that the court thinks is equitable but the party having difficulty in performing does not accept the offer, the party in difficulty can no longer demand termination. As the court has no power to impose a modification, the contract will continue as it was. We will see that because of this the Italian Supreme Court seems to consider article 1467 of the Italian Civil Code to be of limited assistance.

(ii) Priority between remedies

A second difference is that systems which allow a choice between termination and adjustment give different priority as between the two remedies. Given the importance that German jurists have placed on restoring the equilibrium of the contract,[65] it is not surprising that § 313 BGB goes for adjustment as the primary remedy. § 313(3) BGB provides that the disadvantaged party may rescind[66] the contract only if adaptation of the contract is not possible, or if one party cannot reasonably be required to accept it. Article 6:111(3) of the PECL lists the courts'

[63] Another example is art 79 of the United Nations Convention on Contracts for the International Sale of Goods (CISG). With its reference to 'impediments beyond [a party's] control', this was evidently designed to deal with cases of force majeure, but the CISG Advisory Council has issued an Opinion stating that it also applies to cases of 'hardship', ie 'when a change of circumstances beyond the control of a party makes performance excessively onerous, if that party could not reasonably be expected to have taken the change into account or to have avoided or overcome it or its consequences': CISG Advisory Council, *Opinion no 20, Hardship under the CISG* (2–5 February 2020) rule 4. If the affected party does not perform, the other may avoid the contract; there is no duty to renegotiate, and a court or arbitrator may neither adjust the contract nor bring it to an end: ibid rules 11, 12 and 13. On art 79 CISG, see Sergio García Long, 'A Single Theory of Impediments under The CISG: A Latin-American Perspective' in Francesca Benatti, Sergio García Long, and Filippo Viglione (eds), *The Transnational Sales Contract: 40 Years of Influence of the CISG on National Jusrisdictions* (Kluwer 2022) 219.

[64] English translation prepared by the author and editors.

[65] See text to n 35.

[66] Rescission is the translation by the Federal Ministry of Justice (see n 27) of the German word *zurücktreten*. *Rücktritt*, termination of a contract not involving continuing obligations, may lead to the restitution of benefits received: see Markesinis, Unberath, and Johnston (n 17) 420. § 313(3) BGB states that in the case of continuing obligations (where restitution of benefits already received is not appropriate), the right to 'terminate' (a translation of *Küngdigung*—which literally translates as ending the contract for the future) takes the place of the right of rescission.

power to terminate the contract before its power to adjust it, but Comment D to the article states that 'the first aim should be to preserve the contract'. Other systems seem to consider termination to be the primary remedy.[67]

(iii) (Re-)negotiation

Third, there is the question of renegotiation. I suppose everyone hopes that when there has been a change of circumstances, the parties will be able to agree on a way forward. The BGB makes no reference to renegotiation, but some codes seem to be drafted so as to encourage it—see for example article 1195 of the revised French Civil Code:

> If a change of circumstances that was unforeseeable at the time of the conclusion of the contract renders performance excessively onerous for a party who had not accepted the risk of such a change, that party may ask the other contracting party to renegotiate the contract. The first party must continue to perform his obligations during renegotiation.
>
> In the case of refusal or the failure of renegotiations, the parties may agree to terminate the contract from the date and on the conditions which they determine, or by a common agreement ask the court to set about its adaptation. In the absence of an agreement within a reasonable time, the court may, on the request of a party, revise the contract or put an end to it, from a date and subject to such conditions as it shall determine.[68]

Article 6:111(3) of PECL goes so far as to impose a duty to negotiate, and provides that the court may award damages for the loss suffered when a party refuses to negotiate or breaks off negotiations contrary to good faith and fair dealing. Comment D adds that the court should employ any means permitted under national law, such as appointing a mediator to assist the parties. In the Draft Common Frame of Reference,[69] however, the duty became merely what German jurists call an *Obliegenheit*: it is a condition of being able to seek help from the court that 'the

[67] For instance, Vietnam: Do (n 30), citing art 420(3) of the Vietnamese Civil Code.

[68] Translation by John Cartwright, Bénédicte Fauvarque-Cosson, and Simon Whittaker, 'The new provisions of the Code civil created by Ordonnance no 2016-131 of 10 February 2016 and including revisions made to the text by Loi no 2018-287 of 20 April 2018 translated into English' <https://www.justice.gouv.fr/sites/default/files/migrations/textes/art_pix/Translationrevised2018final.pdf> accessed 4 February 2025. Whether the right to ask for renegotiation adds much may be questioned. Muriel Fabre-Magnan, *Droit des obligations*, vol 1 (7th edn, Themis 2024) para 786, remarks that 'there was no need to have a provision to tell us that' (translation by the author). Pédamon and Vassileva (n 28) 28 point out that if there is negotiation, it must be carried out in good faith under art 1104 Cc; but it does not seem that art 1195 Cc imposes a duty to negotiate in the first place.

[69] Christian von Bar and Eric Clive, *Principles, Definitions and Model Rules of European Private Law: Draft Common Frame of Reference* (Sellier 2009) (DCFR).

debtor has attempted, reasonably and in good faith, to achieve by negotiation a reasonable and equitable adjustment of the terms regulating the obligation'.[70]

D. Other legal bases for adjustment

We saw earlier[71] that the German author Windscheid first put forward a theory, based on the doctrine of *rebus sic stantibus*, that was called the theory of pre-supposition. This has found its way into Italian doctrine[72] and case law[73] and seems to provide an alternative approach, though I am told that it is difficult to find cases where the *presupposizione* is positively applied. Something very similar, however, is used in other legal systems. If the parties have agreed on a lease of land that the lessee intends to develop in a way that requires planning permission, though this purpose is not mentioned in the contract, and unexpectedly permission is refused, even in a common law system a court might be persuaded that the lease was conditional on permission being granted.[74] But the result of a failure of presupposition or condition will be failure of the contract rather than adjustment of it.

Danish and Swedish laws also have a doctrine that seems broadly similar, the doctrine of assumptions. This can apply to post-contractual changes that falsify the parties' assumptions as well as to cases of mistake. The remedy will be either termination of the contract or possibly adjustment (in Sweden only a reduction) of the price.[75]

A second alternative is to rely directly on the doctrine of good faith. We saw that in Germany the courts used § 242 BGB as the foundation on which to develop the doctrine of change of circumstances and good faith is also the basis used by courts in civilian systems which have not codified the doctrine. In Germany, however, the doctrine seems to have acquired a life of its own, detached from the doctrine of good faith, even before it was incorporated into the BGB (and § 313 BGB makes no explicit reference to good faith). In Italy the doctrine of change of circumstances is

[70] DCFR art III.-1:110(3)(d).

[71] See text to n 18.

[72] See Coppo (n 57) 610.

[73] Corte di cassazione, sez III, ordinanza no 19144, 23 September 2004. I am grateful to Luisa Antoniolli and Anna Veneziano for this information.

[74] Cf *Sheng Siong Supermarket Pte Ltd v Carilla Pte Ltd* [2011] 4 SLR 1094, though in that case the court held that the purpose was indicated in the contract, which was therefore conditional. Cf also the English cases of *Financings Ltd v Stimson* [1962] 1 WLR 1184 (offer to take car on hire purchase held to be conditional on car remaining in state in which seen by hirer); *HR & S Sainsbury Ltd v Street* [1972] 1 WLR 834 (sale of barley to be grown on seller's land held to be subject to implied condition that seller would be excused to extent that crop produced fell short of contract quantity).

[75] See Hondius and Grigoleit (n 12) 98–106, 112–14. In Denmark it seems that the courts more often deal with changed circumstances by holding that, in light of what has occurred, one or more of the terms of the contract is or are unreasonable and therefore invalid under s 36 of the Danish Contracts Act (Act No 600 of 8 September 1986 as amended by Act No 1098 of 21 December 1994, Act No 389 of 14 June 1995, and Act No 385 of 22 May 1996): ibid 115.

also codified in article 1467 of the Italian Civil Code,[76] but the Supreme Court, in detailed guidance on how courts should treat cases that were expected to arise after the Covid-19 pandemic, said that courts should not use article 1467 because it only gives rise to a right to terminate. Rather, they should rely on the doctrine of good faith, which looks to preservation of the relationship and may require the parties to negotiate; should the parties fail to agree, the court can make adjustments.[77] It seems that in Belgian law before enactment of the new Civil Code, good faith, and specifically the prohibition of abuse of rights, was used to prevent landlords claiming the full rent when a change of circumstances led to rented premises being closed.[78]

Lastly, many systems have particular provisions, pre-dating the pandemic, that in effect can be used to give some relief to a party who is facing difficulties because of a change of circumstances. For example, even before the adoption of a doctrine of change of circumstances in 2016, the French Civil Code gave the court the power to defer payments of sums due for up to two years, and to reduce any interest payable (though not to below the legal rate[79]), 'taking into account the situation of the debtor and the needs of the creditor'.[80] Others have provisions allowing for the adjustment of rent[81] or the price of construction work to be varied if circumstances change. For example, article 1664 of the Italian Civil Code provides:[82]

[76] See text to n 64.

[77] Corte di cassazione, *Relazione tematica no 56 del 2020—Novità normative sostanziali del diritto 'emergenziale' anti-Covid 19 in ambito contrattuale e concorsuale*, 8 July 2020 <https://www.cortedicassazione.it/it/rlc_dettaglio.page?contentId = RLC24205> accessed 18 December 2024. I am most grateful to Federico Pistelli for bringing this to my attention. Eugenia Dacoronia, 'Coronavirus and Its Impact on Contracts in Greece' in Hondius and others (n 11) 743, 751 argues that if the conditions for application of art 388 of the Greek Civil Code (change of circumstances) are not met, a Greek court can fall back on good faith (art 288) 'as an *ultimum refugium*'. In France, in contrast, the *Cour de cassation* has held that good faith does not require a party to renegotiate the contract when there has been a change of circumstances: Pédamon and Vassileva (n 28) 31, citing Cass com 19 June 2019 no 17-29.000, <https://www.legifrance.gouv.fr/juri/id/JURITEXT000038734034> accessed 20 January 2025.

[78] See Michaël de Potter de ten Broeck, 'The Covid-19-Pandemic and the Forced Closure of a Rented Premises: A Belgian Perspective on the Judgment of the Bundesgerichtshof of 12 January 2022' (2023) 31 European Review of Private Law 587, 597–99.

[79] The French government sets statutory rates of interest to be used to calculate interest on money owed to a creditor in the event of late payment of a judgment debt or a loan that does not state the annual percentage rate (*le taux annuel effectif global*), taking into account credit charges, etc: see <https://www.service-public.fr/particuliers/vosdroits/F20688> accessed 16 December 2024. There are two rates, a lower rate for professional creditors and a higher one for individual creditors not acting for professional purposes. See art L313-2 of the French Monetary and Financial Code.

[80] Art 1343-5 Cc. Maintenance payments are excepted. Art 1244 of the Belgian Civil Code is similar: see Philippe (n 25) 534. Cf 'time orders' under Consumer Credit Act 1974 s 129, which is much more limited in scope.

[81] For instance, Italy, art 1623 Italian Civil Code (when there is legislative or governmental interference); Taiwan, Taiwanese Civil Code, art 442 ('In case the thing leased is... real property, either party may apply to the court for an increase or reduction of its rental in proportion to the fluctuation of its value, unless the lease is made for a definite period') and art 457 ('The lessee of... agricultural land may demand... a reduction or release of the rental, if by reason of force majeure, the profits of the thing leased have decreased or totally failed'). Translation on Ministry of Justice website, https://law.moj.gov.tw/ENG/LawClass/LawAll.aspx?pcode = B0000001 (accessed 4 February 2025).

[82] English translation prepared by the author and editors.

> Where, as a result of unforeseeable circumstances, there have occurred increases or decreases in the cost of materials or labo[u]r, such as to result in an increase or decrease exceeding than one-tenth of the total agreed price, the contractor or the principal may request a revision of that price. The revision may be granted only for that difference exceeding one-tenth.
>
> If during the course of the work difficulties arise in the performance arising from geology, water and similar causes, not foreseen by the parties, which make the performance significantly more onerous for the contractor, the contractor shall be entitled to fair compensation.

E. Mandatory?

In some systems it is not possible for the parties to exclude the operation of change of circumstances. In the Netherlands, article 258 of the Civil Code is regarded as mandatory,[83] and in China the courts will not respect any attempt to exclude the doctrine (now embodied in article 533 of the Civil Code), because it is 'based on contractual justice and not contractual freedom'.[84] However, if the parties have agreed on a clause allowing for adaptation, that will be respected.[85] In contrast, in French law, although the doctrine is based on good faith and the duty of good faith itself is seen as mandatory,[86] the operation of the change of circumstances doctrine can be excluded by agreement,[87] and it is reported that French contracts frequently do so.[88]

F. Variations in readiness to apply the doctrine

Perhaps the greatest surprise was to find that courts in some systems appear much readier to apply the doctrine than do others. In Germany the doctrine is presented as coming into play only in exceptional cases.

> The doctrine of *pacta sunt servanda* requires that a subsequent change of the terms of a contract must be restricted to extreme cases.[89] . . . [W]hat is really

[83] Hondius and Grigoleit (n 12) 73.
[84] Wang (n 30).
[85] ibid.
[86] See art 1104(2) Cc.
[87] Olivier Deshayes, Thomas Génicon, and Yves-Marie Laithier, *Réforme du droits des contrats, de régime générale et de la preuve des obligations* (2nd edn, LexisNexis 2018) 440, citing preparatory works and the discussion in the Senate.
[88] Borghetti (n 28) 519. Cf the reaction to the Contracts (Rights of Third Parties) Act 1999, see Hugh Beale, 'A Review of the Contracts (Rights of Third Parties) Act 1999' in Andrew Burrows and Edwin Peel (eds), *Contract Formation and Parties* (OUP 2010) 225.
[89] Markesinis, Unberath, and Johnston (n 17) 325.

> required is such a fundamental and radical change in the relevant circumstances that it would be an intolerable result, quite inconsistent with law and justice, to hold the party to the contract.[90]

In the Netherlands the doctrine is so rarely applied that Hondius and Grigoleit felt Dutch law should be classified as a 'closed' system, in the same category as English law.[91] Cases from Taiwan present a marked contrast. Taiwanese law in this area was heavily influenced by German law (via Japanese law) and introduced a provision on change of circumstances in 1941[92] to deal with disputes arising out of the extreme fluctuation of commodity prices and inflation.[93] Although in principle a 'tremendous change' is required for the doctrine to be triggered,[94] the Taiwanese Supreme Court has applied change of circumstances to a construction contract when the government issued a ban on the collection of sand and rocks from rivers, which brought about a 50 per cent increase in the price of sand and rocks. The Supreme Court has indicated that the doctrine might apply when a construction contract unexpectedly delayed by 'the changed design of a bridge, the delay of acquiring the land for work, the delay of removing things and electronic poles on the site, and inhabitants' opposition=' took twice the expected time;[95] and similarly when a contractor was delayed for more than one thousand days by another contractor unexpectedly suspending work.[96] It seems unlikely that a German court would consider such changes to be sufficiently serious to trigger § 313 BGB.

We know that legal transplants often develop very differently in the host soil.[97] The interesting question now is why the particular differences occur. I think that differences with respect to the seriousness of the effects of the change that trigger the doctrine must be closely connected with variations in the idea of risk. § 313 BGB and German cases restrict change of circumstances to cases where what has happened is outside the risk that the complaining party is normally expected to bear; likewise, the Taiwanese Supreme Court says the effects of the change must

[90] ibid 337 (quoting BGH NJW 1959, 2203–4).

[91] Hondius and Grigoleit (n 12) 644.

[92] Article 20(2) of the Supplemental Rules of Civil Procedure 1941. See now art 227-2(1) Taiwanese Civil Code, which provides: 'If there is [a] change of circumstances which is not predictable then after the [conclusion] of the contract, and if the performance of the original obligation arising therefrom will become obviously unfair, the party may apply to the court [to] increas[e] or reduc[e] his payment, or alter[…] the original obligation.'

[93] Chen (n 30).

[94] ibid.

[95] Supreme Court 103 Tai-shang No. 1363 Civil Judgment (2014), cited and translated by Chen (n 30). I have not been able to find other translations of the decisions of the Supreme Court of Taiwan.

[96] Supreme Court 96 Tai-shang No. 482 Civil Judgment (2007), cited by Chen (n 30). On the other hand, courts in Taiwan seldom granted relief to business tenants who were having great difficulty in paying their rent because of restrictions imposed during the COVID-19 pandemic: see text preceding n 146.

[97] See for example Mindy Chen-Wishart, 'Legal Transplant of Undue Influence: Lost in Translation or a Working Misunderstanding?' (2013) 62 International and Comparative Law Quarterly 1, 1–3.

'go beyond the scope of risks that should be borne under the original outcome of a contract, taking into consideration the social-economic situations, common ideas and any other objective affairs'.[98] Yet the systems seem to reach very different results. One possible explanation is a different understanding of the kind of risk that a party to a particular type of contract is normally expected to bear. It would be interesting to compare typical (presumably standard form) construction contracts, and also actual contract practice, in the two jurisdictions, but I have not been able to do either.

There is another possibility—or perhaps it is an explanation for the different attitudes to risk—that is suggested by an account of scholarly opinion in Japan. Eriko Taoka points out that the concept of contract that lies behind the traditional reluctance to adjust the contract in changed circumstances is a 'static' one, and that some scholars take a different approach, according to which

> the concept of contract is no longer static, but rather fluid in the sense that 'contractual obligations are not finalized at the time of the formation of the contract, but rather changed and re-established through the parties' continuous negotiations'[99] even after the formation of the contract. Since a re-negotiation, as well as an amendment of a contract, is a process of re-defining the contractual obligations, the process is part of keeping a contract, or the principle of *pacta sunt servanda*. In consequence, the doctrine of changed circumstances becomes a rule facilitating the *pacta sunt servanda*, rather than an exception to it.[100]

Taoka links this to the idea of relational contracts, which 'also views the concept of contract as a fluid one[;] the doctrine of changed circumstances is viewed as a rule to support... *pacta sunt servanda*'.[101] To my mind, it might also be linked to the reportedly traditional approach of parties to contracts in Japan: that the contracts tend to be short, defining the rights of the parties in only broad terms and leaving

[98] Supreme Court 104 Tai-shang No. 2413 Civil Judgment (2015), as reported and translated by Chen (n 30).

[99] fn 75 in the text cites Kenji Yamamoto, 'Kēyakukōshōkankē no hōtekikōzō ni tsuite no ichikōsatsu [Some Thoughts on the Legal Structure of Contractual Negotiation] Part 1, (1989).

[100] Taoka (n 30), citing Kenji Yamamoto, 'Kēyakukōshōkankē no hōtekikōzō ni tsuite no ichikōsatsu (1) (2) (3)' ['Some Thoughts on the Legal Structure of Contractual Negotiation (1) (2) (3)'], Part 3, 100(5) Minshōhō zasshi 808, 809; Kazuhiko Matsui, 'Katē shikōteki hōsisutem to saikōshōgimu' ['The Process-oriented Legal System and the Obligation of Renegotiation'] (1996) 115(1) Hitotsubashi Review 250, 270–1; Tomohiro Yoshimasa, *Jijōhenkōhōri to Kēyakukihan* [*The Doctrine of Changed Circumstances and Rules on Contracts*] (Yūhikaku 2014) 74. Accordingly, this school of thought also attempts to substantiate the meanings of the duty of negotiation in order to prevent opportunistic behavior in the negotiation process (see Hiroyasu Ishikawa, '"Saikōshōgimu" ron no kōzō to sono rironteki kiso (2)' ['The Structure and Basis of the Doctrine of Renegotiation (2)'] (2001) 118(4) Journal of Jurisprudence Association 530; Osamu Morita, 'America ni okeru "saikōshōgimu" ron [Discussions on the Duty to Negotiate in American Law]' in Osamu Morita (ed), *Kēyakusekinin no hōgakuteki kōzō [The Legal Structure of Contractual Responsibilities]* (Yūhikaku 2006) 334; Yoshimasa (above) 171).

[101] Taoka (n 30), though she points out that this relaxed view is not the predominant one.

the rest to negotiation between the parties should a conflict arise, while parties to a contract are not seen as having conflicting interests but a mutually beneficial and co-operative relationship, one of mutual trust.[102] If that is, or at least was, the tradition in Japan, it would be very interesting to know whether it had any influence on Taiwanese attitudes and the approach its courts take to change of circumstances.

It would also be interesting to know whether the English judges who have argued for the recognition of a general duty of good faith in relational contracts[103] appreciate that it might lead to not only a doctrine of change of circumstances but a very soft version of it.

V. Covid-19 and Special Measures

To get anything like an accurate picture of how a legal system dealt with disputes that have arisen from the restrictions imposed on economic activities during the pandemic,[104] we have to look not only at general contract doctrine but also at the special measures that were adopted in the various systems—including those that do not recognize change of circumstances, as the special measures might produce results that are not very different from those that could be reached under that doctrine.

The special measures adopted to deal with disputes arising from the restrictions imposed to deal with Covid-19 vary in many respects. Rather than try to give an account of even a few schemes, I will look at just three variables: (1) the degree to which they overrode contract terms, rather than using other, 'non-contractual' mechanisms, (2) the kind of relief made available, and (3) the extent to which the systems attempted to provide balanced relief, so that the interests of both parties had to be considered.

In England and Wales,[105] a major part of the Government's effort went into prevention rather than cure—for example, the furlough scheme for employees and agency workers and a similar scheme for the self-employed. But when contracts were impacted there was relatively little direct interference with the terms of contracts, the main ones being to extend the minimum notice periods (set by statute)

[102] Hiroshi Oda, *Japanese Law* (4th edn, OUP 2021) 160–61, referring to works by Kawashima and Gray, and subsequent discussion by a number of authors. Oda himself seems doubtful that there is much difference between Japan and other countries in this respect (ibid).

[103] For example, *Al Nehayan v Kent* [2018] EWHC 333 (Comm) and *Bates v Post Office Ltd (No.3: Common Issues)* [2019] EWHC 606 (QB). On the English cases see Whittaker's detailed account in *Chitty on Contracts* (n 43) paras 2-071–2-110.

[104] Needless to say, this was not the first time that countries have passed special legislation to deal with the effects of major disruptions: see eg Lorenz (n 17) 359 and Pédamon and Vassileva (n 28) 9–11, referring to French legislation after each of the two World Wars. For special legislation in Italy see the references given by Alpa (n 50) 554.

[105] See Beale and Twigg-Flesner (n 11). For an account of the position in Scotland see Hector L MacQueen, '"Coronavirus Contract Law" in Scotland' in Hondius and others (n 11) 491.

for terminating residential tenancies.[106] Rather, changes were made to protect debtors in two principal ways. One was via civil procedure—the possession proceedings that have to be taken before a tenant can be evicted were suspended save in exceptional cases, and bailiffs were forbidden to execute debts.[107] The other was by changes in industry regulation of credit and other financial contracts (such as insurance) made with consumers. The Financial Conduct Authority relied on its power to require financial institutions to 'treat customers fairly' to insist, for example, that consumers whose ability to pay had been affected by the restrictions be given 'payment holidays' of up to three (and later six) months, unless the firm, '(acting reasonably)', determined that it was obviously not in the customers' interests to do so.[108] Applications for or grants of payment holidays were not to affect the consumer's credit record. But in nearly all cases, interest would continue to mount during the payment holiday. So on the second variable, the landlord's or creditor's rights were not reduced, they were merely postponed.

Other schemes, even in common law jurisdictions, involved potentially greater interference with contractual rights, especially under business-to-business (B2B) contracts. Singapore's COVID-19 (Temporary Measures) Act 2020,[109] which applied to a wide range of B2B contracts[110] made before 1 February 2020, prevented not only the commencement of court or arbitral proceedings and execution of distress, and so on, in relation to the contract but also the repossession of any hired goods or the termination or forfeiture of leases or licences of immoveable property for a prescribed period.[111] There were special provisions for, for example, the inability to perform construction contracts or supply contracts, giving relief against the forfeiture of performance bonds and liquidated damages clauses;[112] and interest charges were limited to the legal rate. To some extent, contract prices could be adjusted, for example the contractor could require the employer to pay additional 'foreign manpower salary' costs.[113]

It was by no means just the common law jurisdictions that introduced special measures: so too did many jurisdictions that already recognize change of circumstances.[114] For example, France, despite having recently adopted the doctrine of

[106] See Coronavirus Act 2020, sch 29. The periods were changed several times during the course of the pandemic.

[107] Initially under Practice Direction 51Z. For further details see Beale and Twigg-Flesner (n 11) 478.

[108] This was FCA, High Level Principle 6. Breach of a Principle did not give a person who had suffered loss as the result any right to compensation, but the offending firm could be disciplined and the FCA could require it to compensate those who had lost. The regulatory scheme has subsequently been changed: see *Chitty on Contracts* (n 43) ch 42.

[109] Act no 14 of 2020 (7 April 2020).

[110] ibid sch 1, para 1. The list includes, for example, construction and supply contracts.

[111] ibid s 5, especially s 5(3)(k), (l), and (m).

[112] ibid s 6.

[113] ibid ss 79A–K.

[114] Vanessa Mak, 'Covid-19 and Long-term Contracts' (2022) 30 European Review of Private Law 419, 424, responding to a suggestion by Pédamon and Vassileva (n 28) 7 that civil law jurisdictions

change of circumstances, also adopted special measures. These were different from the English measures in that they did affect the terms of contracts directly, but interestingly they did not go much further in terms of the kind of relief made available. Rights of termination and penalties for non-performance that would have arisen in certain periods of time were not enforceable, but payment obligations were not reduced.[115]

On the third variable, a feature of the relief given by the English and French measures, and also the Singaporean measures so far mentioned, is that it is essentially one-sided: the affected party gets relief irrespective of the other's interests. Where the affected party is a consumer and the other is a financial institution, that is understandable. In the Singapore Act, however, there is some attempt to balance the interests of the parties. Where a construction contract could not be completed within the extended time permitted, and as a result the contractor incurred 'prolongation costs', such as having to rent equipment or maintain insurance cover for longer,[116] the cost of so doing should be shared with the employer.[117]

Many of the measures adopted in systems that already recognized change of circumstances were also one-sided, for example giving tenants extra time to pay the rent[118] or suspending their repairing obligations. Commentators frequently noted this, arguing that the one-sided measures were justified by simplicity and the need to provide certainty as quickly as possible.[119] But some measures appeared to reflect in a rough-and-ready fashion the kind of adjustment that might be made under change of circumstances. Germany provides an interesting illustration.

In Germany[120] an Act of 27 March 2020 introduced a new Article 240, 'Contractual rules occasioned by the COVID-19 pandemic', into the Introductory Act to the German Civil Code.[121] Article 240 contained a number of measures. Some of these gave relief just to one party: for example, where tenants and lessees

tend to be more open to legislative intervention in contracts by temporary measures than common law systems, argues that government intervention in long-term contracts in England was more extensive than in the Netherlands. That might be expected, given that the courts in the Netherlands already had greater power to adjust contracts. But the detail into which Mak has to go demonstrates just how difficult it is to make generalized comparisons.

[115] Pédamon and Vassileva (n 28) 19–21.

[116] For 'qualifying costs' see s 39D(9) of Singapore's COVID-19 (Temporary Measures) Act 2020. Interestingly, any costs incurred in trying to accelerate the work are not included: ibid s 39D(9)(g).

[117] See ibid s 39D.

[118] For instance, Portugal: see Antunes (n 50) and Ana I Afonso, 'Obligation to Pay Rent for Commercial Premises During the Covid-19 Lockdown: The Portuguese Juridical System Solution' (2023) 31 European Review of Private Law 643.

[119] For instance, Antunes (n 50) 683, 690.

[120] This account is taken from Schmidt-Kessel and Möllnitz (n 40) 699–718.

[121] Act on Mitigation of the Consequences of the COVID-19 Pandemic in Civil, Insolvency and Criminal Proceedings, 27 March 2020, introducing art 240 into the *Einführungsgesetz zum Bürgerlichen Gesetzbuche* (hereafter, 'art 240'). The translation is available at <https://www.gesetze-im-internet.de/englisch_bgbeg/englisch_bgbeg.html#p0237> accessed 4 February 2025.

of real estate had been affected by Covid-19 restrictions, their contracts could not be terminated because of payments missed during April, May, and June 2020,[122] though article 240 did not relieve them from paying the rent or interest on rent arrears.[123] Other sections of article 240 adopted a kind of balancing approach. This can be seen in the case of long-term contracts under which a business had undertaken to supply a consumer or a micro-business (MB),[124] and in essential services such as compulsory insurance, gas, electricity, and telecommunications. If due to Covid-19 restrictions a consumer could not pay without endangering their own or their relatives' reasonable maintenance,[125] or if a MB would face an existential threat, a moratorium was imposed: the consumer or MB could refuse to perform while the other party's performance must continue. However, the supplier could object to the consumer's or MB's refusal if non-performance was unacceptable to it also. In that case the consumer or MB's only right was to terminate the contract. Similarly, for loan agreements and mortgages, Article 240 § 3 provided that if the debtor's loss of income due to Covid-19 made it unreasonable for the debtor to have to pay, interest was deferred and termination was excluded, and the creditor had to offer to negotiate an arrangement to help the debtor. If the creditor did not do so, or the parties failed to reach an agreement, the payment period would be extended by three months and the obligations under the agreement would be deferred by the same period. However, none of this applied

> if it is unreasonable to expect the lender to accept the deferral of payment or the preclusion of termination of the agreement after giving due consideration to all the circumstances of the individual case, including the changes to the general circumstances of life brought about by the COVID-19 pandemic.[126]

Thus, in Germany the special legislation to some extent followed the approach of general doctrine.

Why was it thought necessary to replicate general doctrine, rather than rely on change of circumstances? It may just have been thought desirable to give more precise guidance to businesses and consumers as to what they should expect, but another reason seems to be to fill a possible gap in the application of the change of circumstances doctrine. German lawyers sometimes state a version of the rule that we encountered earlier, that payment of money is always possible. So it is said that the 'dogma of unlimited liability with one's own assets' means that 'economic

[122] ibid art 240 §2.
[123] But §313 BGB might apply, see text to nn 129–139.
[124] As defined by the European Commission in Commission Recommendation of 6 May 2003 concerning the definition of micro, small and medium-sized enterprises, C(2003) 1422, OJ L 124, 20.5.2003, p. 36: fewer than 10 employees, and an annual turnover not exceeding €2m.
[125] By reference to the basic needs set out in the Sozialgesetzbuch (SGB).
[126] ibid art 240 § 3(6).

distress and lack of liquidity are only rarely accepted as relevant circumstances'[127] under change of circumstances. Relief against the effects of the Covid-19 restrictions was evidently not intended to be limited in that way.

VI. Change of Circumstances and Covid-19 Measures

Most authors in *Coronavirus and the Law in Europe* from systems that recognize change of circumstances or a similar doctrine appeared to expect the general law to continue to apply and to be used to deal with the fallout from Covid-19. In Germany, for instance, the general law continued to apply except insofar as the new article 240 of the Introductory Act solved the issue or the remedies under the BGB (eg termination for an important reason, § 314 BGB) would be inconsistent with the specific provisions of article 240.[128] So though termination by the landlord is prohibited, adjustment seemed possible. To make this clear the legislator later added article 240 § 7(1),[129] which states that:

> Where, as a consequence of government measures to combat the COVID-19 pandemic, leased land or leased premises which are not residential premises cannot be used for the tenant's operations or only with significant restrictions, the presumption is made that a circumstance within the meaning of section 313 (1) of the Civil Code which became the basis of the rental contract has significantly changed since the contract was entered into.[130]

There have been at least ninety-seven decisions on § 7,[131] and so it seems that in Germany change of circumstances is being used to deal with pandemic cases. What I do not know is with what success. In one of the early decisions, before the adoption of § 7, the tenant of premises used as a fashion store which had been closed by order argued that the rent should be reduced under § 313 BGB.[132] The claim failed but interestingly, one commentator[133] says that normally the court would have allocated the loss 50–50 between landlord and tenant, though in the individual circumstances, which must always be taken into account when applying

[127] Schmidt-Kessel and Möllnitz (n 40) 705.
[128] ibid 710.
[129] With effect from 31 December 2020.
[130] Act on Mitigation, art 240 § 7(1).
[131] I am grateful to Martin Schmidt-Kessel for this information (email of 4 September 2023).
[132] Munich Regional Court I, 22 September 2020, case no 3 O 4495/20.
[133] Christian Lonquich, Lars Reubekeul, and Coletta Braun, 'Update in Commercial Tenancy Law Once again, the Regional Court of Munich I (Landgericht München I) rules against a commercial tenant's claim to adjust the contract' (DLA Piper, 17 February 2021) <https://www.lexology.com/library/detail.aspx?g = 0e54d1f7-226e-4a8c-ba8a-8213fa6d8a6f> accessed 18 December 2024).

change of circumstances, the court ruled that the tenant could obtain certain advantages through ownership, such as storage possibilities or remodelling work, and so refused to make a reduction. A different comment of 3 March 2021 says that most courts, while admitting that in principle adjustment under § 313 BGB is possible, are refusing to make an adjustment on the ground that 'in a lease, the tenant basically bears the risk of all operational circumstances, i.e. in particular risk to exercise its right to use the rented premises while the landlord is subject to an obligation to grant use'[134]—just the argument that has appeared in the English cases in which tenants have tried to argue that closure of cinemas frustrated the leases.[135] However, subsequently the BGH[136] ruled not only that § 313 BGB applies to this kind of case in principle, but also that there is, and in light of article 240 § 7 continues to be, a rebuttable presumption that the Covid-19 restrictions have changed the circumstances of the contract: there is no reason to believe that the lessee had assumed the sole risk of use were their retail business to be shut down owing to the pandemic, unless there are provisions in the contract showing otherwise.

In this situation, should the pain be shared equally? The approach taken by the lower court in the case (the Dresden Higher Regional Court), and also by the Dutch *Hoge Raad* in a similar case,[137] was to reduce the rent by 50 per cent. That has the merit of predictability,[138] but the BGH considered it to be too simple. The individual circumstances must be considered, for example whether the tenant has received payments from insurance or government support schemes, and so the BGH remitted the case to the Dresden Court.[139]

It is clear that in other jurisdictions it was expected that the courts would have to apply change of circumstances or similar doctrines to deal with the effects of

[134] 'The COVID-19 pandemic and commercial rent' (*Noerr*, 3 March 2021) <https://www.noerr.com/en/insights/the-covid-19-pandemic-and-commercial-rent> accessed 18 December 2024, with references, including to one case that went the other way. The authors said they awaited decisions of the higher courts.

[135] *Bank of New York Mellon (International) Ltd v Cine-UK Ltd* [2022] EWCA Civ 1021.

[136] BGH 12 January 2022, no XII ZR 8/21. See 'Covid-19: Germany's Federal Court of Justice recognizes claim to rent adjustment upon closure of business due to the coronavirus' (*Gleiss Lutz*, 14 January 2022) <https://www.gleisslutz.com/en/rent_adjustment_upon_closure_of_business_due_to_the_coronavirus.html> accessed 18 December 2024; 'Comment on judgement no. XII ZR 8/21 of the German Federal Court of Justice on the obligation to pay rent in the event of a COVID-19 related shop closure' (*Dwf*, 24 January 2022) <https://dwfgroup.com/en/news-and-insights/insights/2022/1/german-federal-court-of-justice-on-the-obligation-to-pay-rent-in-the-event-of-a-corona-shop-closure> accessed 18 December 2024; Olaf Mayer, 'Obligation to Pay Rent for Commercial Premises During the Covid-19 Lockdown: The German Federal Court of Justice on the Distribution of Risk Between Tenants and Landlords' (2023) 31 European Review of Private Law 577. The case is also commented on from the point of view of Belgian law (see n 78).

[137] Hoge Raad, 24 December 2021, ECLI:NL:HR:2021:1974, see Schelhaas (n 29) 621. In the Netherlands, the exact reduction may be adjusted in light of business turnover and government support received: see Mak (n 114) 432–33. The 50–50 approach was also taken by some lower courts in Poland: Zachariasiewicz (n 50) 640.

[138] Mayer (n 136) 585.

[139] BGH 12 January 20 (n 136).

the Covid-19 restrictions. The Italian Supreme Court issued detailed guidance which suggested that the provision of the Civil Code on change of circumstances, article 1467, was not appropriate because the only remedy available is termination of the contract;[140] instead the courts should adjust contracts under the doctrine of good faith. But in an interesting contrast to what seems to be happening in Germany, I am told that not many Italian courts have dealt with cases arising from Covid-19. A few have held that in the changed circumstances, not just of the lockdown but of the post-lockdown economic uncertainty, good faith means the party affected is entitled to have the terms renegotiated,[141] but others have refused.[142] My colleague Federico Pistelli has pointed out[143] that the Grand Chamber of the Supreme Court (Sezioni Unite) has given a decision[144] that, though not related to Covid-19, goes in the second direction. The case involved rent indexed to the Swiss franc. As a consequence of changes in exchange rates caused by the financial crisis, the lessee had to face an increase in cost of more than double. The Supreme Court concluded that the parties are free to determine the content of their agreement and that the court should not intervene to redistribute the losses and gains of an economic arrangement when it is the result of a freely expressed contractual autonomy of the parties. This suggests that despite the guidance issued earlier, in practice the Italian courts are not ready to hold that good faith requires the renegotiation or adjustment of contracts.

Given that in other contexts the courts in Taiwan seem fairly ready to give relief for change of circumstances, for example when a change has affected construction contracts,[145] I was surprised to learn that while there have been nineteen District Court cases in which tenants have sought relief from paying rent, only two tenants were successful. In the other cases relief was denied on one of a number of grounds: that a reduction of the tenant's income for a couple of months was not outside the normal risk taken by the tenant; that having to perform its original obligations was not obviously unfair to the tenant, either because the tenant did not suffer large losses or because the lessor did not gain any benefits arising from the pandemic; or that a two-month interruption was not severe enough; or that there

[140] See text to n 64.

[141] Tribunale di Roma, sez VI, ordinanza, 27 August 2020. Similarly, though not connected to Covid-19, Tribunale Ordinario di Arezzo, 1137/2022, 22 June 2022 held that a contract to provide refrigerated storage should be adjusted in light of the enormous and seemingly long-lasting increase in energy prices. In one case the Tribunal of Milan reduced a tenant's rent by 50% by an analogical application of special measures that gave relief to gyms, swimming pools, and sports centres owned by individuals. Coppo (n 57) 612 notes that this cannot be accepted as a general principle. She argues instead that where the premises could only be used for limited purposes the case should be treated as one of partial impossibility and the rent reduced on that basis (ibid 611–12).

[142] Tribunale di Roma 12, sez VI, sentenza, 12 January 2021.

[143] Email of 15 April 2024 to the author.

[144] Corte di cassazione, Sezioni Unite, 23 February 2023 no 5657, Foro italiano, I, 2023, 1070 ff.

[145] See text to nn 95 and 96.

was no benefit to the lessor.[146] Perhaps the seemingly different approach in the two types of cases is because judges have different ideas of what risks are 'normal' in various kinds of contract. Possibly it merely reflects the fact that businesses in Taiwan were less seriously affected than businesses in many countries in Europe. Whatever the true explanation, the treatment of the effects of the pandemic seems to demonstrate just how hard it is to compare the actual application of apparently similar doctrines in different jurisdictions.

VII. 'Rebalancing' in England and Wales

The special measures in England and Wales that I described earlier are evidently limited, amounting to little more than giving parties extra time to perform and restricting termination of contracts where that required a court order. I have also described the measures as being one-sided: they do not seem to require any balancing of the parties' respective interests. On paper, however, there have been exceptions.

First, in response to the Covid-19 crisis the Government tried to encourage negotiation. It published a *Code of Practice for Commercial Property Relationships During the COVID-19 Pandemic* that stated:

> [I]t is in the interests of both landlords and tenants to do everything reasonable to enable otherwise viable businesses to continue operating through the period of recovery. This means that landlords and tenants must work together collaboratively and many will want to find temporary, and where possible sustainable, arrangements outside of the existing letter of their leases in order to create a shared recovery plan. The aim of this code is to facilitate those discussions by communicating best practice and presenting a unified approach.[147]

In similar vein, in early May 2020 the Cabinet Office issued *Guidance on responsible contractual behaviour in the performance and enforcement of contracts impacted by the COVID-19 emergency.*[148] In this document the government exhorted all individuals and businesses 'to act responsibly and fairly in the national interest in performing and enforcing their contracts'[149] where these are affected by the Covid-19 pandemic. In particular, the contracting parties should be 'reasonable

[146] Chen (n 30). On the question of benefit to the other party, see n 58.

[147] Department for Levelling Up, Housing and Communities and Local Government, *Code of Practice for Commercial Property Relationships During the COVID-19 Pandemic*, para 2, available at https://www.gov.uk/government/publications/code-of-practice-for-the-commercial-property-sector/code-of-practice-for-commercial-property-relationships-during-the-covid-19-pandemic (accessed 4 February 2025).

[148] Cabinet Office, 'Guidance on responsible contractual behaviour in the performance and enforcement of contracts impacted by the Covid-19 emergency' (7 May 2020).

[149] ibid para 3.

and proportionate in responding to performance issues and enforcing contracts', which entails 'acting in a spirit of cooperation and aiming to achieve practical, just and equitable contractual outcomes having regard to the impact on the other party'.[150] This guidance has no legal force, nor indeed any basis in law, and it is in obvious conflict with the general philosophy of English contract law. While parties in a commercial relationship always have the flexibility to depart from their strict contractual obligations in the interests of their commercial relationship, such a decision needs to be weighed up against each party's wider interests and obligations to others (such as shareholders). This may explain the rather dismissive reactions to the document in blogs from law firms and barristers' chambers.[151]

Both documents strike me as ambivalent, because while encouraging negotiation they seem to indicate that there should be no overriding of contractual rights. As the *Code of Practice for Commercial Property Relationships* continued,

> [t]he legal position is that tenants are liable for covenants and payment obligations under the lease, unless this is renegotiated by agreement with landlords. Tenants who are in a position to pay in full should do so.

Contractual rights could be overridden, however, under the Commercial Rent (Coronavirus) Act 2022. This statute aimed to provide relief to business tenants who because of the restrictions had accumulated rent arrears in the period from 21 March 2020 to 18 July 2021. A temporary moratorium was imposed on enforcement proceedings[152] and each party should make a proposal as to how to deal with the arrears. Ultimately an arbitrator could make an award as to how much the tenant should pay, in order to preserve (or where the tenant's business will only be viable if relief is granted, to restore and preserve) the viability of the business of the tenant, so far as that is consistent with preserving the landlord's solvency.[153] For a common law jurisdiction this seems extraordinary. It is reported, however, that there has been very little take-up of the scheme: 'the Act operated within very

[150] ibid para 14.

[151] See eg Charles Samek, 'Freedom of contract: Does it still exist?' (*Littleton*, 11 May 2020) <https://littletonchambers.com/articles-webinars/freedom-of-contract-does-it-still-exist/> accessed 18 December 2024; Katherine Calder and Mark Richard, 'Play fair children!—UK Cabinet Office publishes contract management guidance entreating all parties to act "reasonably" in managing Covid-19 issues' (*JDSupra*, 15 May 2020) <https://www.jdsupra.com/legalnews/play-fair-children-uk-cabinet-office-30763/> accessed 18 December 2024; Fern Schofield, 'Play nicely, children': Cabinet Office guidance on responsible contractual behaviour during the pandemic' (*Falcon Chambers*, 13 May 2020) <https://www.falcon-chambers.com/publications/articles/play-nicely-children-cabinet-office-guidance-on-responsible-contractual-beh> accessed 18 December 2024; 'UK Government publishes guidance on "responsible contractual behaviour" applicable to all contracts impacted by COVID-19' (Norton Rose Fulbright, May 2020) <https://www.nortonrosefulbright.com/de-de/wissen/publications/0a264bcc/uk-government-publishes-guidance-on-responsible-contractual-behaviour-applicable#2> accessed 18 December 2024.

[152] Commercial Rent (Coronavirus) Act 2022, s 23; likewise on insolvency proceedings, ibid s 25.

[153] ibid s 15.

narrow limits because of the limited period of time for which it applied (it only operated between 24 March 2022 and 23 September 2022) and because its requirements were not easy for a tenant to satisfy.'[154]

VIII. Conclusion

The number of jurisdictions that one might consider and the diversity of rules and of approaches within the doctrine of change of circumstances, let alone the diversity within the special measures taken to deal with the effects of restrictions imposed during the pandemic, make it hard to draw general conclusions, but a few points emerge from this brief study.

In terms of general contract doctrine, there is an obvious divide between at least the traditional common law systems, which with one or two possible exceptions[155] do not give relief for change of circumstances, and the civil law systems, most of which now recognize change of circumstances in some form or other. However, where relief for change of circumstances is accepted, there is much less uniformity than I had blithely assumed. A doctrine that clearly reflects its German ancestry[156] may be enshrined in the Civil Code or other legislation or, with varying degrees of certainty, in doctrine and case law, but other notions are sometimes employed to reach similar results. One is economic impossibility;[157] others, the doctrine of shared assumption[158] or simply the general notion of good faith.[159] Even in jurisdictions in which the doctrine is in the civil code, the courts may fall back on the doctrine of good faith in order to provide more flexibility with respect to remedies. Where the doctrine is clearly recognized, there are significant differences in the remedies available.[160]

It also seems that the doctrine does not always work in the same way in the jurisdictions from which it was transplanted as it does in the new hosts. In particular, some jurisdictions seem to require a significantly less serious change of circumstances than does Germany, from where the doctrine originated.[161] This difference seems closely connected to different understandings of the risks that one party or the other should normally bear—indeed, risk and the degree of change required to trigger the doctrine may just be opposite sides of the same coin.

There are important limits on the doctrine of change of circumstances, especially the attitude (or rule?) that payment of money is always possible and/or lack

[154] *Chitty on Contracts* (n 43) para 27-017.
[155] Frustration of the contractual purpose, see text to nn 42–46, and implied conditions, see n 74.
[156] See text following n 20.
[157] See text following n 35.
[158] See text preceding n 75.
[159] See text preceding n 76.
[160] See text following n 61.
[161] See text following n 94.

of resources is never a reason for adjustment.[162] This may be one reason why special measures were thought to be necessary even in jurisdictions where change of circumstances is recognized.

As to dealing with problems that arose as a result of the pandemic, in jurisdictions that recognize change of circumstances in one form or another there have certainly been attempts to obtain the adjustment of contracts via that route; and in Germany the BGH has laid down guidance that seems to give some tenants a good chance of obtaining a reduction.[163] But even in many of these jurisdictions, special measures were also adopted, just as they were in the common law systems of England and Singapore.

The special measures vary greatly, even within common law countries, and employ a variety of mechanisms.[164] My broad impression is that for the most part they had the effect of giving parties affected by Covid-19 restrictions extra time in which to pay, and meanwhile preventing the other party from terminating the contract or taking similar steps. In some cases there was more interference, for example by stopping the accrual of rent or allowing tenants not to carry out repairs, and so on. Many of these special measures were one-sided, in that they gave relief to one party without considering the interests of the other party.[165] The main exception to this that I found was in Germany, when the courts were called on to find a balance between the two parties' interests, not only in cases decided under § 313 BGB but in a rough-and-ready way under some of the special measures.[166]

Despite the absence of any tradition of contract adjustment in the common law, in England and Wales something like it was tried in respect of commercial leases.[167] But there seems to have been little take-up. Why might that be? Possibly landlords, whatever their lawyers may have thought, decided that it was better to make some concession voluntarily, so that the tenant stayed and the landlord got the practical benefit of 'avoiding a void',[168] rather than risk pushing the tenant into insolvency, which might mean the arrears would never be recovered anyway. It may turn out at the end of the day that the impact of Covid-19 does not provide a good test-bed for the doctrine of change of circumstances, because the restrictions may have been a

[162] See text following n 52.
[163] See text to n 136.
[164] See text following n 104.
[165] See text following n 115.
[166] See text following n 119.
[167] Commercial Rent (Coronavirus) Act 2022: text following n 152. It strikes me as odd that the government provided the possibility of compulsory relief for commercial tenants who could not pay but, for residential tenants whose landlords would not agree to a rent reduction, merely put off the day on which the tenant might be evicted. Perhaps the thinking was that residential tenants would never be able to pay off the arrears, so the landlord would in effect have to suffer a reduction in rent. But a former tenant with significant rent arrears outstanding will often be barred from bidding for social housing and will find it very hard to get new accommodation in the private sector.
[168] cf *MWB Business Exchange Centres Ltd v Rock Advertising Ltd* [2016] EWCA Civ 553.

sharp but too short a shock. Either one party will have become insolvent, in which case the doctrine becomes irrelevant, or the parties will have renegotiated their contract in the hope of keeping their commercial relationship going.[169]

This project also reinforced some lessons about comparative study that were far from new but are worth mentioning: for example, that you should not look at any doctrine in isolation, but must look at the interplay of (often many) doctrines in a given system; that transplants develop a life of their own; and that words and phrases may be false friends that do not mean the same thing in different systems.

Most of all I was struck yet again by the difficulty of getting into the mindset of judges and lawyers from other jurisdictions, for example as to what risks parties are expected to bear. I do not believe this to be impossible, but it requires skill and a great deal of effort. Simon Whittaker's work is a wonderful example of what can be achieved by the right person. I hope that his 'retirement' gives him the opportunity and the incentive to do more, not less, comparative work.

[169] See also Menyhárd (n 36) 777, who suggests that parties prefer renegotiation to unpredictable judicial decision-making.

PART II
TORT LAW

7
Violation of a Right and Tort Law

Dorota Leczykiewicz

In recent years, we have witnessed an intense debate in English legal scholarship about the importance and role of rights in private law, in particular in tort law.[1] One group of English tort scholars considers violation of a right a necessary, and sometimes sufficient in itself, basis of liability in tort.[2] The other group disputes this view as a convincing interpretation of the law and argues that liability in tort is multi-faceted.[3] This second group thinks that tort law scholarship, instead of focusing on grand theories, should focus on the exact ways in which judges are developing the common law.[4] In response, the argument of English rights scholars is that a rights-based account not only better fits the existing 'tort law material' but is also superior prescriptively.[5] English rights scholars argue that locating rights at the centre of tort law increases the intelligibility of the scheme and its coherence, and, prospectively, leads to a shared identity for all torts.[6] Infusing tort law with rights-based thinking offers English law the opportunity to move beyond the historical boundaries of particular tortious causes of action, and to rationalize English tort law alongside moral principles.[7] The other side relies on moral arguments too. By emphasizing the collective and forward-looking dimension of tort law, they

[1] Robert Stevens, *Torts and Rights* (OUP 2007); Donal Nolan, 'Rights, Damage and Loss' (2017) 37 Oxford Journal of Legal Studies 255; Donal Nolan and Andrew Robertson (eds), *Rights and Private Law* (Hart Publishing 2014).

[2] Stevens (n 1).

[3] Andrew Burrows, 'Damages and Rights' in Nolan and Robertson (n 1) 275, 291.

[4] Jane Stapleton, *Three Essays on Tort* (OUP 2021) 2.

[5] The 'tort law material' used for the purpose of this 'fit' argument tends to be exclusively tort-law case law, ie common-law tort law, rather than also statutory tort law. See Stevens (n 1) 3 or Allan Beever, *Rediscovering the Law of Negligence* (Hart Publishing 2007) 21.

[6] Stevens (n 1) vii; Beever (n 4) 30 specifically about the law of negligence.

[7] In the English legal system, the task of rationalizing tort law, largely a judicial creation, falls on judges. As a result, academic discussion of the rationalization project focuses not only on substantive questions but also on the source from which judges should derive the principles of tort law constituting its rationalization. Morality tends to occupy the centre ground for English rights scholars. For example, Stevens claims that rights 'sourced in judicial decisions' are 'moral rights' and that the only rights that can be made by judges are those 'derived from moral rights'. Stevens (n 1) 330 and 331. Beever, in a similar vein, insists that tort law should be concerned with a conception of interpersonal wrongdoing encapsulated by Immanuel Kant in his *Metaphysics of Morals* (1797). Allan Beever, *A Theory of Tort Liability* (Hart Publishing 2016) 19.

Dorota Leczykiewicz, *Violation of a Right and Tort Law* In: *Comparative Reflections in Private Law*. Edited by: Marco Cappelletti, Ciara Kennefick, and Dorota Leczykiewicz, Oxford University Press. © Marco Cappelletti, Ciara Kennefick, and Dorota Leczykiewicz 2026. DOI: 10.1093/9780198959168.003.0009

criticize the scholarly focus on rights, which in their view gives 'the ideology' of individual freedom excessive prominence.[8]

Inspired by this recent debate in English private law scholarship, this chapter conducts a comparative inquiry into the role played by violation of a right in German, English, and French tort law. As a work in comparative law, the chapter draws on the methodology exemplified by many of Simon Whittaker's publications, in which the conceptual analysis is accompanied by the historical and the contextual. As Simon Whittaker has usefully outlined in his opus magnum, *Liability for Products*:[9]

> [The] enterprise [of comparative law] is essentially concerned with an attempt at understanding the way in which lawyers in other legal systems see legal questions, attempt to resolve them, deal with the resolution of disputes, and relate legal questions to other types of questions (political, economic or social).[10]

The chapter demonstrates that I share Simon Whittaker's conviction that it is useful to survey broad areas but keep the different fields of law distinct.[11] For this reason, the survey in the present chapter will extend only to those liability regimes which are considered to form part of tort law. Secondly, like Simon Whittaker, I am interested in the lawyer's way of asking questions, which is why the chapter will focus on the choices made by legislators and judges in the three jurisdictions under examination, and, as far as English law is concerned, on the scholarly attempts at reframing these questions by reference to rights.

Finally, while I appreciate that there is a link between the legal systems' choice in using or not using rights in tort law and its political, economic, and social context, in the chapter I focus primarily on what could be described as 'legal institutions', that is, distinctive and structured sets of legal norms, such as individual torts (tortious causes of action) in English law or particular codified bases of non-contractual liability in German and French law, and the networks of concepts, principles, and definitions in which they function.[12] The inquiry thus concerns

[8] Peter Cane, *The Anatomy of Tort Law* (Hart Publishing 1997) 17–18. See also Peter Cane, 'Rights in Private Law' in Nolan and Robertson (n 1) 35, 40 (at fn 20) and 48.

[9] Simon Whittaker, *Liability for Products: English Law, French Law, and European Harmonization* (OUP 2005).

[10] ibid 2–3.

[11] In *Liability for Products* (ibid), Simon Whittaker is keeping categories distinct and discusses separately private, public, and criminal law, and within private law, its different areas; in French law delictual liability, the law of sale, and the law on the provision of services; and in English law the tort of negligence, the law of sale, and the law governing private and public services (Whittaker (n 9) ix–xiv). On the importance of taxonomy in law, see Emily Sherwin, 'Legal Taxonomy' (2009) 15 Legal Theory 25.

[12] On the institutional approach to law, see Joseph Raz, *The Concept of a Legal System: An Introduction to the Theory of Legal System* (OUP 1970) ch 8; Neil MacCormick, *Institutions of Law: An Essay in Legal Theory* (OUP 2007) 13.

the question of whether the institutional networks constituting general tort law[13] in the three jurisdictions include violation of a right in three distinct but possibly related ways: as a shared element offering a unifying feature for all or some instances of tort liability, as a doctrinal justification for the imposition of liability, and as a rhetorical device allowing judges to introduce normative distinctions on what would be perceived as principled or properly legal grounds.

One difficulty which my inquiry is facing is its reliance on the concept of right, whose meaning is generally acknowledged to be system-relative.[14] The methodological approach proposed in the chapter has two elements, terminological and substantive. The English word 'right' has some common roots with German 'Recht' and historically manifested the same duality as that term and the French term 'droit', both of which still mean a body of law, as well as an individual right.[15] More substantively, we can rely on works of scholars who have tried to establish if Roman law included the concept of 'right'.[16] While conclusions of these scholars have diverged or even clashed, their works can provide us with a series of objective criteria that allow us to detect 'rights' whatever the language of the legal system under examination. On this basis, we can arrive at a neutral definition of 'right' as an abstract individual entitlement granted to a person, which is not tied to a specific legal relation or a remedial (procedural) mechanism for enforcement, and is generally an expression of an individualistic philosophy or the idea of personhood presupposing that individuals can possess rights inherently and not merely because of their status or relationships.[17] So, unlike Lawson, I do not propose to

[13] The concept of 'general tort law' refers to those areas within the law of non-contractual liability for harm which constitute the default rules, and which tend to be more open-ended and flexible in their remit, and thus amenable to judicial calibration. Given the level of judicial discretion which tends to arise in the context of general tort law, the need for normative justification for the adopted distinctions is particularly pressing. The term 'bases of liability' is used as a neutral term that intends to incorporate both 'causes of action', as used in English legal parlance, and the various civil code provisions under which non-contractual liability for harm can be imposed in civilian legal systems.

[14] Geoffrey Samuel, '"*Le Droit Subjectif*" and English Law' (1987) 46 Cambridge Law Journal 264. On the difficulty of using Roman law's term *ius* as the common denominator of European legal traditions, see J Finnis, *Natural Law and Natural Rights* (Clarendon Press 1980) 206–09, and Richard Tuck, *Natural Rights Theories: Their Origin and Development* (CUP 2012) 5–31.

[15] Albert Kiralfy, 'Law and Right in English Legal History' (1985) 6 Journal of Legal History 49, 53 and 57. Kiralfy's focus is on the historical usage of 'right' as referring to 'law in general', as contrasted with 'law' understood in a more positivistic sense as statutes and other exercises of law-making authority, but the author also explains why English law has restricted the word 'right' to the notion of 'individual rights based on law' (ibid 57–59).

[16] Tuck (n 14) 7–8. Michel Villey, *Le droit et les droits de l'homme* (PUF 1983) and 'L'idée du droit subjectif et les systèmes juridiques romains', Revue historique de droit français et étranger 1946–7, Quatrième série, vol 24, 201; Giovanni Pugliese, '"Res corporales", "res incorporales" e il problema del diritto soggettivo' in *Studi in onore di Vincenzo Arangio-Ruiz nel XLV anno del suo insegnamento. Volume III* (Jovene 1953) 301.

[17] As Kurki has observed, for 'rights' to emerge, the legal system has first to arrive at the idea of personhood (a human being as a rights-holder) and then sharpen its understanding of right as a legal concept, as a personal entitlement rather than a demand of justice (what is right). In the last step, the theory of right has to be selected as either a 'sphere of external freedom' (referring to Kant) or a protected interest as determined by positive law. Visa AJ Kurki, *A Theory of Legal Personhood* (OUP 2019) ch 1.

focus on interest protection alone,[18] even if consensus exists among most tort law systems that interest protection is one of their explicit or implicit goals.[19] Instead, I discuss those instances of using the concept of right which engage the idea of an individual entitlement. The differences among the three legal systems in which I will be interested concern not just the presence or absence of a 'rights discourse' but also how they are understood. Indeed, rights relevant in tort law can be considered to be either claim-rights themselves and thus directly correlated with duties, or normative positions giving rise to claim-rights. There is also the issue of how general the duty that tort law rights in a given jurisdiction impose is, and, in consequence, when rights will be regarded as 'violated'. What this means is that I will not discriminate between the conception of rights as bundles of entitlements, that is, general rights, and the conception of rights as specific demands. I will be interested in both types of instances of using the concept of right. As long as 'rights' are observed to constitute more than just 'superstructural' elements[20] or a mere inference from the fact that a remedy is available in such and such circumstances,[21] their presence in their respective tort laws will be of relevance to my study.

I. The Three Functions of Rights in Tort Law: Structural, Doctrinal, and Rhetorical

Within this broad framework I intend to examine the role of violation of a right in the three tort laws. I propose to look at the issue through the lens of three potential functions of right violations: structural, doctrinal, and rhetorical.

A legal system will be regarded as assigning a *structural* function to violation of a right if that concept is used to organize the entirety or the default part of its tort law. To establish a structural tendency, the chapter will investigate, first, whether

[18] Frederick H Lawson, '"Das subjektive Recht" in the English Law of Torts' in *Many Laws. Selected Essays*, vol 1 (North-Holland 1977) 176, 183.

[19] James Gordley, 'The Architecture of the Common and Civil Law of Torts: An Historical Survey' in Mauro Bussani and Anthony J Sebok (eds), *Comparative Tort Law. Global Perspectives* (Edward Elgar Publishing 2015) 173, 177; Cees van Dam, *European Tort Law* (2nd edn, OUP 2013) ch 7.

[20] 'Superstructural' rights are rights which are included within a scheme, but which are not in any clear way connected to the imposition of liability, ie they do not function as rights to which courts give enforcement through a tort remedy. See Peter Birks, 'Obligations: One Tier or Two?' in PG Stein and ADE Lewis (eds), *Studies in Justinian's Institutes: in Memory of J. A. C. Thomas* (Sweet & Maxwell 1983) 18; Helge Dedek, 'Of Rights Superstructural, Inchoate and Triangular: The Role of Rights in Blackstone's Commentaries' in Nolan and Robertson (n 1) 183, 195.

[21] Thus, I am interested more in the *ubi ius, ibi remedium* than the *ubi remedium, ibi ius* perspective. Unlike some scholars, I do not think that focusing on the *ubi ius, ibi remedium* perspective begs the question as far as English law is concerned because the view that English law follows the logic of *ubi remedium, ibi ius* does not take account of such factors as the doctrine of precedent, the principle of the incremental judicial development of law, and the binding force of common law principles. Cf Patrick O'Callaghan, 'Reversing *Ubi Remedium Ibi Jus* in the Common Law: The Right of Privacy' (2007) 5 European Review of Private Law 659.

in a given jurisdiction there is a pull towards unity in tort law and whether that unity finds its expression through rights. A legal system will be regarded as ascribing a *doctrinal* function to violation of a right if it is using that concept to limit or expand liability for 'pure negligence';[22] to justify strict liability; to devise the criteria regulating recovery of certain types of harm, such as pure economic loss or emotional distress; or to enable substantive damages without (proof of) loss.[23] Finally, the legal system will be regarded as using violation of a right for *rhetorical* purposes[24] where its judges refer to rights when drawing distinctions which have moral and political undertones and which would otherwise have to be made by reference to substantive, including policy, arguments.[25] In systems where substantive reasoning is not acceptable judicial behaviour, 'rights' can be a way of conducting an equivalent normative inquiry without the reasoning overtly leaving the realm of 'pure' law.[26] Judicial justification has the capacity either to perpetuate or to challenge the accepted modes of legal argumentation.[27] In the face of a regimented approach towards substantive arguments, the introduction of a new entitlement or the decision to circumscribe an existing one frequently forces judges to look for formalistic ways to express their reasons. The language of rights can be a useful tool in that regard because of its perceived alignment with orthodox canons of argumentation.

[22] I am using the term liability for 'pure negligence' to indicate a type of liability where the sanctioned misconduct is not defined by reference to any statutory framework, either because there are no relevant statutes or, if there are, they do not participate in designating the misconduct as 'negligence'.

[23] Throughout the chapter, I use the term 'loss' to refer to a situation where the claimant is worse off, financially or otherwise, ie their situation is worse than it would be had the tort not been committed, whether or not the law allows recovery for every instance of such loss. In contrast, I use the term 'harm' in a more neutral sense as indicating any perceived detriment for which the claimant seeks recovery, whether or not objectively in their situation we can actually speak of their being worse off. The term 'damage', on the other hand, will be reserved for references to a legal requirement, ie where 'damage' is one of the formal criteria of liability.

[24] I am using the term 'rhetorical' in the meaning proposed by MacCormick, where 'rhetoric' is understood as 'the study of good and bad arguments . . . with reference to the "Rule of Law"'. 'Rhetorical' arguments are defined by MacCormick as, on the one hand, persuasive and, on the other, as sound in the light of 'sources of law', which here do not include 'ideology extraneous to law'. Neil MacCormick, *Rhetoric and the Rule of Law* (OUP 2005) 7, 19–20 and 23.

[25] Robert S Summers, 'Two Types of Substantive Reasons: The Core of a Theory of Common-Law Justification' (1978) 63 Cornell Law Review 707. On the definition of policy, see Neil MacCormick, *Legal Reasoning and Legal Theory* (OUP 1978) 263: 'those courses of action adopted by Courts as securing or tending to secure states of affairs conceived as desirable'. According to MacCormick, '[a] "policy argument" for a given decision is an argument which shows that to decide the case in *this* way will tend to secure a desirable state of affairs' (ibid, emphasis in the original text).

[26] There is an ongoing debate in different legal traditions, including English law, as to whether non-formal arguments, such as policy or moral arguments, belong in the realm of law, especially private law. Arguments that leave the realm of 'pure law' are not only those that reveal judges' political involvement but all those that cannot be described as 'authority' reasons. See, for example, Jenny Steele, 'Scepticism and the Law of Negligence' (1993) 52 Cambridge Law Journal 437. For the discussion of 'authority reasons', see Summers (n 25) 724.

[27] John Bell, 'The Acceptability of Legal Arguments' in Neil MacCormick and Peter Birks (eds), *The Legal Mind: Essays for Tony Honoré* (OUP 1986) 45.

II. The Centrality of Rights in German Tort Law

The comparative literature frequently makes us believe that rights are the central feature of German tort law.[28] If we ask the *structural* question of whether violation of a right gives German tort law conceptual unity, the answer will have to be negative. German tort law has three general bases of liability, not one. Only the first of them, § 823(1) BGB, positions violation of a right as a necessary element of tort liability. The other two, § 823(2) BGB (liability for breach of a statute with protective effect) and § 826 BGB (liability for intentional harm caused by breaching good morals), focus on other elements and do not require a finding of a right violation. German scholars often look at this structure through the concept of unlawfulness (*Rechtswidrigkeit*), observing that the three provisions use three different notions of unlawfulness, the first concerning violation of a right, the second violation of a statute, and the third violation of unwritten normative standards ('good morals').[29]

And yet, the impression persists that it is § 823(1) BGB which is the default provision. This impression is reflective of legal reality. When we look at § 823(2) BGB, we can see that it presupposes the existence of a statute whose purpose is to protect the claimant (as a member of a class).[30] 'Fault' (*Verschulden*) is still required for liability, on top of a breach of a statute, but mere negligence (breach of a duty of conduct) does not suffice unless the statute which has been violated imposes a duty of conduct identical with the negligence duty.[31] The proliferation of statutory regulation in the twentieth century has made this basis of tort liability much broader and enabled the overall expansion of protected interests, including by offering greater protection to purely economic interests. However, it has not removed the gatekeeping function of the statutory footprint—liability under § 823(2) BGB can be imposed only where there is a statute which covers the subject matter. § 826 BGB,

[28] See, for example, van Dam (n 19) 167.

[29] Nils Jansen, 'Developing Legal Doctrine: Fault in the German Law of Delict' in Nils Jansen (ed), *The Development and Making of Legal Doctrine* (CUP 2010) 96, 115–17. The role of *Rechtswidrigkeit* in German tort law has historically been to emphasize the position that 'damage as such was not enough to establish unlawfulness of an act'. Patrick Mosler, 'The Discussion on General Clause or Numerus Clausus During the Preparation of German Civil Code' in Eltjo JH Schrage (ed), *Negligence: The Comparative Legal History of the Law of Torts* (Duncker & Humblot 2001) 361, 369. The decision of the First Commission working on the draft of the BGB to link liability to violation of another's right and define rights positively was intended to produce 'a system where liability [was] the consequence of acts rendered unlawful elsewhere in the legal system as encroachments on rights, violations of statutory provisions, and illoyal conduct' (ibid 377).

[30] Basil S Markesinis, John Bell, and André Janssen, *Markesinis's German Law of Torts* (Hart Publishing 2019) 74.

[31] In German law, duties the breach of which establishes negligence are 'duties of conduct' (*Verhaltenspflichten*) and refer to the standard of reasonable care. They are sometimes translated into English as 'duties of care' because like the English concept of duty of care in the tort of negligence, they refer to the idea of reasonable behaviour in the circumstances of a particular situation. Statutory duties may use the form of 'duties of conduct' but can also use other forms, such as prescribing exactly the conduct which should be followed or prescribing a defined course of action. Markesinis, Bell, and Janssen (n 30) 55–56.

on the other hand, is restricted by its insistence that intention to cause harm, as well as violation of good morals, needs to be shown before liability is established.[32] For these reasons, it is § 823(1) BGB that has emerged as the most general (ie the most open-ended) basis of tort liability in German law. And that provision demands that violation of a right be established before liability can be imposed. Some violations are enumerated (of the right to life, bodily integrity, health, freedom, property), but others can be added by judges because the provision refers to 'other rights'.[33]

The wording of § 823(1) BGB explains why the *doctrinal* function of right violations is present in German tort law. The key observation here is that under § 823(1) BGB, harm can be recovered only if it stems from an interference with an entitlement that has been described as a 'right'.[34] So what needs to be identified is not just an 'interest' or 'benefit' that deserves protection. In fact, as will be discussed further below, recovery for pure economic loss runs exactly along the line between a non-right economic interest (which can be protected elsewhere in the law but is not capable of giving rise to a remedy under § 823(1) BGB) and 'rights' recognized under § 823(1) BGB, whose violation entitles the claimant to a remedy under this provision (I will call these latter interests 'tort law rights'). Similarly, non-physical personal injury is compensated under § 823(1) BGB if classified as a violation of a right to health ('injury to health') but, in principle, not otherwise, even though in all instances a victim of emotional distress undoubtedly has an interest in their emotional well-being.[35] Yet, because some forms of distress fall outside the 'injury to health' concept, ie do not constitute a right violation, they will not be recoverable unless one of the exceptions applies. What this means is that, as an expression

[32] 'Anyone who intentionally causes harm to another person in a manner that violates good morals is obliged to repair that harm' (author's own translation). 'Obliged to repair harm' is here used instead of 'obliged to compensate' because the latter suggests a single form of redress (a monetary award calculated by reference to the value of the loss), while German law knows also another form of redress, namely *Herstellung*, which entails restoration of the original position. For more on this point, see text to n 50.

[33] § 823(1) BGB: 'Anyone who intentionally or negligently unlawfully injures the life, body, health, freedom, property or any other right of another person is obliged to repair any resulting loss' (author's own translation, see also n 32).

[34] This has been confirmed in the case law of the highest German courts, the Reichsgericht (RG) and the Bundesgerichtshof (BGH), many times. The earliest judgment dates to the beginning of the twentieth century: RG 27 February 1904, RGZ 58, 29, where liability for unauthorized copying of the claimant's carpet patterns was made conditional on whether it was covered by 'another right' under § 823(1) BGB. The RG held that protection from having one's carpet patterns copied was available under § 823(1) BGB if it was covered by the right to 'an existing independent commercial activity', whose existence was thereby recognized. Because the right to 'an existing independent commercial activity' was found to be, at least in part, a freedom right, it could be recognized to be one of the 'other rights' under § 823(1) BGB. Markesinis, Bell, and Janssen (n 30) 38–40 refer to this right as 'the right to an established and operating business'. In my view, a better term is 'the right to an existing independent commercial activity', which is why I use it in the present chapter.

[35] This is reinforced by § 253(1) BGB, according to which 'damage' other than pecuniary as a category is not recoverable unless it falls within one of the explicitly mentioned exceptions. These exceptions concern situations where recovery is granted for an injury to the body, health, freedom, or sexual self-determination (§ 253(2) BGB).

of their doctrinal function, in German law, rights violations delineate the outer limits of tort liability.[36]

The discretion to identify additional rights whose violation gives rise to liability in negligence has been used by German courts sparingly. The key question is the criteria which a right relevant under § 823(1) BGB needs to meet. It turns out that it cannot be just any right, that is, anything that German law would be prepared to call a right (*Recht*), or more correctly a 'subjective right' (*ein Subjektives Recht*). Only certain subjective rights will qualify. Unlike in English law,[37] one criterion German subjective rights do *not* need to meet is their 'private law' character. While German law knows the distinction between private and public subjective rights,[38] that distinction is not key in identifying rights which are relevant for liability in private law.[39] What seems to matter is whether the right that contends to be a 'tort law right' is an erga omnes right, that is, enforceable against everyone (against the whole world), sometimes confusingly called 'an absolute right'.[40] The prevailing theory of such rights is the 'freedom from' theory (as an offshoot of the will theory of rights) rather than an interest theory.[41] For example, a company's property right includes the entitlement not to have the cost of repair of its power line increased by making access to it more difficult, but it does not include the right to have the most convenient access.[42] The former is a 'freedom from' entitlement (freedom from excessive difficulty and cost), while the latter could only be conceptualized as a right under the interest theory of rights (the company has an interest in the most

[36] Nils Jansen, *The Structure of Tort Law* (Sandy Steel tr, OUP 2021) 341. As the author explains, this has not always been the German understanding. Originally, the view that every tort required violation of a right, held by the Pandectists, was not understood doctrinally (as a reason for imposing tort liability) but merely conceptually (as an abstract definition).

[37] Discussed at text to n 93.

[38] The latter are called *subjektive öffentliche Rechte* and have been traditionally described as rights arising from public law relationships, which are in turn defined as relationships in which at least one party is a public body, or more precisely, a bearer of public authority. Lutz Richter, 'Das subjektive öffentliche Recht', Archiv des öffentlichen Rechts 47 (1925), 1 (3). In practice, the public law character of subjective rights is established by reference to the legal text that recognizes them because the totality of 'objective law' from which subjective rights emerge is itself divided into public and private law.

[39] For example, the right to personality is a constitutional right that has been recognized as protected under § 823(1) BGB. BGH 15 November 1994, VI ZR 56/94, NJW 1995, 861 (*Caroline von Monaco I*). Hein Kötz and Gerhard Wagner, *Deliktsrecht* (Vahlen 2017) 173.

[40] The absolute character of a right does not refer to its content or unlimited character but the question against whom it can be invoked, at least in its negative dimension, that is, in so far as it imposes a duty to refrain from certain action. Thus, in German law, an absolute right is a right which obliges everyone to refrain from conduct that interferes with that right. This is why it is described as 'an area of personal sovereignty'. See Jansen (n 36) 343.

[41] On the distinction between the will theory and the interest theory of rights, see for example, George W Rainbolt 'Rights: Interest and Will Theories' in Mortimer Sellers and Stephan Kirste (eds), *Encyclopedia of the Philosophy of Law and Social Philosophy* (Springer 2023) 3109. These days, subjective rights in German law are generally understood as legitimate interests but, as Jansen (n 36), 353 and 367 explains, in the realm of tort law they have retained their more traditional meaning, as areas of personal sovereignty (see n 40), ie spheres of individual freedom where the individual is protected from interference, even though it is recognized that precisely which liberties an individual enjoys is a consequence of allocative decisions taken by courts.

[42] BGH, 5 June 1990, VI ZR 359/89, NJW-RR 1990, 1172, at 1173.

convenient access to the power line). It thus follows that under the German doctrine of tort law rights, only the former (freedom form excessive difficulty and cost) can be recognized as protected by §823(1) BGB.

The absolute or erga omnes character of 'tort law rights' explains also why in German law breach of contractual rights cannot form the basis of tort liability unless they are subsumed, in selected cases, into the concept of 'property' or the right to 'an existing independent commercial activity'.[43] For example, the right to receive electricity is a contractual right, which means that loss suffered by a business due to interruptions in supply resulting from damage to the power line belonging to another party is not recoverable under § 823(1) BGB.[44] However, where the lost profit can be connected with the business' property and 'existing independent commercial activity', such as profit lost due to boycotts and unlawful competition from other operators, it becomes recoverable. Because the right to an existing independent commercial activity has been held to include the right to maintain a relationship with existing suppliers and the right to existing customers, an act which interferes with these entitlements constitutes a 'violation of a right' for the purpose of § 823(1) BGB.[45] Lost profit is also recoverable if it stems from copyright or patents, or, in the case of boycotts, if it can be linked to a property right, for example, in a situation where the boycott prevented customers from entering the business' premises.[46]

The other doctrinal function, that of justifying strict liability, is not visible in German tort law because of its restrictive attitude towards strict liability, which can only be introduced by a statute explicitly introducing such a form of liability. However, it has been argued by Jansen that stricter liability is imposed not only by statute in German law but also by 'objectivizing' the negligence standard.[47] In his opinion, such a transformation is only permissible where violation of a right is the basis of liability. The normative idea seems to be that without violation of a right, subjective fault would be required to impose liability because in that case it would be the behaviour of the defendant, not the harm suffered by the claimant, which would (morally) ground liability. This is reflected in the structure of German tort law, where the objective standard of care (and thus objectivized negligence) under § 823(1) BGB can be contrasted with § 826 BGB, where the focus remains on the defendant's subjective state of mind.[48]

[43] See n 34.

[44] BGH, 9 December 1958, VI ZR 199/57, *Stromkabel-decision*, NJW 1959, 479.

[45] Ibid.

[46] ibid. Confusingly, German case law uses the distinction between 'direct' and 'indirect' interference with the right to an existing independent commercial activity to determine which losses are covered under this concept and which are not. As the BGH admitted (ibid), the distinction is unclear; it is not intended to be expressive of causal relationships, but instead it is a shorthand way of signalling that not all losses suffered by a business will be seen as flowing from the violation of the right in question.

[47] Nils Jansen, 'Duties and Rights in Negligence: A Comparative and Historical Perspective on the European Law of Extracontractual Liability' (2004) 24 Oxford Journal of Legal Studies 443.

[48] Seemingly, the same observation cannot be made about § 823(1) and (2) BGB. § 823(2) does not make liability dependent on violation of a right and yet, it does not require subjective fault. While the

The *rhetorical* dimension of rights violations is not as prominent as the doctrinal effect but is detectable in German law. As a reminder, what we are looking for is how judges justify their decisions where policy issues are at stake. In German law, this is particularly the case where a judge is departing from what could be described as 'default rules', that is, rules that apply unless a judge deviates from them in the context of a particular case. For example, in German law, it is a rule that (consequential) loss needs to be shown before a tort award can be made.[49] Here, we have to be mindful of the distinction which German law makes between 'restoring' what has been harmed and 'compensating' for the harm. Duties of repair (including to pay the cost of repair) are regarded as restorative, they are 'reparation in kind' (*Herstellung*), which needs to be ensured 'in full'.[50] According to § 249(1) BGB, '[a] person who is under a duty to repair must create the situation that would exist if the circumstance giving rise to a duty to repair had not occurred'.[51] No limits are imposed on the award made as *Herstellung*. In particular, loss is not the measure of the award, although the cost of repair or replacement, which in English law would be regarded as the claimant's 'loss', will determine the level of the defendant's expense as part of the *Herstellung*.[52]

The 'restorative' mode of recovery does not erase the wording of § 823(1) BGB, which clearly requires loss as well as violation of a right. And thus, we can inquire what rhetorical devices have been used in German tort law to justify recovery for harm without loss (sometimes referred to as *injuria sine damno*). For example, German law denies the existence of loss if the ensuing harm is not quantifiable.[53] Such a situation arises in the so-called 'loss of use' cases.[54] And what we find here is

provision mentions 'fault' as a positive requirement, the case law has reversed the burden of proof of fault under § 823(2) BGB with the effect that violation of a protective statute is prima facie sufficient to establish liability. However, the absence of subjective fault does have an exonerating effect under § 823(2) BGB. See Markesinis, Bell, and Janssen (n 30) 73.

[49] § 823(1) BGB requires violation of a right, as well as 'loss' resulting from that right violation (*Schaden*).

[50] I have translated the type of obligation which § 249(1) BGB imposes as 'restoration' or 'reparation in kind', and not 'restitution in kind', to avoid a misclassification of this remedy as a restitutionary remedy, although in some situations the remedy may have such an effect. The idea of *Herstellung* makes reference to '*restitutio in integrum*', ie restoring (creating) the situation that would exist without the tort. According to § 252 BGB, lost profits, which are recoverable only as consequential losses, can be recovered if foreseeable and incurred even where mitigating steps had been taken. Consequential losses, unlike losses flowing directly from a violation of a right, can fall outside of the scope of the duty whose violation constitutes negligence. Markesinis, Bell, and Janssen (n 30) 203–04.

[51] Author's own translation. See also n 32.

[52] Markesinis, Bell, and Janssen (n 30) 201.

[53] Gert Brüggemeier, *Common Principles of Tort Law: A Pre-statement of Law* (BIICL 2004) 201.

[54] 'Loss of use' is the customary way of referring to cases in which the central factual circumstance is the fact that through the defendant's conduct, the claimant has been prevented from using their property or lost access to it for a period of time, primarily where the item of property in question was not used for generating profit or was not intended to be used for this purpose during the relevant time. The harm is not 'quantifiable' because what the court would have to assess is the value to the claimant of the possibility of using the item and not the value of using the item. Physical damage to the item also generates a 'loss of use' type of harm but because there is physical interference with the material substance of the item, the claimant can easily show loss by pointing to the repair or replacement costs. Where the

reliance on rights as a way of explaining why substantive compensation needs to be awarded. As the *Bundesgerichtshof* (BGH) has held in relation to the right of ownership, that is, a property right:

> According to the established case law of the Federal Court of Justice, the violation of [the right of] ownership of an item can occur not only through an impairment of the material substance, but also through other actual interaction with the item itself that affects the owner's powers and which objectively prevents its use . . . This can be assumed, for example, if a vehicle temporarily loses its ability to move, thereby being deprived of its function—e.g. as a means of transport—and deprived of its intended use.[55]

In other contexts, German tort law has developed the doctrine of 'normative loss' (*normative Schaden*), which Brüggemeier describes as 'fictive damage' because it is damage which is taken to exist regardless of whether there is any loss.[56] Because 'normative loss' is taken to exist without a need for proof, it triggers the award of substantive damages. Yet, compensation for 'normative loss' ('normative damages') is an exception to the so-called 'difference principle', whereby the value of the compensatory award is set by calculating the difference in the claimant's assets and liabilities between the situation created by the tort and the one that would exist if the tort had not been committed.[57] It shows an acceptance of rough rather than precise evaluation of a monetary award, where the right violation offers the normative ground justifying a departure from the principle of full (exact) compensation, under which only established and quantifiable losses are recoverable.[58]

Despite these exceptions, it should be emphasized that generally in German law, violation of a right on its own does not entitle the right-holder to reparation. Other conditions, such as negligence and resulting loss (unless 'loss' is presumed under

item is not physically damaged but merely detained and had not been expected to generate profit, the claimant has no way of showing 'loss' as required by law, unless a particular legal system accepts pure loss of use as 'loss' or 'damage'. On how I use the concepts of 'loss' and 'damage', see n 23.

[55] BGH, 21 June 2016, VI ZR 403/14, NJW-RR 2017, 219.

[56] Brüggemeier (n 53) 202. There is a connection between the 'loss of use' situation and the normative loss. The author indicates (ibid, esp fn 1029) that the well-known example of 'normative loss' today is what he describes as 'abstract compensation for loss of use', which is awarded even where the claimant hired no replacement vehicle (in the event of loss of use of a car) or rented no replacement dwelling (in the event of the defendant making their dwelling inhabitable).

[57] BGH recognized that 'normative damages', ie compensation for 'normative loss', are an exception to the difference principle in BGH, 31 May 1994, VI ZR 12/94, NJW 1994, 2357, at 2359, by holding that when they arise the difference in assets and liabilities must be determined 'in the evaluative manner', and also observed that 'the nature and significance of the assets are not limited to their existence, but include also the *possibilities* created by those assets for the asset holder' (emphasis added).

[58] Brüggemeier (n 53) 201. Stathis Banakas, 'Tales of Damage and (Retro-)Causation', Nuovo Diritto Civile 2016, no 2, 275, 282, argues that 'German law has, in the "normative concept of damage", endorsed an idea similar to the Common Law idea of an action for damages as a vindicative remedy of a right (*Rechtsverfolgende Natur des Schadensersatzes*)'.

the doctrine of 'normative loss'), need to be satisfied too. However, it is also the case that, despite attempts, described by Jansen, undertaken by some German scholars, tort law rights have not been reduced to mere 'bundles of duties of conduct'.[59] Thus, rights continue to possess an independent normative import in German tort law. This feature of tort law rights facilitates their rhetorical use. Violation of a right can open the door to doctrinal solutions which would otherwise be perceived as deviations from the requirements of the provisions of the civil code.

III. Fragmentation of English Tort Law

As explained in the opening paragraph of the present chapter, the discussion of the role of rights in English tort law scholarship is dominated by the concern to give all torts a shared identity and improve the system's coherence and intelligibility.[60] This suggests that the *structural* function of violation of a right is recognized in legal writings. However, the impact of legal scholarship on judicial practice is limited. As Stapleton has observed, English judges face constraints that academics do not.[61] English judges do not choose the arguments they consider and are not confronted with a clean slate. Instead, they operate within what Stapleton calls 'the doctrinal past' that 'structures the very issues that court must confront'.[62] In her view, the 'grand theory' of tort law as based on rights, as proposed for example by Stevens,[63] is 'false' in the descriptive sense because it does not fit (all of) the case law.[64]

Indeed, the argument that violation of a right could be the focal point of all tort liability[65] can be considered only if it is first accepted that judicial output is capable of being rationalized, and that judicial decisions rendered in individual cases—with the characteristic common law attention to facts and contextual circumstances—can produce a coherent body of law. That process has produced a system characterized by a multiplicity of tortious causes of action. Not only is English tort law fragmented; also, the different torts are oriented towards different concepts. And thus, some tortious causes of action are oriented towards duties of conduct while others are oriented towards protecting particular interests, for example liberty, bodily integrity, exclusive possession of property, or reputation.[66]

[59] Jansen (n 36) 355.
[60] Text to n 6.
[61] Stapleton (n 4) 3.
[62] ibid 4.
[63] ibid 13.
[64] Stapleton (n 4) 21 and 24–25. The author claims that 'a Grant Theorist . . . when confronted with tort phenomena that cannot be made to fit the descriptive claim . . . attempts to edit out or ignore these phenomena', which in her view reduces grand theories to normative accounts.
[65] Stevens (n 1).
[66] This is reflected in their name, in that the tort of negligence is oriented towards the duty not to act negligently, ie to take reasonable care, although that duty is only owed in distinct situations, while the tort of false imprisonment focuses clearly on physical liberty; trespass to a person is directed to bodily integrity; trespass to land and conversion are oriented towards exclusive possession of property (land

This is the direct consequence of English tort law being historically organized along 'formulary' lines.[67]

In structural terms, the rights-based approach to tort law provides tools to criticize excessively faithful adherence to old tort law forms and facilitate a transformation such as the one which English contract law underwent in the nineteenth century. That transformation involved the law's reorganization around its substantive principles and a move away from the formal requirements.[68] The argument of rights scholars is that the law's focus when deciding matters of liability should be on rights, their existence, and violations, rather than the historical limits of particular tort actions and the requirements that stem from them.[69]

This structural argument sometimes reaches the judicial realm. For example, *Watkins v Home Office*,[70] a case of a prisoner whose mail was maliciously opened by prison officers, was argued from a rights-based perspective. The case was brought in the tort of misfeasance in public office, which is actionable on proof of damage (not actionable per se). What the claimant had put forward as his 'damage' was not considered to be sufficient because it did not amount to loss, according to the evaluative judgment of the first instance court. That meant that on appeal the case had to be argued on different grounds as concerning the legal requirements of the cause of action. The Court of Appeal allowed the claimant's appeal but gave them only nominal damages and granted leave to appeal to the House of Lords to the defendant, the Home Office. Before the House of Lords, the claimant adopted a different strategy. They invited the House of Lords to hold that in the event of a violation of a right, here specifically a constitutional right, there should be liability to pay substantive damages, whether or not any economic loss (or other 'damage')

or personal property respectively); libel and slander protect reputation. On the different orientation of particular torts in English law, see eg Peter Cane, *Key Ideas in Tort Law* (Hart Publishing 2017) 15–16. Even Stevens, who strongly advocates a rights-based conception of the entirety of English tort law, admits that '[t]here is some authority for drawing a distinction between rights-based torts and duty-based torts'. Stevens (n 1) 291.

[67] Cane (n 66) 15. The term 'forms of action' was used by lawyers before the reforms of English civil procedure in the nineteenth century to refer to 'compartments of law and practice' associated with different writs. A writ was a document which a claimant had to obtain from the Chancery to commence the proceedings. They came in different types and included a description of a situation serving a dual function. First, it specified the circumstances in which royal courts had jurisdiction, and secondly, it triggered a decision of liability once the described situation had been factually established. While some manipulation of the factual description of a case was possible, in general terms, if the claimant's situations could not be presented in a way typical for one of the writs, the claim could not be successful. John Baker, *An Introduction to English Legal History* (5th edn, OUP 2019) 64.

[68] AWB Simpson, *A History of the Common Law of Contract: The Rise of the Action of Assumpsit* (Clarendon Press Oxford 1987) ch 7. Because English contract law during the nineteenth century became more focused on substantive principles than the formal requirements of a particular cause of action, judges and scholars were able to articulate its fundamental ideas as independent doctrines. These doctrines include the doctrine of consideration, privity of contract, and a clearer distinction between enforceable and non-enforceable agreements.

[69] Stevens (n 1) 296.

[70] *Watkins v Home Office and Others* [2006] UKHL 17, [2006] 2 AC 395.

has been shown.[71] One way of viewing the case is as an attempt to challenge the 'formulary' lines of English tort law. The claimant's argument before the House of Lords could be presented as redirecting the law's focus away from a fixed list of requirements that attached to the cause of action in question and towards a substantive argument relating to the need to protect a constitutional right.

The House of Lords did not follow this approach. While Lord Walker was less convinced by the 'historical objection',[72] that is, the objection against allowing recovery in misfeasance in public office without proof of loss based on the historical origin of the tort and past judicial descriptions of its constitutive elements, he was not at all open to a reconceptualization of the tort as not based on damage in some instances.[73] Also, Lord Bingham was adamant that compensation, not vindication, was the function of the tort.[74] All in all, the rights-based argument did not manage to dislocate the more traditional approach to liability, focusing on the specific features of the cause of action in question. English tort law was confirmed as a law of causes of action,[75] not a law of substantive principles of liability.

Arguably, an even bigger challenge to the rights-based restructuring of English tort law is posed by the broadest of the tortious causes of action—the tort of negligence. The tort of negligence has a broader scope than § 823(1) BGB[76] because there is no *a priori* restriction on the range of interests it might protect, although it is the case that different interests are not protected equally in that tort. It is also open-ended in its scope in that, even after the UK Supreme Court's judgment in *Robinson*,[77] the new duties of care can in principle be created for novel situations, expanding the range of contexts and behaviours which the tort covers. The extent to which this possibility exists in practice and not only in theory is debatable. Be it as it may, some of the duty tests (for assumption of responsibility or for liability for pure psychiatric injury to primary victims) are formulated broadly enough to enable the imposition of liability in situations which do not have exact counterparts in existing case law (precedents). The tort of negligence is also very generous when it comes to foreseeable physical injury to a person or damage to property. What constitutes negligent conduct is also open-ended given that negligence is to

[71] ibid.

[72] *Watkins* (n 70) [74].

[73] ibid [73].

[74] ibid [9].

[75] See Browne-Wilkinson V-C in *Kingdom of Spain v Christie, Manson & Woods Ltd* [1986] 1 WLR 1120, 1129: 'In the pragmatic way in which English law has developed, a man's legal rights are in fact those which are protected by a cause of action . . . in the ordinary case to establish a legal or equitable right you have to show that all the necessary elements of the cause of action are either present or threatened.'

[76] See text to n 33.

[77] In *Robinson v Chief Constable of West Yorkshire Police* [2018] UKSC 4, [2018] AC 736, the UK Supreme Court held that the duty question in most cases should be answered by reference to 'established principles' (which are in fact case law *rules* for duty and no-duty), not any general test. The open-ended duty test, known as the *Caparo* test, is to be used only in 'novel situations'.

be assessed in all the circumstances, and that judges are expected to evaluate in each case whether the risk that had been created was reasonable and/or stemmed from a useful activity, and whether a reasonable person would have taken steps to reduce or eliminate the risk.[78]

It appears that unless the tort of negligence can be conceptualized as rights-based, it cannot be maintained that English tort law structurally tends towards the concept of right. The particular difficulty which English rights scholars encounter is that the tort of negligence does not overtly use violation of a right as one of its requirements. In justice terms, the imposition of such a requirement would be regarded as too much of a straitjacket, stifling its expansion and conflicting with the compensatory function of the tort of negligence. The response of rights scholars is twofold. First, the tort of negligence is presented as an outlier that should be disbanded and divided into separate torts to which particular rights will give intelligibility.[79] Secondly, they observe that the tort of negligence is based on a 'breach of duty' and, thus, all that is required is to flip the description and say that a breach of duty is equivalent to a violation of a right.[80] This reversal is attractive theoretically and seems to solve the problem of fit for rights scholars. However, the rights which are so teased out are not similar by type to the rights which counted as 'tort law rights' in German law. They are 'claim-rights', not general, freedom-from rights.[81]

English tort law rights, to the extent that they are present in the law, or in the way they are described by rights scholars, are rights not to have one's well-being interfered with *in a certain way*. They are rights correlated with duties of conduct, not with a general obligation not to infringe them, even where they are erga omnes rights.[82] Stevens explains the correlation between tort law rights and duties of conduct by the fact that tort law rights are not and could not be 'absolute', which entails a necessity to define the conduct which will constitute their violation.[83] He calls it the question of 'how boundaries of our primary rights are to be drawn'.[84] Nolan, on the other hand, contrasts tort law rights with what he calls 'general rights', such

[78] *Bolton v Stone* [1951] AC 850; *Overseas Tankship (UK) Ltd v The Miller Steamship Co (The Wagon Mound (No. 2))* [1967] 1 AC 617.

[79] Beever (n 5) 215 speaks of the need to 'translate' the common law, ie the judge-made law, 'into rights language': 'The reason for translating remedies language into rights language in this context is that it enables us better to see and deal with the issues we must confront if we are adequately to resolve the problems of economic loss, liability for omissions, etc.' He adds that 'in translating the question into rights language, we identify the concerns appropriate to providing the necessary answer' (ibid).

[80] As Bagshaw observes, the reversal does not always work because rights scholars do not always accept the right that emerges when the duty is flipped. Roderick Bagshaw, 'Tort Law, Concepts and What Really Matters' in Andrew Robertson and Hang Wu Tang (eds), *The Goals of Private Law* (Hart Publishing 2009) 239, 252–53.

[81] Stevens (n 1) 4–5; Nolan (n 1) 256.

[82] Stevens' list of erga omnes rights whose violation gives rise to liability in tort include property rights in tangible things, intellectual property, rights to bodily safety, freedom of movement, the right to reputation, the power to vote, and the right not to be lied to. See Stevens (n 1) 7–8.

[83] ibid 99–100.

[84] ibid 100.

as property or bodily integrity, which are 'constellations of legal norms, including claim-rights', not claim-rights themselves, and thus not 'tort law rights' (or 'negligence rights' at least).[85]

The fact that in most accounts of English tort law, 'negligence rights' are not freedom-from rights, explains why their violation incorporates the negligence standard. Violation of a right is only regarded as established if the duty to take reasonable care is found to be breached. For this reason, a right cannot be described as infringed merely because there is an interference with a protected interest or a resulting harm. This means that while negligence rights can be identified and defined at the duty stage, that is, the stage in the judicial inquiry that focuses on the relationship between the parties in order to establish whether prima facie negligence liability should arise, violation of the right does not arise until a failure to take reasonable care is found. Both the duty and the breach analysis take account of the interest at stake: the graver the interest violated, the easier it is to establish a duty of care; the graver the harm, the less demanding the duty requirement for the claimant and, in principle, the higher the level of care expected from the defendant. However, there is no independent inquiry into whether the alleged harm stems from a violation of a right.

An alternative to a duty-focused search for violation of a right would be to locate this element within the requirement of 'damage'. It is widely known that the tort of negligence is actionable only on proof of damage; that damage is the gist of the action.[86] As Nolan has explained, there can be two competing approaches to the requirement of 'damage' in the tort of negligence.[87] One approach effectively equates damage with 'loss', understood here as a situation of being worse off. The second approach does not banish loss from the tort of negligence but treats it as relevant not for the question of liability but for the remedial question—how much, if at all, the claimant should receive in damages. On this second approach, 'damage' can encompass or even signify the idea of violation of a right.[88] The tort of negligence would then be rights-based because, rather than loss, it requires 'damage', so understood. As a result, loss, especially loss in financial terms, would be neither necessary nor sufficient to prove 'damage'. English rights scholars believe that this rule is already in place because the tort of negligence, despite being a tort actionable only on proof of damage, already offers substantive damages for 'loss of use' in the absence of actual loss.[89]

[85] Nolan maintains that, unlike in the case of claim-rights, in the case of 'general rights' it is difficult to claim that they 'can form a "rights base" of negligence law'. Nolan (n 1) 268, fn 56.

[86] Jane Stapleton, 'The Gist of Negligence' (1988) 104 Law Quarterly Review 213.

[87] Nolan (n 1).

[88] Nolan supports this second approach and defines 'damage' as a 'more intangible notion of a certain kind of interference with a person's protected interests' (ibid 261) and explains why, so understood, damage, and not loss, is an element of the cause of action.

[89] *The Mediana* [1900] AC 113. See also Stevens' discussion of *Dimond v Lovell* [2000] UKHL 27, [2002] 1 AC 384, in Stevens (n 1) 72, a case in which the cost of hire of a temporary replacement for a damaged item was held to be recoverable by the claimant even though the claimant did not have to

Finally, when we zoom out and look at the role of rights in demarcating the realm of private law, understood as a catalogue of certain remedies, different from public law remedies, we can see what has become known as 'correlativity'. Unlike public law relationships, private law relationships are correlative, which can be expressed as structural correspondence between the right of one party and the duty of another.[90] According to Lord Diplock in *O'Reilly v Mackman*, in cases involving public authorities, judicial review (a public law remedy) should always be preferred over other remedies unless 'the invalidity of the [administrative] decision arises as a collateral issue in a claim for infringement of a right of the plaintiff arising under private law'.[91] To the extent that English public law can even be regarded as embracing the concept of a right, a public law right would be correlated with a duty owed to the public at large.[92] A private law right, on the other hand, is correlated with a duty owed to a particular person or a class of persons.[93] The duty is directed to the person that holds the right, and the right is considered to exist because there is a duty which is owed specifically to the claimant, or a class to which the claimant belongs. So unlike in other legal systems, in English law it is not the identity of the duty-bearer or the context in which harm has occurred (public service) which demarcates public and private law (of remedies), but the character of the duty breached.

The independence of the private law duty (and the resulting private law right) from public law has been emphasized in negligent omission cases, in which it has been stated unequivocally that a public law duty cannot ground a duty of care in the tort of negligence.[94] Specialized tort law tests, not public law tests, need to be

pay the cost of hire. The term 'loss of use' was defined above (n 52). As was discussed in the context of German law, a legal system that makes recovery for 'loss of use' independent from consequential financial loss can be considered to allow substantive damages for 'pure' violation of a right (the right of property).

[90] Cane (n 8) 12.

[91] *O'Reilly v Mackman* [1983] 2 AC 237.

[92] *Michael v Chief Constable of South Wales* [2015] UKSC 2, [2015] AC 1732. A public law right should not be confused with a 'public right', which is a right to use a public good, such as rivers, roads, bridges, etc. The harm created by obstruction (interference with a 'public right') is recoverable in public nuisance if the claimant has suffered 'special damage'.

[93] The distinction between public law and private law rights has also another dimension. It is a popular view that public law rights should only be recognized (or public law remedies only made available) if it is in the public interest. See Lord Woolf extrajudicially: Harry Woolf, 'Public Law–Private Law: Why the Divide? A Personal View' [1986] Public Law 220 and 'Droit Public—English Style' [1995] Public Law 57. See also Jason NE Varuhas, 'The Public Interest Conception of Public Law: Its Procedural Origins and Substantive Implications' in John Bell and others (eds), *Public Law Adjudication in Common Law Systems: Process and Substance* (Hart Publishing 2016) 45.

[94] Lord Hoffmann in *Gorringe v Calderdale MBC* [2004] UKHL 15, [2004] 1 WLR 1057, [23]: 'If a statute actually imposes a duty, it is well settled that the question of whether it was intended to give rise to a private right of action depends upon the construction of the statute . . . If the statute does not create a private right of action, it would be, to say the least, unusual if the mere existence of the statutory duty could generate a common law duty of care'. The statement uses the phrase 'a common law duty of care' to designate a private law duty in the tort of negligence. However, as Lord Hoffmann observes, private law duties (duties opening the possibility of using private law remedies, such as a tortious cause of

used for this purpose. On the flipside, only violations of public law rights give access to public law remedies, in particular judicial review. This reveals an additional structural function of rights in English law, although what is being organized here is the entirety of private law, and not specifically tort law.

Moving to the *doctrinal* function of violations of a right in English tort law, one obvious test case is the already mentioned 'loss of use' situation. Substantive damages awarded in the absence of loss can be taken as evidence of English tort law modifying its standard rules, both substantive and remedial, in order to allow the claimant to vindicate their rights. As has been explained above, a group of tortious causes of action in English law are only 'actionable' on proof of damage. Damage that has to be pleaded to complete the cause of action is referred to as 'special damage'.[95] In addition, on the remedial side, we find a rule according to which the claimant is only entitled to damages which are equivalent to their loss.[96] Loss is the prescribed measure of damages. What this means is that, as Tettenborn points out, 'where no loss has been suffered no substantial damages of any kind can be recovered'.[97] That would suggest that being prevented from using one's property where this fact does not lead to any consequential financial loss is not a circumstance that would attract a substantive award, even though it constitutes a violation of a property right.

However, in 2018, the UK Supreme Court in *One Step (Support) Ltd v Morris-Garner*[98] confirmed the availability in English tort law of 'user damages', that is, seemingly 'compensatory' damages calculated by reference to how much the defendant would have had to pay to the claimant if they hired or rented the property the possession of which they unlawfully deprived the claimant. Somewhat surprisingly, Lord Reed described the harm for which 'compensation' was granted as 'loss', albeit of 'a different kind'. This conclusion permitted Lord Reed to maintain that no departure from orthodox tort law rules was necessary. However, the loss's 'different' character was used to justify a different measure of damages. In Lord Reed's own words:

action) can be also statutory, while the central public law remedy—judicial review—is in fact a common law remedy.

[95] Harry Street, *Principles of the Law of Damages* (Sweet & Maxwell 1962) 18.

[96] Nourse LJ in *Stoke-on-Trent City Council v W & L Wass Ltd* [1988] 1 WLR 1406, 1410: '[t]he general rule is that a successful plaintiff in an action in tort recovers damages equivalent to the loss which he has suffered, no more and no less. If he has suffered no loss, the most he can recover are nominal damages.'

[97] Andrew Tettenborn, *The Law of Damages* (Lexis Nexis 2003) 51. An example can be found in *Constantine v Imperial Hotels* [1944] KB 693, where the defendant's refusal to accommodate the claimant violated his recognized 'common law right'. Although the court agreed that the action may be sustained without the proof of 'special damage', it awarded only nominal damages.

[98] *One Step (Support) Ltd v Morris-Garner* [2018] UKSC 20, [2019] AC 649.

> Where . . . an unlawful use is made of property, and the right to control such use is a valuable asset, the owner suffers a loss of a different kind, which calls for a different method of assessing damages. In such circumstances, the person who makes wrongful use of the property prevents the owner from exercising his right to obtain the economic value of the use in question, and should therefore compensate him for the consequent loss.[99]

Note that Lord Reed surmises that the right to control the use of property is a 'valuable asset' in all situations, presumably even if no profit could have been made from the property in question. 'User damages' are thus awarded without proof of loss and in that sense could be described as vindicating the property right. There is a sense that the concept of 'compensation' is being twisted in *One-Step*,[100] which justifies the claim that what is being protected here is the property right itself, regardless of the consequences of its violation. If this interpretation is accepted, we can conclude that violations of a right sometimes perform a doctrinal function in English tort law.

The doctrinal use of rights is not restricted to justifying substantive damages calculated by reference to measures other than the value of financial loss. Rights scholars use it also to explain particular rules and judicial approaches, such as English law's approach to liability for pure economic loss or emotional distress in the tort of negligence and beyond it.[101] In addition, rights are used critically to evaluate judgments where the claimant is awarded damages for pure economic loss even though there was no factual assumption of responsibility to the claimant. The argument is that only actual, not presumed or deemed, assumption of responsibility is capable of creating a duty not to cause a given pure economic loss and the correlative right in the claimant not to have that loss inflicted by the defendant. For example, *Smith v Bush*,[102] a case in which a purchaser was held to be owed a duty by a property surveyor employed by the building society, who disclaimed all responsibility to parties other than the building society, is easily explainable on the loss-based model of negligence liability because the surveyor's negligence, in stating that the property had not required any repairs, was on the facts historically involved in the claimant's loss (the cost of repair or the difference between the price paid for the property and its value after the defect was discovered).[103]

[99] ibid 671, [30].

[100] ibid.

[101] Stevens argues that economic loss is not recoverable 'sine injuria' also when it is intentionally caused (Stevens (n 1) 22). He also observes (ibid 53) that emotional harm is recoverable where consequent upon infringement of a right, such as in the case of personal injury, seizure of personal property, defamation or even nuisance (as disturbance of the claimant's use of their land). See also Nolan (n 1) 267–68.

[102] *Smith v Eric S Bush* [1990] 1 AC 831.

[103] I am using the term 'historically involved' rather than 'caused' in order to avoid a debate about the nature of causal claims in cases involving human decision-making, where a number of factors may play a role in the claimant arriving at a particular decision, for example, a decision to buy a property. English judges generally accept the claimant's assertion that they had entered a particular transaction

From the perspective of the rights-based model of negligence liability, on the other hand, the judgment can be criticized for allowing the claimant who did not have a right enforceable against the defendant to recover from them for the loss suffered.[104] The resulting loss is not regarded as stemming from a violation of a right enforceable against the defendant because the only circumstance that could generate such a right is a factual assumption of responsibility, that is an undertaking made by the defendant to the claimant to protect them from incurring a loss in the context of a given transaction. In the face of a disclaimer, it could not be maintained that any such responsibility had actually been assumed. So, on the rights-based model, the purchaser's action should have failed because they had no right against the property surveyor to demand from them the taking of reasonable care so that the purchaser not suffer pure economic loss from the transaction. The route chosen by their Lordships in *Smith v Bush*, which involved setting aside the disclaimer as 'unreasonable' under the Unfair Contract Terms Act[105] and then relying on non-factual reasons to impose duty of care, is incompatible with the rights-based model, which is why the judgment has been described by Stevens, a rights scholar, as 'anomalous'.[106]

At the beginning of the chapter, I explained that the doctrinal function of violation of a right is visible also when it is used to justify strict liability, that is where in a given legal system we can observe a tendency to impose strict liability in cases involving infringements of interests regarded as constituting or being protected by 'rights'. We have seen that in the German context, it has been argued that the shift towards stricter liability has been justified by the need to enhance protection of certain rights, such as the rights to life and health.[107] In English law, strict liability is primarily the domain of torts actionable per se, which are oriented towards rights, or protected interests (in this context the difference does not matter), including liberty, bodily integrity, exclusive possession of property and reputation.[108] Torts actionable per se have been described as primarily 'vindicative' in character. 'Vindication' in this context is generally understood as enforcement of rights and

in reliance on the defendant's negligent (and in consequence incorrect) statement, but the defendant can still argue that the negligent statement was not present in the claimant's mind when taking the decision, which would dispute the existence of a causal connection between the negligent statement and the ensuing loss. See, eg, *Leeds City Council v Barclays Bank Plc* [2021] EWHC 363 (Comm), [2021] QB 1027.

[104] Stevens (n 1) 43.

[105] The disclaimer was deemed 'unreasonable' under the Unfair Contract Terms Act 1977, which made it ineffective against the claimant. Today the relevant statute is the Consumer Rights Act 2015.

[106] Stevens (n 1) 43.

[107] Text to n 47.

[108] It is worth noting that English law is also familiar with other strict liability torts, ie those not actionable per se, such as the rule in *Rylands v Fletcher* or the tort of nuisance. These torts can also be conceptualized as protecting the right to (the private use and enjoyment of) land and thus also rights-based. Donal Nolan, '"A Tort Against Land": Private Nuisance as a Property Tort' in Nolan and Robertson (n 1) 459, 465.

can be contrasted with both the compensatory and the regulatory functions of tort law, where the primary focus is on providing access to compensation in the event of harm or on regulating conduct and the associated duties of conduct.[109] Torts actionable per se, that is not requiring proof of damage, cannot be presented as primarily compensatory in their outlook. Nor are they oriented towards duties of conduct, which would make them more 'regulatory' in character.[110] Instead, torts actionable per se have at their centre the right infringement (interference with liberty, bodily integrity, property or reputation).[111] Keating goes so far as to claim that rights at issue in these torts are 'powers of control, not protections against harm',[112] which would suggest a freedom/will conception of rights, rather than the interest conception.[113] Torts actionable per se are 'strict' in the sense that they do not require proof of negligence, but they do require that the right-violating conduct (but not the causation of harm) be 'intentional' in the sense of its being voluntary.[114] Loss might still be relevant in these torts in determining the type of the monetary award, substantive or nominal,[115] and its amount, but not for liability itself. The argument is that 'strict liability torts are wrongs because they involve violations of rights', as they would otherwise lack a justification for being recognized as 'wrongs'.[116] In other words, liability is imposed because the claimant's right has been violated by the defendant's 'voluntary' conduct.

[109] Jason NE Varuhas, 'The Concept of "Vindication" in the Law of Torts: Rights, Interests and Damages' (2014) 34 Oxford Journal of Legal Studies 253 argues that 'vindication' in tort law 'entails attesting to, affirming and reinforcing the importance of those interests that are the subject of the law's protection and their inherent value, and by association the importance of the overlying legal rights'. See also Jason NE Varuhas, *Damages and Human Rights* (Hart Publishing 2016) 17 and 26.

[110] The regulatory character of torts manifests itself through the setting of behavioural standards. The setting of standards can be accomplished more directly where a tortious cause of action includes a duty of conduct as one of its requirements, such as the duty to take reasonable care in the tort of negligence. On standard setting in tort law, see Peter Cane, 'Tort Law as Regulation' (2002) 32 Common Law World Review 305, 313.

[111] In their case, the violation of a right cannot be reduced to a breach of a duty to behave in a certain way, as it is in the context of the tort of negligence when reconceptualized as a rights-based tort. See text to n 85. This is visible in the fact that the wrongfulness of interference is in these torts removed not by showing that the defendant respected a duty of conduct but by showing that there was a justification for the interference.

[112] Gregory C Keating, 'Strict Liability Wrongs' in John Oberdiek (ed), *Philosophical Foundations of the Law of Torts* (OUP 2014) 293, 305. The chapter uses US law as its point of reference, but the claims made are transferable to English tort law.

[113] Text to n 41.

[114] Despite the structural differences between torts actionable per se and torts requiring proof of damage/loss, which might suggest that only the former are rights-based, English rights scholars insist that all torts, including those requiring damage, are rights-based. Stevens (n 1) 89 argues that 'the division between wrongs actionable per se and those only actionable upon proof of consequential loss should reflect a choice between those rights which are, and are not, as a question of social fact sufficiently important to be deserving of protection irrespective of the consequences of the violation'.

[115] *Constantine v Imperial Hotels* [1944] KB 693. However, in certain situations damage is presumed and substantive damages are awarded. *Exchange Telegraph Co v Gregory* [1896] 1 QB 147; *Draper v Trist* [1939] 3 All ER 513; *Nicholls v Ely Beet Sugar Factory Ltd* [1936] Ch 343.

[116] Keating (n 112) 296 and 308. The author observes that the conduct involved in torts actionable per se, while violating a right, 'may be otherwise entirely innocent, entirely justified, and even beneficial' (ibid 308).

Strict liability actionable-per-se torts are evidence that the doctrinal function of rights violations is present in English law, at least implicitly. In my opinion this doctrinal use can only be inferred and not positively confirmed because English judges simply accept the existence of these strict liability torts and, when holding the defendant liable in one of these torts, they do not feel compelled to justify why they are imposing a strict form of liability. Instead, discussion tends to focus on the question of whether a given conduct is actionable under a particular tort actionable per se.[117] The strictness of liability is the consequence of the situation falling within the ambit of a particular tortious cause of action.

In addition to the structural and doctrinal aspects, the English debate about the role of rights in tort law takes a *rhetorical* turn, a turn that is significantly less visible in civilian jurisdictions. The rhetorical superiority of rights stems from the belief that rights-based reasoning is more legitimate than other forms of legal reasoning, especially the one involving reliance on policy.[118] The attack on the judicial use of policy arguments has as its background the concern for the limits of judicial competence and the 'political legitimacy' of decisions based on policy.[119] This is true whether policy is used to expand or restrict liability. For example, *Smith v Bush*, discussed above, which was ultimately based on policy grounds (the desire to protect non-professional purchasers of residential property), is criticized by rights scholars for extending liability for pure negligence to a situation where the defendant did not violate any rights of the claimant.[120] Equally, rights scholars tend to criticize judgments which for reasons of policy place limits on recovery for harm resulting from a violation of a recognized right (for example, the right to mental health).[121]

However, not all English rights scholars display an unequivocally negative attitude towards policy reasoning. For example, McBride and Robertson both independently argue that the public interest might be relevant when defining what private law rights people have, and should be excluded only from the question of

[117] For example, whether direct negligent physical interference with a person is actionable in trespass (actionable per se) or negligence. *Letang v Cooper* [1965] 1 QB 232.

[118] Stevens (n 1) 331 argues 'the only legal rights that can be judge-made are those derived from moral rights', suggesting that only moral arguments can be used when law is developed by judges, while Beever (n 5) 43 argues that judges cannot decide contrary to principle, which he defines as contradicting 'the rules and doctrines of the law itself'.

[119] Donal Nolan and Andrew Robertson, 'Rights and Private Law' in Nolan and Robertson (n 1) 1, 22.

[120] Text to n 104.

[121] Stevens (n 1) 55, discussing *Alcock v Chief Constable of South Yorkshire Police* [1992] 1 AC 310, which established a rule of non-liability in the tort of negligence for all cases of secondary victims of psychiatric injury with the exception of those who cumulatively met three criteria: direct appreciation of the event with one's own senses, proximity in time and space with the incident and the requirement of a close and loving relationship with the primary victim of the incident. Beever (n 5) 408–09 considers these criteria unjustified, even if traceable to an earlier case, *McLoughlin v O'Brian* [1983] 1 AC 410, because their Lordships did not justify each of the criteria individually. A general sentiment that allowing broader recovery for psychiatric injury would extend liability too far does not, according to Beever, explain the specific criteria that have been imposed.

when tort law remedies will be available.[122] According to McBride, English judges adjudicating tort cases, when deciding if the claimant has a right against the defendant, should focus on the claimant's interest and its importance, but also the side effects of recognizing the right and whether it would undermine a voluntary agreement between the claimant and the defendant. The side effects which judges should take into account, according to McBride, include welfare considerations.[123] Which side of the debate a right scholar will fall on depends largely on their view of judicial competence and the constitutional role of the judge as a law maker. Those who continue to be critical of reliance by judges on policy considerations associate rights-based reasoning with a more ethical view of never treating people as means to external ends and with the idea that the source of 'primary rights' resides in individual sovereignty and interpersonal morality.[124]

IV. Looking for Rights in French Tort Law

Violation of a right is famously absent from the wording of the tort provisions of the French Civil Code (Cc).[125] This would suggest a total absence of rights as the idea that gives French tort law *structural* unity, and around which the different bases of liability could be organized. The overt absence of rights from French tort law has been explained by different historical circumstances, the one most frequently mentioned being the influence of Pothier, an eighteenth-century jurist, on the French Civil Code.[126] Pothier is said to have been inspired by Grotius in formulating the general principle of liability for negligence, but chose not to adopt Grotius' concept of recoverable harm (*damnum*).[127] Grotius defined a situation when 'a man has less that what is his', that is, *damnum*, by reference to a list of things which 'a man may regard as his by nature' (life, body, limbs, fame, honour,

[122] Nicholas McBride, 'Rights and the Basis of Tort Law' and Andrew Robertson, 'Rights, Pluralism and the Duty of Care' in Nolan and Robertson (n 1) 331 and 435 respectively.

[123] McBride (n 122) 354.

[124] Beever (n 5) 62–63 and 187–89. In Alan Beever, 'On Our Most Fundamental Rights' in Nolan and Robertson (n 1) 63, 86, Beever argues that in cases in which courts relied on policy to arrive at the outcome, the claimant has been used as 'resources' for external ends. He gives the example of *Hill v Chief Constable of West Yorkshire* [1989] AC 53, 64, where Lord Templeman insisted that '[t]he question for the determination . . . [was] whether an action for damages [was] an appropriate vehicle for investigating the efficiency of a police force'.

[125] Arts 1240–1244 Cc.

[126] Jean-Louis Halperin, *The French Civil Code* (Tony Weir tr, Routledge 2006) 68. Pothier's treatise influenced the drafting of the original civil code provisions on torts (Chapter II of Title IV of Book III: *Des délits et des quasi-délits*, Articles 1382–1386 Cc). These provisions are still part of the French Civil Code, but after *Ordonnance* no 2016-131 of 10 February 2016, the relevant chapter of the Code is called 'general extracontractual liability' (*la responsabilité extracontractuelle en général*) and the numbering of Articles changed to Articles 1240–1244 Cc.

[127] Robert Fenestra, 'Grotius' Doctrine of Liability for Negligence: Its Origin and Its Influence in Civil Law Countries under Modern Codifications' in Eltjo JH Schrage (ed), *Negligence: The Comparative Legal History of the Law of Torts* (Duncker & Humblot 2001) 129, 169.

personal liberty).[128] In contrast, the concept of 'damage' (*dommage*) in Pothier's writings remained unspecified.[129]

Another feature of the French Civil Code is the separation of the law of persons and the law of things from the law of obligations. The latter is seen as the domain of rights in personam only, that is rights that come into existence as a result of an obligation.[130] An obligation, on the other hand, arises from contract, extracontractual liability, administration of the other's affairs (*la gestion d'affaires*), undue payment (*le paiement de l'indu*), and unjustified enrichment.[131] What this means is that, conceptually, extracontractual liability as a source of an obligation is a source of (in personam) rights, not the product of a violation of a right. In personam rights are contrasted with erga omnes rights, including in rem rights governed by the law of property, but also human rights, including personality rights.[132] As far as the structure of French tort law is concerned, we cannot see any apparent role of erga omnes rights and their corresponding 'injuries' (types of harm) in identifying the different tortious bases of liability. Indeed, personal injury is recoverable both under the provision regulating liability for personal fault (article 1240 Cc), as well as the strict liability principle recognized under article 1242 Cc (the so-called liability for the acts of things, *responsabilité du fait des choses*).[133] The same is true of other recognized types of harm, such as 'material' (*dommage matériel*) or 'moral' harm (*dommage moral*).[134]

Also *doctrinally*, we do not see any obvious function of violation of a right in French tort law. Unlike in German law, any presumption in favour of recovery of certain types of harm is not expressed through the language of rights. Equally, liability under articles 1240 and 1241 Cc, which inter alia establish liability for pure

[128] 'Damage, *damnum* (perhaps from *demo*) is when a man has less that what is his, whether it be his by mere nature or by some human act in addition such as ownership, agreement or statute. Things which a man may regard as his by nature are life ... his body, limbs, fame, honour, and his own acts.' Paragraphs II.XVII.1-2 of Hugo Grotius, *De iure belli ac pacis libri tres*, first published probably in 1625, quoted after James Gordley, *Foundations of Private Law* (OUP 2006) 162.

[129] Robert-Joseph Pothier, *Traité des obligations* (first published 1761, Dalloz 2011) § 116.

[130] Jean Carbonnier, *Droit civil. Les obligations* (22nd edn, PUF 2000) 36.

[131] Title II I: *Des sources d'obligations* (arts 1100–1303-4 Cc).

[132] François Chabas, *Introduction à l'étude du droit* (12th edn, Montchrestien 2000) 274 and 279.

[133] Whittaker (n 9) 26 has observed that the reinterpretation of what is now art 1242 Cc (previously art 1386 Cc), which led to the introduction of a strict liability regime for 'acts of things', was motivated by the concern for ensuring access to compensation for victims of personal injuries. It is worth noting that *dommage corporel* refers to physical personal injury only and is juxtaposed with *dommage moral* (which encompasses the non-physical consequences of personal injury as well as pure emotional or mental harm such as grief or stand-alone psychiatric illness) and *dommage matériel* (damage to property or financial assets). See François Terré, Philippe Simler, and Yves Lequette, *Droit civil. Les Obligations* (11th edn, Dalloz 2013) 767–75.

[134] For the discussion of these different types of recoverable harm in French law, see Dorota Leczykiewicz, 'Loss and Its Compensation in the Proposed New French Regime of Extra-contractual Liability' in Jean-Sébastien Borghetti and Simon Whittaker (eds), *French Civil Liability in Comparative Perspective* (Hart Publishing 2019) 181, 183. French tort law is also attached to another distinction, that is between *préjudices patrimoniaux* and *préjudices extrapatrimoniaux*. This distinction, while important for issues such as the extent of third-party payers' (social security funds' and insurance companies') right of recourse, in no way determines the existence or extent of the defendant's liability (ibid 193).

negligence, is in no way limited by the requirement that the recoverable harm be a consequence of a violation of a right. While it is standard for French scholars to define *dommage* as 'a violation of a legitimate legally protected interest' (*la lésion d'un intérêt légitime juridiquement protégé*),[135] judges are not expected to identify explicitly the specific interest that has been violated or verify if the violated interest amounts to a right. Even the traditional emphasis on the legitimacy of the violated interest does not change this conclusion. First, as I observed elsewhere,[136] the legitimacy of the violated interest is a requirement used by judges only selectively to preclude recovery of certain instances of harm, such as loss of illegal gains or, more generally, of something to which the claimant had not been entitled, and has traditionally also been used to restrict the range of secondary victims who could recover against the defendant in addition to the primary victim.[137]

As we have seen with regard to German and English law, the testing ground for the doctrinal significance of a violation of a right tends to be negligence liability for pure economic loss, for which a rights-based tort system tends to give limited recovery only. As it is widely known, French law does not impose any a priori limits on the recovery of pure economic loss. Indeed, French tort law seems to have internalized a view that loss of future profit, if only sufficiently probable, is as much *dommage* as other forms of 'material' damage (*dommage matériel*). Equally, modulation of the level of protection offered to different interests is achieved in French law without relying on rights. Indeed, the series of measures to which French law has resorted to offer greater protection against personal injury include reinterpretation of what was article 1384 Cc (what is now article 1242 Cc) and the development of strict liability for 'acts of things',[138] and the transfer of some of the liability to contract where *obligations de securité*, if found, impose strict liability for what is now to be regarded as contractual breach.[139]

However, there are some curious instances of interferences which are or historically were treated without more as establishing both *dommage* and *faute*. They include 'neighbourhood disturbances' (*trouble de voisinage*), where for actions brought under article 1382 Cc (now article 1240 Cc), abnormal (excessive) disturbance (*trouble anormal*) was sufficient for liability, boundary transgressions

[135] Geneviève Viney, Patrice Jourdain, and Suzanne Carval, *Traité de droit civil. Les conditions de la responsabilité* (4th edn, LGDJ 2013) 19. Legitimacy and legal protection are sometimes combined into a single requirement of 'lawful interest' (*intérêt licite*).

[136] Leczykiewicz (n 134) 188.

[137] Secondary victims who were excluded were 'concubines' because what the law protected was a 'relationship in law' (*lien de droit*), not a factual connection. This changed in 1970, when the *Cour de cassation* held that a relationship in law was not required. Cass ch mixte 27 February 1970, D 1970.201, JCP 1970.II.16305. This change was aided by the creation of a new head of damage: *préjudice d'affection*.

[138] See n 133.

[139] This method works also where French judges want to move liability away from a strict liability regime to a negligence-based regime. Simon Whittaker, 'Privity of Contract and the Law of Tort: The French Experience' (1995) 15 Oxford Journal of Legal Studies 327.

(the same), and *violation de droit de la personalité*.[140] All these instances are significant because they are undisputed cases of violations of a right, even described as such in the case law.[141] Not only is proof of loss regarded as superfluous but, in these cases, the liability imposed is effectively 'strict', even if the legal basis, except for *trouble de voisinage*, which now has its own provision in the Civil Code, continues to be article 1240 Cc, a provision which imposes liability for fault (*faute*). However, some French lawyers would feel uncomfortable describing this form of liability as 'strict' and instead would expand the concept of fault to include violation of a right.[142] Either way, it is violation of a right that seems to be doing the tacit doctrinal work in these types of cases.

Another example, which is frequently used to signal a legal system's doctrinal engagement with a rights analysis, is limited recovery for emotional harm. The argument is that it is rights-based thinking which explains why emotional harm is not recoverable in all instances. Emotional harm is not recoverable in all cases because recovery is permitted only when it stems from a violation of a right. This argument does not overtly apply to French law, where *dommage moral*, once identified, entitles the claimant to receive substantive damages and no requirement of a right violation formally attaches to a successful tort claim. But it would be wrong to claim that all forms of emotional harm are recoverable. Instead, the process of separating recoverable and irrecoverable emotional harm is hidden from view because the issue is considered 'factual' and thus within the sovereign assessment of the *juge du fond*.[143] That is not to say that the space is entirely unregulated and thus discretionary. Indeed, the *Cour de cassation* has been indicating through its judgments in which situations the lower courts are obligated by article 1240 Cc to find *dommage moral*.[144] Legal scholars use these judgments to identify the circumstances in which *dommage moral* will be recoverable, sometimes even choosing to use the language of 'rights' to label these circumstances.[145] This is aided by courts

[140] Cass civ (1) 5 November 1996, Bull Civ I no 378, JCP 1997.II.22805; Cass civ (3) 25 February 2004, Bull Civ II no 41, D 2004.1631. Since 2024, neighbourhood disturbances are regulated expressly in the Civil Code (art 1253 Cc), where 'a disturbance exceeding normal neighbourhood inconveniences' (*trouble excédant les inconvénients normaux de voisinage*) is the only requirement that needs to be met before the identified parties (owner, tenant, occupier, landlord, etc) are liable for the resulting harm; this provision codifies the position that fault (negligence) does not have to be established independently from the excessive disturbance.

[141] For examples, see n 140.

[142] Viney, Jourdain, and Carval (n 135) 454–56.

[143] *Juges du fond* can be translated as 'judges of the facts', that is, judges sitting at the level where both legal and factual issues are settled (trial courts and courts of appeal). They are contrasted with the *Cour de cassation*, which can decide only on legal matters by reviewing the lower courts' application of the law to the 'facts' of the case.

[144] Viney, Jourdain, and Carval (n 135) 60–70.

[145] ibid 60. When describing the situations in which the claimant receives compensation for *dommage moral*, the authors speak about 'the rights recognised for the benefit of natural persons'. Older treatises used in this context the concept of '*atteinte*' (interference), listing the situations in which *dommage moral* was recoverable under the headings of different interest or right violations, such as interference with reputation (*atteinte à la reputation*), interference with bodily integrity (*atteinte à l'intégrité de la personne humaine*), interference with privacy of correspondence (*atteinte à l'inviolabilité de la correspondance*),

offering additional labels for the different instances of emotional harm, such as *préjudice d'affection* (loss of affection), *préjudice d'agrément* (loss of enjoyment of life), *préjudice esthétique* (cosmetic harm).[146]

The tendency to label the different types of recoverable *dommage moral* as *préjudice* could lead us to believe that it is the concept of *préjudice* that expresses French tort law's commitment to rights. There is some support for this claim. As Viney, Jourdain, and Carval observe, the distinction between *dommage* and *préjudice* is inspired by Roman law, where the term *damnum* in the delict of *damnum iniuria datum* meant, according to the authors, interference with bodily integrity, a 'simple fact without legal significance'.[147] In contrast, *préjudice* is a consequence of *dommage* that under law can be an object of compensation.[148] Referring to harm as *préjudice* entails a claim that the harm is legally relevant and thus, if found to be stemming from the defendant's act, it will entitle the claimant to recovery. The distinction between *dommage* and *préjudice* is also used in the context of another proposition made by some French scholars, that is that French law knows two, not one, modes of repairing harm: compensation and reparation in kind.[149] In their view, reparation in kind is available only with respect to *dommage* (here understood as the initial injury), while *préjudice* can only be repaired through a pecuniary equivalent (compensation), and thus, unlike *dommage*, needs to fulfil legal conditions.[150]

These scholarly propositions are not reflected in the case law. *Dommage* is the term used in article 1240 Cc. When accompanied by different adjectives (*moral, matériel*), it is used to categorize harm at a high level of generality, with different *préjudices* constituting the lower-level instantiations of the different types of *dommage*.[151] This explains why *dommage* and *préjudice* are frequently used interchangeably.[152] The amount of the monetary award is based on the totality of harm, whether labelled by a particular judge as *dommage* or *préjudice*.[153] Also the

interference with the right to a name (*atteinte au droit d'une personne sur son nom*), interference with personal liberty (*atteinte à la liberté*), or interference with feelings of affection (*atteinte aux affections*). René Savatier, *Traité de la responsabilité civile en droit français. Tome II. Conséquences et aspects divers de la responsabilité* (first published 1951, LGDJ 2016) 97–105.

[146] For a discussion of the more pragmatic reasons why French judges have introduced these additional categories of recoverable emotional harm, see Leczykiewicz (n 134) 197.

[147] Viney, Jourdain, and Carval (n 135) 4.

[148] ibid.

[149] ibid. See also Geneviève Viney, Patrice Jourdain, and Suzanne Carval, *Traité de droit civil. Les effets de la responsabilité* (4th edn, LGDJ 2017) 85 and 143. Those who argue that the obligation to repair in French tort law takes only the form of the duty to pay damages contrast non-contractual liability with contractual liability, where both modes of reparation are clearly available (ibid 86, fn 2).

[150] Viney, Jourdain, and Carval (n 135) 4.

[151] Leczykiewicz (n 134) 183.

[152] Viney, Jourdain, and Carval (n 135) 4.

[153] According to French case law, the claimant's compensatory award should leave them neither with outstanding loss nor enriched ('*ni perte ni profit pour la victime*'). See Ass plén 19 December 2003 no 02-14.783, JCP 2004.II.10008, and then, the next time in a tort case, Cass civ (3) 12 January 2010 no 08-19.224.

principle that the claimant should not be enriched by the compensatory award—what I have described elsewhere as the principle of 'exact' compensation[154]—covers in equal measure items of harm described as *dommage* and *préjudice*. Moreover, looking from the perspective of allowing recovery without proof of financial loss, it is *dommage* rather than *préjudice* that has the potential to give rise to a more 'normative' understanding of damage under article 1240 Cc.[155] For example, loss of use, discussed above in the context of both German and English law,[156] is recoverable in French law under the principle of *réparation intégrale* as *dommage matériel*.[157]

And thus, the overall conclusion on French law would need to be that, while it is comfortable with using the language of interests, both in legal scholarship, more explicitly, and in cases, through references to the different typified kinds of dommage and préjudice,[158] 'rights' as a distinct legal concept do only localized doctrinal work. Rights are not used at all as an organizing idea of French bases of extracontractual liability, nor are they overtly used as a rhetorical tool. This is partly because they do not form part of the official language of the relevant provisions in the Civil Code and did not feature prominently in the discussions surrounding the preparation of its original provisions. As Graziadei observed, in the post-revolutionary period, interests—especially self-interest—rather than backward-looking rights were considered to be a more appropriate foundation of the new French society.[159]

V. Conclusion

Much has been made of the fact that English law is not familiar with the concept of 'subjective right', which is central to German private *and* public law.[160] Lawson's response to this was that English tort law was not so dissimilar in that it accepted the idea of a protected interest.[161] The multiplicity of torts is to some extent the consequence of English law's desire to offer comprehensive but differentiated protection

[154] Leczykiewicz (n 134) 201.
[155] cf in German law, on which see text to n 56.
[156] See text to n 54 and 89.
[157] Cass civ (3) 23 June 1993, Bull civ III no 102. *Dommage materiél* is a very broad concept which covers any interference with the claimant's patrimony (*l'atteinte au patrimoine)*, where 'patrimony' (*le patrimoine*) is defined as a collection of rights and liabilities, including future ones. Jacques Ghestin, Gilles Goubeaux, and Muriel Fabre-Magnan, *Traité de droit civil. Introduction générale* (4th edn, LGDJ 1994) 156–57.
[158] The main doctrinal tool which is used to restrict recovery for pure economic loss is causation and thus it is more difficult to identify the boundary between recoverable and irrecoverable pure economic loss.
[159] Michele Graziadei, 'Rights in the European Landscape: A Historical and Comparative Profile' in Sacha Prechal and Bert van Roermund (eds), *The Coherence of EU Law: The Search for Unity in Divergent Concepts* (OUP 2008) 64, 69.
[160] Samuel (n 14).
[161] Lawson (n 18).

to a range of interests. Others observe that English law, alongside other common law jurisdictions, does not need to isolate 'subjective rights' because the meaning of the 'subjective right' concept is identical with the term 'right', while in German or French law 'right' and 'law' are referred to by a single word (*Recht*, *droit*), a duality which was visible already in Roman law in the double meaning of the term *ius*.[162] The relationship between subjective and objective *ius* can be conceptualized in two ways. Subjective *ius* can be seen as a product of exclusively objective *ius*: I only have the rights which objective (positive) law gives me. Alternatively, the two instantiations of *ius* can be regarded as independent: the rights I have as an individual may have many sources (positive law, interpersonal morality, custom). On this second account, the import of 'subjective rights' is greater than the sum of all the protection granted to individuals by positive law. With this explanation, it is clear that it is not the subjectivity of German tort law rights that poses a challenge to a comparative lawyer who would like to find similar concepts in English law. Individuals are vested with rights; the sovereignty of individuals is recognized in English law, which accepts the role of tort law (or private law more broadly) in protecting individual autonomy.[163] The problem, as I explained above, is that many 'rights' cannot be regarded as violated independently from evaluating the defendant's conduct. Even where such a possibility exists, as with torts actionable per se, English rights scholars insist that rights give rise to duties of conduct.[164] Actionable harm is harm that stems from a breach of a duty not to behave in a certain way, and in this sense from a violation of a 'claim right', but for most English rights scholars interference with a Hohfeldian power (or liberty) would not qualify.[165] Like in French law, the

[162] Helge Dedek, 'Subjective Right(s)' in Jan Martien Smits, Jaakko Husa, and Catherine Valcke (eds), *Elgar Encyclopedia of Comparative Law* (2nd edn, Edward Elgar Publishing 2023) 449; Thomas Mautner, 'How Rights Became Subjective' (2013) 26 Ratio Juris 111, 127.

[163] See Blackstone's definition of 'wrongs': 'WRONGS are divisible into two sorts or species; *private wrongs*, and *public wrongs*. The former are an infringement or privation of the private or civil rights belonging to individuals, considered as individuals.' William Blackstone, *Commentaries on the Laws of England*, Book the Third, ch 1 (first published 1765–69, OUP 2016) 3 (emphasis in the original). Cf Pierre Legrand, 'European Legal Systems Are Not Converging' (1996) 45 International and Comparative Law Quarterly 52, 70, claiming: '[English law] does not reveal any rational adherence to a legal philosophy that would locate in the legal subject a legally authoritative form of sovereignty so that he would be invested with the power to frame a legal claim in the language of "individual prerogatives".' On English law's familiarity with the idea of right as an individual entitlement, see Kiralfy (n 15) 57. On rights in English philosophical thought, see William E Edmundson, *An Introduction to Rights* (2nd edn, CUP 2012) chs 2 and 4.

[164] See text to n 82.

[165] Wesley Newcomb Hohfeld, 'Some Fundamental Legal Conceptions as Applied in Judicial Reasoning' (1913) 23 Yale Law Journal 16. Tort law rights are discussed in exactly such terms by Stevens (n 1) 4. The distinction between claim-rights and powers/liberties is of great significance to Stevens' analysis. Graziadei (n 159) 73, fn 31, observes that the fact that the English law of property is not centred on the image of *dominium* and the prerogatives of the owner of an asset means that in English law, contrary to what had taken place in the civil law tradition, the notion of an absolute right could not develop, 'despite Blackstone's vision of the right of private property as an "absolute right"'.

frequently mentioned concept of 'interference with a protected interest' does not invoke ideas of private law illegality, which it does in German law.[166]

In German law the reasoning in relation to cases brought under § 823(1) BGB proceeds in two stages. First, judges establish whether the claimant's harm (*Schaden*) stems from a violation of a right recognized by that provision, and only later are they interested in the more factual question of harm's existence. The two-stage analysis is to be found in English and French law too. English law asks about 'actionability of damage'—whether what the claimant has put forward in order to satisfy the requirement of damage meets what the law requires in that regard in a given context. French law does not dwell on the requirement of *dommage* where the factual circumstances include physical harm to the person or property of the claimant. But it expands the concept of *dommage* to address some of the normative questions of tort liability, such as that of the compensability of non-financial harm, recovery for future harm, or the treatment of claims brought by secondary victims. But the first stage of the analysis is either not at all about rights or only occasionally about rights.

Could the difference between German and French law be explained by the different modalities of the Roman law reception?[167] And what about English law? It has been established that the idea of violation of a right was popular among English theoretical writers. German thought had influence on Austin, who, on the other hand, influenced other English writers, including more recently.[168] English tort law seems less receptive to 'general rights', that is, rights that deliver bundles of entitlements. Such bundles, in order to give rise to remedies in English law, need to be decoupled into claim-rights. But any decoupling of the general rights needs also to be followed by the identification of a cause of action, within its established boundaries, that will enforce such a claim right. In that sense, *ubi remedium, ibi ius*.[169] It also explains why in English law rights scholars locate rights of relevance to tort law outside the field of tort law. Rights are imported from 'the common law', here understood more in the sense of customary law rather than pragmatic judge-made rules. Through decisions on recovery in a tort action, they become converted into claim-rights with more defined contours, tort law remaining the gatekeeper of liability.

[166] This is known as 'the result (or outcome) theory of illegality/unlawfulness' in German tort law. Dedek (n 162) 449 goes so far as to say this of German law: 'an entire regulatory set-up . . . constructs positive private law around the "subject", the individual'.

[167] Peter Stein, *Roman Law in European History* (CUP 1999) 83–84 and 88–92.

[168] Helge Dedek, 'From Norms to Facts: The Realization of Rights in Common and Civil Private Law' (2010) 56 McGill Law Journal 77, 84–85.

[169] Simon Whittaker, 'The Terminologies of Civil Protection: Rights, Remedies and Procedures' in Barbara Pozzo and Valentina Jacometti (eds), *Multilingualism and the Harmonization of European Law* (Kluwer Law International 2006) 45; Reinhard Zimmermann, *The Law of Obligations: Roman Foundations of the Civilian Tradition* (OUP 1996) 6.

In that regard German law is similar because while 'tort law rights' may have their origin outside of tort law (including in constitutional law), they need to be recognized as relevant for § 823(1) BGB. In English law, transposition into tort law of rights located in other parts of the law (human rights law) takes place either more or less readily depending on the openness of a given area of the law to the influence of rights.[170] French law is obviously less interested in the incorporation of rights into tort law, but, just like German and English law, gives liability law autonomy in determining instances of liability. However, in a system which leaves evaluative freedom to lower courts and in which the highest court can only condemn what the lower courts have done if presented as a violation of the tort provisions of the Civil Code, ideas will remain unexpressed. Certain circumstances are conventionally taken to give rise to *dommage moral* or *dommage matériel*, the conceptual justification for the categorization being less relevant. These concepts give French lawyers convenient and flexible containers facilitating the finding of the damage element.

Historically, 'damage' in English tort law could be seen as equally flexible. There was ambiguity within it. Sometimes 'injury' (a violation of a right) would be 'damage' or the reason to presume it.[171] In other cases, 'damage' could be used to describe anything with a physical manifestation or amounting to an observable change in a physical state of a person or a thing.[172] In still others, it could be pure economic loss or non-physical harm, as long as it passed a threshold test.[173] 'General damages', initially awarded by juries and later by judges for items lacking the specificity of 'special damage', which has to be proved and estimated more rigorously, offered, not unlike the French concepts of *dommage moral* and *dommage matériel*, convenient ambiguity and flexibility.[174] When rules on setting and calculating damages have been articulated and as tort law damages have become more frequently described as 'compensatory', loss, either financial or in the sense of the claimant being observably worse off, has emerged as the dominant concept of 'damage'.[175] This is true for the tort of negligence and some other torts (nuisance and, although not consistently, misfeasance in public office).[176] The law is still pulling in different

[170] A standard example is privacy, which in English law has led to the transformation of the tort of breach of confidence. However, breach of confidence has not been converted wholesale into a privacy tort. The privacy right has been used only selectively to produce a tort of misuse of private information. *Campbell v MGN Ltd* [2004] UKHL 22, [2004] 2 AC 457.

[171] *Ashby v White* (1703) 2 Ld Raym 938.

[172] Jane Stapleton, 'The Gist of Negligence: Part 1 Minimal Actionable Damage' (1988) 104 Law Quarterly Review 213.

[173] *Rothwell v Chemical & Insulating Co Ltd* [2007] UKHL 39, [2008] 1 AC 281.

[174] Street (n 95) 16.

[175] For example, even in the tort of conversion (a property tort), damages have been described as 'compensatory'. *Kuwait Airways v Iraqi Airways (Nos 4 and 5)* [2002] UKHL 19, [2002] 2 AC 122, [67] (Lord Nicholls).

[176] *St Helen's Smelting Co v Tipping* (1865) 11 HLC 642; *Watkins v Secretary of State for the Home Department* [2006] UKHL 17, [2006] 2 AC 395. See text to n 70 for a discussion of *Watkins* and misfeasance in public office.

directions, on the one hand rejecting interference with bodily integrity (penetration of lungs by asbestos fibres) as 'damage',[177] and on the other allowing 'user damages' without proof of financial loss, or allowing compensation for harm to the risk of which the defendant had not contributed, because the defendant violated the patient's right to information and the underlying right to personal autonomy.[178] That this should happen across different torts would be perhaps understandable, given the division in function between different tortious causes of action. But that it is happening with the same cause of action, the tort of negligence, is perhaps more challenging and, in the vein of French law, seems more casuistic.

The institutional debate, which affects the rhetorical dimension, is also not without significance. What gives judges the authority to determine the scope and limits of tort liability? Are claims about rights or their perceived absence a legitimate ground on which judges could base their rulings? The desire to provide judges with a template that allows them to make allocative decisions, at least seemingly on the basis of law, not policy, is shared across legal systems. Rights have been used to modify German tort law in order to include within its scope recovery for initially neglected pure economic loss or emotional harm.[179] In English law, rights are being used by scholars to break down unhelpful patterns of thinking, challenge the rigidity of historically determined causes of action, or reform precepts of tort liability. They could help bring out the substantive questions of the law, although for some they rather obscure the real questions: individual responsibility, fairness, and the distribution of legal protection.[180] It is doubtful that the making of contentious allocative decisions by judges can be entirely avoided, or that judges will actively and consistently seek to avoid them. The judicial process of inferring claim-rights from general rights or identifying specific duties as arising from recognized rights can be portrayed either as merely expressive or as a deeper, and potentially more controversial, normative search for considerations justifying non-contractual liability.

177 *Rothwell* (n 173).
178 *Chester v Afshar* [2004] UKHL 41, [2005] 1 AC 134.
179 Jansen (n 29) 101 and 105.
180 Peter Cane, 'Distributive Justice and Tort Law' [2001] New Zealand Law Review 401.

8
Foreseeability in the Law of Torts
A Comparative Analysis

*Marco Cappelletti**

I. Introduction

> The universe, cosmology suggests, is comprised largely of 'dark matter,' invisible stuff ubiquitously binding all things together. Lurking deep inside the law of tort, permeating and connecting its various components, a vital ingredient defines and gives moral content to the law of negligence, controlling how each element fits together and, ultimately, whether one person is bound to pay another for harm. Foreseeability is the dark matter of tort.[1]

This metaphor is how David Owen, a leading US scholar, portrays the role of foreseeability in tort law. Owen's view is symptomatic of the way in which foreseeability has traditionally been perceived across common law jurisdictions. In England and Wales, the concept of foreseeability has long constituted one of the main conceptual pillars of tort law, playing a fundamental role in delineating the conditions and scope of liability. First, foreseeability has long characterized many of the ingredients of the most dominant tort of all, negligence: it helps identify the range of potential claimants, it contributes to establishing what constitutes negligent conduct, and it limits the range of compensable harms. Secondly, foreseeability has spread from the tort of negligence to other torts, including those which have traditionally been regarded as imposing strict liability, such as the tort of private nuisance and the rule in *Rylands v Fletcher*. Finally, where the law is unclear and still needs to be settled, the tendency is to see foreseeability as a prima facie attractive solution which can be deviated from only for very good reasons.[2]

* Many thanks to the participants in the workshop 'Comparative Reflections in The Law of Obligations', Oxford, September 2023, for their insightful comments, and to Ciara Kennefick, Dorota Leczykiewicz, and Donal Nolan for written feedback on a draft of the chapter.

[1] David G Owen, 'Figuring Foreseeability' (2009) 44 Wake Forest Law Review 1277, at 1277.

[2] See text to and following nn 120–23.

Marco Cappelletti, *Foreseeability in the Law of Torts* In: *Comparative Reflections in Private Law*. Edited by: Marco Cappelletti, Ciara Kennefick, and Dorota Leczykiewicz, Oxford University Press. © Marco Cappelletti, Ciara Kennefick, and Dorota Leczykiewicz 2026. DOI: 10.1093/9780198959168.003.0010

Given the prominence of foreseeability in English law (and in other common law jurisdictions),[3] it is of considerable interest to ask whether comparable emphasis is placed on this concept in other tort systems, particularly those belonging to the civil law tradition. In this respect, it is surprising to see that, while there are historical studies considering the development of foreseeability in tort law,[4] this concept has received limited attention in the comparative tort law literature.[5]

The purpose of this chapter is to start filling this gap by exploring and comparing, both doctrinally and theoretically, the concept of foreseeability in English and French law. To do so, the analysis proceeds by considering the main elements of a typical tort action in which foreseeability can be found—namely, conduct, causation, and defences—and exploring how foreseeability operates within each. The aim is to start painting a picture of the concept of foreseeability in the English and French tort systems, comparing and contrasting its different uses and significance across them. As will be seen, there is a dramatic difference between the two: while foreseeability is a lead actor in English tort law, it plays a very marginal role on the other side of the Channel. As mentioned above, in England and Wales foreseeability is a fundamental ingredient of many tortious causes of action, particularly in the field of accidental harm, and it profoundly affects the assessment of conduct and causation as well as the availability of defences. In France, by contrast, it will be seen that foreseeability is largely irrelevant to the legal concept of *faute* ('fault'), that its role in causal analyses is occasional and, in any case, controversial, and that its impact at the level of defences is rather modest.

These striking divergences suggest wider differences between the English and French understandings of tort law and its aims: foreseeability aligns well with concerns which are readily identifiable in English law and which focus on the position of the tortfeasor, namely promoting ethical norms of individual responsibility, furthering deterrence goals, or keeping liability exposure under control; by contrast, foreseeability does not align well with the most fundamental aims of French law, namely compensating the victims of accidents and spreading losses in a spirit of social solidarity. A systematic analysis of the relationship between foreseeability and each of these goals within the two systems is beyond the scope of the chapter, but some tentative suggestions are nevertheless offered where possible.

3 Owen (n 1) 1278.

4 See eg David Ibbetson, *A Historical Introduction to the Law of Obligations* (OUP 2001) 164–67, 175–77, 195–96, 200.

5 The main comparative studies discussing foreseeability take either the form of a comparative analysis of case law across jurisdictions, or the form of answers to questionnaires from national reporters: see eg Walter Van Gerven, Jeremy Lever, and Pierre Larouche, *Cases, Materials and Text on National, Supranational and International Tort Law* (Hart Publishing 2000); Bénédict Winiger and others (eds), *Digest of European Tort Law, Volume 4: Essential Cases on the Limits of Liability* (De Gruyter 2024). Studies of this type analyse a vast array of legal issues and a wide variety of jurisdictions, with the result that foreseeability is not the exclusive (or even the main) concern of the analysis and cannot be explored in a systematic or comprehensive way.

The nature and aims of this study are inspired by Simon Whittaker's understanding of the meaning and value of comparative law. As he pointed out, a fundamental aim of comparative law is to deepen our understanding of the legal systems studied and of the ways in which their legal actors—judges, scholars, and legislators—think about the law.[6] Crucially, the existence of differences in ways of thinking across jurisdictions does not pose an obstacle to comparative analysis. On the contrary, 'differences in ways of thinking between lawyers from other legal systems can enrich debates both as to what we would wish to be doing with our laws and how we should be doing it, issues of policy and of technique'.[7] In that spirit, the considerable differences that the chapter uncovers in the use of foreseeability in English and French law can enrich the debate on its role in the two systems and shed light on the ways in which English and French legal actors think about it. As a result, this comparative study can promote both a critical reappraisal of the role and usefulness of foreseeability and a re-assessment of the goals and values shaping the two tort systems—at least insofar as these are reflected in the concept's treatment and significance.

The chapter is organized as follows. In section II, I briefly introduce and explain the concept of foreseeability, which is understood in broadly similar terms in English and French law. Sections III, IV, and V explore foreseeability in conduct, foreseeability in causation, and foreseeability in defences, respectively. Section VI provides some concluding remarks.

II. The Concept of Foreseeability

The concept of foreseeability, or *prévisibilité* in French, can be taken to refer to the ability of a person to anticipate future events, such as the consequences of one's own behaviour, the possible actions of other people, or natural events.

In tort law, the assessment of what is foreseeable is generally conducted by considering the range of events which a reasonable person would envisage.[8] On this basis, a risk of harm may be perceived as 'physically impossible', or 'so fantastic or far-fetched' that no reasonable person would foresee it.[9] Other risks may be small

[6] Simon Whittaker, *Liability for Products: English Law, French Law, and European Harmonization* (OUP 2005) 2–3.

[7] ibid 3.

[8] The foreseeability requirement may sometimes deviate from the reasonable person standard, and a higher level of knowledge may be imputed to the defendant. For example, under the Council Directive 85/374/EEC of 25 July 1985 on the approximation of the laws, regulations and administrative provisions of the Member States concerning liability for defective products, OJ L 210, 7.8.1985, p 29, manufacturers are liable for harms whose risk is foreseeable according to the most advanced level of scientific and technical knowledge available when the product was put into circulation. See art 7(e) of the Directive (establishing the development risk defence); Case C-300/95 *Commission v United Kingdom* [1997] ECR I-2649, esp paras 26–27.

[9] For English law, see eg *Overseas Tankship (UK) Ltd v Miller Steamship Co Pty Ltd (The Wagon Mound) (No.2)* [1967] 1 AC 617, 641–42 (PC). For French law, see Julia Heinich, *Le droit face*

but significant enough to be in the contemplation of the reasonable person, or they could be 'real and substantial', in which case they would clearly qualify as reasonably foreseeable.[10] In short, if the relevant risk is thought to be sufficiently likely on the basis of an ex ante assessment conducted by the reasonable person, it will be deemed to be reasonably foreseeable, or *normalement prévisible*.[11] In a sense, then, whether or not an event is foreseeable depends at least to some extent on an estimation of probability: the less probable an event is thought to be, the more unforeseeable its occurrence is regarded.

The relationship between foreseeability and probability is a complex one, though, and both English and French lawyers are aware of this. Given that there is no established threshold of probability recognized in law as distinguishing the foreseeable from the unforeseeable, knowledge (or accurate estimation) of probabilities will not be determinative of foreseeability issues. For example, is it reasonably foreseeable that a head injury inflicted on an employee by the employer's defective machinery will cause to him post-traumatic stress disorder, leading to severe depression and, ultimately, suicide, knowing that there is a 2–4 per cent chance of this outcome materializing?[12] Reasonable minds may differ, with some thinking that the employee's suicide is a reasonably foreseeable consequence of the employer's negligence,[13] and others believing instead that it is a mere possibility.[14]

Moreover, the ability to estimate probability and, hence, to foresee is affected by a variety of biases characterizing the human mind.[15] For example, while the odds of a fatal shark attack are extremely low,[16] and therefore this event should be judged as unforeseeable as a matter of probability, many would see it as 'eminently foreseeable'.[17] This happens because shark attacks receive a degree of media coverage and are so much part of popular culture[18] that they are seen as much more probable than they actually are, affecting our foresight. More generally, if an event has already occurred, people who know of the event tend to exaggerate the ex

à l'imprévisibilité du fait (PUAM 2015) paras 191–282 (discussing the various degrees of (un) foreseeability).

[10] See *The Wagon Mound (No. 2)* (n 9) 641–42.
[11] See Heinich (n 9) paras 255ff.
[12] This example draws on the English case *Corr v IBC Vehicles Ltd* [2008] UKHL 13, [2008] 1 AC 884.
[13] ibid [13] (Lord Bingham) and [56] (Lord Neuberger).
[14] ibid [28] (Lord Scott). On the vagueness of foreseeability, see also *Page v Smith* [1996] AC 155, 170 (HL) (Lord Keith and Lord Ackner disagreeing as to whether injury by nervous shock to the claimant was a reasonably foreseeable consequence of a car accident in which the claimant suffered no physical injury).
[15] See eg Amos Tversky and Daniel Kahneman, 'Availability: A Heuristic for Judging Frequency and Probability' (1973) 5 Cognitive Psychology 207.
[16] 1 in 4,332,817 in the United States: <https://www.floridamuseum.ufl.edu/shark-attacks/odds/compare-risk/death/> accessed 12 December 2024. To put this figure in perspective, consider that many more people die in the US from fireworks (1 in 340,733), drowning (1 in 1,134), and car accidents (1 in 84).
[17] Helen Scott, 'The History of Foreseeability' (2019) 72 Current Legal Problems 287, 313.
[18] ibid.

ante probability of its occurrence, a phenomenon called 'hindsight bias'.[19] Besides biases, idiosyncrasies too influence the ability to assess probability and our perception of what is foreseeable and what not. For example, a risk-averse person is more likely to consider small risks than risk-takers, and a person with a deeper knowledge of the outside world is more likely to foresee risks than a less knowledgeable person.[20] And while it is true that the courts generally resort to the reasonable person standard to ensure a level playing field, the reasonable person is a *fictio iuris* and the judges' own biases and idiosyncrasies as to what a reasonable person should contemplate will inevitably become decisive.[21]

In sum, the concept of foreseeability is inherently elusive and malleable, and this is clearly acknowledged in both French and English law.[22] Despite this, foreseeability features in the law of torts of both legal systems, although to markedly differing extents. To appreciate how the role and significance of foreseeability varies across the two jurisdictions studied, the discussion below first considers foreseeability in conduct, then moves to foreseeability in causation, and finally considers foreseeability in defences.[23]

III. Foreseeability and Conduct

From the standpoint of conduct, liability in tort is often classified either as strict or as based on fault. This tendency is common across jurisdictions, and neither English nor French law are exceptions to this.[24] Liability for fault is generally taken to rest on a judgment that the tortfeasor should have behaved differently, for

[19] Extensive empirical studies show this. See eg Baruch Fischhoff, 'Hindsight ≠ Foresight: The Effect of Outcome Knowledge on Judgment Under Uncertainty' (1975) 1(3) Journal of Experimental Psychology: Human Perception and Performance 288; Kim A Kamin and Jeffrey J Rachlinski, 'Ex Post ≠ Ex Ante: Determining Liability in Hindsight' (1995) 19 Law and Human Behavior 89. See also Heinich (n 9) para 10-1.

[20] Peter Cane and James Goudkamp, *Atiyah's Accidents, Compensation and the Law* (9th edn, CUP 2018) 39–40.

[21] For English law, See *Glasgow Corp v Muir* [1943] AC 448, 457 (Lord Macmillan) ('What to one judge may seem far-fetched may seem to another both natural and probable'). For French law, see Heinich (n 9) para 10 at p 35 (noting that the notion of foreseeability offers French judges a degree of flexibility, but it also generates uncertainty given its lack of precision); Philippe Le Tourneau, *Droit de la responsabilité et des contrats. Régimes d'indemnisation* (12th edn, Dalloz 2022) [2142.41] at p 734 (making a similar point).

[22] See eg Laurent Aynes, 'L'imprévision en droit privé', Revue de Jurisprudence Commerciale 2005, no 5, 1, para 19 (arguing that 'foreseeability is unseizable'); Heinich (n 9) para 10; Roderick Bagshaw, 'What Is "Reasonable Foreseeability"?' in Kylie Burns and others (eds), *Torts on Three Continents: Honouring Jane Stapleton* (OUP 2024) 145; Cane and Goudkamp (n 20) 39–40.

[23] It is sometimes suggested that foreseeability is in fact used as a cover beneath which judges hide all sorts of policy choices. While this may sometimes be true, the issue is an important and complex one, deserving a study of its own. Hence, it is outside the scope of the present chapter, which instead assumes that, when used, foreseeability has some substantive meaning.

[24] Marco Cappelletti, *Justifying Strict Liability: A Comparative Analysis in Legal Reasoning* (OUP 2022) 3 and 13–63.

instance because they acted with an intention to harm or because they failed to act as a reasonable person would have done in the circumstances. By contrast, strict liability is usually understood as liability which rests on grounds other than a failure in conduct, therefore being widely portrayed as liability without (or regardless of) fault.[25]

Focusing specifically on the question of the tortfeasor's conduct, foreseeability is far more relevant to fault-based liability than to strict liability. In strict liability torts, foreseeability can be of significance only in a particular and tenuous way. A requirement of foreseeability of harm puts people in a position to know, or at least to guess, their potential exposure to liability, should they decide to engage in an activity which is subjected to a strict liability regime. By knowing that liability will be limited to foreseeable harm, these people will be able to make an informed decision as to whether or not to engage in that activity.[26] In this sense, foreseeability surely influences the choices and behaviour of potential tortfeasors. However, once a choice has been made and the potential tortfeasor engages in an activity attracting strict liability, their conduct will be immaterial in the sense that no amount of care will help them escape liability. But if the tortfeasor's conduct is irrelevant, foreseeability as a factor bearing on the evaluation of that conduct would seem irrelevant too, as a matter of logic.

By contrast, foreseeability is prima facie more relevant in liability for fault, and this will be the main focus of the discussion. As will be seen, the different way in which the concept of fault is understood and articulated in English and French law impacts significantly on the role of foreseeability at the level of conduct. Moreover, even where similar understandings of fault are compared, most notably the English concept of lack of reasonable care and the French concept of *imprudence* or *manque de diligence*, striking differences persist between these two legal systems.

A. English law

English tort law features a wide range of distinct torts, each with its own technical rules and requirements, including in relation to the standard of conduct. As a result, a general and legal concept of fault with its own recognizable set of ingredients has never been developed in the English context. This is so true that, as Simon Whittaker persuasively observed, 'the language of "fault" ... serves only to confuse, being too vague and unspecific for the particularity of the English techniques'.[27]

[25] ibid.
[26] See Peter Cane, 'Fault and Strict Liability for Harm in Tort Law' in William Swadling and Gareth Jones (eds), *The Search for Principle: Essays in Honour of Lord Goff of Chieveley* (OUP 1999) 171, 185–86.
[27] See Whittaker (n 6) 201.

While this is certainly true, the language of fault has nevertheless great currency in the English context: as applied to conduct, fault is typically understood as failure to comply with prescribed standards of behaviour and it involves a judgment that the defendant should have acted differently.[28] For present purposes, what is key is that this type of liability for fault requires foreseeability: it is possible to say that a person is at fault in relation to some (risk of) harm, and hence that they should have acted differently in relation to it, only if they could reasonably be expected to foresee the possibility of its occurrence and then act on that basis.[29] This idea has been developed most clearly in the context of the tort of negligence, as this is the tort which has long dominated the scene as far as liability for accidental harm is concerned. As will be seen immediately below, foreseeability plays a key role in the assessment of conduct in negligence law. Moreover, foreseeability seems to have spread to other torts as well, most notably private nuisance, and in this context it has raised questions about its impact on the strict liability nature of the tort, as will be discussed in section III.A(ii) below.

(i) Foreseeability and the standard of reasonable care

Since *Vaughan v Menlove*,[30] the standard of conduct imposed by the tort of negligence has been that of reasonable care. According to this standard, a defendant can be found liable in tort if they failed to take the care which a reasonable person would have taken in the circumstances.[31] This standard can be broken down into two key components: foreseeability and negligence analysis. The negligence analysis assesses whether the defendant acted reasonably in not taking the precaution which the claimant alleges should have been taken. To perform this assessment, a variety of factors are considered and balanced with one another, most importantly the probability of harm, the severity of harm, and the burden of taking an effective precaution against the relevant risk of harm.[32] Crucially, these factors are assessed with *foresight*, meaning that they are all analysed by reference to the information available before or at the time of the alleged negligence.

[28] See eg Cane (n 26) 178ff.

[29] ibid 185.

[30] (1837) 3 Bing NC 468.

[31] In some cases, the standard of reasonable care is adapted to the qualities of certain categories of defendants, such as children, professionals, ordinary skilled people professing to have a special skill, and defendants participating in sports and games: for an overview of these variations, see Jenny Steele, *Tort Law: Text, Cases, and Materials* (5th edn, OUP 2022) 133–51.

[32] This assessment is sometimes couched in terms of cost–benefit analysis, an expression commonly associated with the economic analysis of law. However, it must be borne in mind that the balancing involved in the negligence (or cost–benefit) analysis cannot be easily reduced to an economic calculation, as the three main factors involved—probability of harm, severity of harm, and burden of precaution—are often financially incommensurable. Moreover, there are further factors which may on occasion be relevant to the negligence analysis and which appear impossible to quantify monetarily, ie compliance with common practice (eg *Baker v Quantum Clothing Group Ltd* [2011] UKSC 17, [2011] 1 WLR 1003, [82]) and the social usefulness of the defendant's conduct (eg s 2 of the Social Action, Responsibility and Heroism Act 2015).

English courts have put a lot of effort into elucidating the relationship between foreseeability and the negligence analysis, particularly in relation to the probability and severity of harm. As far as probability of harm is concerned, an excellent illustration is provided by *Roe v Ministry of Health*.[33] In that case, two patients remained severely injured due to a disinfectant which, after seeping into ampoules of anaesthetic through invisible cracks, became mixed with the anaesthetic itself and was administered to them. At the time of the accident, the state of scientific knowledge did not enable the medical community to appreciate that invisible cracks could appear in ampoules because of the anaesthetic they contained and, as a result, the probability that harm could be caused to patients in that way was perceived to be zero. Since the injury in question was totally unforeseeable, there was nothing that the defendant should have done to eliminate that risk, and therefore liability was ruled out. Similarly, it is not expected of the reasonable person to guard against risks of harm which, though theoretically known or knowable, are 'fantastic or far-fetched',[34] for otherwise 'life would be almost impossible'.[35] What is required of the reasonable person is to take precautions against risks which they know or ought to know are reasonably likely to materialize as well as risks which, though small or very small, need to be guarded against because of the weight which the other factors of the negligence analysis have in the circumstances. For example, in *The Wagon Mound (No. 2)*, the probability that oil on water could be set alight was very low, but the foreseeable severity of harm if that happened was great and the precautions which could foreseeably avoid the accident very cheap.[36] In light of this, the defendant's failure to take precautions attracted a finding of negligence. In sum, as applied to probability of harm, the foreseeability requirement excludes negligence in cases of absolute (or quasi-absolute) unforeseeability, while in situations where the probability of harm is characterized as small (or even very small), a finding of negligence is certainly possible if the other factors point in that direction.

This is very clear if attention is paid to the relationship between foreseeability and severity of harm. As emphasized by the Privy Council in *Paris v Stepney*, a reasonable person should be influenced 'not only by the greater or less probability of an accident occurring, but also by the gravity of the consequences if an accident does occur'.[37] In that case, the defendant knowingly employed in their garage a worker with only one good eye, but failed to provide him with goggles, with the result that the good eye was struck by some splinters of steel, causing complete blindness in the worker. The defendant employer was held liable because a reasonable

[33] [1954] 2 QB 66.
[34] *The Wagon Mound (No. 2)* (n 9) 642.
[35] *Bolton v Stone* [1951] AC 850, 863.
[36] *The Wagon Mound (No. 2)* (n 9) 642–44.
[37] *Paris v Stepney Borough Council* [1951] AC 367, 381.

person in that position would have appreciated that, despite the risk of harm to the worker's sight being small, its foreseeable severity was very considerable and the cost of taking an effective precaution (providing a pair of goggles) was negligible. In this case, then, the foreseeability requirement as applied to severity of harm supported a finding of liability, but other cases have gone the other way. In *Harris v Perry*,[38] the defendants hired some equipment for a birthday party for their children, including a bouncy castle. The children and some of their friends were playing on the castle when the claimant, who had just performed a somersault on it, received a hit to the forehead from a taller boy who was also performing somersaults, and suffered severe injuries. The Court of Appeal found that reasonable parents in the defendants' position would foresee that, if children played on a bouncy castle, some minor injury might occur; in relation to that risk, it was found that the defendants had taken adequate precautions. By contrast, in the Court's view the exceptional severity of the injury which occurred to the claimant was not reasonably foreseeable, and therefore the defendants could not reasonably be expected to guard against it. As can be readily appreciated from these cases, the foreseeability of severity of harm can play a role in determining the outcome of negligence claims.

Finally, although it is difficult to find cases discussing this point, it seems fair to say that foreseeability is equally significant when it comes to the burden of precaution as a factor in the negligence analysis. If the existence of a cost-justified and effective precaution was unknowable and thus unforeseeable at the time of the accident, the defendant would not be found negligent for not taking that precaution.[39] Holding the opposite view would mean judging the defendant's behaviour in hindsight—something which would be inconsistent with the way in which all the other factors of the negligence analysis are evaluated.

Overall, it is abundantly clear that foreseeability is key to establishing what constitutes unreasonable conduct. Whether a defendant has been negligent mainly depends on a combination between the foreseeable probability of harm, the foreseeable severity of harm, and the foreseeable burden of precaution, as anticipated by the reasonable person. As shown, English courts have developed a structured approach to the role of foreseeability in the negligence analysis, solidifying foreseeability as a formal requirement and providing general guidelines as to how this requirement should be approached at the conduct stage of the tort of negligence (or of any other tort based on the standard of reasonable care). As will be seen shortly in section III.B below, the position in France is strikingly different.

38 [2008] EWCA Civ 907, [2009] 1 WLR 19.

39 See Benjamin C Zipursky, 'Foreseeability in Breach, Duty, and Proximate Cause' (2009) 44 Wake Forest Law Review 1247, 1257.

(ii) Foreseeability of interference in the tort of private nuisance

Besides the tort of negligence, foreseeability constitutes an important consideration in English law in relation to other torts as well, including torts of strict liability.

If strict liability is liability which does not rest on a failure in conduct, it should be immaterial whether the defendant acted as a reasonable person should have done in the circumstances. This is, or at least has traditionally been, the configuration of liability for the creation of a private nuisance. Indeed, there are many judicial statements of the highest level emphasizing that liability for private nuisance is strict; as Lord Goff observed in *Cambridge Water Co v Eastern Counties Leather*, 'the fact that the defendant has taken all reasonable care will not of itself exonerate him from liability'.[40]

However, the truth of this proposition might be affected by the issue of whether private nuisance requires foreseeability of interference with the claimant's land.[41] This issue has sparked significant controversy among scholars,[42] and much of the recent disagreement seems to turn on the interpretation of statements included in the House of Lords' decisions in *Cambridge Water* and *Transco plc v Stockport MBC*.[43] In *Cambridge Water*, Lord Goff observed that 'foreseeability of harm is . . . a prerequisite of the recovery of damages in private nuisance';[44] in *Transco*, Lord Hoffmann said that 'the general rule of liability for nuisance today' is that the 'discharge' is 'intended or foreseeable'.[45] These remarks have been interpreted in opposite ways: on some accounts, they support the view that no private nuisance can be established unless the interference with the claimant's land is reasonably foreseeable;[46] on other accounts, these statements do not provide any clear support for this proposition, with the result that foreseeability of interference would not be required.[47]

Recently, though, the Court of Appeal seems to have come to a view. In *Northumbrian Water Ltd v Sir Robert McAlpine Ltd*,[48] the defendant construction

[40] [1994] 2 AC 264, 300.

[41] This requirement is distinct from the well-established requirement of foreseeability of the relevant type of harm: see text to nn 107–112.

[42] See eg Gerry Cross, 'Does Only the Careless Polluter Pay? A Fresh Examination of the Nature of Private Nuisance' (1995) 111 Law Quarterly Review 445, 458–73. For a more recent overview of the issue, see Maria Hook, 'Reasonable Foreseeability of Harm as an Element of Nuisance' (2016) 47 Victoria University of Wellington Law Review 267, esp 268, 274 (including fn 36).

[43] [2004] 2 AC 1.

[44] *Cambridge Water* (n 40) 301.

[45] *Transco* (n 43) [26]. Noteworthy, Lord Hoffmann seemed to have in mind cases of isolated (as opposed to repeated) escapes only, for in his view '[i]t is the single escape which raises the question of whether or not it [the escape] was reasonably foreseeable' (ibid [27]). With respect, confining unforeseeable escapes to isolated escapes seems a mistake: isolated escapes may well be foreseeable, and repeated or continuous escapes may well be unforeseeable (as in *Cambridge Water* (n 40) itself).

[46] James Goudkamp and Donal Nolan, *Winfield & Jolowicz on Tort* (21st edn, Sweet and Maxwell 2025) para 15-038.

[47] See eg Cross (n 42) 467–68; Hook (n 42) 270–71, 273–74.

[48] [2014] EWCA Civ 685, [2014] BLR 605.

company poured concrete into an underground shaft as part of their redevelopment works, but the concrete escaped into a private sewer and caused a partial blockage of the claimant's sewerage system. The claimant brought proceedings to recover remediation costs, but the Court of Appeal rejected the claim. Through a reasoning which relied heavily on Lord Goff's and Lord Hoffmann's obiter dicta in *Cambridge Water* and *Transco* respectively,[49] the court held that the defendant was not negligent in failing to discover the risk that the concrete could escape and that they had no reason to foresee the possibility of that escape.[50] In other words, there could be no private nuisance because the interference with the claimant's land was not reasonably foreseeable and thus no failure in the defendant's conduct could be shown. A similar approach had been already adopted in *Network Railway Infrastructure v Morris*, where the claimant complained about the effects that the magnetic field on the defendant's railway line had on the electric guitars he had been using in his recording studio, located approximately 80 metres from the line.[51] The Court of Appeal dismissed the claim on the ground that it was not reasonably foreseeable that the magnetic radiation could cover such a distance and hence reach the recording studio, based on evidence and past experience.[52]

The nature, strict or fault-based, of the tort of private nuisance has long been the subject-matter of intense discussion, and the approach adopted by the Court of Appeal to foreseeability of interference reinvigorates the debate. It is certainly true that foreseeability and fault/negligence can be pulled apart, that is, that an ability to foresee alone does not imply neither fault nor negligence,[53] and hence that requiring foreseeability of interference does not necessarily mean that negligence is also a prerequisite of liability for nuisance. But practically, one might wonder whether the effect of requiring foreseeability of interference would not be to confine liability to negligent conduct:[54] if one is not liable because they could not reasonably foresee an interference with the claimant's land, would they be liable because they could foresee it but not prevent it? On at least some accounts, the answer appears to be negative: it would only make sense to ask about foreseeability of interference if one also asks whether the defendant should have acted to avoid or reduce its risk.[55]

Given its potential implications, that is, turning private nuisance into a tort about unreasonable conduct, the requirement of foreseeability of interference has been met with scepticism.[56] Instead, the critics insist, it would be better to decide nuisance cases on the basis of an ex post evaluation of which property interest,

49 ibid [12]–[18].
50 ibid [18]–[19].
51 [2004] EWCA Civ 172, [2004] Env LR 41.
52 ibid [20]–[28].
53 Allan Beever, *The Law of Private Nuisance* (Hart Publishing 2013) 100–04.
54 Hook (n 42) 277, 282.
55 ibid 277.
56 ibid 277ff; Beever (n 53) 99–105.

the defendant's or the claimant's, takes priority,[57] regardless of any foreseeability of interference. Indeed, this approach would be entirely consistent with the well-established view that nuisance law focuses on the unreasonable effects of an interference with the claimant's property interest, not on the unreasonable character of the defendant's conduct. Be that as it may, what matters for present purposes is that, in light of recent decisions of the Court of Appeal, foreseeability of interference appears to be part of the law of private nuisance. Its inclusion, which is not a logical necessity but a deliberate choice of the lawmaker, shows a remarkable attachment of English law to the concept of foreseeability and, one might add, to the view that liability regardless of foreseeability should be closely scrutinised.[58]

B. French law

In contrast with English law, in French law the assessment of fault is largely independent of the concept of foreseeability. To an English lawyer, there can be negligence only in relation to reasonably foreseeable harm, for it cannot be said that a person should have behaved differently in relation to a risk of harm that could not be anticipated.[59] As seen, this link between negligence and foreseeability permeates the legal concept of reasonable care in English law. The French approach is different. To be sure, (at least some) French lawyers are well aware that, at an abstract level, foreseeability is relevant to the assessment of negligent behaviour. Yet, foreseeability is really not part of the fabric of the *legal* concept of fault in French tort law, revealing a marked contrast with English law. Moreover, as will be explained in the second subsection below, strict liability torts seem to be safe from the influence of fault-friendly ideas such as foreseeability, contrary to what has happened in English law.

(i) The meanings and flexibility of *la faute*: an obstacle to the concept of foreseeability

In discussing the role of fault in tort law, Carval writes that, '[w]hen asking themselves whether the defendant has acted as a reasonable man, judges obviously have regard to a wide range of elements, such as the foreseeability of the harm caused'.[60] Similarly, a leading textbook notes that '[non-intentional] fault consists

[57] This evaluation may be conducted in many different ways: eg compare Beever (n 53) 105–106, with Guido Calabresi and Alvin K Klevorick, 'Four Tests for Liability in Torts' (1985) 14 Journal of Legal Studies 585, 610.

[58] As will be seen in section IV.A.(ii), foreseeability is not limited to the interference element of private nuisance, as it is also a key ingredient of its causation/remoteness element; nor is it confined to the law of nuisance itself, as it has spread to the rule in *Rylands v Fletcher* and could potentially apply to other strict liability torts.

[59] Cane (n 26) 185.

[60] See Suzanne Galand-Carval, 'Fault under French Law' in P Widmer (ed), *Unification of Tort Law: Fault* (Kluwer Law International 2005) 89, para 19. See also Geneviève Viney, Patrice Jourdain,

sometimes in not having foreseen the possibility of harm, sometimes, if it has been foreseen, in not having taken the necessary precautions to avoid its occurrence'.[61] These statements show that the link between foreseeability and fault, particularly if understood as a failure in conduct, does not go unnoticed in France. However, acknowledgments of this type in academic texts are very rare, and it is equally difficult to find references to foreseeability in French judicial decisions.

To understand why foreseeability is perceived as so far removed from fault, it is indispensable to appreciate the distinctive meaning of *faute* in French tort law. Contrary to English law, where there is no category of fault recognized as such, in French law *faute* is a foundational legal concept enshrined in article 1382 (now 1240) of the French Civil Code (Cc). But when has *faute* been committed? Interestingly, *faute* has never received a formal substantive definition. The Civil Code is (still) silent on this, and French courts have generally refrained from defining the concept. As for legal scholars, several different views and formulations have been propounded,[62] and today it is widely agreed that any breach of a norm or duty recognized by the law constitutes fault.[63] Admittedly, given its vagueness, this definition of *faute* is not very helpful, even though some guidance is provided by looking at the range of situations in which *faute* is found to exist. Besides any failure to take reasonable care (*imprudence* or *manque de diligence*), *faute* encompasses the (non-negligent) violation of legislative requirements or administrative regulations, the commission of any criminal offence (however strict), and even the mere infringement of specific rights recognized by the law.[64] As can be readily appreciated, *faute* is a flexible and capacious concept, much broader than negligence. In the light of this, it is not surprising to see that foreseeability is not part of the concept of *faute*; if it were, the scope of application (and, ultimately, meaning) of *faute* would change considerably, as it would need to be restricted to conduct relating to foreseeable risks of harm only. Here, the contrast with English law is

and Suzanne Carval, *Les conditions de la responsabilité. Traité de droit civil* (4th edn, LGDJ 2013) para 344 (in discussing causation, arguing that the use of foreseeability means going back to fault-related issues), para 399 (in discussing defences, noting that unforeseeability is nothing else that the absence of fault in anticipating other causes of harm); Philippe Malaurie, Laurent Aynès, and Philippe Stoffel-Munck, *Droit des obligations* (13th edn, LGDJ 2024) para 42.

[61] Jacques Flour and others, *Droit civil. Les obligations. Le fait juridique* (15th edn, Dalloz 2024) para 134.

[62] See Marie Dugué, 'The Definition of Civil Fault' in Jean-Sébastien Borghetti and Simon Whittaker (eds), *French Civil Liability in Comparative Perspective* (Hart Publishing 2019) 79. A common definition of *faute* is a 'failure to fulfil a pre-existing obligation': see Marcel Planiol, 'Études sur la responsabilité civile', Revue critique de législation et jurisprudence 1905, 277, 287; Viney, Jourdain, and Carval (n 60) para 443.

[63] Jean-Sébastien Borghetti, '*The Definition of* la faute *in the* Avant-projet de réforme' in John Cartwright, Stefan Vogenauer, and Simon Whittaker (eds), *Reforming the French Law of Obligations: Comparative Reflections on the Avant-projet de réforme du droit des obligations et de la prescription ('the Avant-projet Catala')* (Hart Publishing 2009) 271, 278.

[64] See eg Simon Whittaker, 'The Law of Obligations' in John Bell and others (eds), *Principles of French Law* (2nd edn, OUP 2008) 294, 364–81.

sharp: while foreseeability is part and parcel of negligence—and, through that, of fault—in English law, there seems to be little, if any, trace of it in the French concept of *faute*. This is, of course, a reflection of the different understandings of fault in the two legal systems.

But even if one restricts the focus to *imprudence* or *manque de diligence*, the nearest equivalent to lack of reasonable care in English law, the situation does not change. As seen above,[65] English courts assess lack of reasonable care by means of an overt negligence analysis, which has been given a clear structure and content, and, in conducting this analysis, judges use the concept of foreseeability equally overtly. By contrast, French courts say very little if anything about the content of *imprudence* or *manque de diligence*. As their assessment of conduct is unstructured and there is no overt or articulate balancing of the factors which may be relevant to it,[66] it is unsurprising that there is no trace of foreseeability either. To explain this sharp difference between English and French law, two distinct (though related) points are in order.

The first concerns the different nature of English and French adjudication, a point which Simon Whittaker has perceptively identified and explained in his work. The English doctrine of binding precedent mixes fact and law together. As Whittaker explains, 'the facts of previous decisions [are involved] in the construction of the law itself, for the binding aspect of a decision (its *ratio decidendi*) is found in that proposition of law, or those propositions of law, which are necessary for the decision on the facts'.[67]

So, English lawyers pay the utmost attention to the facts of previous decisions and evaluate whether variations of fact may affect the law and its development. Moreover, even where courts must decide an issue of fact (such as fault in the tort of negligence) and hence have discretion in that regard, they structure the exercise of such discretion by providing a framework of analysis, for example guidelines or factors to be taken into account by lower courts in future cases.[68] This is an important aspect of judicial law-making, and it has contributed to the establishment and development of the negligence analysis and of the foreseeability requirement as considerations relevant to the fault issue in the tort of negligence. Where this issue is disputed, both the negligence analysis and the foreseeability requirement may be litigated by the parties, and the courts will decide their relevance to the facts of the case at hand on the basis of factors and guidelines developed through the accretion of previous (binding) case law. In the result, English law has

[65] See section III.A.(i).

[66] See Whittaker (n 6) 42–46 (offering several reasons for this silence in French law).

[67] ibid 192.

[68] See Simon Whittaker, 'Theory and Practice of the "General Clause" in English Law: General Norms and the Structuring of Judicial Discretion' in Stefan Grundmann and Denis Mazeaud (eds), *General Clauses and Standards in European Contract Law: Comparative Law, EC Law and Contract Law Codification* (Kluwer Law International 2006) 57.

developed a *legal* understanding of the negligence analysis as well as of the ways in which foreseeability affects that analysis.[69]

By contrast, none of this happens in France. While the work and activism of the courts have been a formidable force in the development of French tort law, there is no doctrine of binding precedent there. Therefore, the tendency is for the judges to apply the appropriate principles and (legislative) rules in every case and be satisfied that their decision is consistent with them, with no need to link fact and law in the way English judges do.[70] Determinations as to issues of fact such as *imprudence* or *manque de diligence* are left to the sovereign power of assessment of lower courts, which can take into account whichever considerations they prefer and see most appropriate in the circumstances. As Carbonnier put it, '[n]owhere more than in relation to fault do the judges proceed by way of a judgment based on fairness [*équité*] condemning or pardoning in the name of society'.[71] For its part, the *Cour de cassation* is content to review the correctness of such decisions of fact, while it has always refused to set out a definition or at least some guidelines for the evaluation of fault, even though it could very well have done so.[72] The result of all this is that French judges enjoy a very considerable degree of unstructured discretion when deciding what constitutes *imprudence* or *manque de diligence*, and the concept of foreseeability appears to be far away from their minds.

A second, related point explaining why foreseeability is not part of the picture goes to its substantive desirability. As Borghetti has noted, liability for fault is imposed today even in relation to unforeseeable harm.[73] In the exercise of their sovereign power of assessment, judges can pay little attention to issues of foreseeability and prioritize considerations of a very different nature, including the needs of victims, the deep pockets of defendants, or the availability of insurance, especially in cases involving personal injuries.[74] If foreseeability were to become a necessary factor in the assessment of *imprudence* or *manque de diligence*, judges would be forced to ask what a reasonable person in the defendant's position could be expected to know and anticipate, whether in relation to the precautions available or to the relevant risk of harm. In this way, foreseeability would lead to a (re)structuring of the judicial assessment of fault, making it much more difficult for judges to decide the fault issue covertly on the basis of considerations which are at odds with reasonable foreseeability and with a proper evaluation of behaviour. In addition, importing foreseeability into the concept of fault would prevent the imposition of liability on entire categories of defendants, for example individuals lacking

[69] See section III.A.(i).
[70] Whittaker (n 6) 201–02.
[71] Jean Carbonnier, *Droit Civil, Tome 4, Les obligations* (22nd edn, PUF 2000) para 228 (translation by Whittaker (n 6) 44).
[72] Viney, Jourdain, and Carval (n 60) para 440; Borghetti (n 63) 273.
[73] Borghetti (n 63) 284.
[74] See Carbonnier (n 71) para 228; Whittaker (n 6) 201; Dugué (n 62) 93.

discernment such as infants. These are unable to understand their own acts and anticipate the possible consequences of their behaviour.[75] Nevertheless, they are deemed capable of committing a fault in French law, given the resolutely objective understanding of fault as any breach of a legal norm or duty.[76] If foreseeability were adopted as an ingredient of *faute*, this area of French law would be in need of radical reform.

In conclusion, if foreseeability were imported into the French concept of *faute*, it would likely cause an attenuation of the incidence of liability, whether by encouraging a more structured evaluation of the defendant's behaviour or by preventing *tout court* the imposition of liability on certain categories of tortfeasors. Most French lawyers would see these developments as undesirable, for they would result in a reduction in the level of protection afforded to the victims of accidents and hence would conflict with the very reason behind the flexibility of the concept of *faute*. If, as Borghetti noted, 'one of the great strengths of the concept of fault, in French law, is its extreme pliability and flexibility',[77] any foreseeability requirement would be not only unnecessary but also a significant obstacle to the achievement of the fundamental goals of the French system. This contrasts sharply with English law where, as we have seen, foreseeability is widely perceived as an essential requirement of fault and it constitutes a distinctive ingredient of the standard of reasonable care. Whether this so in order to be ethically fair to defendants, to protect them from excessive liability, or to produce outcomes which are attuned to goals of deterrence (how could one avoid harm which was not foreseeable?), the effect is to restrict significantly the range of sanctionable conduct and, hence, of compensable harms. From this perspective, foreseeability contributes to drawing the attention of English law to concerns which are based on a close assessment of the defendant's conduct and which, therefore, are far removed from the victim-centred approach of French law.

(ii) Fault, strict liability, and foreseeability

Unlike English law, where the tort of negligence is the general and main basis of liability for accidental harm, French law relies heavily on strict liability (*responsabilité sans faute*, or *responsabilité de plein droit*).[78] For example, a person can be strictly liable for the harm caused by the deeds of things or animals in their own 'keeping' (*la garde*),[79] for the action of a person for whom they are responsible (eg children, employees),[80] for road accidents in which their own motor vehicle is

[75] Viney, Jourdain, and Carval (n 60) para 444.
[76] ibid.
[77] Borghetti (n 63) 273.
[78] This does not mean that fault has become unimportant. Where there is no other legal ground to seek redress, arts 1240 and 1241 Cc remain available to claimants.
[79] Art 1242(1) and art 1243 Cc, respectively.
[80] Art 1242(1), (4)–(8) Cc.

involved, or for the harm caused by their ruinous buildings.[81] In addition, extensive strict liabilities can be imposed on French public bodies for the harm caused to others in the performance of their activities.[82]

The cumulative scope of application of all these (and other) strict liability rules is very broad, with the result that there is a vast area of accidental damage where fault is not a condition of liability. This means that the concept of foreseeability, understood as a component of the evaluation of conduct, is not part of the picture. A few examples by way of comparison with English law show how this works and reveal a marked difference between English and French law. Consider *Roe v Ministry of Health*, which was discussed before when exploring foreseeability in the English context.[83] As already mentioned, at the time of the accident it was not possible to know that invisible cracks could appear in ampoules because of the anaesthetic they contained, and hence that the phenol in which they had been stored could seep into the ampoules and be eventually administered to the patients. Because of the totally unforeseeable nature of the injury, the defendant was found not liable in English law. Should the same facts arise in France, the claimants may well try to bring an action under article 1242 Cc and establish liability for the deeds of things. The claimants could target phenol as the thing, and they could argue that the phenol was in the hospital's keeping, being in its 'use, direction, and control'.[84] On the facts of the case, according to the rules on causation developed by French courts, a causal link between the thing and the harm would be presumed because the phenol was in motion and it came into contact with the victims.[85] This would be enough for the claimants to get compensation for their injuries and, critically for present purposes, there would be no need for them to show any fault in the defendant, nor to prove foreseeability of harm.

Now take *Harris v Perry*, the English case concerning a child injured while doing somersaults on a bouncy castle.[86] As will be recalled, the parents who hired the bouncy castle were found not negligent because the magnitude of the harm which materialized, a severe head injury, was deemed to be unforeseeable. In French law, it is difficult to say with certainty what the position of a judge would be on the issue of fault, but this would not matter: the injured child could sue the hirers of the bouncy castle as keepers of the thing under article 1242(1) Cc, or he could sue the parents of the taller boy who had injured him and claim their vicarious

[81] Art 1244 Cc. For a more comprehensive list of strict liability rules in French law, see Cappelletti (n 24) 37–49.

[82] See René Chapus, *Droit administratif general, Tome 1* (15th edn, Montchrestien 2001) paras 1450–1519.

[83] See text to and following n 33.

[84] This is how *la garde* is defined in French law: see Ch réun 2.12.1941 (*Franck*), S 1941.1.217, note H Mazeaud.

[85] For a detailed account of causation rules in liability for the deeds of things, see Viney, Jourdain, and Carval (n 60) paras 661–674.

[86] See (n 38).

liability under article 1242(4)(7) Cc. Either way, liability would be imposed on a strict basis and no issue of fault—and in consequence of foreseeability as relevant to conduct—would arise.

These examples (to which countless more could be added) are helpful in establishing a more general point. In the field of non-intentional harm, English law relies primarily on the tort of negligence while French law makes available to claimants a vast array of strict liability rules. This means that, in English law, the defendant's conduct is typically scrutinized, and foreseeability acts as a fundamental condition for the imposition of liability. By contrast, the high number and impressive rigour of strict liability rules in French law means that the defendant's conduct is often not an issue, and hence foreseeability (as relevant to conduct) is immaterial too.

In sum, not only is foreseeability absent from the legal concept of fault, which is where one could expect to find it, but fault itself—understood as negligent behaviour—is comparatively much less prominent in France than in England, this further reducing the significance of foreseeability in French law.

IV. Foreseeability and Causation

As seen above, one question is to ask whether and how foreseeability is relevant to the assessment of tortious conduct, that is to say if the defendant should have foreseen that their behaviour posed a certain risk of harm and that reasonable precautions were available. A different question, which will be the focus of this section, is instead to ask whether foreseeability is relevant to establishing a legally relevant connection between the tortious conduct or event and the claimant's harm. This type of question is typically encountered in the context of the causation element of liability rules. As will be seen, the nature and structure of causal inquiries is controversial and can take a variety of forms, with key differences between English and French law. Most importantly for present purposes, foreseeability may feature in different forms and to different extents in the structure of causal inquiries, and this emerges very clearly by comparing the two tort systems. As will be seen, foreseeability looms large in English law, whereas it has limited relevance in French law.

A. English law

In English law, causation has traditionally been divided into two distinct questions. The first is usually labelled as the question of 'cause in fact', or 'factual causation'. In its basic form, this question asks whether the defendant's conduct was a necessary (or 'but-for') cause of the claimant's harm: absent that conduct, would the harm have still materialized? For present purposes, issues of factual causation can be left to one side, because foreseeability is not relevant there: what matters in factual causation is to decide, retrospectively, whether the defendant's conduct played a role in the history of the harm, and there is no way in which foreseeability can be of assistance in this inquiry.

The second question has traditionally gone under the banner of 'cause in law', 'legal causation', or 'remoteness'. These terms are sometimes used interchangeably (as in this chapter), while at other times they refer to different issues.[87] Fundamentally, though, they all reflect a concern to assess whether there is a connection between the defendant's conduct and the claimant's harm which is regarded as sufficient by the law. It may happen that the defendant's conduct is a cause in fact of the claimant's harm, and yet the law concludes that the two are not sufficiently connected, for instance because the harm could not be anticipated or was not among the risks which made the defendant's conduct negligent, because causal factors other than the defendant's conduct were at work,[88] or because the claimant was not a foreseeable victim of the defendant's conduct.[89] Although many of these issues are sometimes framed in openly causal language,[90] they have little to do with the reconstruction of events and more with a normative judgement about the scope of liability for the consequences of tortious conduct.[91] Perhaps partly because of their role in limiting the scope of liability, remoteness and legal causation issues have attracted considerable attention in legal scholarship, and the courts have put a lot of effort into developing a structured framework of analysis for them. In this respect, the significance of the concept of foreseeability cannot be exaggerated: as will be seen, foreseeability has traditionally played a key role in this context, and its attractiveness has even led to its spreading from the tort of negligence to torts of strict liability.

(i) Remoteness in negligence law

Since *The Wagon Mound (No. 1)*,[92] the starting point of analysis for assessing the remoteness of accidental harm has been reasonable

[87] Compare Steele (n 31) ch 6; Simon Deakin and Zoe Adams, *Markesinis and Deakin's Tort Law* (8th edn, OUP 2019) ch 5; and Goudkamp and Nolan (n 46) para 8-067.

[88] A prime example is *novus actus interveniens*, ie conduct of a third party or of the claimant which, in the eyes of the law, constitutes the sole legal cause of the claimant's harm and hence severs the causal link between that harm and the defendant's conduct. While *novus actus* is often discussed in the context of legal causation, for reasons of exposition I discuss it in the context of defences: see section IV.A.

[89] Traditionally, foreseeability of claimants is an issue considered by English courts when assessing the duty of care element of the tort of negligence. This classification has been questioned and the issue of claimant foreseeability seems more appropriately analysed as part of the remoteness inquiry: see text to and following n 105.

[90] See eg HLA Hart and Tony Honoré, *Causation in the Law* (2nd edn, OUP 1985).

[91] Jane Stapleton, 'Occam's Razor Reveals an Orthodox Basis for Chester v Afshar' (2006) Law Quarterly Review 426, at 426. See also Jane Stapleton, 'Legal Cause: Cause-in-Fact and the Scope of Liability for Consequences' (2001) 54 Vanderbilt Law Review 941.

[92] *Overseas Tankship (UK) Ltd v Morts Dock & Engineering Co Ltd (The Wagon Mound)* [1961] AC 388.

foreseeability,[93] the same test which applies to the assessment of conduct, as seen previously. As Viscount Simonds put it:

> It is a principle of civil liability . . . that a man must be considered to be responsible for the probable consequences of his act. To demand more of him is too harsh a rule, to demand less is to ignore that civilised order requires the observance of a minimum standard of behaviour . . . After the event even a fool is wise. But it is not the hindsight of a fool; it is the foresight of the reasonable man which alone can determine responsibility.[94]

Over the years, the proposition that a defendant can be liable in negligence only for harm which was a reasonably foreseeable consequence of their conduct has undergone considerable refinement. First, the courts have made clear that the decision in *The Wagon Mound (No. 1)* links foreseeability to the *type* of harm, not to its extent: so long as the harm suffered by the claimant is of a type which was reasonably foreseeable, liability will extend to the full extent of that harm, even if such extent was unforeseeable.[95] Secondly, it is not necessary that the exact sequence of events leading up to the accident is foreseeable, so long as the harm inflicted on the claimant is of a type which was reasonably foreseeable.[96]

While these two refinements of the foreseeability principle might seem straightforward, they are not, and the second one in particular looks unstable. Indeed, there are cases where the courts have been clearly concerned with the way in which the damage occurs rather than with the type of damage itself,[97] and where they have been prepared to rule out liability on that basis. For example, in *Tremain v Pike*, the claimant herdsman, while employed on the defendant's farm, contracted Weil's disease as a result of the excessive growth of the rat population on the farm.[98] Even assuming that the defendant had been negligent in not keeping

[93] The qualification 'accidental' is necessary because foreseeability is not an issue for harm deliberately inflicted. Indeed, any loss which is the direct and natural consequence of deliberate or dishonest wrongdoing is compensable, regardless of its foreseeability: see eg *Quinn v Leatham* [1901] AC 495, 537; *Doyle v Olby (Ironmongers) Ltd* [1969] 2 QB 158, 167; *Essa v Laing Ltd* [2004] EWCA Civ 2, [2004] ICR 746, at [39] (per Pill LJ). See also Hart and Honoré (n 90) 259; *Clerk & Lindsell on Torts* (24th edn, Sweet & Maxwell 2024) paras 2-148–2-151.

[94] *The Wagon Mound (No. 1)* (n 92) 423–24. See also *Doughty v Turner Manufacturing Co Ltd* [1964] 1 QB 518.

[95] See *Smith v Leech Brain & Co Ltd* [1962] 2 QB 405: while it was not reasonably foreseeable that a burnt lip could result in cancer and in the death of an employee, it was reasonably foreseeable that the employer's defective equipment could cause the initial injury (burnt lip), with the result that the employer was held liable for the employee's death, even if unforeseeable. See also *Wieland v Cyril Lord Carpets Ltd* [1969] 3 All ER 1006; *Simmons v British Steel PLC* [2004] UKHL 20, [2004] ICR 585; *Corr* (n 12).

[96] *Hughes v Lord Advocate* [1963] AC 837 (while it was not reasonably foreseeable that a dropped paraffin lamp in a manhole could have resulted in an explosion, it was reasonably foreseeable that a person may have burnt themselves on some negligently unattended paraffin lamps).

[97] eg *Jolley v Sutton LBC* [2000] 1 WLR 1082.

[98] [1969] 1 WLR 1556.

the rat population under control, Payne J held that the possibility of contracting Weil's disease was not reasonably foreseeable and hence that the defendant could not be held liable. By contrast, injury resulting from a rat bite or food poisoning from contaminated food would have been a sufficiently foreseeable consequence of the defendant's negligence. In other words, on the facts of the case 'rat-induced disease' was not sufficiently specific as a type of harm to satisfy the foreseeability requirement,[99] and much more was required in terms of foreseeing how rats might spread a disease. As this decision shows, both the meaning of type of damage and the relationship between type of damage and the manner of its infliction can become unclear.

Partly for this very reason, it has been questioned whether foreseeability alone can explain the law on remoteness of damage, and today it is increasingly popular to maintain that the real test is not foreseeability but instead the so-called scope of risk principle.[100] According to this, a harm is too remote if it is not within the scope of the risk that made the defendant's conduct negligent: if a doctor gives negligent advice to a mountaineer as to the fitness of their knee, and the mountaineer gets injured on an expedition because of a rock fall, the doctor will not be liable because, although foreseeable, injury due to a rock fall (as opposed to injury due to a defective knee) was not within the risk which made the advice negligent.[101] While it is still controversial whether scope of the risk is best seen as the true remoteness test or as a framework that complements a foreseeability-based test, it is clear that, ultimately, no liability can be imposed for harm which, though foreseeable, is outside the sphere of risk negligently created by the defendant. In addition, and what matters the most for present purposes, foreseeability remains a key element of remoteness under either approach: whether as the gist of the analysis under a foreseeability-based test, or as a sub-question within the 'scope of risk' test, harm is not recoverable if it was unforeseeable.[102]

Finally, it should be mentioned that the concept of foreseeability is used to restrict the range of potential claimants, as liability for negligence can be imposed only if it was reasonably foreseeable that someone in the position of the claimant could be harmed by the defendant's conduct.[103] The foundational decision is

[99] See Goudkamp and Nolan (n 46) para 8-073.

[100] See Donal Nolan and James Plunkett, 'Keeping Negligence Simple' (2022) 138 Law Quarterly Review 175. Cf *Armstead v Royal & Sun Alliance Insurance Co Ltd* [2024] UKSC 6, [2024] 2 WLR 632, [47](i): 'The test for remoteness in the tort of negligence . . . is that loss is too remote to be recoverable as damages if the type of loss suffered was not reasonably foreseeable at the time of the breach of duty.'

[101] *South Australia Asset Management Corp v York Montague Ltd (SAAMCO)* [1997] AC 191, 213 (Lord Hoffmann). See also *Khan v Meadows* [2021] UKSC 21, [2021] 3 WLR 147. Given that the relevant risk must be assessed *ex ante*, ie in foresight, the 'scope of risk' principle is sometimes thought to overlap with the test of reasonable foreseeability. See the *Restatement (Third) of Torts: Liability for Physical and Emotional Harm*, § 29, comment *j*, and the Reporters' Note on comment *j*.

[102] As mentioned above, harm of unforeseeable extent is recoverable, provided that the initial harm was foreseeable: see text to n 94.

[103] For traditional formulations of this requirement, see *Donoghue v Stevenson* [1932] AC 562, 580; *Bourhill v Young* [1943] AC 92, 104.

Donoghue v Stevenson,[104] where Lord Atkin famously stated that a duty of care is owed to persons which one can reasonably foresee would be likely injured by one's own act or omission.[105] Traditionally, the issue of claimant foreseeability has been considered by English courts when dealing with the element of duty of care in the tort of negligence, but several scholars have persuasively argued that it would be more appropriate to analyse it as part of the remoteness inquiry.[106] Regardless of whether it is best seen as going to duty of care or to remoteness, claimant foreseeability is a key limitation on the scope of liability for negligence. Indeed, the same careless act may foreseeably harm a person and unforeseeably harm another person, triggering liability in relation to the former but not in relation to the latter. A famous decision which is often mentioned in the English context to illustrate this point is the US case *Palsgraf v Long Island Railroad*.[107] There, the defendant's employees assisted a passenger to board a moving train but negligently knocked a package from the latter's arms. Unknown to the employees, the package contained fireworks, which fell upon the rails and exploded. The explosion caused some scales on the other side of the platform to fall and to strike and injure the claimant, Mrs Palsgraf. While harm to the passenger or to his property (the package) was a foreseeable risk of the employees' conduct, and could have therefore led to liability vis-à-vis that passenger, there was nothing in the circumstances to suggest that the same conduct could have injured Mrs Palsgraf, and hence the defendant was held not liable to her. As can be appreciated, by limiting the range of people who can successfully sue the tortfeasor for its negligence, the requirement of claimant foreseeability confirms once again the central role of foreseeability in determining the scope of liability for negligence.

(ii) Remoteness in strict liability torts

Besides the tort of negligence, foreseeability has been adopted as a key element of remoteness of damage in various strict liability torts, and it also attracts support as the best or most natural solution in relation to torts whose remoteness rules are still unclear.

In *The Wagon Mound (No.2)*, the Privy Council introduced the idea that a defendant could not be held liable in nuisance for harm which was not a reasonably foreseeable consequence of the interference,[108] and this view has been adopted by the House of Lords in *Cambridge Water Co v Eastern Counties Leather*.[109] In that case, the defendants used a solvent which seeped into the ground below their

[104] *Donoghue v Stevenson* (n 103).
[105] ibid 580.
[106] See eg Donal Nolan, 'Deconstructing the Duty of Care' (2013) Law Quarterly Review 559, 566 and, 573.
[107] 162 N.E. 99 (N.Y. 1928).
[108] *The Wagon Mound (No.2)* (n 9) 640.
[109] *Cambridge Water* (n 40).

premises and reached a borehole, contaminating the claimants' water. The defendants were found not liable on the ground that it was not reasonably foreseeable that the solvent would pollute the claimant's water. Importantly, Lord Goff observed that 'the development of the law of negligence in the past 60 years points strongly towards a requirement that . . . foreseeability should be a prerequisite of liability in damages for nuisance, as it is of liability in negligence'.[110]

Limiting in this way the scope of liability was not a logical necessity, but rather a choice. Given that liability for the creation of a private nuisance has traditionally been understood as not resting on a failure in conduct, it would have been possible to base remoteness of harm on tests other than reasonable foreseeability.[111] Indeed, while foreseeability is an indispensable ingredient in negligence as a tort concerned with unreasonable risk creation, the same is not true for strict liability torts, whose gist is not the defendant's conduct and whose boundaries may, therefore, be drawn via concepts other than foreseeability. The House of Lords took a different view, however, arguably because of the attractiveness of ideas characterizing the tort of negligence, most notably foreseeability, and of the need to specially justify any departure from them. Taken together with the adoption of the requirement of foreseeability of interference,[112] a test for remoteness based on foreseeability suggests that the tort of private nuisance is heavily influenced by the tort of negligence, and this has even pushed some scholars to argue (perhaps too pessimistically) that private nuisance may be absorbed into negligence.[113]

In *Cambridge Water*, the House of Lords also considered the remoteness element of the rule in *Rylands v Fletcher*,[114] and it equally established that foreseeability of harm of the relevant type is the appropriate test in the event of an escape.[115] This development is even more remarkable than that which occurred in the law of nuisance, for the rule in *Rylands v Fletcher* was, in its early days, distinctively strict and it provided general protection against the use of dangerous things.[116] However, over the course of the twentieth century, the highest judicial authorities have drastically reduced the scope of application of this rule, by confining it to the protection of interests in land and by filling it with controversial and stringent requirements.[117] As a result, *Rylands v Fletcher* is today treated as an extension of private nuisance to cases of isolated escapes; its scope of application is very narrow, and its usefulness to potential claimants rather modest. As for remoteness

[110] ibid 300.

[111] See eg Beever (n 53) 106.

[112] See text to nn 41–58.

[113] Beever (n 53) 105.

[114] (1865) 3 H & C 774 (Court of Exchequer); (1866) LR 1 Ex 265 (Court of Exchequer Chamber); (1868) LR 3 HL 330.

[115] *Cambridge Water* (n 40) 306.

[116] See eg Donal Nolan, 'The Distinctiveness of Rylands v Fletcher' (2005) Law Quarterly Review 421, 432–33.

[117] The key decisions in the history of the demise of the rule in *Rylands v Fletcher* are: *Read v J Lyons* [1947] AC 156; *Cambridge Water* (n 40); and *Transco* (n 43).

of harm, the appropriate test was a controversial issue among scholars, with some supporting foreseeability and others rejecting it;[118] on its part, the House of Lords must have thought it natural to conform the remoteness test in *Rylands v Fletcher* to that used in the tort of private nuisance (and, ultimately, in negligence), given that the rule itself is seen as a sub-species of that tort.[119] In sum, while other paths could have been taken, foreseeability has made its way into the rule in *Rylands v Fletcher* because of a combination of factors, such as its (now very close) relationship with private nuisance, the adoption in private nuisance of a foresight-based remoteness test, and a clear reluctance to adopt broad and rigorous rules of strict liability for accidental harm.[120]

A final indicator of the position of foreseeability in English law can be discerned from the debate surrounding other strict liability torts whose remoteness rules are currently unclear. For example, the Animals Act 1971 says nothing about remoteness of harm caused by animals, and it is therefore unclear whether the test should be reasonable foreseeability or something else. Different views have been expressed on this matter, but the fact that reasonable foreseeability plays a key role in negligence law, in nuisance, and in *Rylands v Fletcher* appears to carry some weight,[121] and it has sometimes been seen as a sufficient reason for applying the same test to liability for animals.[122] Similarly, the Consumer Protection Act 1987 is silent on the remoteness rules to be applied to liability for defective products, and scholars disagree as to what approach should be followed: while some argue that limiting liability by reference to foreseeability is 'out of place in a strict liability action',[123] others note that '[p]erhaps the better view is that a foreseeability test should indeed be applied, since the tendency has been to extend the negligence remoteness rules to other unintentional torts, including those where liability is strict'.[124] Regardless of what the better approach would actually be, what is worth noting is that the debate revolves around reasonable foreseeability as if this were a sort of default position which could be adopted in cases of doubt and from which any departure would need special justification. This is a further testament to the

[118] For a summary of this debate, see *Cambridge Water* (n 40) 304.

[119] ibid 300–06.

[120] On the English approach to strict liability and its justifications, see Cappelletti (n 24) 13–26 (strict liability generally), 103–14 (risk), 137–45 (accident avoidance), 166–70 (the deep-pockets rationale), 205–16 (loss spreading), 234–39 (victim protection), 250–53 (administrative cost reduction), 271–81 (individual responsibility), and 307–310.

[121] See Peter North, *Civil Liability for Animals* (OUP 2012) para 2.60 (on dangerous animals), para 2.75 (on non-dangerous animals), para 3.31 (on straying livestock).

[122] See James Goudkamp and Donal Nolan, *Winfield & Jolowicz on Tort* (20th edn, Sweet and Maxwell 2020) para 17-027. Cf the new edition, Goudkamp and Nolan (n 46) para 11-027, where the reference in the previous edition to 'the principles of foreseeability as developed since *The Wagon Mound*' has been dropped.

[123] *Markesinis and Deakin's Tort Law* (n 87) 613.

[124] Goudkamp and Nolan (n 46) para 12-050. See also Duncan Fairgrieve and Richard Goldberg, *Product Liability* (3rd edn, OUP 2020) para 17.74.

significance of foreseeability in English law and to the influence that this concept has exerted and continues to exert on tort law and its development.

B. French law

As in English law, in French law too the existence of a causal connection (*lien de causalité*) between the defendant's harmful conduct or activity and the claimant's harm is a fundamental condition for the imposition of liability.[125] This requirement is sometimes expressed by saying that only damage (*dommage*) which is a direct consequence of the defendant's conduct is recoverable (*dommage direct*). While *dommage* is distinct from *causalité* in the taxonomical structure of French tort law, arguably in the same way as damage and causation are treated separately in English law, it is uncontroversial that insisting that *dommage* be *direct* is another way of requiring a certain type of the *lien de causalité* between conduct and damage.[126]

When, according to French law, does a causal connection exist? Compared to English law, the French causal inquiry is not clearly divided into different stages of analysis, but it takes the form of a global assessment of causation. As will be seen imminently, this assessment can be based on one or more causal theories and, depending on the approach adopted, the concept of foreseeability may or may not be relevant.

(i) Foreseeability in French causation: the theory of adequate causation

The French approach to causation resembles, in some ways, that to the concept of *faute*. French courts do not provide a specific definition of causation, nor do they pledge allegiance to any particular causal theory. Rather, judges typically content themselves with stating that the defendant caused (or did not cause) the claimant's harm, therefore retaining a very considerable degree of discretion in their causal analyses. In this way, causation represents (together with fault) a key control device in the hands of French courts for drawing the boundaries of liability and for deciding cases in the way they perceive as most equitable.[127] But while causation may be an almost impenetrable concept if analysed through judicial decisions,[128]

[125] See arts 1240 and 1241 Cc.

[126] see eg Flour and others (n 61) para 172; Francois Terré and others, *Droits civil, Les obligations* (13th edn, Dalloz 2022) para 927; Viney, Jourdain, and Carval (n 60) para 359; Malaurie, Aynès, and Stoffel-Munck (n 60) para 159; Philippe Le Tourneau, 'Le préjudice' in Philippe Le Tourneau (ed), *La responsabilité civile* (PUF 2003) 29.

[127] See Muriel Fabre-Magnan, *Droit des obligations. 2—Responsabilité civile et quasi-contrats* (6th edn, PUF 2025) para 234.

[128] Boris Starck, Henri Roland, and Laurent Boyer, *Obligations*, vol 1, *Responsabilité délictuelle* (5th edn, LITEC 1996) para 1066: 'Causation is one of the most obscure issues in the law of torts. Masses of cases shed no further light on the subject-matter, dominated as they are by the individual circumstances of the case and the intuition of the court' (translation by Van Gerven, Lever, and Larouche (n 5) 418).

French scholarly discussions are much more informative. From these, it emerges that two main causal theories hold sway in French law: the theory of equivalence of conditions (*théorie de l'équivalence des conditions*) and the theory of adequate causation, or adequacy theory (*théorie de la causalité adéquate*).

Starting with the theory of equivalence of conditions, this theory mirrors the English but-for test, as they are both concerned with assessing the factual role of the defendant's conduct in the production of the claimant's harm:[129] conduct is a factual cause of the harm if, but for it, the harm would not have occurred. In this theory, there is no place for the concept of foreseeability, as the causal assessment is done retrospectively, ie on the basis of the information available at the time of litigation.

The position looks different in relation to the adequacy theory, according to which an event or action is an adequate cause of harm if it raises the probability of its occurrence.[130] This theory exists in versions of different rigour, depending on the level of information available to the person assessing probability and on the time of assessment. The most rigorous approach maintains that the probability of harm should be estimated at the time of trial (ie in hindsight), and that all the knowledge available to humankind should be relied upon for the estimation.[131] On a less rigorous approach, the probability of harm is estimated in foresight, that is, on the basis of the knowledge available at the time of the conduct. This is the approach that, according to French scholars, characterizes French law: a conduct constitutes an adequate cause of harm if, judged at the time the tortfeasor acted, the harm constituted a probable, and hence foreseeable, consequence of the conduct in the ordinary course of events.[132]

In the context of a foresight-based adequacy theory, different views have been developed as to the appropriate level of knowledge for assessing probability. First, the relevant information may be that available to the particular defendant, taking into account all their idiosyncrasies and limitations. Secondly, it could be that available to the reasonable person; as this approach focuses on whether the claimant's harm was a reasonably foreseeable consequence of the defendant's conduct, it corresponds to the foreseeability test adopted in English law for remoteness of damage. Thirdly, the relevant knowledge may be that available to the most perceptive person, who knows everything that can be known by humankind.[133] Between these alternatives, French law does certainly not focus on the knowledge

[129] Fabre-Magnan (n 127) para 231.

[130] See AM Honoré, 'Causation and Remoteness of Damage' in *International Encyclopedia of Comparative Law, Volume XI: Torts* (1971) para 80.

[131] ibid paras 81–84. See also Florence Gsell-Macrez, *Recherches sur la notion de causalité* (Université Paris I Pantheon-Sorbonne, These 2005) para 103.

[132] Viney, Jourdain, and Carval (n 60) para 340-1; Philippe Brun, *La responsabilité civile extracontractuelle* (6th edn, LexisNexis 2023) para 240; Fabre-Magnan (n 127) para 232.

[133] Honoré (n 130) para 82.

expected of the particular defendant,[134] as this approach is highly individualized and therefore would lead to uncertainty in the administration of the law and to a denial of liability, and hence of compensation, in too many cases. As between the other two approaches, French law seems inclined to prefer that referring to the knowledge imputable to the reasonable person: scholars usually refer to what is *normalement prévisible* (literally, normally foreseeable),[135] and this corresponds to what would be regarded as reasonably foreseeable in the English context.[136] In sum, if foreseeability plays some role in the French law of causation, it does so as an ingredient of the adequacy theory.

(ii) The relevance of foreseeability in causation

The usefulness of the adequacy theory in French law is particularly evident in relation to strict liability torts. There, the absence of a fault requirement accentuates the need for a causal test which can complement or replace the theory of equivalence of conditions.[137] Its role in fault-based liability is instead more controversial, and probably more tenuous, with other causal approaches often coming into play.

In the realm of strict liability torts, the clearest example of the adequacy theory can be found in the liability for the deeds of things. According to article 1242(1) Cc, strict liability is imposed for the harm caused by a thing in the defendant's keeping. As it is very common for a physical thing to be involved in the causative process leading to a person's harm, French courts have developed requirements which allow to overcome the causal over-inclusiveness resulting from the application of the theory of equivalence of conditions. In particular, judges have established that if the thing is in motion and comes into contact with the claimant's body or property, it will be presumed that the thing played an active role (*rôle actif*) in causing the harm; if, however, either the thing is in motion but does not come into contact with the claimant's body or property, or the thing is stationary, there will be no presumption of causation and the claimant will have to establish that the thing had an active role in producing the harm.[138] This will be typically proved by showing that the thing had an internal defect, or that it was in an abnormal position or state. For example, a person who slips on the floor of a supermarket which has been made slippery by the presence of a fallen ice cream can get damages from the defendant supermarket, as what caused the injuries was the abnormal (ie slippery) state of

[134] See Viney, Jourdain, and Carval (n 60) para 340-1.

[135] ibid para 344; Brun (n 132) para 241; Mireille Bacache-Gibeili, *Les obligations, La responsabilité civile extracontractuelle* (3rd edn, Economica 2016) para 497; Fabre-Magnan (n 127) para 232.

[136] Carbonnier (n 71) para 216. Cf Viney, Jourdain, and Carval (n 60) para 340-1 (saying that the assessment of an adequate cause is conducted 'by reference to scientific data', this arguably involving knowledge available to the most perceptive person); but see ibid para 344 (referring to what is *normalement prévisible*). It may often be difficult to draw the line between different degrees of foreseeability, as recognized in Viney, Jourdain, and Carval (n 60) para 344.

[137] Malaurie, Aynès, and Stoffel-Munck (n 60) para 63; Flour and others (n 61) para 212.

[138] See Viney, Jourdain, and Carval (n 60) paras 665–674.

the floor.[139] Similarly, a woman who, walking towards a balcony, does not realize that the sliding glass door is closed, hits it, and breaks it can recover damages for personal injuries, as the very fact that the glass in the door shattered is proof of its fragility and, therefore, abnormality.[140] Many French scholars read these (and similar) cases as applications of the adequacy theory, for the relevant abnormality or defect in the thing is seen as what renders the occurrence of the harm probable and foreseeable.[141] Regardless of whether or not these cases constitute correct applications of the adequacy theory, the key point here is that this theory and, with it, the concept of foreseeability are perceived as especially useful because they can help resolve the problems of causal uncertainty posed by the theory of equivalence of conditions.

Another way in which foreseeability appears to be at work through the adequacy theory is by alleviating the burden of proof borne by claimants, especially in the context of fault-based liability. Claimants may sometimes struggle to prove a sufficient causal link between the tortfeasor's conduct and their harm, and this difficulty has led the courts to develop a variety of facilitating mechanisms. For present purposes, what is most interesting is that French courts sometimes note that the defendant's fault created a dangerous situation and then rely on concepts such as probability or foreseeability to conclude that causation between conduct and harm is established.[142] Used in this way, the adequacy theory is not seen as limiting liability. On the contrary, it works as a means to increase a claimant's chances to obtain redress, because it allows the courts to engage in a probabilistic reasoning leading to a presumption of causation which can only be displaced by a more certain and credible cause.[143]

In sum, as presented in scholarly writings, the adequacy theory and the concept of foreseeability can find application in various ways in the French law of causation. On the other hand, their significance should not be overestimated, for the following reasons.

To begin with, the adequacy theory is heavily criticized. First, the very idea of a foreseeable event would lack rigour, for it is unclear on the basis of what data and of what conception of 'ordinary course of events' such an idea should be worked

[139] Cass civ (2) 24 January 1985 no 83-15.378, Bull civ 1985, II, no. 21. See also Cass civ (2) 25 October 2001 no 99-21.616 (a letter box overhanging by 40 cm on a sidewalk was deemed to be in an abnormal position and therefore to have caused injuries to a pedestrian who collided with it).

[140] Cass civ (2) 24 February 2005 no 03-13.536, RTD civ 2005.407 obs Jourdain.

[141] Viney, Jourdain, and Carval (n 60) para 358-1 (including fn 90 for extensive references to further academic writings), para 674 at p 830.

[142] Viney, Jourdain, and Carval (n 60) para 369 (giving examples about defendants (i) renting out a dangerous thing to a person not capable of controlling the attendant risk; (ii) failing to monitor someone under their surveillance; (iii) marketing dangerous products; (iv) generally creating a situation of danger for others). See also Cass civ (1) 24 January 2006 no 02-16648, RTD civ 2006.323 obs Jourdain; Cass civ (2) 15 March 2012 no 10-15503; Cass civ (1) 22 March 2012 nos 11-10935 and 11-11237.

[143] Viney, Jourdain, and Carval (n 60) para 347; Fabre-Magnan (n 127) para 232.

out.[144] Secondly, the adequacy theory may lead to a denial of compensation in many cases and for no good reason, as vague notions such as probability or foreseeability should not trump the need to protect the victims of accidents.[145] This is particularly so given that some tragic accidents may well occur at the end of an extraordinarily uncommon sequence of events, and denying compensation in these circumstances would run counter to the fundamental function of modern tort law,[146] which is compensating and spreading losses in a spirit of social solidarity.[147] Thirdly, the adequacy theory would confuse fault and causation, as it revolves around ideas, especially foreseeability, which should pertain to the assessment of conduct only.[148]

A second reason suggesting that the significance of the adequacy theory in French law should not be overestimated is its controversial scope of application. The theory is generally presented as a way to select, among the but-for causes of a harm, that which is legally relevant. Using the adequacy theory in this way is certainly possible, but not necessary, in the sense that causation issues can be dealt with without resorting to the adequacy theory. Indeed, contrary to English law where the but-for test is merely the first step in the causal inquiry, in France the corresponding test, the theory of equivalence of conditions, is sometimes seen as exhausting the causal assessment, especially in relation to fault-based liability rules: if it is concluded that the defendant's negligent conduct is a factual, but-for cause of the claimant's harm, then the causal assessment is completed.[149] Moreover, where the theory of equivalence of conditions cannot provide a clear and definitive answer, complementary tests other than the adequacy theory are said to be relied upon: if both the defendant and the claimant (or a third party) were at fault, the degree of severity and immorality of the different faults may be key, in the sense that the gravest fault would absorb the others and constitute the sole legal cause of the harm;[150] in other situations, a criterion of temporal proximity is invoked to explain decisions where the event nearest in time to the occurrence of harm is selected as the legally relevant cause.[151]

[144] Viney, Jourdain, and Carval (n 60) para 344. See also Brun (n 132) para 241.

[145] See eg Brun (n 132) para 241; Bacache-Gibeili (n 135) para 497. See also François Chabas, *L'influence de la pluralité de causes sur le droit à réparation* (LGDJ 1967) paras 113–114.

[146] Viney, Jourdain, and Carval (n 60) paras 344 and 346.

[147] See eg Jean-Sébastien Borghetti, 'The Culture of Tort Law in France' (2012) 3 Journal of European Tort Law 158.

[148] Viney, Jourdain, and Carval (n 60) para 344.

[149] Borghetti (n 63) 284.

[150] See eg Cass civ (2) 7 December 1988 no 87-18917 Bull Civ 1988 no 246, p 133; Fabre-Magnan (n 127) para 235.

[151] Cass civ (3) 19 February 2003 no 00-13253, RTD civ 2003.508 obs Jourdain. Between the first defendant causing a fire which destroys a roof and the second defendant's negligence in repairing the roof, the latter is selected by the court as the cause of the water leak from the roof which damaged the claimant's property. Cf Jourdain, ibid p 509, noting that it was neither probable nor foreseeable that the original fire could result in damage by water leak (and hence the fire was not an adequate cause of the claimant's damage).

Thirdly, and relatedly, the practical impact of the adequacy theory is the object of strong disagreement among legal scholars: some see it as an exception to the theory of equivalence of conditions,[152] while others think of it as the dominant causal paradigm.[153] This uncertainty is due to the fact that the case law on causation is opaque and of difficult interpretation, as French courts often refrain from providing any meaningful elucidation on their approach to causal issues. What seems clear, though, is that, if compared to English tort law, foreseeability has much less to say in the French context. In English law, foreseeability applies to all the main areas of accidental harm, given that it is a remoteness requirement in the tort of negligence. By contrast, in French law it does not apply in a key area such as road accidents,[154] and the extent of its involvement in other strict liability rules as well as in fault-based liability is unclear. To give an example concerning strict liability, consider the English case of *Cambridge Water* and how it would be decided in France. In England, the claim was brought in negligence, nuisance, and under the rule in *Rylands v Fletcher*. The House of Lords held that the claim would fail on all three counts, as it was not reasonably foreseeable that the defendant's solvent could seep into the ground below their tannery and reach the claimant's borehole or that it could irremediably contaminate their water. Should the same facts happen in France, the claimants could rely on liability for the deeds of things under article 1242(1) Cc. The defendants would clearly qualify as keepers of the solvent, as this was in their use, direction, and control. At the level of causation, no issue of foreseeability would arise; the causal link between the action of the thing and the damage could be established simply on the ground that the solvent was in motion and came into contact with the claimant's property (their water).

Overall, then, the concept of foreseeability plays only a timid role in the French law of causation, and it certainly does not enjoy the currency it has in English law. In France, foreseeability works as a key element of the theory of adequate causation, but the role of this theory is controversial, both because the extent of its use in the case law is unclear and because its merits are challenged, particularly on the grounds that it threatens to reduce the degree of protection afforded to the victims of accidents by restricting the range of relevant but-for causes and, hence, of compensable harm. In contrast, in English law foreseeability plays a key role in determining the sufficiency of the link between conduct and harm, both in fault-based torts and in some strict liability torts. If the relevant harm is of a type which was not

[152] Viney, Jourdain, and Carval (n 60) para 356.

[153] Terré and others (n 126) para 1091; Alain Bénabent, *Droit des obligations* (19th edn, LGDJ 2021) para 551.

[154] The *loi* Badinter (*loi* no 85- 677 of 5 July 1985) imposes liability on the driver or keeper of a motor vehicle for any accident arising in connection with the operation of that motor vehicle, and issues of foreseeability of harm bear no relevance in the *loi*. For an overview of this liability regime, see Jean-Sebastien Borghetti, 'Extra-Strict Liability for Traffic Accidents in France' (2018) 53 Wake Forest Law Review 265, esp at 273 (saying that the *loi* Badinter covers 'any *unforeseen* and potentially harmful event arising in connection with the circulation of motor vehicles') (emphasis added).

reasonably foreseeable, then it is too remote to trigger the imposition of liability. By restricting the scope of liability in this way, the foreseeability requirement suggests that English law is less concerned with compensation than French law, and that its remoteness rules may be more attuned to other considerations, for example the promotion of ethical norms of responsibility or the prevention of accidents.[155] In sum, in English law foreseeability limits liability to an extent (and for reasons) which most French lawyers would regard as unacceptable.

V. Foreseeability and Defences

The concept of foreseeability can be an important feature of defences. The term 'defence' can refer to a variety of concepts but, broadly defined, it refers to a fact the existence of which entails that no liability arises or that an established liability is reduced or restricted in some way.[156] This section will consider only defences which operate to negate one or more elements of a tort claim, for these are the defences in which the concept of foreseeability is most visible in both jurisdictions.[157] As will be seen, *un*foreseeability can be a greater or lower barrier to a finding of liability depending on the role it is made to play in these defences. Perhaps unsurprisingly, unforeseeability is much less of an obstacle for claimants in French law than for claimants in English law.

A. Unforeseeability as a reason to reject liability in English law

In English law, unforeseeability features in a number of defences which may be invoked to attack either the conduct element or the causation element of a tort claim, notable examples being act of God and act of a third party. In defences of this type, unforeseeability works as a threshold requirement, in the sense that if a court is satisfied that the relevant act or event was not reasonably foreseeable, the

[155] On the relationship between foreseeability in causation and moral norms of responsibility, see eg Honoré and Hart (n 90) 254–55; Owen (n 1) 1293ff. The link between foreseeability in causation and deterrence is evident from a law-and-economics perspective: see eg Guido Calabresi, 'Concerning Cause and the Law of Torts: An Essay for Harry Kalven, Jr' (1975) 43 University of Chicago Law Review 69; Omri Ben-Shahar, 'Causation and Foreseeability' in Michael Faure (ed), *Tort Law and Economics* (Edward Elgar Publishing 2009) 100.

[156] This understanding of the term 'defence' draws on the taxonomy developed in Sandy Steel, 'Defences to Tortious and Contractual Liability in French Law' in Borghetti and Whittaker (n 62) 285, 285–86. On the disagreement regarding the meaning of the concept of defence, see Andrew Dyson, James Goudkamp, and Frederick Wilmot-Smith, 'Central Issues in the Law of Tort Defences' in Andrew Dyson, James Goudkamp, and Frederick Wilmot-Smith (eds), *Defences in Tort* (Hart Publishing 2015) 3, 5–11.

[157] In English law, defences which negate an element of a tort claim are sometimes called 'denials': see James Goudkamp, *Tort Law Defences* (Hart Publishing 2013) 46–74.

defendant's plea will be accepted without more and hence a finding of no liability will follow.

Starting with act of God, this term refers to natural events 'which involved no human agency and which . . . could not have been prevented by any amount of *foresight*, pains and care, reasonably to be expected of [a human]'.[158] In negligence claims, this defence has been pleaded to negate the conduct element. For example, an exceptionally severe frost[159] or a sudden heart attack[160] have been judged to constitute events which the defendants could not have foreseen and guarded against, therefore shielding them from liability because of lack of fault.[161] In strict liability torts, particularly in relation to the rule in *Rylands v Fletcher*, a plea of act of God has been accepted to negate causation. In *Nichols v Marsland*, an extraordinarily violent rainfall caused a large quantity of water to escape from some artificial embankments, resulting in extensive property damage.[162] The court found that the rainfall was so exceptional that no reasonable person could have anticipated it, although, if anticipated, the escape could have been prevented. The court concluded that the unforeseeability of the rainfall was enough to justify a finding of no liability.

A similar approach can be identified in relation to the act of a third party. This defence has been pleaded primarily in actions under the rule in *Rylands v Fletcher*. For example, in *Perry v Kendricks*, a boy caused an explosion by throwing a match into the patrol tank of a disused coach located in the defendant's parking ground.[163] The defendants were held not liable for the claimant's injuries resulting from the explosion, on the ground that the boy's action was something they could not have anticipated (and guarded against).[164]

A further defence is act of the claimant, according to which the defendant's liability is denied if harm was due wholly to the claimant's own conduct. For example, in *Rylands v Fletcher* it was said that a defendant could be exempted from liability if the escape of the dangerous thing from their land had been caused by the claimant's own conduct.[165] While not much has been said on (un)foreseeability in the context of this defence, it seems clear that the foreseeability (and avoidability) of the claimant's act would be relevant considerations.[166]

[158] *Transco* (n 43) [59] (emphasis added).
[159] *Blyth v Birmingham Waterworks Co* (1856) 11 Ex 781.
[160] *Ryan v Youngs* [1938] 1 All ER 522, 525.
[161] In principle, extraordinary events of a similar type may also be invoked to negate causation: see Goudkamp (n 157) 58–59.
[162] (1876) 2 Ex D 1.
[163] [1956] 1 WLR 85.
[164] ibid 89, 91, 93. See also *Markesinis and Deakin's Tort Law* (n 87) 500 (emphasizing that a defendant sued under *Rylands v Fletcher* can avoid liability by proving that the escape of the dangerous thing 'was caused by the *unforeseeable* act of a stranger') (original emphasis).
[165] (1866) LR 1 Ex 265, 279–80.
[166] *Reeves v Commissioner of Police of the Metropolis* [2000] 1 AC 360, 393–94 (Lord Hobhouse).

Finally, *novus actus interveniens* is sometimes described as a defence, as it can be invoked by the defendant to negate liability.[167] A *novus actus* is an act of a third party or of the claimant which is subsequent to the defendant's conduct and which, in the eyes of the law, constitutes the sole effective cause of the claimant's harm. In assessing whether the intervening act constitutes *novus actus*, foreseeability is often thought to play a role, although its relevance can vary.

First, there is case law suggesting that the unforeseeability of the relevant act is likely to rule out liability. For example, in *Knightley v Johns*, Mr Johns's negligent driving caused the blocking of a busy tunnel, which led the police inspector to order a police constable, Mr Knightley, to drive back against the traffic to close the tunnel. While doing so, Mr Knightley was struck and injured by another driver, Mr Cotton, who was driving too fast into the tunnel.[168] In deciding on the liability of Mr Johns for Mr Knightley's injuries, Stephenson LJ emphasized that 'the question to be asked is . . . whether that whole sequence of events is a natural and probable consequence of [Mr Johns's] negligence and a reasonably foreseeable result of it'.[169] The Court of Appeal concluded that the police actions and Mr Cotton's negligence constituted a sequence of events that was not reasonably foreseeable by someone in Mr Johns's position, and this was enough to break the causal link between Mr Johns's initial negligence and Mr Knightley's injuries.

In other cases, foreseeability has been deemed to be irrelevant. In *McKew v Holland Hannen & Cubitts*,[170] the claimant had temporarily lost control of his left leg because of an injury which had been caused by the negligence of his employers. Sometime later, on leaving a flat, the claimant suffered a severe fracture of the ankle after his leg collapsed as he made to descend some steep stairs which had no handrail. Importantly, the claimant knew of his leg issues and could have descended the stairs in a more careful way or with the assistance of his wife and brother-in-law, but he freely chose not to. On the facts, the House of Lords observed that the chain of causation between the employer's negligence and the claimant's fall had been broken, and that foreseeability did not come into this assessment. To be sure, it was eminently foreseeable that a person in the claimant's position could take some unreasonable risk and that this could result in some injury,[171] but that was neither here nor there: the unreasonableness of the claimant's behaviour was conclusive and did not allow any room for foreseeability-based considerations which could help the claimant.

In yet other cases, foreseeability has been considered as one of the factors bearing on *novus actus* issues. In *Clay v TUI UK Ltd*, the Court of Appeal suggested a multi-factorial balancing exercise that considers the extent to which the

[167] *Stone & Rolls Ltd v Moore Stephens* [2009] UKHL 39, [2009] 1 AC 1391, 1425.
[168] [1982] 1 WLR 349.
[169] ibid 366.
[170] [1969] 3 All ER 1621.
[171] ibid 1623.

conduct in question is reasonably foreseeable, the degree of unreasonableness of the conduct, and the extent to which this conduct is voluntary and informed.[172] Broadly speaking, the idea is that the more unreasonable and voluntary/informed the conduct is, the more likely it is to be a *novus actus*, while the more foreseeable the conduct is, the less likely it is to be a *novus actus*.[173] In *Clay* itself, the claimant inadvertently trapped his family on the balcony of a hotel room due to the defective locking mechanism of the sliding balcony door. In stepping across onto the balcony of an adjacent room to rescue his family, the claimant fell to the terrace below and was seriously injured. In deciding that the claimant's conduct broke the chain of causation between the defendant's negligence (defective locking mechanism) and the claimant's own injury, the Court considered the three factors mentioned above: stepping across balconies was (i) beyond the sensible contemplation of any ordinary hotelier, (ii) a highly unreasonable course of action given the high risk of injury involved, and (iii) a deliberate choice of the claimant.[174]

On the basis of existing case law it is therefore not entirely clear how foreseeability affects *novus actus* issues, particularly where the relevant act is foreseeable; but if the *Clay* approach is followed in the future, then decisions will be based on a balancing exercise with foreseeability as one of the relevant considerations.

Overall, the concept of foreseeability plays a role in defences denying one or more elements of a liability rule. Most importantly for present purposes, if there is an act of God, of a third party, or of the claimant which is not reasonably foreseeable, liability in the defendant is likely to be denied.

B. Unforeseeability as an autonomous requirement of force majeure in French law

While defences have attracted less scholarly attention,[175] they have traditionally been the object of considerable discussion in French law. In a tort system deeply committed to the compensation of losses, working out if and how defences can operate is particularly important because it clarifies and keeps under control the conditions under which a defendant may be able to escape liability or obtain its reduction. In French law, defences are also the legal category where the concept of (un)foreseeability is most visible and controversial.

For present purposes, the focus will be on *les causes d'exonération de la responsabilité* (grounds of exoneration of liability), and more particularly on

[172] [2018] EWCA Civ 1177, [2018] 4 All ER 672, [28].

[173] ibid. However, if the defendant's duty of care includes a duty to prevent the claimant from engaging in that very conduct, liability may well follow even if the claimant's conduct was deliberate/voluntary: see *Reeves* (n 166).

[174] *Clay* (n 172) [46].

[175] Steel (n 156) 291.

la cause étrangère. There are three main types of *cause étrangère*, broadly corresponding to the defences analysed above in relation to English law: *cas fortuit* (which includes both natural events and events such as wars or strikes), *fait du tier* (act of a third party), and *fait de la victime* (act of the claimant). To be a *cause étrangère*, an act or fact must be 'exterior' to the defendant, to their things, or to the people for whom they are liable.[176] For example, the keeper of a thing which caused harm to others cannot plead *cause étrangère* merely because the harm was due to a defect or characteristic in the thing of which the defendant knew (or could know) nothing. Any such defect or characteristic is by definition internal to the thing, and therefore the exteriority requirement will not be met.

Crucially, a *cause étrangère* can amount to a force majeure, which has the effect of exempting completely the defendant from liability, if it possesses two characteristics: unforeseeability and unavoidability.[177] The relationship between these two requirements has sparked a lively debate, particularly as to whether they are both necessary to trigger force majeure. In English law, if an act of God, of a third party, or of the claimant is either unforeseeable or unavoidable, the defendant will generally be able to escape liability.[178] In France, the issue is controversial, but a majority of courts require the act to be both unforeseeable and unavoidable. For example, if a car driver stops between railroad crossing gates and gets killed by an oncoming train, his conduct does not constitute force majeure because, while unavoidable, the presence of vehicles in that position is foreseeable in light of its statistical frequency.[179] Again, if the keeper of a piece of land knows of the risk of a landslide and thus can foresee it, but cannot do absolutely anything to prevent it from occurring and damaging someone else's property, the landslide does not constitute force majeure. The mere fact that the event is foreseeable, even though unavoidable, prevents it from constituting force majeure.[180]

This approach has been heavily criticized by many French legal scholars, who believe that the fundamental point of force majeure is unavoidability.[181] An event is unavoidable if it cannot be prevented through the taking of appropriate measures. On this approach, unforeseeability is certainly a clear indicator of unavoidability: if

[176] Bacache-Gibeili (n 133) paras 530ff.
[177] See Fabre-Magnan (n 127) paras 245ff.
[178] See section IV.A.
[179] See Cass civ (2) 10 November 2009 no 08-20971.
[180] For extensive referencing and discussion of the case law requiring both unforeseeability and unavoidability as conditions of force majeure, see Viney, Jourdain, and Carval (n 60) para 396.
[181] André Tunc, D 1963.674; Valerie Depadt-Sebag, D 2003.2465; Patrice Jourdain, 'L'imprévisibilité de la force majeure: une pomme de discorde entre les première et deuxième chambres civiles', Revue trimestrielle de droit civil 2003, 301; Viney, Jourdain, and Carval (n 60) para 396; Fabre-Magnan (n 127) para 246; Flour and others (n 61) para 352 (in relation to liability for the deeds of things). See also art 1253(2) of the 2017 reform project of the French Civil Code: Ministère de la Justice, *Projet de réforme de la responsabilité civile*, 13 March 2017; Simon Whittaker and Jean-Sébastien Borghetti (trs), *Reform Bill on Civil Liability (March 2017)*, <http://www.textes.justice.gouv.fr/art_pix/reform_bill_on_civil_liability_march_2017.pdf> accessed 12 December 2024.

an act or event is unforeseeable, it is also unavoidable, for it cannot be expected that a defendant takes precautions against something which was not foreseeable. In this case, there is no doubt that the relevant act or event amounts to force majeure. On the other hand, unforeseeability should not be an independent condition of force majeure, in the sense that an action or event which is unavoidable should, without more, constitute force majeure. Excluding force majeure and therefore imposing liability merely because the act or event is foreseeable, even if unavoidable, would be inappropriate. While this type of criticism has not fallen on deaf ears and some courts have stated that unavoidability is enough to give rise to force majeure,[182] recent developments in the case law reaffirm vigorously that unforeseeability remains an autonomous requirement,[183] arguably with a view to ensuring that the victims of accidents are compensated for their harm (particularly in cases of personal injury).[184]

In sum, in contrast with English law, the mere foreseeability of a natural event or of an act of a stranger/claimant defeats the defence of force majeure. At the same time, the mere unforeseeability of that act or event is not enough to rule out a finding of liability in France, as other conditions must be satisfied, namely unavoidability and exteriority.

As a final point, it should be noted that force majeure is not so relevant from a practical standpoint, this affecting the overall significance of (un)foreseeability as a limitation on liability in French law. To begin with, in fault-based liability it would not make any sense for a defendant to seek to establish the triad of requirements of force majeure; it would be much easier to prove absence of fault. Moreover, in the context of strict liability, force majeure does not operate in relation to road accidents, and indeed the desire to get rid of this defence was one of the reasons for enacting the *loi* Badinter.[185] Similarly, it is difficult to find any case on strict parental liability where liability was excluded on the basis of force majeure.[186] Finally, force majeure can certainly apply in the context of liability for the deeds of things, but its significance should not be overestimated: first, the scope of application of this liability rule has reduced substantially after the introduction of the *loi* Badinter as a special regime governing road accidents;[187] secondly, where it still applies, either the claimant does not manage to establish a causal link between the

[182] See eg Cass civ (1) 9 March 1994 no 91-17.459, 91-17.464, Bull Civ I no 91.

[183] See eg Cass civ (2) 5 April 2007 no 06-10797; Cass civ (2) 10 November 2009 no 08-20971; Cass civ (2) 4 February 2010 no 09-65420; Cass civ (2) 16 September 2010 no 09-68849. See also Bacache-Gibeili (n 135) para 534.

[184] See Geneviève Viney, 'La force majeure: une définition spécifique à la matière contractuelle?', Revue des contrats 2006, no 4, 1207, at 1210.

[185] Borghetti (n 154) 271.

[186] See Brun (n 132) para 284, fn 209.

[187] Fabrice Leduc, 'L'état actuel du principe général de responsabilité délictuelle du fait des choses' in Fabrice Leduc (ed), *La responsabilité du fait des choses, Réflexions autour d'un centenaire* (Economica 1997) 35, 35–41.

thing and its harm, in which case there is no need to plead force majeure, or, if the claimant establishes causation, then it will be extremely difficult for the defendant to prove force majeure.[188] Overall, the scope of application of force majeure is relatively limited today, and this means that the ambit of operation of unforeseeability as a reason for excluding liability is also reduced.

To conclude, the role of foreseeability in defences is considerably different in French and English law. In England, the circumstance that an act of God, of a stranger, or of the claimant is unforeseeable appears to be a sufficient reason to bar (or reduce) liability for harm caused by that act; if, instead, the act is reasonably foreseeable, the defendant may still escape liability on various grounds such as *novus actus interveniens*.[189] By contrast, in France the unforeseeability of a *cause étrangère* is not enough to exempt the defendant from liability, as further requirements must be met; and the mere foreseeability of a *cause étrangère* is enough to exclude force majeure as a valid defence. In sum, at the level of defences, (un)foreseeability is used in profoundly different ways in the two tort systems, and it constitutes a far greater barrier to liability in English law than in French law. This is not surprising at all, given that in France the fundamental preoccupation of tort law is to ensure that the victims of accidents are compensated for their harm. The French way of using (un)foreseeability in defences goes precisely in that direction. By contrast, English law is notoriously less sympathetic to the needs of the claimants, and other (often conflicting) considerations play a role in shaping the law, such as not being too harsh on defendants, adhering to ethical norms of personal responsibility, or paying attention to a defendant's ability to avoid accidents. These considerations align well with the role that foreseeability is made to play in the English context at the level of defences.

VI. Conclusions

The comparative picture of foreseeability painted in this chapter shows that the uses and significance of this concept differ sharply between the two legal systems studied.

Foreseeability is prominent in English tort law. This concept acts as one of the gatekeepers of liability for negligence, and hence of vast areas of liability for accidental harm: it contributes to the determination of what counts as negligent conduct, of what constitutes a legally meaningful connection between conduct and harm (including the determination of the category of potential claimants), and of what acts or events amount to valid defences. But foreseeability goes well beyond

188 Brun (n 132) para 284.
189 See text to nn 166–73.

the tort of negligence. The gravitational pull of this tort has pushed English courts to require foreseeability of interference in the tort of private nuisance, at least as far as the creation of a nuisance is concerned. Moreover, as an element of remoteness of damage, foreseeability has spread from negligence law to both private nuisance and the rule in *Rylands v Fletcher*, and it is invoked as an attractive solution in cases where remoteness rules are still unclear, such as in the statutory liabilities for animals and for defective products. Finally, foreseeability plays an important role in defences, as the unforeseeability of a causally relevant agency (eg an act of God or of a third party) is generally enough to bar liability. Overall, then, foreseeability does look like the dark matter of English tort law.

By contrast, foreseeability features only very marginally in French law. While French lawyers are well aware of the concept of foreseeability, they do not show any particular attachment to it. At the level of conduct, foreseeability does not feature in the concept of *faute*, which defies any clear definition and which is deployed flexibly to ensure equitable outcomes. In this context, foreseeability is unnecessary, and its introduction may be even detrimental because it would prevent the imposition of liability in too many cases. At the level of causation, foreseeability plays a role, essentially as an ingredient of the theory of adequate causation. However, given the controversial status of this theory and the use of numerous other approaches to causal issues, the significance of foreseeability looks limited. Finally, if looked at from the perspective of defences, foreseeability (or, better, unforeseeability) is no significant obstacle to the imposition of liability, mainly because of additional and stringent requirements characterizing force majeure. In sum, the role of foreseeability in French tort law as a condition of, and limitation on, the imposition of liability is very modest, particularly if compared to the English approach.

This study has focused on the different ways in which foreseeability is used in the French and English laws of torts and on its varying significance in the two tort systems. It has also been suggested that the reasons for such divergences lie, at least in part, in the different aims and concerns of tort law in the two jurisdictions. French law is characterized by a strong ethos of social solidarity, with the compensation and spreading of losses being the fundamental aims of the tort system. In this context, the concept of foreseeability is understandably marginal. A significant role for it would likely shift the focus from the needs of victims to the behaviour of defendants, and it would therefore reduce the incidence and scope of liability, with an appreciable diminution in the level of attainable compensation and spreading. The English understanding of tort law and of its functions is different. To be sure, English law is to some extent sympathetic to the needs of the victims of accidents; however, the starting point in English tort law is 'why the defendant should be liable', not 'why the victim should bear the loss'. In other words, concerns other than the compensation of losses affect English law and its development. In this context, foreseeability is widely perceived as an attractive condition of liability and as a necessary limitation on its scope. In sum, if foreseeability is treated in a dramatically different way in the English and French tort systems, different visions of tort law and of its aims appear to have a significant role in this. Working out the details of the relationship between foreseeability and each of these aims is left for future research.

9

Justifying the Denial of Compensation for Pure Economic Loss

Jean-Sébastien Borghetti

I. Introduction

Pure economic loss is usually defined as a financial loss—that is, an expenditure or a loss of expected profits—that is neither a consequence of personal injury suffered by the claimant nor a consequence of physical damage caused to a thing belonging to them.[1] It is a classic comparative tort law topic,[2] and one which is discussed in most comparative tort law scholarly works or textbooks.[3] This is probably because it is an issue with respect to which different legal systems adopt strikingly different approaches, at least on the face of it. Whereas English and German law, for example, normally refuse to compensate for such loss under 'ordinary' liability for fault rules,[4] other legal systems, such as French law, see no problem in awarding compensation for it even under the general regime of liability for fault. The contrast between legal systems is all the stronger as, contrary to what happens on other issues, the difference exists not only in principle but also in practice. In other words, not only do different legal systems display diverging principles (as is or was

[1] See, eg, Peter Benson, 'The Problem with Pure Economic Loss' (2009) 60 South Carolina Law Review 823; Helmut Koziol, 'Observations under Art. 2:102. Protected Interests' in European Group on Tort Law (ed), *Principles of European Tort Law. Text and Commentary* (Springer 2005) para 9; Cees van Dam, *European Tort Law* (2nd edn, OUP 2013) 208; Gerhard Wagner, 'Comparative Tort Law' in Matthias Reimann and Reinhard Zimmermann (eds), *The Oxford Handbook of Comparative Law* (2nd edn, OUP 2019) 994, 1006. This definition of pure economic loss has been officially adopted by the Swedish *Skadetsåndslagen* (Tort Liability Act, chap 1, s 2), which seems to be the only piece of legislation to explicitly mention and define this notion: see Thomas Kadner Graziano, *Comparative Tort Law. Cases, Materials, and Exercises* (Routledge 2018) 91–92. Other definitions have been suggested, however, such as 'all loss that is not the consequence of the violation of a legal right': Christian von Bar, *The Common European Law of Torts* (vol 2, OUP 2000) 26.

[2] See, eg, (since 2000) Mauro Bussani and Vernon V Palmer (eds), *Pure Economic Loss in Europe* (CUP 2003); Vernon V Palmer, 'A Comparative Law Sketch of Pure Economic Loss' in Mauro Bussani and Anthony J Sebok (eds), *Comparative Tort Law. Global Perspectives* (Elgar 2017) 300–22; Willem H van Boom, Helmut Koziol, and Christian A Witting (eds), *Pure Economic Loss* (Springer 2004).

[3] See, eg, (since 2000) Kadner Graziano (n 1) 71–114, 419–48; van Dam (n 1) 208–17; Walter van Gerven, Jeremy Lever, and Pierre Larouche, *Cases, Materials and Text on National, Supranational and International Tort Law* (Hart 2000) 168–208; von Bar (n 1) 24–35; Wagner (n 1) 1006–10; Bénédict Winiger, Bernhard A Koch, and Reinhard Zimmermann (eds), *Digest of European Tort Law, Volume 2: Essential Cases on Damage* (De Gruyter 2011) 383–418.

[4] Ie, liability for negligence in English law and liability based on § 823(1) BGB in German law.

Jean-Sébastien Borghetti, *Justifying the Denial of Compensation for Pure Economic Loss* In: *Comparative Reflections in Private Law*. Edited by: Marco Cappelletti, Ciara Kennefick, and Dorota Leczykiewicz, Oxford University Press.
 DOI: 10.1093/9780198959168.003.0011

the case on the issue of specific performance or penalty clauses, for example),[5] but they also produce different outcomes in concrete cases (which is not so clear as far as specific performance or penalty clauses are concerned). This is perhaps best exemplified by the famous 'cable cases', in which contractors have been sued for having negligently cut off the power supply of a factory or economic unit, thus causing a reduction in output and a loss of expected profits, but without damaging physical property belonging to the claimant. Whereas such a loss cannot normally be compensated for under English[6] or German law,[7] it has been compensated for without discussion in French law.[8]

Pure economic loss is also interesting from the perspective of legal thinking and the circulation of legal ideas. In those legal systems which normally refuse to compensate for pure economic loss under 'ordinary' liability for fault rules, the exclusion of pure economic loss has generally been the subject of much discussion. Courts and authors have written at length about the reasons that justify or are said to justify the exclusion of such losses from the ambit of compensation. By contrast, for a long time pure economic loss was not an issue at all in some legal systems such as French law,[9] where the very concept of *préjudice économique pur* (which is the exact and accepted French translation of 'pure economic loss') was ignored by most lawyers,[10] and even civil liability scholars.[11] The reasons for the silence, or perhaps ignorance, will be explained in the next section, but what should be stressed at this point is that it is the example of foreign legal systems that led French scholars to identify the concept of pure economic loss and encouraged them to engage in a reflection on the specificity of this type of loss.[12] It is therefore an example

[5] See, eg, Jens Kleinschmidt, 'Introduction before Art 9:101' in Nils Jansen and Reinhard Zimmermann (eds), *Commentaries on European Contract Laws* (OUP 2018) 1186 (specific performance); Reinhard Zimmermann, 'Art. 9:509: Agreed Payment for Non-performance' in Nils Jansen and Reinhard Zimmermann (eds), *Commentaries on European Contract Laws* (OUP 2018) 1539, 1541–44.

[6] *Spartan Steel & Alloys Ltd v Martin & Co (Contractors) Ltd* [1973] 1 QB 27.

[7] BGHZ 29, 65 VI, Civil Senate, VI ZR 199/57, 67ff.

[8] Cass civ (2) 8 May 1970 no 69-11.446, Bull civ II no 160. See also Conseil d'État, 2 June 1972 no 79597.

[9] Mireille Bacache, 'Le prejudice économique pur. Rapport français' in Association Henri Capitant (ed), *Le préjudice: entre tradition et modernité* (Bruylant LB2V 2015) 39; Jonas Knetsch, *Tort Law in France* (Wolters Kluwer 2021) para 295; Christian Lapoyade Deschamps, 'La réparation du préjudice économique pur en droit français' in Efstathios K Banakas (ed), *Civil Liability for Pure Economic Loss* (Kluwer 1996) 89.

[10] Even though it did play a role in insurance law: see Bacache (n 9) 49.

[11] To the extent that 'tort' can be understood as an implied reference to English law and its system of discrete torts, in the context of French law it is preferable to talk of civil liability (which accurately translates 'responsabilité civile'). Unlike English tort law, French civil liability law heavily relies on general clauses: see Jean-Sébastien Borghetti and Simon Whittaker, 'Principles of Liability or a Law of Torts?' in Jean-Sébastien Borghetti and Simon Whittaker (eds), *French Civil Liability in Comparative Perspective* (Hart 2019) 455. However, since it has become common usage in comparative law to talk of 'tort law' to designate rules on non-contractual liability whether they originate in common law or civil law jurisdictions, this usage has been followed in this contribution, except where only French (or Belgian) law is discussed.

[12] The first article by a French scholar dealing explicitly with the subject is apparently Lapoyade Deschamps (n 9) (the article was also used as a contribution to the 15th International Comparative Law Congress and published with the same title in the Revue internationale de droit comparé, 1998, vol

of comparative law having a real impact on French legal thinking. This is as it should be, but it is unfortunately not so common in the context of French law.

Over the past few years, a few scholars have debated whether French law should continue to compensate for pure economic loss, just like any other kind of damage or loss, or whether it should take a more restrictive approach to it, following the English or German examples.[13] While the policy arguments that have been exchanged are not very original from a comparative perspective, the way in which the debate on pure economic loss has connected with other issues and debates in French civil liability law can perhaps be of interest to comparative lawyers. Pure economic loss has forced French lawyers to reflect on their own system and its conceptual structure—something they do not do very often, engrossed as they tend to be in a very positivistic approach to tort law.

Simon Whittaker's knowledge of French law is remarkable, but—if possible—his understanding of the French legal mind is even more impressive. This understanding goes hand in hand with a profound interest in what French lawyers think of, and how they understand, their own legal system, especially in the field of contract and civil liability law. Therefore, it is only fitting that, in a contribution intended to celebrate Simon Whittaker, something should be said about the French approach to pure economic loss, and how it relates to the structure of French civil liability law, which he has remarkably analysed in several of his works (section II).[14] An attempt at connecting this approach to the larger comparative debate on pure economic loss will then be made (section III).

II. Pure Economic Loss in French Law

The basic provision of French civil liability law, now article 1240 of the Code civil (Cc) and formerly article 1382 of that same code, is famous for its general character: 'Any human action whatsoever which causes harm to another creates an obligation in the person by whose fault it occurred to make reparation for it.'[15]

50, no 2, 367). See also Christophe Radé and Laurent Bloch, 'Compensation for Pure Economic Loss Under French Law' in van Boom, Koziol, and Witting (n 2) 41.

[13] Jean-Sébastien Borghetti, 'Les intérêts protégés et l'étendue des préjudices réparables en droit de la responsabilité civile extra-contractuelle' in Jean-Sébastien Borghetti, Olivier Deshayes, and Cécile Pérès (eds), *Études offertes à Geneviève Viney* (LGDJ 2008) 145, 170; Julie Traullé, 'La réparation du préjudice économique "pur" en question', Revue trimestrielle de droit civil 2018, no 2, 285; Jean-Sébastien Borghetti, 'Le préjudice économique pur et l'atteinte au cours normal des choses' in Geneviève Viney and others (eds), *Mélanges en l'honneur du professeur Suzanne Carval* (IRJS Éditions 2021) 113.

[14] Recounting Simon Whittaker's complete bibliography on French (civil liability) law would be fastidious, but perhaps his most impressive work in that respect is Simon Whittaker, *Liability for Products: English Law, French Law, and European Harmonization* (OUP 2005).

[15] 'Tout fait quelconque de l'homme qui cause à autrui un dommage oblige celui par la faute duquel il est arrivé à le réparer.'

Admittedly, this sentence is not particularly clear,[16] but it has long been accepted that the rule behind this provision is straightforward and can be restated as follows: any person who commits a fault must compensate for the harm caused by that fault.[17]

The Code civil does not define any of the terms contained in article 1240, and the *Cour de cassation*, France's highest court in civil and criminal matters, has also cautiously abstained from doing so. This deliberate lack of definition has fuelled a very broad and flexible understanding of the notions mentioned in article 1240, starting with the two central ones: fault (*faute*) and harm (*dommage*). Concerning harm, the view generally taken by French civil liability lawyers, and confirmed by a wide array of cases, is that almost any detriment can be considered as harm, and can therefore be compensated for under article 1240 (as well as under the other liability regimes existing in French law).[18] This view is often said to reflect that of the drafters of the Code, as expressed in a famous sentence by Tarrible, a French statesman who contributed to the discussion of the future Code civil:

> [Article 1382 of the Civil Code] encompasses in its breadth of scope all kinds of harm and subjects them to a uniform remedy which takes as its measure the value of the loss suffered. From homicide to the slightest injury, from the burning of a building to the collapse of frail building, everything is subjected to the same law; everything is declared capable of an evaluation which will compensate the injured party for whatever harm they have incurred.[19]

This broad conception of harm, and of what ought to be compensated for under civil liability law, is the reason why French law and French lawyers see no problem in awarding compensation for pure economic loss. If any deterioration of the claimant's situation caused by the defendant's fault is compensable, indemnifying a financial loss that is not a consequence of personal injury or of physical damage to property suffered by the claimant is not an issue, provided this loss appears 'sufficiently certain'. This is illustrated by many French judgments, including cable cases.[20] For example, the *Cour de cassation* held that a dredging company could be held strictly liable, on the basis of liability for the action of things (*responsabilité*

[16] For an analysis of this wording and an attempt to identify its original meaning, see Jean-Sébastien Borghetti, 'L'ex-article 1382 du Code civil et le droit de la responsabilité civile: requiem pour une disposition méconnue', Revue de droit d'Assas 2020, no 20, 153.

[17] John Bell, Sophie Boyron, and Simon Whittaker, *Principles of French Law* (2nd edn, OUP 2008) 364.

[18] This is clearly expressed in the reference treatise on French civil liability: Geneviève Viney, Patrice Jourdain, and Suzanne Carval, *Les conditions de la responsabilité. Traité de droit civil* (4th edn, LGDJ 2013) para 248-1.

[19] Jean Tarrible, 'Discours du corps législatif' in *Code Civil* (Firmin Didot 1804) 264, 275.

[20] See n 8.

du fait des choses),[21] for the costs incurred by a shipowner whose vessel's entry into a port had been delayed due to the presence of a sling head that had become detached from the dredger and prevented access to the port.[22] The fact that the defendant, the 'guardian' of the dredger, had committed no fault was therefore irrelevant and was no obstacle to them being held liable for the claimant's pure economic loss.[23] The compensation of pure economic loss under French law is thus clearly not some kind of punishment for the moral wrongdoing of the defendant. Rather, it is an apparently ineluctable consequence of the broad conception of harm.

Another interesting case is the 'Marseilles bus case'. It concerned a traffic accident in Marseilles, which had apparently resulted in a traffic jam. Due to this traffic jam, buses had been delayed, and the Marseilles transport authority brought a claim against the person who had caused the accident, claiming compensation for the loss of revenue in the form of ticket sales that had allegedly resulted from the buses' delay.[24] The appellate court had granted the claim. When challenged before the *Cour de cassation* on the ground that the existence of the loss had not been sufficiently established, the judgment of the appellate court was confirmed.[25] Interestingly, the type of loss for which the transport authority claimed compensation apparently never came under discussion before the court. The only issue was whether that loss was certain enough. The case thus confirms not only the principle that pure economic loss is readily compensable under French civil liability law, but also that pure economic loss was for a very long time a non-issue for French lawyers. There is really nothing special about the Marseilles bus case from a traditional French perspective and the case would now be long forgotten if it had not been drawn to the attention of French lawyers by foreign comparative lawyers,[26] as an example of French law's attitude to pure economic loss.

[21] On which see Bell, Boyron, and Whittaker (n 17) 381–93; Knetsch (n 9) paras 165–73. This liability regime was famously developed by the courts based on art 1384(1) Cc, which has now become art 1242(1).

[22] Cass civ (2) 19 March 1980 no 78-15.838, Bull civ II no 65, cited by Bell, Boyron, and Whittaker (n 17) 389.

[23] Another illustration of the irrelevance of the defendant's conduct as far as compensation of pure economic loss is concerned is Cass civ (2) 26 September 2002 no 00-18.627, Bull civ II no 198. A building hosting a hotel and a restaurant was located at the foot of a cliff. In view of the risk that blocks may fall from the cliff, an administrative order was issued ordering the closure of the hotel and restaurant. The owners of the business brought an action against the owner of the piece of land on which the cliff was situated and claimed damages for the loss of profits resulting from the closure of their business. The *Cour de cassation* accepted that the defendant should be held liable under the rules of liability for the action of things, ie, strict liability. The case confirms that, under French law, compensation for pure economic loss is not connected to the defendant's moral wrongdoing.

[24] It is unclear if the defendant's liability was based on fault or, as was more usual in traffic accident cases at that time, on liability for the action of things, which is strict. The circumstance that this issue is not mentioned in the judgment is of course significant, as it confirms that the basis for the defendant's liability is officially irrelevant when deciding whether the claimant's loss is compensable.

[25] Cass civ (2) 28 April 1965 no 63-13.624, Bull civ II no 373.

[26] See Kadner Graziano (n 1) 99.

Given the very broad approach to compensation adopted in French civil liability law, for a long time there was no need to precisely distinguish different types of damage. Since (almost) everything was compensable,[27] singling out specific types of damage was apparently useless, and French courts were in the habit of awarding to the claimant a global amount of damages intended to encompass all the heads of damage or loss they had suffered.[28] In that context, pure economic loss neither deserved nor received any particular attention. The very concept was unknown to French lawyers and when some of them first noticed that pure economic loss was a concern to some foreign tort or civil liability lawyers, it was difficult for them to fathom why. However, things have been changing over the past two or three decades. (Some) French lawyers better understand why pure economic loss stands apart in other legal systems and, while a majority of them see no reason why such loss should stand apart in the context of French law,[29] a few daredevils have argued, or at least hinted, that unlimited compensation of pure economic loss may not be justified, even in the land of article 1240 of the Code civil.[30]

This debate has developed in the broader context of a reassessment of the damage requirement in French civil liability law. French lawyers famously argued at length over the justification of civil liability (fault or risk?)[31] and their focus was for a very long time the act or fact giving rise to liability (which they call *fait générateur*), rather than the ensuing harm. Things have been changing, though. The centre of gravity of French civil liability seems to have shifted from the conduct of the tortfeasor to the position of the victim.[32] This, in turn, has prompted a new interest in the concept of damage. This evolution is not altogether surprising in a system that is so 'victim-oriented',[33] but it was also prompted by the need to clarify the legal consequences of personal injuries.

[27] It has always been accepted that the deprivation of something to which the claimant had no right (such as revenues from moonshining) could not give rise to compensation: Philippe Brun, *Responsabilité civile extracontractuelle* (6th edn, LexisNexis 2023) 135.

[28] This used to be called compensation 'toutes causes de préjudices confondues'.

[29] See eg Bacache (n 9) 46; Traullé (n 13); Viney, Jourdain, and Carval (n 18) para 251.

[30] See esp Borghetti, 'Le préjudice économique pur' (n 13).

[31] Geneviève Viney, *Introduction à la responsabilité* (4th edn, LGDJ 2019) 121–42.

[32] Borghetti, 'Les intérêts protégés' (n 13) 148.

[33] The French system of civil liability has aptly been described as being governed by a 'compensation ideology' (*idéologie de la réparation*): Loïc Cadiet, 'Les faits et les méfaits de l'idéologie de la réparation' in *Mélanges Pierre Drai* (Dalloz 1999) 495. Another author has spoken of 'victimophily': Pauline Remy-Corlay, 'Damages, Loss and the Quantification of Damages in the *Avant-proejt de réforme*' in John Cartwright, Stefan Vogenauer, and Simon Whittaker (eds), *Reforming the French Law of Obligations: Comparative Reflections on the Avant-projet de réforme du droit des obligations et de la prescription ('the Avant-projet Catala')* (Hart Publishing 2009) 305, 310. As Simon Whittaker pointed out, the fact that French law usually talks of victims (*victimes*), instead of claimants or injured parties (as does German law when referring to *Geschädigte*), is significant and suggests a bias in favour of those who have suffered harm: Simon Whittaker, 'La responsabilité pour fait personnel dans l'Avant-projet de réforme du droit de la responsabilité: donner voix aux silences du Code civil', Revue des contrats 2007, no 1, 89, 99. Admittedly, victims are frequently not the claimants in the litigation, so it is not right to identify 'victims' with 'claimants', but a more neutral term like 'injured person' (*personne lésée*), less suggestive of the existence of a right to compensation, could be used.

When such an injury occurs, social security and other entities, such as private insurance companies, often pay directly for some of its consequences (such as the cost of medical treatment) or pay some sort of compensation to the injured party (such as an indemnity to compensate for the loss of their salary). When the injury has been caused by a fact giving rise to liability, these entities, called 'third party payers' (*tiers payeurs*), may want to bring a claim against the tortfeasor, to be reimbursed for the sums they have had to disburse because of them. These claims by third party payers often compete with the injured party's own claim, whereby the latter seeks compensation for the losses or harm they have suffered (such as pain and suffering) that were not compensated for or taken care of by third party payers. This has often resulted in very complex situations, with third party payers sometimes taking the bread out of the mouths of injured parties. This prompted the legislator, courts, and academics to attempt to classify the legal consequences of personal injuries and to distinguish the consequences of which charge could be taken by third party payers and for which regress claim by those payers against the tortfeasor was admissible, and the consequences for which only the injured party can claim compensation from the tortfeasor.[34]

The clarification process took some time but was eventually successful. Drawing on earlier legal developments and academic work, a classification of the consequences of personal injuries was proposed in 2005 by a commission set up by the Ministry of Justice and headed by Jean-Pierre Dintilhac, a senior judge at the *Cour de cassation*. Though this document, commonly called the Dintilhac nomenclature (*nomenclature Dintilhac*), was never endorsed by the legislator, it has been adopted by courts and now constitutes the undisputed framework for the compensation of personal injuries and their consequences under French law.[35]

The nomenclature rests entirely on the basic distinction between the personal injury itself, called '*dommage corporel*', and its various consequences, called '*préjudices*'. These *préjudices* are then classified using three further distinctions: pecuniary (*patrimonial*) or non-pecuniary (*extrapatrimonial*); temporary (*temporaire*) or permanent (*permanent*); and *préjudices* suffered by 'the direct victim' (*victime directe*, ie, the injured person) or by indirect victims (*victimes indirectes*), such as the injured person's relatives, also called 'ricochet victims' (*victimes par ricochet*). The basic distinction between *dommage corporel* and the resulting *préjudices* is now accepted by all French lawyers in the context of personal injuries, but there is a debate as to whether this distinction should be generalized. As shall be seen, this debate is of importance on the issue of pure economic

34 On this complex issue, see Brun (n 27) 445–52; Dorota Leczykiewicz, 'Loss and its Compensation in the Proposed New French Regime of Extra-contractual Liability' in Borghetti and Whittaker (n 11) 181, 193–98.

35 Brun (n 27) 440–44.

loss because the distinction helps to identify the interests at stake when compensation for such loss is sought.

For a very long time, the words *dommage* and *préjudice* were regarded as synonyms in French law.[36] Over the past decades, some authors have argued that a distinction should be made between the primary harm caused by a damaging act and the negative consequences flowing from that primary harm, and that the word *dommage* should be used to refer to the former and the word *préjudice* to refer to the latter.[37] The distinction can be seen as reflecting the nature of things and has a strong clarifying power.[38] This was brilliantly illustrated by the Dintilhac nomenclature but is also true, for example, in the case of ricochet losses.[39] This explains why the distinction is increasingly present in legislation. There are now several legislative provisions, including in the Code civil, which explicitly distinguish primary harm and its consequences (even though they do not always use the words *dommage* and *préjudice* to do so).[40] Some of these provisions deal specifically with personal injuries and could therefore be seen merely as an implicit endorsement of the Dintilhac nomenclature,[41] but others do not,[42] thus showing that the distinction is not limited to such injuries. Case law still lags a little behind, though. So

[36] Even though, in practice, they were not totally interchangeable, since a convention has emerged of using one word in certain contexts, and the other in other contexts.

[37] The idea was already formulated by René Rodière, note on Cass civ (1) 21 October 1952, JCP G 1953.II.7592, and Francis-Paul Bénoit, 'Essai sur les conditions de la responsabilité en droit public et privé (problèmes de causalité et d'imputabilité)' JCP G 1957.I.1351. It gained momentum after 1980: Loïc Cadiet, *Le préjudice d'agrément* (PhD thesis, University of Poitiers 1983) paras 323ff; Sylvie Rouxel, *Recherches sur la distinction du dommage et du préjudice* (PhD thesis, University of Grenoble 1994); Isabelle Poirot-Mazères, 'La notion de préjudice en droit administratif français', Revue du droit public et de la science politique en France et a l'etranger 1997, no 2, 519.

[38] The position has also been taken, including by myself in earlier works (Borghetti, 'Les intérêts protégés' (n 13) 153), that *dommage* is purely factual, while *préjudice* needs to satisfy legal requirements: see Viney, Jourdain, and Carval (n 18) para 246-1. However, as will be shown later in this chapter, *dommage* is not purely factual. Quite to the contrary, it is the notion that allows a control on what interests are protected by the legal system.

[39] In particular, the fact that the defendant may raise the injured party's comparative negligence as a defence against the claimant seeking compensation for a 'ricochet loss', which is a well-established solution in case law but which some authors have found difficult to explain, can easily be accounted for if one considers that the loss flows from the injured party's harm and that its compensation should therefore be affected by such elements as may limit the reparation of that harm; See Christian Lapoyade Deschamps, 'Quelle(s) réparation(s)?', Responsabilité civile et Assurances, hors-série June 2001, 62, para 23; Rouxel (n 37) 276. That latter work also contains a detailed analysis of most of the practical consequences that could be drawn from the distinction between harm and loss.

[40] For a list of these provisions, see Borghetti, 'Le préjudice économique pur' (n 13) 116–18.

[41] See esp art 2226(1) Cc: 'L'action en responsabilité née à raison d'un événement ayant entraîné un dommage corporel, engagée par la victime directe ou indirecte des préjudices qui en résultent, se prescrit par dix ans à compter de la date de la consolidation du dommage initial ou aggravé' ('An action for liability arising from an event resulting in personal injury, brought by the direct or indirect victim of the resulting injury, shall be barred after ten years from the date of consolidation of the initial or aggravated injury').

[42] See, eg, art 6 of *Loi* no 85-677 of 5 July 1985 (*loi* Badinter): 'Le préjudice subi par un tiers du fait des dommages causés à la victime directe d'un accident de la circulation est réparé en tenant compte des limitations ou exclusions applicables à l'indemnisation de ces dommages' ('Damage suffered by a third party as a consequence of harm caused to the direct victim of a traffic accident is compensated for subject to the limitations and exclusions applicable to the latter's compensation').

far, French courts have not clearly adopted the distinction bewteeen the primary harm and its consequences outside the field of personal injury. They still tend to use the terms *dommage* and *préjudice* quite freely, without always seeking clearly to separate the primary harm from its consequences. Yet, some rulings show that the *Cour de cassation* can make the distinction when it wishes to do so, as it recently did in the field of product liability.[43]

It might be forced to do so in the future if the reform of French civil liability law, which has been on the agenda for twenty years, eventually goes through. The Reform Project published by the Ministry of Justice in March 2017, which is still officially in the pipeline, endorses the distinction between *dommage* and *préjudice*,[44] as had the two rival academic proposals published in 2005[45] and 2011.[46] The distinction is present throughout the Project and is made particularly explicit at article 1235 Cc,[47] which defines *préjudice réparable* as follows: '*Est réparable tout préjudice certain résultant d'un dommage et consistant en la lésion d'un intérêt licite, patrimonial ou extrapatrimonial*' ('any certain *préjudice* is reparable where it results from *dommage* and consists of an injury to a lawful interest, whether patrimonial or extra-patrimonial').[48] The French Senate's Bill of July 2020 on the reform of civil liability, which takes up the main thrust of the Ministry's 2017 Project while eliminating its boldest provisions, does not call into question the distinction between *dommage* and *préjudice* and faithfully follows the Project on this point.[49] Whether one likes it or not (for some authors are still reluctant to endorse it),[50] the distinction between *dommage* and *préjudice* is thus already a feature of French law and cannot be ignored. Interestingly, it has also been adopted by

[43] Cass civ (1) 9 December 2020 no 19-21.390.

[44] On which see Borghetti and Whittaker (n 11).

[45] Pierre Catala (ed), *Avant-projet de réforme du droit des obligations et de la prescription* (La Documentation française 2005) 173, fn 2: 'As far as possible, the group tried to give distinct meanings to the terms "*dommage*" and "*préjudice*", *dommage* referring to an injury to the victim's person or property and *préjudice* referring to the resulting encroachment on economic or non-economic interests' ('Dans toute la mesure du possible, le groupe a essayé de donner des sens distincts aux termes 'dommage' et 'préjudice', le dommage désignant l'atteinte à la personne ou aux biens de la victime et le préjudice, la lésion des intérêts patrimoniaux ou extra-patrimoniaux qui en résulte'). On this academic proposal, see Cartwright, Vogenauer, and Whittaker (n 33).

[46] François Terré (ed), *Pour une réforme du droit de la responsabilité civile* (Dalloz 2011) arts 9 and 49. The proposal makes the existence of *dommage* a condition of liability, while clearly indicating that compensation relates to the *préjudice* resulting from that *dommage*.

[47] On which see Leczykiewicz (n 34) 183–85; Pietro Sirena, 'The Concepts of "Harm" in the French and Italian Laws of Civil Liability' in Borghetti and Whittaker (n 11) 205, 205–07.

[48] The translation is borrowed from Simon Whittaker, 'English Translation of the Projet de réforme de la responsabilité civile' in Borghetti and Whittaker (n 11) 477. The words '*dommage*' and '*préjudice*' have been left in French, as the way in which they should be translated into English is discussed further down.

[49] Art 1235 Cc.

[50] See, eg, Muriel Fabre-Magnan, *Droit des obligations. 2—responsabilité civile et quasi-contrats* (5th edn, PUF 2021) 127–28; Xavier Pradel, *Le préjudice dans le droit civil de la responsabilité* (LGDJ 2004) 10–12.

the recent reform of Belgian civil liability law, albeit using a different language,[51] due to the constraints of the Dutch/French bilingualism.[52]

At this point, an attempt should be made at rendering *dommage* and *préjudice* into English. Always a difficult task, translating legal terms is especially delicate here, since the distinction touches on the very structure of French civil liability law, which is markedly different from English tort law.[53] It can also have an influence on a non-French-speaking lawyer's understanding of French law regarding recovery of pure economic loss. Besides, there is no unanimity among common lawyers about the meaning of the English terms which immediately come to mind when one thinks of translating *dommage* and *préjudice*, namely damage, harm, injury, and loss.[54] Simon Whittaker was faced with this challenge when he translated the 2017 Reform Project and explained the following:

> There is an important distinction in the text between *le dommage* (translated as 'harm' or 'the harm') and *le préjudice* (translated as 'loss' or 'the loss') which the claimant (often in the text, the 'victim') suffers as a result of the infliction of this harm. *Le dommage* is translated as 'harm' rather than 'damage' (which is obviously closer linguistically) as *le dommage* can include a number of non-physical harms (such as the grief or upset included under *le dommage moral*), whereas 'damage' in English is typically (though not exclusively) understood as being physical.[55]

Despite the inevitable ambiguity of the terms 'harm' and 'damage' in the context of English tort law, the translation adopted by Simon Whittaker seems particularly appropriate and will be followed throughout the chapter.

The official adoption of the distinction between harm and loss in French law requires or will require many clarifications. The nature of the link between the harm and the loss is one of them. The Reform Project, like several existing legislative provisions, speaks of the loss 'resulting' (*résultant*) from the harm. The expression undoubtedly expresses the need for a causal relationship between the two. Yet, the legislator is understandably reluctant to speak of causation to designate both the link which must exist between the *fait générateur* and the harm and the link which must exist between the harm and the loss,[56] even though many French judgments

[51] Ar 6.24(1) of the new Belgian Code civil.

[52] Jean-Sébastien Borghetti, 'Le soleil se lève au nord: ou comment la réforme belge de la responsabilité extracontractuelle fait pâlir le projet français', Recueil Dalloz 2024, no 13, 643, 646. See also n 61.

[53] Borghetti and Whittaker (n 11).

[54] See, eg, the discussion in Donal Nolan, 'Rights, Damage and Loss' (2017) 37 Oxford Journal of Legal Studies 255, 259–60.

[55] Whittaker (n 48) 477, fn 2.

[56] This is what some legal systems do, such as German law, where in the context of § 823(1) BGB a distinction is made between *haftungsbegründende Kausalität* (the requirement of a causal link between the act or omission and the infringement of a right) and *haftungsausfüllende Kausalität* (the requirement of a causal link between the infringement of a right and the loss).

dealing with causation concern the connection between the harm and the loss and not that between the *fait générateur* and the harm.[57]

The key question, however, which is closely linked to the issue of pure economic loss, is that of the definition of 'harm' and 'loss'. The existing provisions on civil liability in French law define neither of these terms, even when they rely on the distinction. Article 1235 of the Reform Project contains no definition of harm but describes 'reparable loss' (*préjudice réparable*) as 'resulting from a harm' and consisting 'of an injury to a lawful interest, whether patrimonial or extra-patrimonial'. This provision is arguably flawed. It is 'harm' that should be defined in the first place, and not 'loss'. Besides, the definition of loss that is given should apply to harm.[58] It is harm that consists in the violation of a lawful interest, or rather in the violation of a *protected* interest,[59] as was made clear in the earlier Terré academic draft[60] and as is the case in the new Belgian civil liability law, which defines losses as 'the economic or non-economic repercussions of an infringement of a legally protected interest'.[61]

Defining harm as the infringement of a protected interest makes it clear that harm is (or should be) a central notion of civil liability under French law and that it has (or should have) a controlling function.[62] This is something not easily accepted by French courts and lawyers, who often repeat that everything is compensable.[63]

[57] See, eg, Cass civ (2) 19 June 2003 no 00-22.302, Bull civ II no 203.

[58] See Leczykiewicz (n 34) 189, pointing accurately to the fact that the distinction between *dommage* and *préjudice* suggests that the first notion governs actionability and the second one recoverability of damage, so that the violation of a lawful interest would be better understood as a condition of *dommage*, and not of *préjudice*.

[59] This raises the question of how 'interest' should be defined. Rather unsurprisingly, neither Belgian law nor French law offers a definition. The English word 'interest' and the French word 'intérêt' may or may not be exact equivalents, but they both refer to something which is probably too basic to receive any helpful definition. The reference French legal dictionary defines 'intérêt' as 'that which matters' (translating *ce qui importe*), which is both true and vague: see 'intérêt' in Gérard Cornu (ed), *Dictionary of the Civil Code* (Alain Levasseur and Marie-Eugénie Laporte-Legeais trs, LexisNexis 2014). The present contribution will not attempt to offer a better definition. As some authors have written, 'the legal definitions of *intérêt* are of "little help": too vague when they are right, defective when they aim at precision': François Ost, *Droit et intérêt*, vol 2 (Publications des Facultés universitaires Saint-Louis 1990) 11, citing '*Pandectes Belges* (Larcier 1896) v° 'intérêts (en général)'.

[60] Terré (n 46) art 8(1): 'Harm is any definite violation of an interest of the person recognized and protected by law' ('Constitue un dommage toute atteinte certaine à un intérêt de la personne reconnu et protégé par le droit'). See also Clothilde Grare-Didier, 'Du dommage' in Terré (n 46) 131, 133–35.

[61] In French, art 6.24(1) of the new Belgian Code civil reads: 'Le dommage consiste dans les conséquences économiques ou non économiques d'une atteinte à un intérêt personnel juridiquement protégé.' Since the same Dutch word (*schade*) translates both 'dommage' and 'préjudice', the new Belgian provisions on civil liability speak of 'dommage' where French lawyers speak of 'préjudice', and of 'atteinte' (which can be translated as 'infringement') where French lawyers speak of 'dommage'.

[62] cf Bacache (n 9) 39, who considers that the notion *dommage* is purely factual and has no legal dimension.

[63] For good examples of the reluctance to accept that the concept of protected interest is a relevant one in French civil liability law, see Hadi Slim, 'Les intérêts protégés par la responsabilité civile en droit français' in Groupe de Recherche Européen sur la Responsabilité Civile et l'Assurance (GRERCA) (ed), *Le Droit français de la responsabilité civile confronté aux projets européens d'harmonisation* (IRJS éditions 2012) 113; Luc Grynbaum, 'Point de vue extérieur' in GRERCA (n 63) 791.

However, even in a civil liability system as open-ended as the French one, there are some limits to that which deserves compensation and on that for which compensation is granted.[64]

One of the merits of the distinction between 'harm' and 'loss' is precisely that it elicits an explicit decision about whether the claimant deserves compensation or not. French courts currently make such decisions, but without saying so. When they believe that the interest that has been violated is not worthy of protection, they do not say it openly, but rather resort to causation (a notoriously flexible concept, especially in French law, where it is not defined) to justify their refusal to grant compensation on a seemingly technical ground. This they have done for example when faced with claims by children alleging that harm caused to their parents or grandparents before they were conceived prevented them from having any relationship, or a 'normal' one, with the latter,[65] or when faced with claims for financial loss suffered by 'economic partners' of the person directly injured.[66] Adopting the distinction between harm and loss, and defining harm as the violation of a protected interest, would provide French courts with a tool allowing and even obliging them to make their policy choices explicit. However, it is doubtful if French judges are willing to be given such a tool. The current situation, where policy choices remain hidden behind loose technical reasoning, is very comfortable for them.

Whether or not the tool is wanted, another question is whether it works. Some French authors take the opinion that, while the distinction between *dommage* and *préjudice* is helpful in the case of personal injuries, it is otherwise useless, and even possibly impracticable when the primary harm is non-material, that is, cannot be witnessed as a physical change in the world,[67] as is for example the case where

[64] See, eg, n 27.

[65] Cass civ (2) 24 February 2005 no 02-11.999, Bull civ II no 53; Cass civ (2) 3 March 2011 no 10-16284.

[66] Bacache (n 9) 48. Most of the case law on claims by 'economic partners', which is relatively sparse, is along these lines. See the rulings cited by Marie Dugué, *L'intérêt protégé en droit de la responsabilité civile* (LGDJ 2019) 247–49; Viney, Jourdain, and Carval (n 18) para 312. There are however some exceptions, the most famous one (though not a very authoritative precedent) being probably CA Colmar, 20 April 1955, JCP 1955.II.8741 (*Football club de Metz c Wiroth*), in which the appellate court awarded damages for the financial loss suffered by a football club as a result of the accidental death of their star player. The case is of course reminiscent of the famous Italian case *Meroni*, in which the *Corte di cassazione* adopted substantially the same solution (reversing its previous position in the *Superga* case: Corte di Cassazione, 4 July 1953, no 2085 (*Associazione Calcio Torino v Soc ALI*)), also in relation to the death of a football player: Corte di Cassazione, 26 January 1971, no 174 (*Associazione Calcio Torino v Romero*); on these cases, see Rebecca Spitzmiller, *Selected Areas of Italian Tort Law. Cases and Materials in a Comparative Perspective* (Il Sirente 2011) 115–56. Bell, Boyron, and Whittaker (n 17) 413 cite another French case, illustrative but hardly authoritative, TGI Nanterre, 22 October 1975, Gaz Pal 1976, 1, 392, obs Alain Planqueel (a first instance judgment), in which the court awarded damages to the employees of a hairdresser's salon for wages and tips lost while the salon was closed for renovation due to the defendant's car having crashed into it.

[67] See eg Fabrice Leduc, 'Faut-il distinguer le dommage et le préjudice?: Point de vue privatiste', Responsabilité civile et Assurances 2010, no 3, 10.

there is a pure economic loss.[68] According to that view, the distinction cannot therefore be generalized. Admittedly, when the harm consists in damage caused to someone's body or physical property, the violated interest—namely physical integrity, or the right to property—is obvious, and so is the protection it deserves. By contrast, when the harm does not consist in physical damage, the interest that has been violated may be more difficult to identify. But there must be one, and there is.[69] If the law grants a claim for damages, then there is at least an implied recognition than an interest worthy of protection has been violated.[70] It cannot be otherwise.[71] This is precisely why applying the distinction between harm and loss to pure economic loss is useful. Regardless of whether compensation is available in respect of such loss, the distinction calls for an identification of the interest that stands 'behind' or 'upstream' of the loss.

For pure economic loss is indeed a loss (*préjudice*), and not a harm (*dommage*). Losing expected revenues is not in itself a violation of a protected interest. Only if there was some sort of right or entitlement to these revenues does this loss become compensable. And granting compensation for this loss amounts to saying that the claimant was somehow entitled to them. The same is true for spending money. It deserves compensation only if the expense was made to compensate in some way the violation of an interest deserving protection.

What, then, is the harm in case of pure economic loss? There is not a single answer to that question, because there are different instances of pure economic loss.[72] It would take too long to identify the harm and the underlying interest in all these instances. At this stage, taking one typical case of pure economic loss to show that there is indeed a harm behind it is enough. The above-mentioned Marseilles bus case can be chosen because it is to some extent an extreme example, where the claimant's claim would have been rejected without any hesitation in many legal systems. In this case, the claimant was essentially complaining about a disruption of the usual course of events. According to that course, there should have been no traffic jam in Marseilles on that day, or not such an important one. The harm upstream of the loss claimed by the transport authority can therefore

[68] The view that there can be no distinction between harm (or damage) and loss in the case of pure economic loss has also been taken in other legal systems: see, eg, Donal Nolan, 'Damage in the English Law of Negligence' (2013) 4 Journal of European Tort Law 259, 268.

[69] cf Bacache (n 9) 39, who considers that pure economic loss (*préjudice économique pur*) is a loss (*préjudice*) not flowing from a harm (*dommage*).

[70] Even though the focus there is on the meaning of loss in the specific context of French law, a comparable if not similar approach has been adopted by Tettenborn, for whom the assessment of loss is the valuation of the legally protected interest that has been infringed: Andrew Tettenborn, 'What Is a Loss?' in Jason W Neyers, Erika Chamberlain, and Stephen G A Pitel, *Emerging Issues in Tort Law* (Hart Publishing 2007) 441, esp 457.

[71] Of course, the conceptual framework varies depending on the legal system. For example, in the English tort of negligence, it is the duty concept, not the concept of 'damage' or 'loss', which controls which pure economic loss should be recognized as 'actionable'.

[72] See section III.

be conceptualized as a violation of an entitlement to the usual or expected course of events. The resulting economic loss consisted in a deprivation of the revenues that were expected by the claimant and which it would have earned if events had unravelled as they normally did. It was therefore fundamentally the loss of an expectation.

This analysis shows that it is possible to include cases of pure economic loss within the framework of civil liability based on the distinction between harm and loss. The framework is therefore valid and can safely be generalized if French civil liability is reformed. It should be stressed that applying the framework to all losses, including pure economic loss, would not *per se* change the existing solutions in French law. In itself, the distinction between harm and loss is neutral. It neither demands nor forbids the compensation of any specific harm or loss. Distinguishing harm and loss and identifying the harm 'upstream' of a pure economic loss does not call into question the compensation of such a loss by French courts. Since the latter imposes virtually no restriction on the interests whose infringement constitutes a harm, there is no reason to deny recognition to harm consisting in the alteration of the normal course of things and to refuse compensation for the subsequent losses.

The paradox, however, is that even though French courts see no problem in compensating for pure economic loss, the distinction between harm and loss that is steadily establishing itself in French law provides a framework which can help better understand why other legal systems refuse to compensate for such loss.

III. An Interest-based Approach to Pure Economic Loss

While the rule that pure economic loss should normally not be compensated for in case of 'ordinary fault' is well established in many legal systems, it usually has many exceptions. It is also striking to see how much effort has been devoted to justifying it, and also sometimes to fighting it. Admittedly, the debate seems to be particularly vivid in the common law world, where the rules concerning pure economic loss have been established by the courts and may not be totally settled. However, even in Germany, where the refusal to compensate for pure economic loss in cases of 'ordinary' fault is based on § 823(1) BGB,[73] the rule (and the main exceptions to it) attracts a fair amount of attention. This suggests, and French law confirms, that the refusal to compensate for pure economic loss is neither natural nor inevitable.

[73] Liability based on § 823(1) BGB requires that the tortfeasor acted intentionally or negligently, but an intention to cause damage is not required. By contrast, § 826 BGB, under which liability for pure economic loss is possible, requires that the defendant intentionally caused damage 'in a manner offending common decency'. Likewise, under § 823(2), pure economic loss can be compensated for but only if the defendant, on top of committing a fault, breached a norm intended to protect a certain class of claimants against such loss.

The reasons for refusing compensation for pure economic loss are indeed not entirely obvious. While many justifications have been offered for this refusal, the debate often reverts to policy considerations, at least in comparative law, and two arguments seem to be most often put forward.[74]

The first is the famous 'floodgates argument'. According to many judges and authors, to allow compensation for pure economic loss, and no doubt more generally for 'pure' losses (ie, not resulting from physical material damage to a person or thing), would run the risk of leading to an inordinate extension of liability, which would result both in multiplication of claims and in the submission of economic operators to a potentially unlimited financial burden.[75] As Judge Cardozo famously argued, the risk is of introducing 'liability in indeterminate amount for an indeterminate time to an indeterminate class'.[76] The argument is an old one and predates the emergence of the debate on pure economic loss. It can already be found, for example, in the work of Jhering, who was concerned about the ravages of an overly broad conception of fault.[77] In the case of pure economic loss, it is the absence of an 'anchor' in personal or physical damage that gives rise to fears of an excessive extension of liability. As Bussani and Palmer have written, '[f]inancial harm is assumed to travel far and wide. It has often been pointed out that the laws of Newton do not apply on the road to financial ruin.'[78]

The relevance of the floodgates argument has been challenged, and for good reason.[79] First, the example of legal systems that allow compensation for pure economic loss suggests that an absence of restrictions on the recovery of pure economic loss has not generally led to courts being overwhelmed and liability getting out of control. For instance, French courts do not appear to be flooded with civil liability claims, and the French economic or insurance system has not collapsed as a result of compensation being awarded for pure economic loss.[80] However, this

[74] See, eg, Mauro Bussani and Vernon V Palmer, 'The Notion of Pure Economic Loss and Its Setting' in Bussani and Palmer (n 2) 3, esp 16–24; Willem H van Boom, 'Pure Economic Loss: A Comparative Perspective' in van Boom, Koziol, and Witting (n 2) 1, 31–37; Helmut Koziol, *Basic Questions of Tort Law from a Germanic Perspective* (Jan Sramek Verlag 2012) 194–200. Other types of considerations have also been put forward, however; see, eg, Efstathios K Banakas, 'Tender Is the Night: Economic Loss—The Issues' in Banakas (n 9) 1. In the United States, an argument drawn from the economic analysis of law has also been made, whereby pure economic loss should not be compensated for because it is a purely private loss, and not a 'social' one; but this view is disputed: see, eg, Anita Bernstein, 'Keep It Simple: An Explanation of the Rule of No Recovery for Pure Economic Loss' (2006) 48 Arizona Law Review 773, 774–75.

[75] This is the reason most often put forward in France to explain that many liability insurance contracts do not cover pure economic loss (often called in the insurance context 'dommage immatériel pur'—not a very happy expression in my view): Bacache (n 9) 49.

[76] *Ultramares Corp v Touche* 174 NE 441, 444 (NY 1931), which was a case of negligent misstatement.

[77] Rudolf von Jhering, 'VI. Culpa in contrahendo oder Schadenersatz bei nichtigen oder nicht zur Perfection gelangten Verträgen', Jherings Jahrbücher für die Dogmatik des bürgerlichen Rechts 4 (1861) 1, 12.

[78] Bussani and Palmer (n 74) 17.

[79] See, eg, van Boom (n 74) 33–35.

[80] Jean-Sébastien Borghetti, 'The Culture of Tort Law in France' (2012) Journal of European Tort Law 158, 159.

observation alone is not decisive, as it could be argued that compensation for pure economic loss is of little consequence in France because there are comparatively few liability actions in that country and the compensation awarded for economic losses is notoriously low.[81] In countries where the level of litigation and the average amount of damages are much higher, it cannot be ruled out that a priori unconstrained compensation for pure economic loss would have more serious economic consequences.

That being so, and as several authors have pointed out, there is no reason why economic losses resulting from personal injury or damage to property should be less extensive than pure economic losses.[82] Yet, in all legal systems, the former are generally recognized as compensable. Moreover, the development of mass or toxic torts shows that losses flowing from personal injuries or damage to property can be at least equal in magnitude to that of pure economic losses,[83] and equally unpredictable.[84]

The second policy argument often put forward for rejecting the compensation for pure economic loss relates to the social value of the interests at stake. If one accepts that the wealth which a given society can devote to compensation is limited, or more generally that the law does not have the means to grant the same protection to all interests, it makes sense to rank interests and to prioritize some of them, as does for example § 823(1) BGB.[85] Seen from that perspective, it is understandable that many legal systems should choose to prioritize bodily integrity, certain fundamental rights and freedoms, and the integrity of tangible property. Some add that this choice is an old one and reflects a fundamental choice as to the objective of tort law or civil liability.

On the other hand, as some authors have argued, intangible assets constitute an ever-increasing part of natural and legal persons' assets. In an age of widespread digitalization, is it still justified to privilege tangible property over other forms of wealth?[86] Furthermore, historical studies suggest that the refusal to compensate for pure economic loss, in addition to not being shared by all legal systems, only became established in the nineteenth century in countries such as Germany and England.[87] Incidentally, what has already been said about the floodgates argument

[81] See, eg, Suzanne Carval, 'Les dommages économiques "purs", Rapport français' in Bernard Dubuisson and Patrice Jourdain (eds), *Le dommage et sa réparation dans la responsabilité contractuelle et extracontractuelle, Études de droit comparé* (Bruylant 2015) 779, paras 8 and 13.

[82] See, eg, Gary T Schwartz, 'The Economic Loss Doctrine in American Tort Law: Assessing the Recent Experience' in Banakas (n 9) 103, 126, insisting on product liability.

[83] See eg Edwin Peel and James Goudkamp, *Winfield and Jolowicz on Tort* (19th edn, Sweet & Maxwell 2014) para 5-063; Traullé (n 13) 296–97.

[84] Predictability is of course essential to allow insurance; but even risks of physical damage have not always been adequately anticipated, as the recent example of 'persistent pollutants' (PFAS) shows.

[85] Borghetti, 'Les intérêts protégés' (n 13) 147.

[86] See eg Traullé (n 13) 298–99.

[87] James Gordley, 'The Rule against Recovery in Negligence for Pure Economic Loss: An Historical Accident?' in Bussani and Palmer (n 2) 25.

raises the question of whether the limited resources allegedly available for compensation are really a problem.

The two main arguments traditionally put forward (at least in comparative legal scholarship) to justify the refusal to compensate for pure economic loss do not therefore appear entirely convincing. However, there is probably a more fundamental reason for this refusal, which underlies these two arguments, and which the distinction between harm and loss helps to highlight. That reason is that the concrete interest underlying a claim for pure economic loss is often not worthy of protection in the eyes of the law or the judge.

The above-mentioned Marseilles bus case offers an illustration of that. In that case, and several other typical pure economic loss cases, such as cable cases,[88] the loss for which compensation is sought can be analysed as the consequence of an interference with the usual course of events. Compensating for the loss in such cases thus means accepting, albeit implicitly, that such an interference constitutes harm, and therefore that the claimant had a protected interest in events following their normal course.

This is something which many legal systems do not accept—rightfully, in my view. Be it in England or in Germany, most lawyers would probably agree that events following their usual course is not something to which people have a right and which the law should protect, unless there are some special circumstances (such as a promise made by someone, in which case the claimant will normally have a contractual claim against that person). People are of course free to count on the likelihood that events will follow their usual course, and they very often act on the assumption or expectation that this will be the case. When someone calculates how much time they need to drive to the train station or the airport, they normally do so based on their experience of the usual traffic conditions and likely disruptions. This is a perfectly sensible thing to do, and it usually works, but it may also happen that an exceptional event will totally block the traffic and will result in that person missing their train or plane and suffering a loss because of it. The refusal to allow compensation for this loss can be justified by reference to the floodgates argument, but a better or more straightforward justification seems to be that events following their normal course is not an interest that should be protected,[89] as Lord Denning famously suggested in *Spartan Steel* by pointing to certain 'hazard[s]' for the materialization of which it would not be 'healthy' to blame anyone.[90] This justification is also slightly different from the one deriving from the classical hierarchy

[88] Or the cases which have been described as cases of closure of public markets, transportation corridors, and public infrastructures: Bussani and Palmer (n 74) 12.

[89] Another way to look at it is to say that events not following their normal course is 'an ordinary risk of everyday life', against which tort law offers no protection: Banakas (n 74) 3. German lawyers also refer to the notion of the 'general risk of life' (*allgemeines Lebensrisiko*), although not always in this context: see, eg, Erwin Deutsch, 'Compensation for Pure Economic Loss in German Law' (Tony Weir tr) in Banakas (n 9) 73, 87; Hein Kötz and Gerhard Wagner, *Deliktsrecht* (14th edn, Vahlen 2016) para 216.

[90] *Spartan Steel* (n 6) 38.

of interests argument. The latter argument is very general and suggests that a loss can only be compensated for if it can be related to the violation of an interest from a pre-established list. However, the distinction between harm and loss is substantially neutral, in the sense that it does not rest on any pre-established list of protected interests, and it therefore calls for a concrete analysis of the interest at stake in the case at hand. Looking at the specific interest whose violation resulted in the loss that is being claimed provides a better reason for accepting or refusing to compensate for this loss than general considerations on the aims or limits of tort law.[91]

At first sight, this way of justifying the refusal to compensate for pure economic loss might look very much like the rights-based approach to tort law, which has been forcefully promoted in common law recently.[92] Compensating for pure economic loss means recognizing that there is an underlying harm consisting in the violation of a protected interest. If one accepts that a right is the same thing as, or something very close to, a protected interest, as Jhering famously argued,[93] then compensating for pure economic loss means recognizing an underlying right. In that sense, the interest-based approach to pure economic loss indeed comes close to the rights-based approach. However, they do not coincide exactly.

First, many would dispute that a protected interest amounts to a right. The definition of a right is a notoriously debated question, which becomes even more complex if one tries to encompass several legal systems and to cross the common law–civil law divide.[94] The rights-based approach to tort law that has recently emerged in English law is apparently grounded in the conception of rights developed by Hohfeld in his landmark article of 1913,[95] and the relationship between this conception and that of Jhering is at best uncertain. However, one of the advantages of an interest-based approach is that it does not rest on a pre-defined conception of a 'right' and is compatible with most definitions of that notion.[96]

While there are different rights-based approaches to tort law, the prevailing view seems to be that a claim can be granted only when there has been an infringement of a pre-existing right which the law has chosen to protect independently from tort law. As McBride puts it (criticizing this approach): 'if we are to protect a

[91] This is not to say that such considerations are useless or superfluous. For example, in a system based on precedent, they may be needed to set a framework for future cases.

[92] See, notably, Robert Stevens, *Torts and Rights* (OUP 2007). See also Benson (n 1) 874, arguing that, to be compensable, a loss 'must result from the defendant's interference with something that comes under plaintiff's exclusive rights as against the defendant'.

[93] Rudolf von Jhering, *Geist des römischen Rechts auf den verschiedenen Stufen seiner Entwicklung*, vol 3 (5th edn, Breitkopf & Härtel 1905) 339.

[94] As was notably made clear by Frederick H Lawson, '"Das subjektivc Recht" in the English Law of Torts' in Frederick H Lawson, *Many Laws: Selected Essays*, vol 1 (North-Holland 1977) 176, and Geoffrey Samuel, '"Le Droit Subjectif" and English Law' (1987) 46 Cambridge Law Journal 264.

[95] Wesley N Hohfeld, 'Some Fundamental Legal Conceptions as Applied in Judicial Reasoning' (1913) 23 Yale Law Journal 16.

[96] In the rest of this contribution, when I refer to 'right', I mean a legally recognized interest, but the gist of the argument does not depend on this definition.

given interest of the plaintiff's by requiring a defendant to take care not to damage that interest, we have to show that that interest is *already* protected under the law' (emphasis in the original).[97] In other words, under the prevailing rights-based approach, it is not for tort law to say what interests ought to be protected. Rather, tort law takes note of the protection granted by other branches of the law.

In my opinion, this is not entirely convincing. Admittedly, the law protects some interests very clearly by granting express rights to legal subjects. Proprietary rights are good examples of that. When this is the case, tort law must of course recognize the existence of a protected interest and cannot refuse to compensate for a loss flowing from its violation if the conditions of liability are met. However, many interests do not enjoy such clear legal protection independently from the law of tort. If one takes the example of French law, which is based on legislation (at least officially),[98] it was not until recently that legislative provisions formally recognized one's right to privacy or the value of bodily integrity,[99] and the courts played a great role in the building up of their protection.[100] In Italy, where the courts use the requirement that damage be 'unjust' (*danno ingiusto*) to limit the scope of liability,[101] for example in case of pure economic loss,[102] the *Corte di cassazione* has recognized a right to the integrity of one's patrimony (*diritto all'integrità del proprio patrimonio*), for the purpose of awarding compensation for some instances of such loss.[103] Even in Germany, where § 823(1) BGB sets a list of protected rights, the courts have taken the liberty to recognize two rights that are not listed in that provision.[104]

Even assuming that all rights must first be recognized outside tort law, courts enjoy some discretion when it comes to determining the exact scope and content of a right. This applies to rights that are undoubtedly recognized by the legal system independently from tort law. For example, it is very interesting to see how courts in some countries have interpreted broadly the right of property, so as to include

[97] Nicholas J McBride, 'Rights and the Basis of Tort Law' in Donal Nolan and Andrew Robertson (eds), *Rights and Private Law* (Hart Publishing 2012) 331, 338.

[98] For a reconsideration of the role of legislation in French law, see Jean-Sébastien Borghetti, 'Legal Methodology and the Role of Professors in France—*Professorenrecht* is not a French word!' in Jürgen Basedow, Holger Fleischer, and Reinhard Zimmermann (eds), *Legislators, Judges, and Professors* (Mohr Siebeck 2016) 209.

[99] The right to respect for one's private life was formally recognized in the Code civil in 1970 (art 9 Cc), and the right to respect for one's body in 1994 (art 16-1 Cc).

[100] Viney (n 31) 105–109.

[101] Art 2043 of the Italian Codice civile states: 'Any intentional or negligent act, which causes unjust damage to others, obliges the perpetrator to provide compensation for the damage' ('Qualunque fatto doloso o colposo, che cagiona ad altri un danno ingiusto, obbliga colui che ha commesso il fatto a risarcire il danno').

[102] Sirena (n 47) 215.

[103] Corte di Cassazione, sez III, 4 May 1982, no 2765 (*De Chirico*), in which the claimant was seeking compensation after he had bought a painting on which the famous painter Giorgio De Chirico had put his signature although it was not authentic.

[104] For a detailed presentation in English of that aspect of German tort law, see John Bell, André Janssen, and Colm McGrath, *Markesinis's German Law of Torts* (3rd edn, Hart Publishing 2019) 93–97.

within the category 'damage to property' instances where there was no physical harm and which would otherwise have been categorized as cases of pure economic loss.[105] This is a good illustration of the fact that even the rights recognized most explicitly by the legal system do not have crystal-clear boundaries and that courts enjoy some freedom when delimiting the scope of the interests that are protected through that right.[106] Obviously, this freedom is even greater when the courts establish the existence of a pre-existing right based on a scattered collection of provisions or cases.

What this means is that, even if the courts deciding tort cases pretend to identify pre-existing rights, they enjoy substantial discretion in doing so, whether in a common law or a civil law jurisdiction. In practice, in some cases it can be difficult to tell if the courts are concretizing a pre-existing right or if they are creating a new right. Saying that tort law only recognizes pre-existing rights is a postulate whose truth cannot be established but which does not sound very realistic.[107] While some interests are undoubtedly protected by the legal system independently from tort law, other interests do not enjoy such unambiguous protection and courts, when deciding a tort law issue, have some leeway in determining whether they should indeed be protected.

Pure economic loss cases are precisely those in which the interest that appears to be protected—unlike bodily integrity or tangible property, which are clearly recognized elsewhere in the legal system—cannot be readily identified or located 'upstream' of the loss. This is perhaps why pure economic loss has also been defined as a 'loss that is not the consequence of the violation of a legal right'.[108] If there was a clearly protected interest or 'legal right' upstream of the loss, the latter would not be regarded as 'pure'.[109] And this is why a rights-based approach of tort law is arguably not very helpful in cases of pure economic loss. Insofar as such an approach makes the outcome of a compensation claim depend on the pre-existence of a right, it cannot give a straightforward answer to cases where it is not clear if there is indeed such a right (ie, a protected interest).

105 See, eg, for English law and other common law jurisdictions, Nolan (n 68) 276–80; Peel and Goudkamp (n 83) para 5-058; for German law, Bell, Janssen, and McGrath (n 104) 94; von Bar (n 3) 42–45.

106 The distinction between pure economic loss and physical damage has been described in Scotland as 'Jesuitical': *Colerdige v Miller Construction* [1997] SLT 485, 491.

107 And it has met with strong criticism; see, eg, Peter Cane, 'Rights in Private Law' in Nolan and Robertson (n 97) 35.

108 von Bar (n 3) 30.

109 Admittedly, pure economic loss is usually defined as a financial loss not stemming from physical personal injury or physical damage to property suffered by the claimant themselves: see n 1. Yet, in many legal systems, a financial loss suffered by someone as a consequence of, say, violation of their right to privacy would probably not be categorized as 'pure' economic loss. This suggests that lawyers are not so keen to speak of 'pure' losses when they flow from the violation of an interest that is unambiguously protected by the legal system.

An interest-based approach to pure economic loss does not really contradict a rights-based approach but is perhaps more pragmatic. Speaking of rights adds a layer of complexity in the analysis of tort law. If one accepts that there is no predetermined list of rights defined in or outside tort law which tort law must recognize and protect, granting compensation for a loss can be analysed more simply as the recognition that an interest worthy of protection has been violated. Such an approach is also possibly more dynamic or flexible, in the sense that a right is normally defined rather rigidly and calls for protection as a matter of principle, whereas the extent to which an interest deserves to be protected may depend on the circumstances and the way in which it has been violated.[110]

The key issue, of course, is to determine what are those interests that are not clearly protected by the legal system but deserve to be recognized and protected by tort law. If one accepts that the legal system does not set a clear and complete list of such protected interests (or rights), then one must also accept that the courts enjoy some leeway in that respect, and that policy considerations therefore have a role to play in the courts' decisions. To that extent, an interest-based approach to pure economic loss does not contradict the traditional justifications for not compensating for pure economic loss grounded on policy considerations either. However, such an approach calls for more detailed and tailored justifications than those offered by the traditional theories, in cases where the loss does not flow from the violation of an interest which is undoubtedly protected by the legal system.

Under such an interest-based approach, it makes no sense to set a general rule concerning pure economic loss,[111] because there is no single interest at stake behind the variety of cases involving such loss. Equally, it is not necessary to recognize a hypothetical right not to suffer pure economic loss resulting from another's conduct, the existence of which has been forcefully denied.[112] Cases have been cited where the underlying interest appears to be reliance on the usual course of events, but not all pure economic losses flow from a disruption of that course. For example, in the case of a negligent misstatement, which is a classic instance of a situation causing pure economic loss,[113] the interest upstream of the loss is not the normal course of events, like in the Marseilles bus case, but rather the reliance which the third party had placed on the information provided by the defendant. The protection which this interest deserves can depend in turn on several circumstances, for instance the existence of a 'special relationship' between the parties, as was famously required in *Hedley Byrne*.[114]

[110] See Pietro Trimarchi, *La responsabilità civile: atti illeciti, rischio, danno* (Giuffrè 2017) 26.

[111] See also van Boom (n 74) 39.

[112] See notably Nolan (n 54) 263–97.

[113] As several famous common law cases illustrate: see esp *Glanzer v Shepard* 233 N.Y. 236 (1922); *Ultramares Corp v Touche* 174 N.E. 441 (1931); *Hedley Byrne & Co Ltd v Heller & Partners Ltd* [1964] AC 465; *Caparo v Dickman* [1990] 2 AC 605.

[114] *Hedley Byrne & Co Ltd v Heller & Partners Ltd* [1964] AC 465.

Another interesting example is that of 'ricochet' losses, where the claimant suffers a loss due to personal injury caused to someone else, for example when someone loses financial support due to the death of their spouse or partner. It could be disputed if those are indeed cases of pure economic loss since the loss of the claimant flows from a personal injury and could therefore be seen as consequential loss. This latter view is apparently taken (albeit implicitly) by the French Dintilhac nomenclature, where it distinguishes (and puts on the same level) *préjudices* suffered by the direct victim of the personal injury from those suffered by ricochet victims.

However, this approach is arguably flawed. If it were to be adopted, it would entail systematic compensation for ricochet economic losses, because the interest upstream (bodily integrity) is undoubtedly worthy of protection. But this is not the right way to look at things. In the case of ricochet loss, the interest for which the claimant is implicitly seeking recognition and protection is not the bodily integrity of the direct victim but the relationship which they had with that person. Ricochet economic loss is therefore rightfully viewed as an instance of pure economic loss,[115] and it could be analysed as a type of 'relational economic loss', even though this expression usually designates loss arising out of physical damage caused to a third party's property.[116] Whether or not to compensate for such loss should hinge on whether the underlying relationship deserves protection. This, in turn, can depend on a number of factors, including its duration, whether it is recognized by law, and so on.[117] An interest-based approach to pure economic loss therefore does not discard the various policy considerations which the courts (or authors) may have put forward to justify or deny compensation for such loss. Rather, it offers a framework where these considerations can be weighed against each other.

Accordingly, under an interest-based approach, the fact that pure economic loss is compensated for in some cases and not in others is perfectly understandable, and not the result of some incoherence (as French lawyers might be tempted to think, due to their taste for general rules).[118] This is because, among all the interests that are not clearly protected by the legal system and which can underlie claims for compensation for 'pure' losses, some are worthy of protection and others are not. It is therefore understandable that, in legal systems where there exists a principle against the recovery of pure economic loss, so many exceptions can be found.[119]

[115] See, eg, Schwartz (n 82) 109.

[116] See, eg, Bruce Feldthusen, 'The Recovery of Pure Economic Loss in Canada: Proximity, Justice, Rationality and Chaos' in Banakas (n 9) 131, 143; Benson (n 1) 823.

[117] For instance, in France, the *Cour de cassation* over several decades in the middle of the twentieth century maintained that the ricochet loss of a concubine should not be compensated for because she did not have a 'legally protected legitimate interest' (*intérêt légitime juridiquement protégé*): Viney, Jourdain, and Carval (n 18) para 308. This was another way of saying that only the existence of a legally recognized relationship allowed for compensation of the loss flowing from its unlawful destruction. This approach was reversed in the famous *Dangereux* case: Cass ch mixte 27 February 1970 no 68-10.276, Bull crim no 1.

[118] Borghetti and Whittaker (n 11) 455.

[119] For a comparative overview, see Wagner (n 1) 1008–09.

Conversely, this is also the reason why the French official position accepting the compensation for pure economic loss as a matter of principle is arguably wrong. Taking such a position amounts to saying that all interests are worthy of protection,[120] which cannot be the case. It should therefore come as no surprise that French law has many exceptions (most of them unofficial)[121] to the rule that all losses are compensable, and that most of these exceptions concern 'pure' losses, that is, losses that do not flow from the violation of an interest clearly protected by the French legal system.[122] Besides, French law limits compensation for pure economic loss more indirectly, but rather efficiently,[123] by applying a stricter standard of fault (*faute*) in the context of claims based on disloyal competition,[124] as well as by the famous '*non-cumul*' rule, which forbids the application of tort law rules between contracting parties and thus prevents a situation where a tort claim would upset the balance of interests agreed between them.[125] The doctrine of loss of a chance is yet another way to limit compensation for pure economic loss,[126] since it is frequently used in the context of a loss of expected profits and results in the claimant being granted damages for only a fraction of those profits and not the full amount.[127]

An interest-based approach to pure economic loss therefore calls for a careful analysis of the interest that lies behind the loss for which compensation is being claimed. Indeed, typologies of the different instances of pure economic loss have already been proposed[128]—an approach which can be seen as reflecting this logic. However, the variety of interests potentially at stake is probably greater than the list

[120] Provided they are not unlawful, since French law insists that violation of an interest in pursuing an unlawful activity does not deserve compensation: see n 27.

[121] They can be called unofficial because they are not set out in legislation and have only been accepted by the courts, but without being presented as exceptions to the rule that all types of losses are normally compensable. The courts were able to do so because judgments of the *Cour de cassation* contain only a formal justification for the ruling (although this is now changing), and because the denial of compensation is sometimes deceptively presented as grounded on purely technical grounds, such as the absence of a causal link between the defendant's action and the loss: see n 65 and 66.

[122] See, eg, claims by children complaining that they cannot have a normal relationship with their parents or grandparents (see n 65); claims for financial loss suffered by the 'economic partners' of the person directly injured (see n 66); claims for wrongful life (which are now prohibited by art L 114-5 of the *Code de l'action sociale et des familles*); claims for losing a bet (Cass civ (2) 14 June 2018 no 17-20.046, Bull civ II no 124).

[123] As has been clearly identified by Wagner (n 1) 1006–07.

[124] See Bell, Boyron, and Whittaker (n 17) 380–81; Philippe le Tourneau (ed), *Droit de la responsabilité et des contrats. Régimes d'indemnisation* (12th edn, Dalloz 2020) paras 2214.00–2214.106. While a *faute* can normally consist in mere negligence, as is made clear by art 1241 Cc, only intentional acts are regarded as constituting *faute* in cases of disloyal competition.

[125] See Jean-Sébastien Borghetti, 'La responsabilité du fait des choses, un régime qui a fait son temps', Revue trimestrielle de droit civil 2010, no 1, 1, esp paras 47 and 67.

[126] For a critical analysis of this doctrine and its origins, see Hugo Méral, *La perte de chance en droit privé. Essai critique* (Éditions Panthéon-Assas 2024).

[127] Romain Lorentz, 'Dommage purement patrimonial, rapport français', Revue internationale de droit comparé 2006, vol 58, no 2, 393, 407.

[128] See, eg, Bell, Janssen, and McGrath (n 104) 93–97; Bussani and Palmer (n 74) 10–14; Deutsch (n 89) 84–86; Feldthusen (n 116) 135–47; Palmer (n 2) 302–06; van Boom (n 74) 15–31.

of items in these typologies. What is needed in matters of pure economic loss is a 'typical case' approach, with each discrete case defined by reference to the specific underlying interest.[129]

It should be stressed that the identification of the interest underlying a loss is not always straightforward. There is often room for discussion. Let us take the example of the financial loss suffered by someone due to the death of their spouse, which is usually analysed as an instance of pure economic loss. Assuming the death was accidental, it can be seen merely as a deviation from the normal course of events, in which case no compensation should be granted—if one accepts that the interest which people may have in events following their normal course (which includes other people's dying of old age) should not be protected in the absence of a contractual promise to that effect. However, the interest at stake in this example can also be analysed, perhaps more convincingly, as the continuation of a conjugal relationship, something worthy of protection in the eyes of the law, in which case the claimant should be entitled to compensation.[130]

The fact that there is more than one interest-based way of approaching the question of recovery of pure economic loss in the event of a spouse's death does not disqualify the interest-based approach. Rather, it merely shows that one and the same situation can sometimes be analysed in different ways. The existence of diverging viewpoints on the same situation is the reason why many cases come to court, why lawyers can disagree over the outcome of a case, and why some cases are still being discussed decades or even centuries after they were adjudicated. Pure economic loss is a matter of continuous discussion because many of the cases where compensation has been sought constitute what are known in legal theory as 'hard cases'. By construction, they are cases where no unequivocally protected interest can be identified and where there is room for discussion as to whether the interest at stake deserves protection. There is no miraculous theory or approach that could spare courts and lawyers the effort to engage in such a discussion (at least until a clear solution has been established in case law concerning the specific interest or situation at stake). The challenge is therefore not to give a straightforward answer to all cases of pure economic loss—something which is not possible[131]—but rather to make the discussion both as open and as focused

[129] This approach seems to be adopted by at least some Japanese lawyers: Taro Nakahara, 'Le Préjudice économique pur. Rapport japonais' in Capitant (n 9) 53, 59.

[130] The same would apply to the emotional suffering of that person, which is obviously not economic loss but also falls in the category of 'pure' losses, that is losses not flowing from a violation of an interest undoubtedly protected by the legal system. In cases of emotional suffering, compensation typically depends on whether the relationship between the claimant and the person who was killed or physically injured is regarded as sufficiently close to deserve protection. It is therefore that relationship which constitutes the interest whose 'protection-worthiness' must be assessed.

[131] This, at least, is what the experience of English law seems to suggest.

as is reasonably possible. A discussion in which reasonable minds may differ is unavoidable, but what should be avoided to the extent possible are elements that obscure the discussion or twist the issues at stake. Approaching pure economic loss from the perspective of the specific underlying interest, using the distinction between harm and loss, is arguably a way to go to the point and to avoid unnecessary technical or theoretical complications.

10

A 'Pilfered Ginger'

Tort Claims for Harm Caused by Products Involving Illegality

*Matthew Dyson**

I. Introduction

What happens when a claim for harm from a defective product involves the claimant's own illegal conduct? The chapter explores what law there is, and why there are few reported decisions on this question. The issue might cover illegality in acquiring the product, illegality in the use of the product, and perhaps even illegality in the product itself. It is inspired by Simon Whittaker's path-breaking work in both product liability and comparative law. An example might be this: what would have happened if Mrs Donoghue had stolen the ginger beer in the famous English case of *Donoghue v Stephenson*? In 1932, the House of Lords held for the first time that a producer owed a duty to take reasonable care of the ultimate consumer of a drink where it was sold in an opaque bottle that presented no opportunity for intermediate inspection. The question of legal difficulty arose because she had not bought the drink herself; she had instead been gifted it by the purchaser, and so the normal contractual route was not available. The variants of that fact pattern show the range of issues that can arise.

1. Pilfered ginger: C steals a bottle from the café and the contents make C ill. There is a useful comparison with the situation where the claimant steals the bottle from the producers' warehouse before the product was released into the market.
2. Tippled ginger: C tips a vending machine in order to cause the bottle to fall to the bottom and be obtained for free, a form of theft, but the vending machine tips over and C is injured by the falling machine; vending machines should be secured to prevent injury from machines falling over.

* With particular thanks to the editors; the attendees at the volume's workshop, especially Simon Whittaker; and Margot Calmar, Tripp Haston, and Chadwick Lamar.

Matthew Dyson, *A 'Pilfered Ginger'* In: *Comparative Reflections in Private Law*. Edited by: Marco Cappelletti, Ciara Kennefick, and Dorota Leczykiewicz, Oxford University Press. © Marco Cappelletti, Ciara Kennefick, and Dorota Leczykiewicz 2026. DOI: 10.1093/9780198959168.003.0012

3. Filched ginger: C reaches inside a vending machine in order to steal a bottle from it, and is injured on the internal mechanisms, a risk only engaged when attempting something unlawful.
4. Embezzled ginger: D, a member of staff, sells the drink to another, outside the terms of the employment, such as to a person under the age of consumption or outside of lawful trading hours, and C is injured by its contents.
5. Gin not tonic: C buys the drink lawfully, but the drink has a further interaction that is only relevant for those who have committed illegal acts, such as if the drink produces a harmful side-effect on users of illegal drugs.

These variants highlight that a claimant's illegality does not have to be far-fetched to be legally relevant. But for legally trained readers, it might already be apparent that reported decisions with facts like these are in fact vanishingly rare. This chapter uses 'illegal claims' as a starting point to begin to consider how different forms of reasoning within a legal system interact. Understanding how legal actors conceptualize, consider, and argue about issues is one of the highlights of comparative legal studies.

On the one hand, there is the regime of product liability, a bespoke part of tort law with distinct features prioritizing the consumer. Product liability law has black letter rules, principles, and the approaches and values of lawyers involved, with litigation processed typically through general civil law courts. It is treated as a field of law, with books written about it by academics, and as a practice area separate to others by many practitioners, though this is perhaps most strongly evident in common law countries.

On the other hand, there are ideas which are applied across a legal system, and many represent or are designed to produce uniformity or coherence across the legal system. In effect, they are there to minimize the differences between areas of law. The example that concerns us here is illegality: that illegal conduct by the claimant is relevant to what would otherwise be a valid tort claim.

Product liability is a particularly useful area for examining how forms of reasoning inside a system interact, because liability has been standardized across many legal systems on the basis of strict liability for producers. Since this gives fewer 'moving parts' for illegality to operate under, it has to be accommodated by one of those, or stand alone as a new and explicit ground to deny liability. No such defence has been found so far. For some legal actors it might be that illegality is relevant, for others it might not be; but in either case any work to be done by the concept is carried out through existing components of liability. The interaction between illegality and product liability therefore sets the scene for considering how different forms of reasoning are made to co-exist within a legal system.

Centre stage in that process is how lawyers behave. They have to consider any apparent divergence between rules or outcomes, and how to resolve it. It is hard to piece together that process for the mind of a single lawyer, let alone many, across legal systems. One step will be to see how, if at all, lawyers integrate overlaps between subject matters such as illegality and product liability, especially where there are conflicting approaches or rules. Illegality in product liability is a challenging example, as there are in fact few if any reported cases. That might suggest that the issue has not been one that has been taken before the courts for resolution. Possible reasons for this are canvassed below. They include alternative doctrinal avenues for addressing as much of the illegality is thought relevant, as well as practical problems such as claimants disclosing their own illegal conduct.

The chronology of the issues in this chapter also ties it into this volume in another way: the EU's Product Liability Directive was passed in 1985, becoming law in the UK in the Consumer Protection Act 1987 (CPA 1987); the growth of illegality rules in England began in the 1980s; and, not least importantly, Simon Whittaker began his academic career in the 1980s.

The chapter will look at (2) Product Liability, (3) Illegality, and (4) the Relationship between the two, before turning to (5) How these areas of law can be integrated and (6) a Conclusion.

II. Product Liability

From a career of powerful and scholarly work by Simon Whittaker, it is invidious to pick out just one example. There is a rich collection of work, filled with nuance, insight, and rigour. Nonetheless, it was in connection with *Liability for Products: English Law, French Law, and European Harmonization*[1] that I first engaged with his work in detail, and it remains a work repaying careful attention. It is a book that looks at where ideas and functions sit in a legal system, regardless of the legal category they have been placed into. A legal system can be said to have functions done by objects, such as rules, within a legal system. The legal system applies its own categories. By identifying the function, one might then compare where that work is done in another legal system. It thankfully also sets out much of the law and its development in England and France, and as a result this chapter does not need to.

A. Strict liability

A sketch of the key features of the Product Liability Directive of 1985[2] suffices to set the scene for product liability law in multiple legal systems in Europe. The

[1] Simon Whittaker, *Liability for Products: English Law, French Law, and European Harmonization* (OUP 2005).

[2] Council Directive 85/374/EEC of 25 July 1985 on the approximation of the laws, regulations and administrative provisions of the Member States concerning liability for defective products, OJ L 210,

Directive was enacted to provide minimum consumer protection across the EU. It required member states to have a system of liability without fault for all defective products put into the market, subject to a few relatively narrow defences. The CPA 1987 implemented the Directive in England and Wales. Its implementation was slightly more generous to producers than the wording in the Directive. However, in practice, any discrepancy should be resolved in favour of the Directive, as the obligation to interpret Part I of the CPA 1987 in line with the Directive shows.[3] *A v National Blood Authority*, long the leading case in England and Wales, clearly stated that the Directive was the overriding legal source,[4] endorsing ECJ case law.[5]

The Directive imposes strict liability: in simple terms, the claimant does not need to prove the defendant's fault, only that the defendant was a producer of a defective product, which caused damage actionable under the Directive.[6] A product is defective when 'it does not provide the safety which a person is entitled to expect, taking all circumstances into account' according to article 6 of the Directive. The latest English case on the Directive confirms that, in assessing 'defect', a risk/benefit analysis is normally required.[7] That is, since all products necessarily pose some risk, the issue in order to find a wrong, if any, for the purposes of tort liability under the Directive, is to find which risks the producer should be liable for. To that end, there remain significant questions of whether 'avoidability' and regulatory standards are relevant, and whether any rules of thumb about the product being 'standard' or 'non-standard' are useful.[8] In any case, the phrasing of product liability is not formulated around a relevant wrong. Doing so would most commonly look for the interference with a right of the claimant.[9] While one could describe product liability in those terms, it is not how this is commonly done, perhaps

7.8.1985, p 29. There is another Directive, Council Directive 2001/95/EC of 3 December 2001 on general product safety, OJ L11/4, 15.1.2002, p 4, but that seeks to prevent unsafe products reaching the market, not dealing with the consequences of when they do.

[3] CPA 1987, s 1(1).

[4] [2001] 3 All ER 289 [2], [21].

[5] Case C-300/95 *European Commission v UK*, ECLI:EU:C:1997:255: Opinion of AG Tesauro, para 28; judgment of the Court of Justice of the European Communities (now the Court of Justice of the EU), paras 38 and 21–22.

[6] There are limits on the types of harm, and a minimum threshold of harm, but otherwise implemented according to relatively standard national approaches; most commonly it is personal injury. There are some more difficult questions and points of controversy, for example, potentially distinguishing between design defects, warning defects, manufacturing defects, and aftercare defects.

[7] *Wilkes v DePuy International Ltd* [2016] EWHC 3096 (QB), see especially [15]–[19], [82]–[83] and [133]. This built on academic commentary: see eg C Miller and R Goldberg, *Product Liability* (2nd edn, OUP 2004) esp ch 10.

[8] *Wilkes* (n 7) where Hickinbottom J, in contrast to *National Blood* (n 4) said yes, yes, and no to those three questions. The Court of Justice of the European Union has recently said that having an abnormal potential for damage would be relevant, though the case itself was more about whether a specific product was within a class of those (pacemakers) with a risk of failure: Case C-503/13 *Boston Scientific Medizintechnik GmbH v AOK Sachsen-Anhalt*, ECLI:EU:C:2014:2306.

[9] See eg Peter Birks, 'The Concept of a Civil Wrong' in David Owen (ed), *The Philosophical Foundations of Tort Law* (Clarendon 1997) 31.

because it seems to stretch the English language (at least): that the claimant had a right that all producers not put into the market a defective product that would cause the claimant harm.

B. Defences

There are six defences listed.[10] In their modern, post-Brexit form, they are:

1. the defect is attributable to compliance with a UK or retained EU law obligation;
2. the defendant did not put the product into circulation;
3. the defendant did not supply the product in the course of a business and is either not a producer, or not a for-profit producer;
4. the defect did not exist at the relevant time;
5. the state of scientific and technical knowledge at the time meant that the producer could not have been expected to discover the defect while the product was under his control; and
6. the defect in the product arose from the design of a subsequent product it was integrated into.

The Directive expresses a judgement about which risks individuals should bear and which profit-making entities should bear, something expressly referred to in recitals 2 and 7 to the Directive explaining the Directive as promoting the 'fair apportionment of risk'. One argument is that, as a result of its greater knowledge and expertise, it is normally the producer who can most cheaply prevent the product from being defective. It is therefore the overall cheapest solution for the producer to do so, rather than require every consumer to make the products safe and consequently raising the price of all the units of the product. In most commercial situations, the producer will pass on a tiny fraction of this smaller cost to the consumer. Therefore, strict liability makes the consumer's life a lot simpler, more cheaply, and without significant cost to the producer. There is then a question of whether a finding of liability under the CPA 1987 necessarily amounts to a finding of wrongdoing. Proving a claim in strict liability here proves only that the producer has put onto the market a defective product, not that they did anything wrong by doing so, unless one takes the view that introducing that risk into the market was itself a wrong.

In many legal systems, the Directive added to the law, rather than replaced earlier rules. It is a form of maximal harmonization, but only in respect of a strict

[10] CPA 1987, s 4(1)(a)–(f).

liability regime for defective products governed by extracontractual liability rules, not in respect of contractual rules or fault-based tort rules. In England, this means that the common law still exists underneath the Directive, allowing a product liability claim based on fault. Thus, negligence in a product's manufacture will, paradigmatically, allow a claim to be brought even by an ultimate consumer outside of a contractual relationship with the producer.[11] The test in such cases is based on reasonable care, though one might take the view that some of the cases showed that quite a high standard is expected in fact, particularly where the consumers themselves were unable to use everyday means, such as unaided sight, to assess the safety or quality of the goods.[12]

In practice, judgments under the CPA 1987 are rare. It seems that settlement is particularly common. Liability is more easily established than under other rules, especially than under the tort of negligence. There are also dedicated specialists litigating the cases, aware of the transaction costs and dealing with most cases relatively simply.[13] Defending a product liability claim might bring information into the public domain that would be commercially disadvantageous to release.

The role of defences can be particularly significant under the CPA 1987.[14] The strict liability is otherwise particularly onerous. One of the defences can even undermine the strictness of the liability: the development risks defence. It provides a defence to strict liability on the basis that the expectations of producers at the time the product was put into the market did not include discovery of the defect in the product. In a sense, this unties one of the threads in liability under the CPA 1987, that the safety of the product did not meet expectations: a reasonable producer could not be expected to know of the defect when in the claimant's hands, and as such should not be liable. The implication is that knowing of the defect would have led to taking other measures, whether that it does not go out into the market at all, or its safety be improved. The defence is unlikely to assist unless the defect was totally unknown and unpredictable at the time.[15] In *A v National Blood*,[16] the defence failed: if there is a known risk, then the producer who continues to produce and supply the product does so at his own risk. However, defendants are also incentivized not to rely on the development risk defence in particular. When pleaded, the defence might avoid liability in the case in issue but it involves admitting that the product was defective, but the company was not capable enough to realize that at

[11] The famous case of *Donoghue v Stevenson* [1932] AC 562.

[12] See eg *Donoghue* (n 11); *Grant v Australian Knitting Mills* [1936] AC 562; *Pollard v Tesco Stores Ltd* [2006] EWCA Civ 393.

[13] For example, Henderson Chambers in London are perhaps the leading set of chambers for product liability cases, and directly advertise themselves as such. The same might be said of solicitor firms, with generalists such as Addleshaw Goddard, Baker McKenzie, Herbert Smith Freehills, and Hogan Lovells having strong teams, and some smaller firms, such as Cooley's.

[14] As is easily the case for defences to strict liability more generally.

[15] See eg Case C-300/95 *Commission v United Kingdom* (n 5).

[16] See n 4.

the time. The public relations and media effects of that admission could be significant, perhaps worse than liability in a particular case.

We can therefore see a somewhat standardized strict liability claim, based on defect and with limited and specifically pleaded defences. We turn now to the other half of the problem, the role of illegality in denying civil claims.

III. Illegality

After that brief summary of product liability, and its openness to other defences, we can turn now to the specific way in which product liability interacts with the doctrine of illegality. Examples of doctrines addressing a claimant's illegality seem to be exclusively found in common law legal systems.[17]

A. Types of illegal claims

We can see four types of illegality claims, three types of losses claimed for, and a host of legal responses. These types capture the kinds of conduct already covered in the introduction, though the majority of fact patterns are in the first category, unilateral illegality.

(i) Unilateral illegality

The simplest form is sometimes called 'unilateral' illegality: whether a person, breaking the law, is still entitled to the protection tort law provides. This is normally a question of interpretation, of whether the rule of law being broken means to deprive the wrongdoer of tort law's protection. The illegality in itself is not normally a bar to a claim.[18] The classic nexus is being a trespasser: trespassing is not normally sufficient to mean you lose civil claims you would otherwise have had.[19] A more recent case is a person seeking to evade arrest and suffering serious injuries by doing so.[20]

[17] See Matthew Dyson (ed), Understanding Illegal Tort Claims: Comparative Legal Reasoning in Global Perspective (Hart, forthcoming 2026).

[18] eg *Henwood v The Municipal Tramways Trust (South Australia)* (1938) 60 CLR 438; with *Cross v Kirkby* [2000] EWCA Civ 426 being obiter and less persuasive.

[19] *Bird v Holbrook* (1828) 4 Bing NC 628, 130 ER 911; cf *Katko v Briney*, 183 NW 2d 657 (Iowa 1971). Occupier's Liability Act 1984, s 1(3); *Revill v Newbury* [1996] QB 56; Tony Weir wrote, without enthusiasm for the decisions, Tony Weir, 'Swag for the Injured Burglar' (1996) Cambridge Law Journal 182, 183: 'We must therefore suppose it to be the law that a criminal who would be refused damages if he sued his accomplice is to be granted them if he sues his victim instead.'

[20] *Vellino v Chief Constable of Greater Manchester* [2002] 1 WLR 218; cf participation in an illegal act: *Colburn v Patmore* (1834) 1 CM & R 72, 149 ER 999.

(ii) Joint illegality

A second form is 'joint' illegality: whether one can sue another in tort for injury sustained while both were breaking the law. A famous judicial comment expressed doubt that a robber, cracking open a safe, should be able to sue in tort his accomplice who sets the explosives badly and injures the robber's hand.[21] Road traffic cases are common, such as the getaway driver who drives badly and injures his criminal passengers.[22] Legal systems vary dramatically in how they address such claims.[23] There are also complex cases on the edge of tort law, such as whether persons without the right to work are entitled to wages that should have been paid by an employer who abuses them, knowing of their status.[24] The paradigm fact pattern has shifted over time from illegal fights[25] to road traffic accidents.[26]

(iii) Joint wrongdoers

These are actions by wrongdoers as between themselves for consequences of their wrongdoing. Claims of this type are regulated differently across legal systems, but some kind of action in contribution is now a common answer. One person, who is jointly or solidarily liable for the same harm, brings a simplified action against other wrongdoers whose share that person had had to pay.[27] This is perhaps the least relevant form of illegality to the present discussion as the formal legal rules are now historic. The reasoning seems to be treated as relevant to the next category though.

(iv) Sanction-shifting

The third form is sometimes imperfectly called 'sanction-shifting':[28] whether a person who commits a crime can claim in tort against another whose earlier tort is connected to that crime. Courts are sometimes reluctant to allow the claimant to 'shift' the effect of a criminal sanction by making another person liable in tort as well. That is, all the conditions of tort liability are met, but there is a defence on the basis of illegality. There have been two major variations in fact patterns so far.

[21] *National Coal Board v England* [1954] AC 403, 429.

[22] eg *Ashton v Turner* [1981] QB 137. See also *Joyce v O'Brien* [2013] EWCA Civ 546.

[23] See generally Dyson (n 17).

[24] See eg James Goudkamp and Lorenz König, 'Illegal Earnings' (2018) 9 Journal of European Tort Law 54.

[25] *Lane v Holloway* [1967] 3 All ER 129; cf *Murphy v Culhane* [1977] QB 94.

[26] *Pitts v Hunt* [1991] 1 QB 24.

[27] *Merryweather v Nixan* (1799) 8 TR 186, where the plaintiff and defendant had been held liable for injury to the reversionary interest in a mill, but the plaintiff had the whole damages levied against him; it was held that he could not bring any action for contribution against the defendant. The rule was changed in 1935 by the Law Reform (Married Women and Tortfeasors) Act 1935 and is now governed by the Civil Liability (Contribution) Act 1978.

[28] See eg James Goudkamp, 'Can Tort Law be Used to Deflect the Impact of Criminal Sanctions? The Role of the Illegality Defence' (2006) 14 Torts Law Journal 20.

In one variation, the defendant, who wishes the tort claim to be barred, is the original cause of the claimant's crime. The most common form of the claim begins with a traumatic event. That event causes the claimant to suffer from a psychological condition that changes the claimant's personality, so that the claimant kills another. Later, the claimant sues the person who caused the initial traumatic event. What might be claimed for varies, but the simplest case is perhaps the psychological harm suffered by the claimant. English tort law normally holds that the defendant who negligently caused the traumatic event, such as a largescale train accident causing post-traumatic stress disorder, is liable for its consequences. A significant authority is *Gray v Thames Trains* in 2009.[29] It was said to have been decided largely on the ground of 'coherence', although this concept was not clearly defined. Lord Hoffmann held that there were two forms of the illegality 'rule':

> The wider and simpler version is that . . . you cannot recover for damage which is the consequence of your own criminal act. In its narrower form, it is that you cannot recover for damage which is the consequence of a sentence imposed upon you for a criminal act.[30]

The narrower version was based, importantly, on 'personal responsibility' and 'inconsistency':

> The inconsistency is between the criminal law, which authorizes the damage suffered by the plaintiff in the form of loss of liberty because of his own personal responsibility for the crimes he committed, and the claim that the civil law should require someone else to compensate him for that loss of liberty.[31]

This reasoning often focused on the outcomes, of compensating someone for the fact of imprisonment, but at times it might have been wider: Lord Rodger at one point contrasted not the outcomes of the civil and criminal courts, but their 'policies'.[32]

Where the claimant was criminally liable for the killing (or other prohibited result), English law has decided that no claim exists for the consequences of the criminal conviction: those include everything from deprivation of liberty and fines, to the mere fact of being labelled a criminal by the conviction.[33] Most commonly, cases do not meet the centuries-old and narrow test for the verdict of 'not guilty by reason of insanity', so the defendant (who will become the claimant in any later tort action) is still liable, typically for the still serious offence of manslaughter by reason

[29] [2009] 1 AC 1339.
[30] ibid [32].
[31] ibid [37].
[32] ibid [82].
[33] See eg the UK Supreme Court's decision in *Gray v Thames Trains* (n 29).

of diminished responsibility.[34] This could be relevant to our present enquiry, such as where a product's use to commit a crime was by a person suffering from a mental disorder caused by another tortfeasor.

In the other variation, the defendant fails to prevent the claimant's illegality when they should. A recent example is a hospital trust who admitted they were negligent in failing to take a paranoid schizophrenic into a medical unit.[35] Three days later, the claimant went on to kill her mother, and the question before the court was whether the hospital was liable for the claimant's resulting losses. The losses included the claimant's trauma when lucid, her further medical care, and the portion of her estate she lost by killing her mother. The defendant argued that while they were negligent, they should not have to pay for those losses because of the illegality. An earlier criminal court had convicted the claimant of manslaughter by reason of diminished responsibility. However, it had not ordered any punishment, only hospital care. In addition, the trial judge found that she had no significant personal responsibility for what she had done. Nonetheless, in this case as in *Gray*, the UK Supreme Court rejected 'sanction-shifting' claims.

One of the small twists is that claims featuring illegality seem to be dealt with differently in tort law than in some other areas. A longstanding rule, now in the Forfeiture Act 1982, precludes a person who has unlawfully killed another from acquiring a benefit in consequence of the killing. However, there is a discretion under that Act to vary the rule, particularly taking into account the conduct of the offender and any other relevant circumstances (s 2).[36] In earlier litigation, a judge had applied that discretion to give the claimant half the amount she would have received.[37] In the UK Supreme Court, the court applied tort law to deny her entire claim on exactly the same facts. This highlights that principles which are said to run through the law might not in fact do so, or might be given different effects in different parts of the law.

B. Types of illegality losses

The losses claimed for tend to divide into the physical, the classic forms of personal injury and property damage to the person who behaved illegally, and the financial, the claims for lost profits from illegal endeavours. The first group often include consequential losses, but the focus is on physical harm. The second group arises

[34] As in *Gray* itself; for apparently the first time the contrary has come up (defendants seek to use illegality defence where claimant was not guilty by reason of insanity): *Lewis-Ranwell v G4S Health Services (UK) Ltd* [2024] EWCA Civ 138, [2024] KB 745, on appeal to the UKSC, heard in 2025, awaiting judgment.

[35] *Henderson v Dorset Healthcare University NHS Foundation Trust* [2020] UKSC 43, [2021] AC 563.

[36] ibid [18].

[37] ibid.

during illegal activity, most famously in an illegal transaction.[38] These are the simplest losses for the legal system to deal with.[39] The claimant is generally not entitled to that profit; particularly difficult questions arise relating to whose conduct was illegal in the operation of companies.[40]

It is not a different type of loss, but particularly difficult questions have arisen where losses claimed for are in some way associated with orders of criminal courts. Attempts to get compensation for, for instance, lost earnings while in prison, have been called 'sanction-shifting' since the sanction applied by the criminal law is directly or indirectly reallocated by a civil court. In fact, it would be as accurate to call them 'loss and sanction' cases, since the real question is as much about the allocation of losses as it is about the burden of a sanction; or one could focus on the role of the defendant, as an 'earlier agent' as a cause of the crime being committed. A classic example is *Gray v Thames Trains*,[41] where the claim for lost earnings while in prison for committing manslaughter was dismissed.

C. Types of responses to illegal claims in tort law

If a legal system is going to respond to the illegality in the facts giving rise to a claim, it could do so in a number of ways. The common law position, moving to defence, or a judicial discretion to refuse to grant the remedy claimed,[42] went through many of those paths. Some other legal systems still deal with illegality, if they do so at all, through those other ways. The four general headings those ways could be grouped under match one way of seeing the component parts of tort claims: procedure, unlawfulness (most often in the specific form of wrongfulness), fault, causation, or defences.[43]

Procedurally, claims which show signs of illegality might be restricted in some way before the substantive questions can be addressed. These restrictions might be the purpose of the procedural rules, or they might be side-effects of the purpose of those rules. In some cases, these could be very procedural rules indeed, such as requiring permission to bring a claim, where the claimant has been convicted of a

[38] *Holman v Johnson* (1775) 1 Cowp 341, esp 343; *Hounga v Allen* [2014] UKSC 47, [2014] 1 WLR 2889.

[39] *Everitt v Williams* (1725), reported in (1893) 9 Law Quarterly Review 197.

[40] *Les Laboratoires Servier v Apotex Inc* [2014] UKSC 55; *Bilta (UK) Ltd v Nazir* [2015] UKSC 23, [2016] AC 1.

[41] [2009] 1 AC 1339; it was famously not argued in *Meah v McCreamer* [1985] 1 All ER 367.

[42] It is somewhat unclear whether the court can consider illegality of its own motion; in practice defendants are typically highly incentivized by its nature as a complete defence to raise it where possible, so judges would have less need to raise it themselves. The possible exception is joint illegality, discussed above.

[43] For one of the earliest versions of such a scheme of core questions in tort, see Helmut Koziol, *Basic Questions of Tort Law from a Germanic Perspective* (Jan Sramek Verlag 2012) 109–268.

crime in respect of the same events.[44] It would similarly include, stepping beyond tort for a moment, denial of ex gratia compensation schemes to criminals, or even of the right to vote. There are other mechanisms which are less direct,[45] such as rules delaying a civil action until a prosecution for the same events has taken place. That might be particularly significant where the criminal conviction strips the convicted defendant of resources to compensate once a civil claim can be brought. That is well known as a consequence of imprisonment, for instance, but it is magnified where existing resources are reduced, such as where there are significant confiscation powers.[46] For some legal systems with a rule suspending a parallel civil claim it matters much less because the claimant can and typically does get significant compensation through a process within the criminal court.

While not technically in the procedural category, there is also the simple reality that in a case of joint illegality, defendants would normally have to admit to the same illegal conduct as they allege the defendant engaged in.

The claim might have some requirement relating to unlawfulness that captures the issue of the illegality. Finding the unlawfulness is often in practice done by finding wrongfulness, the defendant's breach of some kind of right or interest held by the claimant. English law has seen this route followed relatively recently, though somewhat tentatively. It has fallen out of favour in one place it was used: to deny that there was a duty of care owed to someone committing a crime.[47] However, it might be what explains the well-established position in many legal systems that you cannot claim in tort for losses which flowed from you committing crimes. For example, a claim that the defendant's tort caused the claimant to lose the income from robbery would fail.[48]

Using the unlawfulness part of the tort calculation is very established in some other legal systems. For example, in the Netherlands a concept of 'relativity' is well established under article 6:163 of the *Burgerlijk Wetboek* (*BW*).[49] In effect, the violated rule must protect the person of the injured party from the kind of damage suffered, and in the way it happened. In effect, otherwise valid claims within the general tort law provisions will fail where claimants are not themselves upholding the duties they seek to sue others for failing to uphold. A further form of illegality

[44] In England, see eg the Criminal Justice Act 2003, s 329 for trespass to the person actions brought in respect of events which led to the claimant being convicted of a crime.

[45] See generally, Matthew Dyson, *Explaining Tort and Crime—Legal Developments across Laws and Legal Systems, 1850–2020* (CUP 2022) chs 6–8.

[46] Technically in England until 1870 all of a felon's property was forfeit to the Crown upon conviction, not just the property connected to the crime; this was removed by the Forfeiture Act 1870, though some other mechanisms were brought in.

[47] *Hillen v ICI (Alkali) Ltd* [1934] 1 KB 455; *Ashton v Turner* [1981] QB 137; *Vellino v Chief Constable of Greater Manchester* (n 20).

[48] *Burns v Edman* [1970] 1 Lloyd's Rep 137; *Hewison v Meridian Shipping Services Pte* [2002] EWCA 1821.

[49] Art 6:98, on causation, which connects the nature of the liability with the loss. See generally, Johannes Bijlsma and Elbert de Jong, 'The Netherlands' in Dyson (n 17).

affecting the nature of a duty is how in Germany the duty might not be owed to an individual who is breaking the criminal law.[50]

Where fault is relevant to a claim, the fault requirement might provide a means to cater for illegal conduct by the claimant. This has largely been unsuccessful in England,[51] but for a period it worked in Australia. One way of framing the issue was in negligence, and to say that the level of care owed to a person engaged in a crime or taking the risk of crime was less than that owed to someone not so engaged.[52]

Fault highlights how interconnected the components of tort liability can be, particularly when unstable or under pressure. Fact patterns seen through fault might be relevant even in some otherwise strict liability torts, though the operation of a defence that denied fault. Similarly, the same kind of issue could be expressed through other means, such as through unlawfulness, causation, or a 'defence' or quantification tool for determining the quantum of liability which in England is captured by contributory negligence.

A further option is to rely on causation as a means to address any illegality: typically by saying the tort was not the cause of the loss, rather, the illegality was. This has not been a common argument in England for denying whole claims. It has been attempted in the USA, particularly in the mid-twentieth century, though without much consistent success.[53] A slight variation is to accept that some consequences from the illegality were within the scope of liability, but others were too remote.[54] Similarly, where the claimant's illegal conduct is said to be deployable to separate out any heads of loss which flow from the illegality, this might remove the significant parts of the claim, as it did in *Gray v Thames Trains*.[55] One legal system that seems to embrace the causation analysis is Argentina. It appears that the framing of causation is a way to connect to a requirement of unlawfulness as well, as among other things, to be compensable, the harm caused must be to a lawful interest.[56] For example, in 2021 the illegal exit route from a trapped train was treated as the adequate cause of why the claimant was injured.[57] The illegality was there on the face of the claim, but within Argentine legal reasoning, causation was the neatest way to address the issue.

The final option is to rely on defences to deal with any illegality that lawyers wish to channel away from liability. Not all legal systems use formal defences on

[50] Sven Asmussen and Gerhard Wagner, 'Germany' in Dyson (n 17).

[51] One interesting variation that was attempted was to argue that the defendant acted reasonably with respect to the claimant's interests in light of the fact that the claimant was acting illegally, as seen in *Marshall v Osmond* [1983] QB 1034.

[52] See eg *Smith v Jenkins* (1970) 119 CLR 397.

[53] See eg *Meador v Hotel Grover* (1942) 9 So 2d 782.

[54] eg illegal conduct seen as too remote: *Meah v McCreamer (No 2)* [1986] 1 All ER 943.

[55] See n 28.

[56] Civil and Commercial Code, art 1739. See further Yanina Pantiga and Martín Hevia, 'Argentina' in Dyson (n 17).

[57] Cámara Nacional de Apelaciones en lo Civil Sala D, Expte. 3159/2013, *Romano, Juan Ignacio c Ministerio del Interior y otro s/ Daños y Perjuicios*, 5 March 2021.

the same scale as in the common law. For some, using the contributory fault of the claimant is not necessarily a formal defence, but might feature elsewhere in the components of liability, such as in quantification of damages, or as a matter of causation. For English law, it is something the defendant must raise, but also operates to reduce the damages claimed. It is an interesting example, as it speaks to both the claimant's fault and the claimant's causal contribution to the harm, and offers the judge significant discretion in deciding how much they contributed to the total loss. Under the Law Reform (Contributory Negligence) Act 1945, it is a pro-rata defence. However, before that the claimant's negligence had been a full defence and could have been even more significant in preventing claims affected by illegality from coming before the courts for resolution. But more conceptually, being at fault and contributing to a harm suffered are not themselves illegal, and vice versa.[58] For legal systems which do not separate out illegality and fault, that distinction will not matter; the same would be true where unlawful conduct is automatically culpable, squaring the circle that way.

In some fact patterns, particularly unilateral and bilateral illegality, consent could in practice be used by many legal systems. In some instances, the application of consent might be hidden in a denial of wrongfulness, though it might be hard to prove that this was what was happening. In some systems, consent might take effect as a formal defence to liability. One of the reasons why road traffic claims appear significantly in the development of illegality rules in English law is that in 1972 the defence of consent was barred from operating in tort claims there.[59]

The final form, adopted in most common law jurisdictions, seems to be a specific defence of illegality, or, as it is sometimes put, *ex turpi causa non oritur actio*. This defence means that an otherwise valid tort claim will be barred on the grounds of the illegal conduct of the claimant. Various restrictions can be imposed, such as a sufficient connection between the illegality and the tort.[60] The defence is binary—a head of loss is barred or not—rather than able to be reduced pro-rata for the role of the illegality in the claim.

We see from these responses to illegality that the components of liability can be manipulated to prevent, or allow, claims featuring illegality to proceed, and the final form which that has taken in English law seems to be a specific defence of illegality. Common lawyers do not openly discuss it a great deal, but the implication is that a defence is accepted as the most transparent, enabling an analysis of the underlying principles and policies openly, without attempting to put them into other components of liability which are not designed to handle them. The result is that tort law now locates its discussion of claims featuring illegality not by saying that there was contributory negligence or consent, but by highlighting the character

[58] See eg *Nettleship v Weston* [1971] 2 QB 691, 710 (Megaw LJ).
[59] Road Traffic Act 1972, s 148(3); see now Road Traffic Act 1988, s 149(3).
[60] See eg *Vellino v Chief Constable of Greater Manchester* (n 20).

of the criminal prohibition infringed. Ultimately, why that form has been selected is unclear, but it seems likely that none of the alternatives attempted or conceived have been as practical or perhaps sufficiently intellectually rigorous. If the defence is indeed to pursue coherence, one implication is that other components of liability have been unable to do that effectively or without distorting their purpose.[61]

D. The current law in England: illegality as a defence to a tort claim

The issues are still live and still difficult, but English law has recently formed a new approach to its way of using a defence to deny tort liability. In 2016, a nine-member panel of the UKSC handed down *Patel v Mirza*[62] as a recasting of how illegality was to be handled by the courts. The case concerned insider trading contrary to section 52 of the Criminal Justice Act 1993, and the recovery of monies which had been paid by the claimant for use in such trading. The case resolved a number of earlier ambiguities between different techniques, notably a discretion-based system and a strict rule-based system.[63] Strict rule-based systems would require firm and overriding rules for coherence, but these are not what has been developed by the common law now. As *Patel v Mirza* shows, the UKSC's position is a discretion to refuse a claim based on illegality applied on top of the existing rules which were otherwise interpreted only from within the field of unjust enrichment. Lord Toulson gave the leading judgment, and identified two key principles, namely not profiting from a wrong, and coherence:

> Looking behind the maxims, there are two broad discernible policy reasons for the common law doctrine of illegality as a defence to a civil claim. One is that a person should not be allowed to profit from his own wrongdoing. The other, linked, consideration is that the law should be coherent and not self-defeating, condoning illegality by giving with the left-hand what it takes with the right hand.[64]

Lord Toulson also, and nicely, highlighted the importance of comparing coherence to other values when he set out the relevant test:

> The essential rationale of the illegality doctrine is that it would be contrary to the public interest to enforce a claim if to do so would be harmful to the integrity of the legal system (or, possibly, certain aspects of public morality, the boundaries

[61] See particularly McLachlin J in *Hall v Herbert* [1993] 2 SCR 159, 181–85, rejecting illegality concerns being located within the duty of care analysis as being a barren analysis.
[62] *Patel v Mirza* [2016] UKSC 42.
[63] As in *Tinsley v Milligan* [1994] 1 AC 340.
[64] ibid [99].

> of which have never been made entirely clear and which do not arise for consideration in this case). In assessing whether the public interest would be harmed in that way, it is necessary (a) to consider the underlying purpose of the prohibition which has been transgressed and whether that purpose will be enhanced by denial of the claim, (b) to consider any other relevant public policy on which the denial of the claim may have an impact and (c) to consider whether denial of the claim would be a proportionate response to the illegality, bearing in mind that punishment is a matter for the criminal courts. Within that framework, various factors may be relevant, but it would be a mistake to suggest that the court is free to decide a case in an undisciplined way. The public interest is best served by a principled and transparent assessment of the considerations identified, rather than by the application of a formal approach capable of producing results which may appear arbitrary, unjust or disproportionate.[65]

The test laid down in *Patel v Mirza* has had mixed success since. Two cases from the UKSC itself highlight that. One example is *Stoffel & Co v Grondona*,[66] concerning a mortgage fraud lying underneath a claim against solicitors for the large financial losses from their negligently failing to carry out conveyancing. The UKSC held that fraud did not bar the claim, taking particular account of the need for solicitors to handle such transactions carefully. In particular, on the proportionality point, the relevant conduct was reprehensible, but the purpose of the claim was to enable the claimant to discharge a liability to another, the 'victim', who had adopted the transaction and there was no risk that the integrity of the legal system would be undermined.

On the other hand, the Supreme Court's use of coherence in *Henderson v Dorset Healthcare University NHS Trust*[67] is open to doubt. Due to the admitted negligence of a community mental health team, the claimant, a paranoid schizophrenic, was not taken into a psychiatric unit, and shortly thereafter she stabbed her mother to death. The claimant pleaded guilty to manslaughter on the ground of diminished responsibility pursuant to section 2 of the Homicide Act 1957, and was ordered to be detained in a secure hospital. She claimed against the relevant NHS Trust for six heads of loss, but all were rejected, applying *Gray v Thames Trains* and the earlier case of *Clunis v Camden and Islington Health Authority*.[68] The heads of loss had included personal injury, loss of amenity and future care costs because of the killing, loss of liberty for being in a mental institution, and the roughly £60,000 loss from a Chancery Master's decision to disapply the forfeiture of her claim to her mother's estate under the Forfeiture Act 1982 to the extent of granting half of her

65 ibid [120]; see also [101] and [107].
66 [2020] UKSC 42, [2021] AC 540.
67 *Henderson* (n 35).
68 *Clunis v Camden and Islington Health Authority* [1998] QB 978.

entitlement. The court held that even where the claimant bore no, or no significant responsibility, for the killing, the claim was still barred on the grounds of illegality on the stated ground that *Gray* required this.

So far, I have been unable to find a single case where a product liability claim was dismissed on the basis of the illegal conduct of the claimant. No such claim was found in tort claims alleging failure to take care and tort claims founded on separate doctrines of product liability. All of the four forms of illegality claims could have been engaged, but none seems to have reached a reported decision in any of the jurisdictions I looked at.[69] The question might be: why?

IV. Illegality and Products

We can now consider how product liability and illegality might interface with each other.

A. The past

We might start by turning back to consider the earlier hypothetical: what would have happened in *Donoghue v Stevenson* had Mrs Donoghue stolen the ginger beer bottle. We should first acknowledge that the case was complex, and picking up one facet to twist might yield artificial results. In particular, *Donoghue v Stevenson* was selected as a test case to challenge the rule in *Winterbottom v Wright* and the limitations on duties of care for products.[70] However, the facts would not have been as suitable for litigation if the claimant had stolen the ginger beer. Had there also been illegality, the case might never have come to court.[71] Indeed, the illegality angle would have been novel if it had come to court. Before 1932, there were almost no cases where a defence of illegality at common law to a claim in tort like this was applied.[72] While such a defence had been known in contract for centuries by then,[73] tort cases applying an overt defence of illegality were not really known in England until the 1980s and 1990s, and only marginally earlier in Australia.[74]

[69] France, Germany, Spain, Italy, Argentina, Brazil, USA, England and Wales, and Canada.

[70] According to it, a product claim outside of common carriers needed contractual privity.

[71] See eg Matthew Dyson and Emily Gordon, 'Stability in Tort' in Joe Sampson and Stelios Tofaris (eds), *Essays in Law and History for David Ibbetson: Querella* (CUP 2024).

[72] There was a case appearing to deal with 'sanction shifting', though it related to a strict liability conviction against the publisher of a libel in a newspaper which would likely not lead to the same result in the modern law: *Colburn v Patmore* (1834) 1 CM & R 72, 4 Tyr 677, 149 ER 999.

[73] *Holman v Johnson* (1775) 1 Cowp 341, esp 343, 98 ER 1120, esp 1121; the case concerned an action in assumpsit, but the principle has been applied across contractual actions to the modern day.

[74] The earliest was *Christiansen v Gilday* (1948) 48 SR (NSW) 352 (NSWSC), but it was more developments in the 1960s that changed how the defence was understood, driven particularly by road traffic fact patterns: *Godbolt v Fittock* (1963) SR NSW 617 (NSWSC); *Bondarenko v Sommers* (1968) 69 SR NSW 269 (NSWSC) 275–78 (Jacobs JA).

Without an overt defence already available, the courts addressing *Donoghue v Stevenson* might have reached for another way to reject an illegal claim, or they might have permitted the claim to go forward regardless of the illegality. Other possible routes to reject the claim were noted above in section III.C. The most plausible seem to be a denial of a duty, as had been the case prior to *Donoghue*; causation; and contributory negligence. These kinds of routes were considered in the decades that followed *Donoghue*, and the final result has been to develop a defence of illegality to deny otherwise valid tort claims. That defence's current form, based in a cluster of decisions of the UK Supreme Court in England, is of a defence which balances the *prohibition* infringed, such as theft in taking the ginger beer, against the *policy* of tort law and the *proportionality* in denying a claim. If we are right in thinking that the defence did not exist in 1932, or was not in common use, there might have been more pressure to develop it on the facts of the claim in *Donoghue v Stevenson.* It certainly seems unlikely to a modern view that Lord Atkin's neighbour principle should not create a duty in many of the types of criminal ginger fact patterns introduced at the start of this article. But that might be reading back modern views of course. The slightly messy majority in *Donoghue v Stevenson* might have been harder to obtain in a case of illegality even if the principles themselves were the same.

B. The present

How different would the position be in the modern law? As we will see, it is hard to be sure. There is almost no academic engagement. Many legal systems, particularly those part of the civilian tradition, do not seem to discuss illegality and certainly do not have a defence based on it. Public policy, comparative fault and other techniques shape some of the doctrine, but without an overarching rejection of claims simply for being related to illegality in some way. The Product Liability Directive itself does not refer to illegality. The rules under the Directive, even more than at common law, have focused on the product, its entry into the market, and the producers involved.

Can the apparent dearth of case law be explained? The answer seems to be that legal actors have not felt the need for an illegality defence within product liability. That means they have not inserted it when legislating and have not read it in from an existing defence outside of legislation. Four factors might be considered.

First, we might question the claim that there is a dearth of cases: such cases might in fact exist but have not been found in my searches. This is certainly possible, and even seems to fit an intuition that the issue must have come before courts, particularly across the whole of the EU and USA. Not all possible jurisdictions within these areas have been accessible, so that risk is clearly present. At the same time, the cases do not appear in searches on the databases that would normally be searched, nor in the works of academics who specialize in the area.[75] Even if some reported cases do exist, they do not seem to be used to provide established answers to the issues.

A second factor might be that the fact patterns involving illegality simply have not happened yet. This seems unlikely, though it is difficult to go beyond educated guesses and intuitions in assessing this. The fact patterns do not seem particularly unusual. Products can easily have small flaws, and there is no shortage of crime, even minor crime. A variation on this second answer is that the fact patterns have happened, but there have not been actionable losses and hence no claims have been brought. This also seems unlikely. That is not just because some legal systems have much wider concepts of actionable loss, such as the French,[76] but also because even systems which limit the claims to specific forms of interferences with rights or interests would not find it hard to find actionable losses.

A third factor might be that while the fact pattern has happened, leading to actionable losses, reported decisions have not been needed to resolve the issue. Claimants might not wish to bring a claim that discloses illegality in their prior conduct. Or, litigation might be brought but not lead to the issue appearing in a report. That might especially be because such cases are settled, replicating a general trend in products liability cases in general. This equates to the procedural grounds for addressing illegality already considered as a response to illegality, in section III.C.

Fourth, relatedly, the fact pattern might be resolved without reference to illegality, so that the cases are reported without reference to the facts grounding the claim. This is certainly possible, and hard to trace. English law at least has had a tradition of allowing claims to be brought so long as no illegal behaviour is alleged, which can lead to inventive pleadings.[77] To work, this reason would require existing components of tort liability, particularly within product liability, to address anything in the underlying illegality that the legal actors inside the system think needs addressing. The ways to respond across legal systems might be grouped across basic questions legal systems answer to generate tort liability, described above already. Some forms of illegality will be caught by other defences. For instance, stealing a product from a manufacturer before it is put out into the market would likely lead to a defence under article 7(a), that the product had not been released into the market (see section II.B above), but that would not apply to a product stolen from the retailer. The use of strict liability for products removes the option of using fault to adjust the claim. Causation is very much available, whether on its own, or mediated through a functional equivalent of the English

75 For example, Westlaw for the US and England and Wales, and specialist texts such as Marshall Shapo, *Shapo on the Law of Product Liability* (7th edn, Edward Elgar Publishing 2017).

76 For example, Jacques Herbots, 'Why It Is Ill-Advised to Translate Consequential Damage by *Dommage Indirect*' (2011) 19(6) European Review of Private Law 931.

77 See eg Dyson (n 45) ch 7.

contributory negligence. Similarly, there might be forms of loss that were recognized, or prohibited, by the general law, which could be doing some of the work.[78]

To test how well these four factors might explain why doctrinal routes to address illegal claims in product liability are hypothetical, we might take an example. If there was a legal system with very developed product liability rules which also recognized illegality as a defence, perhaps the strongest contender would be the USA. However, illegality is not the lens through which these kinds of fact patterns have been addressed. Rather, the main formal reasoning evidence is of foreseeability. That is, illegal use of a product is not itself a defence to a claim for harm from a defective product, but falls instead within the general analysis limiting product liability to foreseeable injuries caused by foreseeable uses. Of course, the USA is made up of more than fifty state jurisdictions, along with federal and other forms of law, but a sketch of the general rules is possible.

In general, a manufacturer may be held liable for placing a defective product on the market if the product causes the plaintiff's injury during a reasonably foreseeable use of the product. A classic example is *Chavez v Glock*.[79] A California Court of Appeal held that it was a question for the jury (on proximate causation grounds) to decide whether a party's potentially criminal failure to store a pistol safely was an unforeseeable misuse of the product that prevented Glock's liability arising. Some states treat unforeseeability as an affirmative defence, such as California did in *Chavez v Glock*, while others treat it as a way to remove the plaintiff's burden of proving causation and an unreasonably dangerous condition, as occurred in Iowa.[80] What would have been a foreseeable use is normally a jury question, and juries should expect a manufacturer to foresee some degree of misuse and abuse of a product, by a user or third party, and to take reasonable precautions to minimize the harm that might result from that.[81] By contrast, a Maryland appellate court held that the improper storage of a handgun in violation of state law and manufacturer-provided warnings about safe storage as a matter of law precluded liability as it was unforeseeable as a matter of law.[82] A New York Court of Appeals held that an eleven-year old's criminal misuse of an aerosol can was, as a matter of law, an unforeseeable use of the product.[83] Key to this reasoning was that the plaintiff had not shown enough evidence that this kind of criminal use had happened enough that the manufacturer should have foreseen it. That suggests that it is possible in principle for criminal acts to be foreseeable, and the court did not consider in any detail what would have happened had that been so. That spray cans could be used in various criminal ways seems highly foreseeable, as does the

78 See particularly, Hevia and Pantiga (n 56).
79 *Chavez v Glock* (2012) 207 Cal App 4th 1283, 1302 (Cal Ct App).
80 *Hughes v Magic Chef Inc*, 288 N.W.2d 542, 545 (Iowa 1980).
81 *Chavez* (n 79) 1308.
82 *Halliday v Sturm Ruger & Co Inc*, 770 A.2d 1072, 1095 (Md Ct Spec App 2001).
83 *Stephenson ex rel Coley v SC Johnson & Son Inc*, 239 A.D.2d 402, 404 (NY App Div 1997).

failure to store a gun properly risk criminal harm resulting. That makes the use of the foreseeability doctrine all the more interesting. It is at least plausible that foreseeable conduct is not being found to be foreseeable, as a way to control liability. The beneficiaries of such an approach would be producers. If true, the concept of foreseeability seems to have been viewed as sufficiently flexible to accommodate these preferences. The use of this doctrinal component also highlights that others, including those mirrored in the EU Directive, were not thought suitable. Illegality, of course, was not thought needed either.

In product liability cases alleging a defect in design, manufacture, or warnings, strict product liability might run alongside negligence. Among other things, this might bring foreseeability of the harm as a key criterion. Foreseeability is commonly phrased as the absence of liability where '[s]tated positively, the general duty imposed on manufacturers and suppliers of products to use ordinary care includes a duty to consider risks of injury created by foreseeable misuse of the product'.[84] That is inherently a fact-dependent question. Thus, in one case in New Mexico, whether a particular gun should have been disabled from firing when the magazine was removed, or should have had a warning that it could, was something that should have been left to a jury. On the strict liability calculation, the issue was whether there was an unreasonable risk, in this case to the minors where one injured another. 'Suppliers are responsible for risks arising from foreseeable uses of the product, including reasonably foreseeable unintended uses and misuses.'[85] On the negligence calculation, the courts have often focused on the design, and the foreseeable uses of it.

It is also possible for product liability to go wider, for example by imposing on the manufacturer a duty to protect others from the criminal use of their products. In some cases, this gives rise to the gun shield laws and similar prohibitions on some claims which form part of the US gun control debate. For example, the Maryland Supreme Court held that a 'gun store owner' did not owe any tort duty 'to third parties to exercise reasonable care in the display and sale of handguns to prevent the theft *and illegal use* of the handguns by others against third parties'.[86] Likewise, some states have considered whether the defendant had any kind of special relationship to the user or the injured third party, but again the issue tends to be hidden within jury determinations, and not formally about criminality/illegality. Courts sometimes express this in terms of avoiding unreasonably creating

[84] *Smith v Bryco Arms* (2001) 33 P.3d 638, [21].
[85] ibid [17].
[86] *Valentine v On Target Inc*, 727 A.2d 947, 948 (Md 1999) (emphasis added). See also *Alston v Caraco Pharma Inc.*, 670 F.Supp.2d 279, 286 (SDNY 2009): 'Manufacturers have a duty to warn of the foreseeable risks posed by their products, but they are under no duty to anticipate or prevent criminal or quasi-criminal conduct'; *Elsroth v Johnson & Johnson*, 700 F.Supp. 151, 164 (SDNY 1988), holding that the consequences of criminal conduct are not something that manufacturers must be forced to take on 'as a cost of doing business'.

foreseeable risks,[87] and liability being more likely where the defendant had some kind of control over the criminal.[88]

C. The future

So far there does not appear to have been the pressure necessary to force a case to apply a defence of illegality to a product claim, but will that always remain the case? What if a truly egregious case arose, perhaps extreme tippled, filched, or embezzled ginger, as introduced at the start of the chapter? This brings back into focus the key question this chapter explores: how wider rules within a legal system interact with product liability, and whether a defence of illegality could be added.

Clearly the CPA, and the Directive, do not contain in their own terms all the rules needed for a tort claim. The phrasing of the Act relies on substantive content, most significantly causation and forms of legally recognized damage from elsewhere in English tort law, as discussed in section II above.[89] It expressly imports contributory negligence, under the Law Reform (Contributory Negligence) Act 1945, in CPA 1987: section 6(4). The Act allows for a reduction in the sum awarded in a tort claim up to just below the amount of the loss caused by the fault of the claimant.[90] Such a 'defence', or rule affecting causation or quantum (depending on your personal and/or legal system preference) uses fault and causation to reduce the claim. In short, the consequences of the claimant's risk-taking is attributed to him, rather than to the defective product. The same section states that 'fault', in the CPA, is to be given the meaning in the 1945 Act, where the 1945 Act does not define the term. There is less clarity about whether there are Directive-derived rules for the capacity of a defendant to be sued. But the civil procedure questions of how to sue seem to be left to the normal rules of tort law, subject to any specific exceptions applied.[91] By contrast, 'defect' is largely established as a special term of art, without reference to other parts of tort law.

Could defences from outside the CPA be used? We might start with the relevant text, and take the CPA as an example. The section in the CPA introducing defences,

[87] *Faverty v McDonald's Restaurants of Or Inc*, 892 P.2d 703, 708, 710 (Or Ct App 1995).

[88] *Warr v JMGM Grp., LLC*, 70 A.3d 347, 355 (Md 2013).

[89] See particularly the text to and in n 6.

[90] Law Reform (Contributory Negligence) Act 1945, s 1(1): 'Where any person suffers damage as the result partly of his own fault and partly of the fault of any other person or persons, a claim in respect of that damage shall not be defeated by reason of the fault of the person suffering the damage, but the damages recoverable in respect thereof shall be reduced to such extent as the court thinks just and equitable having regard to the claimant's share in the responsibility for the damage', with restrictions in later parts of s 1 relating to contract and limitations of losses. On not giving 100%, see *Anderson v Newham College of Further Education* [2002] EWCA Civ 505; [2003] ICR 212 [19].

[91] For this purpose, the nature of limitation does not need to be decided, whether it is procedural or substantive it is nonetheless expressly provided for, with a shorter limitation period, under s 6(6) and Sch 1 of the CPA 1987, amending the Limitation Act 1980.

section 4, does not use exclusive language: 'In any civil proceedings by virtue of this Part against any person ('the person proceeded against') in respect of a defect in a product it shall be a defence for him to show [one of the six listed defences].' The precise words do not exclude reference to other defences. It could have said 'It shall *only* be a defence . . .' (emphasis added) if the drafters had wanted, but it did not. It might be possible to argue that, *expressio unius est exclusio alterius*, by giving one way to provide a defence, other defences are implicitly excluded. There are no other clues in the text itself, so a principled argument will have to be developed.

A defence of consent does not seem to be used within the CPA 1987. It is not one of the defences listed, and despite some claims to the contrary,[92] it does not seem to be a settled understanding of legal practitioners that it is available. It could be debated whether an assumption of risk defence was available separately. The difference between the two formulations is not clear within the common law,[93] but as far as English law goes, it seems likely that if assumption of risk functions like contributory negligence it would be permissible under the 1945 Act. The more difficult question is where it was to operate as a full defence, and where it was to do so, whether it could only do so if consent was itself recognized as a defence as well. Otherwise, a difference between the two would be manifest at least in such cases.

Other defences seem unlikely to be of assistance. Exclusion of liability is expressly prohibited by section 7 of the CPA 1987.

For provisions implemented from a Directive, there is an inherent tension in how much domestic law can vary from the higher norm. Where a legal system has principles of internal coherences expressing an illegality defence, the internally principled position would be that a domestic system could add further defences to those listed in the Directive on grounds of public policy or interference in the scope of the criminal law. Against this position of principle, the preamble of the Directive states its purpose to allocate risks fairly, and it might be argued that criminal law's determination of appropriate risk was not determinative. Dismissing domestic criminal law might not seem too persuasive, but it should be judged against the way the ECJ interpreted the Directive as being one of maximal harmonization in the field of tort.[94]

It is hard to be sure what position the Court of Justice of the EU or the UK Supreme Court would take. One argument against such a defence is the maximal harmonization nature of this Directive. Another argument might be that tort liability itself does not concern itself, in this way at least, with the claimant's illegality; that argument would be less likely to work in many common law jurisdictions.

[92] Cf the Lexisnexis Practice note 'Defences to a claim under the Consumer Protection Act 1987' (LexisNexis, 2025) <https://www.lexisnexis.co.uk/legal/guidance/defences-to-a-claim-under-the-consumer-protection-act-1987> accessed 7 March 2025.

[93] For one US view, see Kenneth Simons, 'Assumption of Risk and Consent in the Law of Torts: A Theory of Full Preference' (1987) 67 Boston University Law Review 213.

[94] See eg Case C-52/00 *Commission v France*, ECLI:EU:C:2002:252, para 24.

Indeed, conceivably now that the UK has left the European Union, it at least will have more reason to consider the potential application of an illegality doctrine to product claims. At least so far, legal actors within civilian legal systems have shown themselves open to using the components of liability to determine liability, and illegality has not been thought to add anything useful. The same arguments might not be as obvious were it a contractual Directive, where it is standard for legal systems to render either void or unenforceable contracts founded on illegality. There, the principles of the system might be recognized in the Directive, but it would seem a harder ask to deny them purchase even if the Directive were absent.[95]

V. The Mechanics of Integrating Areas of Law

This inquiry highlights a wider issue even within England and Wales, and that is whether statutory torts permit or require references to the rest of tort law, particularly on defences. A further example would be a strict liability claim under the Animals Act 1971 for harm caused by a member of a dangerous species or a dangerous member of a non-dangerous species. It is arguable that, in such statutory cases, general defences within tort will apply unless expressly or impliedly excluded by the statute itself. More broadly, this raises questions about how different areas of law are integrated. The more structured and integrated a legal system is, the less need there may be for external mechanisms—such as the recognition of illegality as relevant to otherwise valid tort claims.

We have discussed doctrines of illegality as one way of integrating the effects of two areas of law: here, classically, the criminal and the civil. So far, the focus has been on the technical application of a possible defence to a statutory tort, but we might step back to consider the deeper questions in play. The starting point, that there might be general defences which apply across all of tort law, is itself an open question, with no clear or well-established answer across the world. When a defence integrates material from another area of law, the issues become even more complex. In some legal systems, like the French, legal actors rarely find they need to refer to many distinct grounds for shaping liability, relying predominantly on *la faute* and the *lien de causalité*.[96]

A simple way to integrate norms from outside the purely civil sphere into how civil claims are decided is to use a different building block than the norm itself, such as integrating 'unlawful acts'. Dutch law's key definition of an unlawful act

[95] cf the difference in English law shown in *Henderson* (n 35), comparing tort and equity, which seems certain to be a mistake or to turn on specific statutory interpretation.

[96] For how this developed, see generally, Olivier Descamps, *Les origins de la responsibilité pour faute personnelle dans le Code civil de 1804* (LGDJ 2005); on causation, see Duncan Fairgrieve and Florence G'Sell-Macrez, 'Causation in French Law: Pragmatism and Policy' in Richard Goldberg (ed), *Perspectives on Causation* (Hart Publishing 2011) 111.

is as, among other things, 'an act or omission in violation of a duty imposed by written law' and all criminal laws must be in written form (in addition, breaching social standards of due care generates liability).[97]

A famous example of a narrower general integrative technique is to cross-refer to the relevant rule as a component of liability, seen in § 823(2) of the German Civil Code (*Bürgerliches Gesetzbuch* or BGB). First, § 823(1) BGB requires anyone who intentionally or negligently injures the protected interests of German law, life, body, health, freedom, property or another right, to pay compensation to that person. German law further adds, in § 823(2) BGB, that the same duty to compensate is owed by someone who breaches a norm intended to protect another, so long as it is done with fault. A protective norm, or *Schütznorm*, will be found in many criminal offences which might not otherwise fit within § 823(1) BGB easily. Other legal systems do so in more or less overt ways.[98]

Beyond cross-referring, there are other integrative techniques turning on specific substantive terms. Some torts and crimes share the same requirements: examples in England include public nuisance[99] and harassment;[100] perhaps the most notable example in France is defamation under a special law of 1881.[101] Equally, it should not be forgotten that one area of law might rely on the other not just to close off liability, but to substantiate it. There may be times when criminal law relies on substantive rules of the civil law:[102] a classic example is the definition of property and who has a right to possess it.[103]

At the other end of the liability process, a determination by a criminal court that there cannot be liability might bind a civil court.[104] This is connected to the idea that the duty would be the same across tort and crime, but extends beyond a duty expressly, but on some other component of liability, such as whether there is a justification, or no wrong. English law has not adopted that position in the most

[97] Dutch Civil Code, art 6:162.

[98] See eg art 109(2) of the Spanish Criminal Code: 'The carrying out of an act prescribed by the law as *delito* or *falta* obliges reparation, according to law, for the damage and losses caused by it.' (my translation). *Delito* marks out the more serious crimes, *falta* the less serious ones. See also art 100 Ley de Enjuiciamiento Criminal: see generally, Lorena Bachmaier Winter, Carlos Gómez-Jara Diez and Albert Ruda-González, 'Blurred borders in Spanish tort and crime' in Matthew Dyson (ed), *Comparing Tort and Crime—Learning from across and within Legal Systems* (CUP 2015) 223; Isabel González Pacanowska, 'The Development of Traffic Liability in Spain' in Wolfgang Ernst (ed), *The Development of Traffic Liability* (CUP 2010) 151, 153–58.

[99] See eg JR Spencer, 'Public Nuisance—A Critical Examination' (1989) 48(1) Cambridge Law Journal 55; *R v Rimmington, R v Goldstein* [2005] 3 WLR 982, thought see now Police, Crime, Sentencing and Courts Act 2022, s 78.

[100] Protection from Harassment Act 1997, ss 1–3.

[101] Art 29 of the law of 29 July 1881 'sur la liberté de la presse' (on the liberty of the press). On this, see the PhD thesis of Mathilde Alfrida Groppo, *The Regulation of Defamation in Tort and Criminal Law: A Comparative Study of England and France*, UCL, 2016: https://kclpure.kcl.ac.uk/portal/files/51618253/2016_Groppo_Mathilde_0636483_ethesis.pdf, last accessed 23 March 2025.

[102] See eg JC Smith, 'Civil Law Concepts in the Criminal Law' (1972) 31 Cambridge Law Journal 197.

[103] English law has made some particularly startling departures, eg *R v Hinks* [2001] 2 AC 241. See also Sarah Green, 'Theft and Conversion—Tangibly Different?' (2012) 128 Law Quarterly Review 564.

[104] See, generally, Dyson (n 45) ch 8.

common point where it might arise, self-defence, though some other legal systems have, at least formally.[105]

VI. Conclusion

Trying to understand a difficult question, with little direct evidence, by seeing how the relevant legal actors shape their doctrines, is very much in the line of work at which Simon Whittaker excelled. That he made so many things look so explicable and understandable is a testament to his intellect and hard work, but there remain some things the rest of us can only tease out at the edges.

It seems likely that there are claims based on product liability involving illegality, and that for the most part, potential claimants do not make claims as the losses are small and/or litigation is expensive and risky. But if they do, there are other mechanisms which respond to the claim in a way that legal actors inside the system have so far found sufficient. There has not been enough pressure, by the value of the claim or other claims in the background, or facts of such an extreme character to offend the sensibilities of defendants or their lawyers, to need to highlight or develop a new defence grounded on that illegality. Instead, as far as legal actors seem to be concerned, the existing mechanisms, legal or non-legal, deal with any illegality sufficiently. It might be that perceptions of the integration of different areas of law vary too. Some systems might have a fuller integration in their legal framework, so might not call for more through means of, for example, an illegality defence. In the many mainly civilian legal systems which have not developed a tort defence of illegality, this is perhaps less surprising, as that attitude is the default position, relying on requirements of unlawfulness, fault, causation, or quantification of damages as the mechanism to do any adjustment to the claim. In common law countries, we have had some decades of established use of illegality as a defence, and of a separate stream of product liability.

Perhaps the snail's pace of legal development is down to ginger beer being insufficiently attractive, to criminals at least.

[105] *Ashley v Chief Constable of Sussex Police* [2008] 1 AC 962; cf art 65 Codigo procesal penal de Brazil (Brazilian Code of Criminal Procedure).

PART III

BETWEEN AND BEYOND CONTRACT AND TORT

11
The Subsidiarity of Unjustified Enrichment

*Pietro Sirena**

I. Introduction

A. The bone of contention

In most legal systems, claims for unjustified enrichment are classified as 'subsidiary', whether this qualification arises from statutory provisions, judicial interpretations, or scholarly analysis. The doctrine or rule of subsidiarity that is thus established essentially serves to address the fact that unjustified enrichment has the potential to spill over its natural boundaries, by providing a mechanism to regulate the relationship between the restitutionary claims concerned and the remedies available in the three main areas of private law with which they frequently overlap; that is, contract, torts, and property.

This relationship is thus understood within a hierarchical framework, in which unjustified enrichment occupies a 'lower' or 'inferior' position, while the other areas automatically take precedence. Therefore, where it is more strongly and consistently affected by subsidiarity, unjustified enrichment is put at the bottom of a hierarchy among the sources of obligations, and restitution rarely governs. As a result, courts prioritize remedies based on contract, tort, or property law, while unjustified enrichment is relegated to a sort of storeroom within the legal system—a marginal space where irregular or anomalous cases are haphazardly amassed when they fail to fit within the more structured and 'regular' domains of private law.

Of course, it cannot be denied in principle that unjustified enrichment may have a narrower scope or be otherwise more limited compared to other areas of private law. However, there remains considerable uncertainty as to what precisely justifies its classification as subsidiary and what this alleged subsidiarity entails. In fact, despite the strong pedigree and broad recognition of the subsidiarity of unjustified enrichment across various legal systems, the precise meaning and scope of this doctrine or rule is still a conundrum.[1] Courts and scholars continue to grapple

* For their valuable comments on the manuscript, I owe much gratitude to Luigi Buonanno, Birke Häcker, Robert Stevens, and Reinhard Zimmermann (in alphabetical order). Errors and omissions are my own.

[1] See Peter Schlechtriem, *Restitution und Bereicherungsausgleich in Europa*, vol 1, *Eine rechtsvergleichende Darstellung* (Mohr Siebeck 2000) 8.

Pietro Sirena, *The Subsidiarity of Unjustified Enrichment* In: *Comparative Reflections in Private Law*.
Edited by: Marco Cappelletti, Ciara Kennefick, and Dorota Leczykiewicz, Oxford University Press.
 DOI: 10.1093/9780198959168.003.0014

with what exactly renders such claims subsidiary and in what sense this classification applies. These doubts result in theoretical ambiguities and inconsistencies in practice, ultimately posing a threat to the coherence of the broader framework governing unjustified enrichment. Therefore, a considerable number of specialists in this field are of the view that this doctrine or rule of subsidiarity should be interpreted as narrowly as possible or should, to the extent that this is permissible, even be overcome, abandoned, or repealed.

Fundamentally, one might question whether it would be sufficient simply to define the constitutive elements and prerequisites of unjustified enrichment in order to delineate its scope, thereby also clarifying its relationship with other areas of private law. Indeed, similar issues of coordination arise in other parts of the legal system, such as the interplay between contractual and extracontractual liability,[2] in which, however, they have been resolved without the need to classify one action as subsidiary to the other.[3]

The objective of this contribution is, therefore, to assess whether the theory and practice of private law should move away from the subsidiarity of unjustified enrichment altogether.[4] To this end, a mapping of civil law and common law jurisdictions where this doctrine or rule has been established will be conducted (section I.B). Furthermore, the vast array of different interpretations and applications of this doctrine or rule will be analysed (section I.C), with a particular focus on the two extremes of the spectrum: the strong (or *in abstracto*) and weak (or *in concreto*) versions of subsidiarity. It will then be shown that, in the legal systems considered, there is a general trend towards abandoning (or at least mitigating) the doctrine or rule of subsidiarity of unjustified enrichment, both in theory and in practice. This is due to the perception that this doctrine or rule is inconsistent, superfluous, or at the very least incapable of rationalizing the case law on unjustified enrichment and providing it with a logically satisfactory foundation (section I.D). Subsequently, the chapter will explore the theoretical and practical issues arising from the intersections of unjustified enrichment with the three other core areas of private law, that is, contract (section II), property (section III), and tort (section IV), focusing on the mechanisms that regulate the overlap of remedies within each domain.

The conclusion (section V) is that the doctrine or rule of subsidiarity should be abandoned. It persists merely as a historical remnant of the original foundation

[2] See Stephen Smith, 'Concurrent Liability in Contract and Unjust Enrichment: The Fundamental Breach Requirement' (1999) 115 Law Quarterly Review 245; Stephen Smith, 'The Restatement of Liabilities in Restitution' in Charles Mitchell and William Swadling (eds), *The Restatement Third. Restitution and Unjust Enrichment: Critical and Comparative Essays* (Hart Publishing 2013) 227; Sarah Worthington, 'The Commercial Triple Helix: Contract, Property and Unjust Enrichment' in Peter Devonshire and Havelock Rohan (eds), *The Impact of Equity and Restitution in Commerce* (Hart Publishing 2018) 33.

[3] See section I.D.

[4] See Stephen Waddams, 'Contract and Unjust Enrichment: Competing Categories, or Complementary Concepts?' in Charles Rickett and Ross Grantham (eds), *Structure and Justification in Private Law. Essays for Peter Birks* (Hart Publishing 2016) 167.

of unjustified enrichment on purely equitable grounds. Subsidiarity was formulated in contexts where claims in unjustified enrichment as such were established as exceptional corrective measures to the strict application of the law, rather than as occurrences of a necessary structural principle. However, with the integration of unjustified enrichment into codified law, or its incorporation into legal systems in other forms, a subsidiarity-based approach appears outdated, if not entirely untenable. In other words, the fear that the restitutionary claims at stake might undermine existing legal structures is unfounded, as unjust enrichment is now an integral and regulated part of the law. Concurrently, to prevent unjust enrichment from extending beyond its proper scope, it remains crucial precisely to define its essential elements, especially the requirement of 'at the claimant's expense'.

B. Mapping civil law and common law jurisdictions that establish subsidiarity of unjustified enrichment

Some of the civil codes in which unjustified enrichment ranks as an autonomous source of obligations (besides contract and torts) contain a black-letter rule that, more or less eloquently, establishes the subsidiarity of the action granted to the impoverished party against the enriched party, as is the case with the Italian Codice civile (art 2042) and, after the 2016 reform, the French Code civil (art 1303-3). A cognate feature is to be found in jurisdictions that are without a civil code but nevertheless regulate unjustified enrichment through statutory provisions that are redolent of the civilian tradition, as is the case with section 6 of the Israeli Unjustified Enrichment Act 1979.[5]

Among these provisions, it is Italian law that explicitly refers to 'the subsidiary character of the action',[6] as also does article 474 of the Portuguese Código civil.[7] In contrast, the French Code civil refrains from such terminology,[8] but it is widely

[5] '*Scope of Application and Saving of Remedies.* (a) The provision of this law shall take effect where there are no special provisions in any other law with regards to the matter at hand and where no other agreement between the parties applies [. . .] (c) This law shall not derogate from any other remedy' (translation taken from https://www.wipo.int/wipolex/en/legislation/details/15221).

[6] Art 2042 of the Codice civile (Italian Civil Code). Substantially, this provision was mirrored by art 1955 of the Peruvian Código Civil of 1984, whose heading however omits any specific reference to subsidiarity (see Ricardo Geldres Campos, 'La subsidiariedad del enriquecimiento sin causa', Gazeta civil & procesal civil 2018, 113).

[7] Art 474 Código civil português (Portuguese Civil Code). See Diego Leite de Campos, *A subsidiariedade da obrigação de restituir o enriquecimiento* (Almedina 1974, reprinted 2003). See also section I.C.

[8] Art 1303-3 Code civil. See Philippe Drakidis, 'La "subsidiarité", caractère spécifique et international de l'action d'enrichissement sans cause', Revue trimestrielle de droit civil 1961, 577; Philip Rémy, 'Le principe de subsidiarité de l'*action de in rem verso* en droit français' in *L'enrichissement sans cause* (LGDJ 2007) 57; Alexis Posez, 'La subsidiarité de l'enrichissement sans cause: étude de droit français à la lumière du droit comparé', Revue de droit international et de droit comparé 2014, 185; Antoine Gouëzel, *La subsidiarité en droit privé* (Economica 2013) 60. See also sections I.C. and II.B.

assumed that it mandates the same rule,[9] whose genuine origin can be traced back to French case law between the nineteenth and twentieth centuries.[10] Soon adopted from France by the Italian *Corte di cassazione*, it was later captured in article 2042 of the Codice civile, which, being enacted in 1942, was historically the first to formalize the rule of subsidiarity of unjustified enrichment. In fact, article 1303-3 of the French Code civil, which encapsulates the French case law, was not enacted until 2016,[11] when, in the framework of a broad reform of contract law, the Code civil was finally equipped with a discrete set of rules explicitly addressing unjustified enrichment.[12] In other civil codes, the subsidiarity of this source of obligations is less ostensibly set out, but there is nevertheless broad consensus among courts and scholars that some of the governing provisions are to be interpreted as laying down such a rule, as is the case with article 1494 of the Quebec Code civil of 1991.[13]

By contrast, the German *Bürgerliches Gesetzbuch* (BGB), as well as the Dutch *Burgerlijk Wetboek*,[14] deliberately rejected any rule of the sort. Yet, in these legal systems too, a certain degree of subsidiarity (albeit significantly less than in Italy or France) is accorded to unjustified enrichment by scholars who write reference works on the subject, and this doctrine is also used by courts to govern the case law. Under German law, in particular, it is frequently applied in two-party cases, but even more importantly in three-party cases of unjustified enrichment that are based on the voidness or avoidance/rescission of a contract of sale (or another

[9] See Muriel Fabre-Magnan, *Droit des obligations*, vol 2, *Responsabilité civile et quasi-contrats* (5th edn, PUF 2021) 582–83. For further reference, see Mélodie Combot, *Quasi-contrat et enrichissement injustifié* (LGDJ 2023) 313–29.

[10] See section II.B. For a comparative analysis, see Simon Whittaker, 'The Law of Obligations' in John Bell, Sophie Boyron, and Simon Whittaker (eds), *Principles of French Law* (2nd edn, OUP 2008) 437; Simon Whittaker, 'Performance of Another's Obligation: French and English Law Contrasted' in David Johnston and Reinhard Zimmermann (eds), *Unjustified Enrichment. Key Issues in Comparative Perspective* (CUP 2002) 444.

[11] See Mélodie Combot, 'Unjustified Enrichment and Civil Liability' in Jean-Sébastien Borghetti and Simon Whittaker (eds), *French Civil Liability in Comparative Perspective* (Hart Publishing 2019) 357. On the previous state of French law in this field, see Eric Descheemaeker, 'Quasi-contrats et enrichissement injustifié en droit français', Revue trimestrielle de droit civil 2013, 1. For a comparative analysis, see Valentin Pinel le Dret, *Les quasi-contrats en droit privé français envisagés sous l'angle des rapports entre le contrat, la loi et le juge, avec égards aux droits allemand et anglais* (PhD thesis, Université Paris I Panthéon-Sorbonne 2023–24).

[12] Yet, it is still claimed by some scholars that, despite appearances, unjustified enrichment is not a proper source of obligations under French law. In favour of this view, see Combot (n 9) 203, 468.

[13] See Lionel Smith, 'Property, Subsidiarity and Unjust Enrichment' in Johnston and Zimmermann (n 10) 588, 607ff.

[14] For Dutch law, see Gerrit E van Maanen, 'Subsidiarity of the Action for Unjustified Enrichment—French Law and Dutch Law: Different Solutions for the Same Problem?' (2006) 14 European Review of Private Law 409, 416; Jeroen Chorus, 'Il disegno eclettico del nuovo codice olandese' in Letizia Vacca (ed), *Arricchimento ingiustificato e ripetizione dell'indebito* (Giappichelli 2005) 183. For South African law (but also for an extensive comparative analysis), see Christo Joost and Eltjo Schrage, 'Subsidiarity of the General Action for Unjust Enrichment (part 1)' (2016) Journal of South African Law 1, and 'Subsidiarity of the General Action for Unjust Enrichment (part 2)' (2016) Journal of South African Law 220.

contract aimed at the transfer of property), and it is used to curtail the proliferation of restitution claims by the transferor against the transferee (or, even more importantly, a remote recipient): insofar as the payer of an undue performance is entitled to claim restitution for their performance (*Leistungskondiktion*), they are not entitled alternatively to claim restitution for any other unjustified enrichment that the immediate or a remote recipient may have otherwise obtained from that same performance (*Nichtleistungskondiktion*).[15]

In English case law, on the other hand, the subsidiarity of unjustified enrichment appears to have been of little, if any, practical relevance,[16] but it is far from unfamiliar in other common law jurisdictions.[17] Moreover, scholars who have engaged in this subject are of the view that it is a key feature of unjustified enrichment, which is instrumental to the role it plays as a gap-filler in the legal system and therefore should be emphasized more than it usually is.[18]

In the light of the foregoing, it seems that all jurisdictions have acknowledged a certain subsidiarity of unjustified enrichment, even though it is explicitly articulated by the legislature only in a few.[19] Yet, the scope and the consequences of this rule or doctrine vary considerably from one legal system to another, as will be examined further in the next section.

C. Restrictive and broadening applications of subsidiarity in theory and practice: from 'strong' (*in abstracto*) to 'weak' (*in concreto*) versions

Article 1303-3 of the French Code civil explicitly commands that a claim in unjustified enrichment is ousted by any other remedy that is afforded to the claimant by the law, regardless of whether this other remedy is obstructed by a legal impediment (*obstacle de droit*), such as prescription. This reflects a traditional line of French authorities according to which an action for unjustified enrichment is disallowed by the availability of another claim, even if this alternative is barred by the passage of time (*prescription*, and *déchéance* or *forclusion*) or by *res iudicata* (*autorité de la chose jugée*), and even if it does not determine the case because the

[15] See Gerhard Dannemann, *The German Law of Unjustified Enrichment and Restitution: A Comparative Introduction* (OUP 2009) 52ff. See also section III.C.

[16] For a quick reference, see Viktoria Winzer, '"At the Expense Of" and "Subsidiarity": Two Lessons on Unjust Enrichment' (2022) 138 Law Quarterly Review 524, 528.

[17] A notable example is provided by the Singaporean Court of Appeal in *Esben Finance Ltd v Wong Hou-Lianq Neil* [2022] SGCA(I) 1. See the comment by Winzer (n 16) 524.

[18] Ross Grantham and Charles Rickett, 'On the Subsidiarity of Unjust Enrichment' (2001) 117 Law Quarterly Review 273, 296.

[19] See Konrad Zweigert and Hein Kötz, *Introduction to Comparative Law* (Tony Weir tr, 3rd edn, OUP 1998) 550; Ulrich Magnus, 'Concurrent Claims' in Jürgen Basedow and others (eds), *The Max Planck Encyclopedia of European Private Law*, vol 1 (OUP 2012) 347.

claimant has failed to prove their allegations on the merits.[20] This is also the case law of several other European countries, such as Belgium and, less rigidly, Spain, as well as Hungary and Bulgaria.[21]

Nevertheless, a trend can be identified in French case law,[22] as well as in that of other European countries (such as Portugal),[23] by which courts tend in practice to mitigate the strictness of the subsidiarity rule which is formally spelt out. For example, after failing to prove the existence of a *de facto* partnership, the *Cour de cassation* upheld a claim for restitution of unjustified enrichment brought by one of the partners against the other, for the contribution the claimant had made to the increase of their own assets.[24] In another case, the *Cour de cassation*, holding that it had not been proved that the seller had been aware of the defects of the goods sold (within the meaning of article 1645 of the Code civil), dismissed the buyer's principal claim for damages, but upheld the buyer's alternative action *de in rem verso* against the seller.[25]

In respect of Italian law, it has been argued that the vast majority of the judgments in which courts appeared to apply a 'strong' sense of subsidiarity were misleading in their reasoning. In these cases the claimant had initially brought a different action, and at a certain point of the proceedings they sought to replace it with a claim in unjustified enrichment, thus violating the bars established by the Italian Code of Civil Procedure.[26] A close examination of case law suggests that,

[20] The leading case is Cass civ (3) 29 April 1971, Revue trimestrielle de droit civil 1971, 842 obs Yvon Loussouarn. See also Cass civ (3) 23 June 2010, Revue des contrats 2010, 1370 obs Charlotte Goldie-Genicon. Some scholars have argued that, for a claim of unjustified enrichment to be inadmissible, the burden falls on the defendant to prove that the obstacle to pursuing an alternative action is attributable to the claimant, ie the party allegedly impoverished. For more detail, see Posez (n 8) 225ff.

[21] See Christian von Bar and Stephen Swann (eds), *Principles of European Law on Unjustified Enrichment* (Sellier 2010) 524ff.

[22] Yves-Marie Laithier, 'L'affaiblissement de la règle de la subsidiarité doit-il faire craindre l'envahissement du contrat par l'action *de in rem verso*?', Revue des contrats 2008, no 4, 1138 (note on Cass civ (1) 25 June 2008 no 06-19556); Sophie Gaudemet, 'Subsidiarité de l'enrichissement sans cause, où donc en est-on?', Revue des contrats 2009, no 3, 1177 (note on Cass civ (1) 2 April 2009 no 08-10742); Philippe Rémy, 'Le principe de subsidiarité de l'action *de in rem verso* en droit français' in Vincenzo Mannino (ed), *L'arricchimento senza causa* (Giappichelli 2005) 82; Philippe Rémy, 'Les restitutions dans un système de quasi-contrats: l'expérience française' in Vacca (n 14) 89.

[23] Christian von Bar and Stephen Swann (n 21) 543.

[24] Cass civ (1) 15 October 1996, Revue trimestrielle de droit civil 1997, 657 obs Joseph Mestre, which reversed Cass civ (1) 8 December 1987, Revue trimestrielle de droit civil 1988, 745 obs Joseph Mestre. Similarly, on a case of work performed within the family context, see also Cass civ (1) 14 March 1995, La Semaine juridique-Édition générale 1995.II-22516 obs Frédéric Roussel, according to whom the ruling would represent 'a manifest violation of the principle of subsidiarity'. See also Michel Borysewicz, 'Travail et enrichissement sans cause dans les relations de famille' in *Mélanges en l'honneur de Jean-Pierre Béguet* (Toulon Faculté de Droit 1985) 53.

[25] Cass civ (1) 3 June 1997, La Semaine juridique-Édition générale 1998.II-10102 obs Geneviève Viney.

[26] Donato Carusi, 'Una fonte (inesauribile?) di equivoci: la sussidiarietà dell'azione di arricchimento', Giurisprudenza italiana 2014, 5 (note on Corte di cassazione, 2 August 2013, no 18502); Mauro Grondona, 'Arricchimento senza causa' in Andrea D'Angelo (ed), *Le obbligazioni restitutorie* (Giappichelli 2015) 56.

with some exceptions, courts tend to permit claims for unjustified enrichment where the claimant has failed to prove the allegations underlying their other actions.[27] In this context, subsidiarity is applied in a 'weak' sense (or *in concreto*).

Despite numerous instances of a more lenient application of the subsidiarity rule, these remain largely uncaptured in the dicta of French and Italian authorities, which generally maintain an ostensibly strict interpretation. The alignment between the highest courts of the two legal systems has not been preserved, however, in cases where the claimant seeks payment for a contractual performance, but the claim is found to be ill-grounded due to a lack of evidence of a contract between the parties.

In such cases, an unwavering line of rulings by the French *Cour de cassation* denies a subsidiary claim in unjustified enrichment, particularly where what is at issue is a loan[28] or a contract for services.[29] By contrast, in 2023, the Extended Bench (*Sezioni Unite*) of the Italian *Corte di cassazione* ruled that, although a claim in unjustified enrichment is ousted by the availability of an alternative remedy, the claim nevertheless lies where the claimant is unable to establish the requirements of a contract, a tort, or another source of obligations vis-à-vis the defendant. A claim in unjustified enrichment is, therefore, allowed when other remedies are flawed from the outset (*ab origine*), as is the case when no contract is found to exist between the parties or when the contract exists but is void (unless it violates mandatory rules or contravenes public policy). Conversely, the subsidiary remedy is denied, for example, in cases where a valid contract is found but the claimant fails to prove loss resulting from the defendant's breach.[30]

Hence, the subsidiarity of unjustified enrichment as applied by the Italian *Corte di cassazione* can be described as 'imperfectly strong' or 'semi-strong', while the French *Cour de cassation* adheres to a 'perfectly' or 'entirely strong' version of the rule. The French approach appears consistently to deny restitutionary claims whenever the claimant fails to substantiate the merits of an alternative remedy, whether in terms of its requirements or its consequences.

[27] Donato Carusi, 'Proposizione in via subordinata dell'azione di arricchimento, autorità del precedente giudiziale e stile delle sentenze', Rivista di diritto commerciale 2015, I-247.

[28] One of the last cases in this line is Cass civ (1) 10 January 2024 no 22-10.278. See Cédric Hélaine, 'Caractère subsidiaire de l'enrichissement sans cause et administration de la preuve', Dalloz actualité 2024 (available at https://www.dalloz-actualite.fr/flash/caractere-subsidiaire-de-l-enrichissement-sans-cause-et-administration-de-preuve).

[29] See Laithier (n 22) 1138; Combot (n 9) 318–19.

[30] Corte di cassazione (Sezioni unite civili), 5 December 2023, no 33954. For detailed and insightful comments, see Davide Achille, 'La sussidiarietà dell'azione di arricchimento senza causa: nihil sub sole novum', Nuova giurisprudenza civile commentata 2024, I-374; Geo Magri, 'La sussidiarietà dell'azione di arricchimento senza causa: un'occasione mancata per superare la tradizione, garantendo maggiore equità all'ordinamento', Responsabilità civile e previdenza 2023, 1920; Stefano Gatti, 'La sussidiarietà "in astratto" secondo le Sezioni Unite: meriti e zone d'ombra di un approccio casistico', Responsabilità civile e previdenza 2024, 96.

D. The trend towards the abandonment (or mitigation) of subsidiarity in case law and model rules

In common law jurisdictions, it has been argued that, in all instances in which unjustified enrichment has been classified as subsidiary, this classification was superfluous, as the defendant's enrichment was not unjustified and therefore could not ground by definition any restitutionary claim, be it subsidiary or otherwise. If that is the case, the fundamental requirement of this restitutionary remedy is not satisfied from the outset, and consequently the vocabulary of 'subsidiarity' would be unsuited to serve the purpose it is aimed at, that is, explaining some of unjustified enrichment's relations with other legal categories.[31] Further scepticism has been voiced through the assumption that the common law does not frequently rank different remedies in a hierarchical order,[32] and this stance seems to be reflected in section 1(4) of Lord Burrows' *Restatement of the English Law of Unjust Enrichment*, where it is set forth that 'a right to restitution for unjust enrichment may be claimed concurrently with another claim (for example, for a tort or breach of contract)', with the reservation that 'satisfaction of more than one claim is not permitted where it would produce double recovery'.[33]

As far as German law is concerned, the doctrine of subsidiarity is used by courts to govern cases of unjustified enrichment and is widely recognized in standard works of reference in this field, but it has a very narrow coverage and decidedly plays a lesser role than in French or Italian law.[34] Moreover, this doctrine has been rejected by several scholars,[35] who claim that the depiction of unjustified enrichment as subsidiary is either superfluous or inaccurate as a map of the relevant case law and to provide guidance for its further development.[36] According to some of them, such subsidiarity would do nothing more than reconceptualize the cases

[31] Mat Campbell, 'Against the Subsidiarity on Unjust Enrichment' (2022) Law Quarterly Review 368, 370; Mat Campbell, 'Doubting the Subsidiarity of Unjust Enrichment' (2021) Lloyd's Maritime and Commercial Law Quarterly 535.

[32] *Goff and Jones: The Law of Unjust Enrichment* (Charles Mitchell, Paul Mitchell, and Stephen Watterson eds, 10th edn, Sweet & Maxwell—Thomson Reuters 2022) paras 2-03–2-04. On the possibility of concurrent liability in both tort and contract, the leading case is *Henderson v Merrett Syndicates Ltd* [1994] UKHL 5, [1995] 2 AC 145.

[33] Andrew Burrows, *A Restatement of the English Law of Unjust Enrichment* (OUP 2012) 5.

[34] See also section I.A.

[35] See Claus-Wilhelm Canaris, 'Die Bereicherungsausgleich im Dreipersonenverhältnis' in Gotthard Paulus, Uwe Diederichsen, and Claus-Wilhelm Canaris (eds), *Festschrift für Karl Larenz zum 70. Geburtstag* (Beck 1973) 853, republished in Claus-Wilhelm Canaris, *Gesammelte Schriften*, vol 2 (Jörg Neuner und Hans Cristoph Grigoleit eds, de Gruyter 2012) 717. See also Karl Larenz and Claus-Wilhelm Canaris, *Lehrbuch des Schuldrechts*, vol 2.2 (13th edn, Beck 1994) 215–16.

[36] Larenz and Canaris (n 35) 253 argue that subsidiarity eventually leads to practical outcomes that, in most cases of unjustified enrichment, are acceptable, but the doctrine is dogmatically flawed and must be reconceptualized, above all with regard to the requirement of the lack of a legal basis (which is the very reason why the enrichment is unjustified). Therefore, it can be said that this doctrine provides general guidance in sorting some more problematic cases, but it also engenders a number of contradictions in the legal systems (*Wertungswidersprüche*), which must be addressed with additional arguments and development of the law (*Rechtsfortbildung*).

where one or several of the requirements of unjustified enrichment are not met, either because the defendant's enrichment is not unjustified, being based on either contract or property law,[37] or because that enrichment is only 'indirectly' obtained, that is, not 'at the claimant's expense'. According to some others, the doctrine of subsidiarity obscures a specific prohibition of restitution of the enrichment (indirectly) obtained by the defendant through the intervention of a third party (*Versionsverbot*).[38]

With regard to the jurisdictions in which the subsidiarity of unjustified enrichment is established as a black-letter rule, it is noteworthy that leading commentators on article 1303-3 of the Code civil are of the view that this provision has failed to clarify one of the most nebulous features of unjustified enrichment,[39] both in theory and in practice, and that the longstanding challenges of using subsidiarity to regulate the interplay between restitution of unjustified enrichment and other areas of private law thus remained unsolved.[40] In fact, the case law of the *Cour de cassation* that is encapsulated in article 1303-3 is far from unambiguous. On the one hand, the Court's reasoning adheres to a strict subsidiarity of unjustified enrichment, yet its judgments not infrequently make use of a *de facto* flexibility, subtly leaning towards a milder understanding of the rule.[41] Some scholars engaging with unjustified enrichment echo this pragmatic approach taken by French courts and, even before the 2016 Reform, had suggested that the rule of subsidiarity should be interpreted loosely, if not abandoned altogether.[42]

In respect of Italian law, article 2042 of the Codice civile has been traditionally interpreted by scholarship in a very rigid sense.[43] However, some authors have recently argued that the provision merely aims to prevent double recovery for the same unjustified enrichment and should not bar this restitutionary claim from

[37] Georg Thielmann, 'Gegen das Subsidiaritätsdogma im Bereicherungsrecht' (1987) 187 Archiv für die civilistische Praxis 23.

[38] Chris Thomale and Anton S Zimmermann, 'Der Vorrang der Leistungsbeziehung—eine rechtsrealistische und rechtsdogmatische Kritik' (2017) 217 Archiv für die civilistische Praxis 246.

[39] Olivier Deshayes, Thomas Genicon, and Yves-Marie Laithier, *Réforme du droit des contrats, du régime général et de la preuve des obligations. Commentaire article par article* (2nd edn, LexisNexis 2018) 558.

[40] Combot (n 9) 313–29.

[41] See section II.B.

[42] See Jacques Mestre, Revue trimestrielle de droit civil 1997, 657, who, commenting on Cass civ (1) 8 December 1987, argues that the general action for unjust enrichment should be precluded only when the claimant is protected under the 'legal rule normally applicable to the legal situation', and a similar view is conveyed by Jacques Raynaud, 'À propos de la subsidiarité en droit privé' in *Mélanges Christian Mouly*, vol 1 (Litec 1998) 136. For a more radical perspective, see Viney (n 25), who, commenting on Cass civ (1) 3 June 1997, contends that the identification of such a 'legal rule' is impossible and instead advocates for a full rejection of subsidiarity. See also Eric Descheemaeker, 'The New French Law of Unjustified Enrichment' (2018) 25 Restitution Law Review 77.

[43] Piero Schlesinger, 'Arricchimento (Azione di)' in *Novissimo Digesto italiano*, vol 1, 2 (UTET 1958) 1008; Alberto Trabucchi, 'Arricchimento *b)* Diritto civile' in *Enciclopedia del diritto*, vol 3 (Giuffrè 1958) 74. More recently, see Cesare Massimo Bianca, *Diritto civile*, vol 5, *La responsabilità* (3rd edn, Giuffrè 2021) 799ff, and Francesco Gazzoni, *Manuale di diritto privato* (21st edn, ESI 2024) 712ff.

being brought concurrently with another (eg, for damages).[44] This view has not gained much traction in legal theory, and even less in practice, in which a well-established line of authorities supports a 'strong' interpretation of subsidiarity (*in abstracto*). Nonetheless, Italian courts, including the *Corte di cassazione*,[45] have occasionally leant towards a less strict application (*in concreto*) of article 2042, mitigating the rule to some extent.[46] As a result, a misalignment has inevitably arisen, which was ultimately referred to the judgment of the Extended Bench (*Sezioni Unite*) of the *Corte di cassazione* in 2023.[47]

Interestingly, the Draft Common Frame of Reference (DCFR), which was intended to provide a comprehensive picture of European private law (but which is *de facto* based mainly on German law in this area), does not explicitly provide for any subsidiarity of unjustified enrichment. Some of the issues to which this rule or doctrine is intended to respond have not been left unaddressed but have been dealt with in other ways, as is also made clear in the official comments annexed to the Principles of European Law on Unjustified Enrichment.[48]

II. Subsidiarity of Unjustified Enrichment vis-à-vis Contract

A. Two-party cases

(i) Contractual risk allocation and failure of basis (or consideration)

To the extent that a party to a valid contract confers a benefit upon the counterparty in discharge of a contractual obligation, it is settled across legal systems that the subsistence of the contract will generally preclude any restitutionary claim in respect of that performance. In English law, this has been called the 'obligation rule'.[49] While one might argue that such a claim cannot take precedence over the contractual terms, describing it as 'subsidiary' is ultimately superfluous, since the existence of a continuing contractual regime excludes the possibility that the

[44] Carlo Castronovo, *Responsabilità civile* (Giuffrè 2018) 696ff; Carlo Castronovo, 'La violazione della proprietà intellettuale come lesione del potere di disposizione. Dal danno all'arricchimento', Diritto industriale 2003, I-7; Pietro Sirena, 'Note critiche sulla sussidiarietà dell'azione generale di arricchimento senza causa', Rivista trimestrale di diritto e procedura civile 2005, 105; Pietro Sirena, 'La sussidiarietà dell'azione generale di arricchimento senza causa', Rivista di diritto civile 2018, 379; Pietro Sirena, *La gestione di affari altrui. Ingerenze altruistiche, ingerenze egoistiche e restituzione del profitto* (Giappichelli 1999) 148–49; Marcello Gaboardi, *Il concorso di azioni*, vol 1, *Contratto, impresa e tutela giurisdizionale dei diritti* (Egea 2018) 224–25.

[45] See section I.C.

[46] Donato Carusi, 'Il concorso dei rimedi restitutori con quello risarcitorio' in Pietro Sirena (ed), *La funzione deterrente della responsabilità civile* (Giuffrè 2011) 405; Paolo Gallo, *sub* art 2042, in Enrico Gabrielli (ed), *Commentario del codice civile* (UTET 2015) 356; Paolo Gallo, *sub* art 2042, in Piero Schlesinger and Francesco Donato Busnelli (eds), *Il Codice Civile. Commentario* (Giuffrè 2003) 88.

[47] See section I.C.

[48] Christian von Bar and Stephen Swann (n 21) 524ff.

[49] Graham Virgo, *The Principles of the Law of Restitution* (4th edn, OUP 2024) 40ff, 151ff.

enrichment obtained from the counterparty's performance could be regarded as 'unjustified'. Consequently, no claim in restitution arises at all, rendering the notion of subsidiarity irrelevant. This entails that where one contracting party has assumed the risk of a particular event, they are, as a general rule, precluded from bringing a restitutionary claim against the other party upon the occurrence of that event.[50] In fact, all legal systems enable the parties to a contract to allocate risks and benefits between themselves, and as long as their agreement is valid,[51] unjustified enrichment generally does not apply.

In this respect, it is notable that, in civil law jurisdictions, the parties to the sale of a future thing can assign the risk of its non-existence to either the seller or the buyer. If the seller bears that risk (*emptio rei speratae*), the contract becomes void if the thing does not come into existence, and the buyer may claim unjustified enrichment to recover the payment made. Conversely, if the buyer bears that risk (*emptio spei*), the contract remains valid even if the future thing does not materialize, and the seller's enrichment from the buyer's payment is not unjustified, preventing the buyer from claiming restitution.[52]

As a general matter, a performance—be it inside or outside a contractual context—may be made, explicitly or implicitly, contingent upon the counter-performance of the other party,[53] or also upon a condition involving the existence of an identified state of affairs or the occurrence of an event which involves no promised performance by the recipient.[54] If this basis is shared with the latter, the question typically arises whether, in the event that the condition is not met, or the counter-performance is not rendered, a restitutionary claim becomes immediately available, or whether such claim is instead allowed only after the contract has been terminated. In certain instances of this nature, the doctrine of frustration of contract (in common law systems) or the rules on supervening impossibility of counter-performance (in civil law systems) may allow the party thus impoverished to bring a restitutionary claim,[55] provided that the contract is thereby discharged (or automatically terminated) and thus no longer offers a legal basis for

[50] Virgo (n 49) 39–40. For criticism of the view that a risk-taker cannot recover in unjustified enrichment, see Frederick Wilmot-Smith, 'Replacing Risk-taking Reasoning' (2011) 127 Law Quarterly Review 610, 616.

[51] See Sebastian Lohsse, 'Initial Impossibility' in Nils Jansen and Reinhard Zimmermann (eds), *Commentaries on European Contract Law* (OUP 2018) 653. In case the contract at stake is either void or avoided/rescinded, see section III.A.(ii).

[52] Reinhard Zimmermann, *The Law of Obligations. Roman Foundations of the Civilian Tradition* (OUP 1996) 245ff.

[53] *Stocznia Gdanska SA v Latvian Shipping Co* [1998] 1 WLR 574, 588.

[54] *Barnes v Eastenders Cash and Carry plc* [2014] UKSC 26, [2015] AC 1; *Roxborough v Torthmans of Pall Mall Australia Ltd* [2001] HCA 68, (2001) 208 CLR 516 (HCA).

[55] On frustrated contracts, see *Goff and Jones: The Law of Unjust Enrichment* (n 32) paras 15-01ff. On supervening impossibility, see Jens Kleinschmidt, 'Particular Remedies for Non-performance' in Jansen and Zimmermann (n 51) 1316ff.

the enrichment obtained by the counterparty.[56] The contractual regime does not continue, and the relevant cases, therefore, fall outside the scope of the argument presently under consideration.

In English law, moreover, the recognition of the doctrine of (total) 'failure of basis', or 'failure of consideration', as a ground for claims in unjustified enrichment allows those who have made a conditional payment to seek restitution where the recipient has failed to fulfil a promissory condition stipulated in their agreement or to render their counter-performance,[57] even if the contract has not been terminated by the innocent party.[58] On this ground, exceptional limitations to the abovementioned 'obligation rule' have been recognized by courts,[59] allowing claims in unjustified enrichment to address lacunae in the contractual allocation of risk.[60] In this sense, the law of unjustified enrichment has been understood as complementary, rather than merely subsidiary, to contract law.[61]

These developments raise the challenging question of whether unjustified enrichment claims may operate in the interstices of the agreement between the contracting parties.[62] Although the issue remains in a state of flux, the UK Supreme Court has recently adopted a more restrictive position on the matter.[63] To the extent that such a restitutionary claim is granted to the claimant, there is, in any case, no reason to describe it as 'subsidiary', since it coexists with the continuing contractual regime.

(ii) Voidness, avoidance/rescission, termination, frustration of contract

A restitutionary claim in unjustified enrichment may generally lie between the contracting parties insofar as the contract is void,[64] has been avoided/rescinded or discharged for breach, or is frustrated.[65] In this domain, the depiction of

[56] In English law, the inception of restitution (of an advanced payment) for frustration of contract was marked by the landmark decision in *Fibrosa Spolka Akcyjna v Fairbairn Lawson Combe Barbour Ltd* [1943] AC 32 (HL).

[57] This rule has long been recognized in English law: see *Moses v Macferlan* (1760) 2 Burr 1005, 1012 (Lord Mansfield).

[58] *Anron Bunkering DMCC v Glencore Energy UK Ltd* [2023] EWHC 295 (Comm).

[59] *Dargamo Holdings Ltd v Avonwick Holdings* [2021] EWCA Civ 1149, [2022] 1 All ER (Comm) 1244; *Bank of New York Mellon (International) Ltd v Cine-UK Ltd; London Trocadero (2015) LLP v Picturehouse Cinemas Ltd* [2022] EWCA Civ 1021, [2021] 4 WLR 143; *International Energy Group Ltd v Zurich Insurance Plc* [2015] UKSC 33, [2016] AC 509, 550–52. See Robert Stevens, *The Laws of Restitution* (OUP 2023) 124; Virgo (n 49) 151.

[60] See Jack Beatson, 'The Temptation of Elegance: Concurrence of Restitutionary and Contractual Claims' in William Swadling and Gareth Jones (eds), *The Search for Principle. Essays in Honour of Lord Goff of Chieveley* (OUP 1999) 143, 145ff; Jack Beatson, 'Restitution and Contract: *Non-Cumul?*' (2000) 1 Theoretical Inquiries in Law 83; Niamh Connolly, 'A Common Law Perspective on the Concurrence of Claims in Contract and Unjust Enrichment' (2014) 6 European Review of Private Law 1005, 1012ff.

[61] See Virgo (n 49) 161, 163.

[62] See Waddams (n 4) 143ff.

[63] *Barton v Morris* [2023] UKSC 3, [2023] AC 684.

[64] In English law, the definitive affirmation that the nullity of a contract executed by both parties obliges each of them to return the performances they have respectively received was established in *Kleinwort Benson Ltd v Lincoln City Council* [1999] 2 AC 349.

[65] For restitution grounded on a frustrated contract, see section II.A.(i).

unjustified enrichment as being subsidiary is abundant, for reasons that are, in a sense, the reverse of those considered in the context of a continuing contractual regime. Prior to the contract's being avoided, rescinded, or terminated, the enrichment obtained from the counterparty's performance could not properly be regarded as 'unjustified'.[66] This is not a matter of subsidiarity, however, but rather a question concerning the very definition of the constitutive elements of unjustified enrichment.

In this context, it is also important to note that in cases of contract termination (due to breach), most legal systems have specific rules on restitution,[67] which take precedence over the general rules of unjustified enrichment. Given that contract termination in several legal systems operates retroactively (except for long-term contracts), a key issue arises concerning the destruction or disposal in the interim of the goods which had been delivered and the resulting impossibility of their return by the recipient, who conversely remains entitled to recover the consideration they provided.[68] In legal systems lacking special rules on restitution for such cases,[69] the general rules of unjustified enrichment typically apply. However, these general rules are often adjusted to account for the specific circumstances, particularly with regard to ensuring reciprocal restitution by both parties.[70]

[66] For restitution grounded on failure of basis (or failure of consideration), nevertheless, see section II.A.(i). For restitution grounded on a rescinded contract, see section III.A.(iii). With regard to a terminated contract, it should be noted that common law systems generally do not permit restitution for unjust enrichment where the claimant has fully performed the contract by providing services to the defendant. In such cases, contract law continues to govern the parties' rights and obligations, and the claimant is limited to an action for damages for breach of contract, rather than a restitutionary claim for *quantum meruit*: see Virgo (n 49) 156ff.

[67] See Hein Kötz, *European Contract Law* (Gill Mertens and Tony Weir trs, 2nd edn, OUP 2017) 237ff; Phillip Hellwege, 'Effects of Termination and Restitution' in Jansen and Zimmermann (n 51) 1367.

[68] A long-lasting contribution to the civilian development of this issue was provided by Ernst von Caemmerer, '*Mortuus redhibetur*. Bemerkungen zu den Urteil BGHZ 53, 144 und 57,157', republished in Ernst von Caemmerer, *Gesammelte Schriften*, vol 1, *Rechtsvergleichung und Schuldrecht* (HG Leser ed, Tübingen 1983) 168. For the debate in the aftermath of the 2001–2 reform of the BGB, see Gerhard Wagner, 'Mortuus redhibetur im neuen Schuldrecht?' in Theodor Baums and others (eds), *Festschrift für Ulrich Hubner* (Mohr-Siebeck 2006) 591; Reinhard Zimmermann, 'Restitution after Termination for Breach of Contract: German Law and the Reform of 2002' in Andrew Burrows and Alan Rodger of Earlsferry (eds), *Mapping the Law. Essays in Memory of Peter Birks* (OUP 2006) 323.

[69] This was the case of French law. After the 2016 reform, however, the new arts 1352ff of the French Code civil introduced a specific set of rules governing restitutionary obligations (*Les restitutions*), which supplements the provisions on the recovery of undue payment now set out in arts 1302ff (*Le paiement de l'indu*). The coordination between the two sets of rules, however, is unclear. According to one view, the recovery of undue payment constitutes one species of restitutionary obligations, meaning that the general provisions here addressed would have a broader scope and would also apply to other obligations (of the same kind). See Deshayes, Genicon, and Laithier (n 39) 799ff.

[70] For a comparative analysis, see Elena Bargelli, *Il sinallagma rovesciato* (Giuffrè 2010) 228ff, 271ff; Marie Malaurie, *Les restitutions en droit civil* (Cujas 1991) 130ff. For similar questions arising from illegal contracts, see Sonja Meier, 'Restitution' in Jansen and Zimmermann (n 51) 1921.

B. Three-party cases

Under French law, where the transferee fails to perform the contract of sale entered into with the transferor, the latter is enabled to 'leapfrog' the former and sue remote recipients of their performance, or third parties that have otherwise obtained an unjustified enrichment through it.

The key example is that of the buyer of chattels who, while in default on payment owed to the seller, transfers the goods to a third party or uses them to improve a third party's property. Under French law, this third party, having (indirectly) benefited from the seller's contractual performance, is held liable in unjustified enrichment towards the seller if the buyer is bankrupt or insolvent. French courts have ruled that this claim is not ousted by the contractual action of the seller against the buyer, as the conditions of subsidiarity set forth by article 1303-3 of the Code civil are not considered to have been met. In this respect, it is claimed, on the one hand, that the alternative remedy can be brought by the claimant only against the defaulting party to the contract, but not against the defendant, who is the unjustly enriched third party; on the other hand, the buyer's insolvency is viewed not as a legal impediment (*obstacle de droit*) to the claimant's redress, as required by article 1303-3,[71] but as a factual impediment (*obstacle de fait*), which does not bar unjustified enrichment claims.

Such use of unjust enrichment in three-party cases, where the action against the third party depends on the insolvency or bankruptcy of the claimant's contractual counterparty, was streamlined by the *Cour de cassation* in accordance with the model of the *actio de in rem verso* (*utilis*) from the medieval *ius commune*.[72] This remedy was expressly provided for by only a few civil codes of Germanic countries between the late eighteenth and early nineteenth centuries,[73] but not by the French Code civil. However, a unique combination of historical circumstances and the influence of legal scholarship eventually led to its adoption in French case law.

At the beginning of the nineteenth century, the Code civil was in force on the left bank of the Rhine and in the Grand Duchy of Baden. During this time, Karl Salomo Zachariä von Lingenthal, a professor at the University of Heidelberg,

[71] See section I.B.

[72] Under Roman law, this action was classified among those of 'additional character' (*actiones adiecticiae qualitatis*). However, it was a peculiar type of *actio adiecticiae qualitatis* because its coverage was limited to the defendant's enrichment; the others were more akin to what would be now considered vicarious contractual liability, where the *pater familias* was held accountable for the debts contracted by a *filius* (son) or a *servus* (slave). See Berthold Kupisch, *Die Versionsklage. Ihre Entwicklung von der gemeinrechtlichen Theorie des 17. Jahrhunderts bis zum österreichischen Allgemeinen Bürgerlichen Gesetzbuch* (Heidelberg University 1965) 25ff; Paolo M Vecchi, *L'azione diretta* (CEDAM 1990) 200ff. For further references, see Zimmermann (n 52) 878ff; Helmut Coing, *Europäisches Privatrecht 1500 bis 1800*, vol 1, *Älteres gemeines Recht* (Beck 1985) 498ff.

[73] *Allgemeines Landrecht für die Preußischen Staaten* (§§ 262–280 I 13, *Von nützlichen Verwendungen*), enacted in 1794 (PrALR), and Austrian *Allgemeines Bürgerliches Gesetzbuch* (§§ 1041–1044, *Verwendung einer Sache zum Nutzen des Andern*), enacted in 1811 (ABGB).

taught French law to his students and, to this end, he authored a handbook to deliver his course.[74] Since Zachariä von Lingenthal viewed French law through the lens of his own legal tradition, he sought artificially to reconstruct the Germanic model of the *actio de in rem verso*, which he found absent from the Code civil. To achieve this, he combined various provisions scattered in the Code, ultimately developing a restitutionary remedy based on the *negotiorum gestio (utilis)* in three-party cases and relating not to things as such, but to their role as components of patrimony (*vindicatio rerum singularium*).

Subsequently translated into French, Zachariä's work significantly influenced the development of French law.[75] As a result of his theory, the *Cour de cassation* in 1892 applied the 'principles of the *actio de in rem verso*' for the first time,[76] affirming that this remedy was founded on equity and was not 'subject to any specific condition'.[77] About twenty years later, it clarified that, in order for such an action to be exercised, it was necessary that 'the impoverished party not have any other action based on a contract, quasi-contract, delict or quasi-delict',[78] thus establishing that the remedy was subsidiary.

Ironically, the drafters of the BGB deliberately rejected the model of the *actio de in rem verso (utilis)*,[79] opting instead to base the restitution of unjustified enrichment on a different *ius commune* model, namely the *condictio sine causa generalis*.[80] In Roman law, this remedy had been granted to redress defective transfers of benefits between the parties, but it had been reinterpreted by Savigny as based on the principle that one should not enrich themselves at the expense

[74] Karl Salomo Zachariä (von Lingenthal), *Handbuch des Französischen Civilrechts*, vol 2 (4th edn, Mohr 1837) para 440, 429ff (the first edition dates back to 1808).

[75] The French translation was carried out by Charles Aubry and Frédéric-Charles Rau and first published between 1839 and 1844. In later editions of their *Cours de droit civil français*, the three-party *actio de in rem verso* that Zachariä had conceived, while retaining its denomination, was definitively presented by Aubry and Rau as an action for unjustified enrichment in the modern sense, thus being exercisable not only in three-party but also in two-party cases.

[76] Req 15 June 1892, S 93.I.281 obs Joseph-Émile Labbé (so-called *affaire Boudier*, or case *du merchand des engrais*). A merchant had sold chemical fertilizer to the tenant of a property, who, on the expiry of his contract, had become insolvent. The owner of the property had harvested the natural fruits that had been produced through the use of that fertilizer. The *Cour de cassation* allowed the merchant to claim restitution of the owner's enrichment thus obtained. See Henri and Léon Mazeaud, Jean Mazeaud, and François Chabas, *Leçons de droit civil*, vol 2/1, *Obligations-théorie générale* (9th edn, Montchrestien 1998) 836ff, and for comparative analysis, Whittaker (n 10) 418–19, 433–34.

[77] Shortly beforehand, the *Conseil d'État* had already ruled in this direction. For more information, see Posez (n 8) 190.

[78] Cass civ, 12 May 1914, S 1918.I.41, obs Éliacin Naquet (so-called *arrêt Clayette*); Cass civ, 2 March 1915, D 1920.I.102 (so-called *arrêt Brianaut*). Also in this connection, the *Conseil d'État* had already ruled in the same direction, and for reference see Posez (n 8) 190, n 14. For comparative analysis, see Whittaker, 'The Law of Obligations' (n 10) 433.

[79] *Motive zu dem Entwurf eines Bürgerlichen Gesetzbuches für das Deutsche Reich*, in *Die gesamten Materialen zum Bürgerlichen Gesetzbuch für das Deutsche Reich*, vol 2, *Recht der Schuldverhältnisse* (Benno Mugdan ed, von Decker 1899) para 761, 487ff.

[80] Zimmermann (n 52) 857ff, 871ff.

of another.[81] In line with its original model, the remedy still required a direct transfer of assets between the two parties, thus not covering cases of so-called indirect enrichment.

The requirement of immediacy of the enrichment (*Unmittelsbarkeitserforder nis*) has been explicitly addressed in German case law in order to identify both the impoverished party entitled to bring a restitutionary claim and the enriched party against whom that claim could be brought. Ultimately, this requirement enforces a prohibition against 'leapfrogging' (*Durchgriffsverbot*),[82] indirectly protecting the enriched party from what would ultimately amount to a private penalty.[83] In common law jurisdictions, too, the existence of a contract under which a benefit has been transferred bars a claim in unjustified enrichment against a third party who may have benefited from the contractual performance of either party.[84] This remains true even if the other party to the contract is bankrupt or insolvent and thus not worth suing.[85]

III. Subsidiarity of Unjustified Enrichment vis-à-vis Property

A. Restitution of an asset and vindication of a right

(i) Personal and proprietary remedies

Both common law and civil law jurisdictions generally respond to unjustified enrichment by granting the impoverished party a personal remedy, aimed at the recovery of the asset that the enriched party has obtained at the former's expense.[86]

[81] Friedrich Carl von Savigny, *System des heutigen römischen Rechts*, vol 5, *Beylage*, XIV, *Die Condictionen* (Veit 1840) 525ff. See Zimmermann (n 52) 887ff, 900–901.

[82] For a comparative analysis, see Reinhard Zimmermann, 'Unjustified Enrichment: The Modern Civilian Approach' (1995) 15 Oxford Journal of Legal Studies 403, 408ff; Birke Häcker, *Consequences of Impaired Consent Transfers. A Structural Comparison of English and German Law* (Hart Publishing 2013) 215ff.

[83] An exception can be found in § 822 BGB, which provides as follows: '*Duty to surrender of third parties.* If the recipient bestows the benefit obtained on a third person at no charge, then that third person is obliged to surrender the benefit as if they had received the benefit from the creditor without legal grounds, to the extent that as a result of the bestowal the duty of the recipient to surrender the enrichment is excluded' (translation taken from https://www.gesetze-im-internet.de/englisch_bgb/englisch_bgb.html#p4188). This provision, however, does not apply to restitution after termination for breach of contract.

[84] *Pan Ocean Shipping Co Ltd v Creditcorp Ltd (The Trident Beauty)* [1994] 1 WLR 161, [1994] All ER 470 (HL).

[85] *MacDonald Dickens and Macklin v Costello* [2011] EWCA Civ 930, [2012] QB 244. See Virgo (n 49) 162ff.

[86] If unjustified enrichment is a proper source of obligations, the defendant is to be held liable to pay damages for a failure to make restitution. In common law jurisdictions, however, this assumption is challenged by the view that the defendant's liability would depend on the court making an order, rather than arising from a primary duty. See Stephen A Smith, 'Unjust Enrichment: Nearer to Tort than Contract' in Robert Chambers, Charles Mitchell, and James Penner (eds), *Philosophical Foundations of the Law of Unjust Enrichment* (OUP 2009) 181, 188.

Yet, the object of restitution thus granted to the claimant differs substantially between the civil law and the common law traditions.[87]

In civilian jurisdictions, the enriched party is first and foremost obliged to return the asset unjustly obtained,[88] including any secondary benefits derived from it,[89] and therefore the restitution that is granted to the claimant is primarily specific or in kind.[90] Only to the extent that such restitution is not possible either from the start,[91] or due to circumstances that have subsequently arisen,[92] is the defendant obliged to pay a sum of money representing the objective value of their unjustified enrichment, and in that case the restitution that is awarded is that value.[93] The claimant is also entitled to interest at the statutory rate, insofar as the defendant is not considered to be in good faith, whether because they knew of the lack of legal cause or because the action for surrender has become pending against them.[94]

By contrast, the personal remedy (action *in personam*) granted by common law jurisdictions to the claimant is a pecuniary order, by which the defendant is liable to pay the value of the benefit to the claimant rather than return the benefit itself,

[87] For a comparative analysis, see Whittaker (n 10) 421; Daniel Visser, 'Unjustified Enrichment in Comparative Perspective' in Mathias Reimann and Reinhard Zimmermann (eds), *The Oxford Handbook of Comparative Law* (2nd edn, OUP 2019) 969, 980ff.

[88] § 812(1)(1) BGB, and also § 816(1)(1) BGB, all the more in connection with § 818(2) BGB.

[89] § 818(1)(1) BGB; art 1352-3 Code civil. However, where the claimant is the owner of property and seeks restitution of secondary benefits (*Nutzungen, fruits, frutti*) that the defendant acquired from the thing held in their possession, the law of unjustified enrichment does not apply. Traditionally, civil codes have separately addressed restitution between the owner of property and the possessor, as well as damages that the latter may owe to the former, and these rules fall within the law of property (and possession) (§§ 987–993 BGB; arts 549–550 Code civil; arts 1148–1152 Codice civile). This conceptual framework is particularly developed in German law, where legal scholarship has added extensive details, ultimately articulating a complex legal relationship between the owner and the possessor (*Eigentümer-Besitzer-Verhältnis*), to which unjustified enrichment is subsidiary: for the detail, see Dieter Reuter and Michael Martinek, *Ungerechtfertigte Bereicherung*, vol 2.2 (2nd edn, Mohr Siebeck 2016) 483ff. However, this is largely an unnecessary and excessively complex overlap, as the restitution and compensation obligations considered here are, ultimately, fully compatible with the general rules on unjustified enrichment (and *negotiorum gestio*). For this critique on the projects of European model laws, see Reinhard Zimmermann, 'The Present State of European Private Law' (2009) 57 American Journal of Comparative Law 479, 483–84 and 498–99.

[90] It follows that, in civil law jurisdictions, the claimant is entitled to benefit from any increase in the value of the asset, subject to the reimbursement of (certain) expenses incurred by the defendant in the meanwhile. The distinction between necessary and useful expenses generally matters, with the reimbursement of useful expenses typically being of a lesser magnitude.

[91] eg where the thing to be returned to the claimant is not tangible.

[92] eg where the thing to be returned to the claimant has, in the meantime, been disposed or destroyed by the defendant.

[93] § 818(2) BGB; art 1352 Code civil; art 2037 Codice civile. The defence of change of position is generally allowed to the defendant, provided that they are in good faith.

[94] Under German law, the connection between § 818(4) BGB and § 819(1) BGB establishes that, if the defendant was in good faith at the time of receiving unjustified enrichment but later became aware of the lack of legal grounds for it, interest at the statutory rate is owed from the moment of this supervening knowledge. In contrast, art 1352-7 Code civil and art 2033 Codice civile seem to rule that bad faith, arising after the receipt of the benefit, does not make the defendant liable for interest (*mala fides superveniens non nocet*), though they are held responsible for interest from the date of the judgment against the defendant. The French and Italian approach is thus based on the assumption that bad faith on the part of the defendant and judgment against the defendant do not need to be treated alike.

and therefore the restitution is not specific or in kind, but equivalent (or monetary).[95] Additionally, (pre-judgment) interest is not owed on the basis of unjust enrichment,[96] but 'in proceedings (whenever instituted) before the High Court for the recovery of a debt or damages there may be included in any sum for which judgment is given simple interest, at such rate as the court thinks fit or as rules of court may provide'.[97]

On a different note, it must be said that in civil codes, unjustified enrichment qualifies as a (general) source of obligations, which, next to contract and torts, creates a relationship of creditor and debtor between the parties.[98] Hence, the impoverished party is entitled to claim for restitution (be it specific or equivalent) only from the recipient of their asset, and not from any third party, and the claimant's credit is unsecured and does not generally take priority over the rights of other creditors of the defendant. Civil law jurisdictions also grant restitutionary remedies that operate *in rem*, that is, that are proprietary, but these are not grounded in unjustified enrichment in a substantive sense. While unjustified enrichment may be recognized as the rationale behind the rules governing proprietary restitutionary remedies, it is widely assumed that such remedies are provided by, and belong to, the law of property and are aimed at the vindication of the claimant's rights. The distinction between personal restitutionary remedies (governed by the law of unjustified enrichment) and proprietary restitutionary remedies (governed by the law of property) prevents civilian jurisdictions from establishing a unified framework of restitution.

By contrast, in common law jurisdictions it has been argued that unjustified enrichment can give rise not only to personal, but also to proprietary remedies,[99] and this view appears to be supported by a considerable number of authorities that are seen as foundational to the law of restitution, with *Lipkin Gorman* being the

[95] Virgo (n 49) 4. For a different view, see Robert Chambers, 'Two Kinds of Enrichment' in Chambers, Mitchell, and Penner (n 86) 242.

[96] See *Prudential Assurance Co Ltd v Commissioners for Her Majesty's Revenue and Customs* [2018] UKSC 39, [2019] AC 929, which departed from *Sempra Metals Ltd v Inland Revenue Commissioners* [2007] UKHL 34, [2008] 1 AC 561, which, in turn, had overruled *Westdeutsche Landesbank Girozentrale v Islington LBC* [1996] UKHL 12, [1996] AC 669. For an account of the developments in case law on this issue and some criticism on its current state, see Virgo (n 49) 32–36; Andrew Burrows, *The Law of Restitution* (3rd edn, OUP 2011) 21ff; Charles Mitchell, 'Recovery of Compound Interest as Restitution or Damages' (2008) 71 Modern Law Review 290; Tatiana Cutts, 'Use Value and Interest in Unjust Enrichment' (2019) 3 Lloyd's Maritime and Commercial Law Quarterly 410. It remains uncertain whether the same rule applies to equitable restitutionary remedy, such as an account of profits for breach of a fiduciary duty, or whether, in these cases a court still holds the discretionary power to award (compound) interest.

[97] Senior Courts Act 1981 (UK), s 35A.

[98] Unjustified enrichment is often regarded as the third pillar of the law of obligations, as it plays a relatively minor role compared to contract and tort law and has historically developed much more recently. See section V.

[99] Peter Birks, *Unjust Enrichment* (2nd edn, OUP 2005) 33; Peter Birks, 'Misnomer' in William E Cornish and others (eds), *Restitution. Past, Present and Future. Essays in Honour of Gareth Jones* (Hart Publishing 1998) 1; Burrows (n 96) 172ff.

first and most authoritative case,[100] followed by *Chase Manhattan Bank.*[101] Except for a line of cases involving the remedies of subrogation, however, this analysis of English law has been fiercely contested by some scholars,[102] who argue that the proprietary restitutionary remedies at stake are not based on unjustified enrichment as a cause of action, but on the vindication of the claimant's rights. As far as the reversal of unjustified enrichment is concerned, the law of restitution on this view provides only personal remedies, whereas the restitutionary remedies that operate *in rem*—that is, proprietary remedies—are available only to claimants who have 'retained' or 'obtained' a proprietary interest, whether at law or in equity.[103] Thus, these remedies would then aim not at the reversal of the defendant's unjustified enrichment, but at the vindication of the claimant's property.

In civil law jurisdictions, cases such as *Lipkin Gorman*, *Sinclair*, or *Chase Manhattan Bank* are typically concerned with issues of unjustified enrichment and do not involve vindication of the claimant's property rights. This is because the claimant does not retain ownership of the property and, upon losing it, does not acquire an equitable title. Civil law systems do not recognize legal devices such as constructive trusts and the like, and therefore they do not allow remedies that operate *in rem* in such cases, but only remedies that operate *in personam*. In a case such as *Lipkin Gorman*, therefore, the money unlawfully withdrawn from the joint bank account and gambled away at a casino by an (unfaithful) employee could not have been recovered by the employer on the grounds of ownership. Although it was the claimant who had deposited that money, the employer had irrevocably lost any title to the ownership of that sum and therefore the right to claim restitution.[104]

In respect of the common law as such, it must be emphasized that the very foundations of the law of unjust enrichment have been laid down by the House of Lords in *Fibrosa* and *Lipkin Gorman*, by equating this body of general rules with that governing restitution,[105] and this approach has subsequently been endorsed by a

[100] *Lipkin Gorman (a firm) v Karpnale Ltd* [1991] 2 AC 548.

[101] *Chase Manhattan Bank v Israel-British Bank* [1981] Ch 105. Furthermore, it is noteworthy that some prominent scholars, such as Peter Birks, 'Restitution and Resulting Trust' in Stephen R Goldstein (ed), *Equity and Contemporary Legal Developments* (Hebrew University of Jerusalem 1992) 335, argue that while the outcomes of certain cases traditionally addressed in terms of constructive or resulting trusts are correct, they should be reinterpreted as awarding a proprietary remedy based on unjust enrichment, and notable examples include *Sinclair v Brougham* [1914] AC 398. This could be also the case of *Westdeutsche Landesbank Girozentrale* (n 96), as suggested also by *Goff and Jones: The Law of Unjust Enrichment* (n 32) paras 8-67–8-77, but for a different view see Virgo (n 49) 18ff and 652ff. For further reference, see Kit Barker, 'Rescuing Remedialism in Unjust Enrichment Law: Why Remedies are Right' (1998) 57 Cambridge Law Journal 301.

[102] See Virgo (n 49) 14ff.

[103] See however section III.A.(iii).

[104] See Sonja Meier, 'Bona fide Purchase as a Defence in Unjust Enrichment' in Andrew Dyson, James Goudkamp, and Frederick Wilmot-Smith (eds), *Defences in Unjust Enrichment* (Hart Publishing 2016) 255.

[105] See section V. The 'quadration' of restitution and unjust enrichment was initially advocated by Peter Birks, *An Introduction to the Law of Restitution* (rev edn, OUP 1989) 26.

number of authorities.[106] This approach has been clearly accompanied and supported by influential scholarship in this field,[107] so much so that today it can be said that, according to the perspective labelled as 'orthodox',[108] restitution law is the same as the law of unjustified enrichment.[109]

However, this issue remains highly controversial, not least because while the outcome in what is perhaps the leading common law precedent in this area, *Lipkin Gorman*, has been subsequently affirmed, the House of Lords has reinterpreted the restitutionary remedy in proprietary terms.[110] Several leading scholars have also argued that the 'orthodox' view is too simplistic and that the law of restitution is not based solely on the reversal of unjustified enrichment, but also on two other principles: preventing wrongdoers from benefiting from their wrong, and vindicating property rights with which the defendant has interfered.[111]

Yet, this three-pronged approach may appear too eclectic and heterogenous to ensure the integrity of the law of restitution. Whereas the two principles of the reversal of unjustified enrichment and disgorgement of profits from a wrongdoer can be rather easily seen as akin and thus belonging to one area of the legal system,[112] the vindication of the claimant's rights is, as such, clearly not amenable to a common denominator with them, unless 'restitution' is used in a merely descriptive sense.

It must, therefore, be acknowledged that the unity of the law of restitution is properly based on the principle of unjust enrichment,[113] although it undoubtedly includes some specific variations (most importantly, for wrongs).[114] This unified framework was developed by judges and scholars over the course of recent decades,[115] and its disruption would undermine the integrity and the coherence of

[106] Notable examples include *Woolwich Equitable Building Society v Inland Revenue Commissioners* [1993] AC 70, 170 (Lord Goff); and *Bank of Cyprus UK Ltd v Menelaou* [2015] UKSC 66, [2016] AC 176.

[107] Birks, *Unjust Enrichment* (n 99) 4.

[108] Virgo (n 49) 7.

[109] Birks, *Unjust Enrichment* (n 99) 33; Andrew Burrows, 'In Defence of Unjust Enrichment' (2019) 78 Cambridge Law Journal 521; Burrows (n 96) 172ff; *Goff and Jones: The Law of Unjust Enrichment* (n 32) paras 37-01ff.

[110] See section III.A.(iii).

[111] Virgo (n 49) 8. This view has been extensively criticized by Burrows (n 96) 13.

[112] Birks (n 105) 4–5.

[113] Indeed, the foundational relevance of this assumption becomes particularly evident in the recent radical theoretical revision of this subject achieved by Stevens (n 59) 3ff, who, in rejecting unjust enrichment as its overarching principle, concludes (quite consistently with his premises) that 'there is no unified area of law called "restitution" or "unjust enrichment"'. For a critical and confrontational perspective on Stevens' work, see Andrew Burrows, 'A View from the Orthodox Camp' (Symposium held at Keble College, Oxford, October 2023). See also Burrows (n 109) 521.

[114] Birks (n 105) 26, who, however, subsequently changed his approach and argued in favour of a more marked distinction between restitution of unjust enrichment and restitution for wrongs. See Peter Birks, 'Unjust Enrichment and Wrongful Enrichment' (2001) 79 Texas Law Review 1767; Birks, 'Misnomer' (n 99) 1ff; Birks, *Unjust Enrichment* (n 99) 20ff.

[115] For a detailed account and reference, see Andrew Burrows, 'Unjust Enrichment and Restitution' in Andrew S Gold and others (eds), *The Oxford Handbook of the New Private Law* (OUP 2020) 293; Burrows (n 96) 5ff.

the law of restitution, thus dismantling a feature that has proven invaluable for enhancing understanding of the legal system and guiding its evolution in a consistent and reasoned manner.[116] Moreover, the unified construction of the law of restitution, while fully expressing the particularities of the common law,[117] facilitates meaningful comparison with the civilian tradition, thereby promoting mutual enrichment and improvement between the two families of legal systems.

(ii) Civil law jurisdictions

In civil law jurisdictions, it is widely agreed that, to the extent that the impoverished party holds title to the asset unjustly obtained by the enriched party, the former are able to vindicate their right (proprietary restitution) and, alternatively or concurrently, to claim in unjustified enrichment (personal restitution). In particular, the claimant can seek surrender by means of a proprietary remedy (*rei vindicatio*) or, concurrently, restitution of the asset by means of a personal remedy (unjustified enrichment), insofar as the requirements of both remedies are met.[118] If the return of the thing is not possible in kind, personal restitution is to be made in monetary terms (equivalent to its use value),[119] but in either case the defendant in an unjustified enrichment claim (unless in bad faith) can raise a defence of change of position.

The scope of the *condictio possessionis* is however different depending on whether the system of transferring property is causal or abstract.[120] Where such system is causal, the voidness or avoidance/rescission of the sale, or gift, between the contracting parties does not *per se* prevent the claimant from holding title to the asset that is in the defendant's possession. The defendant has to surrender the asset to the claimant both on the basis of the law of property (proprietary restitution) and of unjustified enrichment (personal restitution),[121] but the claimant will preferably opt for the latter in any case where the defendant is the first recipient of

[116] Burrows (n 96) 5, 9ff, but in conclusion also Virgo (n 49) 20. Cf the different view of Stevens (n 59) 9, who contends that: 'The reality [of the law(s) of restitution] is of different kinds of claim—some are the subject of litigation every day, whilst others have only ever arisen in a few cases and so are of limited practical importance. Many are intimately related to other areas of law that a work of this size cannot adequately encompass (eg all of contract, Equity, property, and agency law)'. For similar scepticism on the unity of restitution (or unjust enrichment law), see Steve Hedley, 'Unjust Enrichment. Looking for a Role' in Warren Swain and Sagi Peari (eds), *Rethinking Unjust Enrichment: History, Sociology, Doctrine, and Theory* (OUP 2023) 275.

[117] Notably, the title of the leading book by Goff and Jones, initially being 'The Law of Restitution', has been changed in 'The Law of Unjust Enrichment'. For arguments against this change, however, see Burrows (n 96) 11–12.

[118] See section III.A.(i).

[119] If the defendant committed a tort, however, and is, therefore, liable for damages, under French and Italian law the victim is not able to bring a claim in unjustified enrichment, due to the statutory subsidiarity of this remedy vis-à-vis compensation. See section IV.

[120] For a comparative analysis, see Rodolfo Sacco, 'Introduzione al diritto comparato' in Rodolfo Sacco (ed), *Trattato di diritto comparato* (UTET 1992) 106; Uwe Kischel, *Comparative Law* (OUP 2019) 273ff.

[121] See section III.A.(i).

the benefit: the *probatio diabolica* of the claimant's title, which affects *rei vindicatio*, will be thus avoided, and the burden of proof lying on the claimant will be more manageable. Instead, if restitution of an asset is claimed from a remote recipient or another party who indirectly benefited from the claimant's performance, no personal action can be generally brought against them, since an obligation to surrender the asset arose only against the first recipient.[122]

Conversely, the question arises as to whether personal restitution is owed when title to an asset passes to the defendant, or when, even though it was not voluntarily transferred to them by the claimant, the defendant is a *bona fide* purchaser. While this mechanism of a *non domino* purchase rarely operates in respect of land, it is frequent with chattels, and the question of whether the previous owner is entitled to a claim in unjustified enrichment is generally to be answered in the negative, since insofar as title to an asset passes to the defendant, the corresponding enrichment cannot be said to be unjustified, unless otherwise determined by law (as is the case with money, whose title is peculiarly fragile as it can be readily lost, either through mixing or by a transfer of currency).

The concurrent use of the *rei vindicatio* and a claim in unjustified enrichment has inevitably less traction under German law, insofar as German law adopts an abstract system of transferring property. In such a system, the voidness or the avoidance/rescission of the sale, or gift, between the contracting parties do not, *per se*, prevent the title from passing to the defendant, and therefore no proprietary remedy will be granted to the claimant, but they will necessarily have to bring an action in unjustified enrichment.[123] According to the celebrated definition by Savigny, the action in unjustified enrichment is a substitute of *rei vindicatio* (*Vindikationsersatz*), insofar as the latter is of no use to the claimant.[124] Since only personal restitution is owed, the claimant cannot pursue a claim against a remote recipient of their performance or anyone else who indirectly benefited from the claimant's performance, and the claimant is treated like any other unsecured creditor of the defendant, that is, the initial recipient, particularly in the event of their bankruptcy or insolvency.[125] It remains the case that no personal restitution is generally owed insofar as the defendant purchases *a non domino*, that is, acquires title that the law of property commands be superior and beneficial (§ 932 BGB).

[122] However, a personal restitutionary claim can be granted against a remote recipient who did not provide value for the benefit received under a void or avoided/rescinded contract. For a comparative analysis, see Birke Häcker, 'Direct and Indirect Enrichment at the Claimant's Expense in Three-Party Cases' in Mitchell and Swadling (n 2) 31. See section III.A.(i), especially with reference to § 822 BGB (at n 83).

[123] Birke Häcker, 'Contract and Conveyance: The Further Repercussions of Different Transfer Systems' in John Cartwright and Ángel M López y López (eds), *Property and Contract: Comparative Reflections on English Law and Spanish Law* (Hart Publishing 2021) 114.

[124] Savigny (n 81) 525ff.

[125] See section III.A.(i).

(iii) Common law jurisdictions

On the footing that the claimant retains their title to an asset in the defendant's possession, they are entitled to vindicate their right and make use of a proprietary remedy, consisting either in a mechanism of recovery,[126] or of payment of the asset's value *in lieu*.[127]

However, the question arises whether, as strongly advocated for by some scholars in this field,[128] such orders, which are also available against third parties, can be appropriately described as remedies for unjustified enrichment. According to other scholars, that question should be answered in the negative, since if the claimant retains title to an asset in the defendant's possession, they are simply entitled to vindicate their right, and there should be no need to resort to the principle of reversing unjust enrichment.[129] First and foremost this is because, as a matter of principle, property rights are of such importance that they deserve a particular protection,[130] but also (and accordingly) for practical reasons, if the claimant vindicates their right, no defence of change of position can be pleaded successfully by the defendant.[131] In addition, the requirement that the enrichment be 'at the expense of the claimant' would not be met.[132]

Starting from the leading case of *Lipkin Gorman*,[133] it seems that the common law grants the claimant a personal right of restitution, based on the law of unjustified enrichment in such cases.[134] Yet, the reasoning behind this authority has been debated among scholars,[135] and while its outcome has gained consensus, subsequent authorities have rewritten and reinterpreted its reasoning in terms of proprietary remedies.[136] Various compromise solutions have also been proposed,

[126] However, it is commonly acknowledged that the common law, unlike the civil law, lacks any general proprietary remedy to enable the claimant to recover property from the defendant.

[127] Virgo (n 49) 701ff.

[128] Birks, *Unjust Enrichment* (n 99) 33; Burrows (n 96) 172ff; *Goff and Jones: The Law of Unjust Enrichment* (n 32) paras 37-01ff.

[129] Virgo (n 49) 175. For reference, see Peter Jaffey, *Private Law and Property Claims* (Hart Publishing 2023) 211ff.

[130] Virgo (n 49) 19.

[131] ibid.

[132] William Swadling, 'Ignorance and Unjust Enrichment: The Problem of Title' (2008) 28 Oxford Journal of Legal Studies 627. However, for a different view, see Peter Birks, '"At the Expense of the Claimant": Direct and Indirect Enrichment in English Law' in Johnston and Zimmermann (n 10) 493.

[133] See section III.A.(i).

[134] The explanation given by Lord Goff is that the cash withdrawn from the claimant's bank account by a dishonest agent, who became owner of it, represented the traceable substitute for the chose in action of which the claimant was owner. For some criticism on this opinion, however, see *Goff and Jones: The Law of Unjust Enrichment* (n 32) paras 8-87 and 8-98–8-103.

[135] See Virgo (n 49) 703–704, and Lionel Smith, 'Simplifying Claims to Traceable Proceeds' (2009) 125 Law Quarterly Review 338.

[136] *Foskett v McKeown* [2001] 1 AC 102, 115 (misapplication of trust fund), and in the wake of this authority, *Armstrong v Winnington Networks Ltd* [2012] EWHC 10 (Ch), [2013] Ch 156 (transfer of intangible asset by a third party who, by means of an email phishing, usurped the claimant's authentication procedures). For a critique on (the reasoning of) these rulings, see *Goff and Jones: The Law of Unjust Enrichment* (n 32) paras 8-21–8-26, but for an alternative viewpoint, see Virgo (n 49) 16–17.

suggesting that the remedy is based on a 'proprietary' or 'title' link underlying unjustified enrichment.

Concurrently, in cases of rescission of contract, it remains uncertain whether the claimant has first to rescind the contract in order to be revested with the title they previously held, or whether an 'immediate interest' (under a trust) remains with them from the outset—and if so, in which cases.[137] As a rule, unjustified enrichment governs when the claimant seeks to recover the exchange or use value of their property.[138] In any case, a claim can lie to recover (restitutionary) damages for the defendant's trespass to the claimant's land, or for the former's conversion of or trespass to the latter's goods, and so on. If that is the case, it remains questionable whether a personal claim in unjustified enrichment lies as an alternative, without the need to prove a wrong committed by the defendant. A negative answer tends to prevail, particularly with regard to land.[139]

In some cases, furthermore, the claimant acquires an equitable interest in the asset that is now in the defendant's hands, and this equitable interest is enforced by a (constructive or resulting) trust, or by a lien, which is imposed by the law. In those cases, the claimant's equitable interest in the asset generally binds all subsequent transferees other than *bona fide* purchasers for value of a legal interest without notice,[140] unless overreached by later dispositions. The property is thus recoverable and traceable in equity, meaning that the beneficiary can invoke the rules of following and tracing to identify property either in the hands of the trustee (following) or in the hands of a subsequent recipient as representing their original property.[141] Unless the recipient is a *bona fide* purchaser, the claimant can then obtain an order for conveyance of title, obliging the defendant to surrender the property in question. In other cases of misappropriated assets that have been traceably used to pay secured debts owed to a third party, the claimant is entitled

[137] Birke Häcker, 'Minority and Unjust Enrichment Defences' in Dyson, Goudkamp, and Wilmot-Smith (n 104) 195; Häcker (n 82) 100ff, 215ff; Birke Häcker, 'Proprietary Restitution after Impaired Consent Transfers: A Generalised Power Model' (2009) 68 Cambridge Law Journal 324; William Swadling, 'Rescission, Property and the Common Law' (2005) 121 Law Quarterly Review 123. See Virgo (n 49) 26–27.

[138] As stems from the classic dictum of Lord Mansfield in *Hambly v Trott* (1776) 1 Cowp 371, 375; 98 ER 1136, 1138: '[I]f a man take a horse from another, and bring him back again; an action for trespass will not lie against his executor; though it would against him; but an action for the use and hire of the horse will lie against the executor.'

[139] *Armstrong v Winnington Networks Ltd* [2012] EWHC 10 (Ch), [2013] Ch 156. For a critique, see *Goff and Jones: The Law of Unjust Enrichment* (n 32) paras 8-43–8-52.

[140] *Goff and Jones: The Law of Unjust Enrichment* (n 32) para 38-12.

[141] Where unauthorized substitutes for the original trust assets are in the hands of a third party (who is neither a trustee nor another fiduciary), the leading authority is *Foskett* (n 136). In that case, the majority of the House of Lords emphatically rejected the application of the law of unjustified enrichment, holding instead that the claimants could elect between (proportionate) beneficial ownership and an equitable lien—whichever was more advantageous. However, according to *Goff and Jones: The Law of Unjust Enrichment* (n 32) paras 8-154–8-165, the decision in *Foskett* could also be expressed in terms of unjust enrichment.

to the equitable remedy of subrogation to the discharged creditor's extinguished security interest and associated rights.[142]

Additionally, in cases in which someone else's property is transferred by a third party who thus is in breach of their fiduciary duty to the former, knowing recipients are personally liable.[143] It is now suggested that this personal liability for 'knowing receipt' is a form of personal liability in unjustified enrichment.[144]

Knowing receipt arises in numerous cases of fiduciary misconduct,[145] including misapplications not only of trust assets by trustees,[146] but also of other fiduciaries,[147] such as directors misusing corporate assets.[148] Some authorities hold that, in addition to being liable for 'knowing receipt', the defendant is also liable for being unjustly enriched: unlike the equitable liability, which is fault-based, this additional liability in unjust enrichment would be strict (subject to defences), not depending 'upon knowledge that the receipt [was] improper in some way'.[149] A parallel has been drawn with the '*Re Diplock* personal claim': the charities to which the money forming part of a deceased's estate was wrongly distributed by the executor were held liable for the restitution of the sum they respectively gained, though subject to the proviso that the claimants (ie next-of-kin entitled under the rules of intestate succession) have first exhausted their claims against the personal representatives.

Some scholars not only emphasize precedents of this kind,[150] but also seek to expand their scope, aiming to establish general rules governing the concurrence of the remedies involved. In this regard, it is argued that, where the trustee or the board's director has acted outside their authority, their 'lack of authority' makes the defendant liable for the restitution of what they have received at the expense of the claimant, ie the beneficiary or principal. As far as the '*Re Diplock* personal claim' is concerned, however, several features of the authority do not square with those of unjustified enrichment, and it is difficult to understand whether it is possible (and desirable) to reconcile them.[151] This applies especially to the condition

[142] For reference, see *Goff and Jones: The Law of Unjust Enrichment* (n 32) paras 8-142–8-148.

[143] For a recent development, see *Byers and others v Saudi National Bank* [2023] UKSC 51, [2024] AC 1191.

[144] *Goff and Jones: The Law of Unjust Enrichment* (n 32) paras 8-199–8-200. For a different view, see Lionel Smith, 'W(h)ither Knowing Receipt?' (1998) 114 Law Quarterly Review 394.

[145] See *Goff and Jones: The Law of Unjust Enrichment* (n 32) paras 8-166–8-180.

[146] For reference, see ibid paras 8-181–8-192.

[147] ibid paras 8-193–8-195.

[148] The directors are not technically trustees, but in the common law they are deemed to be subject to liabilities and duties equivalent to those available against trustees. See ibid paras 8-27ff.

[149] *Relfo Ltd (In Liquidation) v Varsani* [2012] EWHC 2168 (Ch), [2014] EWCA Civ 360, [2015] BCLC 14. See *Goff and Jones: The Law of Unjust Enrichment* (n 32) paras 8-75 and 8-103; Virgo (n 49) 714ff.

[150] *Goff and Jones: The Law of Unjust Enrichment* (n 32) paras 8-132–8-141.

[151] For a positive answer, see Lionel D Smith, 'Three-Party Restitution: A Critique of Birks' Theory of Interpretative Subtraction' (1991) 11 Oxford Journal of Legal Studies 481, esp 487ff. For the different view subsequently taken by the same author, however, see Lionel Smith, 'Unjust Enrichment, Property and the Structure of Trusts' (2000) 116 Law Quarterly Review 412. On his revisited opinion, see the criticism by *Goff and Jones: The Law of Unjust Enrichment* (n 32) fn 266 (para 8-125). See also

that the claimant must first exhaust their remedies against the personal representatives responsible for the improper distribution and, further to that, that that claim is limited to such amounts, to the extent that they could not be recovered from the personal representatives.[152]

It remains uncertain, therefore, whether the strict liability of the recipient of a trust asset constitutes a general rule and how it relates to the '*Re Diplock* personal claim'. Additionally, it remains uncertain whether either claim appropriately falls within the scope of unjustified enrichment, and if so, whether it can be generalized.

B. Two-party cases

With regard to common law jurisdictions, it has been argued that unjustified enrichment would enable the transferor to repudiate or reverse the title acquired by the transferee of a right. Hence, this remedy would be reflective of restorative or corrective justice,[153] challenging the fundamental values of choice and consent that underpin the liberal and democratic political tradition of Anglo-American countries. Therefore, unjustified enrichment should be characterized as subsidiary, operating in the interstitial spaces between the doctrines of contract and property, as well as of torts, since they are imbued with the primacy of choice and consent. The grounds for restitution of unjustified enrichment should be confined to the defectiveness of the transferor's subjective consent,[154] as would be the case with lack of capacity, mistake or coercion, or failure of basis (or of consideration).[155]

The starting assumption of the foregoing is that a characteristic value of Anglo-American law is freedom of choice, so that once consent has been given, it can no longer be challenged or revoked. It follows that, in the province of private law, the law of contract (and other voluntary obligations), the law of tort, and the law of property play a primary role because they are based precisely on the primacy of consent. Conversely, unjustified enrichment would be based on an antagonistic value, that of corrective justice, and therefore should be restrictively contained in cases where the other areas of private law explicitly or implicitly allow the transfer of a right to be challenged by the transferee.

Timothy Liau, *Standing in Private Law: Powers of Enforcement in the Law of Obligations and Trusts* (OUP 2023) 141ff.

[152] *Goff and Jones: The Law of Unjust Enrichment* (n 32) paras 8-123–8-126.
[153] ibid paras 8-127–8-131.
[154] This is not the terminology used by the authors, who instead refer to the presence of objective consent, but not subjective consent. This choice of terminology is probably aimed at ensuring consistency with the traditional, corrective-justice based understanding of unjustified enrichment.
[155] Grantham and Rickett (n 18) 279–80.

These preliminary assumptions—namely, the primacy of freedom of choice in private law and corrective justice as the value underpinning unjustified enrichment—will not be discussed in this chapter, as they appear uncontroversial and applicable across legal systems within the Western legal tradition, although they are framed in terms which are intended to be lenient to the 'unjust factor' approach as opposed to the 'lack of legal basis' approach, which is seen as redolent of the civilian tradition. More importantly for present purposes, it must be noted that some developments of the common law of unjustified enrichment of the past decades, both in theory and practice, are surreptitiously abandoned or, even worse, disregarded, and the 'unjust factors' are identified in strict accordance with the list Lord Mansfield drew up in *Moses v Macferlan*:[156] capacity,[157] mistake or coercion,[158] failure of consideration (or of basis).[159]

Ultimately, the stance under consideration is based on a concept of unjust enrichment that is excessively narrow on several counts, as it allows a restitutionary claim only to the extent that the defendant is vested with a right to enjoy the possession.[160] This assumption necessarily implies that the asset, or title to the asset, belonged to the claimant, who voluntarily transferred it to the defendant. In light of the foregoing, the law of unjustified enrichment would not apply where the 'subtraction' of wealth to the detriment of the claimant results from a conduct of the defendant, not of the claimant themselves (or of a third party).[161]

This view is certainly foreign to the civilian tradition, according to which restitution of unjustified enrichment is owed not only by the recipient of an undue performance from the claimant, but also where the defendant has otherwise been (unjustly) enriched 'at the claimant's expense', whether by their own conduct or through the intervention of a third party. In the common law context, a line of authorities supports the view that a claim in unjustified enrichment may lie where the defendant has received an asset, or title to an asset, that did not previously belong to the claimant and that, *a fortiori*, cannot have been voluntarily transferred by the claimant to the defendant[162]—as is the case when the defendant engages

[156] *Moses v Macferlan* (1760) 2 Burr 1005. See Grantham and Rickett (n 18) 277.

[157] Grantham and Rickett (n 18) 279.

[158] ibid 280.

[159] ibid.

[160] ibid 282. In case of money, the transfer of possession to the defendant (either by the claimant or by intermediation of a third party) generally leads to the (immediate or subsequent) loss of the claimant's title, either by mixing, or by transfer as currency (for civil law jurisdictions, see also section III.A.(iii)). This is the reason why the action for money had and received historically arose; it was specifically used for the restitution of sums of money paid under a contract that was void or rescinded: see John Baker, 'The History of Quasi-Contract in English Law' in William E Cornish and others (eds), *Restitution. Past, Present and Future. Essays in Honour of Gareth Jones* (Hart Publishing 1998) 37, 49, fn 56.

[161] Restitution for wrongs, as such, will not be specifically addressed in this chapter.

[162] A further—though related—objection to allowing unjustified enrichment claims in both two-party and (especially) three-party cases, is that the requirement of enrichment 'at the claimant's expense' would not be satisfied. See section III.A.(iii).

in unauthorized 'interceptive subtractions' of sums owed by a third party to the claimant,[163] or in the unauthorized receipt of services rendered by the claimant.[164]

In a different vein, it may be said that, despite some uncertainty, a similar understanding also applies to cases of unauthorized inter-account funds transfers, whether 'in-house' or 'inter-bank'—even when the transaction was initiated by a third party on whose instruction the bank was authorized to act. In that respect, however, it must be emphasized—as has been noted[165]—that where a customer's account is in credit, an inter-account funds transfer does not involve an assignment of the transferring customer's rights to the transferee. Rather, it consists in a matched adjustment of the relative indebtedness between the transferring customer and their bank, and between the transferee customer and their bank.[166] Therefore, these fact patterns are to be addressed as two-party cases of restitution based on unjustified enrichment, not on the claimant's title.[167] Furthermore, it is largely uncontroversial that a claim in unjustified enrichment lies in cases involving the unauthorized receipt of a tangible monetary asset, where, notwithstanding the absence of the claimant's consent or proper authority, the defendant gains, and the claimant loses, title to that asset—which therefore might not be said to have been transferred from the latter to the former.[168] Similar reasoning applies to intangible assets as well.[169]

It seems that these developments in the English law of unjustified enrichment may now be regarded as established, whereas it is irrelevant here whether they necessarily imply the adoption of a 'lack of legal basis' approach, or whether they may also be explained by an extension of the 'unjust factors'.[170] From a different (but connected) viewpoint, it will not be discussed whether, in the relevant cases, the grounds for restitution are better explained in terms of 'lack of consent' or 'want of authority',[171] or in terms of 'ignorance',[172] supplemented by 'powerlessness'.[173]

[163] Birks (n 132) 506ff. However, for a critique, see Lionel D Smith (n 151) 481; Mitchell McInnes, 'Interceptive Subtraction, Unjust Enrichment and Wrongs–A Reply to Professor Birks' (2003) 62 Cambridge Law Journal 697.

[164] This case draws on the historical origins of the *indebitatus assumpsit* for *quantum meruit*.

[165] *Goff and Jones: The Law of Unjust Enrichment* (n 32) para 8-66.

[166] *R v Preddy* [1996] AC 815. Of course, it is possible that the bank of the transferee is the same as that of the transferor (inter-account funds transfers are 'in-house').

[167] *Goff and Jones: The Law of Unjust Enrichment* (n 32) para 8-66.

[168] For reference, ibid paras 8-36–8-38.

[169] ibid para 8-39.

[170] Especially since *Westdeutsche Landesbank Girozentrale* (n 96), a question that arises in relation to some of the cases considered here is whether equity might treat the defendant—like a thief—a trustee of the original asset for the claimant. See *Goff and Jones: The Law of Unjust Enrichment* (n 32) paras 8-67–8-77.

[171] *Goff and Jones: The Law of Unjust Enrichment* (n 32) paras 8-05–8-26. This view has been taken from the 8th edition of the book (Sweet & Maxwell 2011).

[172] Birks (n 105) 406; Ewan McKendrick, 'Restitution, Misdirected Funds and Change of Position' (1992) 55 Modern Law Review 377. For a critique, however, see Swadling (n 132) 627.

[173] Burrows (n 96) 406; Burrows (n 33) 92ff, followed by James Edelman and Elise Bant, *Unjust Enrichment* (2nd edn, Hart Publishing 2016) 291–92, 298–99.

C. Three-party cases

In three-party cases in which the transferee of an asset retransfers it to a remote recipient, the role of unjustified enrichment's subsidiarity is largely dependent on the approach to the transfer of property that is taken by each legal system, and particularly on whether such system is abstract or causal.[174]

According to the principle of abstraction (*Abstraktionsprinzip*) that is adopted by German law, the voidness or avoidance of a sale and, more generally, of a contract (*Kausalgeschäft*) does not hinder the transfer of ownership but implies only a personal liability of the first recipient. The seller is then enabled to bring an action for the recovery of the undue performance (*Leistungskondiktion*) against the buyer, but not a general action for unjustified enrichment (*Nichtleistungskondiktion*) against a remote recipient, not even when, following several intermediate sales, the latter has, effectively, acquired the property directly from the initial seller.[175] It is only to the extent that the validity of the conveyance is expressly made conditional upon the effectiveness of the contract, or both 'transactions' suffer from the same defect, that the question may arise whether the initial seller is able to bring a general action for unjust enrichment (*Nichtleistungskondiktion*) against remote recipients.

Thus, following the leading view in legal scholarship,[176] the case law of the *Bundesgerichtshof* affirmed that, on the one hand, a claimant who is entitled to bring an action for the recovery of an undue performance (*Leistungskondiktion*) against the immediate recipient cannot rely on a general unjust enrichment claim (*Nichtleistungskondiktion*) against more remote recipients;[177] and, on the other hand, that the recipient of a performance, precisely because they are liable to make restitution of an undue performance (*Leistungskondiktion*), cannot be sued under the general action for unjust enrichment (*Nichtleistungskondikt ion*).[178]

[174] The separation between contract and conveyance does not imply *per se* that the latter is abstract, ie 'decoupled' from the former. This applies particularly to Austrian and Spanish law, in which the principle of separation applies, but not that of abstraction (as it was presumably under classical Roman law).

[175] Yet, § 816(1) BGB provides as follows: '*Disposition by an anauthorized person.* If an unauthorized person disposes [of] an object and the disposition is effective in relation to the authorized person, then they are obliged to surrender to the authorized person the benefit obtained by the disposition. If the disposition is gratuitous, then the same duty applies to a person who as a result of the disposition directly gains a legal advantage' (translation taken from https://www.gesetze-im-internet.de/englisch_bgb/englisch_bgb.html#p4188). See Larenz and Canaris (n 35) para 70.

[176] Joseph Esser, *Schuldrecht* (2nd edn, Beck 1960) paras 190 and 195. For reference, see Friederike Wallmann, *Die Geltung des Subsidiaritätsgrundsatzes im Bereicherungsrecht* (Lang 1996) 32ff.

[177] BGHZ 40, 272, 278 VII, Civil Senate, VII ZR 285/61 (*Einbaufall*), NJW 1964, 34.

[178] BGHZ 56, 228 VII, Civil Senate,VII ZR 43/61 (*Materiallieferantenfall*), NJW 1962, 1200.

In that context, the conceptual framework of subsidiarity risks being misleading,[179] particularly in regard to three-party legal relationships.[180] Due to the principle of abstraction, title generally passes to the buyer upon conveyance—even if the sale is void or avoided—and it therefore passes also to remote recipients. However, only the buyer is liable in unjustified enrichment to the initial seller; remote recipients are not.

Where the system of transferring property is causal—as is the case with French and Italian law, but also with the DCFR[181]—the voidness or avoidance of the contract generally affects not only the buyer but also remote recipients. Despite some scholarly uncertainty,[182] the initial seller can therefore claim from any remote recipient,[183] unless the law allows title to an asset to pass to the defendant even though it has not been voluntarily transferred to them by the claimant (*a non domino* purchase), most typically (but not exclusively) because of their usucaption and/or because they are *bona fide* purchasers.

In both abstract and causal systems of property transfer, where a remote recipient acquires title to an asset irrespective of a conveyance from the previous holder, it is for the law of property to determine whether the enrichment they have 'subtracted' from the former owner is justified. In case where the contract is void, the enrichment of a remote recipient is generally justified to the extent that the acquisition is a *bona fide* purchase for value—though exceptions may apply, for instance, where the asset was stolen or lost.[184] By contrast, if the recipient did not provide value, they are generally liable for unjustified enrichment.[185] Conversely, a claim in unjustified enrichment lies against the first recipient even if they have since disposed of the asset to which the claimant holds title; in this case, they may be liable for the proceeds or the exchange value, subject to a defence of change of position.[186]

[179] See section I.C.

[180] Stephan Lorenz, in *J. von Staudingers Kommentar zum BGB*, Buch 2, *Recht der Schuldverhältnisse, §§ 812-822* (15th edn, de Gruyter 2007) para 64.

[181] Art VIII.-2:102.

[182] Umberto Breccia, 'Il pagamento dell'indebito' in Pietro Rescigno (ed), *Trattato di diritto privato*, vol 9-I, *Obbligazioni e contratti* (2nd edn, UTET 1999) 1009; Pietro Trimarchi, *L'arricchimento senza causa* (Giuffrè 1962) 104.

[183] Pietro Sirena, 'L'azione generale di arricchimento senza causa' in Nicola Lipari, Pietro Rescigno, and Andrea Zoppini (eds), *Diritto civile*, vol 3, *Obbligazioni*, I, *Il rapporto obbligatorio* (Giuffrè 2009) 564.

[184] § 935 BGB; art 2276(2) Code civil.

[185] § 816 BGB. Under French and Italian law, this rule is not written in the respective civil codes but advocated for by some scholars: see Andrea Nicolussi, *Lesione del potere di disposizione e arricchimento. Un'indagine sul danno non aquiliano* (Giuffrè 1998) 119ff.

[186] § 816 BGB; art 1352-2 Code civil; art 2038 Codice civile. A similar conclusion must be reached in cases where, instead of reselling the goods, the first buyer transforms or uses them in such a way that a third party acquires the ownership by way of amalgamation, merger, incorporation, etc. See Werner Lorenz, 'Bereicherungsausgleich beim Einbau fremden Materials' in Ulrich Huber and Erik Jayme (eds), *Festschrift für Rolf Serick* (Recht und Wirtschaft 1992) 255.

IV. Unjustified Enrichment vis-à-vis Tort

A. French and Italian law

Under French and Italian law, a strong subsidiarity (*in abstracto*) of claims in unjustified enrichment prevents their use when a wrong has been committed, as the action for compensation for damages can be pursued instead. This rule is applied quite strictly in French case law, while recent Italian case law has taken a more lenient approach.[187]

The reason given to justify this subsidiarity lies in the need to prevent unjustified enrichment claims from being used to circumvent the law, particularly when it comes to the limitation period applicable to the action for compensation of damages, which is shorter than that applicable to restitution of unjust enrichment. However, these solutions are difficult to accept, as the two remedies are designed to address distinct types of harm: respectively, the loss sustained by the claimant and the enrichment obtained by the defendant. There is, therefore, no inherent inconsistency in treating the two types of claims differently.

Fundamentally, the initial premise that the action for unjust enrichment might circumvent the law is no longer tenable. This remedy is no longer an extraordinary, discretionary measure grounded in equity; rather, it is now recognized by the positive law, and as such it cannot be regarded as a threat to it.[188]

B. German and English law

The concurrence of the action for unjust enrichment with the action for compensation is well established in German law.[189] Since the 'stowaway case' of 1971 (*Flugreiseentscheidung*), the German Federal Court of Justice (*Bundesgerichtshof*) has clarified that it is up to the injured party to decide whether to pursue an action for damages or an action for unjust enrichment, provided the conditions for both remedies are met.[190] Regarding the statute of limitations, § 852(1) BGB stipulates that, if the party causing the damage has been unjustly enriched at the expense of

[187] See section I.C.

[188] See section V.

[189] For a comparative analysis with English law, see Dannemann (n 15) 151.

[190] BGHZ 55, 128 II, Civil Senate (II ZR 23/70)—*Flugreisefall*, NJW 1971, 609. The case can be summarized as follows. A passenger, not yet of legal age, boarded a flight from Munich to Hamburg and then illegally boarded a further flight from Hamburg to New York. It was determined that the passenger was incapable of understanding his actions (§ 828(2) BGB), and he was ordered to pay the price of the relevant ticket as restitution for unjust enrichment (§§ 819(1), 818(4), 292 BGB). Since the New York airport police refused him entry into the United States, and the airline consequently arranged to return him on a flight back to Hamburg on the same day, he was also ordered to pay the price of that ticket, this time as reimbursement of expenses incurred for the useful management of another's affairs (*Geschäftsführung ohne Auftrag*) (§ 683 BGB).

the injured party, the former is obliged to compensate the latter according to the rules of unjust enrichment, even when the action for damages has become time barred.[191]

In common law jurisdictions, the choice between damages and restitution of unjustified enrichment has also been allowed to the claimant,[192] in that they have been traditionally entitled to 'waive the tort' and thus bring an action for money had and received instead of damages.[193] The claimant must choose between the two remedies, and a double award is clearly not allowed.[194]

V. Concluding Remarks

The subsidiary nature of the action for unjustified enrichment developed primarily as a response to the equitable (and historically fragile) origins of this remedy and the fear that it could undermine or alter settled law. In fact, without being a proper novelty in private law, unjustified enrichment has been only recently granted the status of a general doctrine or principle, and its historical roots are more tender than those of contract, torts, and property.[195]

In civil law jurisdictions, unjustified enrichment has traditionally been viewed as a gap-filler, potentially capable of interfering with the formal legislative system by imposing equitable solutions where statutory law did not explicitly provide for them. Furthermore, the conceptualization of unjustified enrichment has developed significantly later than in other legal areas, and judge-made law is still being adjusted and re-categorized accordingly.[196] As a matter of fact, a law of unjustified enrichment as such may not be said to have existed in Roman law, but rather emerged in medieval scholarship through continuous reinterpretation of the sources and doctrinal generalization of disparate cases. Although these materials

[191] For the opinion according to which this provision would represent a sort of obvious repetition, lacking any autonomous normative content, see Ernst von Caemmerer, 'Bereicherung und unerlaubte Handlung' in Hans Dölle, Max Rheinstein, and Konrad Zweigert (eds), *Festschrift für Ernst Rabel*, vol 1, *Rechtsvergleichung und internationales Privatrecht* (Mohr 1954) 394ff, republished in von Caemmerer (n 68) 209ff. For a different view, however, see Larenz and Canaris (n 35) para 83 V, who see in § 852(1) BGB an independent legal basis on which to found restitution for wrongs as such.

[192] On restitutionary (and disgorgement) damages, see *Clerk and Lindsell on Torts* (Andrew Tettenborn ed, 24th edn, Sweet & Maxwell 2023) paras 26-196–26-197; *McGregor on Damages* (Jason Varuhas, Andrew Higgins, and James Edelman eds, 22nd edn, Sweet & Maxwell, 2025) paras 14-001ff.

[193] *Lamine v Dorrell* (1705) 2 Ld Raym 1216. This solution was adopted and endorsed by subsequent cases of the House of Lords, which, in particular, held that the exercise of the action for money had and received against the person who had cashed a bank cheque of which they were not the payee did not preclude the latter from subsequently pursuing an action in tort against the bank (*United Australia Ltd v Barclays Bank Ltd* [1941] AC 1). See Jack Beatson, 'The Nature of Waiver of Tort' in Jack Beatson, *The Use and Abuse of Unjust Enrichment. Essays on the Law of Restitution* (OUP 1991) 206ff.

[194] *Humbly v Trott* (1776) 1 Cowp 375 (Lord Mansfield).

[195] For a comparative analysis, see Ciara Kennefick, 'La faute de l'appauvri: comparaisons anglo-françaises sur l'enrichissement injustifié', Revue des contrats 2015, no 4, 961.

[196] See sections I.B, I.C, and I.D.

had been addressed in quite different contexts, they were unified on the basis of a solemn adage of Pomponius, which, reiterated twice (with minor differences in the wording) in Justinian's Digest, commands that no one be enriched at the expense of another.[197]

In the common law, the establishment of unjust enrichment as a general principle arguably dates back to 1943, when it was acknowledged by Lord Wright in *Fibrosa*,[198] but it was not until 1991 that, under the leadership of Lord Goff in *Lipkin Gorman*,[199] the House of Lords allowed a personal restitutionary claim ostensibly founded on that principle and transcending the constellation of previous cases which hinged on quasi-contracts.[200]

The history of unjustified enrichment demonstrates that, at its inception as a general doctrine or principle, it was closely linked to notions of equity (understood as substantive fairness, if not a distinct jurisdiction) and even to concepts of justice or *ius naturale*. Initially, these ideas aimed to correct positive law *ex aequo et bono*, whether established by statutes or courts. In common law jurisdictions, it is noteworthy that unjust enrichment was first recognized as a principle rooted in 'conscience'.[201] As early as 1760, Lord Mansfield famously held that a defendant must refund money received if, 'upon the circumstances of the case, [the defendant] is obliged by the ties of natural justice and equity'.[202] This approach has been consistently followed in many cases up to the present day.[203]

Consequently, legal theory and practice have often adopted prudent, even defensive, approaches to unjustified enrichment, which at times have led to extreme caution, or even outright hostility, in handling it. A notable example of such approach can be found in French law, in which unjustified enrichment was historically developed by courts, not being provided for by the Code civil (or other written sources of law).[204] To address this gap, the judiciary applied principles of equity, and due to its judicial origins, unjustified enrichment has always been seen as a potential source of conflict with the legislature,[205] to the extent that it was described

[197] D. 12.6.14 (*aequum est neminem cum alterius detrimento fieri locupletiorem*) and D. 50.17.206 (*ius naturae aequum est neminem cum alterius detrimento et iniuria fieri locupletiorem*). See Carlo A Cannata, '*Cum alterius detrimento et iniuria fieri locupletiorem*. L'arricchimento ingiustificato nel diritto romano' in Vacca (n 14) 13ff.

[198] *Fibrosa* (n 56) 32.

[199] *Lipkin Gorman* (n 100).

[200] See Baker (n 160) 37–38; John H Langbein, 'The Later History of Restitution' in Cornish and others (n 160) 57.

[201] *Fibrosa* (n 56) 32, 61 (Lord Wright). See Stephen Waddams, *Sanctity of Contract in a Secular Age. Equity, Fairness and Enrichment* (CUP 2019) 131ff.

[202] *Moses v Macferlan* (1760) 2 Burr 1005, 1012. For further reference on this language and 'unconscionable retention' in English case law, see Virgo (n 49) 62ff, 712ff.

[203] Among others, see *Banque Financière de la Cité v Parc (Battersea) Ltd* [1999] 1 AC 221, 237 (Lord Clyde).

[204] See section II.B.

[205] Paul Esmein, in *Travaux des Journées internationales de l'Association Henri Capitant*, vol 4, *L'enrichissement sans cause* (Dalloz 1949) 91.

as 'a kind of incendiary device capable of blowing up the entire legal edifice'.[206] As a result, a legal mechanism was needed to prevent claimants from using restitution to circumvent statutory law.[207]

All these reasons of historical sensitivity and equitable origin coalesced and converged in the subsidiarity of unjustified enrichment, which therefore came to be understood in both theory and practice as a remedy of last resort—operating only to the extent that the normative body of the law otherwise permits. However, once unjustified enrichment was 'transposed' into positive law, whether provided for in civil codes or recognized as general doctrine or principle of private law, the significance of its subsidiarity became unclear. This is because subsidiarity had historically and inherently served to limit the expansion of an equitable remedy granted by courts *praeter legem*, that is, beyond the scope of the written law. This explains the judicial uncertainties and misalignments evident in French and Italian law, where the subsidiarity of unjustified enrichment is regularly challenged by scholars, and courts struggle to develop consistent and reliable case law.[208]

The issues of coordinating unjustified enrichment with property and contract law can be resolved by more precisely determining when the defendant's enrichment lacks a legal basis, or by identifying the relevant unjust factors that apply. In addition, a clear application of the 'at someone else's expense' requirement is crucial, along with a clarification of the limits within which each legal system permits restitution for indirect enrichments. These refinements—enhancing the precision with which the constitutive elements of unjustified enrichment are formulated—certainly contribute to delineating its scope more clearly (whether broadly or narrowly) in relation to other areas of private law, that is, contract, property, and tort. Yet for that very reason, they render any additional concept of subsidiarity in restitutionary claims entirely superfluous. It is sufficient to state that such claims are available insofar as their constitutive requirements are satisfied—just as with any other legal cause of action.

With respect to the coordination between unjustified enrichment and tort law, it is true that French law, alongside Italian law and other legal systems, adheres to a strict prohibition on the concurrence of restitutionary and compensatory claims. However, this approach is not only unknown to both German and English law, it also lacks a convincing normative foundation. Restitutionary and compensatory claims are directed at redressing different forms of harm, each of which deserves legal redress. Specifically, restitutionary claims aim to reverse the defendant's unjustified enrichment, whereas compensatory claims seek to make good the claimant's loss. Accordingly, restitution and damages should not be viewed as

[206] André Rouast, 'Les obligations dont la source n'est ni le contrat ni la faute' in *Répétitions écrites de droit civil approfondi et comparé* (Dalloz 1933–34) 78.

[207] Barry Nicholas, 'Unjust Enrichment and Subsidiarity' in *Scintillae iuris. Studi in memoria di Gino Gorla*, vol 3 (Giuffrè 1994) 2041.

[208] See sections I.C and I.D.

mutually exclusive remedies, but rather as distinct responses to separate dimensions of injustice within the law of obligations.

It follows that the French and Italian rule on the subsidiarity of unjustified enrichment should be repealed or, at the very least, interpreted in the most restrictive terms possible: namely, as a prohibition against double recovery. Double recovery would occur if the defendant were required to pay for both the (entire) detriment resulting from the enrichment and, in addition, the (entire) damage caused to the claimant—an outcome that would be unduly advantageous to the claimant. By contrast, recognizing in principle the concurrence of restitution and compensation, and permitting their integrated application where appropriate, would bring these systems into closer alignment with the vast majority of European legal systems.

12

Harmonizing Contract Law without a Common Terminology

Comparative Law Perspectives

Barbara Pozzo

The chapter examines the various forces at play in the harmonization of European contract law. After briefly recalling the efforts of the EU institutions to harmonize contract terminology, the chapter examines the different choices made by national legislators in relation to EU law-derived contract law, mainly consumer law. It examines the choice made by the German legislator, which attempted to bring all consumer law under the umbrella of the Civil Code, comparing it with other civil law systems, in particular the French, Italian, and Spanish ones, where different choices were made. Finally, particular attention is paid to the UK. The chapter also focuses on the attitude of national interpreters to European directives and their terminology. It further looks to the criteria developed by the CJEU in interpreting multilingual legislation and the attitudes of national judges to them, and the different perspectives of legal scholars working in different jurisdictions. It further deals with the attitude of national judges to multilingual interpretation in the implementation of EU law, which may depend on several variables. Finally, the chapter focuses on the role of the English language in developing common terminology for harmonized EU contract law, a role which may change after Brexit.

I. The EU Initiatives to Harmonize European Contract Law

Since the 1990s, European Union institutions have developed a series of initiatives that have had a strong impact on the contract law of the Member States. Consumer contracts have been the primary object of attention, but also outside this field, EU law has played an important role.[1] Outside the consumer context, specific

[1] Guido Alpa, 'The Future of European Contract Law: Some Questions and Some Answers' in Katharina Boele-Woelki and Willem Grosheide (eds), *The Future of European Contract Law* (Kluwer Law International 2007) 3; Barbara Pozzo, 'Multilingualism, Legal Terminology and the Problems of Harmonising European Private Law' in Barbara Pozzo and Valentina Jacometti (eds), *Multilingualism and the Harmonisation of European Law* (Kluwer Law International 2006) 3.

Barbara Pozzo, *Harmonizing Contract Law without a Common Terminology* In: *Comparative Reflections in Private Law*. Edited by: Marco Cappelletti, Ciara Kennefick, and Dorota Leczykiewicz, Oxford University Press.
 DOI: 10.1093/9780198959168.003.0015

directives have introduced new rules governing commercial agency contracts[2] and particular aspects of commercial contracts.[3] Further, the public procurement directives have had a major impact on the process of public contracting,[4] while a series of employment directives have created or reshaped the rights of employees in many respects.[5] Altogether, EU legislation has remained piecemeal, targeting particular situations or particular aspects of the rules governing contracts.[6]

In the last decades, harmonization of consumer and contract law[7] has become the focus of Community (now EU) institutions. Simultaneously, the project of constructing a European contract law has become the focus of legal scholarship.[8] Since then, scholars have often pointed out that the lack of a common terminology and the absence of clear legal definitions in EU texts have hindered the harmonization process.[9] The lack of universally applicable definitions for the legal terms used in the directives has led national lawyers to give them different meanings depending on the different legal contexts. One example is the term 'contract', which lacks a clear definition even in the context of the directive on unfair terms.[10]

Among the most perilous types of consumer contracts are, without a doubt, contracts for the supply of electricity, water, or gas; in other words, those necessary to gain access to a supply network. This is because the provider frequently has a monopolistic position, which means the consumer has no choice and must accept

[2] Council Directive 86/653/EEC of 18 December 1986 on the coordination of the laws of the Member States relating to self-employed commercial agents, OJ L 382, 31.12.1986, p 17.

[3] Directive 2000/35/EC of the European Parliament and of the Council of 29 June 2000 on combating late payment in commercial transactions, OJ L 200, 8.8.2000, p 35.

[4] Directive 2004/18/EC of the European Parliament and of the Council of 31 March 2004 on the coordination of procedures for the award of public works contracts, public supply contracts and public service contracts, OJ L 134, p 114; Directive 2004/17/EC of the European Parliament and of the Council of 31 March 2004 coordinating the procurement procedures of entities operating in the water, energy, transport and postal services sectors, OJ L 134, 30.4.2004, p 1.

[5] For example, Council Directive 2000/78/EC of 27 November 2000 establishing a general framework for equal treatment in employment and occupation, OJ L 303, 2.12.2000, p 16.

[6] Simon Whittaker, 'A Framework of Principle for European Contract Law?' (2009) 125 Law Quarterly Review 616.

[7] Stefan Grundmann, 'European Contract Law(s) of What Colour?' (2005) 1 European Review of Contract Law 184; Jürgen Basedow, 'A Common Contract Law for the Common Market' (1996) 33 Common Market Law Review 1169.

[8] See the Preliminary draft of a European Contract Code based on the work of the Academy of European Private Lawyers of Pavia (Giuseppe Gandolfi, 'Pour un code européen des contrats', Revue trimestrielle de droit civil 1992, 707); the General Principles of Contract Law of the Lando Commission (Ole Lando, 'Principles of European Contract Law—An Alternative or a Precursor of European Legislation' (1992) 56 Rabels Zeitschrift für ausländisches und internationales Privatrecht 261); and the UNIDROIT Principles (Michael Joachim Bonell, 'Das UNIDROIT Projekt für die Ausarbeitung von Regeln für internationale Handelsverträge' (1992) 56 Rabels Zeitschrift für ausländisches und internationales Privatrecht 274).

[9] Ana M Lopez-Rodriguez, 'Towards a European Civil Code without a Common European Legal Culture: The Link between Law, Language and Culture' (2003) 29 Brook Journal of International Law 1195; Susan Šarčević, 'Creating a pan-European legal language' in Maurizio Gotti and Christopher Williams (eds), *Legal Discourse across Languages and Cultures* (Peter Lang 2010) 23.

[10] The example is drawn from Simon Whittaker, 'Unfair Contract Terms, Public Service and the Construction of a European Conception of Contract' (2000) 116 Law Quarterly Review 95.

even the most unfair terms. Therefore, a directive which deprives such clauses of any legal effect would be very useful, particularly in contracts with public utilities. However, this can only happen when the legal instrument on the basis of which the consumer is gaining access to the service network is in fact a 'contract', because when this is not the case under the local national law, the directive does not apply, and the consumer does not receive the directive's protection.

In reviewing this problem in 1993, the *Rapport sur l'application de la Directive 93/13/1993*, prepared by the French Institut National de la Consommation and the UK National Consumer Council, revealed that the legal relationship between public service providers and consumers—particularly in relation to services such as the supply of water, electricity, and gas—is classified in different ways across Member States.[11] For example, in the case of water supply, only nine states treated the relationship as contractual.[12] By contrast, in two Member States (Denmark and the UK), it was described as clearly non-contractual; in one state (Belgium), the classification was unclear, in another one (Austria) it differed according to the locality, and in yet another one (Sweden) it depended on the circumstances.

The European Commission took an important step to resolve problems connected with terminology in July 2001 by issuing the Communication on European Contract Law.[13] This document launched a process of consultation and discussion about the way in which problems resulting from divergences between national contract laws in the EU should be dealt with at the European level. It is noteworthy that the Communication was for the first time emphasizing the importance of arriving at a common terminology in European contract law, as different terms and concepts create an obstacle to reaching harmonized results.[14]

In a further Communication of 2003,[15] the Commission launched an Action Plan for a more coherent European contract law. The Commission subsequently financed the work of an international academic network, which carried out the preparatory legal research. This research work was finalized at the end of 2008 and led to the publication of the Common Frame of Reference (CFR)[16] as an academic text. In parallel to this, analytical work was also being carried out by the

[11] See ibid 100–101 (discussing the *Rapport sur l'application de la Directive 93/13/1993 du Conseil du 5 avril 1993 concernant les clauses abusives dans les contrats conclus avec les consommateurs aux prestations de service public* (eds Hall and Tixador), published by the European Commission on the internet (1997)).

[12] Whittaker (n 10) 101.

[13] Communication from the Commission to the Council and the European Parliament on European contract law, COM(2001) 398 final.

[14] ibid paras 36–38.

[15] Communication from the Commission to the European Parliament and the Council—A More Coherent European Contract Law—An Action Plan, COM(2003) 68 final.

[16] Christian von Bar, Eric Clive, and Hans Schulte-Nölke (eds), *Principles, Definitions and Model Rules of European Private Law: Draft Common Frame of Reference (DCFR)* (Sellier European Law Publishers 2009).

Association Henri Capitant des Amis de la Culture Juridique Française and the Société de Legislation Comparée drafting the *Principes Contractuels Communs*.[17]

The CFR aimed to provide the best solutions for a common terminology and rules.[18] This task was to be achieved by defining fundamental concepts and abstract terms such as 'contract' or 'damage' and laying down the rules that apply to them, for example, in the case of non-performance of contracts.[19] The ultimate version of the document, deceptively called the Draft Common Frame of Reference (DCFR), was approved and published in 2009.[20] It had a dual purpose. First, it was intended to serve as a tool for improving the *acquis* by providing clear definitions of legal terms, fundamental principles, and coherent model rules of contract law which draw on the existing *acquis* and best solutions found in the legal systems of the Member States. Secondly, it was said that the DCFR could serve as the basis for an optional instrument on European contract law.[21] Indeed, the initial Proposal for a Common European Sales Law (CESL), published by the Commission in 2011 in the form of a regulation,[22] was aimed at introducing an optional regime with a uniform set of contract rules for the cross-border sale of goods between businesses and consumers. As the Proposal for a CESL was withdrawn in December 2014, the potential of these initiatives cannot be fully evaluated.

Nonetheless, we can conduct an interesting analysis of the linguistic choices made by the authors of the DCFR, given the fact that the language in which the document was drafted is English.[23] In the context of the DCFR, English has become a neutral or descriptive language of provisions the background of which is civil law rather than English law. Thus, it was not used to express common law concepts but rather as a vocabulary for an emerging legal order, the European private law system, as influenced by the various cultural and legal traditions of the Member States.[24]

[17] Bénédicte Fauvarque-Cosson and Denis Mazeaud (eds), *European Contract Law: Materials for a Common Frame of Reference: Terminology, Guiding Principles, Model Rules* (Sellier European Law Publishers 2008). On the choice between the various options on legal terminology, cf Barbara Pozzo, 'Le principes directeurs en droit comparé', Revue des contrats 2013, no 1, 400.

[18] Communication from the Commission to the European Parliament and the Council—European Contract Law and the Revision of the Acquis: the Way Forward, COM(2004) 651 final.

[19] Carlo Marchetti, 'Legal Categories and Legal Terms in the Path towards a European Private Law: The Experiment of the DCFR' (2012) 20 European Review of Private Law 1265.

[20] von Bar, Clive, and Schulte-Nölke (n 16).

[21] Reiner Schulze and Thomas Wilhelmsson, 'From the Draft Common Frame of Reference towards European Contract Law Rules' (2008) European Review of Contract Law 154; Yehuda Adar and Pietro Sirena, 'Principles and Rules in the Emerging European Contract Law: From the PECL to the CESL, and Beyond' (2013) 9 European Review of Contract Law 1.

[22] European Commission, Proposal for a Regulation of the European Parliament and of the Council on a Common European Sales Law, COM(2011) 635 final.

[23] See Ingemar Strandvik, 'On Quality in EU Multilingual Lawmaking' in Susan Šarčević (ed), *Language and Culture in EU Law: Multidisciplinary Perspectives* (Routledge 2015) 141.

[24] Barbara Pozzo 'Comparative Law and the New Frontiers of Legal Translation' in Šarčević (n 23) 73.

Since the emerging European legal order is multilingual, the drafters made painstaking efforts to create a neutral language, devoid of legalese and technicalities, that could be 'readily translated without carrying unwanted baggage with it'.[25] For this reason, terms such as 'rescission', 'tort', and 'delict' are avoided and replaced by descriptive paraphrases.[26] For instance, 'torts' ('delicts') are described as 'non-contractual liability arising out of damage caused to another'.[27] The injured party is referred to as 'a person who suffers legally relevant damage' and the tortfeasor as 'a person who caused the damage' (Book VI.—1:101). For greater concision, neologisms have been created whenever possible, some of which are descriptive while others are literal translations. For example, the rule on force majeure is called an 'event beyond control' (Book VI.—5:302), the German *Rücktritt* is translated as 'unilateral withdrawal', and *Rechtsgeschäft* is translated as 'juridical act' (Book II.—1:101). Latin phrases are also avoided. For instance, instead of using the usual Latin term *negotiorum gestio*, the civilian concept *Geschäftsführung ohne Auftrag* is called 'benevolent intervention in another's affairs' (Book V).

The evaluation of the language of the DCFR conducted by a scholar of English law, none other than Simon Whittaker, confirms that the drafters have generally managed 'to express its rules in terminology which is comprehensible in English, but which is not too tied to the technical concepts of English law itself'.[28] Nonetheless, despite the neutral, descriptive language of the DCFR, Whittaker remarks that 'some significant problems of terminology' remain, which 'will become apparent in the translation of the CFR into all the official languages of the EU'.[29] In fact, using English as the lingua franca for defining European terminology seems to be a necessary choice, but it is a choice not without costs. On the one hand, English is the most widely spoken language in the European Union, but on the other hand, it is the least suitable for translating legal concepts originating from civil law jurisdictions, which make up the majority of EU legal systems. Furthermore, we must remember that the English terminology of the DCFR was meant to be translated into all the other official EU languages, and that all these translations would coexist with the original English version.

Regarding this phenomenon, the following points should be observed. First, translation in a multilingual context must pursue the same purposes as the multilingual legislation, and particularly that of the harmonization of law. The problem is different from that which arises when translating one language to another. Here convergence of meaning needs to be sought between English and the other twenty-three official languages of the EU, the former having been *reinvented* precisely

[25] von Bar, Clive, and Schulte-Nölke (n 16) 29ff.
[26] ibid 29.
[27] ibid 395.
[28] Simon Whittaker, *The Draft Common Frame of Reference: An Assessment* (Assessment commissioned by the Ministry of Justice, 2008) 102.
[29] ibid.

to act as a go-between. Secondly, when translating from this version of 'English' into other EU languages, in order to appreciate the features of the legal ideas to which reference is made by a particular term, one cannot rely on English law or the common law tradition. Instead it is necessary to identify the civil law ideas to which the drafters intended to refer by using the reinvented English terminology. Only then can one search for a corresponding functional term within each other official language of the EU.

In conclusion, the challenges that legal translation poses with respect to this new 'lingua franca', created with the aim of harmonizing European law, were therefore manifold. But the necessity to carry out the translation was removed with the withdrawal of the CESL.

II. The National Reactions to the EU Efforts to Harmonize European Contract Law

Notwithstanding the different EU initiatives aimed at harmonizing national contract laws,[30] and in particular consumer law, the absence of a common contractual terminology across the EU[31] had to be overcome in the solutions developed in the different Member States.[32] The experience so far has shown that the implementation of EU directives into the national legal systems has followed different paths, determined by a variety of factors.[33]

First, we must bear in mind that according to Article 288 TFEU, a directive is 'binding, as to the result to be achieved, upon each Member State to which it is addressed, but shall leave to the national authorities the choice of form and methods'. Directives specify a result to be achieved, but Member States are free to choose the appropriate 'form and methods' for achieving a directive's objective and ensuring the effectiveness of its individual provisions. In implementing directives, domestic laws can copy the text word-for-word, but the terminology used in a particular

[30] See nn 13, 15, and 18.

[31] More than 20 years ago, I published an article with the following title: Barbara Pozzo, 'Harmonisation of European Contract Law and the Need of Creating a Common Terminology' (2003) 11 European Review of Private Law 754, in which I explained the difficulties arising from the lack of a common terminology in contractual matters in the process of harmonizing EU contract law. More recently, I dealt with the problem in Barbara Pozzo, 'Language Diversity and the Future of European Private Law, or: "Why the Language of Europe is Translation"' in André Janssen, Matthias Lehmann, and Reiner Schulze (eds), *The Future of European Private Law* (Nomos 2023) 105.

[32] Michele Graziadei, 'Fostering a European Legal Identity through Contract and Consumer Law' in Christian Twigg-Flesner (ed), *Research Handbook on EU Consumer and Contract Law* (Edward Elgar Publishing 2016) 73, 83.

[33] On these problems, see Barbara Pozzo (ed), *The Impact of Multilingualism on the Harmonization of European Private Law* (2012) 20 European Review of Private Law 1181; see further Barbara Pasa, Piercarlo Rossi, and Martin Weitenberg (eds), *Diritto contrattuale europeo tra direttive comunitarie e trasposizioni nazionali: materiali per lo studio della terminologia giuridica* (Giappichelli 2007).

directive must not be taken literally by national legislators.[34] The Court of Justice has confirmed that the use of terminology which differs from a directive is permissible when it does not constitute a substantive departure from it.[35] This means that national implementations do diverge from the text of the directive.

As will be shown below, the underlying reasons for different attitudes towards the implementation of EU directives may lie in the different legal mentalities embodied by each national system. These include, for instance, the greater emphasis placed on the centrality of civil codes in building a coherent system of concepts in some systems compared to others, the aspiration to present one's own civil code as a model for Europe as a whole, and the criteria of legal interpretation developed within each system. The choices made at the level of individual Member States to meet EU obligations have varied, hindering effective harmonization of contract law.

It seems important to examine them from a comparative law perspective in order to understand the deep-seated reasons for the different approaches among the Member States. They concern not only issues of legislative techniques, but also other aspects of national traditions. The comparative law approach is used here as an important tool to achieve the intended purposes of EU law. EU law is expected to be the instrument through which European citizens can enjoy equal rights and equal guarantees. However, harmonized law must come to terms with the different legal contexts of each Member State,[36] the different *mentalités* of national lawyers,[37] and different reactions to the idea of creating an 'autonomous legal order'.[38] A comparative law approach can contribute to the analysis of divergences and convergences, helping to uncover obstacles in different legal systems that prevent the achievement of harmonization.

III. The Centrality of the Civil Code

Among the various European national systems that we will examine, the German approach to the implementation of European directives is certainly the one that relied most on the centrality of its civil code, the *Bürgerliches Gesetzbuch* (BGB), in building a coherent system of concepts.[39] It has often been pointed out that the

[34] As noted by Christian Twigg-Flesner, 'The (Non-)Impact of Harmonising Measures on English Legal Terminology' (2012) 20 European Review of Private Law 1369.

[35] Case C-283/81, *Srl CILFIT and Lanificio di Gavardo SpA v Ministry of Health*, [1982] ECR 3415.

[36] Thijmen Koopmans, 'The Birth of European Law at the Crossroads of Legal Traditions' (1991) 39 American Journal of Comparative Law 493.

[37] Pierre Legrand, 'European Legal Systems Are Not Converging' (1996) 45 International and Comparative Law Quarterly 52.

[38] Christina Eckes, 'The Autonomy of the EU Legal Order' (2020) 4 Europe and the World: A Law Review 1; Theodor Schilling, 'The Autonomy of the Community Legal Order: An Analysis of Possible Foundations' (1996) 37 Harvard International Law Journal 389.

[39] Peter Rott, 'Legal Terminology: One Reason for Frictions between German and European Consumer Laws' (2012) 20 European Review of Private Law 1353.

attempt to rationalize German private law has had to contend with numerous changes that have taken place over the more than 100 years of its application by courts and with the various innovations introduced by European directives into German consumer contract law.[40]

From a historical perspective, two phases may be distinguished in the integration of EU consumer law into German private law. The first corresponds to the period until the end of 2001, when directives were implemented by way of special legislation[41] outside the German Civil Code. The second corresponds to the period after the enactment of the *Schuldrechtsreform*,[42] the Reform of the Law of Obligations, that modified the Second Book of the BGB and introduced special legislation into the Civil Code.[43]

We might say that in the first phase, while German private law scholars were very careful to point out the conceptual and other inconsistencies of the terminology used in directives, the German legislator did little to define or clarify the doctrinal concepts.[44] It was only with the implementation of the Distance Selling Directive 97/7/EC that the German legislator began to conceptualize consumer law by establishing a first set of common rules for the various rights of withdrawal that were enshrined in EU consumer law at the time.[45] The *Schuldrechtsreform* of 2002 changed this approach: it transposed EU legislation into the BGB in a more coherent way, it took care of the terminological issues entailed by that legislation, and, by creating a coherent set of concepts valid for all German private law, it reinstated the centrality of the German Civil Code.[46]

[40] Reinhard Zimmermann, 'Schuldrechtsmodernisierung?', JuristenZeitung 2001, 171; Beate Gsell, 'Kaufrechtsrichtlinie und Schuldrechtsmodernisierung', JuristenZeitung 2001, 65; Barbara Dauner-Lieb, 'Die geplante Schuldrechtsmodernisierung—Durchbruch oder Schnellschuß?', JuristenZeitung 2001, 8; Simone Jorden and Michael Lehmann, 'Verbrauchsgüterkauf und Schuldrechtsmodernisierung: Zur geplanten Umsetzung der Richtlinie 1999/44/EG im Rahmen eines Gesetzes zur Modernisierung des Schuldrechts', JuristenZeitung 2001, 952.

[41] eg the Doorstep Selling Act of 1986 (Haustürwiderrufsgesetz; HausTWG), the Consumer Credit Act of 1990 (Verbraucherkreditgesetz; VerbrKrG); the Timesharing Act of 1996 (Teilzeitwohnrechtegesetz; TzWrG) and the Distance Selling Act of 2000 (Fernabsatzgesetz; FernAbsG).

[42] On the relationship between the German Reform of the Law of Obligations and EU law, cf Hans Schulte-Nölke and Reiner Schulze (eds), *Die Schuldrechtsreform vor dem Hintergrund des Gemeinschaftsrechts* (Mohr Siebeck 2001).

[43] Rott (n 39) 1354.

[44] ibid 1356.

[45] Peter Rott, 'Widerruf und Rückabwicklung nach der Umsetzung der Fernabsatzrichtlinie und dem Entwurf eines Schuldrechtsmodernisierungsgesetzes', Verbraucher und Recht 2001, 78; Katharina von Koppenfels, 'Das Widerrufsrecht bei Verbraucherverträgen im BGB—eine Untersuchung des § 355 Abs 1 BGB-RegE', WM-Zeitschrift für Wirtschafts- und Bankrecht 2001, 1360.

[46] On the integration of consumer law into the BGB, see Klaus Dörner, 'Die Integration des Verbraucherrechts in das BGB' in Reiner Schulze and Hans Schulte-Nölke (eds), *Die Schuldrechtsreform vor dem Hintergrund des Gemeinschaftsrechts* (Mohr Siebeck 2001) 177, 178; Stefan Grundmann, 'Generalreferat: Internationalisierung und Reform des deutschen Kaufrechts' in Stefan Grundmann, Dieter Medicus, and Walter Rolland (eds), *Europäisches Kaufgewährleistungsrecht: Reform und Internationalisierung des deutschen Schuldrechts* (Carl Heymanns Verlag 2000) 281; Thomas Pfeiffer, 'Die Integration von "Nebengesetzen" in das BGB' in Wolfgang Ernst and Reinhard Zimmermann

The reform of the BGB operated on a number of distinct levels.[47] First, it introduced in the General Part (*Allgemeiner Teil*) of the BGB certain legal concepts developed in academic writings and in case law, such as the principle of changed circumstances,[48] a regime for precontractual liability,[49] and the so-called *positive Vertragsverletzung*, which refers to any breach of contract other than late performance or impossibility (complete non-performance),[50] which became part of the new concept of breach.[51] Secondly, the German Reform implemented the Consumer Sales Directive 1999/44/EC by introducing the relevant norms into the BGB. Thirdly, the Doorstep Selling Law, the Consumer Credit Law, the Timesharing Law, and the Distance Selling Law were all repealed, and their substance transferred to the BGB. Fourthly, the reform of the BGB introduced provisions on general contract terms (*Allgemeine Geschäftsbedingungen*) in a dedicated chapter of the Second Book.[52] Fifthly, the legislator tried to clarify the central concepts of consumers' contracts as emerging from EU legislation. § 355 BGB now provides in a general way for the 'right of withdrawal of the consumer' (*Widerrufsrecht*), establishing that in 'consumer contracts' (*Verbraucherverträgen*) the consumer who exercised the right to withdraw in a manner provided for by the law should no longer be bound by the contract. In addition, the reform introduced a new definition of 'consumer' (*Verbraucher*) in the General Part of the BGB, at § 13. Overall, the main aim of the reform was to put the BGB in line with the European *acquis* and at the same time exert influence on future developments of contract law at EU level.[53]

IV. Implementing Directives outside the Civil Codes

In some other Member States belonging to the civil law tradition, for example France, Spain, and Italy, the transposition of EU directives into national laws has taken place outside the civil codes. The reasons for this are manifold. First, it was felt that the consumer had some characteristics that distinguished them from the intended addressee of the civil code. They were vulnerable, in a weaker position, and in need of additional protection, for which a special regulation

(eds), *Zivilrechtswissenschaft und Schuldrechtsreform: Zum Diskussionsentwurf eines Schuldrechtsmo dernisierungsgesetzes des Bundesministeriums der Justiz* (Mohr Siebeck 2001) 481.

[47] Pozzo (n 31) 761.

[48] '*Wegfall der Geschäftsgrundlage*', new § 313 BGB.

[49] *Culpa in contrahendo*, new § 311(2) BGB.

[50] § 280 BGB.

[51] Stefan Grundmann, 'Germany and the Schuldrechtsmodernisierung 2002' (2005) 1 European Review of Contract Law 129.

[52] BGB, Buch 2, § 305ff.

[53] See, in particular, the former Minister of Justice Herta Däubler-Gmelin, 'Die Entscheidung für die so genannte Große Lösung bei der Schuldrechtsreform', Neue Juristische Wochenschrift 2001, 2281.

was needed. Secondly, the legislation produced by the EU legislator has increased a great deal in volume over the years, covering different areas of contract law, and making it difficult to introduce legislation into the architecture of a civil code.

In France, consumer law has been the object of a separate codification, the Code de la consommation[54] (Consumer Law Code), launched in the 1990s.[55] Such a move was motivated by the need to organize the relevant legal norms in a way that would facilitate their use by, and accessibility to, citizens.[56] The discussion of the benefits of codifying consumer law has never subsided,[57] especially in the light of what is called codification of established law (*codification à droit constant*). This type of codification is defined as a technique aimed at gathering and reorganizing existing law relating to a specific field within a single text validated by the public authorities; it must be carried out without any modification to the substance of the standards.[58] In particular, the aim of the Consumer Law Code was to bring together in one document all the legal texts governing a particular subject matter, regardless of the terminology of the Civil Code.[59] The idea of codifying consumer law, with its own terminology, outside the Civil Code has provoked much scholarly discussion, especially regarding the introduction of the so-called *droit de repentir*,[60] which has no exact equivalent in English, but could be translated as the 'right to reconsider', corresponding to the 'right of withdrawal' granted to the consumer.

A different path was taken by the Spanish legislator, where the transposition of EU Directives has been carried out by enacting special laws, which were to coexist

[54] *Loi* no 93-949 of 26 July 1993.

[55] Jean Calais-Auloy, *Propositions pour un droit de la consommation* (La Documentation française 1985); Jean Calais-Auloy, 'Le projet de code de la consommation', Revue française d'administration publique 1990, no 56, 1, 643.

[56] Jérôme Julien, *Droit de la consommation* (LGDJ 2015) 17ff.

[57] Guy Braibant, 'La problématique de la codification', Revue française d'administration publique 1997, no 82, 165; Philippe Stoffel-Munck, 'Les résultats de la codification', Revue juridique de l'Océan Indien 2004, no 4, 121; Remy Cabrillac, 'Les enjeux de la codification en France', Les Cahiers de droit 2005, no 46, 1, 533.

[58] In 1989, in order to relaunch the slowing codification process, the French government set up the *Commission Supérieure de Codification*, tasked with codifying the law in a number of areas using a 'constant law' approach. It involves changing the form and structure of codes, and the numbering of laws and regulations, without altering the overall content of the law. The aim is to harmonize the codes with each other and with the hierarchy of norms. The work of the *Commission Supérieure de Codification* has resulted in the creation of several dozen new codes. See Pierre Catala, 'Les techniques de codification: l'expérience française', Revue juridique de l'Océan Indien 2004, no 4, 77. For a general overview of how the *Commission Supérieure de Codification* works, and its impact on the Consumer law Code, see Guy Braibant, Christian Vigouroux, and Frédéric Scanvic, 'Cinquieme Rapport Annuel de la Commission Supérieure de Codification (Année 1994)', La Revue administrative 1995, no 48.285, 308.

[59] Denis Mazeaud, 'Le droit européen des contrats et ses influences sur le droit français' (2010) 6 European Review of Contract Law 1.

[60] Valentina Jacometti, 'The "Terminological" Vicissitudes of the Consumer *ius poenitendi* in Community Directives and in the French Legal System' in Gianmaria Ajani and Martin Ebers (eds), *Uniform Terminology for European Contract Law* (Nomos 2005) 241; see further Pozzo (n 31) 767.

with the general law on consumer protection: the General Law 26/1984 for the Protection of Consumers and Users.[61] This fragmentary situation was reorganized by the Royal Legislative Decree 1/2007,[62] which introduced a new consolidated text of the General Law for the Protections of Consumers and Users, containing some of the most important and previously distinct consumer protection laws. The idea behind the reform was to consolidate, integrate, and coordinate the chaotic legislation in the field of consumer protection. Nevertheless, the Royal Legislative Decree 1/2007 is not exhaustive. It is accompanied by a series of other important measures, including the Royal Decree on General Product Safety,[63] the Law on Unfair Competition,[64] the Law on General Conditions in Contracts,[65] the Regulation on Transparency and the Protection of Banking Services Customers,[66] and the Law on Real Estate Loans.[67]

The influence of EU directives on the legal terminology of Spanish consumer protection law is undeniable. Remarkably, most of Spanish law in this area is a direct and immediate consequence of the transposition of directives, which has sometimes occurred without a prior process of reflection or integration. These directives have become the source of many legal terms and, in some cases, of fundamental concepts of Spanish consumer protection law. On other occasions, the usage or meaning of legal categories in Spanish law needed to be adapted or adjusted after the directives' transposition.[68]

A third example may be taken from the Italian experience, where in 2005 the consumer protection legislation of European origin was collected and rearranged into a consolidated text called 'Codice del Consumo' (the Consumer Code).[69] The Consumer Code was initially considered a milestone in the law of consumer protection because it aimed to put order in a field where special laws were previously adopted from time to time, without coordination, mostly to implement EU Directives.[70] Nevertheless, more recent EU directives have not yet been

[61] Ley 26/1984 of 19 July 1984.
[62] Real Decreto Legislativo 1/2007 of 16 November 2007.
[63] Real Decreto 1801/2003 of 26 December 2003.
[64] Ley 3/1991 of 10 January 1991.
[65] Ley 7/1998 of 13 April 1998.
[66] Orden EHA/2899/2011 of 28 October 2011.
[67] Ley 5/2019 of 15 March 2019.
[68] Natalia Álvarez Lata, 'The Impact of the Terminology of the European Directives on Consumer Rights on the Spanish Law: The Construction of a New Legal Language' (2012) 20 European Review of Private Law 1305, 1309.
[69] Decreto Legislativo no 206 of 6 September 2005.
[70] Guido Alpa, 'I contratti dei consumatori e la disciplina generale dei contratti e del rapporto obbligatorio', Rivista di Diritto Civile 2006, no 6, 351, 352; Alessandro Palmieri, 'Arriva il codice del consumo: riorganizzazione (tendenzialmente) completa tra addii ed innovazioni', Il Foro italiano 2006, vol 129, no 2, 77–82; Guido Alpa, 'La codificazione del diritto dei consumatori. Aspetti di diritto comparato', Economia e diritto del terziario 2009, no 1, 69–83.

incorporated into the Consumer Code, and EU legislation on electronic documents[71] has been implemented through a separate text,[72] further fragmenting the system.[73]

The criticism in Italy has been directed primarily at the legislative technique of incorporating entire bodies of legislation into positive law without first attempting to coordinate the various legislative interventions, despite their complexity and fragmentary nature. This style of transposing directives has often been called 'cut and paste' legislation, and has resulted in the emergence of legal texts, like the Italian Consumer Code, which do not have a guiding thread: they lack homogeneity. The failure to coordinate with the Italian Civil Code represented a missed opportunity for a true codification, and not simply a collection of norms of EU origin. Inevitably, with the increasing number of EU directives and regulations related to consumer law, the consequence is that the Consumer Code has been subjected to numerous amendments.[74]

This choice is not without consequences for the search for a coherent system of concepts at the national level. This is because even within a single jurisdiction, we can observe distinct conceptual systems, which are not only not integrated, but can also contradict each other. The implementation of EU directives has, in some jurisdictions, distorted the national terminologies; the meaning of traditional civil law concepts is no longer respected in the field of consumer law. In Italian law, this issue has arisen in particular in relation to the concept of 'unilateral withdrawal' (*recesso*), which had been regulated in the Italian Civil Code but took a different meaning in the Consumer Code, as required by EU directives.[75] *Recesso* is regulated by article 1373 of the Italian Civil Code and refers—in general terms—to the possibility of exiting a contract. The article in question specifies:

> If one of the parties is granted the right to withdraw from the contract, this right can be exercised until the performance of the contract has started.

[71] Notably Regulation (EU) No 910/2014 of the European Parliament and of the Council of 23 July 2014 on electronic identification and trust services for electronic transactions in the internal market and repealing Directive 1999/93/EC, OJ L 257, 28.8.2014, p 73.

[72] The EU legislation on the electronic document was transposed into Italian law by the Decreto del Presidente della Repubblica no 445 of 28 December 2000 and by the Decreto Legislativo no 82 of 7 March 2005.

[73] Criticisms of the Italian Consumer Code have been expressed since its early days. See Giovanni De Cristofaro, 'Il "Codice del consumo": un'occasione perduta?', Studium iuris 2005, 1337, 1148; Giovanni De Cristofaro, 'Il "codice del consumo"', Leggi civili commentate, 2006, no 5, 747, 749 and 755ff; Aurelio Gentili, 'Codice del consumo ed esprit de géométrie', I Contratti 2006, no 2, 159; Lucia Delogu, 'Leggendo il Codice del consumo alla ricerca della nozione di consumatore', Contratto e impresa Europa 2006, no 1, 87, 89.

[74] Maria Giovanna Falzone Calvisi, 'Il "taglia e incolla" non si addice al legislatore', Contratto e impresa Europa 2006, 104.

[75] See eg Giovanni De Cristofaro, 'La disciplina unitaria del "diritto di recesso": ambito di applicazione, struttura e contenuti essenziali' in Giovanni De Cristofaro (ed), *I "princìpi" del diritto comunitario dei contratti. Acquis communautaire e diritto privato europeo* (Giappichelli 2009) 351.

> In contracts for continuous or periodic performance, this right may also be exercised subsequently, but the withdrawal shall not affect performance which has already occurred or that is in the process of occurring.

This form of *recesso* is general and applies to various types of contracts (eg, some partnership agreements, leases, and other contractual relationships). However, since the implementation of EU consumer directives, the concept of *recesso* has been used in a different way. In Italian consumer law, *recesso* refers to the right of withdrawal within a set period after the purchase or agreement, which allows consumers to cancel a contract or return goods purchased without needing to provide a specific reason. This *recesso* typically applies in the context of distance contracts (like online purchases) or off-premises contracts (eg, door-to-door sales). Under the Italian Consumer Code, consumers generally have fourteen days from the moment they receive the goods or sign the contract to exercise their right of *recesso*. After exercising the right, consumers are usually entitled to a full refund but have to return the goods.

In conclusion, there are important differences between the *recesso* of the Civil Code and the *recesso* of the Consumer Code, as far as their purpose, conditions, and scope are concerned. *Recesso* under consumer law is designed to protect consumers from impulsive purchases, while the one under the Civil Code applies to a range of contractual relationships and may not always favour the consumer. The right of *recesso* in consumer law has a set timeframe (usually fourteen days) and generally does not involve penalties, while *recesso* in the Civil Code may involve conditions such as penalties or notice periods. Finally, *recesso* in consumer law is a statutory right, whereas the one in the Civil Code is dependent on there being a contractual term to this effect. Considering all these differences, the use of the same term has often been criticized.[76]

Not surprisingly,[77] a vastly different approach has been taken by the UK, where most of contract, tort, and property law is judge-made, although there are also a number of acts of Parliament dealing with specific and usually quite narrow issues.[78] Some of these statutes have been adopted to deal with concerns relating to the state of the common law,[79] rather than to codify aspects of contract or tort law. As Whittaker has pointed out,

[76] De Cristofaro (n 73).

[77] Karl Riesenhuber, 'English common law versus German Systemdenken? Internal versus external approaches' (2011) 7 Utrecht Law Review 117.

[78] Christian Twigg-Flesner, 'Consolidation Rather than Codification–or Just Complication? The UK's Consumer Rights Act', Zeitschrift für Europäisches Privatrecht 2015, 170.

[79] See the Law Reform (Frustrated Contracts) Act 1943, the Misrepresentation Act 1967, or the Contracts (Rights of Third Parties Act) 1999.

for the UK legislator, the absence of a civil code (and of other codes, such as a consumer law code) means that some of these problems do not arise in the same form. Indeed, the English law applicable to contracts generally remains dominated by the common law, and so the idea of legislation intervening specially and for particular purposes (and sometimes using tailor-made terminology) fits within the traditional view of statutes as 'isolated irruptions' in the common law.[80]

There are only a few areas of English private law where more detailed legislation can be found, most notably the Sale of Goods Act 1979.[81] There is no coherent codification of general contract law in England. Nor is there any comprehensive codification of English consumer law.[82] Measures were adopted to deal with specific problems, but they did not contain provisions dedicated to consumer contracts. For example, the Sale of Goods Act 1979—which, in relation to consumer contracts, has been mostly superseded by the Consumer Rights Act 2015—did not contain separate provisions for consumer sales contracts, although it did apply to such contracts. The statute of 1979 was also not comprehensive because it did not deal with contracts other than sales.

A second significant piece of legislation is the Unfair Contract Terms Act 1977, now replaced as far as consumer contracts are concerned by the Consumer Rights Act 2015. One aim of the former was to provide strong protection for consumers with respect to some exclusion and limitation clauses. Nevertheless, it did not at that time provide a general fairness test so that many unfair contract terms could not be challenged under the Act.[83] Also, the Consumer Protection Act 1987,[84] despite its promising title, only dealt with three broad aspects of consumer law: product liability, price indications, and product safety. What this means is that before 2015 there has been no comprehensive, or even semi-comprehensive, statute on consumer law, meaning that there was no coherent terminology in the field of consumer law either.[85] We also need to bear in mind that UK implementations of EU directives were regulating areas which were largely unregulated by statutory law. In the rare cases where statutes existed and overlapped with a directive, new free-standing legislation was adopted to implement the directive, with

80 Whittaker (n 6) 626.
81 Sale of Goods Act 1979.
82 Twigg-Flesner (n 34).
83 Twigg-Flesner (n 78) 171ff.
84 The Act was 'to make provision with respect to the liability of persons for damage caused by defective products; to consolidate with amendments the Consumer Safety Act 1978 and the Consumer Safety (Amendment) Act 1986; to make provision with respect to the giving of price indications; to amend Part I of the Health and Safety at Work etc. Act 1974 and sections 31 and 80 of the Explosives Act 1875; to repeal the Trade Descriptions Act 1972 and the Fabrics (Misdescription) Act 1913; and for connected purposes'; Consumer Protection Act 1987. The Act has not been integrated into the Consumer Rights Act 2015.
85 Twigg-Flesner (n 34).

the existing statutes left unamended. This is what happened, for example, with the implementation of the Unfair Contract Terms Directive of 1993.[86] The Unfair Contract Terms Act 1977 was left untouched, while the provisions of the Directive were implemented by the Unfair Terms in Consumer Contracts Regulations 1994 (and later their 1999 replacement). As might have been expected, the coexistence of two regimes proved problematic.

In 2001, the Department of Trade and Industry asked the Law Commission (for England and Wales) and the Scottish Law Commission to rewrite the law of unfair contract terms as a single regime and in a clearer and more accessible language. The project faced the problem of an unnecessarily complicated body of law on unfair contract terms,[87] and had to contend with the infiltration of EU terminology into domestic private law.[88] The consequence of the Law Commission's work was a reform of English consumer contract law undertaken between 2012 and 2015.[89] These reforms were introduced by the following regulations and statutes: the Consumer Contracts (Information, Cancellation and Additional Charges) Regulations 2013 ('Consumer Contracts Regulations' or '2013 Regulations'), which impose a series of duties on traders to provide information to consumers, which grant consumers rights of cancellation and which make further particular provision in relation to consumer payments; and the Consumer Protection (Amendment) Regulations 2014, which introduce a form of 'rights to redress' for consumers in respect of certain types of unfair commercial practices by traders by amending the earlier Consumer Protection from Unfair Trading Regulations 2008 (2008 Regulations). In 2015 the Consumer Rights Act 2015 was enacted, which includes, inter alia, a series of provisions related to 'goods contracts', 'digital content contracts', and 'services contracts', and also makes general provision for the control of unfair terms in consumer contracts. Finally, it is worth mentioning the Consumer Insurance (Disclosure and Representations) Act 2012 (as amended by the Insurance Contracts Act 2015), which rewrites the law governing disclosure and representations by consumers in insurance contracts.

What is the relationship between UK legislation and EU law? As Whittaker has pointed out,[90] much of it has a close relationship with EU law, but the nature of that relationship varies. In some cases, UK law faithfully implements the requirements of EU secondary law albeit frequently across different statutory regimes,[91] while

[86] Council Directive 93/13/EEC of 5 April 1993 on unfair terms in consumer contracts, OJ L 95, 21.4.1993, p 29.

[87] Law Commission and Scottish Law Commission, *Unfair Terms in Contracts* (Law Com No 292 and Scot Law Com No 199, 2005).

[88] Twigg-Flesner (n 34) 1370.

[89] Simon Whittaker, 'Distinctive Features of the New Consumer Contract Law' (2017) 133 Law Quarterly Review 47.

[90] ibid 48.

[91] As in the case of the Consumer Contracts Regulations and many of the provisions on sales contracts and unfair contract terms in the Consumer Rights Act 2015. Some provisions in the 2015 Act

in others the EU legislative scheme is implemented with small modifications.[92] In some cases, the new law adds an extra dimension to an EU legislative scheme (as in the case of the rights to redress against traders in respect of certain prohibited commercial practices even though the Unfair Commercial Practices Directive does not affect 'contract law') or the former applies (suitably amended) an EU legislative scheme to contracts to which the latter does not itself apply (as in the case of the special consumer remedies as regards goods contracts other than sale, digital content contracts, and services contracts).[93]

Moreover, some UK consumer legislation enacted before Brexit had no connection at all with EU law. For example, a number of provisions in the Consumer Rights Act 2015 or the law governing consumer insurance reflected earlier domestic law or was the consequence of the Law Commission's own proposal.[94] Perhaps for this reason, the legislative project, which was initiated in order to simplify UK consumer law and make it more accessible, did not succeed, and in fact introduced a highly complex regime with cumbersome and counterintuitive terminology.[95]

In conclusion, to understand the possible impact of EU terminology on English legal terminology in the field of consumer law, it is necessary to trace the transposition of each directive as it has been carried out. For example, the implementation of the Consumer Sales Directive (99/44/EC)[96] dealt with a subject matter

implement the Consumer Sales Directive (Directive 1999/44/EC of the European Parliament and of the Council of 25 May 1999 on certain aspects of the sale of consumer goods and associated guarantees, OJ L 171, 7.7.1999, p 12), notably, the provisions in ss 9 and 10 governing the statutory term that the goods be of satisfactory quality and fit for purpose, the scheme of special remedies in ss 19–20, 23–24, and the provisions in s 30 on goods under guarantee. Other sections implement aspects of Directive 2011/83/EU of the European Parliament and of the Council of 25 October 2011 on consumer rights, amending Council Directive 93/13/EEC and Directive 1999/44/EC of the European Parliament and of the Council and repealing Council Directive 85/577/EEC and Directive 97/7/EC of the European Parliament and of the Council, OJ L 304, 22.11.2011, p 64. Notably, ss 11(4)–(6), 12, 36(3)–(4), 37 and 50(3) (giving contractual force to information supplied by a trader to a consumer as required by the 2013 Regulations) and ss 28–29 (governing the delivery of goods and the passing of risk, respectively, and implementing arts 6(5), 18 and 20 of the 2011 Directive). Part 2 of Consumer Rights Act 2015 re-implements the 1993 Directive on unfair terms in consumer contracts (see n 87), formerly implemented by The Unfair Terms in Consumer Contracts Regulations 1999. Cf Whittaker (n 89) at fn 6.

[92] Whittaker (n 89) 49 gives the following examples: the addition of the consumer's short-lived right to reject non-conforming goods or the apparent narrowing of the 'core exclusion' from fairness control of contract terms.

[93] Directive 2005/29/EC of the European Parliament and of the Council of 11 May 2005 concerning unfair business-to-consumer commercial practices in the internal market and amending Council Directive 84/450/EEC, Directives 97/7/EC, 98/27/EC and 2002/65/EC of the European Parliament and of the Council and Regulation (EC) No 2006/2004 of the European Parliament and of the Council ('Unfair Commercial Practices Directive'), OJ L 149, 11.6.2005, p 22, in particular art 3(2).

[94] Whittaker (n 89) 48.

[95] ibid 59 (noting that 'the terminology of rights and remedies in the 2008 Regulations and 2015 Act is, to say the least, unhelpfully complicated and at times inconsistent', as 'no clear position is adopted as to the relationship between the consumer's substantive rights under the contract . . . and the consumer's remedy or remedies when these substantive rights are not met by the trader').

[96] For a detailed discussion, see Robert Bradgate and Christian Twigg-Flesner, *Blackstone's Guide to Consumer Sales and Associated Guarantees* (OUP 2003).

already covered in the Sale of Goods Act 1979, except for the remedies of repair, replacement, and price reduction. These remedies were required by Article 3 of the Consumer Sales Directive, so when it came to transposing the Directive, the UK government decided to amend the Sale of Goods Act to the extent that it was necessary to bring it into line with the Directive. This meant the retention of the 'satisfactory quality' test and the introduction of the remedial scheme from the Directive's Article 3 into a separate part of the Act. This solution has been subjected to considerable criticism, partly because it resulted in a very complex set of remedies for English consumers, but also because it resulted in a clash between different terminologies.[97]

Finally, it is necessary to consider how UK courts have resolved the terminological issues present in domestic legislation giving effect to EU directives. As Twigg-Flesner has observed, English courts have had to deal with a range of situations.[98] The first concerns cases where some of the terminology used in domestic legislation specifically adopted to transpose a directive had previously been used in other contexts and carried pre-existing meanings. The second situation concerns cases where domestic legislation relied on new terminology, not previously used in English law. And finally, there have been cases where existing legislation was regarded as a sufficient reflection of a directive's requirements. Here, UK courts have considered it necessary to review the meaning in which some of the legislative terms were used in order to ensure conformity with the Directive.[99]

V. Different Attitudes of National Lawyers towards the Europeanization of National Laws

Beyond the existence or non-existence of a consumer code, other divisive factors have emerged, this time stemming from the attitudes of legal scholars and national case law responding to the Europeanization of national laws. Despite the increasingly conspicuous EU legislation relating to contractual matters harmonizing the law in this area and the initiatives taken to create a common terminology, different legal mentalities persist within the various national legal systems. Legal mentality, that is, the way of thinking about law and its concepts, varies depending on the kind of legal education received, and is reflected in beliefs about which sources of law are considered more important and about the role of judges and scholars. To understand how harmonized EU contract law is received, it is important to take

[97] Twigg-Flesner (n 34) 1373.
[98] ibid 1374.
[99] ibid.

account of the different attitudes of judges and scholars, including to the idea of the harmonization of European law and the language and terminology used by it.

The research I have conducted, aimed at understanding the attitudes of legal scholars across different jurisdictions, reveals differences in the reactions to the terminology used by the Community legislator.[100] French legal scholars have, for example, emphasized that the national legislator, when transposing EU consumer protection directives, was influenced by the fact that national rules had often preceded EU legislation. The French legislator decided to maintain its legal system's lexical and conceptual heritage by containing the influence of EU rules.[101] Similarly, Belgian scholars reported having closely scrutinized the terminology used in EU directives.[102]

For example, the Unfair Commercial Practices Directive introduced a European notion of 'commercial practices' (or, more specifically, of business-to-consumer commercial practices),[103] a concept which clashed with that of 'market practices' used by national law.[104] This situation sparked an interesting debate among legal scholars. Initially, the implementation of the Unfair Commercial Practices Directive into Belgian law used the concept of 'commercial practices' and introduced its definition in article 93(5) of the law on commercial practices and the information and protection of the consumer.[105] However, in 2010, this text was replaced by the Statute on market practices and consumer protection,[106] article 2(29) of which defines a 'commercial practice' as 'any act, omission, course of conduct or representation, commercial communication including advertising and marketing, by a trader, directly connected with the promotion, sale or supply of a product'. Interestingly, the concept of 'market practices', which is used in the title of the statute and its article 95, is not defined. Its location within the statute suggests that it is a wider concept than 'commercial practices', which in turn could be interpreted as limited to practices directed at consumers. This limitation is not, however, mentioned explicitly in the Belgian definition of commercial practices, as included in

[100] See Barbara Pozzo, 'The Impact of Multilingualism on the Harmonization of European Private Law' (2012) 20 European Review of Private Law 1181. The aim of the research was to understand if Europeanization of the law has taken place and to what extent a consistent 'European' terminology exists. The field of research covered five legal systems, taking into consideration France, Spain, Belgium, Germany, and England.

[101] Marie-Laure Mathieu, 'La transposition des directives en droit français: maîtrise des mots, maîtrise sur les mots' (2012) 20 European Review of Private Law 1277, 1279–80.

[102] Caroline Cauffman, 'The Impact of EU Law on Belgian Consumer Law Terminology' (2012) 20 European Review of Private Law 1325, 1351.

[103] Unfair Commercial Practices Directive (n 93), art 2(d): 'any act, omission, course of conduct or representation, commercial communication including advertising and marketing, by a trader, directly connected with the promotion, sale or supply of a product to consumers.'

[104] Cauffman (n 102) 1352.

[105] Law of 5 June 2007 modifying the law of 14 July 1991 on commercial practices and the information and protection of the consumer.

[106] Law of 6 April 2010 on Market Practices and Consumer Protection ('LPPC'), *Belgisch Staatsblad*, 12 April 2010, p 20803.

article 2(29) of the statute. For this reason, scholars have argued that there was no need to use the additional concept of 'market practices' on top of 'commercial practices'. However, given the maximum harmonization aim of the Unfair Commercial Practices Directive, it is not certain that the CJEU would allow Member States to give the concept of 'commercial practices' a wider scope (covering practices also not directed at consumers) than that for which the Directive provided. On the one hand, the broadening of the concept is irrelevant given the limited scope of the Unfair Commercial Practices Directive. The Court could thus see the part of the Belgian concept which falls outside the scope of the Directive as neutral from the perspective of the Directive's aims. However, if the EU Court sees Belgian legislation as extending the scope of the Directive's binding effect by modifying the definition of 'commercial practices' used in the Directive, it is more likely to oppose the legislation and deem it non-compliant with EU law. Perhaps for these reasons, the Belgian legislator played it safe by implicitly limiting the concept of 'commercial practices' to those aimed at consumers, while introducing a wider concept of 'market practices' that can be interpreted to encompass practices directed at both consumers and non-consumers.

Another example is provided by Spanish law. Spanish consumer law is to a greater degree than French or Belgian law a direct and immediate consequence of the transposition of EU directives. Spanish scholars have observed that the implementation of EU directives in the field of consumer protection has taken place without a preceding process of reflection or integration.[107] EU consumer law has become a source of many legal terms and foundational concepts of Spanish consumer protection law, inducing the adaptation or adjustment of old categories.[108] Furthermore, the sentiment among Spanish scholars is that it is the case law of the CJEU which has achieved the true Europeanization of Spanish consumer law.[109]

VI. The Role of the Court of Justice of the European Union

The opinion of Spanish scholars on the contribution of the CJEU to the European consumer law harmonization project can only be understood if we appreciate the unique position which the EU Court occupies in the EU legal order. We might recall here that the law made by the EU is multilingual, and that EU legislation is published in all official languages and is equally authoritative in each language.[110]

[107] Álvarez Lata (n 68) 1305.

[108] Luz M Martínez Velencoso, 'The Impact of Harmonized European Private Law and the Acquis Communautaire on Spanish Law' (2018) 11 Journal of Civil Law Studies 152.

[109] Palacios González, 'Tribunal de Justicia de la Unión Europea y derecho del consumo en España' in Paz Andrés Sáenz de Santamaría (ed), *Una contribución a la europeización de la ciencia jurídica: Estudios sobre la Unión Europea* (Thomson Reuters 2019) 397, 398.

[110] Elina Paunio, 'The Tower of Babel and the interpretation of EU law-implications for equality of languages and legal certainty' in Thomas Wilhelmsson, Elina Paunio, and Annika Pohjolainen

The CJEU is known to have made use of the multilingual character of EU legislation, including in cases involving consumer protection issues.[111]

At the same time, multilingualism is a source of numerous problems, both in the drafting of the documents, and then later in their application.[112] For this reason, it has often been said that translating into and from each official language is no longer a practical proposition as today it is necessary to navigate among more than 500 possible language combinations.[113] In this context, the CJEU plays a major role both because of its duty to ensure that 'in the interpretation and application of the Treaty, law is observed' (article 19 TEU), and because the preliminary ruling procedure allows it to influence a case while it is still being heard by the national court, before it is conclusively resolved.[114] One important context in which the Court had to tackle the problem of multilingualism was the application of its *acte clair* doctrine, which allows a national court from whose judgment there is no further judicial remedy to refrain from referring the case to the CJEU, even though this duty is prescribed by Article 267 TFEU.

The relevant judgment is *CILFIT*,[115] where the Court established several exceptions to the obligation to refer currently laid down in the third paragraph of Article 267 TFEU. More particularly, its holding was the following: a court or tribunal against the decisions of which there is no judicial remedy under national law is required, where a question of EU law is raised before it, to comply with its obligation to bring the matter before the EU Court, unless the court or tribunal

(eds), *Private Law and the Many Cultures of Europe* (Kluwer Law International 2007) 385; Elina Paunio, *Legal Certainty in Multilingual EU Law: Language, Discourse and Reasoning at the European Court of Justice* (Routledge 2016); Lawrence M Solan, 'The Interpretation of Multilingual Statutes by the European Court of Justice' (2008) 34 Brook Journal of International Law 277; Karen McAuliffe, 'Creating Multilingual Law: Language and Translation at the Court of Justice of the European Union' in Malcolm Coulthard, Alison May, and Rui Sousa-Silva (eds), *The Routledge Handbook of Forensic Linguistics* (Routledge 2020) 64.

[111] Fabrizio Vismara, 'The Role of the Court of Justice of the European Communities in the Interpretation of Multilingual Texts' in Pozzo and Jacometti (n 1) 61; Barbara Pozzo, 'L'interpretazione della Corte del Lussemburgo del testo plurilingue: una rassegna giurisprudenziale' in Barbara Pozzo and Marina Timoteo (eds), *Europa e Linguaggi Giuridici* (Giuffrè 2008) 383.

[112] Barbara Pozzo, 'Multilingualism and the Harmonization of European Private Law: Problems and Perspectives' (2012) 20 European Review of Private Law 1185.

[113] Barbara Pozzo, 'Multilingualism as a Value in the European Union' in Gianmaria Ajani and others (eds), *The Multilanguage Complexity of European Law: Methodologies in Comparison* (European Press Academic Publishing 2007) 133.

[114] Stefaan Van der Jeught, 'Current Practices with Regard to the Interpretation of Multilingual EU Law: How to Deal with Diverging Language Versions' (2018) 11 European Journal of Legal Studies 5.

[115] *Srl CILFIT and Lanificio di Gavardo SpA v Ministry of Health* (n 35). For a discussion of the case law, see Paul Craig, 'The Classics of EU Law Revisited: *CILFIT* and *Foto-Frost*' in Luis Miguel Poiares Pessoa Maduro and Loïc Azoulai, *The Past and Future of EU Law: The Classics of EU Law Revisited on the 50th Anniversary of the Rome Treaty* (Hart Publishing 2010) 185; Jacobien van Dorp and Pauline Phoa, 'How to Continue a Meaningful Judicial Dialogue about EU Law: From the Conditions in the CILFIT Judgment to the Creation of a New European Legal Culture' (2018) 34 Utrecht Journal of International and European Law 73; François-Xavier Millet, 'Cilfit Still Fits' (2022) 18 European

has established that the question raised is irrelevant, or that the provision of EU law in question has already been interpreted by the EU Court, or that the correct application of EU law is so obvious as to leave no scope for any reasonable doubt. In that case, the Court insisted that the clarity of the EU law which would relieve the national court from the duty to ask for a preliminary ruling is to be assessed against all language versions of the EU law measure. This case is an example of the more general attitude of the Court, which, despite the difficulties which multiple language versions generate and the increasing number of official languages of the EU, has staunchly maintained a rule that the meaning of an EU text needs to be arrived at by comparing its different language versions.[116] While this is mostly the case where a single language version differs from all the others, thus making it easy for the Court to choose 'the' solution,[117] it is still striking that, unlike elsewhere, the Court has not relied on a directive's objective as an indication of what the meaning of a provision should be in the light of its divergent language versions.

So, for example, in *Gubisch Maschinenfabrik AG v Giulio Palumbo*, the Court simply stated that the German version had to be 'construed in the same manner as the other language versions'.[118] In *United Kingdom of Great Britain and Northern Ireland v Commission of the European Communities*, the Commission submitted, and the Court agreed, that, 'in accordance with the established case law of the Court, the need for a uniform interpretation of Community legislation requires that this version [ie, the English version] should not be considered in isolation and that where doubt arises it should be interpreted and applied in the light of the other language versions'.[119] In *Firma Schmid v Hauptzollamt Stuttgart-West*, the Court drew the solution from the 'comparison of the different language versions', interpreting the imprecise definition contained in the German version in the light of the provisions of the other official languages.[120]

What these cases suggest is that the Court was of the view that the textual difficulties can be resolved by means of mere comparison of the wording of the different language versions. This is also true about cases where the Court makes specific references to 'the majority of the language versions' to achieve its interpretative goal. In *Stanley*

Constitutional Law Review 533; Mattias Derlén, *Multilingual Interpretation of European Union Law* (Kluwer Law International 2009).

[116] See, for example, Case 144/86 *Gubisch Maschinenfabrik AG* v *Giulio Palumbo* ('*Palumbo*') [1987] ECR 4861; Case 114/86 *United Kingdom of Great Britain and Northern Ireland v Commission of the European Communities* [1988] ECR 5289; Case 357/87 *Firme Schmid v Hauptzollamt Stuttgart-West* [1988] ECR 6239.

[117] On the different interpretation criteria of the Court, see Pozzo (n 113) 415.

[118] *Palumbo* (n 116) para 14.

[119] *United Kingdom of Great Britain and Northern Ireland v Commission of the European Communities* (n 116) para 3.

[120] *Firme Schmid* (n 116) paras 8–9.

Charles Atkins v Wrekin District Council and Department of Transport, for example, the Court stated:

> interpretation is borne out by the fact that, *in most language versions* of the Directive, the singular is expressly used in Article 1 in stating that the purpose of the Directive is the progressive implementation of the principle of equal treatment for men and women in the field of social security and other elements of social protection provided for in Article 3.[121]

It is only in some cases that the Court moves to considering the Directive's objective when the comparison does not prove sufficient to reconcile the multilingual divergences.[122]

This analysis reveals that it is difficult to formulate an unequivocal theory which the Court is using when arriving at a meaning of EU multilingual texts. The Court has to bear in mind that some linguistic divergences can be the result of translation errors, which the technicality of EU law, the pressure of time, and the large daily workload of lawyer-linguists and translators in European institutions make all too likely. However, there can also be divergences caused by the difficulty of finding equivalent concepts in the different legal traditions that have developed their own 'reference contexts'.[123] Such divergences are not errors but differences in the deeper meaning of the legislative measure in question.

The Court's task goes beyond just reconciling the different language versions. It is aimed at developing uniform concepts and a value system for EU law. European legal scholars should assist the Court in this effort.[124] The Court's effort in fostering law that can be uniformly applied across national jurisdictions sheds light on the Court's case law relating to the manner in which EU legislation should be implemented at the national level. For example, in *Commission v the Netherlands*,[125] the Court insisted that even where legislative action on the part of each Member State was not necessary in order to implement a directive, it was essential for national law to be sufficiently precise and clear and for individuals

[121] Case C-228/94 *Stanley Charles Atkins v Wrekin District Council and Department of Transport* [1996] ECR I-3633, para 30 (emphasis added).

[122] Case 90/83 *Michael Paterson and others v W Weddel & Company Limited and others* [1984] ECR 1567, paras 10–11; Case 19/83 *Knud Wendelboe and others v L.J. Music ApS, in liquidation* [1985] ECR 457, para 13; Case 300/86 *Luc Van Landschoot v NV Mera* [1988] ECR 3443, para 18; Case 55/87 *Alexander Moksel Import und Export GmbH & Co. Handels-KG v Bundesanstalt für landwirtschaftliche Marktordnung* [1988] ECR 3845, paras 14–19.

[123] See Barbara Pozzo, 'Comparative Law and Language' in Mauro Bussani and Ugo Mattei (eds), *Cambridge Companion to Comparative Law* (CUP 2013) 88, 94.

[124] See Barbara Pozzo, 'Comparative Law and the New Frontiers of Legal Translation' in Šarčević (n 23) 73.

[125] Case C-144/99 *Commission of the European Communities v Kingdom of the Netherlands* [2001] ECR I-3541.

to be made fully aware of their rights so that they could rely on them before the national courts.[126] In other cases, the Court intervened to determine the content of concepts that were not defined by EU legislation. This was the case with the concept of 'consumer', which is not defined in the same way in the different Member States.[127] Thus, in *Idealservice*,[128] a case which concerned the meaning of 'consumer' in the context of the Unfair Terms Directive,[129] the Court took a firm stance that the concept covers only natural persons. Even more explicitly, in *Di Pinto* the CJEU gave an even narrower interpretation of 'consumer', stating that for the purposes of the Doorstep Selling Directive[130] a 'trader' is not to be regarded as a 'consumer' protected by the directive even if they are in a position similar to that of a consumer.

Sometimes it is not the concept of 'consumer' but that of 'contract' that is used to narrow the scope of a Directive. This is what happened in the *Dietzinger* case,[131] where the Court addressed the issue of whether a *Bürgschaft* (a surety or personal guarantee) under German law given by an individual to a bank outside the bank's premises would fall under Directive 85/577. Article 1 provides that 'This Directive shall apply to contracts under which a trader supplies goods or services to a consumer'. As it is noted in the Opinion of Advocate General Jacobs, the Directive does not define the concept of 'contract', and, given the different language versions of the Directive, it would be possible to conclude that it also regulated other transactions where one of the parties is a supplier of goods and services.[132] However, after scrutinizing the different language versions of the Directive, the Court inquired about the purpose of the protection afforded by the text and concluded that a guarantee given to a financial institution by an individual who is not acting in the course of their trade or profession, in order to secure a loan by that institution to a third party, is not within the scope of Council Directive 85/577/EEC.

[126] Nenad Gavrilovic, 'The Unfair Contract Terms Directive through the Practice of the Court of Justice of the European Union: Interpretation or Something More?' (2013) 9 European Review of Contract Law 163.

[127] Martin Ebers, 'The Notion of "Consumer"' in Hans Schulte-Nölke, Christian Twigg-Flesner, and Martin Ebers (eds), *EC Consumer Law Compendium. The Consumer Acquis and its Transposition in the Member States* (Sellier 2008) 456.

[128] Case C-541/99 *Cape Snc v Idealservice Srl* and case C-542/99 *Idealservice MN RE Sas v OMAI Srl* [2001] ECR I–9049.

[129] Council Directive 93/13/EEC on unfair terms in consumer contracts (n 86).

[130] Council Directive 85/577/EEC of 20 December 1985 to protect the consumer in respect of contracts negotiated away from business premises, OJ L 372, 31.12.1985, p 31.

[131] Case C-45/96 *Bayerische Hypotheken- und Wechselbank AG v Edgard Dietzinger* [1998] ECR I–1199.

[132] Case C-45/96 *Bayerische Hypotheken- und Wechselbank AG v Edgard Dietzinger* [1998] ECR I–1199, Opinion of AG Jacobs, paras 11 and 17.

VII. The Attitude of National Judges

What is the response of national courts charged with the daily application of EU law?[133] The process of European integration is characterized by centralized legislative power and a decentralized enforcement structure of national courts.[134] Only a subset of cases involving the application of EU consumer law reach the CJEU. Thus, it is the attitudes of national judges that determine how the issue of the multilingual interpretation of EU law is treated in the European legal order. From a more practical point of view,[135] the attitude of national judges to EU law depends on different variables, such as generational differences, legal education, and judicial career paths, and not just the official stance of the EU Court regarding their interpretative duties under EU law.[136]

Significant differences among judges from different Member States arise already in relation to the function and the appropriate use of the preliminary ruling procedure. Research reveals that many factors play a role in the national courts' decisions to refer the case to the CJEU.[137] Equally important are the precise domestic circumstances under which national courts decide whether to request a preliminary ruling from the CJEU.[138] In that regard, it is difficult to assess what role, if any, is played by conceptual divergences among the language versions of the EU legislation that the national court is tasked to apply.

For example, Derlén reports that national courts do not consistently turn to foreign language versions when contemplating a referral to the CJEU and when applying EU law independently.[139] Even assuming that national judges check how

[133] Bruno Nascimbene and Patrizia De Pasquale, 'Il diritto dell'Unione. Il sistema giurisdizionale. La Corte di giustizia e il giudice nazionale' in Giorgio Lattanzi and others (eds), *Il Diritto Europeo e il Giudice Nazionale* (Giuffrè 2023) 3.

[134] Celestina Iannone, 'L'autonomia procedurale dei giudici nazionali nella giurisprudenza della Corte di giustizia dell'Unione europea' in Lattanzi and others (n 133) 25, 25–26.

[135] Giulia Gentile, Monika Glavina, and Tobias Nowak, 'The Application of EU Law from the National Judge's Perspective: A Plea for an Interdisciplinary Approach' in Rossana Deplano and others (eds), *Interdisciplinary Research Methods in EU Law* (Edward Elgar Publishing 2024) 225.

[136] Juan A Mayoral, Urszula Jaremba, and Tobias Nowak, 'Creating EU Law Judges: The Role of Generational Differences, Legal Education and Judicial Career Paths in National Judges' Assessment Regarding EU Law Knowledge' (2014) 21 Journal of European Public Policy 1120. The CJEU has created extensive obligations for national courts brought together under the umbrella of the principle of the primacy of EU law, which today also includes the obligation to interpret domestic law in conformity with EU law (Case C-573/17 *Criminal proceedings against Daniel Adam Popławski*, ECLI:EU:C:2019:530) with particular emphasis on legislation that requires the pursuit of common European goals even before and during the transposition process. Gerrit Betlem, 'The Doctrine of Consistent Interpretation: Managing Legal Uncertainty' (2002) 22 Oxford Journal of Legal Studies 397.

[137] Mattias Derlén, *A Castle in the Air—The Complexity of the Multilingual Interpretation of European Community Law* (Doctoral dissertation, Umeå University 2007).

[138] Monika Glavina, 'To Refer or Not to Refer, That Is the (Preliminary) Question: Exploring Factors which Influence the Participation of National Judges in the Preliminary Ruling Procedure' (2020) 16 Croatian Yearbook of European Law & Policy 25; Arthur Dyevre, Monika Glavina, and Angelina Atanasova, 'Who Refers Most? Institutional Incentives and Judicial Participation in the Preliminary Ruling System' (2020) 27 Journal of European Public Policy 912.

[139] Derlén (n 137).

the provision expressed in their language is formulated in other language versions, there is no guarantee that they compare all language versions. Indeed, it would be interesting to know which other versions are consulted, if at all; that is, which and how many foreign language versions national courts use, especially in situations where they intend to diverge from reading the national language version in isolation. According to recent data, it appears that national courts in many cases only consult a few, more widely known languages.[140]

Finally, it would also be important to know how national courts act in situations where the meanings of the language versions which they have examined deviate from each other. It appears that national courts use different methods of reconciliation, but they often display significant loyalty to the multilingual character of EU law by allowing the meaning of the domestic language version to be determined by one or more foreign language versions.[141]

VIII. Conclusions

The harmonization of European contract law will not be successful without constant monitoring of the evolution of legal taxonomies at the European and national levels. Ensuring the harmonious evolution of legal terminology in twenty-seven countries with twenty-four official languages is a very difficult task. Even limiting the field to contract law alone, the monitoring operation would require a huge effort. An infrastructure that would deliver the monitoring operation appears difficult to set up. In Canada, where a bilingual and bi-juridical system has been established in a relatively efficient way, the investment made to translate, in a coherent way, the common law terminology into French was huge.[142] Could we afford to do the same with twenty-four official languages?

Another firm point relates to the position of the English language after Brexit. English will certainly remain central, as it is the most commonly spoken second language of European citizens and the language that facilitates communication with the rest of the world.[143] But despite the benefits of using English, we cannot

[140] ibid 29.

[141] ibid.

[142] Emmanuel Didier, 'La common law en français. Étude juridique et linguistique de la common law en français au Canada' (1991) 43 Revue internationale de droit comparé 7; JA Clarence Smith, 'La common law en français' (1983) 61 Canadian Bar Review 595; Donald Poirier and Marie-Claude Desrosiers, 'Les axes de recherche de la common law en français' (2003) 5 Revue de la common law en français 193.

[143] Manfred Herbert, 'On the Role of English in the post-Brexit European Union' (2023) 12 International Journal of Language and Law 31; Melvina Melvina, 'The Future of English after Brexit in European Union' in Eri Kurniawan and others (eds), *Proceedings of the Eleventh Conference on Applied Linguistics (CONAPLIN 2018)* (Atlantis Press 2019) 25; Marko Modiano, 'English in a post-Brexit European Union' (2017) 36 World Englishes 313; Kingsley Bolton and Daniel R Davis, 'Brexit and the Future of English in Europe' (2017) 36 World Englishes 302; Ushma Chauhan Jacobsen, 'English in

forget the difficulties of harmonizing different civil law legal systems through a language that represents the common law tradition, which has a completely different history from that of civilian jurisdictions. Most probably, English will become a bridge language between different national languages, gaining specific characteristics connected with the EU jargon.[144]

A third firm point that needs to be emphasized concerns legal education. We should invest in the generation of lawyers to come, to teach them that the dialogue should be not only between each Member State and the European institutions but also between states, to understand how a legal proposition regulated at the European level is translated into the national contexts, and how the problems arising from it have been addressed as part of these contexts. And it is likely that the university programmes we offer our law students today are not well suited to respond to these circumstances. This is not the place to argue for the central role of comparative law in the creation of European private law. However, it is clear that if law faculties in Europe devoted more space to comparative law in their curricula, it would be possible, on the one hand, to lay the foundations for a better understanding of the diverse legal mentalities that exist, and, on the other hand, to deepen the impact of EU law in achieving harmonization in areas where, despite EU legislative rules, it has remained ephemeral.

How will it end? If our 'European House' survives, it will still take a long time for a European consciousness to emerge. The EU legislative institutions could choose to accelerate this process by deciding to define the concepts used in the legislation they enact. Perhaps, we should take inspiration from *Alice in Wonderland*, which illustrates well that the meaning of words depends on who controls them:

> 'I don't know what you mean by "glory," ' Alice said.
>
> Humpty Dumpty smiled contemptuously. 'Of course you don't—till I tell you. I meant "there's a nice knock-down argument for you!" '
>
> 'But "glory" doesn't mean "a nice knock-down argument," ' Alice objected.
>
> 'When I use a word,' Humpty Dumpty said in rather a scornful tone, 'it means just what I choose it to mean—neither more nor less.'
>
> 'The question is,' said Alice, 'whether you CAN make words mean so many different things.'
>
> 'The question is,' said Humpty Dumpty, 'which is to be master—that's all.'[145]

the European Union after Brexit: Inclusion Effects of a Language Without an Owner' (2017) 2 Culture, Practice & European Policy 9.

[144] See Barbara Pozzo, 'The Myth of Equivalence in Legal Translation' in Barbara Pasa and Lucia Morra (eds), *Translating the DCFR and Drafting the CESL: A Pragmatic Perspective* (Sellier European Law Publishers 2014) 29, 41–42.

[145] Lewis Carroll, *Through the Looking Glass and What Alice Found There* (Macmillan 1872) 124.

List of Publications by Simon Whittaker

Books (authored and edited)

1. S Whittaker, *Liability for Products: English Law, French Law and European Harmonisation* (OUP 2005)
2. J Bell, S Boyron, and S Whittaker (eds), *Principles of French Law* (OUP, 1st edn (1998); 2nd edn (2008))
3. R Zimmermann and S Whittaker (eds), *Good Faith in European Contract Law* (CUP 2000) (This work was translated into Chinese and published by the Law Press of China under the EU-China Legal and Judicial Co-operation Programme (2005))
4. J Cartwright, S Vogenauer, and S Whittaker (eds), *Reforming the French Law of Obligations* (Hart Publishing 2009)
   (This work was published in French as *Regards Comparatistes sur l'avant-projet de réforme du droit des obligations et de la prescription* (Soc de lég comp 2010))
5. S Whittaker (ed), *The Development of Product Liability* (CUP 2010)
6. J Cartwright and S Whittaker (eds), *The Code Napoléon Rewritten, French Contract Law after the 2016 Reforms* (Hart Publishing 2017)
   (This work was published in French as J Cartwright, B Fauvarque-Cosson, et S Whittaker, *La Réécriture du Code civil, Le droit français des contrats après la réforme de 2016* (Soc de lég comp 2018))
7. J-S Borghetti and S Whittaker (eds), *French Civil Liability in Comparative Perspective* (Hart Publishing 2019)
   (The majority of the chapters in this book were published in French in the *Revue des contrats*, December 2019, no 4)

Contributions to References Works

8. *Chitty on Contracts* (26th edn of 1989—35th edn of 2023 (Sweet & Maxwell/Thomson Reuters). AG Guest was general editor for the 26th and 27th editions; H Beale was/is general editor for the 28th to 36th editions. Simon Whittaker has been an editor of chapters in this work from the 26th edition; the chapters edited by him in the 36th edition are:
   In Volume I. General Principles:
   Chapter 1. Contract Law and 'Contracts'
   Chapter 2. Freedom of Contract, Good Faith, Fairness and Reasonableness
   Chapter 3. Contract Law and Other Legal Categories
   Chapter 8. Form
   Chapter 12. Personal Capacity
   Chapter 18. Exemption Clauses
   In Volume II. Specific Contracts:
   Chapter 41. Consumer Contracts
   Chapter 48. Suretyship

9. Benjamin's Sale of Goods
   Chapter 14, 'Consumer Protection' in M Bridge (ed), *Benjamin's Sale of Goods* (10th edn of 2017 and 12th edn of 2024) (Sweet & Maxwell/Thomson Reuters)

Journal articles

10. 'Retaining European Union Law in the United Kingdom' (2021) 137 Law Quarterly Review 477
11. 'Unfair Terms in Commercial Contracts and the Two Laws of Competition: French Law and English Law Contrasted' (2019) 39 Oxford Journal of Legal Studies 404
12. 'Un cadre commun pour la responsabilité civile?' (2019) 4 Revue des contrats 145
13. (with J-S Borghetti) 'Principes généraux de responsabilité ou droit des délits?' (2019) 4 Revue des contrats 347
14. 'Distinctive Features of the New Consumer Contract Law' (2017) 133 Law Quarterly Review 47
15. 'Opting for Tort' (2015) 6 Journal of European Tort Law 209
16. '"General Principles" and "Underlying Principles" in the Proposed Common European Sales Law and Their Role in its Interpretation' (2013) 2 Osservatorio del diritto civile e commerciale 361
17. 'The Proposed "Common European Sales Law": Legal Framework and the Agreement of the Parties' (2012) 75 Modern Law Review 578
18. 'The Optional Instrument of European Contract law and Freedom of Contract' (2011) 7 European Review of Contract Law 371
    (Also published in French as 'L'instrument facultatif du droit européen des contrats et la liberté contratuelle' (2011) 2 Revue des contrats 579)
19. 'On the Development of European Standard Contract Terms' (2006) 2 Journal of European Contract Law 51 (Also published in H Collins (ed), *Standard Contract Terms in Europe, A Basis for and a Challenge to European Contract Law* (Wolters Kluwer 2008))
20. 'Contractual Control and Contractual Review in England and France' (2005) 13 European Review of Private Law 757
21. 'A Framework of Principle for European Contract Law' (2009) 125 Law Quarterly Review 616
22. 'The Elaboration of the Common Frame of Reference: Translating the "Tool-box"' (2009) 2 Revue des contrats 807
23. 'Clauses abusives et garanties des consommateurs: la proposition de directive relative aux droits des consommateurs et la portée de l'"harmonisation complète"' (2009) 17 Recueil Dalloz 1152 (Also published in English as 'Unfair Terms and Consumer Guarantees: the Proposal for a Directive on Consumer Rights and the Significance of "Full Harmonisation"' (2009) 3 European Review of Contract Law 223), and in German as 'Missbräuchliche Vertragsklauseln und Garantien für Verbrauchsgüter, Der Vorschlag für eine Richtlinie über Rechte der Verbraucher und die Auswirkungen der "Volharmonsisierung"' in M Reiffenstein and B Blaschek (eds), *KosumentenPolitisches Jahrbuch 2007–2008* Vol 40 (Verlag Osterreich 2009) 25
24. 'Burden of Proof in the Consumer *Acquis* and in the Draft Common Frame of Reference: Law, Fact and Things in Between' (2008) 3 European Review of Contract Law 411
25. 'Form and Substance in the Reception of EC Directives into English Contract Law' (2007) European Review of Contract Law 381
26. 'Form and Substance in the Harmonisation of Product Liability in Europe' (2007) 3 Zeitschrift für Europäisches Privatrecht 858
27. 'Precedent in English Law: A View from the Citadel' (2006) 14 European Review of Private Law 705 (Also published in English and in translation into Serbian in (2007) European Law

Journal 9 (Bosnia); translated into Spanish by C Banfi del Rio and published as 'El precedente en el Dercho ingles: una vision desde la ciudadela' (2008) 35 Revista Chilena de Derecho 37)

28. 'Un droit à la prestation plûtot qu'un droit à l'exécution? Réflexions sur l'exécution en nature et réparation en droit anglais' (2005) 1 Revue des contrats 49
29. 'Assessing the Fairness of Contract Terms: The Parties' "Essential Bargain," Its Regulatory Context and the Significance of the Requirement of Good Faith' (2004) 12 Zeitschrift für Europäisches Privatrecht 75
30. 'Judicial Review in Public Law and in Contract Law: The Example of "Student Rules"' (2001) 21 Oxford Journal of Legal Studies 193
31. 'Public and Private Law-making: Subordinate Legislation, Contracts and the Status of "Student Rules"' (2001) 21 Oxford Journal of Legal Studies 103
32. 'The Application of the "Broad Principle of *Hedley Byrne*" as between Parties to a Contract' (1997) 17 Legal Studies 169
33. 'How Does French Law Deal with Anticipatory Breaches of Contract?' (1996) 45 The International and Comparative Law Quarterly 662
34. 'Privity of Contract and the Tort of Negligence: Future Directions' (1996) 16 Oxford Journal of Legal Studies 191
35. 'Privity of Contract and the Law of Tort: The French Experience' (1995) 15 Oxford Journal of Legal Studies 327
36. 'European Product Liability and Intellectual Products' (1989) 105 Law Quarterly Review 125
37. 'An Historical Perspective to the Special Equitable Action in *Re Diplock*' (1983) 4 Journal of Legal History 3

Chapters in books

38. 'The Nature and Purpose of Default Rules in English Consumer Contract Law' in B Häcker and J Ungerer (eds) *Default Rules in Private Law* (Hart Publishing 2025) 137
39. '"Contractual Purpose" in English Contract Law' in G Albers, F Paolo Patti, and D Perrouin-Verbe (eds), *Causa Contractus* (Mohr Siebeck 2022) 871
40. 'La réforme du droit de la consommation au Royaume-Uni et les contrats portant sur un bien meuble corporel ("goods contracts")' in H Boucard, J Lete, R Pazos, E Savaux, and R-N Shütz (eds), *Les recodifications du droit de la vente en Europe* (Presses universitaires juridiques de Poitiers diff LGDJ Lextenso éditions, 2021) (collection de la Faculté de droit et des sciences sociales) 231
41. 'A Common Framework for Civil Liability?' in J-S Borghetti and S Whittaker (eds), *French Civil Liability in Comparative Perspective* (Hart Publishing 2019) 16
42. (with J-S Borghetti) 'Principles of Liability or a Law of Torts?' in J-S Borghetti and S Whittaker (eds) *French Civil Liability in Comparative Perspective* (Hart Publishing 2019) 455
43. 'Contracts, Contract Law and Contractual Principle' in J Cartwright and S Whittaker (eds), in *The Code Napoléon Rewritten, French Contract Law after the 2016 Reforms* (Hart Publishing 2017) 29
44. 'The Roles of *la prestation* in the New French Contract Law' in G Mattei, A Candian, B Pozzo, A Monti, and C Marchetti (eds), *Studi in onore di Antonio Gambaro* (Giuffrè 2017) Tome II, 1319
45. 'L'amende civile et *punitive damages*: Réflexions comparatives d'un juriste anglais sur le projet de réforme de la responsabilité civile' in D Fenouillet (ed), *Flexibles notions—La responsabilité civile* (Editions Panthéon-Assas 2020) 173
46. 'Le contrôle des clauses abusives dans le Projet d'ordonnance portant réforme du droit des contrats, du régime général et de la preuve des obligations' in P Stoffel-Munck (ed), *Réforme du droit des contrats et pratique des affaires* (Dalloz 2015) 157

47. 'Variation and Termination of Consumer Contracts' in L Gullifer and S Vogenaeur (eds), *English and European Perspectives on Contract Law and Commercial Law, Essays in Honour of Hugh Beale* (Hart Publishing 2014) 199
48. (with K Reisenhuber) 'Conceptions of Contract' in G Dannemann and S Vogenauer (eds), *The Common European Sales Law in Context: Interactions with English and German Law* (OUP 2013) 120
49. 'The Notion of Damage in EU Consumer Contract Law' in E Terryn, G Straetmans, and V Colaert (eds), *Landmark Cases of EU Consumer Law in Honour of Jules Stuyck* (Intersentia 2013) 559
50. 'Le rayonnement de René David' in Association Henri Capitant des amis de la culture juridique française, *Hommage René David* (Dalloz 2012) 65
51. 'Who Determines What Civil Courts Decide? Private Rights, Public Policy and EU Law' in D Leczykiewicz and S Weatherill (eds), *The Involvement of EU Law in Private Relationships* (Hart Publishing 2013) 89
52. 'Traduire les concepts, c'est interpréter les différences: la structure analytique du droit des obligations, les sanctions de l'inexécution et "Remedies for Breach"' in P Catala (ed), *L'art de la traduction, L'accueil international d l'avant-projet de réforme du droit des obligations* (Editions Panthéon-Assas 2011) 75
53. 'The Product Liability Directive and Rome II Article 5: "Full Harmonisation" and the Conflict of Laws' in C Barnard and O Odudu (eds), *Cambridge Yearbook of European Legal Studies* (Hart Publishing 2011) 435
54. 'Contract Networks, Freedom of Contract and the Restructuring of Privity of Contract' in F Cafaggi (ed), *Contractual Networks, Inter-Firm Cooperation and Economic Growth* (Edward Elgar 2011) 179
55. 'Contracts for Services in English Law and in the DCFR' in R Zimmermann (ed), *Service Contracts* (Mohr Siebeck 2010) 115
56. 'Introduction to Fault in Product Liability' in S Whittaker (ed), *The Development of Product Liability* (CUP 2010) 1
57. 'The Development of Product Liability in England' in S Whittaker (ed), *The Development of Product Liability* (CUP 2010) 51
58. '"Termination" for Contractual Non-performance and Its Consequences: French Law Reviewed in the Light of the *Avant-projet de réforme*' in J Cartwright, S Vogenauer, and S Whittaker (eds), *Reforming the French Law of Obligations* (Hart Publishing 2009) 187
59. (with J Cartwright) 'Translating the *Avant-projet de réforme*' in J Cartwright, S Vogenauer, and S Whittaker (eds), *Reforming the French Law of Obligations* (Hart Publishing 2009) 425
60. 'Price Variation Clauses' in M Fabre-Magnan, J Ghestin, and P Jourdain (eds), *Liber Amicorum, Etudes offertes à Genevieve Viney* (LGDJ 2008) 891
61. 'A "Period of Grace" for Contractual Performance?' in M Andenas, SD Alabart, B Markesinis, H Micklitz, and N Pasquini (eds), *Liber Amicorum Guido Alpa, Private Law Beyond the National Systems* (British Institute of International and Comparative Law 2007) 1083
62. 'The Interpretation of Concepts in European Private Law' in K Boele-Woelk and W Grosheide (eds), *The Future of European Contract Law, Essays in Honour of Ewoud Hondius* (Wolters Kluwer 2007) 333
63. 'Termination Clauses' in A Burrows and E Peel (eds), *Contract Terms* (OUP 2007) 253
64. 'Can the Contract Control the Contract? Entire Agreement Clauses in English Law' in F Addis (ed), *Le Clausole di Forma nelle Condizioni Generali di Contratto* (Università di Brescia 2008) 179
65. 'Contributory Fault and Mitigation, Rights and Reasonableness: Comparisons between English and French Law' in L Tichy (ed), *Causation in Law* (Eva Rozkotová 2007) 149
66. 'La responsabilité pour le fait personnel dans l'avant-projet de réforme du droit de la responsabilité: donner voix aux silences du Code civil?' in Pierre Catala (ed), *L'avant-projet de réforme du droit de la responsabilité* (Editions Les Manuscrit 2006) 163
67. 'The Relationship of the Unfair Commercial Practices Directive to European and National Contract Laws' in S Weatherill and U Bernitz (eds), *The Regulation of Unfair Commercial Practices under EC Directive 2005/29: New Rules and New Techniques* (Hart Publishing 2006) 139

68. 'The Language or Languages of Consumer Contracts' (2006) 8 Cambridge Yearbook of European Studies 230
69. 'La Terminologia della Tutela Civile: Diritti, Rimedi e Procedure' in B Pozzo and V Jacometti (eds), *Le politiche linguistiche delle istituzioni comunitarie dopo l'allargamento* (Giuffrè 2006) (Also published in English as 'The Terminologies of Civil Protection: Rights, Remedies and Procedures' in B Pozzo and V Jacometti (eds), *Multilingualism and the Harmonization of European Law* (Wolters Kluwer 2006) 45)
70. 'A Few Observations on the Plurality of Debtors and on Their Release' in A Vaquer (ed), *La Tercera Parte de Los Principios de Derecho Contractual Europeo, The Principles of European Contract Law Part III* (Tirant lo blanch 2005) 23
71. 'Theory and Practice of the "General Clause" in English Law: General Norms and the Structuring of Judicial Discretion' in S Grundmann and D Mazeaud (eds), *General Clauses and Standards in European Contract Law* (Wolters Kluwer 2006) 57
72. 'Consumer Law and the Distinction between Public and Private Law' in J-B Auby and M Freedland (eds), *La distinction du droit public et du droit privé: regards français et britanniques/* The Public Law/Private Law Divide: *une entente assez cordiale* (Editions Panthéon-Assas 2004) 233 (Also published in English in M Freedland and J-B Auby (eds), *The Public Law/Private Law Divide: une entente assez cordiale* (Hart Publishing 2006) 243)
73. 'Taking Time and Giving Time for Performance: A Comparison of Aspects of the English and the French law' in AS Espiau and A Vaquer (eds), *Bases de un Derecho Contractual Europeo/ Bases of a European Contract Law* (Tirant lo Blanch 2003) 261
74. 'The Reformulation of Contractual Formality' in P Birks and A Pretto (eds), *Themes in Comparative Law in Honour of Bernard Rudden* (OUP 2002) 199
75. 'I problemi posti dal recepimento della direttiva 1999/44/CE del maggio 1999, concernente taluni aspetti della vendita di beni di consumo e delle garanzie ad essi relative. Prospettive del diritto inglese' in G Cian (ed), *L'attuazione della Direttiva 99/44/CED in Italia e in Europa* (CEDAM 2002) 293
76. 'Performance of Another's Obligation: French and English Law Contrasted' in D Johnston and R Zimmermann (eds), *Unjustified Enrichment: Key Issues in Comparative Perspective* (CUP 2002) 433
77. 'Contracts which Harm Third Parties: English Law' in L Vacca (ed), *Gli effetti del contratto nei confronti dei terzi nella prospettiva storico-comparatistica* (Giappichelli 2001) 127
78. 'Les sanctions de l'inexécution des contrats, droit anglais' in M Fontaine and G Viney (eds), *Les sanctions de l'inexécution des obligations contractuelles, Etudes de droit comparé* (Bruyant and LGDJ 2001) 977
79. 'Reciprocity beyond Privity' in P Kincaid (ed), *Privity, Private Justice or Public Regulation* (Ashgate 2001) 259
80. 'Le contrat: la loi unique des parties?' in P Legrand (ed), *Common Law: d'un siècle l'autre* (Blais 1992) 119
81. 'The EEC Directive on Product Liability' (1985) Yearbook of European Law 232

Case notes and similar

82. 'Good Faith, Implied Terms and Commercial Contracts' (2013) 129 Law Quarterly Review 463
83. 'Comments on "Abuse of Law" in European Private Law' in R de la Feria and S Vogenauer (eds), *Prohibition of Abuse of Law, A General Principle of EU Law?* (Hart Publishing 2011) 253
84. 'Unfair Contract Terms, Unfair Prices and Bank Charges' (2011) 74 Modern Law Review 106
85. 'Judicial Interventionism and Consumer Contracts' (2001) 117 Law Quarterly Review 215
86. 'Defective Products and Economic Loss' (1986) 49 Modern Law Review 369
87. (with S Lee) 'Rights, Wrongs, Law and Non-Law: Miner Examples' (1986) 102 Law Quarterly Review 35
88. 'Retention of Title and Specification' (1984) 100 Law Quarterly Review 35

Translations

89. Translation with J Cartwright of Pierre Catala, *Proposals for the Reform of the Law of Obligations and the Law of Prescription*. It may be found at http://www.justice.gouv.fr/art_pix/rapportcatatla0905-anglais.pdf
90. '*The Law of Contract, the General Regime of Obligations and Proof of Obligations*', *The new provisions of the Code civil created by Ordonnance no. 2016-131 of 10 February 2016* (with J Cartwright and B Fauvarque-Cosson). This translation was commissioned by the *Direction des affaires civiles et du sceau* of the Ministry of Justice of the French Republic and published on its website in 2016 at http://www.textes.justice.gouv.fr/art_pix/THE-LAW-OF-CONTRACT-2-5-16.pdf
91. *Reform Bill on Civil Liability*, translation into English in consultation with J-S Borghetti of *Projet de réforme de la responsabilité civile* undertaken at the request of the *Direction des affaires civiles et du sceau*, Ministry of Justice, French Republic and published in 2017 at Microsoft Word - REFORM BILL ON CIVIL LIABILITY MARCH 2017 translated into English by S. Whittaker in consultation with J.-S. Borghetti 5.5.17

Commissioned Reports

92. *Unfair Contract Terms: Towards a Unified Regime of Control* (1999), report commissioned by the Department of Trade and Industry. The DTI subsequently referred the issue of the unification of the regime to the English and Scottish Law Commissions, whose joint report, *Unfair Contract Terms* Law Com No 292 (2005) acknowledges its use of this earlier work
93. *The Draft Common Frame of Reference: An Assessment Commissioned by the UK Ministry of Justice* (published 2008 and available at http://webarchive.nationalarchives.gov.uk/20110201125714/http://www.justice.gov.uk/publications/eu-contract-law-common-frame-reference.htm

Index

For the benefit of digital users, indexed terms that span two pages (e.g., 52–53) may, on occasion, appear on only one of those pages.